SYMBOLIC COMPUTATION

Computer Graphics – Systems and Applications

Managing Editor: J. Encarnação

Editors: K. Bø J. D. Foley R. A. Guedj
P. J. W. ten Hagen F. R. A. Hopgood M. Hosaka
M. Lucas A. G. Requicha

Springer-Series
SYMBOLIC COMPUTATION
Computer Graphics — Systems and Applications

J. Encarnação, E.G. Schlechtendahl:
Computer Aided Design, Fundamentals and System
Architectures. IX, 346 pages, 183 figs., 1983

G. Enderle, K. Kansy, G. Pfaff:
Computer Graphics Programming. GKS — The Graphics
Standard. Second, revised and enlarged edition, XXIII,
651 pages, 100 figs., 1987

J. Encarnação, R. Schuster, E. Vöge (eds.):
Product Data Interfaces in CAD/CAM Applications.
Design, Implementation and Experiences. IX, 270 pages,
147 figs., 1986

U. Rembold, R. Dillmann (eds.):
Computer-Aided Design and Manufacturing. Methods and
Tools. Second, revised and enlarged edition, XIV,
458 pages, 304 figs., 1986

Y. Shirai:
Three-Dimensional Computer Vision. XII, 297 pages,
313 figs., 1987

G. Enderle K. Kansy G. Pfaff

Computer Graphics Programming

GKS – The Graphics Standard

Second, Revised and Enlarged Edition

With 100 Figures, Some in Color

Springer-Verlag
Berlin Heidelberg New York
London Paris Tokyo

Dr. Günter Enderle†
Standard Elektrik Lorenz AG
Lorenzstraße 10, 7000 Stuttgart 40, FRG

Dr. Klaus Kansy
Gesellschaft für Mathematik und Datenverarbeitung
Schloss Birlinghoven, 5205 St. Augustin 1, FRG

Dr. Günther Pfaff
GTS-GRAL Graphische Standards für Computer-Systeme GmbH
Alsfelder Straße 7, 6100 Darmstadt, FRG

ISBN-13: 978-3-642-71081-0   e-ISBN-13: 978-3-642-71079-7
DOI: 10.1007/ 978-3-642-71079-7

Library of Congress Cataloging-in-Publication Data.
Enderle, G. (Günter), Computer graphics programming. (Symbolic computation. Computer graphics)
Bibliography: p. Includes index. 1. Computer graphics — Standards. I. Kansy, K. (Klaus)
II. Pfaff, G. (Günther)   III. Title.   IV. Series.   T385.E53   1986   006.6′0218   86-20370

© Springer-Verlag Berlin Heidelberg 1984, 1987
Softcover reprint of the hardcover 2nd edition 1984, 1987

Typesetting : Universitätsdruckerei H. Stürtz AG, Würzburg

2145/3140-543210

In Memoriam Günter Enderle

Shortly before the second edition of this book went into print, we received the message that our friend and co-author of this book, Günter Enderle, died in a car accident on January 13, 1987, at the age of 42.

Günter Enderle received his Dipl.-Ing. (M.S.) in 1971 and Dr.-Ing. (Ph.D. in Engineering) in 1975 from the University of Karlsruhe. He was with the Karlsruhe Nuclear Research Centre from 1971 and became group leader for Computer Graphics and CAD. From 1984 onwards, he was responsible for software development at Standard Elektrik Lorenz (SEL) in Stuttgart. He was a member of EUROGRAPHICS from 1980. He held the position of editor-in-chief of the journal Computer Graphics Forum and inaugurated the book series Eurographic Seminars — Tutorials and Perspectives in Computer Graphics.

The Graphical Kernel System GKS was a focal point of his professional interests. He contributed significantly to its design as a member, from 1979, of the editorial board and by creative participation in the international review process. From 1981 he was chairman of the German Standardization Committee DIN-NI-5.9 (later renamed DIN-NI-21.2) "Computer Graphics" and head of the German delegation to the ISO Working group ISO/TC 97/SC 5/WG 2 (later renamed ISO/TC 97/SC 21/WG 2). Günter Enderle performed these tasks with great energy. He had the gift of motivating people participating in the different committees as volunteers to put all their force into the promotion of a common goal. Therefore, the success of the Graphical Kernel System GKS is closely related to his name.

For nearly ten years, the undersigned collaborated closely with Günter Enderle. For the second author (K.K.), this cooperation started 1978 within the Coordinating Committee "Computer Graphics" of the West German Association of National Research Centres (AGF) with the definition of the so-called AGF-Plotfile, a predecessor of the GKS Metafile.

All three authors came together through their membership of the GKS editorial board and had a very fruitful and productive time with the development of numerous versions of the GKS proposal and in dealing with the bulk of comments which came in when GKS was presented to the international standardization bodies and which had to be handled before GKS was accepted as an ISO work item. In this task, Günter Enderle proved his ability in finding solutions for difficult problems and in realizing solutions within a short time.

The work around GKS included numerous meetings, national and international. These meetings were primarily devoted to hard technical work. Besides and through this technical work, "a network of deep friendship and common understanding has been established", as Günter Enderle himself expressed it on page 59 of this book. Therefore, we have not only lost a creative and dedicated colleague, but also a close friend, with whom we shared work and leisure time for many years. We are sure that our sorrow will be shared by all the colleagues who met Günter Enderle in the various German and international standardization committees for Computer Graphics.

Bonn, Darmstadt, February 1987   *Klaus Kansy*
                                                        Günther Pfaff

FOREWORD TO THE SECOND EDITION

When this book was published in 1983, the process of designing the Graphical Kernel System (GKS) was in its final stages. The final version of the first international standard for Computer Graphics was expected before the end of 1983. However, finalizing a standard is a complex and time-consuming process, so that the International Standard version of GKS appeared in August 1985. Before, the final letter ballot on GKS had been conducted. Comments raised in the ballot by the National Standardization Bodies have led to a number of small changes in the document. The final version of the GKS document was prepared in 1984 and forwarded to ISO central office for publication as an ISO standard. A number of GKS language bindings have also reached a stable and reliable status, and their ISO standard versions are expected soon.

Once GKS had been accepted and recognized as the cornerstone of a family of compatible graphics standards, a number of new projects were started with the aim of standardizing additional important graphics interfaces. The changes in GKS, the finalization of the GKS language bindings, the new projects in the computer graphics field, and last but not least, the extraordinary success of the first edition of this book, have led us to prepare this second edition.

The main differences from the first edition are as follows:

— All changes incorporated in GKS as a result of the final ISO letter ballot have been included.
— The language bindings, primarily FORTRAN and Pascal, have been updated to reflect the latest versions of the GKS Language Bindings Standard.
— The Pascal examples have been modified to reflect the traditional printed appearance of Pascal programs (e.g., keywords of the language are printed in bold letters).
— The three-dimensional (3D) extension of GKS has been completely revised. A new part (Part IV) presents in detail the proposed GKS-3D Standard which adds a complete set of 3D functions to GKS.

— The new projects on a Computer Graphics Metafile (CGM) and on Computer Graphics Interfaces for graphical devices (CGI) have been taken into consideration, where appropriate.

We are confident that this second edition will reinforce the original goal of this book, namely to offer a complete reference for understanding, using, learning, teaching, and implementing the Graphical Kernel System and its environment.

Karlsruhe, Bonn, Darmstadt, November 1986   *Günter Enderle*

Klaus Kansy

Günther Pfaff

FOREWORD TO THE FIRST EDITION

For several years the authors of this book have been involved
in the design and the national and international review of the
forthcoming graphical standard. When it became apparent that
this process was coming to an end and the International Standard
"Graphical Kernel System" (GKS) was cast into its final form,
an urgent need arose to provide the graphics community with
detailed information on the new standard, and to educate graphics programmers in GKS. One major goal of GKS, besides the
portability of graphical application programs and device independence, is "programmer portability" which it aims to achieve by
establishing a common basis for the training of graphics programmers. Having taken part in the development of GKS from the
very early stages of defining the basic concepts and designing
its first versions up to the final draft of the International Standard, we felt it would be worthwhile embarking on the venture
of writing a text book on computer graphics programming based
on GKS.

This book is aimed, on the one hand, at graphics users, experts
and managers who want to gain an overview of the new standard
and a better understanding of its concepts. On the other hand,
it addresses graphics programmers who want to use GKS for
realizing their graphical applications. It can serve as a basis for
teaching and studying the functions, concepts and methods of
GKS. Additionally, it will be a valuable source of information
for implementors of GKS.

One of the main areas of application of computer graphics
is Computer Aided Design (CAD). GKS can serve as an excellent
base upon which portable CAD systems can be built. A thorough
introduction to CAD is presented in another book in the SYM-
BOLIC COMPUTATION series: "CAD — Fundamentals and
System Architectures", by J. Encarnação and E.G. Schlechtendahl [ENCA 82a].

The standard document defining GKS has to be complete
and consistent, it uses formal descriptions where possible, and
it has to adhere to certain formal rules for the specification of
the standard. Only rarely does it give informal introductions,
examples, or explanations for the decisions taken. For an over-

view such as this book aims to provide, however, an informal and less complete presentation is more suitable and examples, figures and explanations are essential for teaching purposes. We want to offer easy access to GKS and to the graphics environment in which it is situated.

It is of course inevitable in a book describing a standard that some material from the standard document will be used. The authors were members of the editorial team which designed GKS up to version 4.8 [DIN 79], and since then have taken part in the development of further versions of the GKS document up to the GKS standard. However, the GKS document is the result of combined contributions from many different people. We feel that the quality of the document is very high, and that there is no better way of describing some aspects of the GKS standard. Accordingly, in such cases the relevant parts of the document are reproduced in this book with little or no alteration.

The book is divided into five main parts. In Part I, an overview of the integration of GKS into the Computer Graphics framework is given and the principles and basic concepts of GKS are introduced and explained. Part II describes the design process of GKS in the committee NI/UA-5.9 of the Deutsches Institut für Normung (DIN), and the extensive international review and refinement carried out by the experts of working group TC97/SC5/WG2 of the International Organization for Standardization (ISO). The groups participating in this process, important events, and major design decisions, are presented, as well as the methods used for handling the review and the revision of the standard draft and for resolving conflicts.

Part III of the book is devoted to explaining the GKS functions and their applications. All GKS functions and their parameters are described, both in the language-independent form presented in the standard document and in the FORTRAN subroutine version. Various examples are given in the programming languages FORTRAN and Pascal. Exercises are provided in order to deepen the reader's understanding of the functions and to assist in the teaching of Computer Graphics programming on the basis of GKS. In Part IV, the 3D extensions to GKS are described.

The last part of the book covers the various interfaces of the standard within the Computer Graphics environment. Before a standardized graphics system can be used, it has to be implemented on existing hardware and operating systems. It is of course desirable that such implementations be validated and that their conformity to the standard be certified. The implementation of the standard in a given programming language is made possible by adapting the standard functions to the rules of that language. We describe the FORTRAN binding of GKS. Further interfaces exist with graphical input and output devices, and with graphics metafiles for storage of pictures. Communication between members of the graphics community is facilitated by a common graphics terminology developed in parallel with the GKS standard.

Newcomers to the Computer Graphics field and readers who want an overview of GKS concepts should read Part I and then use the table of contents or the index at the end of the book to find information of special interest to them. Part II addresses itself to those interested in standards and how they are created. Programmers and scientists designing graphics applications will find a detailed description of the GKS functions in Part III. This part will also be the main reference for learning Computer Graphics programming on the basis of GKS. Part V will be of special importance to GKS implementors.

We hope this book will help to disseminate the application of the Graphical Kernel System, to explain its principles and concepts, and to promote Computer Graphics education on the basis of the first standard in Computer Graphics.

Karlsruhe, Bonn, Darmstadt, July 1983   *Günter Enderle*
                                                Klaus Kansy
                                                Günther Pfaff

DEDICATION

The subject of this book — the Graphical Kernel System — was developed in a long process starting in 1976 and has finally evolved as an International Standard. This book is dedicated to the graphics experts who designed GKS under the auspices of the Deutsches Institut für Normung (DIN), and who played a part in its evolution through the international review process within the working group TC97/SC5/WG2 "Computer Graphics" of the International Organization for Standardization (ISO) and various national standardization organizations. Over 100 scientists from all over the world invested more than 50 man-years in this venture, making GKS the consistent and complete graphics standard it is today, developing a concise terminology for Computer Graphics, establishing the firm basis of a methodology for Computer Graphics, and cooperating in a spirit of mutual confidence and friendship.

Members and experts of DIN-NI/UA-5.9 "Computer Graphics" 1975—1982:

R. Anderl, E. Bauböck, H. Borik, H.-G. Borutka, L. Brandenburger, H. Brüggemann, P. Dobrowolski, R. Eckert, P. Egloff, J. Encarnação, G. Enderle, B. Fink, H. Flegel, R. Gnatz, M. Gonauser, H. Grauer, I. Grieger, Th. Johannsen, E. Jungmann, K. Kansy, R. Karg, W. Klingenberg, R. Konkart, H. Kuhlmann, G. Lang-Lendorff, St. Lewandowski, G. Mittelstraß, G. Nees, H. Nowacki, D. Otto, K. Pasemann, G. Pfaff, F.-J. Prester, K. Reumann, J. Rix, H.-J. Rosenberg, F.-K. Roth, E.G. Schlechtendahl, J. Schönhut, R. Schuster, D. Stroh, D. Völkel, J. Weiss, J. Weskott, H. Wetzel, P. Wißkirchen.

Members and experts of ISO TC97/SC5/WG2 "Computer Graphics" 1977—1982:

J. Bettels (CH), K. Bö (N), P. Bono (USA), H.-G. Borutka (D), K. Brodiie (UK), L. Brown (NL-C), F. Canfield (USA), St. Carson (USA), J. Chin (USA), U. Cugini (I), J. Daabeck (DK), G. Dettori (I), F. de Witte (NL), D. Duce (UK), A. Ducrot (F), R. Dunn (USA), R. Eckert (D), P. Egloff (D), J. Encarnação (D), G. Enderle (D), J. Ero (NL), D. Fisher (UK), A. Francis (UK), J. Gallop (UK), P. Gauriat (F), R. Gnatz (D), T.H. Gossling (UK), I. Grieger (D), R. Guedj (F), Y. Gueniot

(F), Ch. Hatfield (USA), W. Herzner (A), B. Herzog (USA), F.R.A. Hopgood (UK), M. Hosaka (J), K. Kansy (D), R. Kessener (NL), F. Kimura (J), J. Kivi (SF), A. Kotzauer (GDR), G. Krammer (H), H. Kuhlmann (D), R. Langridge (UK), M. Lucas (F), V. Lvov (USSR), J. Matthijs (B), J. Michener (USA), L. Moltedo (I), G. Nees (D), H. Newman (C), Ch. Osland (UK), Ch. Pellegrini (CH), G. Pfaff (D), A. Planman (SF), M. Polisher (USA), F.-J. Prester (D), R. Puk (USA), T. Reed (USA), K. Reumann (D), J. Rix (D), D.S.H. Rosenthal (UK), J. Rowe (USA), J. Schönhut (D), B. Shepherd (USA), E. Sonderegger (USA), R. Spiers (UK), D. Stroh (D), R. Sulonen (SF), D. Sutcliffe (UK), Z. Tolnay-Knefely (H), P. ten Hagen (NL), J. van der Star (NL), H. van Velden (NL), A. Warman (UK), M. Wein (C), J. Weiss (A), M. Whyles (USA), K. Willet (USA), A. Williams (UK), G. Williams (C), R. Williams (USA), P. Wißkirchen (D).

CONTENTS

INTRODUCTION TO COMPUTER GRAPHICS BASED ON GKS

Part I gives an introduction to basic concepts of computer graphics and to the principles and concepts of GKS. The aims of this part are twofold: to provide the beginner with an overview of the terminology and concepts of computer graphics, based on GKS, and to give the computer graphics expert an introduction to the GKS standard. In the early chapters of this part, the main areas of computer graphics, the various classes of computer graphics users, the interfaces of GKS and its underlying design concepts are discussed and important terms are defined. The later chapters give an informal introduction to the main concepts of GKS and their interrelationships: output, attributes, coordinate systems, transformations, input, segments, metafile, state lists, and error handling. This introduction to the GKS framework will prepare the ground for the detailed description of 2D GKS functions in Part III and the 3D extensions to GKS in Part IV.

1 WHAT IS COMPUTER GRAPHICS?

1.1 Definition of Computer Graphics

The Data Processing Vocabulary of the International Organization for Standardization (ISO) [ISO 84] defines Computer Graphics as follows:

> "Methods and techniques for converting data to and from a graphic display via computer."

This definition refers to three basic components of any computer graphics system — namely "data", "computer", and "display". However, the most important aspect of computer graphics, and the main reason for the recent explosive increase in computer graphics applications, is not mentioned in the above definition:

> Computer graphics is the most versatile and most powerful means of communication between a computer and a human being.

Visually presented information can be accessed by human perception in a most natural way: complex structures and relationships can be perceived in less time, in greater number, and with fewer errors than in any other way. Indeed, human beings hardly ever think about models of the real world or models of abstract concepts without resorting to visual representations. This is the reason why computer graphics is first and foremost a means of adapting the interface between computers and man to the specific needs of man. Even when human beings communicate about data which has originated from a computer or has been processed by a computer, computer graphic representations are an important vehicle for transmitting information.

1.2 Areas of Computer Graphics

Depending on the direction in which data is converted and transferred between the computer and the visual representation and on the types of objects dealt with by the computer graphics system, three areas can be identified within computer graphics:
— generative computer graphics;
— picture analysis;
— picture processing.

Table 1.1 gives an overview of these areas. The table follows a scheme set up by Giloi [GILO 78].

In generative graphics, pictures are created from picture descriptions given by computer programs and data. The data can originate from primary input given by a user, it can be generated by computations, or it may originate from the commands and actions of an operator at a graphical workstation. Basic objects like lines, raster elements (pixels), text strings, or filled polygons (areas)

Table 1.1 Main areas of computer graphics

	Computer Graphics		
area	generative computer graphics	picture analysis	picture processing
input:	formal description	visual presentation	visual presentation
output:	visual presentation	formal description	visual presentation
objects:	lines, pixels, areas, texts or sets thereof	generated or scanned pictures	scanned pictures
purpose:	picture generation, presentation, segmentation, transformation	pattern analysis, structure analysis, scene analysis	picture enhancement

are created and their visual representations displayed on the display surface of a graphical output device. Pictures may be divided into parts (segments), and pictures or parts thereof can undergo transformations. For the purpose of interaction with an operator, generative computer graphics also includes methods for handling operator input and identification of picture segments.

In picture analysis, basic objects and their relationships are extracted from a picture given in unstructured form. Normally, the pictures to be analysed are passed to the graphics system by digitizing (scanning) a photographic or television picture. Examples of picture analysis include the recognition of written characters and the analysis of the type and situation of a mechanical part on a conveyer belt by the scene analysis system of a robot.

Picture processing is used to change the visual presentation of a picture in such a way that human perception of the data contained in the picture is improved. Typical methods used include filtering, contrast improvement and noise suppression. An example is the replacement of the grey scale values of a radiograph by corresponding colour hues. In this way the structures within the pictures can be more easily perceived by human beings.

Of course, there are various transitions between the three areas of computer graphics, and systems designed for one area may well have functional capabilities useful for one of the other areas. One common aspect of the whole field of computer graphics is that it deals with pictures, and that pictures have to be presented on a device for human perception. Thus a picture analysis system might well use a generative computer graphics system to present both the pictures to be analysed and the results of the analysis.

1.3   Impact of the Graphical Kernel System on Computer Graphics

The Graphical Kernel System (GKS) [GKS85], which is the subject of this book, covers the most significant parts of the area of generative computer graphics. It also lends itself to use in applications from the areas of picture analysis and picture processing. The Graphical Kernel System is the first international standard for programming computer graphics applications. It provides functions for picture generation, picture presentation, segmentation, transformations and input. However, the extent of its functional capabilities is not the only important aspect of the Graphical Kernel System. An even more significant advantage of the standardization provided by GKS is the following:

> For the first time, a methodological framework for the various concepts within the field of computer graphics has been developed. This forms the basis for a common understanding and a common terminology for creating computer graphics systems, for using computer graphics, for talking about computer graphics and for educating students in computer graphics methods, concepts and applications.

2   AIMS AND CONTENTS OF PART I

Part I of this book gives an overview of principles and concepts of computer graphics on the basis of the Graphical Kernel System. Although the concepts described are closely related to GKS, most of them are in fact common to a wide spectrum of computer graphics systems. This is true of interfaces, including the computer graphics user interface, and of the principles and goals of computer graphics standards as well as of the basic concepts of GKS. A discussion of concepts and methods has to be based on a common understanding, which in turn requires a suitable terminology. The terminology used in this book is taken from the ISO Data Processing Vocabulary [ISO84]. The set of terms defined in the GKS standard document [GKS85] overlaps with the ISO definitions for computer graphics to a great extent. The terms from both documents that are most important in our context are defined and explained in the following chapters. Most of the definitions are taken literally from the GKS document.

The aims of this part are twofold: to provide the beginner with an overview of the terminology and concepts of computer graphics, and to give the computer graphics designer, user or teacher an introduction to the GKS standard. The integration of the particular functionality of GKS into the general context of computer graphics will be illustrated, and a sound framework established for the detailed description of GKS functions and their applications in Parts III and IV.

3   THE COMPUTER GRAPHICS USER

Computer graphics is "used" in many different ways, for different purposes and by people with different skills and educational backgrounds. A person struggling with space invaders in a video game arcade is a computer graphics user, as is a programmer calling plotting routines in order to generate a diagram on a plotter. Broadly speaking, however, three important classes of users can be identified: system implementors, application programmers, and graphical workstation operators. Figure 3.1 shows the relationships between the different types of computer graphics users.

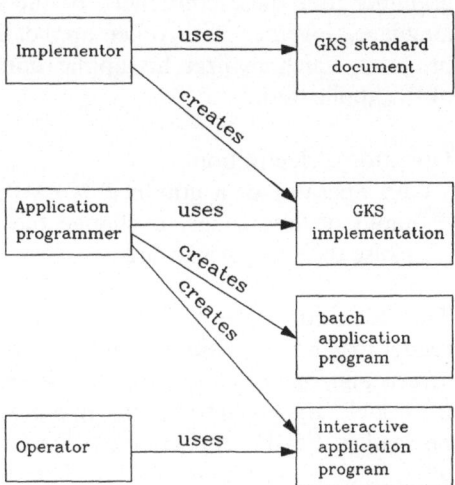

Figure 3.1 Computer graphics users

Implementor — Definition
   The implementor of a graphics system realizes the system defined by a specification. He uses basic software such as programming language processors, linkers and loaders, and input/output routines. He makes the capabilities of graphics hardware (e.g., plotters or displays) available to the application programmer.

In GKS, the specification for the system design is given by the standard documents. The GKS functions are grouped in levels of increasing functionality, ranging from minimal capabilities to the complete set of functions. The implementor has to choose the GKS level he wishes to realize and to specify the implementation-dependent aspects of the system. In so doing, however, he must stay within the bandwidth which the standard leaves open for the implementor. In particular, the requirements of the GKS level structure must be respected (cf. Chapters I.6, III.2), and system interfaces that are not explicitly defined in the standard must be designed. Implementation guidelines and implementation dependencies are summarized in Chapter V.3.

Application programmer — Definition
In the context of this book, we shall restrict the use of the term "application programmer" to applications containing computer graphics tasks. An application programmer uses a computer graphics system by writing programs which use computer graphics functions.

In most cases, computer graphics systems are realized in the form of subroutine packages callable from one or more programming languages (e.g., [GINO 75, GSPC 79, BOS 77, BO 82]). GKS itself is also defined as a set of subroutines or procedures. By contrast, in some graphics systems, graphics capabilities are integrated into the constructs (data types, operations, statements) of the language (e.g., [HURW 67, SMIT 71, SOOP 72, GILO 72]). The application programmer uses these constructs, or the subroutine calls within a programming language, together with other application-specific program parts to create a program which realizes his application needs, including the graphics aspects of the application.

Operator — Definition
An operator of a graphical workstation is a person manipulating physical input devices so as to change the measures of logical input devices and cause their triggers to fire.

This definition is taken from the GKS standard document. At this point, the reader may simply visualize the operator as a person sitting in front of a display screen and manipulating input devices, such as a crosshair cursor moved by a joystick. By his actions, the operator changes logical input values that can be read in by the application program. The terms "measure" and "trigger" are explained in Chapter III.8. The set of input devices which the operator is allowed to manipulate, and the order in which he may do so, are defined by the application program that calls input functions for this purpose.

4   INTERFACES
OF THE GRAPHICAL KERNEL SYSTEM

The GKS standard document defines in a language-independent way a set of functions for performing graphical tasks. However, in an implementation of the system these functions have to be realized as subroutines (or procedures) in a given programming language. Such a language-specific realization, in which the language-independent system nucleus is embedded, is called a language layer. Language layers for FORTRAN and Pascal are available (see examples in Part III, Part IV and Chapter V.4). The functions provided by the language layer can be used by the application programmer, together with operating system functions. In addition, special application-dependent layers can be built on top of the GKS language layer. An example using an application layer for data representation graphics is shown in Figure C7 (page 620), while Figure C8 (page 621) shows a mapping application and Figure C3 (page 619) a CAD application.

The layer model represented in Figure 4.1 illustrates the role of GKS within a graphical system. Each layer may call the functions of the adjoining lower layers. Thus, an application program will have access to a number of application-oriented layers, the language-dependent GKS layer, and operating system resources. All graphical tasks should be performed exclusively by using GKS functions.

The top interface of the GKS nucleus is the language-independent application interface and is defined by the GKS standard. The interface between the language-dependent layer and the application layers is the language-dependent application interface, e.g., the FORTRAN or Pascal interface. These interfaces are currently under consideration for national and international standardization.

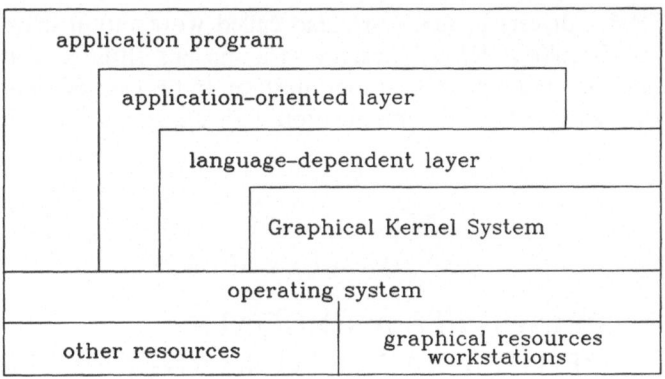

Figure 4.1 Layer model of GKS

GKS is a system nucleus not only in the sense that it provides basic graphical capabilities for many different applications but also because it defines the graphical functions without reference to specific graphical devices. Therefore, an important interface exists between the system nucleus and the various graphical devices attached to it. In GKS, a graphical output device and the input devices connected to it are called a graphical workstation (cf. Chapter 9). The translation of the device-independent representations of functions within the nucleus to and from the different workstation-specific representations is performed by device drivers.

Device driver — Definition
    A device driver is the device-dependent part of a GKS implementation intended to support a graphics device. The device driver generates device-dependent output and handles device-dependent interaction.

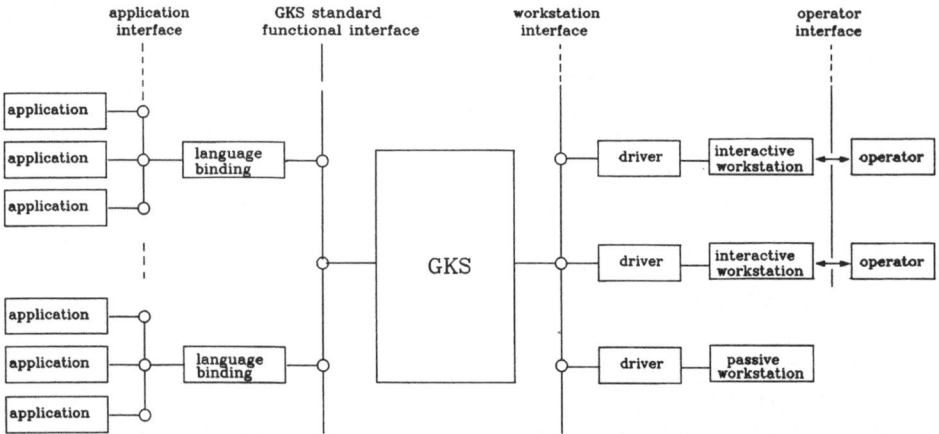

Figure 4.2 GKS interfaces

Device drivers in GKS are also called workstation drivers. Figure 4.2 shows the Graphical Kernel System as a nucleus situated between the application interface and the workstation interface. In the case of an interactive workstation with an operator, communication with the system is achieved via the operator interface.

5   PRINCIPLES AND GOALS
OF THE GRAPHICAL KERNEL SYSTEM

The information contained in this chapter was first presented in a paper of the DIN Computer Graphics group [ENDE 81], based on work done by the ANSI Computer Graphics group ANSC X3H3. It was later included in the GKS draft standard in order to offer explanations and justifications for design decisions taken during the development of GKS. GKS was designed to provide a set of functions for computer graphics programming which can be used in the majority of applications that produce computer generated pictures.

The main reasons for introducing a standard for basic computer graphics are:

— to allow application programs involving graphics to be easily portable between different installations;
— to aid the understanding and use of graphics methods by application programmers;
— to serve manufacturers of graphics equipment as a guideline for the provision of useful combinations of graphics capabilities in a device.

In order to reach these main objectives, GKS was designed on the basis of the following requirements:

— the system must encompass all the essential capabilities from the whole spectrum of graphics, from simple passive output to highly interactive applications;
— the system should be able to support in a uniform way the whole range of graphics devices, including vector and raster devices, microfilm recorders, storage tube displays, refresh displays and colour displays;
— the system should provide all the capabilities required in most applications without becoming unduly large or complex.

These requirements led to the formulation of a number of principles which were used to judge specific design alternatives. This made it possible to contribute to the overall design objectives while focusing on certain aspects. Five design aspects were identified, each associated with a particular group of principles: design goals, functional capabilities, user interface design, graphics devices, and implementation.

Design Goals

The following principles should not be violated by any technical design:

consistency: none of the mandatory requirements of the system should be mutually contradictory;

compatibility: no other standards or commonly accepted rules of practice should be violated;

orthogonality: either the functions or modules of the system should be independent of each other, or else any dependencies should be structured and well defined.

Functional Capabilities

The following principles were used in defining the extent of GKS:

completeness: all functions which are used by most applications at a given level of functionality should be included;

minimality: no functions which are unnecessary for applications at a given level of functionality should be included;

compactness: an application should be able to achieve a desired result by using a set of functions and parameters that is as small as possible;

richness: a rich set of functions offers an extensive range of facilities that stretches beyond the basic functions and includes higher order capabilities.

It is obvious that there must be a trade-off between the principles in this group. For this reason, the functions of GKS are grouped into levels. While the lowest level contains only a minimal set of functions, higher levels are allowed to extend beyond the basic needs towards greater richness.

User Interface Design

The following principles were used in defining the user interface design:

user friendliness: the system should allow the design of a desirable user interface;

clarity: the concepts and functional capabilities of the system should be easily understandable, especially to the application programmer;

error handling: any failure of system functions or modules, whether caused by errors in the system itself or by the application program, should be handled in such a way that the system's reaction is clearly understandable and informative to the application programmer and that the impact on the system and the application program is as small as possible.

Clarity and sound error handling are essential parts of user friendliness. The specification of error handling is an integral part of GKS. As an aid to clarity, the system and its state are presented to the user in an easily comprehensible manner.

The principle of clarity applies not only to the system design but also to the system description. In order to achieve this, the GKS specification is divided into a general description, a description of the underlying logical data structures representing the state of the system, and a description of the functions and their effects on these data structures.

Graphics Devices

The following principles are associated with the range of graphics devices that can be addressed by GKS:

device independence: the system functions should be designed to allow an application program, using these functions, to address different types of graphics output and input devices without modification of the program structure;

device richness: the full capabilities of a wide range of different graphics output and input devices should be accessible via the functions of the system.

These principles led to a fundamental concept underlying the GKS architecture: the concept of multiple independent graphical workstations connected to and driven by GKS. The application program can inquire the capabilities of every workstation.

Implementation

The last group of principles is related to the implementation of GKS:

implementability: it should be possible to support the system functions in most host languages, on most operating systems and with most graphics devices;

language independence: it should be possible to approach the standard facilities of the system from all standard programming languages;

efficiency: the system should be capable of being implemented via efficient algorithms;

robustness: the operator and the application programmer must be protected in the best possible way from hardware or software failures in the system.

The above five groups of principles are interconnected. For example, design goals and functional capabilities both contribute to user friendliness. Efficiency is also important when considering response time in an interactive environment. Some principles may be conflicting, such as richness versus minimality, comprehensive error handling versus efficiency, and compactness versus device richness.

Compromises need to be made in order to achieve the overall design objective: GKS should have an easily comprehensible structure and a set of functions that enables the vast majority of computer graphics users to design portable, device-independent application programs addressing the whole range of computer graphics equipment.

6 MAIN CONCEPTS
OF THE GRAPHICAL KERNEL SYSTEM

The main concepts of a graphics system are closely related to the tasks which such a system is intended to perform. Among these tasks are:

— the generation and representation of pictures;
— routing parts of pictures created in various user coordinate systems to different workstations and transforming them into the respective device coordinate systems;
— controlling the workstations attached to the system:
— handling input from workstations;
— allowing the structuring of pictures into parts that can be manipulated (displayed, transformed, copied, deleted) separately;
— the long-term storage of pictures.

Further concepts, which result from the need to present the standard in a concise manner and to ease the implementation and application of the system, are the representation of system states in state lists, the grouping of functions into distinct levels, and error handling. An important aspect of a graphics system is the dimensionality of the graphical objects it processes. The current GKS standard defines a purely two-dimensional (2D) system. However, a consistent extension of the standard into three dimensions (3D) is presently being defined.

Output: One of the basic tasks of a graphics system is to generate pictures. The concept corresponding to this task is graphical output. The objects from which a picture is built up are called output primitives; their visual appearance on the display surface of a workstation is controlled by a set of attributes (e.g., colour, linewidth).

Coordinate systems and transformations: The output primitives are created in one or more user coordinate systems. It should be possible for these primitives to be placed on the display surface of varying workstations which have different device coordinate systems. The path taken by graphical output from the application program to the display surface of a graphical device is called the "viewing pipeline". The routing and the transformation of output primitives along the viewing pipeline is performed by the graphics system. By using appropriate functions, the output transformations can be controlled by the application program. In 3D systems, a 3D viewing pipeline is used.

Workstations: Output devices and certain input devices can be assembled into groups called "graphical workstations" or just "workstations". They are usually operated by a single operator. A workstation might, for example, consist of a plotter or a display with a keyboard or a tablet connected to it. The workstation concept is one of the original contributions of GKS to the methodology of graphics system design.

Input: In order to be able to communicate with a workstation operator, the application program has to be provided with a means of obtaining input from a workstation. Besides dealing with input that is specific to graphical applications (coordinate data or the identification of a part of a picture), GKS also handles alphanumeric input, selection devices like function keys, and value-delivering devices like potentiometer dials. GKS handles input in a device-independent way by defining logical input devices.

Segmentation: The task of manipulating parts of pictures leads to the concept of segmentation. A picture is composed of parts, called segments, which can be displayed, transformed, copied, or deleted independently of each other. Segments can be identified by an operator and their identification passed to the application program. GKS contains a very powerful segment facility, primarily because it provides a workstation-independent segment storage together with functions for sending copies of segments to workstations or into other segments.

Metafile: The metafile is a means of storing pictures for archiving purposes and of transferring pictures to a different location or different system. The GKS metafile interface allows the long-term storage and retrieval of pictures. It adds considerably to the flexibility of the system.

State lists: At any point in time, GKS is in an operating state represented by the values in a number of state lists. These values are changed by GKS functions called by the application program. The state description includes such information as the set of workstations connected to the system at a given time and the set of segments in existence. The concept of states and state lists was developed during the design of GKS to make a clear and precise description of the effects of functions possible and to give assistance to implementors.

Levels: The 2D GKS functions are grouped into nine different levels. At the lowest level there is only a minimal set of output functions present, while the highest level includes all GKS functions. This allows an implementor to realize only that level of functionality that is needed for his range of applications. In GKS-3D, additional levels are introduced.

Error handling: Along with its functions, GKS defines a number of error conditions which might occur during the processing of each function. The application program can either define its own treatment of error handling or use a standard built-in error handling.

Dimensionality: For the majority of computer graphics applications a 2D system, such as GKS in its present form, will be sufficient. All output and input coordinates are then two-dimensional. Some applications, however, require 3D output primitives, such as lines or areas in 3D space, and even 3D coordinate input. An extension of GKS to three dimensions, involving adding a set of 3D functions, contained in separate levels, to the system, is currently being defined: this is described in Part IV. In the remainder of the book, only the 2D GKS standard is treated.

7   CREATING GRAPHICAL OUTPUT

7.1   Line Graphics and Raster Graphics

Pictures which are produced solely by output functions, without interaction with an operator, are referred to as passive output. The application programmer checks the result of his graphics program by looking at the output picture and changing the program if he wishes to have a different result. The opposite of passive output is interactive computer graphics (see Chapter 10). According to the type of output device used, output can be classified as line graphics or raster graphics.

Line graphics — Definition
    Computer graphics in which display images are generated from display commands and coordinate data.

The basic elements of line graphics pictures are usually vectors or sequences of vectors. Examples of line graphics devices include pen plotters and random scan displays. A typical feature of line drawing devices is a writing instrument (e.g., a pen or an electron beam) that can be positioned arbitrarily on the display surface. It can be moved to a different position with the writing instrument enabled or disabled (e.g., pen up or down), thus creating a visible vector or not. Refresh vector devices continuously rewrite all vectors in the picture in order to present a stable image to the human observer. The picture has to be stored for this purpose in a memory called the display file. GKS has output primitives for the convenient use of line graphics devices.

Raster graphics — Definition
    Computer graphics in which a display image is composed of an array of pixels arranged in rows and columns.

Pixel — Definition
    The smallest element of a display surface that can be independently assigned a colour or intensity.

The basic elements of a raster graphics picture are single dots of the display surface that can be addressed independently of each other. Examples of raster devices include raster colour displays (similar to television monitors) and electrostatic plotters. Usually, a raster device creates the picture line by line. Refresh raster devices repeatedly write all pixels on the screen at a given refresh rate (e.g., 25, 30, 50, or 60 times a second). Due to this the picture has to be stored in a memory called the pixel store or frame buffer.

GKS has special output primitives for addressing raster device capabilities. However, raster primitives can also be displayed on line graphics devices, just as line primitives can be displayed on raster devices.

Text can be displayed on both line and raster graphics devices. The graphical representation of characters will be broken down into the basic elements of the device (vectors or pixels) by a piece of hardware or software called a character generator. Figure 7.1 shows characters built up from vectors and pixels.

Character generator — Definition
    A functional unit that converts the coded representation of a character into the graphical representation of the character for display.

Characters built up   Characters built up from
from vectors   pixels

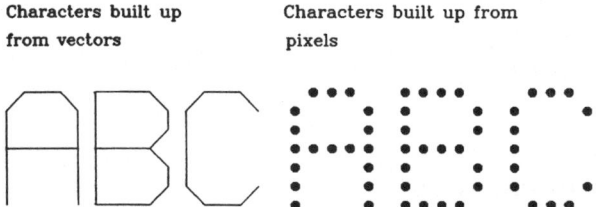

Figure 7.1 Character generation from vectors and pixels

7.2   Output Primitives and Attributes

The basic elements from which a picture is built up at the functional interface of a graphics system are called output primitives. They are specified by their geometry and by the way they appear on the display surface of a workstation. These aspects are controlled by a set of attributes belonging to the primitive. Certain attributes may vary from one workstation to another: e.g., a line may appear on one workstation black and dashed, and on another red and solid. These aspects of a primitive are called workstation-dependent attributes. In GKS, there are functions which create primitives and others which determine their attributes. For certain attributes, the application program can select whether or not the attribute (e.g., linetype or polyline colour) is to be set in a workstation-dependent way.

Output primitive — Definition

A basic graphic element that can be used to construct a display image. Output primitives in GKS are POLYLINE, POLYMARKER, TEXT, FILL AREA, CELL ARRAY, and GENERALIZED DRAWING PRIMITIVE.

Display image — Definition

A collection of display elements or segments that are represented together at any one time on a display surface.

Attribute — Definition

A particular property that applies to an output primitive or a segment. (N.B.: In GKS some properties of workstations are called workstation attributes.)

7.2.1 Output Primitives

GKS provides six output primitives: one line-primitive, one point-primitive, one text-primitive, two raster-primitives and one general purpose primitive serving as an entry point for specific workstation capabilities.

Line-primitive

POLYLINE: GKS generates a set of straight lines connecting a given point sequence.

Point-primitive

POLYMARKER: GKS generates symbols of a particular type centred on given positions. The symbols are called markers; these are glyphs with specified appearances which are used to identify a set of locations.

Text-primitive

TEXT: GKS generates a character string at a given position.

Raster-primitives

FILL AREA: GKS generates a polygon which may be hollow or filled with a uniform colour, a pattern, or a hatch style.

CELL ARRAY: GKS generates an array of rectangular cells with individual colours. This is a generalization of an array of pixels on a raster device. However, the cells of this primitive need not correspond one-to-one with the pixels defined by the display hardware.

General Purpose Primitive

GENERALIZED DRAWING PRIMITIVE (GDP): GKS addresses special
   geometrical output capabilities of a workstation, such as the drawing of
   spline curves, circular arcs, and elliptic arcs. The objects are characterized
   by an identifier, a set of points and additional data. GKS applies all transformations to the points but leaves the interpretation to the workstation.

Examples of the various output primitives are shown in Figure 7.2. This figure
was produced on a vector type workstation. Examples of the output primitives
generated on a raster type workstation are shown in Figure C1 (page 618).

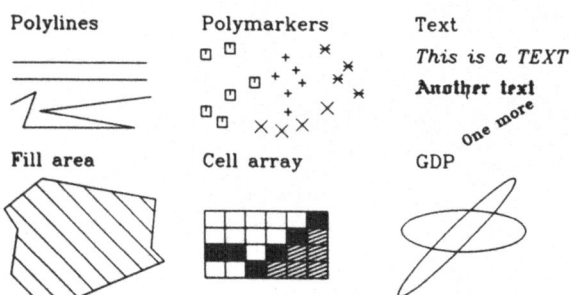

Figure 7.2 Examples of GKS
output primitives

7.2.2   Output Primitive Attributes

Table 7.1 lists, for each output primitive, the set of attributes which govern
its appearance.

The attributes describe the following aspects of output primitives:

Pick identifier — Definition
   A number assigned to individual output primitives within a segment and
   returned by the pick device. The same pick identifier can be assigned to
   different output primitives.

Pick identifiers only have significance in conjunction with the input functions
used for identification of segments by an operator (see Chapter 10).

Linetype — Definition
   Linetypes are used to distinguish different styles of lines. A line may be,
   e.g., solid, dashed, or dashed-dotted. Some examples of linetypes are illustrated in Figure 7.3.

Linewidth scale factor — Definition
   The actual width of a line is given by a nominal linewidth multiplied by
   the linewidth scale factor. Examples of different linewidths are shown in
   Figure 7.3.

Table 7.1 Output primitive attributes

Primitive	Attributes	
POLYLINE	PICK IDENTIFIER LINEWIDTH SCALE FACTOR	LINETYPE COLOUR
POLYMARKER	PICK IDENTIFIER MARKER SIZE SCALE FACTOR	MARKER TYPE COLOUR
TEXT	PICK IDENTIFIER CHARACTER HEIGHT CHARACTER UP VECTOR CHARACTER EXPANSION FACTOR CHARACTER SPACING	TEXT PATH TEXT FONT TEXT PRECISION TEXT ALIGNMENT COLOUR
FILL AREA	PICK IDENTIFIER PATTERN SIZE PATTERN REFERENCE POINT PATTERN ARRAY	INTERIOR STYLE HATCH STYLE COLOUR
CELL ARRAY	PICK IDENTIFIER	COLOUR
GENERALIZED DRAWING PRIMITIVE	PICK IDENTIFIER dependent on the type of GDP	

Colour — Definition
    The colour is specified by the Red, Green, and Blue intensities (RGB values)
    defining a particular colour.

The RGB colour model can be visualized by means of a colour cube (cf.
Figure C5, page 620). The three axes of a 3D coordinate system whose origin
coincides with one corner of the cube represent the red, green, and blue intensities. Each intensity can vary between 0 and 1. Every point within the cube
(including its surface) represents a unique colour. RGB values (0,0,0) represent
black, and (1,1,1) white.

Marker type — Definition
    The marker type is a number specifying the particular glyph used for identifi-
    cation of the polymarker positions.

Marker size scale factor — Definition
    The actual marker size is given by a nominal marker size multiplied by
    the marker size scale factor.

Various different marker types and marker sizes are shown in Figure 7.3.

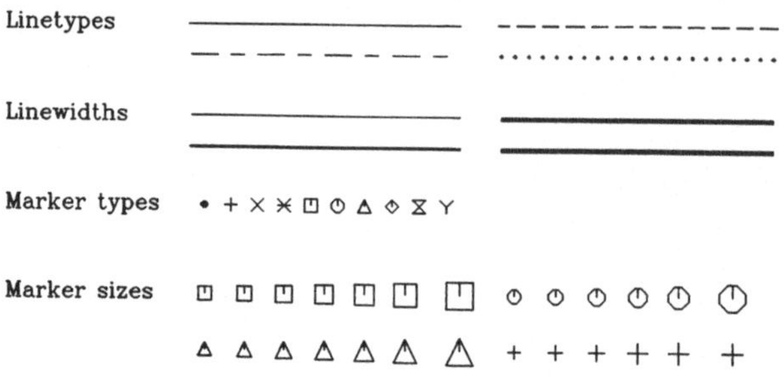

Linetypes

Linewidths

Marker types   • + × ✳ □ ☉ △ ◇ ⅀ Y

Marker sizes   □ □ □ □ □ □ □   ○ ○ ○ ○ ○ ○

△ △ △ △ △ △ △ + + + + + +

Figure 7.3 Examples of polyline and polymarker attributes

Text font — Definition
The text font is a number selecting one representation for the text string characters from the options available on a given workstation. Examples of text fonts are shown in Figure 7.4.

Text precision — Definition
An attribute describing the fidelity with which the character position, character size, character orientation, and text font of text output match those requested by an application. In order of increasing fidelity, the precisions are string, character, and stroke.

Normally, text generated by hardware character generators will only be available in restricted sizes or orientations. If, for example, text can only be displayed horizontally in one of three different character sizes, the text precision is STRING. STROKE text precision usually requires a software character generator.

Character height — Definition
The vertical extent of a character.

Character up vector — Definition
The "Up" direction of a character.

Character expansion factor — Definition
The deviation of the width/height ratio of a character from the ratio defined by the text font designer.

Text path — Definition
The writing direction of the character sequence. The normal path as used in this book is "right", i.e., the text you are reading is written from left to right. GKS also allows the text path values left, up, and down.

Character spacing — Definition
Space to be inserted between adjacent characters of a text string, in addition to the space defined by the font designer.

Text alignment — Definition
> A text attribute describing how the text string is positioned relative to the reference point of the text primitive (e.g., left aligned or centred).

Figure 7.4 gives examples of different values of character height, character up vector, expansion factor, path, spacing, and alignment.

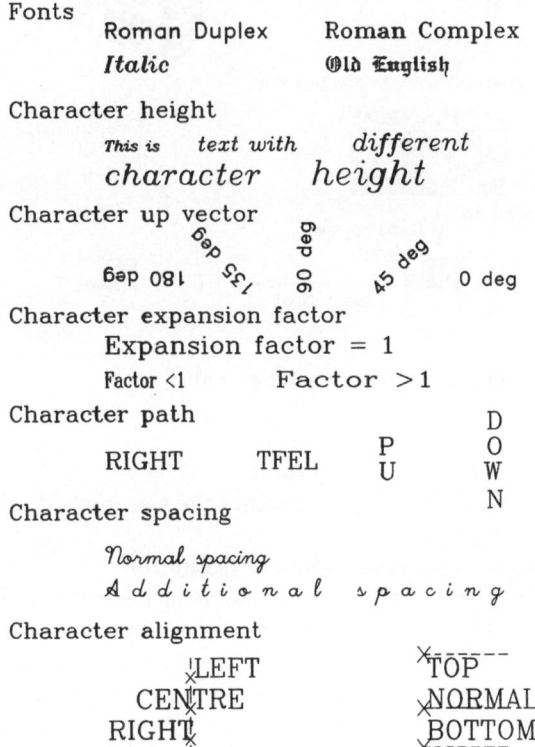

Figure 7.4 Examples of text attributes

Interior style — Definition
> The interior style is used to determine the style in which an area should be filled. It has one of the values hollow, solid, pattern, or hatch.

Figure 7.5 gives examples of different interior styles. This figure was generated on a black and white raster plotter. Examples of fill areas of different interior styles generated on a colour raster workstation are shown in Figure C2 (page 618). Fill areas with interior style SOLID were used to create Figures C4 (page 619) and C5 (page 620). In the case of the interior style PATTERN, a pattern defined by the pattern size, the pattern reference point and the pattern array is repeated until it fills the area.

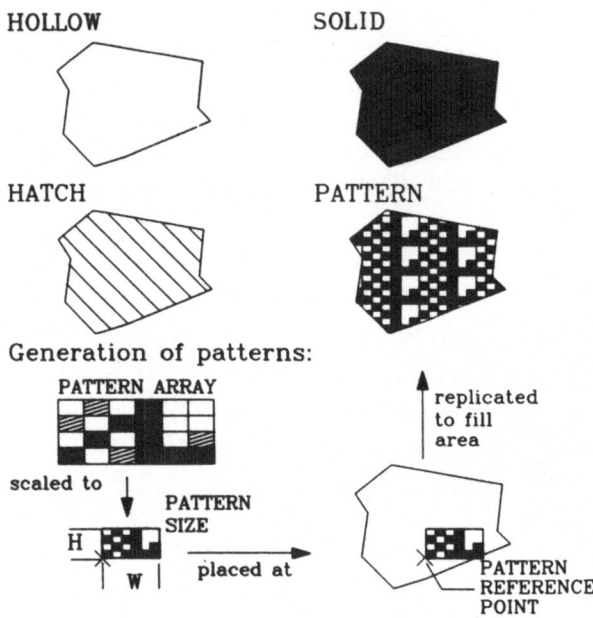

Figure 7.5 Examples of fill area attributes

Pattern size — Definition
   The pattern size specifies the size of the basic pattern rectangle.

Pattern reference point — Definition
   The pattern reference point specifies the origin of the basic pattern rectangle.
   The lower left corner of the rectangle is placed at the reference point, and
   the pattern is then repeated in both directions until the whole area is filled.

Pattern array — Definition
   A pattern is defined by an array of rectangular cells, each having a colour
   assigned to it. These values are used to assign colours to the basic pattern
   rectangle and to all replications of it. Figure 7.5 gives an example of a
   fill area primitive with a pattern.

Hatch style — Definition
   Hatching is specified by a number selecting a hatch style defined by the
   implementor and available on a workstation.

7.3   Indices, Bundles, and Tables

Some attributes are always specified in a workstation-independent way, whereas
others are always workstation-dependent. For most attributes, however, the
application program can specify whether or not it chooses to make the attributes

workstation-dependent. The workstation-independent attributes are modally set by GKS functions, i.e., after an attribute has been set, it is used for all subsequently generated primitives as long as it is not changed.

Example:

SET CHARACTER HEIGHT (hvalue)   {stores the value "hvalue"}
TEXT (point, 'ABC')   {this text will be generated using character height "hvalue"}

The workstation-dependent attributes (with the exception of colours and patterns) are specified by using an index associated with the primitive. This index points into a table available at each workstation for different types of primitives. The set of workstation-dependent attributes for each primitive type is called a bundle, and the table that contains the attributes is called a bundle table. For example, in the case of polylines, the POLYLINE INDEX points to a polyline bundle table which contains linewidth, linetype and a colour index (cf. Figure 7.6). The indices POLYLINE INDEX, POLYMARKER INDEX, TEXT INDEX, and FILL AREA INDEX can be set modally, and they are then used for displaying subsequently created primitives of each respective type.

For each of those attributes that can be workstation-dependent or not there is a global switch called an "aspect source flag (ASF)". These flags can have either one of two values, BUNDLED (workstation-dependent) or INDIVID-UAL (workstation-independent). Thus, they select the "attribute binding mode".

Bundle index — Definition
An index pointing to a bundle table for a particular output primitive. It defines the workstation-dependent aspects of the primitive.

Bundle table — Definition
A workstation-dependent table associated with a particular output primitive. Entries in the table specify all the workstation-dependent aspects of a primitive. In GKS, bundle tables exist for the following output primitives: polyline, polymarker, text, and fill area.

Polyline bundle table — Definition
A table which associates specific values for all workstation-dependent aspects of a polyline primitive with a polyline bundle index. In GKS, this table contains entries for linetype, linewidth scale factor, and colour index.

Polymarker bundle table — Definition
A table which associates specific values for all workstation-dependent aspects of a polymarker primitive with a polymarker bundle index. In GKS, this table contains entries for marker type, marker size scale factor, and colour index.

Text bundle table — Definition
A table of specific values for all workstation-dependent aspects of a text

primitive. In GKS, this table contains entries for text font, text precision, character expansion factor, character spacing, and colour index.

The entries in the bundle tables are predefined by the system implementor, according to the capabilities of the workstation. However, the entries can be changed by GKS functions. Furthermore, the initial setting of the attribute source flags is implementation-dependent. They can be reset individually at any time by the application program. An important property of workstation-dependent attributes is that they can be used to vary the picture already present on the display surface. If the value of an attribute is changed, e.g., an RGB value in the colour table, the primitives already in existence and using these attributes will change their appearance accordingly. (This only works properly for primitives contained in segments.) Attributes assigned to primitives in the INDIVIDUAL attribute binding mode cannot be changed at a later stage.

Colour is a workstation-dependent attribute which is addressed via a colour index in the attribute bundle tables. The colour index points to a colour table which associates RGB values with the colour indices. If entries in the colour table are changed while a picture is being displayed on a workstation, the colours of the primitives being displayed will change accordingly. An example of this is given in Fig. C6 on page 620.

Colour table — Definition
A workstation-dependent table, the entries of which specify the values of the red, green, and blue intensities which thus define a particular colour.

Figure 7.6 shows the set of attributes and their interrelation for polyline output primitives, when all the attribute source flags for the polyline primitive are set to BUNDLED. A similar figure could be drawn for polymarkers and texts.

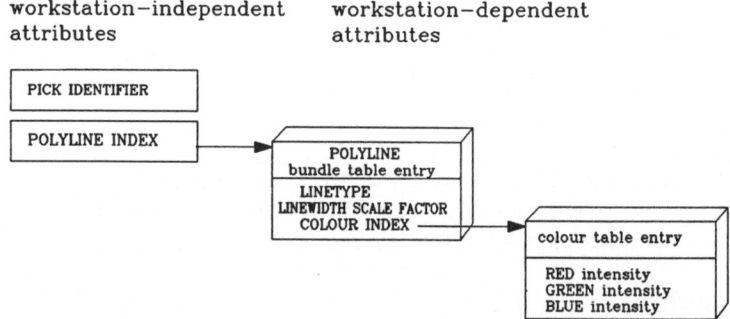

Figure 7.6 Relationship between polyline attributes for the BUNDLED attribute binding mode

Figure 7.7 shows the set of attributes and their interrelation for polyline output primitives when all the attribute source flags for the polyline primitive are set to INDIVIDUAL.

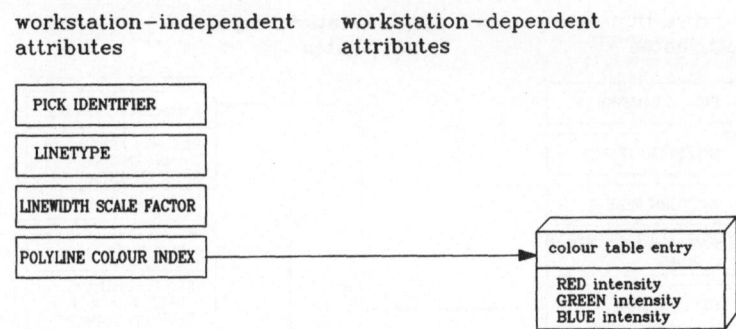

Figure 7.7 Relationship between polyline attributes for the INDIVIDUAL attribute binding mode

The basic scheme for the fill area primitive is similar, although here, the fill area bundle (and the alternate set of individual attributes) contains a style index which is used to select a pattern or a hatch style. In the case of the interior style "pattern", the style index points to a table containing dimensions and colour indices of pattern arrays. The pattern thus identified by the style index will be used, together with the modal fill area attributes, pattern size and pattern reference point, to fill the area. If the interior style is "hatch", the style index is used to select one of the hatch styles supplied by the implementation. Apart from the implementation-defined hatch styles, no other hatching is available.

Fill area bundle table — Definition

A table which associates specific values for all workstation-dependent aspects of a fill area primitive with a fill area bundle index. In GKS, this table contains entries for interior style, style index, and colour index.

Figure 7.8 gives an overview of the relationship between the different fill area attributes when all the attribute source flags for the fill area primitive are set to BUNDLED. Figure 7.9 gives an overview of the fill area attributes, when

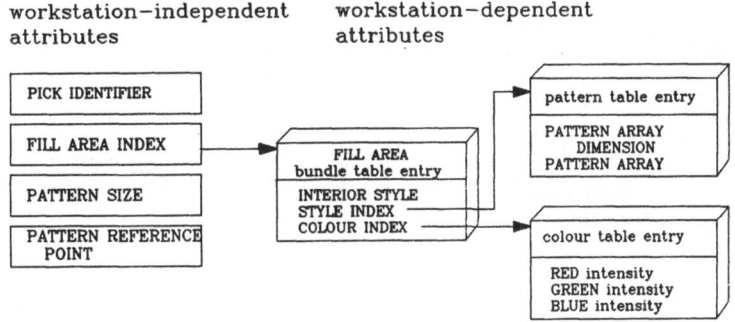

Figure 7.8 Relationship between fill area attributes for the BUNDLED attribute binding mode

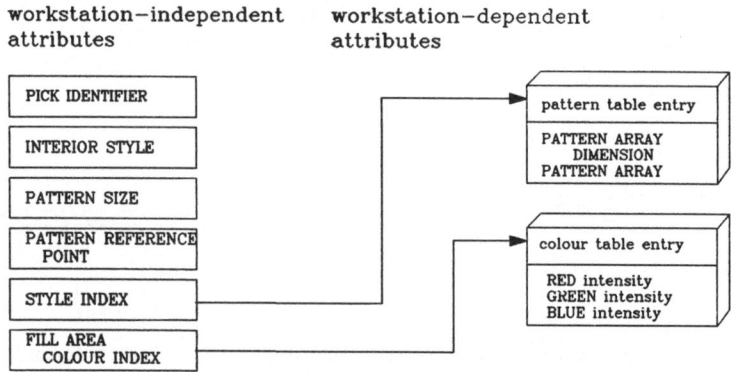

Figure 7.9 Relationship between fill area attributes for the INDIVIDUAL attribute binding mode

all the attribute source flags for the fill area primitive are set to INDIVIDUAL.

The scheme for cell arrays is different: here there is a set of colour indices together with the primitive function. These colour indices refer directly to a colour table as seen in Fig. 7.10. Figure C3 on page 619 shows a cell array generated on a colour raster workstation.

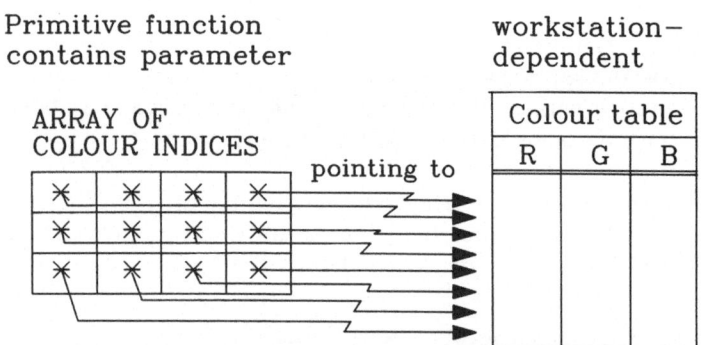

Figure 7.10 Colour specification for the cell array primitive

The generalized drawing primitive (GDP) uses whatever attribute bundles or individual attributes the implementor of a specific GDP chooses. There is no special GDP bundle.

8   COORDINATE SYSTEMS AND TRANSFORMATIONS

8.1   Coordinate Systems

The application programmer wants to define his graphical elements in a coordinate system that is related to his application. However, the devices that are available for presenting a visual image of these elements normally need to use a device-specific coordinate system. In order to meet these requirements while maintaining device independence, three coordinate systems have been defined in GKS. Firstly (the following information is related to 2D GKS), there is the world coordinate (WC) system which the application programmer uses to specify the elements of the picture. The world coordinate system is the standard user coordinate system.

World coordinates (WC) — Definition
   A device-independent Cartesian coordinate system used by the application program to specify graphical input and output.

If the application program wants to use other kinds of coordinate systems (e.g., polar coordinates), it must complete the necessary transformations before entering GKS. In principle, every output primitive is defined with its own world coordinate system.
   Since different output devices have different device coordinate systems, GKS defines, as an abstraction of these device coordinate systems, one single normalized device coordinate (NDC) space. The relative positioning of output primitives is defined by mapping all the defined world coordinate systems onto the NDC space.

Normalized device coordinates (NDC) — Definition
   A device-independent intermediate coordinate system, normalized into a range which in GKS is normally 0 to 1.

Although NDC space in principle extends to infinity, the part of NDC space in which the viewport must be located and that can be viewed at a workstation is the bounded region $[0,1] \times [0,1]$. The normalized picture in NDC space can be stored and manipulated via the segment mechanism; it can also be stored on a metafile.
   The NDC space is mapped onto the device coordinates (DC) of every workstation which is to display the picture. Every type of workstation may have a different device coordinate space and a different mapping. The device coordinate space is always a bounded space since it represents the extension of the display surface of a physical, and hence bounded, device. The DC unit is normally the metre. In GKS, however, functions are available to find the relationship between the specific device units and metres.

Device coordinates (DC) — Definition
A device-dependent coordinate system. N.B.: In GKS, the DC unit is the metre on devices capable of producing a precisely scaled image. If this is not the case an appropriate workstation-dependent unit can be chosen.

8.2   Transformations

A set of normalization transformations map the world coordinate systems onto the single NDC space. A set of workstation transformations map NDC space onto every one of the active workstations. These transformations define the viewing pipeline from the application program onto the display surface of the workstation and the input pipeline for locator input devices from the locator position in DC to the application program. Other types of transformations can be applied to segments; these transformations take place in the NDC space. Figure 8.1 shows the coordinate systems and the applicable transformations. The normalization transformation is explained below, the workstation transformation in Section 9.3, and the segment transformations in Section 11.4.

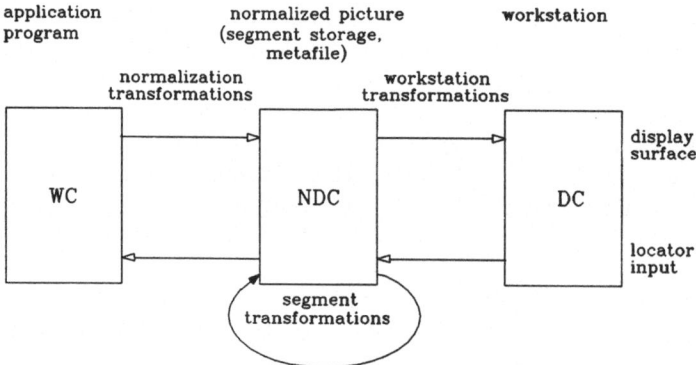

Figure 8.1 Coordinate systems and transformations

8.3   The Normalization Transformation

During output, a single normalization transformation is active at any one time and this is used to transform world coordinates, specified in output primitives or geometric attributes, into normalized device coordinates. A normalization transformation is specified by defining the limits of the area in the world coordinate system (window) which is to be mapped onto a specified area of the normalized device coordinate space (viewport), as shown in Figure 8.2.

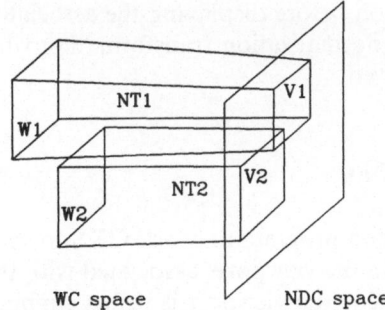

W=Window,V=Viewport,NT=Normalization Transformation

Figure 8.2 Normalization transformation

Normalization transformation — Definition

A transformation which maps the boundary and interior of a window to the boundary and interior of a viewport. N.B.: In GKS, this transformation transforms world coordinates into normalized device coordinates.

Window — Definition

A predefined part of a virtual space. N.B.: In GKS, this definition is restricted to a rectangular region within the world coordinate space used for the definition of the normalization transformation.

Viewport — Definition

An application-program-specified part of normalized device coordinate space. N.B.: In GKS, this definition is restricted to the rectangular region within the normalized device coordinate space used in the definition of the normalization transformation.

Window and viewport limits specify rectangles parallel to the coordinate axes in WC and NDC. A normalization transformation includes translation and differential scaling with positive scale factors for the two axes. A number of normalization transformations can be defined in GKS at any one time. One of these is selected whenever graphical output is to be generated. Each normalization transformation is identified by a transformation number which is an integer between 0 and an implementation-dependent value n. The normalization transformation with the transformation number 0 is the unity transformation which maps $[0,1] \times [0,1]$ in world coordinates onto $[0,1] \times [0,1]$ in normalized device coordinates. It cannot be reset.

Initially, all other normalization transformations are set to a default transformation which is the same as transformation number 0. They may be reset to different transformations at any time when GKS is open. Since GKS provides a number of different normalization transformations, it is possible for the application program to specify them prior to graphical output being produced. The separate parts of the picture are produced by selecting a particular normalization transformation before displaying the associated graphical primitives. However, redefining a normalization transformation while the graphical output is taking place is allowed.

8.4 Clipping

The application program may ask GKS to show only those parts of the picture that lie within the viewports associated with the picture elements. Cutting away all parts outside the viewport is called clipping (another type of clipping takes place at the workstation, cf. Section 9.3). Clipping can be turned on or off by the application program.

Clipping — Definition
>   Removing the parts of the display elements which lie outside a given area, which is usually a window or a viewport.

Clipping does not take place while the normalization transformation is being performed but is delayed until the output primitives are to be displayed on the view surface of a workstation. Output primitives which are stored in segments will have had their coordinates transformed to NDC and the associated clipping rectangle will have been stored with the primitives.

9 THE GRAPHICAL WORKSTATION

In GKS, the graphical workstations are an abstraction of physical devices. An abstract graphical workstation can have the following set of properties (in practice, the workstation may or may not be equipped with all of these capabilities):

— it has one addressable display surface with a fixed resolution;
— it allows only rectangular display spaces (the display space cannot consist of a number of separate parts);
— it permits the specification and use of smaller display spaces than the maximum, while guaranteeing that no display image is generated outside the specified display space (this guaranteed behaviour is referred to as "workstation clipping");
— it provides several linetypes, text fonts, character sizes, etc., so that output primitives can be drawn with different attributes;
— it has one or more logical input devices for each input class and permits different input modes (cf. following chapter);
— it stores segments and provides facilities for changing and manipulating them (cf. Chapter 11).

In GKS, it is possible for the appearance of the output primitives to vary between workstations so that advantage can be taken of their differing capabilities. The facilities which allow this variation are the attribute bundles (described in Section 7.5), the indices pointing to the bundle entries, and the workstation transformation which can be set individually for every workstation. A deferral state allows the operator to be able to control the point in time when an updating of the display surface is required (e.g., a plotter may be driven by buffered output, while an interactive workstation will display picture changes as soon as possible).

At a workstation, display images will be presented within the display space on the display surface of a display device (e.g., a picture will be displayed within that part of the screen defined as the workstation viewport of a storage tube display).

Display device — Definition
    A device (e.g., a refresh display, a storage tube display, or a plotter) on which display images can be presented.

Display image (picture) — Definition
    A collection of display elements or segments which are presented together at any one time on a display surface.

Display surface — Definition
    In a display device, the medium on which display images may appear.

Display space — Definition
    That portion of the device space which corresponds to the area available for displaying images.

9.1 Routing Output to Workstations

The workstations are identified by the application program by using a workstation identifier. In order to establish a connection between the application program and a workstation, that workstation has to be opened. The connection is broken and interactions are no longer possible if the workstation is closed. Output primitives are sent to an open workstation only after it has been activated for output. A function is available for clearing the display surface, i.e., erasing the display image. After deactivation, output will no longer be sent to the workstation. Input can be performed at all open workstations.

The following sequence of functions illustrates how workstations are selected. It also includes the functions for opening and closing GKS.

```
OPEN GKS;                          {start working}
  OPEN WORKSTATION (N1,...);        {open workstations}
  OPEN WORKSTATION (N2,...);
    ACTIVATE WORKSTATION (N1);      {allow output on N1}
```

Output functions;	{generated only on N1}
Input functions;	{possible on N1, N2}
ACTIVATE WORKSTATION (N2);	{output also on N2}
Output functions;	{generated on N1, N2}
DEACTIVATE WORKSTATION (N1);	{no more output on N1}
Output functions;	{generated only on N2}
Input functions;	{possible on N1, N2}
DEACTIVATE WORKSTATION (N2);	{no more output}
CLOSE WORKSTATION (N2);	{close workstations}
CLOSE WORKSTATION (N1);	
CLOSE GKS;	{finish working}

9.2   Types of GKS Workstations

Each type of workstation falls into one of six categories:

— output workstation, which has a display surface for displaying output primitives (e.g., a plotter);
— input workstation, which has at least one input device (e.g., a digitizer);
— output/input workstation, which has a display surface and at least one input device (this is also called an interactive graphical workstation);
— workstation-independent segment storage (WISS, cf. Section 11.5);
— metafile output (cf. Chapter 12);
— metafile input (cf. Chapter 12).

The last three (workstation-independent segment storage, metafile output, and metafile input) are special GKS facilities which provide a means of temporarily or permanently storing graphical information. They are treated as workstations for the purposes of control, but otherwise have quite different characteristics. The metafiles treated by GKS are the GKS Metafile (GKSM) and the Computer Graphics Metafile (CGM).

9.3   The Workstation Transformation

At every open workstation, the application program can independently select any part of the NDC space within the range $[0,1] \times [0,1]$ which is to be displayed anywhere on the workstation display surface. A workstation transformation is a uniform mapping from NDC space onto the device coordinates (DC) specific to that workstation. Figure 9.1 elaborates on Figure 8.2 by including the workstation transformation.

Whereas the normalization transformation is used to compose a picture, the workstation transformation allows different aspects of the composed picture to be viewed at different workstations. For example, a drawing can be sent to a plotter on the correct scale and simultaneously a particular part of the

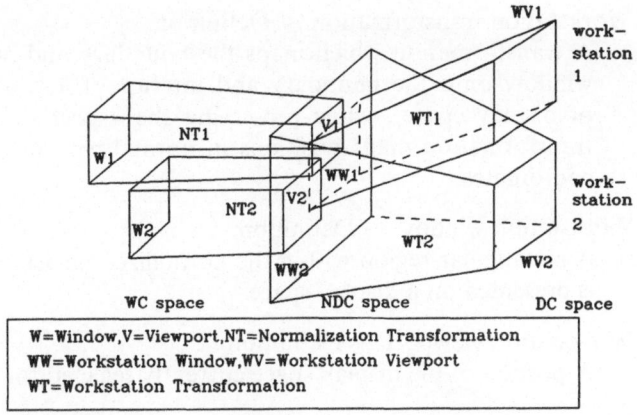

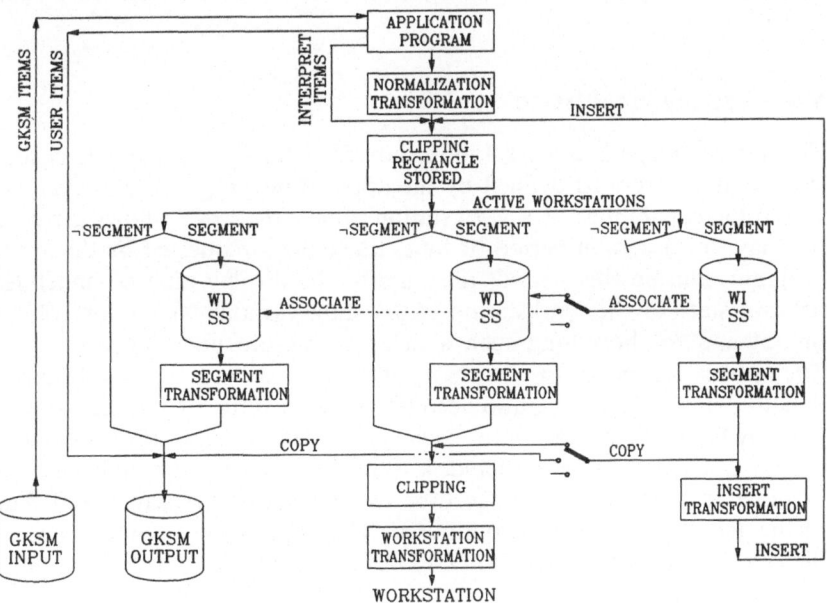

Figure 9.1 Normalization transformation and workstation transformation

Figure 9.2 Data flow chart for GKS output

drawing can be displayed on the full display surface of an interactive workstation. The workstation transformation can be reset at any time after the workstation has been opened.

A workstation transformation is specified by defining the limits of the area in the normalized device coordinate system within the range $[0,1] \times [0,1]$ (workstation window) which is to be mapped onto a specified area of the device coordinate space (workstation viewport). The workstation window and workstation viewport are rectangles parallel to the coordinate axes in NDC and DC, respectively.

Workstation transformation — Definition

A transformation which maps the boundary and interior of a workstation window onto the boundary and interior of a workstation viewport (part of display space), while preserving the aspect ratio. N.B.: In GKS, this transformation maps positions in normalized device coordinates to device coordinates.

Workstation window — Definition

A rectangular region within the normalized device coordinate system which is presented on a display space.

Workstation viewport — Definition

A portion of the display space currently selected for the output of graphics.

A complete data flow chart for graphical output is given in Figure 9.2. This is taken from the GKS standard document. For more information about the parts of this figure related to segments and metafiles, refer to Chapters 11 and 12.

9.4   The Deferral State

The display image at a workstation should, as far as possible, reflect the actual state of the picture as defined by the application program. However, in order to use the capabilities of a workstation efficiently, GKS allows a workstation to delay, for a certain period of time, the actions requested by the application program. During this period, the state of the display may be undefined. The deferral state of the workstation is the state variable which controls whether or not and for how long such a delay of picture updating can be allowed. The application program can change the deferral state. However, appropriate default values which take into account the workstation characteristics are supplied by the implementation for each type of workstation. For example, plotter output can normally be buffered, a refresh display can be updated as quickly as possible, and with a storage tube the erasing of the screen and redrawing of the actual picture can be optimised. The application program can force the display to be updated (using the UPDATE WORKSTATION function).

9.5   Addressing Special Workstation Capabilities

Some present workstations may provide more capabilities than those listed in the workstation description table. These cannot be used by GKS. However, if the workstation itself provides sufficient intelligence, the additional capabilities may be accessed via some special functions. One such function, already introduced, is the GENERALIZED DRAWING PRIMITIVE (GDP) that can be used to create geometrical output at a workstation. Another such function is the ESCAPE function which provides the standard way of addressing nonstandard features. It cannot be used for geometrical output. It could be used, for example, to ring a bell at the workstation or to address raster-op hardware.

Escape — Definition
   A function within GKS which provides the only access to non-GKS func-
   tions which are supported by the implementation of a particular device.
   It cannot be used for graphic output.

Another function which is realized in a workstation-specific way is the MES-
SAGE function. It allows a character string to be sent to a workstation. The
application program has no control over the position and appearance of the
character string, but nevertheless, the message must definitely reach the operator.

10   INPUT

10.1   Interactive Computer Graphics

If a graphics system can not only generate pictures on the display surface of a
graphical output device, but can also receive input that an operator has entered
at a graphical workstation, a new dimension is added to the computer graphics
world. It is this new dimension of interaction that has resulted in the ever
faster growing use of computer graphics devices and systems. The actions of
pointing, selecting, sketching, placing or erasing in a direct manner and the
instantaneous system response to these actions are truly adapted to the way
humans deal with their environment. Interactive computer graphics makes such
interactions possible. It is the most powerful instrument in adapting the human–
computer interface to human needs.
   GKS contains functions that allow the input of values from different classes
of input devices in different operating modes. The characteristics of different
types of physical input devices are mapped onto logical input devices in order
to address a wide range of equipment in a device-independent way. GKS uses
an input model which describes input devices in terms of logical and physical
input devices and the mappings between them. This model (including measures
and triggers of logical input devices) is explained completely in Chapter III.8.

10.2   Logical Input Device Classes

A logical input device provides the application program with a logical input
value. The type of input value is determined by the input class.

Logical input device — Definition
   A logical input device is an abstraction of one or more physical devices.
   It delivers logical input values to the program.

Logical input value — Definition
This is a value associated with a logical input device. It is determined by one or more physical input devices, together with a mapping from the values delivered by the physical devices.

Input class — Definition
A set of input devices that are logically equivalent to each other with respect to their function is an input class.

Input classes — Definition

LOCATOR: provides a position in world coordinates. The position is provided by an operator positioning a locator input device (e.g., moving a crosshair with a joystick or positioning a pen on a tablet).

STROKE: provides a sequence of positions in world coordinates. The positions are provided by an operator positioning a locator input device at a number of different locations.

VALUATOR: provides a real number. This value is provided by an operator operating a valuator input device (e.g., by adjusting a potentiometer or by entering a number into a keyboard).

CHOICE: provides a non-negative integer which represents a selection from a number of choices. A choice value is provided by an operator choosing one possibility at a choice input device (e.g., by pressing one of a number of buttons or by pointing at one of the items of a menu).

PICK: provides a segment name and a pick identifier. A segment is picked by an operator pointing to a part of the picture displayed to him by the system (e.g., he may use a lightpen or may position the crosshair with a joystick to point to a primitive on the screen). Pick identifiers are explained in Chapter 11.

STRING: provides a character string. A character string is entered by an operator using a string input device (the most common string input device being an alphanumeric keyboard).

Of these logical input device classes, only the locator, the stroke, and the pick input can be called truly graphical. However, for the design of a powerful interactive communication interface between an application program and an operator, all the classes of input defined above will probably be needed. Therefore, they have been included in the GKS functionality so that no other additional system is required for handling non-graphical interactions.

10.3   Operating Modes

Each logical input device can be operated in one of three different operating modes. The operating mode is selected by the application program. Only one of the modes can be used to obtain input from a given logical input device at one time. The three operating modes are REQUEST, SAMPLE and EVENT. Depending on the mode, input values can be entered by the operator and passed to the application program in different ways:

Operating modes — Definition

> *REQUEST:* When an input function is called in REQUEST mode an attempt is then made to read a logical input value from a specified logical input device. GKS waits until either the input is entered or a break action is performed by the operator. The break action depends on the logical input device and on the implementation.

> *SAMPLE:* When an input function is called in SAMPLE mode it causes GKS to return the current logical input value of a specified logical input device, without waiting for the operator to act. The device must be in SAMPLE mode.

> *EVENT:* GKS maintains one input queue containing temporally ordered event reports. An event report contains the identification of a logical input device and a logical input value from that device. Event reports, which can only be created by the actions of the operator, are generated asynchronously from the input devices in EVENT mode. The application program can remove the oldest event report from the queue and examine its contents. The application program can also flush from the queue all event reports from a specified logical input device.

The request input mode reads input from a graphical workstation in very much the same way as a normal FORTRAN READ would read text input from the terminal. The application program can only request an input from one specific input device at a time. This leads to a dialogue which is completely controlled by the application program, e.g., an operator is not free to enter a locator or a choice at a given point in time, while using request input. The operator can interrupt the input request by performing an implementation-dependent break action. This could mean pressing a "break" key at the workstation. In this case, the application program will be notified that a break has occurred and no valid input value will be supplied.

With the sample and event input modes, the operator can choose to operate any one of several input devices. All logical input devices in sample or event mode are open to the actions of the operator. The difference between the two is that in sample mode the current value of the device can be determined by the application program, irrespective of whether the operator has changed the value (or even touched the device), while in event input mode, distinct operator actions are needed to transfer the value of a device to the event queue.

For example, in sample mode, an operator uses a joystick to change the value of a locator input device. The application program can read this value in a loop and use it to generate a new transformation matrix, which is then applied to a group of segments. If the loop is executed quickly enough, the operator will have the impression that the segment transformations have been directly caused by his operating the joystick. If at the same time the keyboard and a function keyboard are in event mode, the operator can notify the program via these input devices whether he wants to modify or finish the ongoing operation. To make this possible the application program will inspect the event queue every time the loop is executed.

10.4   Echoes, Prompts, and Input Device Initialisation

When the application program wants the operator to feed in an input value, it has to notify him that an action is expected (in request mode) or possible (in sample or event mode). This signal to the operator, telling him to do something, is called a prompt. Prompting could be done by displaying graphics primitives (e.g. the text "enter value") on the display surface, or the message function. However, there are special prompting capabilities associated with graphical input devices. These capabilities can be controlled by the application program. For locator devices, the prompt may be the appearance of a crosshair or tracking cross, for text, the appearance of the alphanumeric cursor, or for a choice device realized by a function keybord, it may be the flashing of the prompting lights.

Prompt — Definition
   Output to the operator, indicating that a specific logical input device is available.

When an interaction with an input device is taking place, the input device has a value which can be changed by the operator. The operator has to be notified about the current value. This notification is called an echo. For locator and stroke input devices, an echo could be a crosshair or a tracking cross positioned at the current locator position, for text, the visual presentation of the text string characters on the screen, for a pick input device, the blinking of the currently picked segment. Examples for locator and valuator echoes are shown in Figure 10.1.

Echo — Definition
   The immediate notification of the operator at the display console about the current value provided by an input device.

In the case of request input, the current value must be transferred to the application program by a distinct action on the part of the operator, for example, he presses a button after having positioned the locator. In the case of event output, a distinct action is again necessary to cause the transfer of the current value to the event queue. The echo notifying the operator that such a distinct action has been received is called an acknowledgement.

Acknowledgement — Definition
   Output to the operator of a logical input device stating that an operator action to indicate a distinct point of time has been received.

The echo and the acknowledgement, as well as the prompt, are realized by logical input devices mapped onto physical input devices. The application pro-

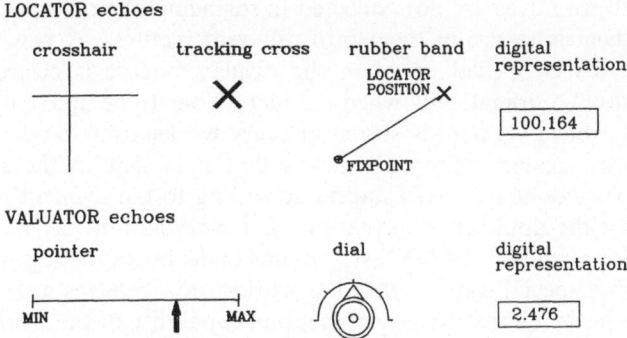

Figure 10.1 Examples for locator and valuator echoes

gram can control these indicators because it can turn echoes and prompts on or off and select one of different echo/prompt types available at a particular input device. However, it cannot generate its own new echo/prompt types. If an echo is generated by displaying output primitives after the application program has interpreted the input value, such an echo is called feedback. In the example in the previous section, where segment transformations are derived from a locator input value, the change of the size, orientation, or position of the segments on the screen is feedback about the locator movements.

Feedback — Definition
   Output indicating to the operator the application program's interpretation of a logical input value.

When interaction with an input device starts, i.e., an input is requested or sample or event mode is enabled, the logical input value is given an initial value. This value can be set by the application program. If echoing or prompting is turned on, it will reflect this initial value until it is changed by the operator's actions.

11   SEGMENTS

11.1   Structuring Pictures

A picture is composed of output primitives. These can be grouped together in parts which can be addressed and manipulated as a whole. These picture parts are called segments.

Segment — Definition
   A collection of output primitives which can be manipulated as a unit.

If primitives are not collected in segments, the only possible way of structuring them is to group them into different pictures. A new picture is started when GKS is opened or when the display surface is cleared (the latter may also result automatically when the picture has to be updated).

Each segment is stored at every workstation active at the time the segment was created. "Stored" means that it is sent to the workstation and that it behaves at that workstation according to the segment manipulations requested by the application program. If a workstation has no real storing capability for segments, the GKS system has to deal with the segments for this workstation in a special way, so that the workstation behaves as if it had a segment store. This is referred to as a conceptual capability of the workstation.

Each segment is identified by a unique name called a segment name. All output primitives are collected in a segment once it has been created and until it is closed. Once a segment is closed, no primitives can be added to or deleted from it. No new segment can be created until the previous one is closed. The output primitives within a segment can have an additional identification that need not be unique. This identification is called a pick identifier and it is part of the input value delivered by a pick input device when a segment is picked. The segment names are specified by the application program when a segment is created. The pick identifiers for the primitives inside the segment are chosen by a modally set output primitive attribute. The following example illustrates creation and closing of segments, as well as the specification of pick identifiers:

```
SET PICK IDENTIFIER (pi4);
CREATE SEGMENT (sega);
    Output functions;                {segment = sega, pick identifier = pi4}
SET PICK IDENTIFIER (pi2);
    Output functions;                {segment = sega, pick identifier = pi2}
CLOSE SEGMENT;
    Output functions;                {primitives not pickable}
                                     {pick identifier = pi2}

SET PICK IDENTIFIER (pi5);
    Output functions;                {primitives not pickable}
                                     {pick identifier = pi5}

CREATE SEGMENT (segb);
    Output functions;                {segment = segb, pick identifier = pi5}
SET PICK IDENTIFIER (pi3);
    Output functions;                {segment = segb, pick identifier = pi3}
CLOSE SEGMENT;
```

11.2 Manipulating Segments

Segments can be manipulated as a whole by:

— changing their transformation (cf. Section 11.4);
— changing their priority or by turning their visibility, detectability, or high-lighting on or off (cf. Section 11.3);

— sending copies to different workstations or inserting them into other segments (cf. Sections 11.5, 11.6);
— deleting them;
— renaming them.

A segment can be deleted from either all workstations at which it is stored
or from only a specific workstation. If a segment is deleted from all workstations,
it is no longer known to GKS or a workstation and its name may be re-used.
Renaming a segment involves replacing its name with a new one which is not
already being used for an existing segment.

11.3 Segment Attributes

Segment attributes are state values which affect all the primitives in a segment
as a whole. The segment attributes are: visibility, highlighting, detectability,
segment priority, and segment transformation. For each segment the attributes
are unique and cannot vary between workstations. The attributes can be changed
for any existing segment, including the open segment.

Segment attributes — Definition
    Attributes that apply only to segments.

Highlighting — Definition
    A device-independent way of emphasising a segment, by modifying its visual
    attributes.

Detectability — Definition
    A segment attribute, indicating whether or not a segment is eligible for
    selection by the pick input function.

Visibility — Definition
    A segment attribute, indicating whether or not a segment is being displayed
    on the display surface of workstations. Invisible segments cannot be picked.

Segment priority — Definition
    A segment attribute used to determine which of the several overlapping
    segments takes precedence for graphic output and input.

Segment priority only affects segments being displayed. If parts of primitives
in one segment overlap with others in another visible segment with a higher
priority, these former parts may be made invisible. The realization of this feature
is implementation-dependent. When primitives of segments overlapping each
other are picked, the segment with higher priority is selected. A sensible evaluation of the segment priority is most important in the case of filled or patterned
areas, displayed on raster devices. On these devices the picture is composed
of an array of pixels and each pixel can only belong to one segment.

11.4   Segment Transformations

Segment transformations are mappings from NDC onto NDC. They comprise translation, scaling, and rotation.

Segment transformation — Definition
   A transformation which causes the display elements defined by a segment to appear at a different position (translation), with a different size (scale), and/or with a different orientation (rotation) on the display surface.

Translation — Definition
   A constant displacement of all or part of a picture to a different position. N.B.: In GKS, this capability is restricted to segments.

Scaling — Definition
   Enlarging or reducing all or part of a picture by multiplying the coordinates of the display elements by a constant value. N.B. For different scaling in two orthogonal directions two constant values are required. N.B.: In GKS this capability is restricted to segments.

Rotation — Definition
   Turning all or part of a picture about an axis. N.B.: In GKS, this capability is restricted to segments.

Segment transformations are specified by a transformation matrix which is associated with the segment. The transformation matrix is a 2×3 matrix consisting of a 2×2 scaling and rotation portion and a 2×1 translation portion. Utility functions are available for the application program to set up the transformation matrices. Initially, the transformation will be set to the identity mapping. Because the transformation matrix has been stored as part of the segment state, the original state can be restored by resetting the transformation matrix back to identity.
   The segment transformation takes place after the normalization transformation, but before any clipping. If clipping is turned on, the primitives of the transformed segment are clipped around the viewport (of the normalization transformation) which was selected when the primitives were put into the segment (cf. Figure 9.2 on page 31).

11.5   Workstation-Dependent and Workstation-Independent Segment Storage

The (conceptual) segment storage in an output or output/input workstation is called the workstation-dependent segment storage (WDSS). It enables the segment attributes, including the transformation, to be changed, and segments to be deleted. In order to allow primitives within a segment to be transferred from one workstation to another or to be inserted into the open segment, a single workstation-independent segment storage (WISS) is defined in which segments can be stored for use by the copying and insert functions. Only one WISS is permitted in a GKS implementation. The implementor has the choice of either realizing the WISS in the workstation-independent part of GKS or of utilizing the capabilities of an appropriate physical workstation.

The point in the viewing pipeline at which primitives are recorded in the WISS immediately follows the point at which data is distributed to workstations (cf. Figure 9.2 on page 31). This is one of the reasons for treating the WISS like a workstation, as far as control functions are concerned. The other reason is that no special functions are needed to control the WISS, and the programmer does not need to remember another set of function names. Segments are stored in the WISS as long as the WISS is open and active. They are eligible for copying by copy functions as long as the WISS is not closed (in which case, all stored segments will be deleted). As well as functions for opening and closing, activating and deactivating the WISS workstation, there is also a clear function for the WISS. It will delete all stored segments.

Primitives are transformed from world coordinates into NDC before they are recorded in the WISS. The clipping rectangle (viewport of the normalization transformation) is stored together with the primitives contained in a segment. When the segment is sent to a workstation for display, the recorded clipping rectangles are used to clip the primitives of the segment, if the clipping is on.

11.6   Copying Segments

Three functions can use the data contained in the segments in the WISS. None of these functions modify the contents of the segments to which they are applied.

COPY SEGMENT TO WORKSTATION makes a copy of each primitive and its associated clipping rectangle in a segment in the WISS and transforms the primitives using the segment transformation. It then puts the clipping rectangles and the transformed primitives into the viewing pipeline at a place equivalent to the one where the segment was removed, but on the pathway to the workstation specified in the function call.

ASSOCIATE SEGMENT WITH WORKSTATION sends the segment to the specified workstation in order to create the situation that would have come about had the workstation been active when the segment was created.

INSERT SEGMENT copies the primitives in a segment from the WISS and applies the segment transformation followed by a special transformation specified in the insert function. This second transformation is called the insert transformation. The primitives are then inserted into the viewing pipeline at a point immediately before data is distributed to the workstations. Thus, such inserted information may re-enter the WISS, if the WISS is active and a segment is open. All clipping rectangles in the inserted segment are ignored. Each (processed) primitive is assigned a new clipping rectangle which is the viewport of the currently selected normalization transformation if the clipping is on,

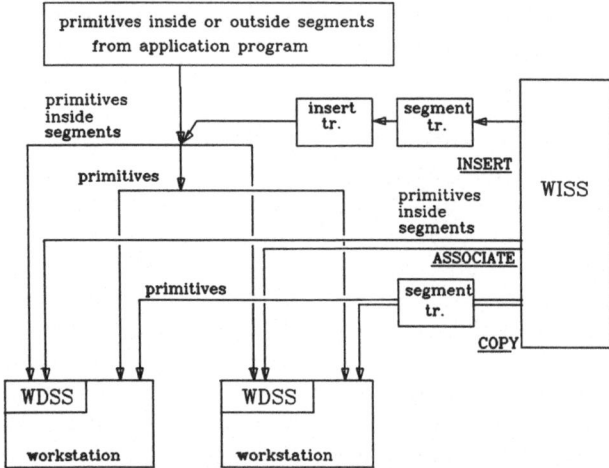

Figure 11.1 COPY, ASSOCIATE, and INSERT functions

i.e., with respect to clipping, the inserted primitives are treated like directly generated primitives.

Figure 11.1, which is an excerpt from Figure 9.2, shows the data flow for the copy functions available in GKS.

12   THE GKS METAFILE

12.1   Graphics Metafiles

GKS offers functions for storing pictures on an external file and for retrieving them from there as an integral part of the system. Files which are used to store pictures are called graphics metafiles. Within the International Organization for Standardization (ISO), the working group TC97/SC5/WG2 "Computer Graphics" has set up a metafile subgroup which defines graphics metafiles as follows [ISO81a]:

Graphics metafile — Definition
   A graphics metafile is a mechanism for the transfer and storage of graphics data that is both device- and application-independent.

The metafiles which can be used by GKS are called the GKS Metafile, GKSM, and the Computer Graphics Metafile, CGM.

GKS metafile (GKSM) — Definition
A sequential file that can be written to or read from by GKS; used for long-term storage (and for transmittal and transferral) of graphical information (this definition applies to the CGM as well).

The main reasons for the introduction of graphics metafiles in connection with graphics systems are:

— The graphics data should be presentable on a number of different display devices. The user should be able to choose between different plotters, output on microfilm, or display screens to display his pictures.
— Graphics data should be retainable for later use. It should be stored in a device-independent way, so that the output device can be chosen after the data has been generated.
— Graphics data should be transportable, both via lines and on a storage medium, e.g., a tape.
— Several sources of graphics data exist in most computing environments. Pictures produced as a result of picture processing techniques, simulation computations or experimental records, with different graphics packages, must be merged together into a uniform presentation.
— Finally, a way should be provided for editing graphics data which have been previously produced and stored. Editing means that parts of pictures are changed, deleted, added to, their visualization is modified, and whole pictures are merged together.

The main impact of graphics metafiles is due to the fact that they are able to interconnect various graphical devices and graphics systems in a standardized and straightforward way. They allow cost-efficient use and sharing of expensive graphical equipment.

The Graphical Kernel System GKS has an interface to the metafile. As part of the standard, the GKS document contains a complete definition of the interface to and from the metafile. However the contents and the format of the GKSM are described in an appendix which is not part of the standard. This division was made to let the standardized graphics metafile develop independently of any particular systems or devices and without any time pressure. Meanwhile the specification of the CGM (Computer Graphics Metafile for Transfer and Storage of Picture Definition Information) is at a very advanced stage.

12.2   GKSM and CGM

The main reason for two different metafile definitions is a purely historical one. When GKS was designed, the need for an interface to a metafile was obvious. The GKS designers concentrated on specifying the metafile interface for GKS. The specification of the contents and the format of the metafile itself was expected to take such an amount of effort and time that it was feared that a metafile standardization at that time would slow down the standardization of GKS. Therefore, the decision was taken to concentrate on GKS and leave the metafile standardization to a later date.

Meanwhile, a metafile format was needed so that GKS could be implemented. To meet this urgent requirement, the DIN metafile proposal, called GKS metafile (GKSM), was included in the GKS standard as an appendix. This appendix is clearly marked as being "not part of the standard".

In 1983, when the GKS was approaching its final state, a concentrated effort was made to standardize an ISO metafile. The result is the metafile proposal called "Computer Graphics Metafile for Storage and Transfer of Picture Definition Information (CGM)" [ISO 85c].

The main characteristics of the two metafile versions are:

GKSM: Practically all output-oriented GKS functions are recorded in the GKSM. Thus GKSM becomes a *protocol file*. The GKSM functionality and one way of coding it are described in an annex of the GKS document, labelled as not being part of the standard.

CGM: Contains items which describe a static picture. No functions which change a picture are included (e.g. no GKS segment functions). In this way, the CGM is a *picture description file*. The CGM is described in a multipart standard (currently 4 parts).
      Part 1 describes the CGM *functionality,* Part 2 contains a character coding, based on ASCII (ISO 2022) code extension techniques. Part 3 defines a binary coding. Part 4 contains a clear text coding which can be understood by humans and edited using a normal text editor. It has a format-free notation, comparable to modern, high-level programming language syntax.

In GKS at output level 0, GKSM and CGM are functionally equivalent. A simple translator can be constructed to translate from one metafile format into the other. At higher levels, the GKSM contains the segment structure of the picture and the segment functions, whereas in the case of the CGM, a GKS system must perform all segment functions to create the final picture, which is then recorded on the CGM.

Two developments can be expected that will remove these present incompatibilities between GKSM and CGM:
— Extending the CGM to include segment functions would bring the CGM up to the level of GKSM functionality.
— Processing the GKSM into an ISO standard would lift it to the same formal status as the CGM.

The attainable goal is to have both GKSM and CGM as standards, so that both contain consistent pictures at level 0 and both present a protocol file at level 1.

12.3 The Metafile Interface

The graphics items in the metafile are generated as a result of calling graphical GKS functions. The user records are written by the function WRITE USER ITEM TO GKSM. Reading the metafile is performed by GKS under user control. The items are passed to the application program where they can be completely processed or be skipped. The interpretation of the graphics metafile records can also be left to GKS. In this case, the application program passes them back to GKS and GKS will perform the function that originally generated the metafile record (cf. Figure 12.1). The flexibility and the generality of GKS has been vastly increased by the addition of the metafile interface.

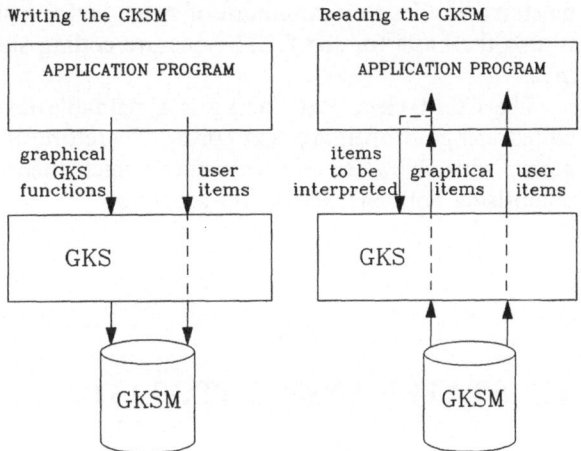

Figure 12.1 Writing and reading the GKSM

12.4 The Metafile Formats

The GKSM and the CGM both contain two-dimensional pictures. Every picture is represented by a series of data records ("items") which are generated as a result of GKS functions being invoked. The metafiles contain items for output primitives and attributes. In addition, the GKSM contains items which represent segment functions. Its control information is contained in the file header, picture header, and the end record. The CGM has its control information in a number of control items, such as

BEGIN PICTURE or END PICTURE.

In addition to the graphical items, both metafiles contain non-graphical, application-dependent data.

The GKSM is built up from a sequence of logical data records of variable length. Every record starts with a key denoting the record type. It is followed by the length of the data record, so that it can be easily skipped if an interpreter is not interested in a particular record type. The data format for the data values in the GKSM can be chosen in a flexible way by using either internal machine code representation or formatted representation by ASCII strings. Which format a given GKSM uses is specified in the file header, which is the first record of each metafile. The logical data records are arranged one after the other on physical records which may have a card image format.

In the case of the CGM, three different codings are specified. The most important ones are the character coding and the clear text coding. The character coding uses ASCII characters to represent the information. ISO 2022 code extension techniques are used to define the coding for metafile functions and their parameters. The character coding is a very compact representation which can be stored in files in a minimum of space and transmitted via lines. This coding is also the basis for the CCITT picture coding standards now under development.

The CGM clear text coding is a readable text which can be created and edited using an ordinary text editor. Therefore, it can easily be integrated, together with character text, into files, which then contain complete documents comprising both characters and graphics.

13   STATES AND STATE LISTS

13.1   The GKS Operating State

At any time during the execution of a program using GKS, GKS will be in a precisely defined state. This state is defined by the operating state and by the values of the state variables contained in a number of state lists, present in a GKS system. When GKS functions are called this can change the values in the state lists: these changes are part of the definition of the functions. The operating state has one of the following five values:
— GKS closed;
— GKS open;
— at least one workstation open;
— at least one workstation active;
— segment open.

A transition from one state to another comes about when control functions are called by the application program. For example, the function OPEN GKS will change the GKS state from "GKS closed" to "GKS open" if the state is "GKS closed" when the function is called. Whether a particular GKS function can be called or not depends on the operating state. Figure 13.1 summarizes the state transitions and the functions which can be called in every one of the states.

13.2   The State Lists

Whereas the GKS operating state is a global value which is available even if GKS is closed, the other state variables are allocated, initialised, and freed as a result of calling GKS functions. The following state lists are present in GKS:

GKS state list: Allocated and initialised by OPEN GKS, deleted by CLOSE
    GKS, present once in a GKS implementation;
Segment state list: Allocated and initialised by CREATE SEGMENT, deleted
    when the segment is removed, present for every existing segment;
Workstation state list: Allocated and initialised by OPEN WORKSTATION,
    deleted by CLOSE WORKSTATION, present for every open workstation;
Error state list: Allocated and initialised by OPEN GKS, deleted by CLOSE
    GKS, present once in a GKS implementation;
Input queue: Allocated and initialised by OPEN GKS, deleted by CLOSE GKS,
    present once in a GKS implementation which has event input capabilities.

The values in the state lists describe the state of GKS at any one time. In the course of a GKS application, the state list values will change. In addition to these, GKS contains description tables with static values that will not change during a GKS application. The GKS description table contains information about the GKS implementation, for example, the GKS level. The workstation description tables contain information about the workstations available in an implementation:

GKS description table: Static table set up by the implementation, present once;
Workstation description table: Static table set up by the implementation; there
    is one for every available workstation type (except WISS and GKSM work-
    stations).

13.3   Inquiry Functions for State List Values

All values contained in any one of the GKS state lists or in one of the description tables can be inquired by the application program. The functions used for this purpose are called inquiry functions. As an example, a subroutine that belongs to the application layer of a program package can find out about the state of the system and save the state variables. It can then change the state, e.g., by altering the attribute values. Before returning to the program from which it has been called, it can use the saved variables to reset the system to the previous state.

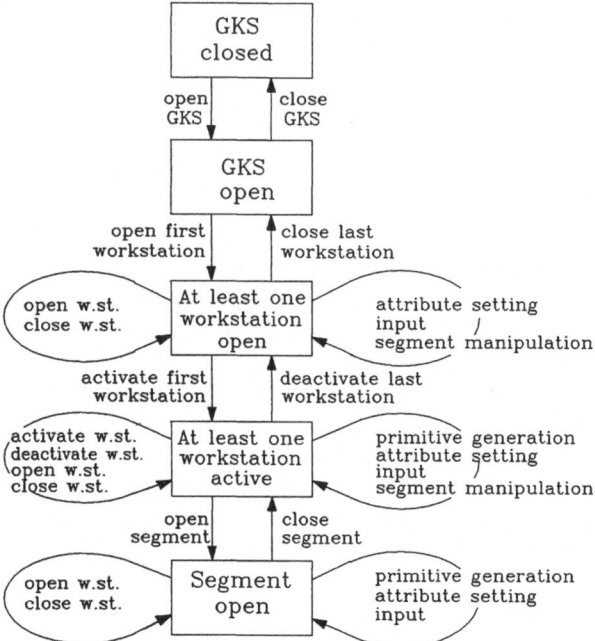

Figure 13.1 Transitions between operating states and possible functions

14   ERROR HANDLING

The description of every GKS function contains a list of the anticipated errors. Every GKS implementation must realize an error handling facility which is able to discover these errors and record at least one of the errors which have occurred in a message file. There the identification of the error and the identification of the GKS function detecting the error will be filed. The application program can replace the standard error handling procedure by its own routine which can react to specific errors. The user error procedure is supplied by GKS with the identification of both the error and the GKS routine which has detected it. It can also inspect the GKS state list by using inquiry functions.

15   THREE-DIMENSIONAL EXTENSIONS TO GKS

Most computer graphics applications only need two-dimensional (2D) pictures. This is why the GKS effort first concentrated on standardization of a 2D graphics system. Now, GKS is well developed and the GKS working group can devote more effort to a three-dimensional (3D) extension of GKS. In important application areas, 3D graphics are needed to represent 3D geometrical objects. Computer aided design is an important example, but also such areas as chemistry or medicine often require 3D graphics. A major influence has come from presentation graphics (3D bar charts, 3D geographic representations) and from computer animation.

A 3D extension of GKS (GKS-3D) has been in the process of being designed since 1983 within the ISO working group for computer graphics. The main characteristics of GKS-3D are:

— GKS-3D is an extension of GKS which does not alter the behaviour of the 2D GKS functions.
— GKS-3D functions are logical generalizations of 2D functions.

Therefore, 2D GKS applications will run without modifications in a GKS-3D system. Being a major means of making geometrical models, GKS-3D provides 3D areas, together with methods for hidden line/hidden surface removal. In Part IV, GKS-3D is explained in detail.

THE PROCESS
OF GENERATING
A STANDARD

Part II describes the way GKS was designed. Chapter 1 traces the development of computer graphics to the point where it was possible to make a successful attempt at standardization. Chapter 2 lists in detail the series of steps taken in developing and processing GKS, until it attained the status of a standard. This development was far from straightforward. Concepts and functionality, laid down in existing graphics systems and in the literature, were examined carefully to select those which could be included in the standard kernel system. Chapter 3 attempts to describe the major points of discussion and the design decisions which were taken in establishing the contents of GKS. This chapter gives useful background information as to why some features were included in GKS, why other useful concepts and features were omitted, and why some features were included in a particular way.

1 THE EVOLUTION OF COMPUTER GRAPHICS

Before a standard can be established, a subject must be ready for it. This means that:
— there must be a sufficiently large number of interested parties to justify all the effort;
— there must be a common understanding of the subject and commonly accepted practices must have developed to form a basis for standardization.

Computer graphics has existed for a long time without formal standards. In the early days of computers, cathode ray tubes and plotters were the only graphics devices. Cathode ray tubes only had limited capabilities and were expensive and were, therefore, rare. The users of plotting devices managed with the software provided by the manufacturers. The software interface provided by the main manufacturers became a 'de facto' standard in computer graphics.

With the advent of low-cost interactive graphics devices in the 1960s, the situation changed drastically. These new devices offered interesting capabilities but it was not yet clear how these capabilities should be addressed. For many research workers it became a challenge to discover how graphics could be integrated into interactive programming, and this led to the development of a variety of graphics systems. This point in time can be regarded as the beginning of computer graphics as a discipline.

1.1 Graphical Devices

The first interactive display devices were cathode ray tubes (CRT) with a vector generator for output and a lightpen or tablet for input. These *vector refresh displays* possess deflection and intensity control circuitry which permits a vector to be drawn between any two addressable points on the screen. To get a stable image, the whole drawing has to be refreshed at least every 1/30th second. Therefore, the number of vectors is limited to that number which can be generated within 1/30th second. In order to increase this number, fast vector generators had to be constructed which made the systems very expensive. Furthermore, the need to refresh requires high data transfer rates which can only be provided by expensive, high-speed channel interfaces. Therefore, vector refresh display systems were usually used for special applications where the price was not the decisive factor, e.g., in turn-key systems for computer aided design (CAD) and in the automobile and aerospace industries.

In the late 1960s, inexpensive *storage tubes* came onto the market which meant many people could now afford interactive graphics. Storage tubes also use CRTs but the displayed image is stored in the form of electrostatic charges on a mesh within the tube, which makes it unnecessary to refresh the image. Slower vector generator circuitry can be used as there is no need to generate the whole image within 1/30th second. Furthermore, inexpensive terminal interfaces with low baud rates connected to a timesharing computer system are quite sufficient. The number of displayable vectors is no longer limited and vectors can be drawn with a higher degree of precision. The main disadvantage of storage tubes is that information on the screen can only be removed by erasing the whole screen and redrawing the information which is to be retained. As a consequence of the slow interfaces, the redrawing may take some time. Dynamic manipulations in real time are not possible.

In the mid 1970s, *raster displays* based on television technology appeared which added new features to computer graphics. Whereas vector refresh displays and storage tubes are calligraphic devices which build up an image from line elements, raster displays use a matrix of intensity values. These values are stored in a frame buffer from which they are continuously read out; a video signal is generated from the intensity values and fed to a standard television monitor. With raster devices it is possible to display solid areas and provide a full colour facility. Colour can be manipulated dynamically by using a colour table. Line drawings have to be converted into raster format before they can be stored in the frame buffer. Raster devices can accept an arbitrary number of vectors limited only by the resolution of the device, which is usually lower than that of other device types. The capabilities for dynamic image manipulation are better than with storage tubes, as the frame buffer can be updated locally. Changes which affect the whole frame buffer, however, still take some time and cannot be done within one refresh cycle.

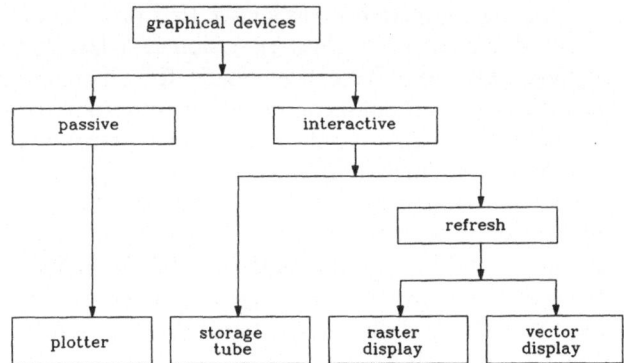

Figure 1.1 Major types of graphical devices

1.2   Graphics Software

The different types of graphics hardware offer a variety of capabilities, which, at a first glance, seem to be incompatible. At the outset, it was not clear what the primitive functions of each device were and how these primitive functions could be correlated. Therefore, the graphics software developed for different types of equipment looked quite different, as peculiarities of equipment became

apparent at the functional interface. For reasons of efficiency, application-specific requirements were implemented within the graphics system and special features of an operating system were also integrated into it. The lack of a common model for a graphics system and its functional capabilities gave rise to the formation of different "schools" of graphics system design [NEWM 78]. The graphics systems at that time tended to be:
— device-dependent;
— application-dependent;
— environment-dependent.

As a consequence, graphics software could only be used with the computer system on which it had been developed. The introduction of graphics devices with new features often involved large parts of the graphics software having to be rewritten.

A further point of divergence was the way the application program could access graphics functions. Three main strategies were used:
— designing a graphics language;
— designing a graphics extension of an existing high-level language;
— designing a subroutine package which can be called from existing high-level languages.

If a new graphics language were designed, then one would, of course, have the freedom to include everything which would make the programmer's task easier. However, the introduction of a new programming language is a difficult task as a sufficiently large number of people must be found who support the new language. Experience has shown that this way does not work.

The design of a graphics extension is a less complicated task. Therefore, language extensions have been made for all major programming languages. The inclusion of graphics commands in a programming language has the advantage that a thorough error check at compile time is possible and that the compiler has more possibilities to optimise the code.

However, this creates the problem that the compiler has to be modified. This can only be reasonably done by a compiler designer as future compiler versions should include the additional functionality. It is not easy to persuade the users of a programming language to accept new features as the overhead has to be paid by all users, whether they use graphics or not. The programming language BASIC is an example of where an attempt has been made to include graphics features as part of the standard definition.

A subroutine package is a less elegant solution. To define graphical objects and operations using a parameter list is not very appealing, errors will mainly be detected at run time only, and the performance will not be optimal. However, this strategy is the only one which can be adapted without interfering with other interests. Therefore, this strategy was borne in mind when designing the standard.

At the beginning of interactive graphics, it was usual that each owner of a graphics device developed his own graphics software with the intention of using the available resources in an optimal way. Graphics conferences were overwhelmed with presentations of new graphical systems. A typical question from the audience was: "Are you the only living user of your system?", a question which often had to be affirmed [NAKE 72]. This waste of software was tolerable only as long as the software investment was smaller than the expenses for hardware, as long as each new language really did offer some slight improvements, and as long as there was no common agreement about the functionality of graphics systems.

However, with the advent of low cost devices and with a widespread use of graphics devices, this situation was no longer tolerable. People wanted to use their graphics devices instead of having to develop graphics systems. Furthermore, they wanted to exchange their programs with their colleagues rather than having to rewrite each routine for their local installation. This was reasonable as, in the meantime, a convergence in graphics systems functionality had become visible. Graphics seemed to be ready for standardization.

The standardization efforts started with a discussion about the objectives of standardization. Two alternatives were considered [ENCA 81b]:

— to standardize output primitives, input primitives and data structures, starting from the current body of knowledge;
— to develop a common model and a design methodology before standardizing the details of a graphics system.

The first approach meant considering the main interfaces within a graphical system. It would surely be possible to reach some agreement which would improve portability of graphics programs.

The second approach naturally would take more time. However, a common model and terminology would facilitate the task of defining primitives and data structures and would ensure a higher degree of consistency.

1.3   SEILLAC I

In this situation, the Graphics Subcommittee WG 5.2 of the International Federation for Information Processing (IFIP) began an attempt at establishing a graphics methodology. Some 25 experts from Europe and North America were invited to participate in a workshop about "Methodology in Computer Graphics" which took place in Seillac (France) and became known under the title SEILLAC I[GUED 76]. This workshop discussed a series of issues central to graphics standardization and formulated some principles which influenced the subsequent standardization efforts.

The discussion about the objectives of a standard led to a more precise definition of the term 'portability'. Portability can be achieved in at least four different areas:

— portability of application programs;
— device independence;
— portability of picture data;
— the training of students, teachers, etc. in computer graphics.

The portability of application programs was the primary target of the standardization attempt. This can be achieved by standardizing the interface between the kernel system and the application program. By defining logical input/output primitives as abstractions of the available device capabilities, it is possible to specify a second interface, i.e., the interface between kernel system and device driver. This makes the kernel system device-independent (cf. Figure 1.2). Devices may be exchanged without any disastrous consequences.

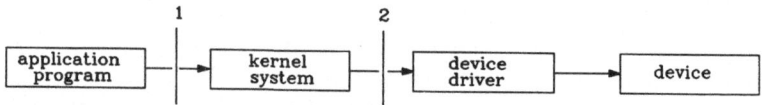

Figure 1.2 Interfaces of a graphics system

Another discussion took place about what functions should be included in the kernel and what functions in the application program area. The distinction was characterized by the terms:
— graphics system and
— modelling system.

The modelling system allows objects to be defined in their own coordinate system. A model of the viewed object is generated in a reference coordinate system called the world coordinate system (WC). The task of the graphics system is to map this model onto a display surface.

When discussing the functionality of the graphics system in detail, two strategies can be adopted:
— define a basic graphics system;
— define a rich graphics system.

In the first case, only a minimum set of functions, necessary to gain access to the facilities of the graphics devices, are included. In the latter case, graphics functions are included according to the principle of "what is good for most programmers and most interactive displays most of the time" [NEWM 78].

Another important issue discussed at SEILLAC I was whether a formal specification technique should be adopted for the specification of the planned standard. The value of such techniques was well understood and further work in this area was encouraged (cf. Part V, Chapter 7).

The SEILLAC I workshop gave a strong impulse to the standardization work being untertaken in the Graphics Standard Planning Committee of ACM-SIGGRAPH and in various national and international standardization bodies.

2   COMMITTEES, PEOPLE, AND EVENTS

2.1   Graphics Standardization Committees

Based on the evolution of different graphics packages and a desire to get started, working groups and formal committees have been working in the field of computer graphics standardization since about 1975. Major efforts were undertaken in the United States, in Germany, in the United Kingdom, and at an international level in the International Organization for Standardization (ISO).

Influenced by the hardware and the software developments in the computer graphics area and by international discussions on computer graphics methodology and terminology, the Standardization Committee for Information Processing (Normenausschuß Informationsverarbeitung, NI) of the DIN (Deutsches Institut für Normung) founded the subcommittee DIN-NI/UA-5.9 "Computer Graphics" in 1975. It was instructed to promote the development of Computer Graphics standards [ENCA 81b]. At the start, this committee had 13 members, whose first chairman was José Encarnação. He was the moving force behind the GKS development — accompanying, directing and protecting it with dedication and persistence until it had been fully developed (he truly can be called the "Kernel of the Kernel System"). José Encarnação held this office until October 1981. He was followed by Günter Enderle. DIN-NI/UA-5.9 presented the first draft of GKS in 1977 and since then the committee has invested enormous effort in redesigning, extending and reviewing GKS. The history and the background of the committee is best documented by the contributions in [ENCA 81a].

In the United States, standardization efforts were first concentrated in the Special Interest Group "Computer Graphics" of the Association for Computing Machinery (ACM-SIGGRAPH). In 1974 it founded the "Graphics Standards Planning Committee" (GSPC) which has been chaired since then by Bob Dunn, Robert Heilmen and Bert Herzog. In the years from 1975 to 1979, GSPC designed two versions of a three-dimensional graphical system called GSPC or "Core System" [GSPC 77, GSPC 79]. In 1979, the graphics standardization activities in the United States were taken over by the American National Standards Institute which set up the Committee ANSI X3H3 "Computer Graphics" with Peter Bono as chairman. The transfer of activities from SIGGRAPH to ANSI caused an interruption in graphics standardization in the United States. However, the SIGGRAPH know-how was transferred to the ANSI X3H3 committee by a group of experts who had been members of GSPC and became members of X3H3. X3H3 was one of the major contributors to the long, and sometimes controversial, reviewing process of GKS.

In the United Kingdom, graphics standardization is the task of the working group OIS/5/WG5 "Computer Graphics" (formerly DPS/13/WG5) of the British Standards Institute (BSI). The working group was established in 1978, chaired by David Fisher. In 1980, David Rosenthal was appointed chairman of OIS/5/WG5. The committee coordinates UK opinions on graphics standards and is one of the important contributors to the work on computer graphics within the ISO. BSI made a large contribution to the GKS review and editing process, moulding the GKS document into an excellent form.

Many other standardization bodies have contributed to the GKS design and review process. This process was mainly dealt with by a working group of the International Organization for Standardization (ISO) which was established in 1977. The working group TC97/SC5/WG2 "Computer Graphics" in the ISO was then founded, having been mainly influenced by the Seillac I workshop on Computer Graphics Methodology [GUED76], by the SIGGRAPH Graphics Standards Planning Committee, and by the work started in the DIN-NI/UA-5.9 (in the context of this book: DIN). TC97 is the ISO Technical Committee for Data Processing, TC97/SC5 is the subcommittee which covers all aspects of programming, and the scope of TC97/SC5/WG2 (in the context of this book: WG2) is computer graphics. The founding chairman of WG2 was David Fisher (UK), followed by Paul ten Hagen (NL) in August 1977. He led the working group until 1983, and without his outstanding leadership, his integrity and devotion, we would not have a graphics standard today. Since 1983, Jürgen Schönhut (D) has been the convenor of WG2.

In 1984, a major reorganization of ISO TC97 took place. The working group for Computer Graphics is now part of SC21 "Open Systems" and is designated TC97/SC21/WG2 "Computer Graphics".

The member countries of WG2 are: Austria, Canada, Finland, France, Germany F.R.G., Hungary, Italy, Netherlands, Norway, Switzerland, United Kingdom, and United States of America. In addition, experts from the following countries participated: Belgium, Denmark, Germany G.D.R., and Japan.

In 1978, WG2 reviewed both the GSPC and GKS proposals, and then, in 1979, GKS was selected as the starting point for an international standard (however, many concepts and functions of GKS originate from the GSPC proposal). Since then, WG2 has been the focal point of computer graphics standardization.

In order to create an international standard, certain formal rules must be adhered to. A standard is developed in several successive steps; formal voting is required before the next step towards a standard can be taken. The voting is done by letter ballot. Only official member bodies of the ISO committees are allowed to vote. In the case of GKS, these are the member bodies of ISO TC97 and of ISO TC97/SC5 (now SC21). The following steps are necessary to reach an international standard [HAGE81]:

1. *Exploration:* The need for a standard in some area is recognized, and the state of the art is analysed.
2. *Work Item:* A subject for standardization has to be accepted by a letter ballot. In most cases, a first draft is already available.
3. *Working Draft:* A draft is available. A national body (the sponsoring body) is responsible for updating, changing and distributing the draft.
4. *Draft Proposal (DP):* A working group (e.g., WG2) considers the draft to be sufficiently complete for a standard. The subcommittee (e.g., SC21) asks the ISO secretariat to register the draft as a DP.
5. *Draft International Standard (DIS):* All technical objections against a DP have been resolved. There are no violations of existing standards. A letter ballot on the subcommittee level is required (e.g., within SC21).

6. *International Standard (IS)*: All comments received on the DIS letter ballot have been answered. The DIS is approved in a final letter ballot both on the subcommittee and the technical committee level (e.g., SC21 and TC97). The draft is registered as an ISO standard. The draft must be available in English and French.

In order to continue from one of these steps to the next, it is necessary for the bodies concerned to agree. Obviously, it is not an easy matter trying to reach agreement amongst the international community in such a quickly developing and expanding field.

2.2 People

About 100 experts from 16 nations participated in the GKS design and review. However, it was an active core of about 30 persons who actually developed GKS to be an international standard. An enormous amount of work was invested in the design and review process of GKS. In the initial years, this work was conducted primarily by the editorial subgroup of the DIN committee. Later the GKS review subgroup of WG2 and, in the final stage, the editorial subgroup of WG2, assisted by the English language and typesetting experts of BSI, were doing the bulk of the work. Most of the group meetings were characterized by working until well past midnight and a common commitment to producing a result acceptable to all participants in time. Conflicts arose where one participating country or another declared it impossible to support the standard if certain technical changes were not incorporated in the draft. It was an outstanding achievement on the part of experts within WG2 that they managed to create a standard acceptable to all, which was still consistent and based on clear and clean concepts.

There is another aspect of international cooperation within WG2 during the GKS design process which undoubtedly deserves our attention, but which cannot be dealt with in a technical book like this. We mean by this the personal and group relationships among a group of people who over the years worked hard together on a subject which often gave rise to conflicts. The stories about the GKS people, their ups and downs, their interrelation in the technical and in the non-technical field, their victories and defeats and their endeavours to humanize the work, could well fill another book. A network of deep friendship and common understanding has been established between the WG2 experts, spanning frontiers and oceans. This was one basis for resolving conflicts, removing obstacles and achieving results leading towards the first international standard in computer graphics.

2.3 Overview of the Main Events

The following is a schedule of meetings, major events and decisions in the development of the Graphical Kernel System (partly taken from [ENCA81b]). Whereas in the initial years, the main activities were concentrated on the DIN-

NI/UA-5.9, since 1979, the GKS design has centred more around ISO TC97/SC5/WG2.

April 1975 DIN-NI/UA-5.9 founded	The DIN subcommittee 5.9 is instructed to promote computer graphics standardization and to develop computer graphics concepts, based on existing computer graphics systems.
1976 Seillac I workshop (France)	In Seillac (France), IFIP working group WG5.2 organizes a workshop on computer graphics methodology. A reference model for a computer graphics system is developed. The separation of "core" and "modelling" capabilities is advocated.
1977 ISO TC97/SC5/WG2 founded	Working group "Computer Graphics" of ISO is established. First chairman: D. Fisher (UK).
July 1977 GKS version 1	GKS version 1 is presented to an international community. It contains output only.
August 1977 WG2 meeting Toronto (Canada)	Proposals considered by WG2 are GSPC, GKS and IDIGS (proposed by Norway). Paul ten Hagen is elected chairman.
September 1978 WG2 meeting Bologna (Italy)	GKS version 2, containing output and event input is presented. An editorial board is established. Principles and concepts for evaluating computer graphics system proposals are formulated.
November 1978 GKS version 3	GKS version 3, containing output and request input is distributed within WG2.
February 1979 WG2 Editorial Board meeting, Amsterdam (The Netherlands)	Evaluation of GSPC and GKS version 3; 24 recommendations are made to GKS, 10 to GSPC.
March 1979 DIN workshop Pulvermühle (Bavaria/Germany)	GKS version 4.8 is designed on the basis of version 3, following WG2 recommendations, and DIN decisions. Inclusion of levels, inquiry functions, GDP, raster-primitives, two-stage transformation, metafile, event and sample input.
June 1979 ANSI X3H3 founded	The ANSI committee "Computer Graphics" is established. Chairman: Peter Bono. Takes GSPC as a basis for computer graphics standardization.
October 1979 WG2 meeting Budapest (Hungary)	WG2 recommends DIN forward the GKS proposal as a work item to the ISO. BSI starts certification efforts. Level 0 GKS is introduced. As a result of the Budapest meeting, DIN prepares GKS version 5.2.
Early 1980 GKS version 6.0	DIN receives 307 international comments about GKS version 5.2. They are used to create GKS version 6.0.

June 1980 WG 2 meeting Tiefenbach (Bavaria/Germany)	GKS review based on version 6.0 and the international comments. As a result of agreed changes, DIN prepares GKS version 6.2.
July 1980 WG 2 Editorial Board meeting Seattle (USA)	A procedure is agreed on to make GKS into an international standard. The GKS review subgroup of WG 2 is established. Chairmen: Rens Kessener (NL) and David Rosenthal (UK).
October 1980 GKS is a Work Item	ISO/TC 97 "Computers and Information Processing" accepts GKS in a letter ballot with no votes against as an ISO Work Item.
Fall 1980 German translation of GKS 6.2	Version 6.2 of GKS is translated into German in order to prepare a DIN national standard.
December 1980 GKS Association founded	The GKS Association (GKS-Verein) is founded in Germany (F.R.G.) to provide a users' organization to promote the distribution of GKS and to educate people in it.
January 1981 WG 2 review meeting Melbourne (Florida/USA)	The GKS review subgroup of WG 2 processes 165 comments ("issues") raised by the WG 2 member bodies about GKS version 6.2.
May 1981 working draft	GKS version 6.4 is registered by SC 5 as the first working draft.
May 1981 GKS version 6.6	Based on the resolved issues of the WG 2 review meeting in Melbourne, the new GKS version 6.6 is prepared by DIN and finalized at an editorial meeting in Amsterdam.
October 1981 WG 2 meeting Abingdon (UK)	GKS 6.6 is reviewed with regard to 152 international issues. All issues are resolved and this meeting results in GKS version 7.0. This version is the basis for the DIS letter ballot.
March 1982 DIN FORTRAN Interface for GKS 7.0	DIN prepares a proposal for a FORTRAN binding of GKS 7.0. This FORTRAN interface is distributed by WG 2 to be commented on.
March 1982 French Translation of GKS 7.0	The French translation is started. This is required in addition to the English version for every ISO standard.
May 1982 GKS is DIS	In a letter ballot, ISO TC 97/SC 5 approves GKS as a Draft International Standard (ISO DIS 7942).
June 1982 WG 2 meeting Steensel (The Netherlands)	WG 2 considers and answers 71 comments received through the DIS letter ballot. Final changes to the GKS document are agreed on (dual attribute binding model, stroke input, character alignment).

June 1982 German translation of GKS 7.0	In the DIN, the German translation of GKS is updated to version 7.0.
July 1982 GKS is DIN Draft	The original English version 7.0 of GKS is issued as a DIN Draft Standard (Entwurf DIN ISO 7942).
October 1982 GKS accepted for ANSI standardization	The American National Standards Institute committee X3H3 "Computer Graphics" votes to forward GKS as a draft proposed American National Standard.
December 1982 GKS DIS document	The DIS version of the GKS standard is prepared at Ruth- erford Laboratories (UK).
1983 DIS Letter Ballot	The letter ballot procedure for the GKS International Stan- dard is started. All member bodies of ISO TC97 and TC97/ SC5 have the opportunity to vote.
September 1983 WG2 meeting Gananoque (Canada)	Comments to DIS letter ballot are processed.
June 1984 WG2 meeting Benodet (France)	Final GKS text is accepted. GKS-3D is processed.
1985 GKS-3D is DIS	GKS-3D is accepted in a letter ballot as a DIS.
August 1985 GKS is IS	On August 15, 1985 GKS is published as the ISO Interna- tional Standard ISO 7942.

3   GKS REVIEW —
PROBLEMS AND THEIR SOLUTIONS

At the beginning, the GKS document was developed in the DIN in the following
way:

— The DIN committee, comprising some 20 people, discussed the major design
  issues in the GKS concept and gave directives to an editorial board.
— An editorial board, comprising four persons from the DIN committee, discussed the consequences of the global decisions and worked out in detail
  the changes to the document.
— The document was compiled and kept up to date by one person.

This scheme gave the DIN committee a means of controlling the global direction of the GKS design. It gave sufficient freedom to the editorial board to choose the best way of implementing the concepts. If new aspects or implications became visible during elaboration, the editorial board had the authority to decide on its own. Thus, as only four people had to reach a common position, the document could be developed relatively easily, while its conceptual homogeneity was guaranteed by one person having exclusive access to it.

However, this scheme had some disadvantages:

— The only response the DIN committee got to its directives was a document. This was feasible as long as the document was not too large. However as the document grew from version to version, it became more and more difficult to see how a specific feature had been implemented and what parts of the document had been affected.
— When new people became involved in GKS, many decisions had to be rediscussed because they did not know the background to the decision making, i.e. the alternatives which had been considered and the arguments which led to the final decision.

These problems became more pronounced when GKS was discussed in the WG2. In ISO, much work is done by correspondence and meetings take place once a year. Furthermore, ISO attaches some importance to reaching a unanimous agreement. When processing a standard, each member is asked to submit his comments on the draft. Each comment must be processed and a satisfactory (not necessarily a positive) answer must be given to the member who made the comment.

In order to assist this commenting process, a formal reviewing procedure was established [ROSE80b], which helped to structure the discussion within WG2 and made the decisions taken transparent to everybody. The reviewing procedure was adopted from a scheme which had proved successful in developing the GSPC CORE proposal.

To start with, the right of the sponsoring body (i.e., the national standardization body submitting the document) to change the document arbitrarily was restricted: One version of the document was declared by WG2 to be the *current draft* which was used as a basis to work on and which, therefore, had to remain unchanged until it had been passed by the next stage of the reviewing procedure and WG2 explicitly requested the sponsoring body to create a new version.

After a current draft had been established, all interested individuals were invited to comment on the document. To ensure the comments were of the right quality, an individual's comments had to be filtered by a national body, before they could be passed to WG2. The comments were collected in an *active issues list*. Each entry in this list had to conform to a given format, containing the following items:

1. a title expressed as a question which briefly described the issue;
2. at least one search key taken from the established graphics terminology (cf. Chapter V.8) which identified the subject area;

3. a category selected from:

   disagreement: the commentator prefers to change the content of the document

   omission: the commentator suggests the addition of some feature or description to the document;

   inconsistency: the commentator identifies conflicting features in the document;

   ambiguity: the commentator believes that some parts of the document can be interpreted in multiple ways;

   question: the commentator asks to have incomprehensible parts of the document clarified;

4. a detailed explanation of the issue;
5. an enumeration of possible alternatives open for solving the issue;
6. a list of arguments for or against some alternative solutions;
7. originator and date.

Items 4, 5, and 6 were optional.

When all comments had been collected, WG 2 had a technical discussion of all the issues. The originator, as well as other parties, were invited to add material and bring forward arguments about any issue and improve it until a decision was taken. The decision taken was added as item 8 to the issue and the issue then moved from the active issues list to the *resolved issues list*. All changes in the document made necessary by the solution of an issue had to be written down explicitly in the *change list*.

The resolved issues list documented all areas where a consensus had been reached. It contained all the arguments considered before taking a specific decision. People with different opinions had the possibility to inspect this list and see whether all relevant aspects had been taken into account. At a later stage, this list helped to avoid rediscussion of resolved issues. A resolved issue could only be rediscussed if completely new arguments could be provided.

The aim of the technical discussion was to move as many issues as possible from the active issues list to the resolved issue list. After a round of discussions, WG 2 requested the sponsoring body to create a new version of the document, containing all the changes from the change list. This new version then became the current draft and was subject to another commenting phase. This process was repeated until the active issues list was empty.

While GKS was being processed in WG 2, 307 issues were raised in the exploratory stage; 165 and 152 issues were discussed at two stages of formal reviewing; 71 comments were produced during the formal voting procedure for GKS. Sets of issues partially overlapped, because unresolved issues automatically reappeared at the subsequent stage. All issues were processed successfully.

To have a good understanding of the background of the GKS concept, it is very helpful to have a look at the development of GKS. In the following sections, some major issues discussed during GKS design will be looked at. The alternatives inspected and the arguments taken into consideration, together with the final decisions taken, will clarify the underlying concepts of GKS and explain how a specific solution was found.

More information will be found in DIN and ISO documents. An overview of the people and the application areas contributing to the GKS design is given by [ENCA81a]. Major parts of the GKS design were evaluated by an early GKS implementation [WISS78], the experiences of which stimulated the development of GKS. For example, the possibility of removing the current position, the inclusion of primitives outside segments, and a two-stage transformation pipeline were demanded in [WISS79]. The major steps of the ISO GKS review are documented in [HAGE79, ISO80, ISO81b,c,d]. As GKS has many features in common with the GSPC CORE proposal, the issues discussed in this context [GSPC77, GSPC79, MICH78] will mostly apply for GKS as well, although some issues were decided in a different way.

3.1   Scope of the Standard

The initial points of discussion focused around the problem of how to define the scope of the intended standard. Criteria like "what is good for most programmers, on most existing interactive displays, most of the time" [GSPC77] gave guidelines but no strict rules for the inclusion or exclusion of concepts.

Graphics versus modelling: How can the graphics system be separated from application-specific parts?

An important result of the SEILLAC I workshop [GUED76] was the distinction made between a *graphics system* and a *modelling system*. The modelling system allows objects to be defined in their own coordinate system and a model to be created in world coordinates. This modelling will depend to a great extent on the data structures and operations used in a specific application area. Therefore, different modelling systems will be required. The graphics system is responsible for the mapping of the model onto the display surface. To describe its functionality, the paradigm of a synthetic camera is used in the GSPC CORE proposal [GSPC77].

However, as useful as this distinction between graphics system and modelling system was at the beginning of standardization, as impeding were the long discussions as to whether a function was a modelling or graphics one each time a new function was to be included. It was discovered that the modelling issue could not be kept completely separate from graphics design [NEWM78]. As a result, some basic modelling functions are included in the kernel and the questions "what is modelling?" and "what is graphics?" were postponed until the design of the kernel was finished. Then a precise definition of modelling and graphics could be given: everything inside the kernel is graphics; everything outside is modelling.

2D versus 3D: Should GKS support three-dimensional primitives?

Another important issue at the beginning was whether the intended standard should serve 2D graphics only, or should include 3D graphics as well. It was agreed that in the future compatible standards for both were required. However, it was not clear whether 2D should be standardized first and then a 3D extension subsequently, or whether a 3D standard was needed first from which a 2D subset could easily be extracted. Some arguments from this discussion are:

Pro 2D:
— The majority of applications require 2D only; this majority should not pay the extra cost for 3D.
— Almost all display surfaces are 2D; when at last a 2D display system is used, 3D can be built as a modelling system on top of a 2D graphics system.
— There are many 3D applications where the application-dependent part extends to the 2D interface.
— Agreement can be more easily achieved for 2D graphics than for 3D.

Pro 3D:
— The amount of people or bodies interested in 3D graphics is growing rapidly and will be a majority within the next few years.
— Defining 3D first ensures full compatibility between 2D and 3D.

Contra 2D:
— How can it be ensured that the 2D standard could be extended to 3D?

It was decided to deal with 2D only and postpone 3D. The work of GSPC on the 3D CORE proposal provided sufficient information about the requirements of 3D, which could be considered while defining the 2D standard.

3.2   Output Primitives

Should GKS support the concept of a current position (CP)?

Many graphics systems maintain a register containing the current position of the drawing utensil. Primitives may be defined relative to this position, e.g., LINE TO (X, Y) draws a line from the current position to the specified position, which is then stored in the register as the new current position. Some arguments extracted from this discussion are:

Pro CP:
— CP is accepted practice.
— CP makes an easy concatenation of character strings possible.
— CP takes advantage of the capabilities of vector devices where a CP is defined by the device.
— CP permits the use of relative coordinates. In particular, a subroutine for drawing symbols can profit from this feature.
— CP is useful when mixing 2D and 3D output primitives.
— CP decreases the number of parameters needed for output primitives.

Contra CP:
— CP can be defined in many different ways: a CP can be maintained in WC, NDC, or DC and, furthermore, a CP can be taken from the clipped or unclipped primitive. Most effective is a clipped CP in DC. However,

there will be a different CP for different devices. An unclipped CP in WC is well defined. However, this CP gives no access to the device's CP; it is a syntactic abbreviation rather than a semantic concept.
— CP means some additional overhead for non-vector devices where the CP has to be calculated, rather than being taken from a device's register.
— CP is not clearly defined after TEXT, FILL AREA, or CELL ARRAY primitives. If the CP is not affected by these primitives, it cannot be used, e.g., to concatenate character strings, which invalidates one 'pro' argument.
— A change of transformations may affect the CP.
— With a CP, one output primitive influences subsequent output primitives. Provision must be taken that this side effect does not extend over segment boundaries as the deletion of a segment must not influence other segments.
— CP is equivalent to an accumulator in assembly language programming. However, output primitives should be defined at a higher level. The definition of a primitive should be more self-contained.

It was agreed that having no CP is cleaner, more consistent, and less confusing. Therefore, GKS does not include the concept of a CP.

Should GKS have optional output primitives like a CIRCLE and INTERPOLATING CURVE?

From the very beginning of GKS, people had required more output primitives than GKS provided. Circle and interpolating curve are two prominent examples of primitives requested by sufficiently large user groups.

However, it takes some effort to implement these functions if they are not provided by the workstation. A circle may degenerate into an ellipse through transformations. It would thus be more appropriate to have an implementation of ellipses rather than circles. Interpolation usually requires the solution of systems of linear equations. As well as the implementation cost arguments, another argument against the introduction of new primitives was the difficulty of then being able to refuse further requests.

On the other hand, these particular primitives cannot easily be built on top of the kernel system. An approximation of these curves using POLY-LINE has to be done in a workstation-dependent way, depending on the current setting of transformations and the resolution and type of the display surface (a low quality approximation for interactive workstations and a high quality approximation for plotters).

The compromise which involved having optional output primitives for some workstations contradicted several design principles of GKS and reduced the portability of the programs. However, it was decided to adopt this compromise, as it is better to have limited portability with well-identified incompatibilities, than programs totally ignoring the standard. The optional primitives were collected into one output primitive called the GENERALIZED DRAWING PRIMITIVE (GDP). Due to this decision, any possible incompatibilities were concentrated into one primitive. If new optional primitives are required, the GDP can easily be extended.

Strict rules were drawn up to ensure that the optional primitives behave like the other output primitives with respect to transformations, clipping, and segment storage.

Should CELL ARRAY be an output primitive?

The CELL ARRAY primitive had been introduced as a response to the growing importance of raster devices within computer graphics. CELL ARRAY is the basic raster primitive. However, it cannot be simulated very well on non-raster devices. This would infer that CELL ARRAY should be just another optional primitive within GDP to be accepted only from specific workstations. Furthermore, FILL AREA together with the PATTERN attribute could provide the whole functionality of CELL ARRAY.

Another objection was that, usually, the cells defined by CELL ARRAY are mapped one-to-one onto the pixels of the raster device, as otherwise unwanted effects may occur, due to pixel rounding. This implies that CELL ARRAY has to be defined in DC rather than in WC, in which the other primitives are defined.

Due to the importance of raster graphics, it was decided to include the CELL ARRAY primitive. It was made clear that CELL ARRAY is defined in WC, like other primitives, and that transformations (including rotation) and clipping are applied. It is left up to the application program to inquire into the raster resolution of a workstation and to set the transformations appropriately in order to avoid unwanted pixel rounding effects (e.g., by securing integer mapping of CELL ARRAY cells to pixels on the display surface).

How should attributes be assigned to primitives?

Output primitives are associated with a set of attributes controlling the appearance of the primitive, e.g., the attributes linetype, linewidth, and colour apply to POLYLINE primitive. The attribute concept of GKS was under continual discussion during the whole reviewing process. In these discussions, many aspects of attribute definition and binding were considered.

An attribute can be specified:
- directly, i.e., the value itself is bound to the primitive;
- indirectly, i.e., an index is bound to the primitive which points to a value stored in a table. In this case, the attribute is called table driven.

An attribute may be:
- static, i.e., the specified attribute cannot be changed retroactively;
- dynamic, i.e., the specified attribute may be changed retroactively.

Usually, direct attributes will be static and indirect attributes will be dynamic.

In GKS, several workstations may be active simultaneously. In this case, an attribute may be specified to be:
- workstation-dependent, i.e., the value can be set independently for each workstation;
- workstation-independent or global, i.e., one value is valid for all workstations.

A further distinction can be made whether attributes are specified:
— individually, i.e., one attribute at a time;
— bundled, i.e., a set of related attributes is specified by one call.

GKS started with a concept which included two non-overlapping sets of attributes:
— static global attributes specified directly and individually;
— dynamic workstation-dependent attributes which were table driven and were collected in one bundle called a 'pen'.

One discussion considered whether there should be workstation-dependent attributes at all. In cartography, for instance, there are strict rules, governing in which colour or in which linetype a particular line has to be drawn, and it makes no sense to have these attributes dynamic. Nevertheless, if a picture which uses such well-defined colours has to be drawn on a black and white display, the missing capabilities have to be simulated. The workstation concept of GKS states that all workstation-dependencies should be under the control of the application program. This means that the simulation of colour on a black and white display device ought to be able to be specified by the application program rather than be determined by some implicit algorithm.

Grouping the attributes into workstation-dependent and workstation-independent attributes turned out to be very difficult. The initial distribution was done according to the experience of the people involved. During the review the following rule was established: geometric attributes should be global; non-geometric attributes should be workstation-dependent. This ensured that all geometrical information about a primitive was available at the time of its generation, so that it could be specified in WC and a proper performance of transformations and clipping was possible. Unfortunately, it was discovered that this rule could not be used to decide all cases, as there were attributes which could not be properly classified. Text font, for example, is clearly a non-geometric attribute, as long as all characters are equally spaced. For proportionally spaced character sets, the character width may differ from character to character and, thus, the font will affect the geometry.

The pen concept had been introduced to keep a proper separation between device-dependent and device-independent aspects of primitives. In this concept, a symbolic attribute, the 'pen', was first bound to the primitive which made it possible to distinguish between different classes of primitives. For each of these classes it was then possible to specify explicitly, on a workstation basis, which attributes were to be assigned to it. The pen concept with some overhead included the functionality of direct attributes, whereas direct attributes could not cover the full functionality of the pen concept.

During the course of discussion, the pen concept was refined. Instead of one pen governing all types of primitives, one bundle for each of the primitives POLYLINE, POLYMARKER, TEXT, and FILL AREA was introduced. This gave greater independence to the different types of primitives and avoided the difficulty that some aspects of the pen did not apply to all types of primitives. However, it was not clear whether all these bundles should be table driven. Table driven attributes are more complicated than direct attributes and have higher implementation costs, even for moderate applications. Tables need a storage capacity, the size of which cannot be precisely estimated a priori. The bundle approach worsens this situation. If several aspects of one bundle are used simultaneously, a multiplication effect occurs, e.g., if POLYLINES are to be drawn with 32 colours, 8 linetypes and 2 linewidths, a table of size 512 is necessary to allow all possible combinations of these aspects in the polyline bundle. The tables have to be maintained even if the entries are never re-used or redefined later on. This puts a heavy burden on some applications. Furthermore, if entries in such a table are changed, this means a retroactive change of attribute values which must be performed by the driver, if the workstation has no appropriate facilities. As the program cannot know a priori whether a retroactive change will occur later or not, it must be prepared for it. This extra cost must be paid for by all applications, whether they use retroactive change or not.

These problems were solved by making it possible for all bundled attributes to be used as unbundled static attributes as well.

3.3   Segmentation

Should segmentation be optional?

Segmentation is a powerful facility within GKS which must be paid for in terms of complexity and implementation costs. There are classes of applications which will not use GKS segmentation because it is not needed or is not adapted to the specific requirements of an application. In such cases, the picture will be directly generated from a data structure maintained by the application program. For these applications, GKS segmentation is only a burden, of no use, and a GKS level without segmentation is preferable.

On the other hand, it had been proposed to allow primitives to be generated within segments only. The arguments in favour of this strict segmentation were:
— segmentation corresponds to structured programming and, therefore, would improve programming style;
— explicit opening and closing is used elsewhere within GKS and, therefore, should also be used for graphical output.

If the concept of a current position (cf. Section 3.2) had been included in GKS, more arguments could have been be added.

It was decided to make segmentation optional so that GKS levels with and without segmentation would be possible. If segmentation is present, primitives may be generated inside and outside segments. It is left to the application program to decide whether to stick to strict segmentation or not.

What is the purpose of segment storage?

Segmentation is a means of structuring a picture so that structural elements can be manipulated. As interactive graphics is gaining more and more in importance, it has been clear from the very beginning that segmentation would be an important part of the graphics standard.

A segment storage is needed for the following purposes:

re-use of segments on the same workstation: redrawing of segments on a series of frames, deletion of segments, setting visibility, detectability and highlighting attributes, transforming segments;

re-use of segments on another workstation: transfer of a picture generated at an interactive workstation to a plotter;

symbol facility: definition of symbols, such as resistors, transistors or capacitors, as separate segments, in order to be able to generate several instances of the same symbol when composing a picture (e.g., drawing a circuit).

Re-use on the same workstation was readily accepted. It simulates the functionality available with the display files of high performance interactive workstations. This functionality is needed by interactive graphics and cannot be built on top of GKS, as response time requirements demand an implementation on or close to a workstation (a workstation-dependent segment storage, WDSS).

The transfer of graphics data to a second workstation, as well as a symbol facility, could be built on top of GKS, as the real time requirements are less important. Furthermore, data must be stored in workstation-independent format, as the content of a segment has to be accessed in order to perform the proper transformations on the coordinates and attributes. If segments are transferred to another workstation, coordinates must be mapped onto the respective device coordinates and attributes onto the available attributes. If multiple instances of a symbol are generated, they will differ in size, location, and attributes. This shows that in both cases the purpose is to provide high-level facilities, which could be regarded as 'modelling' and which, therefore, should be left outside the standard.

The transfer of graphical data to another workstation was accepted as a valid requirement in a graphical kernel system. However with WDSS capabilities only, this is difficult to realize. If a picture is to be edited at an interactive workstation and only the final result is to be sent to a plotter workstation to make a hard copy, both workstations have to be active during the whole session. The interactive workstation is supposed to react immediately to each command, whereas the plotter workstation is supposed to record all commands in the segment storage without generating any visible output. When the session is finished an UPDATE command allows the plotter workstation to draw the current state of the picture, skipping all intermediate states and the respective commands. Such a scheme is difficult to explain and to understand. It seemed more natural to have the plotter deactivated as long as the picture was being edited at the interactive workstation and to allow segments to be copied from the interactive workstation and sent to the plotter when needed.

Both approaches are expensive. In the first case, all intermediate states of the picture and all interactive segment operations have to be carefully performed in the segment storage of the plotter although only the last state is needed.

In the second case, segments have to be kept in workstation-independent format which may be less efficient than keeping them in workstation-dependent formats.

It was decided to enable segments to be copied from one workstation to another. The argument of the high costs of storing all segments in a workstation-independent form was met by introducing a special workstation, called the workstation-independent segment storage (WISS). Only segments generated for this workstation are eligible for transfer to another workstation.

With segment transfer now possible, a limited symbol facility is present. One segment can be transferred several times to the same workstation. However, not all meaningful manipulations of the content of a copied segment are possible. For example, the bundle representation cannot be changed. As the bundle index is bound to the primitives in the WISS, all instances of a segment use the same bundle indices and, therefore, the same way of representation. This means that it is impossible to have one instance red and another instance green in one frame.

At what position should information leave and rejoin the transformation pipeline for segment storage?

Coordinates can leave the transformation pipeline:
— before the normalization transformation is applied. Coordinates are in WC.
— after the normalization transformation and before the clipping associated with the normalization transformation have been applied. Coordinates are unclipped in NDC.
— after the normalization transformation and clipping have been applied. Co-ordinates are clipped in NDC.

Storing coordinates in WC is an acceptable high-level storage. It ensures that the user knows precisely which coordinates are stored. However, it is difficult for a workstation to handle such data efficiently as the current setting of the GKS state list is needed to interpret the data. There is also the argument that a WC segment storage could be built on top of GKS.

Storing coordinates after transformation and before clipping gives valuable flexibility in clipping. If the clipping rectangle is stored rather than being applied immediately:
— segment transformation can be applied, without data leaving the clipping rectangle;
— clipping at the clipping rectangle can be combined with the clipping at the workstation window;
— if segments are used as a symbol facility, the stored clipping rectangle can be discarded and be replaced by the current clipping rectangle, which is exactly what people would expect in this case.

Storing transformed and clipped coordinates improves the performance of a workstation. However, the transformation of clipped segments may generate curious effects. If a segment is expanded, it will go beyond the clipping rectangle and if a segment is scaled down, it will only fill part of the clipping rectangle.

Primitives which have previously been clipped away will not become visible, although they now fit inside the clipping rectangle.

It was decided to store data after transformation and before clipping.

Should INSERT SEGMENT allow the redefinition of primitive attributes?

As long as the segment storage is used for the storage of complete pictures, there is no need to have access to primitive attributes. The bundle concept for attributes gives sufficient freedom to manipulate attributes on the same workstation or to select different attributes for different workstations.

However, when used as a symbol facility, the segment storage needs more flexibility in redefining primitive attributes. With a symbol facility, several instances of the same segment may be displayed on the same display surface. These instances may differ in size and primitive attributes. For example, if a segment describes a resistor symbol, it should be possible to draw this symbol in different sizes and colours.

The segment transformation in GKS provides for segments to be copied with different scaling. But there is no means of having two instances of a segment with different attributes on the same display surface, e.g., having a red and a green resistor. On top of this the PICK identifier cannot vary for different instances of the same segment. Therefore, it was proposed that a facility should be introduced to enable bundle indices and the PICK identifier to be redefined when a symbol was inserted.

One proposal was to specify an offset with the insert function which was to be added to the bundle index and the PICK identifier in order to generate new values. The proposal was rejected as it presented an ad hoc solution which complicated the GKS attribute model considerably, without providing a fully satisfactory facility. A complete symbol facility was considered to be outside the scope of GKS.

Should INSERT SEGMENT act like a macro or like a subroutine?

When a segment is to be inserted into another segment, this can be realized in one of two ways:
— copying the content of the segment;
— providing a pointer to the specified segment.

The first way can be compared with a macro facility of programming languages whereas the second way can be compared with a subroutine. When constructing a symbol facility, a pointer with appropriate attribute redefinition capabilities would be the best solution, because all instances of a symbol should refer to the same definition. If the definition of a symbol is modified, all instances should be modified accordingly. However, the macro facility puts less burden on an implementation and seems to be sufficiently powerful for a kernel system.

How can a segment storage be structured?

The benefit of having a segment storage can be increased if a structure present in a picture can be mapped onto a corresponding structure in a segment storage.

If nesting of segments is possible, a tree structure can be generated. If INSERT SEGMENT merely inserts a reference to a segment rather than a copy of the segment's content, linked structures can be built up. However, it was felt that however useful such structures would be, they nevertheless lay outside the scope of a kernel system and should be included in a modelling system. Therefore, only a one-level segment structure was included in GKS.

3.4   Input

For graphical input, a lot of devices with different characteristics may be used. For coordinate input these include a lightpen, a crosshair cursor, a mouse, a stylus on a tablet, etc. Although these physical input devices must be handled in different ways, it was clear from the very beginning that the application program should address logical input devices only and that it was the task of GKS to map the logical input devices onto the available physical input devices. Logical input devices can be distinguished by the types of data they deliver to the application program. Physical devices delivering the same type of data are grouped together to form one logical input device. Wallace [WALL 76] proposed the following five input classes:

> PICK, delivering segment names;
> LOCATOR, delivering positions;
> VALUATOR, delivering real numbers;
> STRING (keyboard), delivering character strings;
> BUTTON, delivering no data.

Starting from this concept, the following issues were discussed:

Should CHOICE or BUTTON input be provided?

The BUTTON device is the only input device which delivers no data value but only the fact of whether the device was touched or not. This indicated that the BUTTON device was defined on too low a level compared with the other input devices. For example, if the keyboard device were split into some 50 devices, one for each key, they would be on the same low level also. To find out the logical data value behind BUTTON applications, the main uses of BUTTON devices were identified as being:
- trigger for another input device, which allows the identification of a specific value to be transmitted to the application program;
- program control or menu selection via programmable function keyboards or light buttons.

The first use as a trigger was rejected, since a trigger should be part of the particular device anyway rather than something that is addressed as a separate input device. In the second case, buttons are always grouped. By pressing a specific button, the operator selects one entry from a menu containing commands, symbols, etc. To indicate this use, the corresponding logical input device was named CHOICE. The data value delivered is a positive integer giving the number of the alternative chosen.

Having defined a CHOICE input device, good programming style requires that all menu handling and command input be done via the CHOICE input device. Menu handling and command input are important tasks within interactive programs. In existing programs, comfortable facilities to handle elaborate menus with graphical symbols have been built on top of a PICK input device, and command interpreters with syntax checking have been built on top of a STRING input device. It seemed very difficult to subsume such facilities into a CHOICE device which at the same time would have to support simple programmable function keyboards. The solution found was to include the comfortable command/menu handling in the form of special prompt/echo techniques (cf. Section III.8.3).

Should GKS support STROKE input?

A STROKE device is capable of returning a sequence of positions as a single input whereas a LOCATOR device can only deliver a single position at a time. When digitizing curves, a series of positions which describe its shape has to be delivered. Should these points be collected individually by a sequence of LOCATOR invocations or as an entity by a single STROKE invocation?

Pro STROKE:
— STROKE is an inherently graphical input device. GKS should work on graphical input at least as much as it does on non-graphical input.
— STROKE corresponds to POLYLINE output, thus upholding the input/output symmetry.
— STROKE conveys more semantics than a series of LOCATOR inputs. Within a series of LOCATORs, it may be meaningful to digitize the same point twice, consecutively. With STROKE input, however, data reduction may be performed at device driver level to eliminate points lying too close to the previous point. When STROKE is simulated by LOCATOR, data reduction can only be performed outside GKS, so that efficiency is considerably reduced. It may even hinder the processing of continuous input from a tablet if sufficient computing power is not available to empty the buffers in real time.
— STROKE enables efficient operation in a stand-alone or fixed-function environment.

Contra STROKE:
— Where there are environments with no tablets, implementation of STROKE with other input classes may be unsatisfactory.
— STROKE could be built on top of the LOCATOR device. This would, however, contradict the minimality principle of GKS. Thus, only one of the two should be present in GKS.
— STROKE input will jump when it leaves the viewport of the normalization transformation used for coordinate transformation from NDC to WC.

It was decided to include STROKE input in addition to LOCATOR input.

Are EVENT and SAMPLE input disjoint classes?

In SAMPLE mode, GKS reads the state of a device register. This is the usual way to work with continuous input devices like potentiometers. Potentiometers are often used for LOCATOR and VALUATOR devices.

In EVENT mode, the operator generates an interrupt to enter a specific input value to the application program. This is the usual technique when working with discrete input devices like STRING, PICK, CHOICE, STROKE.

These facts would indicate that LOCATOR and VALUATOR should only be used in SAMPLE mode and the other devices only in EVENT mode.

Pro disjoint classes:
— Reading of STRING, PICK and CHOICE in SAMPLE mode is not very meaningful.
— EVENT is difficult to realize with potentiometer based devices.
— Disjoint classes would allow the association of several SAMPLE devices with one EVENT device.

Contra disjoint classes:
— Physical characteristics should not interfere with the concept of logical input devices.
— If an operating mode is accepted, it should be acceptable for all devices.
— Uniform treatment of all devices is more elegant.
— A lightpen LOCATOR is an EVENT device.
— LOCATOR and VALUATOR usually possess a button (integrated in hardware or assigned by software) to generate an EVENT. This button should be regarded as part of the respective device.

It was decided that all operating modes should be applicable to all input devices.

Should it be possible to build up compound input devices?

GKS provides segments as compound output for output primitives. Thus, for symmetry reasons, compound input should be supported as well. Compound input is demanded by many interactive applications where the input does not consist of one single input primitive, but where a set of actions is required to define a graphical object or a complex manipulation. The quality of interaction could be increased considerably if compound input facilities were to be provided.

As long as the set of actions can be split up into a sequence of input primitives, a compound input device can easily be built on top of GKS. In this case, GKS should not carry the burden of additonal input capabilities. However, there are compound input devices which cannot be built on top of GKS. For example, when editing a drawing, a common technique is to use one input device such as a mouse with some buttons which by one action alone:
— identifies a line (PICK),
— inputs a position (LOCATOR) to distinguish between the beginning and the end of the line,
— selects the desired kind of manipulation by pressing a specific button (CHOICE).

Such a compound input device PICK + LOCATOR + CHOICE, which by one action of the operator generates three inputs, usually cannot be built on top of GKS. In this case, GKS can only issue a series of three input function calls. This only works properly if it can be guaranteed that no noticeable time delay will occur between the different function calls. Otherwise, a LOCATOR value, sampled after the PICK input, may deliver a value different from that valid at the time of PICK input. If a compound input device were to be a part of GKS, the device driver would do the task of collecting the different input values which usually can be done with negligible time delay.

It was found that there was not enough experience of advanced input concepts to allow standardization of a general mechanism for defining compound input devices at the application program interface. However, compound input devices may be implemented at a workstation to serve the needs of a particular application. From the GKS point of view, these compound input devices are equivalent to a set of single input devices. However, when EVENTS are stored in the input queue, a flag signals whether some input primitives have been generated simultaneously. Thanks to this feature, an implementor has sufficient freedom to implement compound input devices, without putting additional conceptional burden on the GKS design.

3.5   Transformations

Can the normalization transformation be changed while a segment is open?

The GSPC CORE [GSPC77, GSPC79] uses a 'synthetic camera' analogy to describe the functionality of the viewing pipeline. In this conceptual framework, the transformation process can be compared to taking a 'snapshot' of an object. The snapshot can only be taken of the object as a whole. The only picture parts known to GKS are segments. Therefore, the parameters for the snapshot should be valid for the whole segment. Further arguments supporting this opinion are:
— If transformation parameters can only be set outside of segments, the consistency of the transformation parameters can be checked at the beginning of a segment instead of for each output primitive individually.
— Segment transformations apply for whole segments. Other transformations should behave accordingly for reasons of consistency.

Arguments against this concept were:
— Segmentation and transformation are independent concepts and should be kept apart.
— Segments are units for manipulation. This does not necessarily imply that they have to be constructed with the same normalization transformation.
— Resetting the normalization transformation between primitives does not yield surprising results, as the current position has not been included in GKS.

It was decided to keep segmentation apart from transformation and allow setting of the normalization transformation at any time.

How should normalization transformation clipping be defined?

There was no doubt that clipping should be available with the normalization transformation. Although some applications require clipping along an arbitrary outline, it was agreed that a kernel system should only clip around rectangles parallel to the axes. However, there was a long discussion of whether:
— the clipping rectangle should be defined by the window of the current normalization transformation (window clipping), or whether
— the clipping rectangle should be specified independently of the normalization transformation.

Arguments in favour of window clipping were:
— window clipping is accepted practice;
— in the synthetic camera analogy, clipping and transformation are also combined;
— less data must be kept by GKS;
— the setting of a separate clipping rectangle would demand an extra function.

Arguments for a separate clipping rectangle were:
— transformation and clipping are independent concepts which should be kept apart,
— linking of clipping and transformation together may confuse the user.

Following accepted practice, window clipping was adopted. This decision was taken early on in the discussion of GKS. Later on, it was decided to separate transformation from clipping and to postpone clipping until primitives have been displayed on a workstation. Perhaps a different decision may have been taken, had both options been discussed at the same time.

What coordinate system should be used to pass LOCATOR/STROKE input data to the application program?

Coordinates delivered by a LOCATOR or STROKE device must be converted from DC to some device-independent coordinate system. In the GKS concept, coordinates can be delivered in WC or NDC.

Pro WC:
— Symmetry of input and output. The application defines output in WC and, therefore, will also expect coordinate input in WC.
— Most applications need WC data.
— NDC can be regarded a special case of WC.

Pro NDC:
— Compatibility with 3D. In a 3D system a position in DC cannot be transformed into WC because there is no unique transformation from 2D to 3D. (This applies to a 2D LOCATOR, not to a 3D LOCATOR.)

Contra NDC:
— GKS is based on the principle that as little as possible should be specified in NDC.

It was decided to transform LOCATOR and STROKE input data by the inverse of a normalization transformation.

Should GKS be able to use several normalization transformations simultaneously?

The original GKS design included only one normalization transformation which, however, could be redefined at any time. The normalization transformation was used for input and output. This simple scheme seemed to be sufficiently flexible for most applications. Other applications could use the default normalization transformation, which provided NDC values, and could create more comfortable transformation mechanisms outside GKS.

In the discussion about this issue, it was proposed to have several normalization transformations defined simultaneously, which could serve different purposes:

— To facilitate switching between normalization transformations.
  The normalization transformations which were to be used could be defined once. If a specific normalization transformation was required, it could be referenced by number rather than by repeating the full definition of window and viewport.
— To have all normalization transformations used for output available for transformation of coordinate input.
  Output primitives are generated by different normalization transformations. All these normalization transformations could be candidates for transforming back coordinate input. By storing all normalization transformations, GKS can choose the normalization transformation whose viewport contains the position to be transformed. If viewports overlap, a viewport input priority attribute provides a scale of preference.
— To introduce a shielding capability.
  Shielding is the opposite of clipping: while clipping removes everything outside a clipping rectangle, shielding removes everything inside a shielding rectangle. Shielding is used extensively for technical drawings to suppress any drawing in areas where an inscription is to be inserted, thus ensuring legibility.
  Shielding can be introduced in the following way. A priority is assigned to the output primitives, e.g., the priority of the current normalization transformation. Output primitives are transformed by the current normalization transformation. The viewports of all normalization transformations with higher priority will serve as a shield, viewports with the same priority will serve for clipping, viewports with lower priority will be ignored.

Allowing the normalization transformation to change at any time enables the application program to construct complex pictures from different world coordinate spaces. This can be regarded as a modelling facility which should not be supported by GKS. The major point at issue in the discussion was whether to remove this modelling facility altogether or to provide a rich capability, as described above.

The modelling aspect could be removed, for instance, by not allowing the normalization transformation to change at any time but only between segments or between pictures. In the latter case, a resetting of the normalization transformation would result in a CLEAR WORKSTATION operation. Such a restriction would mean that the functionality would be less than that present in most graphics systems. Therefore, a rigid position which would restrict the normalization transformation was rejected.

On the other hand, it was decided not to include shielding as it was recognized that applications usually require shielding for hundreds of inscriptions and that this surely went beyond the capabilities provided by a kernel system.

The main argument for a single normalization transformation was simplicity of concept and simplicity of implementation.

The main argument for multiple normalization transformations was that many applications generate graphical output from different WCs in non-overlapping areas of the display surface. These applications expect that coordinate input be delivered in the correct WC. This can be achieved without too large an overhead using the concept described above. If only one normalization transformation could be used for input, the resulting coordinates would sometimes be in the correct WC and sometimes not and this could be worse than having no transformation at all.

It was decided to make a compromise. Multiple normalization transformations may be defined. One of them will be selected explicitly by the application program for output. One of them will be selected automatically on a viewport priority basis for input. The details are given in Chapter III.5.

3.6   Workstation Concept

Should GKS support only one workstation at a time?

The first GKS versions allowed only one workstation at a time to be addressed. Arguments in favour of this concept were:
— Most applications only use one workstation at a time.
— Simplicity. Multiple workstations need multiple transformation pipelines; device drivers must be resident simultaneously. This increases the complexity and the costs of implementation considerably.
— The parameter 'workstation identifier' can be removed from the parameter list of many GKS functions. Otherwise, all applications would have to refer to the workstation explicitly in all workstation-relevant GKS functions, although only one workstation was being used.
— One idea behind the definition of a kernel system was to implement it on a chip inside the graphics workstation. This can be achieved more easily if GKS addresses only one workstation at a time.

Although only one workstation at a time is required in many cases, interactive programs will use at least two workstations in succession: an interactive workstation for the generation and editing of a drawing and a passive workstation (plotter, metafile) for saving the final result. A facility had to be provided to transfer graphical data from one workstation to the other. The segment storage had already been designed to store a description of the drawing for interactive manipulation. In order to let graphical data be transferred to other workstations, an INSERT function was defined, which could send copies of segments to any workstation (including the same workstation).

The INSERT function was attacked from many sides. The arguments were:

— INSERT requires the maintenance of all segments in workstation-independent format, whether they will be copied or not. Considerable overhead is thus imposed on the kernel system.
— INSERT allows generation of several instances of a segment at the same workstation. This is a high-level (modelling) function which should not be present in a kernel system.
— INSERT provides three different functions which should be kept separate:
  a) copying of segments from one workstation's segment storage into another workstation's segment storage;
  b) copying of primitives within a segment to the display surface of another workstation, without touching the segment storage;
  c) generation of several instances of a segment on the same display surface.

Another discussion, independent of the INSERT issue, came to the conclusion that multiple workstations are not that uncommon (e.g., training programs with teacher and student in front of separate displays, control of film plotter output on a display, or games). It was stated that it should be possible to address multiple workstations on a lower level than INSERT and without having to store segments in workstation-independent format.

It was finally decided that multiple workstations be accepted. This decision was facilitated by the evolution of the workstation concept for GKS which made evident all the workstation dependencies which, beforehand, had been hidden within an implementation.

The INSERT function was kept and split into three functions, INSERT SEGMENT, ASSOCIATE SEGMENT WITH WORKSTATION, and COPY SEGMENT TO WORKSTATION, each serving exactly one purpose as indicated above. The application program can open several workstations if simultaneous output really is required, or can use one of the above functions if a transfer of a picture to another workstation is desired.

PART III

GRAPHICAL KERNEL SYSTEM PROGRAMMING

Part III gives a detailed description of the functional capabilities of 2D GKS. It is the basic reference book for the application programmer using GKS, as well as for teachers and students. For every one of the different areas of the system, a detailed explanation of the concept is given. Every GKS function and every GKS data structure relevant to that area is explained extensively. For all the functions, both the language-independent definition from the GKS standard and the FORTRAN programming language interface are given. Examples used to clarify the GKS functions are presented both in Pascal and FORTRAN. Exercises are included in order to help in the teaching of GKS. The 3D extensions are dealt with in Part IV.

1 FORMAT AND STRUCTURE OF PART III

1.1 Contents of Part III

Whereas Part I of this book presented a general overview of the principles and concepts of the Graphical Kernel System, and Part II described the process of creating this standard, Part III gives a detailed description of the functional capabilities of GKS. Therefore, this part provides the basic reference for the application programmer using GKS. It also serves as a framework for teaching and learning computer graphics on the basis of GKS. For every one of the different areas of the system, a detailed explanation of the concept is given. Every GKS function and every GKS data structure relevant to that area is explained extensively. For all functions, both the language-independent definition from the GKS standard and the FORTRAN programming language interface are given.

Examples are used extensively throughout Part III to clarify the application of GKS functions. They are an important complement to the definition of the functions, both for the application programmer and for the novice learning to use GKS. The examples are presented in two versions which correspond to each other: one version uses Pascal as a programming language and the second version uses FORTRAN. In the Pascal version, the GKS functions are spelled as in the GKS standard document (e.g., OPEN GKS) rather than being presented in the short forms as specified in the Pascal language binding (see Section V.4.3). In the FORTRAN version, the function names are taken from the FORTRAN language interface (e.g., CALL GOPKS). Since the program constructs in Pascal are more powerful and allow for a presentation of examples according to the principles of structured programming, they are generally more easily readable than the FORTRAN examples. Therefore, the Pascal version is valuable not only to the Pascal programmer but also to the FORTRAN programmer and the GKS student. However, it is possible to work with the following chapters without looking at the language-independent functional definitions or at the Pascal version of the examples.

At the end of the following chapters, further examples have been added, covering typical tasks within the particular GKS area. They are also given in two language versions. These examples are meant primarily for teachers and students. Exercises are added at the end of each chapter in order to help in the teaching of GKS. Most, but not all, of the examples and the exercises have been tested by students during computer graphics courses at Darmstadt Technical University. Since the GKS implementations could not always keep up with the latest alterations to the GKS document, some examples could not be tested in their final versions.

1.2 Format of GKS Function Definitions

The definition of functions is given in two versions. The language-independent definition is taken almost literally from the GKS standard document [GKS85].

The FORTRAN binding for the given function is taken from the GKS FORTRAN binding DP8651/1 [ISO85a]. Section V.4.2 gives the complete FORTRAN binding. It is based on the FORTRAN 77 standard [FORT77].

1.2.1   Example of the Definition of GKS Functions

REQUEST CHOICE		WSOP, WSAC, SGOP	L0a

Parameters:

Input	workstation identifier		N
Input	choice device number	(1..n)	I
Output	status	(OK, NONE, NOCHOICE)	E
Output	choice number	(1..n)	I

Effect:
GKS performs a REQUEST on the specified CHOICE device. If the break facility is invoked by the operator, the returned status will be NONE, otherwise OK is returned, together with the logical input value which is the current measure of the CHOICE device. The choice number zero means 'no choice'.

Errors:

7	GKS not in proper state: GKS should be in one of the states WSOP, WSAC or SGOP
20	Specified workstation identifier is invalid
25	Specified workstation is not open
38	Specified workstation is neither of category INPUT nor of category OUTIN
140	Specified input device is not present at the workstation
141	Input device is not in REQUEST mode

———————————————— *FORTRAN Interface* ————————————————

CALL GRQCH (WKID,CHDNR,STATUS,CHNR)

Parameters:

Input	WKID	workstation identifier		INTEGER
Input	CHDNR	choice device number	(1..n)	INTEGER
Output	STATUS	status	(0=NONE,1=OK, 2=NOCHOICE)	INTEGER
Output	CHNR	choice number	(0..n)	INTEGER

1.2.2   Format of Language-Independent Definition

The language-independent definition, taken from the GKS document, contains a heading, the parameters of the function, a description of its effect, and the errors that may occur when the function is called.

The heading of the function specifies:
— the function's name in the GKS document;
— the GKS states in which the function may be used (cf. Chapter 3);
— the GKS level up to which the function is available in a GKS implementation (cf. Chapter 2).

The parameter list indicates for each entry:
— whether the entry is an input (Input) or an output (Output) parameter (input parameters are passed from the application program to the function, output parameters are returned by the function to the application program);
— in the case of coordinate data, the coordinate system (WC, NDC, DC) to be used in the function call (cf. Chapter 5);
— either, in the case of enumeration type data, the permitted values, or in the case of real and integer data, any restriction on their value range;
— the data type.

The effect of the function is described informally by sentences in English. However, when developing the GKS standard document, the description was laid down as concisely as possible.

The error list contains the errors which can occur when the function is called. Both the error number and the meaning of the error are given. There are additional errors which can occur during evaluation of any GKS functions. Errors and error handling in GKS are described in Chapter 9.

Data types in the definition of functions are either simple types or a combination of simple types. Simple types are:

I integer: whole number;

R real: floating point number;

S string: number of characters and character sequence;

P point: 2 real values specifying the x- and y-coordinates of a location in WC, NDC or DC space;

N name: identification (used for error file, workstation type, escape function identification, GDP identifier, pick identifier, segment name and identification of a GKS workstation);

E enumeration type: a data type comprising an ordered set of values. The ordered set is defined by enumerating the identifiers which denote the values. This type is mapped, for example, onto scalar types in Pascal, or onto integers in FORTRAN.

D record: storage space of a given length.

A combination of simple types can be one of the following:
— a vector of values, for example, $2 \times R$;
— a matrix of values, for example, $2 \times 3 \times R$;
— a list of values of one type; the type can be a simple type or a vector, for example, $n \times I$ and $n \times 4 \times R$;
— an array of values of a simple type, for example, $n \times n \times I$;
— an ordered pair of different types, for example, $(I; E)$.

The occurrence of an n here merely indicates a variable integer value which does not necessarily have anything to do with other occurrences of n.

Permitted values or value ranges can be specified by:
— a condition, for example, >0 or $[0,1]$; the latter implies that the value lies between 0 and 1 inclusive;
— a standard range of integer values, for example, $(1..4)$;
— a range of integer values in which the maximum is determined by implementation or other constraints, for example $(32..n)$. Note that the occurrence of an n does not necessarily imply any relationship with other occurrences of n: it merely denotes a variable integer in this context;
— a list of values which constitute an enumeration type, for example, (SUPPRESSED, ALLOWED);
— an ordered list of any of the above.

1.2.3   Format of FORTRAN Definition

The FORTRAN interface for a GKS function contains a prototype function call and a description of the parameters. The effect and the errors are not repeated, since they can be taken from the language-independent definition of the function. Also, the GKS states in which the function may be called and the GKS levels at which it is available are the same as in the language-independent definition.

The prototype function call contains the FORTRAN keyword CALL, the FORTRAN name of the function, and the parameter list enclosed in parentheses. The parameters are identified by symbolic names.

The parameter description contains for every parameter:
— whether it is an input (Input) or output (Output) parameter;
— its symbolic name;
— its name in the language-independent definition;
— its value range;
— its FORTRAN data type (REAL, INTEGER, CHARACTER or arrays thereof).

The FORTRAN parameters do not in all cases correspond one-to-one with the language-independent parameters. For example, the GKS data type 'point' is mapped onto two FORTRAN REAL values, 'name' is mapped onto INTEGER, and 'enumerated value' is mapped onto INTEGER. The mapping of the GKS data type 'data record' may differ from function to function. Thus the mapping is described together with the function. The mapping of the permitted values of enumeration type parameters represents a one-to-one correspondence of the values given in the language-independent and the FORTRAN definitions. In the example above (Section 1.2.1), the INTEGER values (0, 1, 2) correspond to the enumerated values (NONE,OK,NOCHOICE).

1.3 Format of Examples

The examples given in Part III are all presented in two versions, i.e., the Pascal version and the FORTRAN version. In the Pascal version the syntax described in the Pascal User Manual and Report [WIRT71] is followed as closely as possible. However, in most cases the examples are not complete Pascal programs, procedures or functions, but parts thereof. In many instances, declarations and definitions have been omitted. GKS functions are referred to in the Pascal examples by using the names in the GKS standard document rather than the short forms of the Pascal language binding.

The FORTRAN version will have the same basic effect as the Pascal version. However, the statements of both versions will not correspond one-to-one in every case. Whereas the Pascal version of the examples is used primarily to clarify GKS functions and to teach computer graphics on the basis of GKS, the FORTRAN version should be readily executable on any implementation of the appropriate GKS level that realizes the GKS FORTRAN language interface.

Line numbers are used in the examples for two reasons:
— they show how the Pascal version and the FORTRAN version correspond, as identical line numbers are used for corresponding parts of the examples;
— they serve as a reference for parts of the examples in the explanatory text.

1.3.1 Example of an Example

Example 1.1   GKS Control

Opening and closing GKS.

———————————————————— *Pascal* ————————————————————

L10   OPEN_GKS (error_file, buffer);   {GKS is set into state GKS OPEN}
L20   CLOSE_GKS;   {GKS is set into state GKS CLOSED}

———————————————————— *Fortran* ————————————————————

L10   CALL GOPKS(ERRFIL,BUFA)
         C   *** sets GKS into state GKS OPEN
L20   CALL GCLKS
         C   *** sets GKS into state GKS CLOSED

1.3.2 Format of Pascal Examples

The Pascal examples consist of line numbers and a Pascal part. The Pascal part may be a complete Pascal program, procedure or function, a part thereof or even a fragment thereof. A line number consists of the letter 'L' followed by a decimal number. They are in the left-hand margin of the example in ascending order. GKS functions are spelled as in the GKS standard document. The function names used in the Pascal language binding can be found in Section V.4.3. If the function name consists of several words, the separating blanks are replaced by underscores (e.g., OPEN_GKS). Parameters of GKS functions are given in the same order as in the GKS document and in a one-to-one correspondence. The keywords of the Pascal language are printed in lower case bold letters and variable identifiers are printed in lower case letters. Comments are given to explain the statements of each example. In the Pascal version, they are enclosed between '{' and '}'.

1.3.3   Format of FORTRAN Examples

The FORTRAN version of an example consists of the line numbers and the FORTRAN source part. The FORTRAN source may be a complete main program, a complete SUBROUTINE or FUNCTION or a part thereof. A statement that corresponds to a Pascal statement has been given the identical line number. If a series of FORTRAN statements corresponds to one Pascal statement, the first line number of the FORTRAN sequence will be identical to the Pascal line number. Function names, parameter sequence and parameter types are taken from the FORTRAN language definition. Comments are inserted in between other statements. According to FORTRAN rules they start with the letter C. For easier reading the comment text is preceded by '***', and within the comment text, lower case characters are used together with capital letters.

1.4   Exercises

Exercises are added to the chapters describing the major areas of GKS. They are arranged in order of increasing complexity. This also implies that the time needed to complete them may range from a few minutes to several hours. The exercises can serve as intensive training for students in computer graphics programming on the basis of the Graphical Kernel System. In order to do the exercises in the most profitable way, an implementation of the appropriate GKS level should be available.

2   LEVELS

2.1   Overview

GKS, as a general-purpose graphical kernel system, is designed to address most of the existing graphics devices as well as most graphics applications. GKS implementations have to serve a wide range of applications, from static plotting to dynamic motion and real time interaction. In addition, GKS systems have to support a large variety of graphics devices, from simple plotters, microfilms, and storage tubes, to highly sophisticated vector devices and real time raster-scan devices. Furthermore, they have to be installed on various processors which differ in aspects such as their word length (starting from 8 bits/word) and storage handling facilities (restricted memory size, slow external storage media, up to virtual memory management).

Obviously, it is not sensible to use one fixed GKS system for all these different purposes. On the contrary, it is desirable to tailor GKS to fit the special qualities of the specific environments which exist at any one time. An important means of adapting a GKS system is provided by the definition of suitable subsystems, called levels.

The level concept was based on the following guidelines:

Generation of application-oriented subsets. For a representative set of application classes a suitable subset of graphics functions was selected; thus, no extra burden in acquiring, installing, learning, memorizing, and handling unnecessary functions is placed upon the system and application programmers.

Implementation feasibility. The capabilities of GKS are distributed among the levels in such a way that subsystems with considerably smaller program sizes can be implemented. This is achieved by isolating specific concepts and assigning them to the single levels; thus, concepts can be integrated or omitted as a whole. This reduces compilation, linkage editor, and program performance times and supports the usage of small-memory machines.

Upward-compatibility. All GKS functions are defined so that they have identical effects on all levels in which they exist. Regardless of which GKS level an application program is written for, it will run on every higher level, achieving the same results.

In GKS, capabilities are expressed by functions and by ranges of parameters.

There are three different types of capability at each level:

an explicitly defined and required capability. Every GKS implementation at a specific level must support the capability at that level.
an explicitly defined but not required capability. A GKS implementation may support the capability and, if it does, it must be implemented according to the explicit function definitions.
a conceptually defined but not required capability. A GKS implementation may provide this capability. Its implementation has to follow the general rules laid down by the GKS concepts and functional definitions.

Explicitly defined and required capabilities

Obviously an application program using GKS has to rely on the existence of certain capabilities in every GKS implementation, regarding both functions and possibilities within the functions addressed by parameters. To meet these requirements, GKS defines exactly the minimal support which must be provided at each level by every implementation. All the functions in one level belong to this type of capability at this specific level. Further examples are: the four linetypes "solid", "dashed", "dotted", and "dash-dotted", the marker types 1 to 5, text precision STROKE for the output levels 1 and 2 and a minimum of 10 definable normalization transformations at all levels higher than 0.

Table 2.2 specifies exactly the minimal support which must be provided at each level.

Explicitly defined but not required capabilities

The minimal required capabilities are defined in such a way that a significant number of applications are supported sufficiently in the respective levels. Of course, certain applications may need considerably more facilities, such as a large number of attribute bundles or simultaneously available workstations, a set of hatch styles for filling polygons or certain prompt/echo types for logical input devices, if they are to improve support for human operators with given interactive application problems. The set of explicitly defined but not required capabilities includes: text precision STROKE at the output level 0, the interior styles SOLID, PATTERN, HATCH, and prompt/echo types above 1.

General purpose implementations should provide a means of extending their features by application-required facilities within the same concept. If, for example, high quality text fonts are implemented in a system on a stroke basis, then an extension by other stroke-based fonts should be easily possible. In general, it should be possible to describe the application requirements to a GKS system and to adjust the implementation to give optimal support. This, of course, calls for some sophisticated design decisions and special implementation structures. Existing approaches to design configurable adaptive systems can be found in [PARN75] for the operating systems area and in [PFAF82a] for the field of computer graphics. Furthermore, Part V describes implementation structures which allow for flexible implementations.

Conceptually defined but not required capabilities

An application may need GKS facilities which are not explicitly defined in the standard; they are only conceptually provided and general rules for their effects are given. Examples are: implementation-dependent linetypes and marker types, specific generalized drawing primitives such as circle, ellipse, arcs, splines, etc., prompt/echo types above the defined set, and specific escape functions.

All of these features must not violate the GKS design, e.g., using a special linetype to draw invisible lines seems not to be a valid interpretation of the concept of linetypes. Moreover, it should be mentioned that the use of these features may decrease the portability of programs to a great extent.

In many cases, GKS capabilities which are conceptually defined use an integer type parameter to select a specific instance of that capability. Linetypes, for example, are selected by numbers. In all cases, only part of the number range is explicitly made use of in GKS standard definitions (for linetypes 1 to 4 only). In all these cases, the remaining positive number range is reserved for future standardization or registration and may not be used by an implementation. A registration authority will be set up (under the management of the

U.S. National Bureau of Standards) which will register graphical items at the request of a National Standards Institution and be directed by the ISO Working Group for Computer Graphics. The negative number range, on the other hand, is freely available to implementors for implementation-specific or application-dependent purposes.

2.2   Functionality of the GKS Levels

In this section, the capabilities of each GKS level are described. Some application classes for each of the levels are illustrated and typical graphical devices and hardware configurations for specific applications and levels are listed.

The functional capabilities of GKS can be grouped into the following major areas:

a) output (minimal performance, full performance);
b) input (no input, REQUEST input, full input);
c) number of workstations (one workstation, multiple workstations);
d) attributes (predefined bundles and direct attributes, full attribute concept);
e) segmentation (none, basic segmentation, full segmentation).

If an arbitrary combination of capabilities were considered to be a valid GKS implementation, an almost unlimited number of different standard dialects would result (each one being a combination of one alternative in each axis). This would markedly reduce the portability of application programs since every application uses a different set of capabilities. Therefore, nine valid levels of the GKS system have been defined which can address the most common classes of equipment and applications.

As shown in Table 2.1, GKS separates its facilities into two independent axes which basically can be described as "input" and "all the other functions" summarized as "output". The output level axis has the three possibilities:

0: Minimal output;
1: Basic segmentation with full output;
2: Workstation-Independent Segment Storage (full segmentation).

The input level axis also has three possibilities:

a: No input;
b: REQUEST input;
c: Full input.

Before describing the functionality of each level, the overall structure of Table 2.1 needs a few comments. Each box represents a valid GKS level. It contains a description of the main capabilities of the level in a few keywords. In order to obtain all the capabilities of a specific level, one has to add the functions of the lower levels (previous boxes of the same row and the same column) to the ones described in the specific box. This also expresses the functional compatibility: each function can automatically be used at all the higher levels.

Table 2.1 Capabilities of the levels

	NO INPUT	REQUEST INPUT	FULL INPUT
Minimal Output	All five output primitives; all direct attributes; GDP, if workstation support is available; predefined bundles; at least 5 polyline, 5 polymarker, 2 text, and 5 fill area bundles; multiple normalization transformation facility (at least 1 settable transformation); metafile functions optional; multiple workstation concept, at least 1 output workstation.	Request input functions for LOCATOR, STROKE, VALUATOR, CHOICE and STRING; initialise and set device mode functions; SET VIEWPORT INPUT PRIORITY function; at least one input workstation available.	SAMPLE and EVENT input concept; event queue concept.
Full Output and Basic Segmentation	Multiple workstations; full bundle concept (redefinition of predefined bundles possible, and at least 20 user-settable bundles required); metafile functions and metafile workstations required; basic segmentation.	Request PICK input; initialise PICK device; set PICK device mode.	SAMPLE and EVENT input for PICK device.
Segment Storage Output	Workstation-independent segment storage; INSERT SEGMENT; COPY SEGMENT TO WORKSTATION; ASSOCIATE SEGMENT WITH WORKSTATION.		

2.2.1 The Minimal or Lowest Level of GKS (Level 0 a)

Functionality

The lowest GKS level only contains a subset of the GKS functions, but it can address quite a large community of graphics users. Its capabilities cover all output primitives, normalization transformations, predefined bundles and direct attributes, restricted control of workstations, and associated inquiry functions.

One of the aims of this level is to provide an adequate set of graphics functions for "data representation graphics". Implementations of this level

Table 2.2 Minimum support required at each level

CAPABILITY	Level								
	0a	0b	0c	1a	1b	1c	2a	2b	2c
Foreground colours (intensity)	1	1	1	1	1	1	1	1	1
Linetypes	4	4	4	4	4	4	4	4	4
Linewidths	1	1	1	1	1	1	1	1	1
Predefined polyline bundles	5	5	5	5	5	5	5	5	5
Settable polyline bundles	—	—	—	20	20	20	20	20	20
Marker types	5	5	5	5	5	5	5	5	5
Marker sizes	1	1	1	1	1	1	1	1	1
Predefined polymarker bundles	5	5	5	5	5	5	5	5	5
Settable polymarker bundles	—	—	—	20	20	20	20	20	20
Character heights (cf. note 1)	1	1	1	1	1	1	1	1	1
Character expansion factors (cf. note 1)	1	1	1	1	1	1	1	1	1
String precision fonts	1	1	1	1	1	1	1	1	1
Character precision fonts	1	1	1	1	1	1	1	1	1
Stroke precision fonts	0	0	0	2	2	2	2	2	2
Predefined text bundles	2	2	2	6	6	6	6	6	6
Settable text bundles	—	—	—	20	20	20	20	20	20
Predefined patterns (cf. note 2)	1	1	1	1	1	1	1	1	1
Settable patterns (cf. notes 2 and 5)	—	—	—	10	10	10	10	10	10
Hatch styles (cf. note 3)	3	3	3	3	3	3	3	3	3
Predefined fill area bundles	5	5	5	5	5	5	5	5	5
Settable fill area bundles	—	—	—	10	10	10	10	10	10
Settable normalization transformations	1	1	1	10	10	10	10	10	10
Segment priorities (cf. note 4)	—	—	—	2	2	2	2	2	2
Input classes	—	5	5	—	6	6	—	6	6
Prompt/echo types per device	—	1	1	—	1	1	—	1	1
Length of input queue (cf. note 5)	—	—	20	—	—	20	—	—	20
Maximum string buffer size (characters)	—	72	72	—	72	72	—	72	72
Maximum stroke buffer size (points)	—	64	64	—	64	64	—	64	64
Workstations capable of output	1	1	1	1	1	1	1	1	1
Workstations capable of input	—	1	1	—	1	1	—	1	1
Workstation-independent segment storage	—	—	—	—	—	—	1	1	1
Metafile output workstations	0	0	0	1	1	1	1	1	1
Metafile input workstations	0	0	0	1	1	1	1	1	1

0 indicates explicitly defined but not required at that level
— indicates not defined at that level

Notes:
1) Relevant only for character and string precision text
2) Relevant only for workstations supporting pattern interior style
3) Relevant only for workstations supporting hatch interior style
4) Relevant only for workstations supporting segment priorities
5) Since available resources are finite and entries vary in size, it may not always be possible to achieve the minimal values in a particular application.

should produce small systems that are simple, easy to learn and memorize, and easy to handle even for unskilled, occasional users. The lowest level supports the drawing of polygons, lines, markers, and texts using attributes such as colour, linetype, marker and character size, font, pattern and hatch style. Furthermore, higher, more application-specific graphics functions, such as "axes", can easily be constructed using the basic GKS primitives POLYLINE, POLY-MARKER, TEXT, FILL AREA, and CELL ARRAY, and the GENERAL-IZED DRAWING PRIMITIVE (GDP).

Workstation-dependent predefined bundles exist as combinations of work-station attributes. These can be selected by the application program. Dynamic changes are prevented because the bundles cannot be redefined. Furthermore, level 0a includes all the direct output primitive attributes. To take advantage of the colour tables of many colour raster displays, a SET COLOUR REPRE-SENTATION function is also provided at this level. This makes it possible to modify colour entries, which are addressed by indices.

Level 0a requires only one graphics workstation. To support special applica-tion needs, metafile functions and metafile workstations may be available at this lowest level. If, however, a metafile input workstation is present, then at least one output workstation must also be available. This makes it possible to generate and interpret metafiles and to transport pictures between suitable level 0a installations.

Level 0a systems include the concept of multiple normalization transforma-tions. However, they are permitted to implement only one definable normaliza-tion transformation in addition to the default transformation 0.

Finally, the inquiry functions should be mentioned. Application programs may ask for information, such as predefined bundle contents and the maximum display size, so that they can adjust themselves to actual workstation qualities and control the precise picture scale. Furthermore, there is a function which asks for the extent of the text for a given text output primitive at a specific workstation. It can be used to place and concatenate text strings within a picture.

Applications

Applications of level 0a can be characterized as gathering data from some source (external files or program) and displaying them in a graphical form on a screen or on a plotter device. After a picture has been generated, its colours can be changed if the connected workstation is equipped with a colour look-up table. Other changes in the picture, or in parts of it, can only be performed by the application program: this has to erase the contents of the display surface (CLEAR WORKSTATION) and to regenerate the picture. Other applications may use a GKS level 0a system for low-level output purposes where they utilize GKS as a device-independent graphics driver. Examples of this are image pro-cessing systems (supported by INQUIRE PIXEL, INQUIRE PIXEL ARRAY) and three-dimensional output packages built on top of GKS.

Configurations

Level 0a (L0a) implementations can be installed on a variety of computers, starting from 8 bit microprocessors with integer arithmetic, simple operating systems, and slow external storage devices. They normally support output-only devices without any display files, such as grey-scale or colour vector and raster plotters, microfilm devices, storage tube devices, and also simple raster and vector refresh displays.

2.2.2 Level 0b

Functionality

Level 0b was designed to make simple interaction possible for roughly the same graphics community which uses level 0a systems, at only slightly higher costs. It contains all the functions of L0a and in addition provides REQUEST input functions. The input of positions (LOCATOR), of point sequences (STROKE), of real values (VALUATOR), of integer-coded alternatives (CHOICE), and of texts (STRING) is therefore possible. Furthermore, there are INITIALISE and SET DEVICE MODE functions to control how and where the echoes of the logical input devices appear as well as the display of prompting and echoing. The locator/stroke coordinate transformations from device to world coordinates can be controlled (details about input are explained in Chapter 8).

Applications

With the help of this level, it is possible to enter the data (e.g., for diagrams and charts) via the graphical workstation while the program is being executed. If the echo facilities are applied in a suitable way, even simple correction facilities are available. Bar charts, for instance, may be constructed interactively using locator prompt/echo type 5, i.e., a rectangle is drawn from an initial point to the current locator position while the operator is using the input device.

Configurations

Suitable configurations for level 0b must include workstations that have some input facilities. Alphanumeric and function keyboards are standard equipment. Extensions could be:
— thumb wheels;
— tracking balls;
— joysticks;
— lightpens connected to display devices;
— tablets;
— the positioning and input facilities of plotters, etc.

Most of these devices can be used to implement the five logical input devices of this level.

Table 2.3 Applications listed according to levels

Level	Applications
L0a	Business graphics; microfilm and metafile output; metafile input and interpretation; low-level output driver for higher graphics systems such as three-dimensional drawing systems
L0b	Interactive business graphics; process control; simple picture generating systems; input supply for higher graphics systems.
L0c	Input-based systems with large interaction requirements, such as digitizing applications; optimal usage of physical input device qualities using predefined multiple input device associations.
L1a L1b L1c	Multiple workstation systems; display of several pictures simultaneously; interaction with and manipulation of picture subparts; design applications and simulation systems.
L2a L2b L2c	Design and drafting systems with maximal usage of GKS facilities; re-use of previously defined segments for picture construction; copying of workstation contents to other workstations; office automation systems; graphical editors; CAD systems.

2.2.3 Level 0c

Functionality

By increasing the capabilities of the input component, we come to level 0c. EVENT and SAMPLE input expand the application range to input-oriented systems with strong requirements for interaction processing. Stress is placed on the real time input of large data sets which must not be obstructed by other computation tasks. The requirements for graphical output are considerably smaller than the input requirements at this level.

An input buffer (EVENT QUEUE) compensates the differing processing speeds of the application program, which takes the data from the queue and processes it, and the operator who enters the data into the queue.

An additional major aspect of the event and sample concept at this level is the possibility it gives of connecting several logical input devices to one or more physical devices. Such a device enables the operator to generate several input reports simultaneously and put them into the queue with one action. This level of input should be chosen for high quality interactive applications, so that full advantage may be taken of existing input devices, and good operator tools should be provided. The crosshair device of some digitizers may serve as an example: it enables locator position and an integer value (choice) to be generated simultaneously, when one of the available cursor buttons is pressed.

Applications

Typical examples are digitizing applications in cartography, architecture, and similar areas, where the speed and sequence of input actions is controlled by a human operator.

Configurations

A typical configuration for a level 0c system and a digitizing application consists of a 16 bit processor with a multitasking operating system, a digitizer, and a storage tube or an alphanumeric raster device for displaying the data entered on the digitizer as graphical feedback.

Table 2.4 Processors and graphical devices listed according to levels

Level	Processors	Graphical Devices
L0a	Starting with 8 bit processors (8,16,20,32,36... bits/word); static memory handler; slow external storage media sufficient.	Microfilm, raster and vector plotters, alphanumeric displays and printers, TV monitors, simple storage tubes, simple raster and vector refresh devices.
L0b	As in L0a	Output devices as in L0a; input devices such as alphanumeric and function keyboards, tracking balls, lightpens, tablets, thumb wheels, joysticks.
L0c	Starting with 16 bit processors; multitasking facilities or programmable interrupt handling; possibly dynamic storage handling for event queue.	as in L0b; plus digitizers, shape sampling devices.
L1a L1b L1c	Starting with 16 bit processors; dynamic storage or virtual memory management; fast access to secondary memory desirable.	Vector devices with segmented display file; sophisticated features such as clipping and transformations desirable; storage tubes with refresh components; raster devices with several picture planes; fast raster scan displays with microcomputer intelligence for, e.g. hidden surface elimination; for 1b and 1c systems, lightpens which deliver segment identifiers calculated from display file addresses or by coordinate comparison on raster scan displays.
L2a L2b L2c	As in level 1 systems with emphasis laid on effective storage management.	

2.2.4   Levels 1a, 1b, 1c

Functionality

If we continue by increasing the output capabilities, we come to the levels 1a, 1b, and 1c. These levels cover all GKS concepts except the workstation-independent segment storage. The bundling concept of attributes is completed. Different combinations of attributes can be defined for the presentation of polylines, polymarkers, texts, and fill areas; it is possible to select which one is to be currently in use. If the attributes which have already been used for output are changed, this is done retrospectively, i.e., the appearance of output on a specific workstation changes according to the new attributes either dynamically or after an image regeneration.

Finally, the segmentation feature is introduced. Segments can be created, deleted, transformed, and manipulated. This level, however, restricts the usage of segments: no transportation from one workstation to another and no insertion of previously defined segments into new ones is possible. Of course, the application program (or a system on top of GKS) may generate output at one workstation, check it, and generate (corrected) output at a second workstation. This restriction may avoid the potential overhead of a workstation-independent segment storage, which has to keep the graphics primitives in a device-independent format.

Looking at Table 2.1, if one proceeds from left to right, it is apparent that, firstly, request input and, secondly, event and sample input are added. The input facilities of the levels 1b and 1c differ from those of 0b and 0c only by having the PICK input function. This difference is caused by the segmentation facility of these levels: segments and primitive groups within segments which are separated by PICK IDENTIFIERs can be identified by the PICK input function.

Applications

Typical level 1 applications require one or several of the following features:
— full attribute facilities (i.e., the bundling concept);
— simultaneous use of multiple workstations;
— graphical structures.

Multiple workstations are needed for:
— using several screens when displaying an overview and details of one picture at the same time;
— generating pictures interactively and finally redrawing them on a plotter;
— using several planes of certain raster devices in order to display and manipulate different pieces of graphical information independently;
— displaying the same information at several workstations simultaneously, e.g., in teacher-student systems.

Segment structure is needed to identify and manipulate subparts of pictures. This is necessary, for example, for the design of printed circuit board layout, shipbuilding design, and generally in CAD systems.

Configurations

In general, the same devices as in level 0 systems can also be used for level 1 implementations. Some extra facilities are desirable and can be utilized by efficient GKS implementations, in order to avoid expensive software simulations:

— The ability to keep and identify segments, and possibly perform segment manipulations by hardware without having to regenerate the picture. This is provided by many vector display devices and the up-and-coming raster scan devices which keep a coordinate-oriented display file.
— Sophisticated hardware (or local firmware) facilities such as clipping, coordinate transformations, hidden line and hidden surface elimination for two-dimensional (and 2.5 dimensional) applications.
— The maintenance of attribute tables (for colours, linetypes, patterns, etc.), in order to perform retroactive attribute changes dynamically.

It should be noted that all missing device capabilities can be simulated by the GKS system. The differences between this and the hardware (or firmware) solutions become obvious when looking at performance time and memory requirements.

2.2.5   Levels 2a, 2b, 2c

Functionality

The highest GKS levels 2a, 2b, and 2c integrate the workstation-independent segment storage and the level 1 facilities. There are three new functions, INSERT SEGMENT which re-uses segments which have already been defined to create new segments, COPY SEGMENT TO WORKSTATION which displays primitives of a segment on a workstation, and ASSOCIATE SEGMENT WITH WORKSTATION which transports segments from the segment storage to a workstation.

Applications

Applications of the highest GKS levels differ from those of level 1 systems because they use the GKS facilities more extensively. Basically, there are two application types. The first one is completely or largely supported by GKS: two-dimensional pictures are generated interactively or read in from a metafile, edited using the input and segmentation functions, and finally copied to a plotter device and stored on a metafile for long-term storage.

The other application type uses higher graphics systems such as three-dimensional design and drawing systems, simulation systems, etc. which themselves use GKS as a basis. Unstructured GKS input data is mapped onto structured application data and the application object structure is mapped onto GKS segments and primitives. In contrast to applications which only use level 0 output functions and perform the modelling solely in the higher system, in this case the object structure is realized by both GKS segments and structural information in the modelling system. The manipulation task is split into firstly modelling this structural information and then using GKS segment manipulation functions to create the visual effect.

Configurations

Level 2 systems can be implemented on the same types of processors and graphical devices as level 1 systems. Some more emphasis is laid on the handling of the device-independent segment storage; fast storage handling is needed either in the form of a direct access file or by a large main memory. The latter can be supplied by a virtual memory management.

2.3 The Impact on Writing Portable Application Programs

Every GKS application program needs a specific set of capabilities, expressed by a set of functions and a set of parameters for each function. The function of the highest level which is used by the application program determines the required GKS level. The set of capabilities required by the application program defines the support which a GKS implementation has to provide.

If a program is to be transported to another GKS implementation, it has to be ensured that all the capabilities needed are available there. In order to avoid erroneous program executions, either the required capabilities are described in an accompanying documentation and checked by an operator, or — more conveniently — an "Inquire Facility Program" is supplied. In the most simple case, this consists of the instructions given in Example 2.1:

Example 2.1   Check GKS level

––––––––––––––––––––––––––––––––––– *Pascal* ––––––––––––––––––––––––

```
L10      required_level: = ..... ;
L20      INQUIRE_LEVEL_OF_GKS (error,level);
L30      if (level < required_level) then begin
L40         write ("available GKS level too low for program requirements");
L50         goto lend;
L60      end {end if block};
L...
L...     {program code};
L...
L9999    lend: end {end of program};
```

––––––––––––––––––––––––––––––––––– *Fortran* ––––––––––––––––––––––––

```
L10              REQLEV = ....
L20              CALL GQLVKS (ERRIND,LEVEL)
L30              IF (LEVEL .GE. REQLEV) GOTO 70
L40              WRITE (ERRFIL,1)
L50              GOTO 9990
L55      1       FORMAT (53H available GKS level too low for program requirements)
L70      70      CONTINUE
L...
L...             {program code}
L...
L9990    9990    STOP
L9999            END
```

Example 2.2   Check GKS facilities

If more than the minimal required support of Table 2.2 is required to perform the application program, then Example 2.1 has to be extended, e.g. as follows.

———————————————————— *Pascal* ————————————————————

```
L70    INQUIRE_MAXIMUM_NORMALIZATION_TRANSFORMA-
       TION_NUMBER (error,number);
L80    if (number < required_number) then begin
L90       write ("number of available norm. transformations too small");
L100      goto lend;
L110   end {end if block};
L...
L...   {program code};
L...
L9999  lend: end {end of program};
```

———————————————————— *Fortran* ————————————————————

```
L70           CALL GQMNTN (ERRIND,MAXTNR)
L80           IF (MAXTNR .GE. REQNB) GOTO 20
L90           WRITE (ERRFIL,1)
L100          GOTO 9990
L105   1      FORMAT (52H number of available norm. transformations too small)
L120   20     CONTINUE
L...
L...          {program code}
L...
L9990  9990   STOP
L9999         END
```

2.4   Exercises

Exercise 2.1   Checking the capabilities of a GKS implementation

Assume an application program uses, among other functions, the following GKS capabilities:
— POLYLINE, SET POLYLINE INDEX (indices 1 to 6);
— SET WINDOW, SET VIEWPORT for keeping 5 normalization transformations simultaneously;
— REQUEST LOCATOR via LOCATOR device 2;

Which GKS level is needed? Write a check program which decides whether the application program can be performed on a given GKS implementation. It should also generate a message which lists the GKS capabilities which are required but not available.

Exercise 2.2   Determining the required GKS level

Write a program which automatically scans FORTRAN GKS programs, to decide the required level of a GKS implementation. Restrict yourself to inspecting GKS subroutine calls.

3   STATES AND STATE LISTS

This chapter deals with the states of GKS and the data structures describing them. The operating states of GKS form a central concept within GKS and make a strict structure in graphics programming necessary. For example, a workstation can be accessed only after a certain sequence of initializing functions has been invoked; output can be generated only after a workstation has been activated; workstation attributes can be set only after the workstation has been allocated. Therefore, the novice should read Sections 3.2 and 3.3 carefully. There the different operating states are introduced and those functions listed which are allowed in the respective operating states. Section 3.4 describes the content of some state lists. It is aimed primarily at implementors and experienced users of GKS. Section 3.5 introduces the first two GKS functions: OPEN GKS and CLOSE GKS.

3.1   Introduction

GKS contains some 100 functions which affect its state in one way or another. Output functions modify the state of the display surfaces; attribute setting functions change the state of the GKS nucleus or of a workstation and thus influence the appearance of output primitives; input functions set and inquire into the state of the input devices.

In order to make the GKS states clear, GKS has explicitly defined some data structures which define the major aspects of GKS states and help users and implementors in understanding the effect of each GKS function and the relationship between different GKS functions. These data structures are grouped into the following subsets:
— operating state;
— error state list;
— GKS description table;
— GKS state list;
— workstation description table for every existing workstation type;
— workstation state list for every open workstation;
— segment state list for every existing segment.

The description tables contain entries which describe implementation restrictions or workstation characteristics. The table entries remain constant within one implementation but may differ from one implementation to another. They will be set by the implementor rather than by the users of GKS. The state lists contain state variables which can be set by GKS functions. The state lists are initialised using the description tables or as specified by the implementor.

All values in the above state lists and tables may be inquired into by an application program. The description tables allow an application program to adapt its behaviour to the capabilities of an implementation or a workstation. The state lists reflect the current state of GKS. They are of importance, for example, for complex application systems where subsystems use GKS independently. By inquiring into and storing the current state of all affected state variables when entering the subsystem and by resetting them to these values before leaving it, a subsystem can use GKS without having any side-effects on other subsystems.

Some very important data structures are not contained in any state list: the data structures describing graphical output. Generally, graphical output cannot be retrieved after it has been generated. However, for raster devices with a readable pixel store, the state of the individual pixels can be inquired into. For output contained in segments, a data structure will be generated internally. The segment as a whole may be retrieved, but there is no access to the primitives within the segment. However, GKS contains an interface to a graphics metafile. This metafile can be used to store graphical output and to retrieve individual primitives and attributes.

3.2   Operating States

GKS functions will usually refer to entries of some state lists and, therefore, can only be invoked if the corresponding state list is available. In order to clarify when which particular functions are allowed, five different operating states of GKS have been defined:

GKCL = GKS closed;
GKOP = GKS open;
WSOP = at least one workstation open;
WSAC = at least one workstation active;
SGOP = segment open.

GKS is always in exactly one of these operating states. The operating states differ in the state lists that are available and the data structures that can be built up. State lists and description tables made available in one operating state are also available in the subsequent ones.

The above five operating states of GKS cannot, naturally, cover all aspects of GKS. They only cover overall aspects but do not characterize the individual state of a workstation. Each workstation may be opened and activated individually. The GKS states can only reflect this precisely if, at most, one workstation is addressed. Otherwise, only the highest state reached by some workstation is reflected. Furthermore, each workstation may have several input devices which can be in one of the operating modes REQUEST, EVENT, and SAMPLE. The operating states only reflect whether a workstation has been chosen and, therefore, input is possible but not whether input devices are available or what the operating mode of an individual input device is.

The initial state of GKS is *GKCL (GKS closed)*. If a dynamic allocation of resources is possible, all the graphical resources, state lists and description tables are deallocated. Only the operating state and the error state list exist. The operating state indicates that GKS is closed.

Usually, the first GKS function to be invoked will be OPEN GKS, which moves GKS to the state *GKOP (GKS open)*. OPEN GKS generates and initialises the GKS state list and makes it possible to inquire into the GKS description table and the workstation description tables for all available workstation types. In state GKOP some global attributes (workstation-independent primitive attributes and normalization transformations) may be set and will be recorded.

If input or output capabilities are to be used, a workstation with the desired capabilities has to be addressed. By OPEN WORKSTATION a specified workstation is allocated. OPEN WORKSTATION is invoked individually for each workstation. Each call generates and initialises a workstation state list. When the first workstation is opened, GKS moves from state GKOP to *WSOP (at least one workstation open)*. Subsequent calls do not change the operating state. Such calls occur in the states WSOP, WSAC or SGOP.

After a workstation has been opened, its input devices are immediately available for input in REQUEST mode. Each input device can be set independently to one of the operating modes REQUEST, EVENT, and SAMPLE by SET <input class> MODE. However, these substates are not considered to be separate GKS states.

The output capabilities of a workstation are enabled by ACTIVATE WORKSTATION. ACTIVATE WORKSTATION can be invoked individually for each open workstation. Output is then routed to all active workstations. When the first workstation is activated, GKS moves from state WSOP to *WSAC (at least one workstation active)*. No new state list is generated or made available. Subsequent calls of ACTIVATE WORKSTATION do not change the operating state. Such calls may occur in the state WSAC only.

CREATE SEGMENT moves GKS from state WSAC to *SGOP (segment open)*. In the state SGOP, graphical output is recorded in segments which may be manipulated as described in Chapter 7. CREATE SEGMENT generates and initialises the segment state list for the specified segment.

CLOSE SEGMENT moves GKS back from state SGOP to *WSAC*. The segment data structure is finished. No more output may be added to the segment. The segment state list, however, containing global attributes for the whole segment is still available for manipulations. More segments may be generated by reentering the state SGOP.

Each call of DEACTIVATE WORKSTATION disables output at the corresponding workstation. Only the deactivation of the last workstation moves GKS from state WSAC to *WSOP*. No more output can be generated. The output primitives contained within segments, however, are still available and they can be manipulated. Their visible effects, for example, when a segment is made visible, will also appear at open workstations.

Each call of CLOSE WORKSTATION disables input at the corresponding workstation and deletes the corresponding workstation state list. The workstation identifier is deleted from the lists of associated workstations for every segment. The input queue is flushed of all events from all devices at the workstation being closed. Only the closing of the last workstation can move GKS from state WSOP to *GKOP*. No more input may be generated at all. The segment storage is deleted and the input queue in the GKS state list is set at empty.

CLOSE GKS moves GKS from state GKOP to *GKCL*. The GKS state list is deleted. The GKS description table and all workstation description tables are no longer accessible. GKS can be reopened by invoking the function OPEN GKS.

Table 3.1 lists all the functions which control the state of GKS. Table 3.2 gives a summary of all the state lists and description tables in which they are available and the functions allocating or deallocating each list or table. Figure I.13.1 on page 48 illustrates the transitions within and between states.

Table 3.1 Functions changing the state of GKS

OPEN GKS	GKCL → GKOP	
OPEN WORKSTATION		
(first workstation)	GKOP → WSOP	
ACTIVATE WORKSTATION		
(first workstation)		WSOP → WSAC
CREATE SEGMENT		WSAC → SGOP
CLOSE SEGMENT		WSAC ← SGOP
DEACTIVATE WORKSTATION		
(last workstation)		WSOP ← WSAC
CLOSE WORKSTATION		
(last workstation)	GKOP ← WSOP	
CLOSE GKS	GKCL ← GKOP	

Table 3.2 Availability of state lists and description tables

operating state (exists always)	GKCL, GKOP, WSOP, WSAC, SGOP
error state list (exists always)	GKCL, GKOP, WSOP, WSAC, SGOP
GKS description table (made available by OPEN GKS, deallocated by CLOSE GKS)	GKOP, WSOP, WSAC, SGOP
workstation description table (made available by OPEN GKS, deallocated by CLOSE GKS)	GKOP, WSOP, WSAC, SGOP
GKS state list (generated by OPEN GKS, deallocated by CLOSE GKS)	GKOP, WSOP, WSAC, SGOP
workstation state list (one list generated by each call of OPEN WORKSTATION; one list deallocated by each call of CLOSE WORKSTATION)	WSOP, WSAC, SGOP
segment state list (one list generated by each call of CREATE SEGMENT; deallocated individually by calling DELETE SEGMENT, etc.; all deallocated by calling CLOSE WORKSTATION for last workstation)	WSOP, WSAC, SGOP

3.3   The Functions Allowed in Individual States

GKS functions can only be invoked in certain operating states which are indicated in the description of the individual function. This section gives an overview of the functions allowed in the five operating states.

Most GKS functions may be invoked in several states. However, the effect may be different in different states. For example, if output functions are invoked in state WSAC, output will be created only once and then will be discarded. If the same functions are invoked in state SGOP however, output will be recorded in a segment and will be regenerated automatically on all subsequent frames until the respective segment is deleted or made invisible.

In *any state,* the inquiry functions and the error handling functions may be invoked. The inquiry functions, however, can only provide data if the respective data structure is available. The operating state is the only value properly set in all states. The GKS state list and the GKS description table and the workstation description tables are available in states GKOP, WSOP, WSAC and SGOP. However, some entries of the GKS state list are meaningful in certain states only: the set of segment names in use and the input queue can only be non-empty if at least one workstation is open (WSOP, WSAC, SGOP); the name of the open segment only can be set in state SGOP. The other tables and state lists are available in states WSOP, WSAC and SGOP.

In state *GKCL,* OPEN GKS may be invoked.

In state *GKOP,* CLOSE GKS, OPEN WORKSTATION and some functions setting entries of the GKS state list (workstation-independent primitive attributes and normalization transformations) may be invoked. The ESCAPE function, as a standard way of performing non-standard functions within GKS, can also be used. INTERPRET ITEM is possible but may result in an error if the item corresponds to a GKS function not allowed in this state.

In the states *WSOP, WSAC and SGOP,* most of the GKS functions can be invoked. Therefore, it is more meaningful to list the functions not permitted in each of these states.

In state *WSOP,* the functions OPEN GKS, DEACTIVATE WORKSTATION and CLOSE SEGMENT are meaningless and are therefore not admitted. CLOSE GKS requires all workstations to be closed properly. CREATE SEGMENT needs at least one workstation to be active for output. All output functions, INSERT SEGMENT and WRITE ITEM TO METAFILE generate output which is only possible in states WSAC and SGOP. It should be noted that ASSOCIATE SEGMENT WITH WORKSTATION and COPY SEGMENT TO WORKSTATION are considered to be segment manipulations rather than output generation and can therefore be called in this state.

In state *WSAC,* the functions OPEN GKS, CLOSE GKS and CLOSE SEGMENT are not admissible, as above. Except for these three functions, all the other GKS functions can be used in state WSAC.

In state *SGOP,* the functions OPEN GKS and CLOSE GKS are not meaningful and are, therefore, not admissible.

In SGOP, one segment is generated for all active workstations. ACTIVATE/ DEACTIVATE WORKSTATION enables/disables output at a workstation.

Table 3.3 Table of GKS functions and corresponding states

Control Functions	
OPEN GKS	GKCL
CLOSE GKS	GKOP
OPEN WORKSTATION	GKOP, WSOP, WSAC, SGOP
CLOSE WORKSTATION	WSOP, WSAC, SGOP
ACTIVATE WORKSTATION	WSOP, WSAC
DEACTIVATE WORKSTATION	WSAC
CLEAR WORKSTATION	WSOP, WSAC
REDRAW ALL SEGMENTS	
ON WORKSTATION	WSOP, WSAC, SGOP
UPDATE WORKSTATION	WSOP, WSAC, SGOP
SET DEFERRAL STATE	WSOP, WSAC, SGOP
MESSAGE	WSOP, WSAC, SGOP
ESCAPE	GKOP, WSOP, WSAC, SGOP
Output Functions	WSAC, SGOP
Output Attributes	
Workstation-Independent Primitive Attributes	GKOP, WSOP, WSAC, SGOP
Workstation Attributes (Representations)	WSOP, WSAC, SGOP
Transformation Functions	
Normalization Transformation	GKOP, WSOP, WSAC, SGOP
Workstation Transformation	WSOP, WSAC, SGOP
Segment Functions	
Segment Manipulation Functions	
CREATE SEGMENT	WSAC
CLOSE SEGMENT	SGOP
RENAME SEGMENT	WSOP, WSAC, SGOP
DELETE SEGMENT	WSOP, WSAC, SGOP
DELETE SEGMENT FROM WORKSTATION	WSOP, WSAC, SGOP
ASSOCIATE SEGMENT WITH WORKSTATION	WSOP, WSAC
COPY SEGMENT TO WORKSTATION	WSOP, WSAC
INSERT SEGMENT	WSAC, SGOP
Segment Attributes	WSOP, WSAC, SGOP
Input Functions	WSOP, WSAC, SGOP
Metafile Functions	
WRITE ITEM TO GKSM	WSAC, SGOP
GET ITEM TYPE FROM GKSM	WSOP, WSAC, SGOP
READ ITEM FROM GKSM	WSOP, WSAC, SGOP
INTERPRET ITEM	GKOP, WSOP, WSAC, SGOP
Inquiry Functions	Allowed in all states but meaningful only in:
Inquiry Function for Operating State Value	GKCL, GKOP, WSOP, WSAC, SGOP
Inquiry Functions for GKS Description Table	GKOP, WSOP, WSAC, SGOP

Table 3.3 (continued)

Inquiry Functions for GKS State List	GKOP, WSOP, WSAC, SGOP
except:	
INQUIRE NAME OF OPEN SEGMENT	SGOP
INQUIRE SET OF SEGMENT NAMES IN USE	WSOP, WSAC, SGOP
INQUIRE MORE SIMULTANEOUS EVENTS	WSOP, WSAC, SGOP
Inquiry Functions for Workstation State List	WSOP, WSAC, SGOP
Inquiry Functions for Workstation Description Table	GKOP, WSOP, WSAC, SGOP
Inquiry Functions for Segment State List	WSOP, WSAC, SGOP
Pixel Inquiries	WSOP, WSAC, SGOP
Inquiry Function for GKS Error State List	WSOP, WSAC, SGOP
Utility Functions	GKOP, WSOP, WSAC, SGOP
Error Handling	GKCL, GKOP, WSOP, WSAC, SGOP

If this were permitted in state SGOP, the content of a segment could differ at different workstations. As the content of a segment should be the same for all associated workstations, it is not allowed to activate or deactivate a workstation in state SGOP. N.B.: The opening and closing of workstations is permitted, as it does not affect active workstations.

CLOSE WORKSTATION and CLEAR WORKSTATION delete all segments at one workstation. If they are invoked in state SGOP, this may delete an open segment and for systematic reasons this is not allowed. If it were possible to delete an open segment, a subsequent CLOSE SEGMENT would generate an error although it had been correctly called. For the same reason, DELETE SEGMENT and DELETE SEGMENT FROM WORKSTATION in state SGOP may address all segments except the open one.

Likewise, the function CREATE SEGMENT is not allowed in the state SGOP as a nesting structure of segments could be generated which is not supported by GKS.

ASSOCIATE SEGMENT WITH WORKSTATION and COPY SEGMENT TO WORKSTATION move graphical output data to a workstation. These data will not be included in a segment and, therefore, the corresponding functions are not permitted in state SGOP.

Table 3.3 gives a summary of all GKS functions together with the permitted states. A rough overview is also given in Figure I.13.1 on page 48.

3.4   State Lists

In this section, the content of the
— operating state;
— error state list;
— GKS description table;
— GKS state list;
will be discussed. The remaining
— workstation description table (cf. Table 4.1, page 123);

— workstation state list (cf. Table 4.2, page 129);
— segment state list for every existing segment (cf. Table 7.2, page 242);
are discussed in later chapters in their respective context.

The information for each entry in the state lists and description tables includes:
— the name of the entry;
— the coordinate system (if appropriate);
— the permitted values;
— the data type;
— the initial value (if appropriate).

The notation used is the same as is used in the description of the parameters of GKS functions which set the corresponding entries (cf. Section 1.2.2 for details). In an additional column, an initial value is specified for each entry, if applicable. The abbreviations used in this column are:

i.d.:   Implementation-dependent. The respective value is determined when designing a specific implementation. This applies to the description tables.

w.d.t.:   Value is derived from the workstation description table.

undef: Undefined value, indicating that the corresponding entry has not yet been set.

empty: A value indicating that the respective set is empty.

The *operating state* (cf. Table 3.4) contains only one value indicating the current state of GKS. The initial value is GKCL = "GKS closed" which is available before GKS has been opened. The operating state is set by the state changing functions listed in Table 3.1.

Table 3.4 Operating state

Operating state value	(GKCL, GKOP, WSOP, WSAC, SGOP)	E	GKCL

The *error state list* (cf. Table 3.5) contains some data relevant to error situations. When GKS detects an error, it calls the ERROR HANDLING procedure which may be replaced by the user's own procedure (cf. Section 9.3). The main information about an error, i.e.,
— the identification of the error condition;
— the identification of the GKS function which called the ERROR HANDLING procedure
is not stored in the error state list but passed directly to this procedure. However, to avoid a recursive call of this ERROR HANDLING procedure, only some of the GKS functions which are not generating error messages can be called during error handling. This condition is controlled by the entry 'error state' which indicates whether error handling is in progress or not.

The next entry contains the name of an error file, as defined by OPEN GKS. Error messages will be printed onto this error file by the ERROR LOGGING procedure.

The next entry can be used if an input queue overflow occurs. As this error occurs asynchronously, it cannot be reported immediately to the ERROR HANDLING procedure and, therefore, is stored in the error state list. When the error can be reported to the application program, it may obtain the information by calling INQUIRE INPUT QUEUE OVERFLOW which removes the respective entry.

Table 3.5 Error state list

error state	(ON, OFF)	E	OFF
error file		N	i.d.
identification of one of the logical input devices			
that caused an input queue overflow:			
workstation identifier		N	undef
input class	(LOCATOR, STROKE, VALUATOR,		
	CHOICE, PICK, STRING)	E	undef
device number	(1..n)	I	undef

The *GKS description table* (cf. Table 3.6) describes the overall characteristics of the implementation. It contains the level of GKS indicating which subset of GKS functions is available in this implementation (cf. Chapter 2).

The following two entries describe the set of workstation types admissible for this implementation. The capabilities available on a specific workstation type may be determined by using the corresponding workstation description table. The names of the workstation types may be chosen arbitrarily by the implementor.

Implementations may differ as to how many workstations may be used simultaneously. The following three entries say precisely how many workstations may be simultaneously open, active in state WSAC, and active in state SGOP. In the lowest GKS level, 0a, only one workstation may be used at a time.

The final entry describes how many normalization transformations may be defined simultaneously. For GKS levels 0a, 0b, 0c one definable normalization transformation is sufficient; otherwise, at least 10 normalization transformations have to be supported. The range of admissible normalization transformation numbers goes from 0 to the maximum normalization transformation number.

Table 3.6 shows the content of the GKS description table.

Table 3.6 GKS description table

level of GKS	(0a, 0b, 0c, 1a, 1b, 1c, 2a, 2b, 2c)	E	i.d.
number of available workstation types	(1..n)	I	i.d.
list of available workstation types		n × N	i.d.
maximum number of simultaneously open workstations	(1..n)	I	i.d.
maximum number of simultaneously active workstations	(1..n)	I	i.d.
maximum number of workstations associated with a segment	(1..n)	I	i.d.
maximum normalization transformation number	(1..n)	I	i.d.

The *GKS state list* (cf. Table 3.7) contains state variables referring to the global state of GKS rather than to the state of a particular workstation.

Whereas the GKS description table records which workstation types are available in the implementation, the first two entries of the GKS state list indicate which workstations are currently open or active.

Furthermore, the GKS state list contains the last setting of each normalization transformation. Each implementation has a fixed number of normalization transformations as specified in the GKS description table. When initialising the GKS state list by OPEN GKS, all transformations are set equal to the identity transformation, i.e., all windows and viewports are set equal to the unit square, the viewport input priority is assigned to give a transformation with a lower number precedence over a transformation with a higher number. Clipping is initially switched on. However, as long as all viewports are equal to the unit square, this has no effect.

The next entries contain the current setting of all workstation-independent primitive attributes (cf. Chapter 6 for details about the meaning of these attributes).

If segmentation is available (depending on the GKS level), the name of the open segment is recorded. This name is defined only when GKS is in state SGOP. However, in any of the states WSOP, WSAC and SGOP, a record is kept of the set of names for all the defined segments (including the open segment). For each segment a segment state list is kept. The content of the segment state list is described in Section 7.5.

If EVENT input is possible, an input queue is generated. The function AWAIT EVENT moves the oldest entry from the input queue into the entry 'current event report' of the GKS state list from where it can be obtained by the respective GET <class> function.

Table 3.7 shows the content of the GKS state list.

Table 3.7 GKS state list

set of open workstations		$n \times N$	empty
set of active workstations		$n \times N$	empty

normalization transformation			
current normalization transformation number	(0..n)	I	0
list of transformation numbers ordered by viewport input priority (initially in numerical order with 0 as the highest)			
for every entry:			
normalization transformation number	(0..n)	I	entry number
window	WC	$4 \times R$	0,1,0,1
viewport	NDC	$4 \times R$	0,1,0,1
clipping indicator	(CLIP, NOCLIP)	E	CLIP
clipping rectangle	NDC	$4 \times R$	0,1,0,1

Table 3.7 (continued)

POLYLINE

current polyline index	(1..n)	I	1
current linetype	(−n.. −1, 1..n)	I	1
current linewidth scale factor	≥0	R	1.0
current polyline colour index	(0..n)	I	1
current linetype ASF	(BUNDLED, INDIVIDUAL)	E	note 1
current linewidth scale factor ASF		E	note 1
	(BUNDLED, INDIVIDUAL)		
current polyline colour index ASF		E	note 1
	(BUNDLED, INDIVIDUAL)		

POLYMARKER

current polymarker index	(1..n)	I	1
current marker type	(−n.. −1, 1..n)	I	3
current marker size scale factor	≥0	R	1.0
current polymarker colour index	(0..n)	I	1
current marker type ASF	(BUNDLED, INDIVIDUAL)	E	note 1
current marker size scale factor ASF		E	note 1
	(BUNDLED, INDIVIDUAL)		
current polymarker colour index ASF		E	note 1
	(BUNDLED, INDIVIDUAL)		

TEXT

current text index	(1..n)	I	1
current text font and precision	(−n.. −1, 1..n;		
	STRING, CHAR, STROKE)	(I;E)	1;STRING
current character expansion factor	>0	R	1.0
current character spacing		R	0.0
current text colour index	(0..n)	I	1
current text font and precision ASF		E	note 1
	(BUNDLED, INDIVIDUAL)		
current character expansion factor ASF		E	note 1
	(BUNDLED, INDIVIDUAL)		
current character spacing ASF	(BUNDLED, INDIVIDUAL)	E	note 1
current text colour index ASF	(BUNDLED, INDIVIDUAL)	E	note 1
current character height	WC >0	R	0.01
current character up vector	WC	$2 \times R$	0,1
current character width	WC >0	R	0.01
current character base vector	WC	$2 \times R$	1,0
current text path	(RIGHT, LEFT, UP, DOWN)	E	RIGHT
current text alignment (horizontal and vertical)		$2 \times E$	(NORMAL;
	(NORMAL, LEFT, CENTRE, RIGHT;		NORMAL)
	NORMAL, TOP, CAP, HALF, BASE, BOTTOM)		

Table 3.7 (continued)

FILL AREA			
current fill area index	(1..n)	I	1
current fill area interior style		E	HOLLOW
(HOLLOW, SOLID, PATTERN, HATCH)			
current fill area style index	(−n.. −1, 1..n)	I	1
current fill area colour index	(0..n)	I	1
current fill area interior style ASF		E	note 1
(BUNDLED, INDIVIDUAL)			
current fill area style index ASF		E	note 1
(BUNDLED, INDIVIDUAL)			
current fill area colour index ASF		E	note 1
(BUNDLED, INDIVIDUAL)			
current pattern width vector	WC	$2 \times R$	1,0
current pattern height vector	WC	$2 \times R$	0,1
current pattern reference point	WC	P	(0,0)

current pick identifier	N	language binding dependent

segments		
name of open segment	N	undef
set of segment names in use	$n \times N$	empty
set of segment state lists (one state list for every segment)		empty

input queue	
input queue (one entry for each event report)	empty

each event report containing:			
workstation identifier		N	
device number		I	
input class	(LOCATOR, STROKE,	E	
VALUATOR, CHOICE, PICK, STRING)			
if LOCATOR			
normalization transformation number	(0..n)	I	
position	WC	P	
if STROKE			
normalization transformation number	(0..n)	I	
number of points	(0..n)	I	
points in stroke	WC	$n \times P$	
if VALUATOR			
value		R	
if CHOICE			
status	(OK, NOCHOICE)	E	undef
choice number	(1..n)	I	
if PICK			
status	(OK, NOPICK)	E	
segment name		N	
pick identifier		N	

Table 3.7 (continued)

if STRING			
string		S	
more simultaneous events	(NOMORE, MORE)	E	
(a single event is indicated by NOMORE)			

current event report containing:

input class	(NONE, LOCATOR,		
	STROKE, VALUATOR, CHOICE, PICK, STRING)	E	NONE
if LOCATOR			
normalization transformation number	(0..n)	I	
position	WC	P	
if STROKE			
normalization transformation number	(0..n)	I	
number of points	(0..n)	I	
points in stroke	WC	$n \times P$	
if VALUATOR			
value		R	
if CHOICE			
status	(OK, NOCHOICE)	E	
choice number	(1..n)	I	
if PICK			
status	(OK, NOPICK)	E	
segment name		N	
pick identifier		N	
if STRING			
string		S	
more simultaneous events	(NOMORE, MORE)	E	NOMORE
(a single event is indicated by NOMORE)			

Note 1: All the initial ASF values are the same. It is implementation-dependent whether the initial ASF values are all BUNDLED or are all INDIVIDUAL.

3.5   Basic Control Functions

The basic control functions comprise all the GKS functions necessary to generate graphical output in the lowest GKS level, 0a:
— OPEN GKS
— OPEN WORKSTATION
— ACTIVATE WORKSTATION
— CLEAR WORKSTATION
— DEACTIVATE WORKSTATION
— CLOSE WORKSTATION
— CLOSE GKS

OPEN GKS will normally be the first GKS function called by the application program. In the parameter list, an error file is specified. If an error is detected by GKS, the standard error reaction will include printing an error message to this error file. The second parameter restricts the amount of memory space which GKS can allocate dynamically. This parameter is only meaningful in programming environments in which independent processes can be loaded dynamically and then compete for memory space. If one process is allocated all the available memory space, no other process can be started subsequently. OPEN GKS allocates and initialises the GKS state list; the entry 'error file' in the GKS error state list is set; all workstation description tables are made accessible.

CLOSE GKS will be the last GKS function called by the application program so that GKS can be left properly. All tables and state lists, except the operating state and the error state list, are deallocated. Therefore, the sequence
— CLOSE GKS
— OPEN GKS
may be used to reset all GKS parameters to their default value and to clear all buffers.

The functions OPEN WORKSTATION, ACTIVATE WORKSTATION, CLEAR WORKSTATION, DEACTIVATE WORKSTATION, CLOSE WORKSTATION are presented in the subsequent chapter.

OPEN GKS   GKCL   L0a

Input	error file	N
Input	amount of memory units for buffer area	I

Effect:
GKS is put into the operating state GKOP="GKS open". The GKS state list is allocated and initialised as indicated in Table 3.7. The GKS description table and the workstation description tables are made available. The entry 'error file' in the GKS error state list is set to the value specified by the first parameter. The permitted buffer area which can be used by GKS for internal purposes is limited.

N.B.:
Certain environments may not permit dynamic memory management. In this case, the buffer area may be limited in a static way which will be described in the installation documentation.

Errors:
   1   GKS not in proper state: GKS should be in the state GKCL
200   Specified error file is invalid

────────────────────── *FORTRAN Interface* ──────────────────────

CALL GOPKS (ERRFIL, BUFA)
Parameters:

Input	ERRFIL	error message file	INTEGER
Input	BUFA	amount of memory units (implementation-dependent)	INTEGER

CLOSE GKS   GKOP   L0a

Parameters: none

Effect:

GKS is put into the operating state GKCL = "GKS closed". The GKS state list and the workstation description tables become unavailable. All GKS buffers are released and all GKS files are closed.

N.B.:

GKS can be reopened by invoking the function OPEN GKS.

Errors:

2   GKS not in proper state: GKS should be in the state GKOP

————————————————— *FORTRAN Interface* —————————————————

CALL GCLKS

Parameters: none

3.6 Examples

Example 3.1   Use of basic control functions

This example illustrates the use of the state changing functions listed in Table 3.1. The workstation functions are introduced in Chapter 4 and the segment functions in Chapter 7. The comments show the main function groups callable at the particular position in the program. See Table 3.3 for a complete list.

———————————————————— *Pascal* ————————————————————

```
L10   const error_file = 'GKS_ERRORS';
L11       display = 'T4014';
L12       connection_identifier = '';
L13       type = 'STORAGE_TUBE';
L14       segmax = 100;
L15   var index: integer;
L16       segnr: array [1..100] of name;      {Names must be initialised to distinct values}

          {GKS in state GKCL which allows}
          {Opening or reopening of GKS}
          {Inquiring into the operating state, Error handling}

L20   OPEN GKS (error_file, memory_limit);
          {GKS in state GKOP which allows}
          {Setting of workstation-independent primitive attributes}
          {Setting of normalization transformations}
          {Inquiring into the GKS state list and all description tables}

L30   OPEN WORKSTATION (display, connection_identifier, type);
          {GKS in state WSOP which in addition allows}
          {Setting of workstation attributes}
          {Setting of workstation transformation}
          {Input functions}
          {Inquiring into the state list of workstation 'display'}
```

L40 ACTIVATE_WORKSTATION (display);
        {GKS in state WSAC which in addition allows}
        {Output functions}

L50 **for** index:=1 **to** segmax **do**
L60 **begin**

L70 CREATE_SEGMENT (segnr[index]);
        {GKS in state SGOP which in addition allows}
        {Output functions with output stored}
        {Setting of segment attributes of segment 'segnr'}
        {Inquiring into the state list of segment 'segnr'}

L80 CLOSE_SEGMENT;
        {GKS in state WSAC which allows}
        {Handling of existing segments}
        {Input/output functions}

L90 **end**

L100 DEACTIVATE_WORKSTATION (display);
        {GKS in state WSOP which allows}
        {Handling of existing segments}
        {No more output}

L110 CLOSE_WORKSTATION (display);
        {GKS in state GKOP}
        {All segments deleted}
        {State list of workstation 'display' deleted}

L120 CLOSE_GKS;
        {GKS in state GKCL}
        {Description table of all workstations deallocated}
        {GKS state list deleted}

──────────────────────── *Fortran* ────────────────────────

L10		INTEGER ERRFIL,BUFA, DISPL,CONID,TYPE,
	+	SEGMAX,SEGNR
L11		DATA ERRFIL/27/,DISPL/3/,CONID/0/,TYPE/3/,SEGMAX/100/
L20		CALL GOPKS (ERRFIL,BUFA)
L30		CALL GOPWK (DISPL,CONID,TYPE)
L40		CALL GACWK (DISPL)
L50		DO 90 SEGNR=1,SEGMAX
L70		CALL GCRSG (SEGNR)
L80		CALL GCLSG
L90	90	CONTINUE
L100		CALL GDAWK (DISPL)
L110		CALL GCLWK (DISPL)
L120		CALL GCLKS

4   WORKSTATIONS

4.1   Introduction

GKS provides a set of output functions for computer graphics which may generate output on any device in the whole range of graphics devices, including plotter and interactive devices, vector and raster displays, storage tube and refresh displays, black-and-white and colour displays.

The set of GKS functions has been designed in such a way that all essential capabilities of graphical devices can be addressed. However, the capabilities of the individual devices differ significantly, e.g.,

— black-and-white devices cannot generate colour images;
— storage tubes cannot generate images which move in real time;
— vector displays may have difficulties in displaying solid areas.

The fundamental contradiction between the comprehensive functionality offered at the application program interface and the restricted capabilities of an individual device cannot be eliminated. However, the workstation concept of GKS provides a means of localizing the workstation dependencies and putting them under the full control of the application program.

GKS introduces the concept of an abstract graphical workstation with maximum capabilities which:

— has one addressable display surface of fixed resolution;
— allows only rectangular display spaces (the display space cannot consist of a number of separate parts);
— permits the specification and use of display spaces smaller than the maximum, while guaranteeing that no display image is generated outside the specified display space;
— supports several linetypes, text fonts, character sizes, etc., allowing output primitives to be drawn with different attributes;
— has one or more logical input device for each class of input;
— permits REQUEST, SAMPLE and EVENT type input;
— allows logical input devices to be set in REQUEST, SAMPLE or EVENT mode independently of each other;
— stores segments and provides facilities for changing and manipulating them.

In practice, the workstation may or may not be equipped with all of these capabilities. The available capabilities are documented in the workstation description table, which may be determined by the application program in order to adapt its behaviour to the existing environment.

A workstation possesses, at least, one display surface or one input device. With regard to the output and input capabilities, the following categories of workstations are possible:

OUTPUT: output workstation,
INPUT: input workstation,
OUTIN: output/input workstation.

An output workstation has only output capabilities. It can display all output primitives with the possible exception of the GDP, which is optional. The appearance of output primitives may vary between workstations with respect to the workstation-specific aspects of primitive attributes and the workstation transformation. Workstation-specific aspects and the minimal requirements for the display of the individual primitives are described in detail in Chapter 6. An example of an output workstation is a plotter.

An input workstation has at least one logical input device. An example of an input workstation is a digitizer. In a GKS implementation which supports input, there must be at least one logical input device of each class. However, it is not necessary for any workstation to have more than one logical input device. Input devices may be assigned arbitrarily by the implementor to the individual workstations. Input class PICK must be present only in GKS implementations supporting both input and segmentation.

An output/input workstation has the characteristics of both an output and an input workstation. All interactive devices are output/input workstations.

The conjunction of output and input within one workstation not only reflects a physical conjunction of a display surface with some input devices but also enables one to make use of the fact that input usually refers to the output on one specific display surface, e.g., PICK input only makes sense in conjunction with visible output primitives. Also, LOCATOR input is usually given relative to visible output primitives. The workstation concept is a means of establishing such relationships.

Segments are created for specific workstations. However, the storage of segments is not a capability of an individual workstation which it may or may not have. On the contrary, it is a capability of a specific output level of GKS and if present, it must therefore be supported by all output and output/input workstations. There may be differences between workstations as to whether segment storage is provided locally or whether the workstation uses the capabilities of the GKS nucleus. As these differences only affect the efficiency but do not interfere with the functionality, they are not visible at the application program interface. Segments are explained in Chapter 7.

In addition to the three workstation categories listed above, GKS has three special facilities which provide a means of storing graphical information either temporarily or permanently:

WISS: workstation-independent segment storage;
MO: GKS metafile output;
MI: GKS metafile input.

They are treated as workstations for the purpose of control and, therefore, could be regarded as special workstations. With respect to other GKS functions, however, they have quite different characteristics. For example, these special workstations only possess a very restricted workstation description table and, with the exception of the GKS metafile output, only a shortened workstation state list. The WISS is discussed in detail in Section 7.7. The metafile concept is explained in Chapter 11.

The capabilities of workstations are described in detail by workstation description tables (cf. Section 4.2). One table may characterize a whole class of devices with similar features. The current state of an individual workstation is recorded in a workstation state list (cf. Section 4.3). The six workstation categories mentioned above are best characterized by the set of functions which can be applied to them (cf. Section 4.4). Sections 4.2 − 4.4 give valuable information to the advanced programmer but may be left out by the novice reader.

4.2   Workstation Description Table

The implementor of GKS will classify all workstations according to their characteristics and capabilities. For each workstation type available in a given implementation, a *workstation description table (w.d.t.)* must be implemented, containing a description of all workstation features relevant to GKS. Several workstations may be described by one workstation description table as long as their relevant features do not differ. The entries in the workstation description table may be inquired into, but, naturally, may not be set by the application program.

The first entry is the name of the workstation type. This name will be generated by the implementor of GKS. The second entry indicates the workstation category to which all the workstations of this workstation type belong. The special workstations (WISS, MO, MI) have a workstation description table consisting only of these two entries as their behaviour is fully defined by GKS.

The next entries describe the device coordinate system (DC). The maximum display surface, i.e., the maximum value for the device coordinates, is given in width and height, measured in metres. However, there may be devices where a precise measurement of the display surface is not possible, for example, when the operator is able to scale the display surface without notifying GKS. In this case, the implementor can use a unit of average length and indicate by the value 'OTHER' that the unit of length is not necessarily a metre.

For input workstations the extent of the available input area (e.g., size of a tablet) will determine the maximum value of the device coordinates. If both a display surface and a tablet are present in an output/input workstation, both must be assigned the same device coordinate system.

Furthermore, the resolution of the display surface will be given by two integers. For raster devices, these are the numbers of pixels corresponding to the width and height of the maximum display surface. Pixels do not have to be quadratic.

The rest of the table describes output or input capabilities. Entries exist only for workstations having the particular capability.

The next entry indicates whether the workstation possesses a vector display, a raster display, or perhaps another type of display. This value should be determined before using the CELL ARRAY output primitive as vector displays are bound to make only a very poor simulation. For the FILL AREA primitive as well, this entry may be useful as it helps to select an appropriate interior style.

The subsequent entries describe capabilities with respect to the individual output primitives (cf. Chapter 6 for details on primitives and primitive attributes).

The available linetypes, marker types, font/precision pairs, interior styles, hatch styles, and generalized drawing primitives are given in the form of a list. This has the advantage that the defined numbers on an individual workstation may be non-contiguous. Thus, the implementor may uniquely assign linetypes, marker types, etc. within an implementation without being forced to implement the full set at each individual workstation.

The available linewidths, marker sizes, and character heights are characterized by a minimum and maximum value and the number of available values. If the number of available values is 0, all values between the limits are valid. If the number of available values is positive, some discrete values are available. It cannot be concluded that these values are equally spaced in the interval. GKS will round unavailable values up to the next available value. The table gives a nominal linewidth and marker size in DC to which the linewidth and marker size scale factor refer. Linewidth and marker size are not transformable. They can only be changed by resetting the corresponding scale factor. The given ranges for available character heights and character expansion factors are valid for font 1 at that workstation. Other fonts may have different values.

For the bundle tables related to the output primitives a maximum size and predefined entries are given. These predefined entries have a contiguous set of indices starting from 1 (colour table: 0).

The list of available generalized drawing primitives contains a set of primitive attributes, individually selected by the implementor for each generalized drawing primitive.

The next group describes the colour capabilities. One entry indicates whether colour is available at the workstation or whether the output device is monochrome. The entry 'number of colours' gives the number of different definable colours. This may differ from the 'maximum number of colour indices' which indicates the size of the colour table. If the number of colours is less than or equal to the size of the colour table, the available colours presumably will all be predefined.

The colour table is of use for non-colour devices also. Monochrome devices may use it to specify intensities or, at least, the background colour (entry 0) and the foreground colour (entry 1). Therefore, the colour table has at least length 2.

Segment priority controls the overlapping of segments. This feature primarily is intended for raster devices with multiple bit planes. The entry 'number of segment priorities supported' indicates how far a specific workstation can control overlapping segments.

The behaviour of the workstation in displaying primitives and in changing the display dynamically is described by the following entries. The deferral mode controls the buffering of output functions, for example to optimise data transfer. The implicit regeneration mode indicates whether a picture may be regenerated at any time when required by some function or whether it is suppressed until requested explicitly. This suppression of implicit regeneration is of great importance, for example, when working interactively with storage tubes. The entries 'dynamic modification accepted for ...' indicate in detail which actions may lead to an implicit regeneration. The entries 'deferral mode' and 'implicit regeneration mode' contain values selected by the implementor so that the device's capabilities are used optimally and most applications served in the best way.

The last entries indicate which input devices are available and what the initial settings of these devices are.

Table 4.1 shows the content of the workstation description table. The information for each entry includes:

— the name of the entry;
— the coordinate system (if appropriate);
— the permitted values;
— the data type;
— the initial value (if appropriate).

The notation used is explained in Section 3.2.

Table 4.1 Workstation description table

Entries exist for all workstation categories				
workstation type			N	i.d.
workstation category	(OUTPUT, INPUT, OUTIN, WISS, MO, MI)		E	i.d.
Entries exist for categories OUTPUT, INPUT, OUTIN				
device coordinate units		(METRES, OTHER)	E	i.d.
maximum display surface				
(visible area of the display surface or				
available area on tablet for input only workstations)				
in length units	DC	>0	2 × R	i.d.
in device units	(integer by integer)	>0	2 × I	i.d.
(for vector displays, for example, the device units				
give the highest possible resolution; for raster displays,				
the number of columns and lines of the raster array)				
Entries exist for categories OUTPUT, OUTIN				
DISPLAY TYPE				
raster or vector display (for output)	(VECTOR, RASTER, OTHER)		E	i.d.
(VECTOR = vector display, RASTER = raster device,				
OTHER = other device, e.g., vector + raster)				
POLYLINE				
number of available linetypes		(4..n)	I	i.d.
list of available linetypes		(−n.. −1, 1..n)	n × I	i.d.
number of available linewidths		(0..n)	I	i.d.
(if the workstation supports continuous linewidth,				
the number will be zero)				

Table 4.1 (continued)

nominal linewidth	DC >0	R	i.d.
minimum linewidth	DC >0	R	i.d.
maximum linewidth	DC >0	R	i.d.
maximum number of polyline bundle table entries	(5..n)	I	i.d.
number of predefined polyline indices (bundles)	(5..n)	I	i.d.
table of predefined polyline bundles,			
for every entry:			
linetype	(−n.. −1,1..n)	I	i.d.
linewidth scale factor		R	i.d.
polyline colour index	(0..n)	I	i.d.
(within range of predefined colour indices)			

POLYMARKER

number of available marker types	(5..n)	I	i.d.
list of available marker types	(−n.. −1,1..n)	n × I	i.d.
number of available marker sizes	(0..n)	I	i.d.
(if the workstation supports continuous marker sizes, the number will be zero)			
nominal marker size	DC >0	R	i.d.
minimum marker size	DC >0	R	i.d.
maximum marker size	DC >0	R	i.d.
maximum number of polymarker bundle table entries	(5..n)	I	i.d.
number of predefined polymarker indices (bundles)	(5..n)	I	i.d.
table of predefined polymarker bundles, for every entry:			
marker type	(−n.. −1,1..n)	I	i.d.
marker size scale factor		R	i.d.
polymarker colour index	(0..n)	I	i.d.
(within range of predefined colour indices)			

TEXT

number of available character heights	(0..n)	I	i.d.
(if the workstation supports continuous character heights, the number will be zero)			
minimum character height	DC >0	R	i.d.
maximum character height	DC >0	R	i.d.
number of font/precision pairs	(1..n)	I	i.d.
list of font/precision pairs	(−n.. −1,1..n; STRING,CHAR,STROKE)	n × (I;E)	i.d.
number of available character expansion factors	(0..n)	I	i.d.
(if the workstation supports continuous character expansion factors, the number will be zero)			
minimum character expansion factor	DC >0	R	i.d.
maximum character expansion factor	DC >0	R	i.d.
maximum number of text bundle table entries	(2..n)	I	i.d.
number of predefined text indices (bundles)	(2..n)	I	i.d.

Table 4.1 (continued)

table of predefined text bundles,			
for every entry:		at least one entry	
text font	$(-n..-1,1..n)$	I	i.d.
text precision	(STRING, CHAR, STROKE)	E	i.d.
character expansion factor	>0	R	i.d.
character spacing		R	i.d.
text colour index	$(0..n)$	I	i.d.
(within range of predefined colour indices)			

FILL AREA

number of available fill area interior styles	$(1..4)$	I	i.d.
list of available fill area interior styles			
(HOLLOW, SOLID, PATTERN, HATCH)		$n \times E$	i.d.
number of available hatch styles	$(0..n)$	I	i.d.
list of available hatch styles	$(-n..-1,1..n)$	$n \times I$	i.d.
maximum number of fill area bundle table entries	$(5..n)$	I	i.d.
number of predefined fill area indices (bundles)	$(5..n)$	I	i.d.
table of predefined fill area bundles,			
for every entry:		at least one entry	
fill area interior style (HOLLOW, SOLID, PATTERN, HATCH)		E	i.d.
fill area style index	$(-n..-1,1..n)$	I	i.d.
(for interior style PATTERN must be			
within range of predefined pattern indices;			
for interior style HATCH must be			
within range of available hatch styles)			
fill area colour index	$(0..n)$	I	i.d.
(within range of predefined colour indices)			
maximum number of pattern indices	$(0..n)$	I	i.d.
number of predefined pattern indices (representations)	$(0..n)$	I	i.d.
table of predefined pattern representations,			
for every entry:			
pattern array dimensions	$(1..n)$	$2 \times I$	i.d.
pattern array	$(0..n)$	$n \times n \times I$	i.d.

GENERALIZED DRAWING PRIMITIVE

number of available generalized drawing primitives	$(0..n)$	I	i.d.
list of available generalized drawing primitives (may be empty):			
for every GDP:			
GDP identifier		N	i.d.
number of sets of attributes used	$(0..4)$	I	i.d.
list of sets of attributes used			
(POLYLINE, POLYMARKER, TEXT, FILL AREA)		$n \times E$	i.d.

COLOUR TABLE

number of available colours or intensities	$(0,2..n)$	I	i.d.
(if workstation supports a continuous range of colours,			
the number will be zero)			

Table 4.1 (continued)

colour available	(COLOUR, MONOCHROME)	E	i.d.
maximum number of colour indices	(2..n)	I	i.d.
number of predefined colour indices (representations)	(2..n)	I	i.d.
table of predefined colour representations,			
for every entry:	at least entries zero and one		
colour (red/green/blue intensities)	[0,1]	$3 \times R$	i.d.

SEGMENT PRIORITY

number of segment priorities supported	(0..n)	I	i.d.
(a value of 0 indicates that a continuous range			
of priorities is supported)			

DYNAMIC CAPABILITIES

default value for:			
deferral mode	(ASAP, BNIL, BNIG, ASTI)	E	i.d.
implicit regeneration mode	(SUPPRESSED, ALLOWED)	E	i.d.
dynamic modification accepted for:			
polyline bundle representation	(IRG, IMM)	E	i.d.
polymarker bundle representation	(IRG, IMM)	E	i.d.
text bundle representation	(IRG, IMM)	E	i.d.
fill area bundle representation	(IRG, IMM)	E	i.d.
pattern representation	(IRG, IMM)	E	i.d.
colour representation	(IRG, IMM)	E	i.d.
workstation transformation	(IRG, IMM)	E	i.d.
segment transformation	(IRG, IMM)	E	i.d.
visibility (visible → invisible)	(IRG, IMM)	E	i.d.
visibility (invisible → visible)	(IRG, IMM)	E	i.d.
highlighting	(IRG, IMM)	E	i.d.
segment priority	(IRG, IMM)	E	i.d.
adding primitives to open segment			
overlapping segment of higher priority	(IRG, IMM)	E	i.d.
delete segment	(IRG, IMM)	E	i.d.
where:			
IRG: implicit regeneration necessary (may be deferred)			
IMM: performed immediately			

Entries exist for categories INPUT and OUTIN

LOCATOR

for every logical input device of class LOCATOR:			
locator device number	(1..n)	I	i.d.
default initial locator position	WC	P	i.d.
number of available prompt and echo types	(1..n)	I	i.d.
list of available prompt and echo types	(−n.. −1, 1..n)	$n \times I$	i.d.
default echo area	DC	$4 \times R$	i.d.
default locator data record		D	i.d.

Table 4.1 (continued)

		STROKE	
for every logical input device of class STROKE:			
stroke device number	(1..n)	I	i.d.
maximum input buffer size	(64..n)	I	i.d.
number of available prompt and echo types	(1..n)	I	i.d.
list of available prompt and echo types	(−n.. −1,1..n)	n × I	i.d.
default echo area	DC	4 × R	i.d.
default stroke data record containing at least:		D	i.d.
input buffer size	(1..n)	I	i.d.
		VALUATOR	
for every logical input device of class VALUATOR:			
valuator device number	(1..n)	I	i.d.
default initial value		R	i.d.
number of available prompt and echo types	(1..n)	I	i.d.
list of available prompt and echo types	(−n.. −1,1..n)	n × I	i.d.
default echo area	DC	4 × R	i.d.
default valuator data record containing at least:		D	i.d.
low value		R	i.d.
high value		R	i.d.
		CHOICE	
for every logical input device of class CHOICE:			
choice device number	(1..n)	I	i.d.
maximum number of choice alternatives	(1..n)	I	i.d.
number of available prompt and echo types	(1..n)	I	i.d.
list of available prompt and echo types	(−n.. −1,1..n)	n × I	i.d.
default echo area	DC	4 × R	i.d.
default choice data record		D	i.d.
		PICK	
for every logical input device of class PICK:			
pick device number		I	i.d.
number of available prompt and echo types	(1..n)	I	i.d.
list of available prompt and echo types	(−n.. −1,1..n)	I	i.d.
default echo area	DC	4 × R	i.d.
default pick data record		D	i.d.
		STRING	
for every logical input device of class STRING:			
string device number	(1..n)	I	i.d.
maximum input buffer size	(72..n)	I	i.d.
number of available prompt and echo types	(1..n)	I	i.d.
list of available prompt and echo types	(−n.. −1,1..n)	n × I	i.d.
default echo area	DC	4 × R	i.d.
default string data record containing at least:		D	i.d.
input buffer size	(1..n)	I	i.d.
initial cursor position	(1..n)	I	1

4.3   Workstation State List

When accessing an individual workstation via OPEN WORKSTATION, a
workstation state list is created which contains all the aspects of a workstation
which may be changed directly or indirectly by the application program. The
main part of the workstation state list consists of tables describing the POLY
LINE,POLYMARKER,TEXT, and FILL AREA bundles, together with
the pattern and colour table. Furthermore, the state of each input device is
recorded in the workstation state list. The main source of initial values for
this list is the workstation description table as is indicated by w.d.t. in the
last column.

One such workstation state list exists for every open workstation including
the special workstations WISS, MO and MI. In the case of MI and WISS
however, only the first three or five entries exist, respectively. In the case of
MO all entries exist except those describing input capabilities. The values marked
w.d.t. are undefined for MO as its workstation description table does not include
these entries.

The first three entries of the workstation state list are initialised by OPEN
WORKSTATION (cf. Section 4.5).

The workstation state indicates whether the workstation is ready for output.
A set of stored segments describes the content of the WDSS or the WISS
respectively (cf. Section 7.7). This entry only exists in GKS levels which support
segments. Both entries only exist for workstations with output capabilities.

The next entries describe the bundle tables and the pattern and colour table.
Their initial values are taken from the workstation description table.

The entries 'deferral mode' and 'implicit regeneration mode' allow control
of any possible delay of output or changes in the display. Since the application
program can stop the deferral when needed by UPDATE WORKSTATION
(cf. Section 4.4), it will be unnecessary in most cases to change the initial values
determined by an implementor using the workstation description table.

The entries 'workstation transformation update state' and 'new frame action
necessary at update' give more information about what actions have been de
ferred.

As a change in the workstation transformation could lead to an implicit
regeneration which may be deferred, the transformation parameters are stored
twice: firstly, as the requested values, specified by the application program, and
secondly, as the current values corresponding to the actual display. The re
quested and current values are initially set equal to the maximum possible
values. If the current values specify rectangles with a different aspect ratio
the workstation viewport is reduced internally to a rectangle with the correct
aspect ratio, in order to achieve a workstation transformation with uniform
scaling. This shrunken rectangle, however, is not stored in the workstation
state list.

In the case of workstations with input devices, the last entries record the
current state of all input devices. Refer to Chapter 8 for more details about
input.

Table 4.2 Workstation state list

Entries initialised by OPEN WORKSTATION for all workstations

workstation identifier		N	
connection identifier		N	
workstation type		N	

Entries for workstations of categories OUTPUT, OUTIN, MO, WISS

workstation state	(ACTIVE, INACTIVE)	E	INACTIVE
set of stored segments			
for this workstation		$n \times N$	empty

Entries for workstations of categories OUTPUT, OUTIN, MO

POLYLINE

number of polyline			
bundle table entries	(5..n)	I	w.d.t.
table of defined polyline bundles containing:			
polyline index	(1..n)	I	w.d.t.
linetype	$(-n..-1, 1..n)$	I	w.d.t.
linewidth scale factor	≥ 0	R	w.d.t.
polyline colour index	(0..n)	I	w.d.t.

POLYMARKER

number of polymarker			
bundle table entries	(5..n)	I	w.d.t.
table of defined polymarker bundles containing:			
polymarker index	(1..n)	I	w.d.t.
marker type	$(-n..-1, 1..n)$	I	w.d.t.
marker size scale factor	$\geq$	R	w.d.t.
polymarker colour index	(0..n)	I	w.d.t.

TEXT

number of text bundle			
table entries	(2..n)	I	w.d.t.
table of defined text bundles containing:			
text index	(1..n)	I	w.d.t.
text font and precision	$(-n..-1, 1..n;$	(I;E)	w.d.t.
	STRING, CHAR, STROKE)		
character expansion			
factor	>0	R	w.d.t.
character spacing		R	w.d.t.
text colour index	(0..n)	I	w.d.t.

FILL AREA

number of fill area			
bundle table entries	(5..n)	I	w.d.t.
table of defined fill area bundles containing:			
fill area index	(1..n)	I	w.d.t.

Table 4.2 (continued)

fill area interior style			
	(HOLLOW, SOLID, PATTERN, HATCH)	E	w.d.t.
fill area style index	$(-n.. -1, 1..n)$	I	w.d.t.
fill area colour index	$(0..n)$	I	w.d.t.
number of pattern table entries	$(0..n)$	I	w.d.t.
table of pattern representations containing:			
pattern index	$(1..n)$	I	w.d.t.
pattern array dimensions	$(1..n)$	$2 \times I$	w.d.t.
pattern array	$(0..n)$	$n \times n \times I$	w.d.t.

COLOUR TABLE

number of colour table entries	$(2..n)$	I	w.d.t.
table of colour representations containing:			
colour index	$(0..n)$	I	w.d.t.
colour (red/green/blue intensities)	$[0,1]$	$3 \times R$	w.d.t.

DEFERRAL MODE

deferral mode	(ASAP, BNIL, BNIG, ASTI)	E	w.d.t.
implicit regeneration mode	(SUPPRESSED, ALLOWED)	E	w.d.t.
display surface empty	(EMPTY, NOTEMPTY)	E	EMPTY
new frame action necessary at update	(YES, NO)	E	NO

Entries exist for categories OUTPUT, OUTIN, INPUT, MO

WORKSTATION TRANSFORMATION

workstation transformation update state		E	NOT-
	(NOTPENDING, PENDING)		PENDING
requested workstation window	NDC	$4 \times R$	0,1,0,1
current workstation window	NDC	$4 \times R$	0,1,0,1
requested workstation viewport	DC	$4 \times R$	0, xd, 0, yd
current workstation viewport	DC	$4 \times R$	0, xd, 0, yd
where (xd, yd) is the maximum display surface in length units from w.d.t.			

Entries for workstations of categories INPUT, OUTIN

LOCATOR

for every logical input device of class LOCATOR:			
locator device number	$(1..n)$	I	w.d.t.
operating mode	(REQUEST, SAMPLE, EVENT)	E	REQUEST
echo switch	(ECHO, NOECHO)	E	ECHO

Table 4.2 (continued)

initial normalization transformation number	(0..n)	I	0
initial position	WC	P	w.d.t.
prompt/echo type	(−n.. −1,1..n)	I	1
echo area	DC	4 × R	w.d.t.
locator data record		D	i.d.

STROKE

for every logical input device of class STROKE:

stroke device number	(1..n)	I	w.d.t.
operating mode	(REQUEST,SAMPLE,EVENT)	E	REQUEST
echo switch	(ECHO,NOECHO)	E	ECHO
initial normalization transformation number	(0..n)	I	undef
initial number of points	(0..n)	I	0
initial points in stroke	WC	n × P	empty
prompt/echo type	(−n.. −1,1..n)	I	1
echo area	DC	4 × R	w.d.t.
stroke data record containing at least:		D	i.d.
input buffer size	(1..n)	I	w.d.t.

VALUATOR

for every logical input device of class VALUATOR:

valuator device number	(1..n)	I	w.d.t.
operating mode	(REQUEST,SAMPLE,EVENT)	E	REQUEST
echo switch	(ECHO,NOECHO)	E	ECHO
initial value		R	w.d.t.
prompt/echo type	(−n..−1,1..n)	I	1
echo area	DC 4 × R		w.d.t.
valuator data record containing at least:		D	i.d.
low value		R	w.d.t.
high value		R	w.d.t.

CHOICE

for every logical input device of class CHOICE:

choice device number	(1..n)	I	w.d.t.
operating mode	(REQUEST,SAMPLE,EVENT)	E	REQUEST
echo/prompt switch	(ECHO,NOECHO)	E	ECHO
initial status	(OK,NOCHOICE)	E	NOCHOICE
initial choice number	(1..n)	I	undef
prompt/echo type	(−n.. −1,1..n)	I	1
echo area	DC	4 × R	w.d.t.
choice data record		D	i.d.

Table 4.2 (continued)

PICK

for every logical input device of class PICK:

pick device number	(1..n)	I	w.d.t.
operating mode	(REQUEST, SAMPLE, EVENT)	E	REQUEST
echo switch	(ECHO, NOECHO)	E	ECHO
initial status	(OK, NOPICK)	E	NOPICK
initial segment		N	undef
initial pick identifier		N	undef
prompt/echo type	(−n.. −1, 1..n)	I	1
echo area	DC	4 × R	w.d.t.
pick data record		D	i.d.

STRING

for every logical input device of class STRING:

string device number	(1..n)	I	w.d.t.
operating mode	(REQUEST, SAMPLE, EVENT)	E	REQUEST
echo switch	(ECHO, NOECHO)	E	ECHO
initial string		S	" "
prompt/echo type	(−n.. −1, 1..n)	I	1
echo area	DC	4 × R	w.d.t.
string data record containing at least:		D	i.d.
buffer size	(1..n)	I	w.d.t.
cursor position	(1..n)	I	w.d.t.

4.4   GKS Functions Which Involve Workstations

The characteristics of the different workstation types, especially the characteristics of the special workstations, are best described by the set of functions applicable to them.

Only four functions can be applied to all workstation types:
— OPEN WORKSTATION
— CLOSE WORKSTATION
— INQUIRE WORKSTATION CONNECTION AND TYPE
— ESCAPE

Output workstations are affected by all functions generating or controlling output. *Input workstations* are affected by all functions generating or controlling input with the exception of PICK input. *Output/input workstations* are affected by both groups of functions and, additionally, by all functions relating to PICK input. The special position of PICK is due to the fact that PICK input operates on images shown on the display surface and, therefore, requires output capabilities.

Metafile output is affected by the same functions as output workstations, with the exception of INQUIRE TEXT EXTENT. This function does not evaluate an entry in the workstation state list but rather uses the information associated with a certain font. For example, character width for proportionally spaced fonts depends on the design of the font. As the assignment of a certain font is postponed for metafile output until metafile records are sent to an output/input workstation (which might happen at a different place with a different implementation of GKS), the text extent is not available for metafile output. Furthermore, as metafile workstations do not possess a workstation description table, all corresponding inquiry functions do not apply to metafile output. However, there is one function which can only be applied to metafile output: WRITE ITEM TO GKSM.

Metafile input is only affected by two special functions: GET ITEM TYPE FROM GKSM and READ ITEM FROM GKSM in addition to the four functions mentioned on the previous page.

The *workstation-independent segment storage (WISS)* behaves like an output workstation except that all functions relating to a display surface such as: REDRAW ALL SEGMENTS ON WORKSTATION, UPDATE WORKSTATION, SET DEFERRAL STATE or specifying workstation attributes and workstation transformation do not apply. CLEAR WORKSTATION applies in so far as there are segments to be deleted. The clearing of the display surface is, of course, not relevant to the WISS. COPY SEGMENT TO WORKSTATION needs the WISS as a source but cannot use it as a destination as this would have no effect. Furthermore, most entries in the workstation state list and the entire workstation description table do not exist for the WISS. Consequently, the respective inquiry functions do not apply either.

All the GKS functions with the workstation categories to which they directly or indirectly apply are listed in Table 4.3.

Table 4.3 List of all GKS functions and corresponding workstation types

GKS Function	applicable to					
Control Functions						
OPEN GKS			non-applicable			
CLOSE GKS			non-applicable			
OPEN WORKSTATION	WISS	MO	O	OI	I	MI
CLOSE WORKSTATION	WISS	MO	O	OI	I	MI
ACTIVATE WORKSTATION	WISS	MO	O	OI		
DEACTIVATE WORKSTATION	WISS	MO	O	OI		
CLEAR WORKSTATION	WISS	MO	O	OI		
REDRAW ALL SEGMENTS ON WORKSTATION		MO	O	OI		
UPDATE WORKSTATION		MO	O	OI		
SET DEFERRAL STATE		MO	O	OI		
MESSAGE		MO	O	OI	I	
ESCAPE	WISS	MO	O	OI	I	MI
Output Functions						
POLYLINE	WISS	MO	O	OI		
POLYMARKER	WISS	MO	O	OI		

Table 4.3 (continued)

TEXT	WISS	MO	O	OI
FILL AREA	WISS	MO	O	OI
CELL ARRAY	WISS	MO	O	OI
GENERALIZED DRAWING PRIMITIVE (GDP)	WISS	MO	O	OI

Output Attributes

SET POLYLINE INDEX	WISS	MO	O	OI
SET LINETYPE	WISS	MO	O	OI
SET LINEWIDTH SCALE FACTOR	WISS	MO	O	OI
SET POLYLINE COLOUR INDEX	WISS	MO	O	OI
SET POLYMARKER INDEX	WISS	MO	O	OI
SET MARKER TYPE	WISS	MO	O	OI
SET MARKER SIZE SCALE FACTOR	WISS	MO	O	OI
SET POLYMARKER COLOUR INDEX	WISS	MO	O	OI
SET CHARACTER HEIGHT	WISS	MO	O	OI
SET CHARACTER UP VECTOR	WISS	MO	O	OI
SET TEXT PATH	WISS	MO	O	OI
SET TEXT ALIGNMENT	WISS	MO	O	OI
SET TEXT INDEX	WISS	MO	O	OI
SET TEXT FONT AND PRECISION	WISS	MO	O	OI
SET CHARACTER EXPANSION FACTOR	WISS	MO	O	OI
SET CHARACTER SPACING	WISS	MO	O	OI
SET TEXT COLOUR INDEX	WISS	MO	O	OI
SET FILL AREA INDEX	WISS	MO	O	OI
SET FILL AREA INTERIOR STYLE	WISS	MO	O	OI
SET FILL AREA STYLE INDEX	WISS	MO	O	OI
SET FILL AREA COLOUR INDEX	WISS	MO	O	OI
SET PATTERN SIZE	WISS	MO	O	OI
SET PATTERN REFERENCE POINT	WISS	MO	O	OI
SET ASPECT SOURCE FLAGS	WISS	MO	O	OI
SET PICK IDENTIFIER	WISS	MO	O	OI
SET POLYLINE REPRESENTATION		MO	O	OI
SET POLYMARKER REPRESENTATION		MO	O	OI
SET TEXT REPRESENTATION		MO	O	OI
SET FILL AREA REPRESENTATION		MO	O	OI
SET PATTERN REPRESENTATION		MO	O	OI
SET COLOUR REPRESENTATION		MO	O	OI

Transformation Functions

SET WINDOW	WISS	MO	O	OI	I
SET VIEWPORT	WISS	MO	O	OI	I
SET VIEWPORT INPUT PRIORITY	WISS	MO	O	OI	I
SELECT NORMALIZATION TRANSFORMATION	WISS	MO	O	OI	I
SET CLIPPING INDICATOR	WISS	MO	O	OI	
SET WORKSTATION WINDOW		MO	O	OI	I
SET WORKSTATION VIEWPORT		MO	O	OI	I

Table 4.3 (continued)

Segment Functions

CREATE SEGMENT	WISS	MO	O	OI
CLOSE SEGMENT	WISS	MO	O	OI
RENAME SEGMENT	WISS	MO	O	OI
DELETE SEGMENT	WISS	MO	O	OI
DELETE SEGMENT FROM WORKSTATION	WISS	MO	O	OI
ASSOCIATE SEGMENT WITH WORKSTATION	WISS	MO	O	OI
COPY SEGMENT TO WORKSTATION	(WISS)	MO	O	OI
INSERT SEGMENT	WISS	MO	O	OI
SET SEGMENT TRANSFORMATION	WISS	MO	O	OI
SET VISIBILITY	WISS	MO	O	OI
SET HIGHLIGHTING	WISS	MO	O	OI
SET SEGMENT PRIORITY	WISS	MO	O	OI
SET DETECTABILITY	WISS	MO	O	OI

Input Functions

INITIALISE LOCATOR	OI	I
INITIALISE STROKE	OI	I
INITIALISE VALUATOR	OI	I
INITIALISE CHOICE	OI	I
INITIALISE PICK	OI	
INITIALISE STRING	OI	I
SET LOCATOR MODE	OI	I
SET STROKE MODE	OI	I
SET VALUATOR MODE	OI	I
SET CHOICE MODE	OI	I
SET PICK MODE	OI	
SET STRING MODE	OI	I
REQUEST LOCATOR	OI	I
REQUEST STROKE	OI	I
REQUEST VALUATOR	OI	I
REQUEST CHOICE	OI	I
REQUEST PICK	OI	
REQUEST STRING	OI	I
SAMPLE LOCATOR	OI	I
SAMPLE STROKE	OI	I
SAMPLE VALUATOR	OI	I
SAMPLE CHOICE	OI	I
SAMPLE PICK	OI	
SAMPLE STRING	OI	I
AWAIT EVENT	OI	I
FLUSH DEVICE EVENTS	OI	I
GET LOCATOR	OI	I
GET STROKE	OI	I
GET VALUATOR	OI	I
GET CHOICE	OI	I

Table 4.3 (continued)

	WISS	MO	O	OI	I	MI
GET PICK				OI		
GET STRING				OI	I	

Metafile Functions

	WISS	MO	O	OI	I	MI
WRITE ITEM TO GKSM		MO				
GET ITEM TYPE FROM GKSM						MI
READ ITEM FROM GKSM						MI
INTERPRET ITEM	WISS	MO	O	OI	I	

Inquiry Functions

	WISS	MO	O	OI	I	MI
INQUIRE OPERATING STATE VALUE	non-applicable					
INQUIRE LEVEL OF GKS	non-applicable					
INQUIRE LIST OF AVAILABLE WORKSTATION TYPES	non-applicable					
INQUIRE WORKSTATION MAXIMUM NUMBERS	non-applicable					
INQUIRE MAXIMUM NORMALIZATION TRANSFORMATION NUMBER	non-applicable					
INQUIRE SET OF OPEN WORKSTATIONS	non-applicable					
INQUIRE SET OF ACTIVE WORKSTATIONS	non-applicable					
INQUIRE CURRENT PRIMITIVE ATTRIBUTE VALUES	non-applicable					
INQUIRE CURRENT PICK IDENTIFIER VALUE	non-applicable					
INQUIRE CURRENT INDIVIDUAL ATTRIBUTE VALUES	non-applicable					
INQUIRE CURRENT NORMALIZATION TRANSFORMATION NUMBER	non-applicable					
INQUIRE LIST OF NORMALIZATION TRANSFORMATION NUMBERS	non-applicable					
INQUIRE NORMALIZATION TRANSFORMATION	non-applicable					
INQUIRE CLIPPING	non-applicable					
INQUIRE NAME OF OPEN SEGMENT	non-applicable					
INQUIRE SET OF SEGMENT NAMES IN USE	non-applicable					
INQUIRE MORE SIMULTANEOUS EVENTS	non-applicable					
INQUIRE WORKSTATION CONNECTION AND TYPE	WISS	MO	O	OI	I	MI
INQUIRE WORKSTATION STATE	WISS	MO	O	OI		
INQUIRE WORKSTATION DEFERRAL AND UPDATE STATES		MO	O	OI		
INQUIRE LIST OF POLYLINE INDICES		MO	O	OI		
INQUIRE POLYLINE REPRESENTATION		MO	O	OI		
INQUIRE LIST OF POLYMARKER INDICES		MO	O	OI		
INQUIRE POLYMARKER REPRESENTATION		MO	O	OI		
INQUIRE LIST OF TEXT INDICES		MO	O	OI		
INQUIRE TEXT REPRESENTATION		MO	O	OI		
INQUIRE TEXT EXTENT			O	OI		
INQUIRE LIST OF FILL AREA INDICES		MO	O	OI		
INQUIRE FILL AREA REPRESENTATION		MO	O	OI		
INQUIRE LIST OF PATTERN INDICES		MO	O	OI		
INQUIRE PATTERN REPRESENTATION		MO	O	OI		

Table 4.3 (continued)

	WISS	MO	O	OI	I	MI
INQUIRE LIST OF COLOUR INDICES		MO	O	OI		
INQUIRE COLOUR REPRESENTATION		MO	O	OI		
INQUIRE WORKSTATION TRANSFORMATION		MO	O	OI	I	
INQUIRE SET OF SEGMENT NAMES ON WORKSTATION	WISS	MO	O	OI		
INQUIRE LOCATOR DEVICE STATE				OI	I	
INQUIRE STROKE DEVICE STATE				OI	I	
INQUIRE VALUATOR DEVICE STATE				OI	I	
INQUIRE CHOICE DEVICE STATE				OI	I	
INQUIRE PICK DEVICE STATE				OI		
INQUIRE STRING DEVICE STATE				OI	I	
INQUIRE WORKSTATION CATEGORY	WISS	MO	O	OI	I	MI
INQUIRE WORKSTATION CLASSIFICATION			O	OI		
INQUIRE DISPLAY SPACE SIZE			O	OI	I	
INQUIRE DYNAMIC MODIFICATION OF WORKSTATION ATTRIBUTES			O	OI		
INQUIRE DEFAULT DEFERRAL STATE VALUES			O	OI		
INQUIRE POLYLINE FACILITIES			O	OI		
INQUIRE PREDEFINED POLYLINE REPRESENTATION			O	OI		
INQUIRE POLYMARKER FACILITIES			O	OI		
INQUIRE PREDEFINED POLYMARKER REPRESENTATION			O	OI		
INQUIRE TEXT FACILITIES			O	OI		
INQUIRE PREDEFINED TEXT REPRESENTATION			O	OI		
INQUIRE FILL AREA FACILITIES			O	OI		
INQUIRE PREDEFINED FILL AREA REPRESENTATION			O	OI		
INQUIRE PATTERN FACILITIES			O	OI		
INQUIRE PREDEFINED PATTERN REPRESENTATION			O	OI		
INQUIRE COLOUR FACILITIES			O	OI		
INQUIRE PREDEFINED COLOUR REPRESENTATION			O	OI		
INQUIRE LIST OF AVAILABLE GENERALIZED DRAWING PRIMITIVES			O	OI		
INQUIRE GENERALIZED DRAWING PRIMITIVE			O	OI		
INQUIRE MAXIMUM LENGTH OF WORKSTATION STATE TABLES			O	OI		
INQUIRE NUMBER OF SEGMENT PRIORITIES SUPPORTED			O	OI		
INQUIRE DYNAMIC MODIFICATION OF SEGMENT ATTRIBUTES			O	OI		
INQUIRE NUMBER OF AVAILABLE LOGICAL INPUT DEVICES				OI	I	
INQUIRE DEFAULT LOCATOR DEVICE DATA				OI	I	
INQUIRE DEFAULT STROKE DEVICE DATA				OI	I	
INQUIRE DEFAULT VALUATOR DEVICE DATA				OI	I	
INQUIRE DEFAULT CHOICE DEVICE DATA				OI	I	
INQUIRE DEFAULT PICK DEVICE DATA				OI		

Table 4.3 (continued)

INQUIRE DEFAULT STRING DEVICE DATA			OI	I
INQUIRE SET OF ASSOCIATED WORKSTATIONS	WISS	MO	O	OI
INQUIRE SEGMENT ATTRIBUTES	WISS	MO	O	OI
INQUIRE PIXEL ARRAY DIMENSIONS			O	OI
INQUIRE PIXEL ARRAY			O	OI
INQUIRE PIXEL			O	OI
INQUIRE INPUT QUEUE OVERFLOW		non-applicable		

Utility Functions

EVALUATE TRANSFORMATION MATRIX	non-applicable
ACCUMULATE TRANSFORMATION MATRIX	non-applicable

Error Handling

EMERGENCY CLOSE GKS	non-applicable
ERROR HANDLING	non-applicable
ERROR LOGGING	non-applicable

Key:		
	WISS	workstation-independent segment storage
	MO	GKS metafile output
	O	output workstation
	OI	output/input workstation
	I	input workstation
	MI	GKS metafile input
	(WISS)	workstation-independent segment storage is fundamental to the operation of this GKS function, but the workstation identifier parameter cannot be workstation-independent segment storage

4.5   Workstation Control

Before the application program may use a workstation, the latter must be allocated by the GKS function OPEN WORKSTATION. This function assigns the workstation a name, the workstation identifier, for later reference.

The workstation is selected by a connection identifier which enables the operating system to establish a connection. The connection identifier may be a unit number in FORTRAN, a file name or a link name, etc. depending on the programming environment. The valid connection identifiers will be described in the installation manual.

A further parameter of OPEN WORKSTATION specifies the workstation type according to which the appropriate workstation driver and the workstation description table are selected. The latter is used when initializing the workstation state list. The workstation types available are listed in the GKS description table (Table 3.5). They are all implementation-dependent except for three mandatory workstation types for metafile input, metafile output, and workstation-independent segment storage. Their names are defined with each language-dependent layer.

The selection of a workstation by means of a connection identifier and workstation type offers a flexibility which may be unnecessary (e.g., if only one workstation of a given type exists) or which may not be supported by an operating system (e.g., if the connection has to be determined prior to the program starting). The installation manual will describe which combinations of both parameters are valid or whether a parameter can be totally ignored.

OPEN WORKSTATION allocates the workstation and the workstation state list which is now available for inquiry. Input devices may be used and segments may be manipulated at an open workstation.

To allow graphical output to be sent to an open workstation, the workstation has to be activated by the function ACTIVATE WORKSTATION. Output primitives are sent to, and segments are stored on, all active workstations and no others. Naturally, only workstations possessing output capabilities may be activated.

A workstation must be opened before it can be activated. ACTIVATE WORKSTATION enables output only at an open workstation. It is possible for open (i.e., not active) and active workstations to exist at the same time.

An active workstation is made inactive by the function DEACTIVATE WORKSTATION; an open workstation is closed by the function CLOSE WORKSTATION; the workstation state list is cancelled and the connection to the workstation is broken. Whether the workstation is actually deallocated and made available for another user depends on the capabilities of the operating system.

Example 4.1 in Section 4.8 shows the use of the above functions. The functions OPEN/CLOSE GKS, OPEN/CLOSE WORKSTATION, and ACTIVATE/DEACTIVATE WORKSTATION have been defined as separate functions in order to make the transitions of states in GKS clear and to provide full flexibility for all environments. However, it is common for a graphics workstation to be a terminal which is used for alphanumeric dialogue with the operating system and for graphics at the same time. In this case, there is no need to inform the operating system which workstation is to be addressed, as this workstation has been already allocated and is therefore active at the time of OPEN GKS. For such environments, it may be useful to have one single function which opens GKS and opens and activates this workstation in one step. Such a function can easily be built on top of GKS.

OPEN WORKSTATION   GKOP, WSOP, WSAC, SGOP   L0a

Parameters:

Input	workstation identifier	N
Input	connection identifier	N
Input	workstation type	N

Effect:

If GKS is in operating state GKOP, it will be put into the state WSOP = "at least one workstation open". GKS requests the operating system to establish the specified connection to a workstation characterized in the workstation description table by the 'workstation type'. The workstation state list is allocated and initialised as indicated in Section 4.3. The workstation identifier is added to the set of open workstations in the GKS state list. OPEN WORKSTATION ensures that the display surface is clear, but does not clear the surface needlessly.

N.B.:

The connection identifier is given in a form suitable to the application program language (for example, a 'unit number' in FORTRAN or a 'file identifier' in PL/1). There are three workstation categories, 'metafile input', 'metafile output' and 'workstation-independent segment storage', which are mandatory at certain levels of GKS.

Errors:

8	GKS not in proper state: GKS should be in one of the states GKOP, WSOP, WSAC or SGOP
20	Specified workstation identifier is invalid
21	Specified connection identifier is invalid
22	Specified workstation type is invalid
23	Specified workstation type does not exist
24	Specified workstation is open
26	Specified workstation cannot be opened
28	Workstation-Independent Segment Storage is already open
42	Maximum number of simultaneously open workstations would be exceeded

———————————————— *FORTRAN Interface* ————————————————

CALL GOPWK (WKID, CONID, WTYPE)

Parameters:

Input	WKID	workstation identifier	INTEGER
Input	CONID	connection identifier	INTEGER
Input	WTYPE	workstation type	INTEGER

CLOSE WORKSTATION   WSOP, WSAC, SGOP   L0a

Parameters:

Input   workstation identifier   N

Effect:

An implicit UPDATE WORKSTATION is performed for the specified workstation. The workstation state list is deallocated. The workstation identifier is deleted from the set of open workstations in the GKS state list and from the set of associated workstations in the segment state list of every segment. If the set of associated workstations of a segment becomes empty, the segment is deleted. The input queue is flushed of all events from all devices at the workstation being closed. If the 'identification of one of the logical input devices that caused an input queue overflow' entry in the GKS error state list refers to this workstation identifier, then all the contents of that entry become undefined. The connection to the workstation is broken. GKS is put into operating state GKOP if no workstations remain open. The display surface need not be cleared when CLOSE WORKSTATION is invoked, but it can be.

Errors:

7	GKS not in proper state: GKS shall be in one of the states WSOP, WSAC or SGOP
20	Specified workstation identifier is invalid
25	Specified workstation is not open
29	Specified workstation is active
147	Input queue has overflowed

——————————————— *FORTRAN Interface* ———————————————

CALL GCLWK (WKID)
Parameters:
Input   WKID   workstation identifier   INTEGER

ACTIVATE WORKSTATION   WSOP, WSAC   L0a

Parameters:
Input   workstation identifier   N
Effect:
GKS is put into the operating state WSAC = "At least one workstation active". The
specified workstation is marked active in the workstation state list. The workstation
identifier is added to the set of active workstations in the GKS state list.
N.B.:
Output primitives are sent to and segments are stored at all active workstations.
Errors:

6	GKS not in proper state: GKS should be either in the state WSOP or in the state WSAC
20	Specified workstation identifier is invalid
25	Specified workstation is not open
29	Specified workstation is active
33	Specified workstation is of category MI
35	Specified workstation is of category INPUT
43	Maximum number of simultaneously active workstations would be exceeded

——————————————— *FORTRAN Interface* ———————————————

CALL GACWK (WKID)
Parameters:
Input   WKID   workstation identifier   INTEGER

DEACTIVATE WORKSTATION   WSAC   L0a

Parameters:
Input   workstation identifier   N
Effect:
The specified workstation is marked inactive in the workstation state list. The worksta-
tion identifier is deleted from the set of active workstations in the GKS state list.
GKS is set into the operating state WSOP = "At least one workstation open" if no
workstation remains active.
N.B.:
While a workstation is inactive, primitives are not sent to it nor does it store new
segments. Segments already stored at this workstation are retained.
Errors:

3	GKS not in proper state: GKS should be in the state WSAC
20	Specified workstation identifier is invalid
30	Specified workstation is not active
33	Specified workstation is of category MI
35	Specified workstation is of category INPUT

——————————————— *FORTRAN Interface* ———————————————

CALL GDAWK (WKID)
Parameters:
Input   WKID   workstation identifier   INTEGER

To generate several images at the same workstation, a command is necessary which indicates the start of a new image. GKS provides the function CLEAR WORKSTATION which entirely deletes the previously generated primitives and allows the start of a new image on a cleared display surface. By calling this function, a series of pictures can be generated within one session (cf. Example 4.2).

If a clearing of the display surface by CLEAR WORKSTATION is requested, two capabilities for clearing it are available, namely:
— clear the display surface, even if it is empty;
— ensure that the display surface is clear without clearing the display surface unnecessarily.

The first capability allows the generation of empty images which is needed, for example, when creating a break in a film.

The second capability means that the display surface is only cleared when needed — this would normally be when the display surface was not clear. However, it is no trivial matter to find out whether the display surface is clear or not, because, for example, a circle may have been generated by using GDP with its centre within the display surface and have then been clipped to non-existence. Therefore, GKS will avoid clearing a device unnecessarily only if this does not involve an unreasonable amount of effort.

CLEAR WORKSTATION   WSOP, WSAC   L0a
Parameters:
   Input   workstation identifier   N
   Input   control flag   (CONDITIONALLY, ALWAYS)   E
Effect:
All of the following actions are executed in the given sequence:
a) All deferred actions (cf. Section 4.4) for the specified workstation are executed (without intermediate clearing of the display surface).
b) The display surface is set to a clear state according to the control flag as follows:
   CONDITIONALLY: it is ensured that the display surface is clear without clearing it needlessly;
   ALWAYS: the display surface is cleared.
c) If the 'workstation transformation update state' entry in the workstation state list is PENDING, the 'current workstation window' and 'current workstation viewport' entries in the workstation state list are assigned the values of the 'requested workstation window' and 'requested workstation viewport' entries; the 'workstation transformation update state' entry is set to NOTPENDING.
d) For all segments stored at the specified workstation, the workstation identifier is deleted from the 'set of associated workstations' in the segment state list. If the 'set of associated workstations' of a segment becomes empty, the segment is deleted. The 'set of stored segments for this workstation' in the workstation state list is set to 'empty'.
e) The 'new frame action necessary at update' entry in the workstation state list is set to NO.
f) The 'display surface empty' entry in the workstation state list is set to EMPTY.
Errors:
    6   GKS not in proper state: GKS should be either in the state WSOP or in the state WSAC

20   Specified workstation identifier is invalid
25   Specified workstation is not open
33   Specified workstation is of category MI
35   Specified workstation is of category INPUT

———————————————— *FORTRAN Interface* ————————————————

CALL GCLRWK (WKID,COFL)
Parameters:
  Input   WKID   workstation identifier   INTEGER
  Input   COFL   control flag   (0 = conditionally, 1 = always)   INTEGER

4.6   Deferring Picture Changes

The generation of pictures is a complicated and expensive task. Low performance devices will have difficulties in generating pictures fast enough, which is a particular problem for interactive sessions. In this section the function SET DEFERRAL MODE is introduced which enables a workstation to be tuned in such a way that to some extent the available resources are best used for a specific application.

The novice may leave this section out, as the default setting will serve the most common needs best. Some knowledge of the input and segment functions will be useful for understanding this section.

The display of a workstation should reflect as far as possible the actual state of the picture as defined by the application program. However, to use the capabilities of a workstation efficiently, GKS allows a workstation to delay, for a certain period of time, the actions requested by the application program. During this period, the state of the display may be undefined.

The function SET DEFERRAL STATE allows the application program to choose that deferral state which takes into account the capabilities of the workstation and the requirements of the application program. The deferral state of a workstation is controlled by two attributes: deferral mode and implicit regeneration mode.

Deferral mode controls the possible delay of output functions. For example, data sent to a device may be buffered to optimise data transfer. The deferral mode can be specified as follows:

ASAP: The visual effect of each function will be achieved at the workstation As Soon As Possible (ASAP).

BNIG: The visual effect of each function will be achieved at the workstation Before the Next Interaction Globally (BNIG), i.e., before the next interaction with a logical input device gets under way at any workstation (cf. Section 8.1). If an interaction at any workstation is already in progress, then the visual effect will be achieved as soon as possible.

BNIL: The visual effect of each function will be achieved at the workstation Before the Next Interaction Locally (BNIL), i.e., before the next interaction with a logical input device gets under way at the same workstation (cf.

Section 8.1). If an interaction at that workstation is already in progress, then the visual effect will be achieved as soon as possible.

ASTI: The visual effect of each function will be achieved at the workstation At Some TIme (ASTI).

Deferral applies to the following functions which generate output:
POLYLINE
POLYMARKER
TEXT
FILL AREA
CELL ARRAY
GENERALIZED DRAWING PRIMITIVE
INSERT SEGMENT
ASSOCIATE SEGMENT WITH WORKSTATION
COPY SEGMENT TO WORKSTATION
INTERPRET ITEM

Deferred output functions will be executed:
— when a local or global interaction is initiated (for deferral mode BNIL and BNIG);
— when end of output for the current picture is indicated by the GKS functions CLEAR WORKSTATION or CLOSE WORKSTATION;
— before a new picture is initiated by REDRAW ALL SEGMENTS ON WORKSTATION;
— when required explicitly by UPDATE WORKSTATION or by setting the deferral mode to ASAP.

As long as none of these cases occurs, the workstation driver or GKS may decide arbitrarily when to send deferred output to a workstation's display surface.

Implicit regeneration mode controls the suppression of the implicit regeneration of the whole picture. For example, change of colour by SET COLOUR REPRESENTATION may be performed immediately on a colour raster display by setting an entry in the device's colour table; the same function may be performed on a plotter merely by putting new paper on it and redrawing the whole picture. The latter case is called implicit regeneration and is controlled by the implicit regeneration mode. The mode can be specified as follows:
— implicit regeneration of the picture is SUPPRESSED;
— implicit regeneration of the picture is ALLOWED.
Suppression of implicit regeneration does not prevent an explicit regeneration initiated by REDRAW ALL SEGMENTS ON WORKSTATION or, possibly, by UPDATE WORKSTATION.

The purposes of the implicit regeneration mode are:
— the efficient use of devices with poor dynamic capabilities like storage tubes;
— the precise control of frames produced on hard copy devices.

For such devices, the initial setting of the implicit regeneration mode will be SUPPRESSED which secures that a new frame will be initiated only by an explicit function call to REDRAW ALL SEGMENTS ON WORKSTATION or UPDATE WORKSTATION.

The following functions change the picture and may induce an implicit regeneration:

SET POLYLINE REPRESENTATION
SET POLYMARKER REPRESENTATION
SET TEXT REPRESENTATION
SET FILL AREA REPRESENTATION
SET PATTERN REPRESENTATION
SET COLOUR REPRESENTATION
SET WORKSTATION WINDOW
SET WORKSTATION VIEWPORT
SET SEGMENT TRANSFORMATION
SET VISIBILITY
SET HIGHLIGHTING
SET SEGMENT PRIORITY
DELETE SEGMENT
DELETE SEGMENT FROM WORKSTATION
ASSOCIATE SEGMENT WITH WORKSTATION
INTERPRET ITEM

In addition, the output of primitives (including INSERT SEGMENT), when segment priority is important, may cause implicit regeneration; for example, if primitives are generated within a segment overlapping another segment with lower priority.

These functions can be performed immediately at some workstations, but on others it may be necessary to regenerate the whole of the picture to achieve the function's effect. The entries under 'dynamic modification accepted' in the workstation description table indicate which changes:
— can be performed immediately;
— lead to an implicit regeneration.

The effect of dynamic changes is only guaranteed for primitives within segments. The effect on primitives outside segments may be workstation-dependent. If changes can be performed immediately, those changes may affect primitives outside segments in addition to those inside segments. For example, changing the colour table will affect primitives inside and outside segments. On the other hand, if changes are performed by using an implicit regeneration, only primitives inside segments will show the required attribute change. Primitives outside segments will be merely deleted from the display surface during regeneration. Therefore, for applications using primitives outside segments, it is advisable to suppress implicit regeneration and to control the deletion of primitives outside segments and the regeneration of the picture explicitly.

The concept of deferral refers only to the visible effects of GKS functions. Effects on the segment storage or on the state of the workstation cannot be (conceptually) deferred. In none of the deferral states is it necessary to delay the addition of graphical data, or attribute changes. If this is required, it should be achieved by using the segment storage facility and the visibility attribute.

This restriction means that the buffer for deferred actions can be chosen in an implementation-dependent manner.

If segments of different priority are created at workstations which permit one segment to hide another, even the addition of data may cause an implicit regeneration, which can be deferred. In this case the buffer size may also be limited. Since only segments can have priority, this deferral may only happen to primitives inside segments which are already stored in the segment storage. Primitives outside segments need not be deferred on such workstations.

SET DEFERRAL STATE   WSOP, WSAC, SGOP   L1a

Parameters:

Input	workstation identifier		N
Input	deferral mode	(ASAP, BNIG, BNIL, ASTI)	E
Input	implicit regeneration mode	(SUPPRESSED, ALLOWED)	E

Effect:

The entries 'deferral mode' and 'implicit regeneration mode' for the specified workstation are put in the workstation state list. Depending on the new value of 'deferral mode', deferred output may be unblocked. If in the workstation state list the new values of 'implicit regeneration mode' and 'new frame action necessary at update' are ALLOWED and YES respectively, then an action equivalent to REDRAW ALL SEGMENTS ON WORKSTATION is performed.

Errors:

7	GKS not in proper state: GKS should be in one of the states WSOP, WSAC or SGOP
20	Specified workstation identifier is invalid
25	Specified workstation is not open
33	Specified workstation is of category MI
35	Specified workstation is of category INPUT
36	Specified workstation is Workstation-Independent Segment Storage

——————————————— *FORTRAN Interface* ———————————————

CALL GSDS (WKID, DEFMOD, REGMOD)

Parameters:

Input	WKID	workstation identifier		INTEGER
Input	DEFMOD	deferral mode	(0 = asap, 1 = bnil, 2 = bnig, 3 = asti)	INTEGER
Input	REGMOD	implicit regeneration mode	(0 = allowed, 1 = suppressed)	INTEGER

The function SET DEFERRAL STATE should be used with care, as a change in the values preset by the implementor may strongly influence the performance of the workstation. To ensure that the display of a workstation shows the actual state at certain points in time, the function UPDATE WORKSTATION should be used.

UPDATE WORKSTATION performs two steps:
— If the deferral mode enables the delay of output functions and there are some functions which have actually been delayed, they will now be executed.
— If an implicit regeneration has been suppressed, the actual picture will now be generated on the display surface.

The first step ensures that all output under way to the workstation actually is generated on the display surface. Thus, UPDATE WORKSTATION defines an ultimate point until which output may be deferred. The second step enables changes to be performed which could not be made on the current picture because they require a full regeneration of the picture. If the second step is performed, the first step might seem unnecessary. This may be true for interactive devices but for hard copy devices, however, it is essential to finish the current picture before initiating the next one.

UPDATE WORKSTATION   WSOP, WSAC, SGOP   L0a

Parameters:

Input   workstation identifier   N
Input   regeneration flag   (PERFORM, POSTPONE)   E

Effect:

All deferred actions for the specified workstation are executed (without intermediate clearing of the display surface). If the regeneration flag is set to PERFORM and the 'new frame action necessary at update' entry in the workstation state list is YES, then the following actions are executed in the given sequence.

a) The display surface is cleared only if the 'display surface empty' entry in the workstation state list is NOTEMPTY. The entry is then set to EMPTY.

b) If the 'workstation transformation update state' entry in the workstation state list is PENDING, the 'current workstation window' and 'current workstation viewport' entries in the workstation state list are assigned the values of the 'requested workstation window' and 'requested workstation viewport' entries; the 'workstation transformation update state' entry is then set to NOTPENDING.

c) All visible segments stored at this workstation (i.e. contained in the 'set of stored segments for this workstation' in the workstation state list) are redisplayed. This action usually causes the 'display surface empty' entry in the workstation state list to be set to NOTEMPTY.

d) The 'new frame action necessary at update' entry in the workstation state list is set to NO.

N.B.:

If the regeneration flag is PERFORM, UPDATE WORKSTATION suspends the effect of SET DEFERRAL STATE. In that case, it is equivalent to the following sequence of functions:

INQUIRE WORKSTATION DEFERRAL AND UPDATE STATES;

save deferral state;

SET DEFERRAL STATE (ASAP, ALLOWED);

set deferral state to saved value.

If the value of the 'new frame action necessary at update' entry is NO or the regeneration flag is POSTPONE, UPDATE WORKSTATION merely initiates the transmission of blocked data. If the value of the entry 'new frame action necessary at update' is YES and the regeneration flag is PERFORM, UPDATE WORKSTATION behaves as REDRAW ALL SEGMENTS ON WORKSTATION.

The 'new frame action necessary at update' entry in a workstation state list is set to YES during deferral of an action if both of the following are true:

a) an action causing modification of the picture is actually being deferred at the same workstation;

b) the workstation display surface does not allow modification of the image without redrawing the whole picture (for example, plotter, storage tube display).

Errors:

7	GKS not in proper state: GKS should be in one of the states WSOP, WSAC or SGOP
20	Specified workstation identifier is invalid
25	Specified workstation is not open
33	Specified workstation is of category MI
35	Specified workstation is of category INPUT
36	Specified workstation is Workstation-Independent Segment Storage

——————————————— *FORTRAN Interface* ———————————————

CALL GUWK (WKID,REGFL)
Parameters:

Input	WKID	workstation identifier		INTEGER
Input	REGFL	regeneration flag	(0 = postpone, 1 = perform)	INTEGER

4.7   Addressing Workstation Capabilities Not Covered by GKS

By setting the workstation state list, the application program may access and use a lot of workstation-specific features. However, some particular features will always remain outside the scope of GKS. Knowing this limitation of GKS, some functions have been provided to give the application program a standardized way of accessing non-standard features. The use of these functions will reduce the portability of programs. Their use should, therefore, be avoided as much as possible and be reserved for cases where important capabilities are available but their use is not provided for within GKS.

These additional functions are:
— GDP, to access additional output primitives on a workstation, such as a circle, spline interpolation, etc.
— MESSAGE, to address a human operator at a workstation and to give him instructions such as changing the paper on a plotter or the camera in a microfilm recorder.
— ESCAPE, to call any installation- or hardware-specific features of a workstation or of the whole system.

GDP is discussed in detail in Section 6.7. The syntax of GDP is defined within GKS. This enables all GKS transformations to be applied to the geometrical parameters, thus leaving the interpretation of the data to the individual workstation.

The MESSAGE function allows a character string to be sent to a workstation. The character string sent by MESSAGE will be interpreted by an operator whose reaction is outside the scope of GKS. The application program has no control over the position and appearance of the character string. An implementation can place the string on a device, distinct from but associate to the workstation, for example, on an alphanumeric terminal. The character string is not regarded as output like the TEXT primitive which belongs to the graphics output. Therefore, MESSAGE may also apply to input workstations. The WISS is the only workstation category which does not accept the MESSAGE function.

MESSAGE   WSOP, WSAC, SGOP   L1a
Parameters:
Input   workstation identifier   N
Input   message   S
Effect:
The message function:
a) may display a message at an implementation-dependent location on the workstation viewport or on some separate device associated with the workstation;
b) does not alter the GKS state list;
c) may affect the workstation in a purely local way (for example, by requesting the operator to change the paper). Possible effects on the execution of the application program or on subsequent commands sent to the workstation by GKS must be stated explicitly in the implementation dependencies manual.
Errors:
7   GKS not in proper state: GKS should be in one of the states WSOP, WSAC or SGOP
20   Specified workstation identifier is invalid
25   Specified workstation is not open
36   Specified workstation is Workstation-Independent Segment Storage

——————————————— *FORTRAN Interface* ———————————————

CALL GMSG (WKID, MESS)
Parameters:
Input   WKID   workstation identifier   INTEGER
Input   MESS   message   CHARACTER*(*)

A standard cannot cover all the requirements of all graphics applications. Nevertheless, it is desirable that all application programs should stick as closely as possible to the standard functionality. For this purpose, an ESCAPE function is provided as a standard way of being non-standard, thus enabling the functionality of GKS to be extended. Such an ESCAPE function has naturally negative consequences for the portability of programs. Therefore, it should only be used if important capabilities are needed which GKS does not supply.

ESCAPE allows one to address all the features of a GKS implementation and any of the hardware, except that ESCAPE may not generate output. The generation of non-standard output primitives is solely reserved for GDP so that GKS has at least a minimal control of output. ESCAPE can be useful, for example, on a raster device which has firmware for performing logical operations (AND, OR, EXCLUSIVE OR) on raster matrices in order to generate a raster image ("raster-op").

ESCAPE   GKOP, WSOP, WSAC, SGOP   L0a
Parameters:
Input   specific escape function identification   N
Input   escape input data record   D
Output   escape output data record   D

Effect:
> The specified non-standard escape function is invoked. The form of the escape data records may vary for different functions. Also, the GKS states which allow a specific escape function to be called may be restricted. The following rules govern the definition of a new specific escape function:
> a) the GKS design concept is not violated;
> b) the GKS state lists are not altered;
> c) the function does not generate geometrical output;
> d) any side effects must be well documented.
>
> Specific escape functions may apply to more than one workstation, for example all open workstations or all active workstations. The escape data record can include a workstation identifier where this is required.

N.B.:
> Examples of specific escape functions anticipated at present are:
> a) support of raster devices which allow the display of more than one frame buffer;
> b) use of raster-op hardware to manipulate output data previously produced by CELL ARRAY.

Errors:

8	GKS not in proper state: GKS should be in one of the states GKOP, WSOP, WSAC or SGOP
180	Specified function is not supported
181	Specified escape function identification is invalid
182	Contents of escape data record is invalid

———————————————— *FORTRAN Interface* ————————————————

CALL GESC (FCTID, LIDR, IDR, MLODR, LODR, ODR)

Parameters:

Input	FCTID	function identification	INTEGER
Input	LIDR	length of input data record	INTEGER
Input	IDR(LIDR)	input data record	CHARACTER*80
Input	MLODR	maximum length of output data record	INTEGER
Output	LODR	length of output data record used	INTEGER
Output	ODR(MLODR)	output data record	CHARACTER*80

The functions mentioned above enable the application program to access non-standard features. As well as this, additional features of a workstation may be used locally by the workstation operator without notifying GKS. For example, if a workstation has two display surfaces, the operator may switch locally from one to the other. More than one display surface can be controlled by GKS only by defining a separate workstation for each display surface. Of course, such a local extension of functionality does not affect program portability but rather operator portability.

4.8 Examples

Example 4.1 Workstation selection for input and output

This example illustrates how two workstations 'disp' and 'digi' can be selected independently for input and output. It should be noted that OPEN_WORKSTA-

TION can be called for any workstation, whereas ACTIVATE_WORKSTA-
TION needs output capability at that workstation.

—————————————————————————————*Pascal*—————————————————————————————

```
L10    OPEN_GKS (error_file, memory_limit);
L20    OPEN_WORKSTATION (disp, conid1, vector_refresh_type);
          {Input possible on disp}
L30    OPEN_WORKSTATION (digi, conid2, digitizer_type);
          {Input possible on disp, digi}
L40    ACTIVATE_WORKSTATION (disp);
          {Input possible on disp, digi; Output generated on disp}
L50    ACTIVATE_WORKSTATION (digi);
          {Input possible on disp, digi; Output generated on disp, digi}
L60    DEACTIVATE_WORKSTATION (disp);
          {Input possible on disp, digi; Output generated on digi}
L70    CLOSE_WORKSTATION (disp);
          {Input possible on digi; Output generated on digi}
L80    DEACTIVATE_WORKSTATION (digi);
          {Input possible on digi}
L90    CLOSE_WORKSTATION (digi);
L100   CLOSE_GKS;
```

———————————————————————— *Fortran* ————————————————————————

```
L10        CALL GOPKS (ERRFIL, BUFA)
L20        CALL GOPWK (DISP, CONID1, VECT)
      C    *** Input possible on DISP
L30        CALL GOPWK (DIGI, CONID2, DIG1)
      C    *** Input possible on DISP, DIGI
L40        CALL GACWK (DISP)
      C    *** Input possible on DISP, DIGI; Output generated on DISP, DIGI
L50        CALL GACWK (DIGI)
      C    *** Input possible on DISP, DIGI; Output generated on DISP, DIGI
L60        CALL GDAWK (DISP)
      C    *** Input possible on DISP, DIGI; Output generated on DIGI
L70        CALL GCLWK (DISP)
      C    *** Input possible on DIGI; Output generated on DIGI
L80        CALL GDAWK (DIGI)
      C    *** Input possible on DIGI
L90        CALL GCLWK (DIGI)
L100       CALL GCLKS
```

Example 4.2   Generating a sequence of independent pictures

Assume that a procedure DRAW_PICTURE reads a file which contains data
describing a series of numbered pictures. This example shows the control functions which allocate and deallocate a plotter workstation and advance paper
for each picture.

—————————————————————————————*Pascal*—————————————————————————————

```
L10    OPEN_GKS (error_file, memory_limit);
L20    OPEN_WORKSTATION (plot, connection, plotter_type);
```

L30   ACTIVATE_WORKSTATION (plot);
L40   **for** i: = 1 **to** max **do**
L50   **begin**
L60   CLEAR_WORKSTATION (plot, CONDITIONALLY);
L80   DRAW_PICTURE (i);   {procedure draws i-th picture}
L90   **end;**

L100   DEACTIVATE_WORKSTATION (plot);
L110   CLOSE_WORKSTATION (plot);
L120   CLOSE_GKS;

———————————————————————— *Fortran* ————————————————

L10   CALL GOPKS (ERRFIL, BUFA)
L20   CALL GOPWK (PLOT, CONNEC, TYPE)
L30   CALL GACWK (PLOT)

L 40   DO 90 I = 1, MAX
L60   CALL GCLWK (PLOT, CONDIT)
L80   CALL DRPICT (I)
    C   *** DRPICT draws i-th picture
L90   90 CONTINUE

L100   CALL GDAWK (PLOT)
L110   CALL GCLWK (PLOT)
L120   CALL GCLKS

4.9   Exercises

Exercise 4.1   Workstation description table

Write a workstation description table for one of the graphical input or output devices available at your computing centre. Indicate which capabilities are immediately available on the device and which must be provided by additional software. It should be noted that the minimal requirements depend on the GKS level (cf. Table 2.2) and that furthermore, some requirements are valid for the set of all workstations rather than for each individual workstation.

Exercise 4.2   Workstation state list

Describe in detail what the workstation state list of the workstation in Exercise 4.1 looks like immediately after initialisation. What entries apply and which values are taken from the workstation description table?

5 TRANSFORMATIONS

5.1 Coordinate Systems

Pictures to be generated by GKS will be derived from data provided by the application program. This data may include results from measurements with arbitrary physical dimensions, such as temperature, weight, time, etc. By digitizing an object, data with metrical dimensions will be generated. Numerical calculations may generate data without units. These *user coordinates* have to be mapped onto the device coordinates which describe the display surface of a workstation.

GKS only accepts Cartesian coordinates which only need linear scaling with positive scale factors and shifting to be transformed to device coordinates. These user coordinates are called *world coordinates (WC)*. Other user coordinates, such as polar or logarithmic coordinates cannot be dealt with by GKS and they must therefore be transformed by the application program before being given to GKS.

World coordinates are not transformed directly into device coordinates, but rather they are mapped firstly onto an abstract display surface with *normalized device coordinates (NDC)*. This abstract display surface now has a workstation-independent representation of the picture. This intermediate step has been introduced to separate clearly workstation-dependent from workstation-independent parts of a picture definition. Each workstation may show a different view of the workstation-independent picture. Furthermore, NDC are used for the segment storage (cf. Chapter 7) and for the metafile (cf. Chapter 11). Conceptually the NDC space is unlimited. However, as long as no segment transformations are available, only that part of a picture lying in the range $[0,1] \times [0,1]$ can be displayed on a display surface. If segment transformations are available, parts of a picture can be moved from outside the range $[0,1] \times [0,1]$ back inside it and thus become visible. If real numbers are used when storing coordinate data in segments there will be no difficulties in providing a sufficiently large NDC space. For smaller implementations using integer number representation, NDC space of at least size $[-7,+7] \times [-7,+7]$ must be supported. The number 7 has been selected somewhat arbitrarily. It takes into account the resolution of common graphics devices and the word length of 16 bits used in many small computers.

The display space of each workstation is described in Cartesian coordinates called *device coordinates (DC)*. DC are in metres on a device capable of producing a precisely scaled image and if not, in other appropriate units. The dimension 'metre' for DC makes it very easy to specify a transformation with a prescribed scale. This is a major use of DC in application programs. Whereas the NDC space is quadratic, the display space of each workstation may be an arbitrary rectangle, the size of which can be determined from the workstation description table. The origin of the DC system is in the lower left-hand corner of this rectangle.

DC values, usually, will be different from those of the original device units which often depend on the resolution of a device. For example, raster displays with non-quadratic pixels will have different device units for the two axes. A GKS programmer can ignore such peculiarities except when he wants to address the single pixels in a display by CELL ARRAY.

5.2 Normalization Transformation

The application program can compose a picture from different sources which will have their own WC system. The *normalization transformation* is a means of relating the different coordinate systems by scaling and positioning the different parts of a picture to form a picture in a single NDC space. As WC systems may have axes with different dimensions, a different scaling may be specified for each axis. The normalization transformation is said to perform non-uniform scaling in such cases. The effect of non-uniform scaling is shown in Figure 5.1. The right-hand picture is obtained by non-uniform scaling of the left-hand picture with the x-axis scaled by 1 and the y-axis scaled by 0.7.

A normalization transformation is defined by two rectangles, a *window* within WC space and a *viewport* within the range [0,1] × [0,1] of NDC space. Window and viewport define a transformation which maps the contents of the window onto the viewport.

The window/viewport values of the normalization transformation are stored in the GKS state list. For high output levels, a minimum of ten normalization transformations may be specified and stored. The different transformations are identified by a normalization transformation number. This is an integer between 0 and n, where n is an implementation-specific number which can be determined from the workstation description table. By default, all normalization transfor-

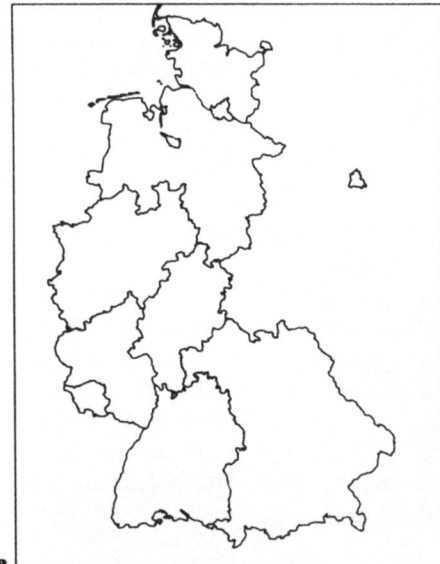

Figure 5.1 Effect of a non-uniform normalization transformation

mations are set to identity, i.e., window and viewport are set equal to the unit square.

Although several normalization transformations can be defined, only one of them can be active for output of primitives at any one time. Initially, normalization transformation 0 is active. Any arbitrary normalization transformation can be activated by SELECT NORMALIZATION TRANSFORMATION. As far as output is concerned, the stored normalization transformations do not provide any additional functionality but merely make it more convenient for an application to switch between a number of fixed transformations. The purpose of this concept is to transform LOCATOR input back into WC. As different normalization transformations are used to generate a picture, it is reasonable to expect LOCATOR in the appropriate WC space. This can be done only if all the transformations used for picture generation are still available. Section 5.5 describes in detail how the transformation which is to be used for coordinate input is selected.

Different normalization transformations can also be obtained by redefining the window and/or viewport of the current normalization transformation. All normalization transformations (except transformation 0) may be redefined at any time, thus enabling the definition of an unlimited number of transformations. This facility will be adequate for many applications and, in output level 0, is the only way of defining different normalization transformations.

SET WINDOW   GKOP, WSOP, WSAC, SGOP   L0a

Parameters:

Input	transformation number	(1..n)	I
Input	window limits XMIN < XMAX, YMIN < YMAX WC		4 × R

Effect:

The window limits entry of the specified normalization transformation in the GKS state list is set equal to the value specified by the parameter.

Errors:

8	GKS not in proper state: GKS should be in one of the states GKOP, WSOP, WSAC or SGOP
50	Transformation number is invalid
51	Rectangle definition is invalid

———————————————— *FORTRAN Interface* ————————————————

CALL GSWN (TNR, XMIN, XMAX, YMIN, YMAX)

Parameters:

Input	TNR	transformation number	(1..n)	INTEGER
Input	XMIN, XMAX, YMIN, YMAX window limits			
	XMIN < XMAX, YMIN < YMAX		WC	4 × REAL

SET VIEWPORT   GKOP, WSOP, WSAC, SGOP   L0a

Parameters:

Input	transformation number	(1..n)	I
Input	viewport limits XMIN < XMAX, YMIN < YMAX NDC		4 × R

Effect:

The viewport limits entry of the specified normalization transformation in the GKS state list is set equal to the value specified by the parameter.

Errors:

8	GKS not in proper state: GKS should be in one of the states GKOP, WSOP, WSAC or SGOP
50	Transformation number is invalid
51	Rectangle definition is invalid
52	Viewport is not within the Normalized Device Coordinate unit square

———————————————— *FORTRAN Interface* ————————————————

CALL GSVP (TNR, XMIN, XMAX, YMIN, YMAX)
Parameters:
Input   TNR   transformation number   (1..n) INTEGER
Input   XMIN, XMAX, YMIN, YMAX viewport limits
           XMIN < XMAX, YMIN < YMAX   NDC   4 × REAL

SELECT NORMALIZATION TRANSFORMATION
                                        GKOP, WSOP, WSAC, SGOP   L0a
Parameters:
Input   tranformation number   (0..n)   I
Effect:
The 'current normalization transformation number' entry in the GKS state list is set equal to the value specified by the parameter. The 'clipping rectangle' entry in the GKS state list is set to the viewport limits of the specified transformation number.
Errors:

8	GKS not in proper state: GKS should be in one of the states GKOP, WSOP, WSAC or SGOP
50	Transformation number is invalid

———————————————— *FORTRAN Interface* ————————————————

CALL GSELNT (TNR)
Parameters:
Input   TNR   transformation number   (0..n) INTEGER

5.3   Workstation Transformation

The NDC space can be regarded as a workstation-independent abstract display surface. For display on a real workstation, the NDC must be mapped onto the coordinate space of the specific workstation. This transformation is called *workstation transformation.*

As different workstations may have different coordinate systems, the workstation transformation may be different for each workstation. The default setting of this transformation ensures that the range $[0,1] \times [0,1]$ in NDC is mapped onto the largest square which fits onto the workstation's display surface. The application program can dynamically reset any workstation transformation. The resetting of the workstation transformation requires a new frame action at the respective workstation. Therefore, in contrast to the normalization transformation, the workstation transformation cannot be used to compose pictures with different workstation transformations on the same display surface. Furthermore, a new frame action deletes all primitives outside segments. For applications not using the segment storage facility, it is only advisable to reset the

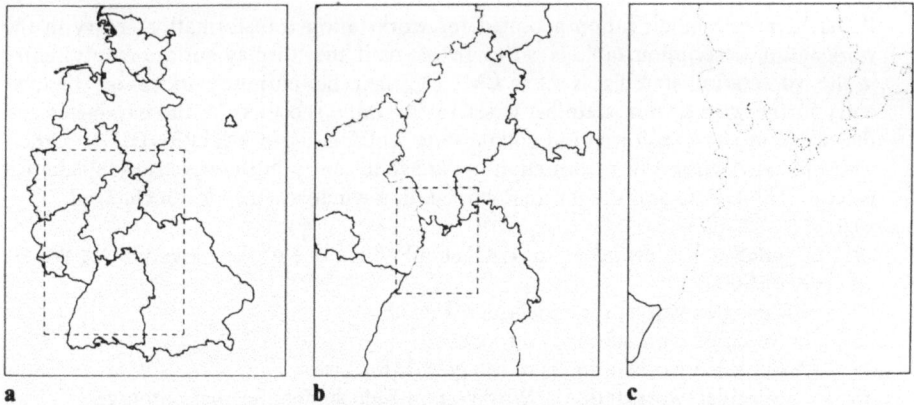

a   b   c

Figure 5.2 Zooming in by resetting the workstation window

workstation transformation as long as no primitives are being displayed, i.e., immediately after CLEAR WORKSTATION.

The workstation transformation is specified in a similar manner as the normalization transformation, i.e., by a window within the range $[0,1] \times [0,1]$ in NDC, the *workstation window*, and by a viewport within the display surface, the *workstation viewport*. The workstation viewport is specified in DC, i.e., the extent is measured in metres (at least in those cases where a display surface has a fixed size and scale). This allows a proper definition of the size and aspect ratio of the resulting picture. Workstation window and workstation viewport are both rectangles which can be set independently. Hence, both rectangles can have different aspect ratios. However, the workstation transformation allows only uniform scaling. Therefore, GKS automatically will reduce the workstation viewport to a rectangle with the same aspect ratio as the workstation window. This rectangle is then positioned in the lower left-hand corner of the workstation viewport leaving any unused space either at the top or right-hand side of the workstation viewport.

The major aims of setting the workstation transformation are:

— to use non-square display surfaces completely by selecting a workstation window in NDC with the same aspect ratio as the display surface;
— to zoom in on part of the picture by selecting a smaller workstation window in NDC for display;
— to draw a picture to the proper scale by setting the appropriate size of the workstation viewport in DC.

SET WORKSTATION WINDOW   WSOP, WSAC, SGOP   L0a
Parameters:

Input	workstation identifier		N
Input	workstation window limits		
	XMIN < XMAX, YMIN < YMAX	NDC	$4 \times R$

Effect:
The 'requested workstation window' entry in the workstation state list of the specified workstation is set equal to the value specified by the parameter.

If the 'dynamic modification accepted for workstation transformation' entry in the workstation description table is set to IMM, or if the 'display surface empty' entry in the workstation state list is set to EMPTY, then the 'current workstation window' entry in the workstation state list is set to the value specified by the parameter and the 'workstation transformation update state' entry is set to NOTPENDING. Otherwise the 'workstation transformation update state' entry in the workstation state list is set to PENDING and the 'current workstation window' entry is not changed.

Errors:

7	GKS not in proper state: GKS should be in one of the states WSOP, WSAC or SGOP
20	Specified workstation identifier is invalid
25	Specified workstation is not open
33	Specified workstation is of category MI
36	Specified workstation is Workstation-Independent Segment Storage
51	Rectangle definition is invalid
53	Workstation window is not within the Normalized Device Coordinate unit square

———————————— *FORTRAN Interface* ————————————

CALL GSWKWN (WKID, XMIN, XMAX, YMIN, YMAX)

Parameters:

Input	WKID workstation identifier		INTEGER
Input	XMIN, XMAX, YMIN, YMAX workstation window		
	limits XMIN < XMAX, YMIN < YMAX	NDC	4 × REAL

SET WORKSTATION VIEWPORT   WSOP, WSAC, SGOP   L0a

Parameters:

Input	workstation identifier		N
Input	workstation viewport limits		
	XMIN < XMAX, YMIN < YMAX	DC	4 × R

Effect:

The 'requested workstation viewport' entry in the workstation state list of the specified workstation is set equal to the value specified by the parameter.

If the 'dynamic modification accepted for workstation transformation' entry in the workstation description table is set to IMM, or if the 'display surface empty' entry in the workstation state list is set to EMPTY, then the 'current workstation viewport' entry in the workstation state list is set to the value specified by the parameter and the 'workstation transformation update state' entry is set to NOTPENDING. Otherwise the 'workstation transformation update state' entry in the workstation state list is set to PENDING and the 'current workstation viewport' entry is not changed.

Errors:

7	GKS not in proper state: GKS should be in one of the states WSOP, WSAC or SGOP
20	Specified workstation identifier is invalid
25	Specified workstation is not open
33	Specified workstation is of category MI
36	Specified workstation is Workstation-Independent Segment Storage
51	Rectangle definition is invalid
54	Workstation viewport is not within the display space

———————————— FORTRAN Interface ————————————

CALL GSWKVP (WKID,XMIN,XMAX,YMIN,YMAX)
Parameters:
  Input   WKID   workstation identifier   INTEGER
  Input   XMIN,XMAX,YMIN,YMAX workstation viewport
                  limits XMIN<XMAX,YMIN<YMAX   DC   4×REAL

5.4 Clipping

GKS provides a mechanism to clip graphical output around a clipping rectangle.
All parts of the primitives within or on the boundary of the clipping rectangle
will be displayed, while everything else will be discarded (cf. Figure 5.3). This
applies to all output primitives.

In the case of the POLYMARKER and the TEXT primitive, GKS relaxes
the requirement for exact clipping as hardware facilities may be involved which
cannot clip parts of a marker or a character. In the case of POLYMARKER,
the marker is visible if, and only if, the marker position is within the clipping
rectangle. The clipping of partially visible markers can be done in a workstation-
dependent way. In the case of TEXT there is a text precision attribute which
specifies whether:
— clipping is done exactly (precision STROKE);
— clipping is done on a character body basis (precision CHAR);

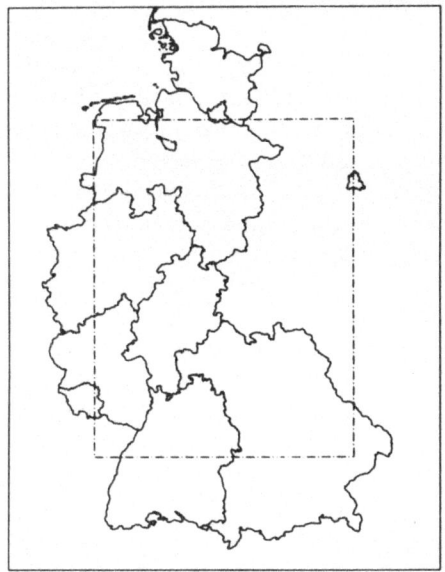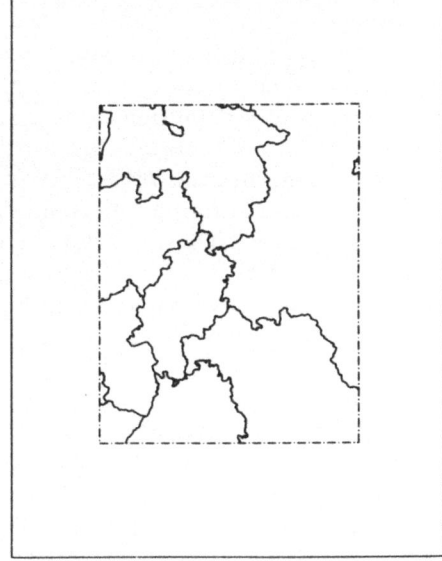

Figure 5.3 Effect of clipping within a clipping rectangle

— clipping is done in an implementation- and workstation-dependent way (precision STRING).

GKS allows both the normalization transformation and the workstation transformation to be associated with clipping. The respective clipping rectangles are the viewport and the workstation window. However, this does not imply that the clipping procedure has to be performed twice, because any clipping associated with the normalization transformation is postponed. The clipping rectangle is sent like an attribute with the output primitives down the transformation pipeline and, if required, into the segment storage as well. Clipping is performed when output is displayed at a workstation. Thus, the clipping processes can be combined by clipping around the intersection of the viewport and workstation windows.

The normalization transformation clipping is done around a 'clipping rectangle' stored in the GKS state list. Usually, this 'clipping rectangle' coincides with the value of the viewport of the current normalization transformation. When the normalization transformation is changed by selecting another transformation number or by resetting the viewport of the current transformation, the 'clipping rectangle' entry changes accordingly. The current value at the time of primitive generation will be applied to the primitive. This allows the clipping of individual primitives around different clipping rectangles and a building up of complex pictures from clipped subpictures. When input is read from a metafile (cf. Section 11.4), it is possible to set the 'clipping rectangle' entry in a different way. By interpreting an item 'clipping rectangle' with the GKS function INTERPRET ITEM, the current 'clipping rectangle' is reset without affecting the viewport of the current normalization transformation. There is a global switch, called a 'clipping indicator', which enables and disables normalization transformation clipping for primitives subsequently generated.

The clipping associated with the workstation transformation clips around the workstation window. It cannot be switched off and, thus, ensures that no output is displayed outside the workstation window and that no more space on the display surface is used than has been asked for.

When segment transformations are applied, they affect the coordinate data and geometrical attributes of output primitives but have no effect on the stored clipping rectangle. Thus, the clipping rectangle appears invariantly at the position it had when primitives were generated. This means that a segment can be zoomed in on within a given clipping rectangle without interfering with the rest of the picture. There is one segment function which does affect the stored clipping rectangles: INSERT SEGMENT. When this function is being performed, all stored clipping rectangles in the respective segment are replaced by the current clipping rectangle.

Some applications, such as cartography, require more complicated clipping facilities, for example, clipping to an arbitrary polygon or shielding. Shielding is the inverse of clipping, ensuring that there is no drawing inside a given rectangle. This is useful when creating readable legends on maps. Such facilities, if necessary, must be provided on top of GKS.

SET CLIPPING INDICATOR	GKOP, WSOP, WSAC, SGOP L0a

Parameters:

Input   clipping indicator   (CLIP, NOCLIP)   E

Effect:

The 'clipping indicator' entry in the GKS state list is set equal to the value specified by the parameter.

Errors:

8   GKS not in proper state: GKS should be in one of the states GKOP, WSOP, WSAC or SGOP

———————————————— *FORTRAN Interface* ————————————————

CALL GSCLIP (CLSW)

Parameters:

Input   CLSW   clipping indicator   (0=noclip, 1=clip)   INTEGER

5.5   Transformation of LOCATOR and STROKE Input

When generating graphical output, GKS accepts coordinate data in several WC systems, and transforms it via NDC onto the display space of a workstation. When defining positions for the LOCATOR or STROKE input device, the operator points to a position within the display space or tablet area. For reasons of symmetry, these DC positions are transformed back via NDC to WC before handing them over to the application program. This scheme enables the immediate use of LOCATOR or STROKE input for output primitive generation at the same position the operator has pointed to. Furthermore, this transformation to WC conforms to the GKS design principle that all coordinate data, as far as is possible and reasonable, is specified in WC at the application program interface.

At any one time, precisely one workstation transformation is in effect for all primitives visible at a specific workstation. Therefore, the transformation between NDC and DC is always well defined and permits transformation of positions in DC back to positions in NDC. To ensure that positions do not leave the range $[0,1] \times [0,1]$ in NDC, input is restricted to the image of the workstation window which is equal to or smaller than the workstation viewport.

The mapping between WC and NDC cannot be done in such a similar trivial way as, generally, several normalization transformations have been used to generate a picture. GKS arbitrates between concurring normalization transformations by comparing their viewports with the input positions. A normalization transformation will be chosen whose viewport contains the NDC value of the LOCATOR position or the NDC values of all the STROKE positions (cf. Figure 8.1, page 280).

However, this test is not sufficient to find one normalization transformation exactly as the viewports of different normalization transformations may overlap. For this reason, GKS has introduced the *viewport input priority* attribute which lays down a strict hierarchy among viewports. The priority of a normalization transformation is specified relative to another so-called reference normalization transformation, so that it is in series immediately below or above this transformation in the priority scale. By default, all normalization transformations are given viewport input priorities according to their transformation number in decreasing order, giving the highest priority to the normalization transformation 0. If an input position is to be mapped by a different normalization transformation, the priority of such a normalization transformation must be set explicitly.

Thus, by testing all viewports in order of decreasing priority, a viewport containing all input positions can be uniquely determined. It is obvious that only stored transformations can participate in this test. If a transformation has been redefined, the previous setting is lost and cannot be considered for input transformation.

As long as input is generated synchronously (REQUEST or SAMPLE mode; cf. Section 8.1.3), there can be no doubt as to what the last setting of transformations is. If, however, input is generated in EVENT mode (cf. Section 8.1.3), positions are generated, transformed, and stored in an input queue asynchronously to the retrieval of the data by the application program. If transformations are reset while a LOCATOR or STROKE device is in EVENT mode, the application program has no control of which data is being transformed according to the old setting and which data is being transformed according to the new. To ensure that the desired WC value is returned to the application program, transformations should not be reset while a LOCATOR or STROKE device is in EVENT mode or while there are entries still in the queue.

Resetting the workstation transformation will cause no problems, as the operator will be aware of any change. Resetting the normalization transformations can be avoided as long as the number of storable transformations is not exceeded. A viewport input priority, however, cannot be used in EVENT mode although it was intended to be a dynamic facility which could give precedence to a transformation of immediate interest in certain situations.

As the selection of a normalization transformation for input transformation depends on positions and priorities, it is not obvious to the application program which transformation has been applied. Therefore, GKS delivers the corresponding transformation number together with the respective WC values to the application program.

To ensure that at least one viewport is always available for LOCATOR and STROKE transformation, there exists a normalization transformation 0 which maps the WC unit square onto the NDC unit square. This viewport contains all the possible NDC values of LOCATOR and STROKE input. The normalization transformation 0 cannot be reset; however, it may be selected and its viewport input priority may be changed.

Output primitives in segments may be subject to segment transformations before being displayed. These transformations are not considered for input transformation.

SET VIEWPORT INPUT PRIORITY	GKOP,WSOP,WSAC,SGOP	L0b

Parameters:

Input	transformation number	(0..n)	I
Input	reference transformation number	(0..n)	I
Input	relative priority	(HIGHER,LOWER)	E

Effect:
The viewport input priority of the specified normalization transformation in the GKS state list is set to the next higher or next lower priority relative to the reference transformation, according to the specified relative priority.

Errors:

8	GKS not in proper state: GKS should be in one of the states GKOP, WSOP, WSAC or SGOP
50	Transformation number is invalid

───────────────────── *FORTRAN Interface* ─────────────────────

CALL GSVPIP (TNR,RTNR,RELPRI)

Parameters:

Input	TNR	transformation number	(0..n)	INTEGER
Input	RTNR	reference transformation number	(0..n)	INTEGER
Input	RELPRI	relative priority	(0=higher, 1=lower)	INTEGER

5.6   Examples

Example 5.1   Composition of a picture using one normalization transformation number

In this example, only normalization transformation 1 is used. Firstly, transformation 1 is set and used to transform OUTLINE properly; then transformation 1 is reset and used to transform PIE.

───────────────────────── *Pascal* ─────────────────────────

```
L10   SELECT_NORMALIZATION_TRANSFORMATION (1);

L20   SET_WINDOW (1, 0.0, 5000.0, 0.0, 5000.0);
      {SET_VIEWPORT (1, 0.0, 1.0, 0.0, 1.0)                    set by default}
L30   OUTLINE;                                      {Procedure draws outline}

L40   SET_WINDOW (1, 0.0, 1.0, 0.0, 1.0);
L50   SET_VIEWPORT (1, 0.2, 0.3, 0.7, 0.8);
L60   PIE;                 {Procedure draws pie showing some statistical numbers}
```

───────────────────────── *Fortran* ─────────────────────────

```
L10        CALL GSELNT (1)

L20        CALL GSWN (1, 0.0, 5000.0, 0.0, 5000.0)
      C    CALL GSVP (1, 0.0, 1.0, 0.0, 1.0)                    set by default
L30        CALL OUTLIN
      C    *** Procedure draws outline

L40        CALL GSWN (1, 0.0, 1.0, 0.0, 1.0)
L50        CALL GSVP (1, 0.2, 0.3, 0.7, 0.8)
L60        CALL PIE
      C    *** Procedure draws pie showing some statistical numbers
```

Example 5.2   Composition of a picture using different normalization transformation numbers

In this example, normalization transformation 1 is solely used for OUTLINE and transformation 2 for PIE. Therefore, both transformations are available for coordinate input.

——————————————————— *Pascal* ———————————————————

```
L10   SET_WINDOW (1, 0.0, 5000.0, 0.0, 5000.0);
      {SET_VIEWPORT (1, 0.0, 1.0, 0.0, 1.0)                           set by default}

L20   SET_WINDOW (2, 0.0, 1.0, 0.0, 1.0);
L30   SET_VIEWPORT (2, 0.2, 0.3, 0.7, 0.8);

L40   SELECT_NORMALIZATION_TRANSFORMATION(1);
L50   OUTLINE;                                          {Procedure draws outline}

L60   SELECT_NORMALIZATION_TRANSFORMATION (2);
L70   PIE;                    {Procedure draws pie showing some statistical numbers}
```

——————————————————— *Fortran* ———————————————————

```
L10        CALL GSWN (1, 0.0, 5000.0, 0.0, 5000.0)
      C    CALL GSVP (1, 0.0, 1.0, 0.0, 1.0)                         set by default
L20        CALL GSWN (2, 0.0, 1.0, 0.0, 1.0)
L30        CALL GSVP (2, 0.2, 0.3, 0.7, 0.8)

L40        CALL GSELNT(1)
L50        CALL OUTLIN
      C    *** Procedure draws outline

L60        CALL GSELNT (2)
L70        CALL PIE
      C    *** Procedure draws pie showing some statistical numbers
```

Example 5.3   Layer which only allows uniform normalization transformations

For many applications, e.g., applications with metric user coordinates, only mappings with uniform scaling are meaningful. In this example, two functions
— SET_WINDOW_WITH_UNIFORM_SCALING
— SET_VIEWPORT_WITH_UNIFORM_SCALING
are defined which ensure that the viewport always has the same aspect ratio as the window. This is done by reducing the viewport, if necessary. The GKS function INQUIRE_NORMALIZATION_TRANSFORMATION is used to obtain the current values of windows. More details about this inquiry function can be found in Chapter 10.

——————————————————— *Pascal* ———————————————————

```
L10   var listvw: array [1..4,1..20] of real;      {listvw stores the requested viewports}

L20   procedure ADAPT_VIEWPORT (trnum: integer;
          wxmin, wxmax, wymin, wymax, rxmin, rxmax, rymin, rymax: real);
```

{ADAPT_VIEWPORT calculates a new viewport from the requested viewport
and the window given in the parameter list}

```
L30    var nxmin,nxmax,nymin,nymax,ratiow,ratiov,factor: real;
L40    begin                          {Assume that the x-extent has to be adapted}
L50      dx:=(wxmax−wxmin) * (rymax−rymin)/(wymax−wymin);
                {The adapted viewport will be centred within the requested viewport}
L60      nxmin:=(rxmin+rxmax−dx)/2.0;

L70      if nxmin > rxmin then begin
L80        nxmax:=nxmin+dx;
L90        nymin:=rymin;
L100       nymax:=rymax;
L110     end

L120     else begin                        {The y-extent has to be adapted}
L130       dy:=(wymax−wymin) * (rxmax−rxmin)/(wxmax−wxmin);
L140       nymin:=(rymin+rymax−dy)/2.0;
L150       nymax:=nymin+dy;
L160       nxmin:=rxmin;
L170       nxmax:=rxmax;
L180     end;

L190     SET_VIEWPORT (trnum,nxmin,nxmax,nymin,nymax);
L200   end {ADAPT_VIEWPORT}

L210   procedure SET_WINDOW_WITH_UNIFORM_SCALING
              (trnum: integer; wxmin,wxmax,wymin,wymax: real)
L220   var rxmin,rxmax,rymin,rymax: real;
L230   begin
L240     SET_WINDOW (trnum, wxmin,wxmax,wymin,wymax);
L250     rxmin:=listvw[1,trnum];           {get requested viewport rxmin,... from listvw}
L260     rxmax:=listvw[2,trnum];
L270     rymin:=listvw[3,trnum];
L280     rymax:=listvw[4,trnum];

L290     ADAPT_VIEWPORT
              (trnum,wxmin,wxmax,wymin,wymax,rxmin,rxmax,rymin,rymax);
L300   end {SET_WINDOW_WITH_UNIFORM_SCALING};

L310   procedure SET_VIEWPORT_WITH_UNIFORM_SCALING
              (trnum: integer; rxmin,rxmax,rymin,rymax: real)
L320   var wxmin,wxmax,wymin,wymax,dummy: real;
L330   begin
L340     listvw[1,trnum]:=rxmin;
L350     listvw[2,trnum]:=rxmax;
L360     listvw[3,trnum]:=rymin;
L370     listvw[4,trnum]:=rymax;
                              {enquire window wxmin,... from GKS state list}
L380     INQUIRE_NORMALIZATION_TRANSFORMATION
              (trnum,error_indicator,
              wxmin,wxmax,wymin,wymax,dummy,dummy,dummy,dummy);
```

L390   ADAPT_VIEWPORT
          (trnum, wxmin, wxmax, wymin, wymax, rxmin, rxmax, rymin, rymax);
L400 end {SET_VIEWPORT_WITH_UNIFORM_SCALING};

──────────────── *Fortran* ────────────────

```
L20              SUBROUTINE ADPTVP (TRNUM,WXMIN,WXMAX,
         +     WYMIN,WYMAX,RXMIN,RXMAX,RYMIN,RYMAX)
      C          *** ADPTVP calculates a new viewport from the requested viewport and
      C          *** the window given in the parameter list.

L30              INTEGER TRNUM
L31              REAL WXMIN,WXMAX,WYMIN,WYMAX,
         +          RXMIN,RXMAX,RYMIN,RYMAX,
         +          NXMIN,NXMAX,NYMIN,NYMAX,DX,DY

      C          *** Assume that the x-extent has to be adapted
L50              DX=
         +     (WXMAX-WXMIN) * (RYMAX-RYMIN)/(WYMAX-WY-
                 MIN)
      C          *** The adapted viewport will be centred within the requested viewport
L60              NXMIN=(RXMIN+RXMAX-DX)/2.0
L70              IF (NXMIN.LT.RXMIN) GOTO 330
L80              NXMAX=NXMIN+DX
L90              NYMIN=RYMIN
L100             NYMAX=RYMAX
L110             GOTO 390
      C          *** The y-extent has to be adapted
L130     330     DY=
         +     (WYMAX-WYMIN) * (RXMAX-RXMIN)/(WXMAX-
                 WXMIN)
L140             NYMIN=(RYMIN+RYMAX-DY)/2.0
L150             NYMAX=NYMIN+DY
L160             NXMIN=RXMIN
L170             NXMAX=RXMAX
      C          *** Set adapted viewport for normalization transformation TRNUM
L190     390     CALL GSVP (TRNUM,NXMIN,NXMAX,NYMIN,NYMAX)
L200             RETURN
L201             END

L210             SUBROUTINE SWNUS
         +     (TRNUM,WXMIN,WXMAX,WYXMIN,WYMAX)
      C          *** Set window WXMIN,... and adapt viewport of normalization trans-
      C          *** formation TRNUM to the window's aspect ratio.

L220             INTEGER TRNUM
L221             REAL WXMIN,WXMAX,WYMIN,WYMAX,RXMIN,RXMAX,
         +          RYMIN,RYMAX,LISTVW(4,20)
L222             COMMON LISTVW

L240             CALL GSWN (TRNUM,WXMIN,WXMAX,WYMIN,WYMAX)
      C          *** Get requested viewport RXMIN,... from LISTVW
L250             RXMIN=LISTVW(1,TRNUM)
L260             RXMAX=LISTVW(2,TRNUM)
```

```
L270            RYMIN = LISTVW (3, TRNUM)
L280            RYMAX = LISTVW (4, TRNUM)
L290            CALL ADPTVP (TRNUM, WXMIN, WXMAX, WYMIN, WYMAX,
           +    RXMIN, RXMAX, RYMIN, RYMAX)
L300            RETURN
L301            END
L310            SUBROUTINE SVPUS
           +    (TRNUM, RXMIN, RXMAX, RYMIN, RYMAX)
       C        *** Store requested viewport RXMIN, ... and adapt this viewport to the
       C        *** aspect ratio of the window of normalization transformation
       C        *** TRNUM.

L320            INTEGER TRNUM
L321            REAL W (4), RXMIN, RXMAX, RYMIN, RYMAX
L322            REAL DUMMY (4), LISTVW (4, 20)
L323            COMMON LISTVW

       C        *** Store the required viewport
L340            LISTVW (1, TRNUM) = RXMIN
L350            LISTVW (2, TRNUM) = RXMAX
L360            LISTVW (3, TRNUM) = RYMIN
L370            LISTVW (4, TRNUM) = RYMAX
       C        *** Inquire window WXMIN, ... from GKS state list
L380            CALL GQNT (ERRIND, TRNUM, W, DUMMY)
L390            CALL ADPTVP (TRNUM, W (1), W (2), W (3), W (4),
           +    RXMIN, RXMAX, RYMIN, RYMAX)
L400            RETURN
L401            END
```

Example 5.4   Drawing to a given scale

A map of size 0.7 m × 0.9 m has been digitized. The digitizer delivers the data according to its resolution in units of 1/10 mm, i.e., data is in the space 7000 × 9000. This data is to be mapped onto the display surface of an interactive workstation, by using as much as possible of the available display space while preserving the aspect ratio. The same data is to be drawn on a plotter to the same scale as the source map. The statements below show the required setting of transformations. Window describes the space 7000 × 9000 of the digitized data. Viewport and workstation window are set to a rectangle within [0,1] having same aspect ratio as the window in order to preserve aspect ratio and to select the full map for display. The workstation viewport is left undefined for workstation display to allow automatic adaptation to the available display surface; for a workstation plotter, it gives the size of the plot in metres. Procedure DRAW_FILE is described in Example 6.1.

──────────────── *Pascal* ────────────────

```
                {Set normalization transformation such that aspect ratio is preserved}
L10   SELECT_NORMALIZATION_TRANSFORMATION (1);
L20   SET_WINDOW (1, 0.0, 7000.0, 0.0, 9000.0);
```

L30   SET_VIEWPORT (1, 0.0, 7.0/9.0, 0.0, 1.0);

{Generate picture on display}
L40   ACTIVATE_WORKSTATION (display);
{The setting workstation_window = viewport ensures that the whole map is mapped onto the display; by not setting the workstation viewport, GKS is enabled to use as much as possible of the display space.}
L50   SET_WORKSTATION_WINDOW (display, 0.0, 7.0/9.0, 0.0, 1.0);
L70   DRAW_FILE(FRG);   {cf. Example 6.1}
L120 DEACTIVATE_WORKSTATION (display);

{Generate picture on plotter with precise scaling and using different colours}
L130 ACTIVATE_WORKSTATION (plotter);
{Workstation_window is set as above; workstation_viewport is set to the desired size of the map measured in metres}
L140 SET_WORKSTATION_WINDOW (plotter, 0.0, 7.0/9.0, 0.0, 1.0);
L150 SET_WORKSTATION_VIEWPORT (plotter, 0.0, 0.7, 0.0, 0.9);
L170 DRAW_FILE(FRG);   {cf. Example 6.1}
L220 DEACTIVATE_WORKSTATION (plotter);

─────────────────────────────── *Fortran* ───────────────────────────────

```
        C    Set normalization transformation such that aspect ratio is preserved
L10          CALL GSELNT(1)
L20          CALL GSWN(1, 0.0, 7000.0, 0.0, 9000.0)
L30          CALL GSVP(1, 0.0, 7.0/9.0, 0.0, 1.0)

        C    *** Generate picture on display using different linetypes
L40          CALL GACWK (DISPL)
        C    The setting workstation_window = viewport secures that the whole map is
        C    mapped onto the display; by not setting the workstation viewport, GKS
        C    is enabled to use as much as possible of the display space.
L50          CALL GSWKWN (DISPL, 0.0, 7.0/9.0, 0.0, 1.0)
L70          CALL DRFILE(FRG)
L120         CALL GDAWK (DISPL)

        C    Generate picture on plotter with precise scaling and using different colours
L130         CALL GACWK (PLOTTR)
        C    Workstation_window is set as above; workstation_viewport is set to
        C    the desired size of the map measured in metres
L140         CALL GSWKWN (PLOTTR, 0.0, 7.0/9.0, 0.0, 1.0)
L150         CALL GSWKVP (PLOTTR, 0.0, 0.7, 0.0, 0.9)
L170         CALL DRFILE(FRG)
L220         CALL GDAWK (PLOTTR)
```

───

See Figure 5.1 a for a sample of output.

Example 5.5   Clipping mechanism

The normalization transformation seen in Example 5.4 is now defined by a smaller window and viewport which, nevertheless, define the same transformation. If the clipping indicator is NOCLIP, the same picture is generated; if the clipping indicator is CLIP, however, the results differ as the window of the normalization transformation is used as a clipping rectangle.

──────────────────────────── *Pascal* ────────────────────────────

L90   SELECT_NORMALIZATION_TRANSFORMATION(1);
L100 SET_WINDOW (1, 1400.0, 5600.0, 1800.0, 7200.0);
L110 SET_VIEWPORT (1, 0.155, 0.622, 0.2, 0.8);   {viewport:=window limits/9000}

L120 SET_CLIPPING_INDICATOR (NOCLIP);
L130 DRAW_FILE (FRG);   {See Figure 5.3a}

L140 SET_CLIPPING_INDICATOR (CLIP);
L150 DRAW_FILE (FRG);   {See Figure 5.3b}

──────────────────────────── *Fortran* ────────────────────────────

L90   CALL GSELNT(1)
L100   CALL GSWN (1, 1400.0, 5600.0, 1800.0, 7200.0)
L110   CALL GSVP (1, 0.155, 0.622, 0.2, 0.8)
         C   *** Viewport=window limits / 9000

L120   CALL GSCLIP (NOCLIP)
L130   CALL DRFILE (FRG)
         C   *** See Figure 5.3a
L140   CALL GSCLIP (CLIP)
L150   CALL DRFILE (FRG)
         C   *** See Figure 5.3b

──

Example 5.6   Setting of viewport input priority

Part of a map is zoomed onto a display surface of an interactive workstation. In addition, in the upper right-hand corner of the display surface, a global view of this map is drawn. Regardless of whether the operator points to the zoomed part of the map or to the global view, the correct user coordinates will be returned (cf. also Exercise 5.5).

User data is the same as in the above examples.

──────────────────────────── *Pascal* ────────────────────────────

                        {This transformation zooms part of map onto full display}
L20   SET_WINDOW (1, 300.0, 6300.0, 300.0, 6300.0);
L30   SET_VIEWPORT (1, 0.0, 1.0, 0.0, 1.0);
L40   SELECT_NORMALIZATION_TRANFORMATION (1);
L50   DRAW_FILE (FRG);   {see Example 6.1}

                        {This transformation maps whole map onto a small viewport}
L60   SET_WINDOW (2, 0.0, 7000.0, 0.0, 9000.0);
L70   SET_VIEWPORT (2, 0.72, 1.0, 0.64, 1.0);
L80   SELECT_NORMALIZATION_TRANSFORMATION (2);
L90   DRAW_FILE (FRG);   {see Example 6.1}

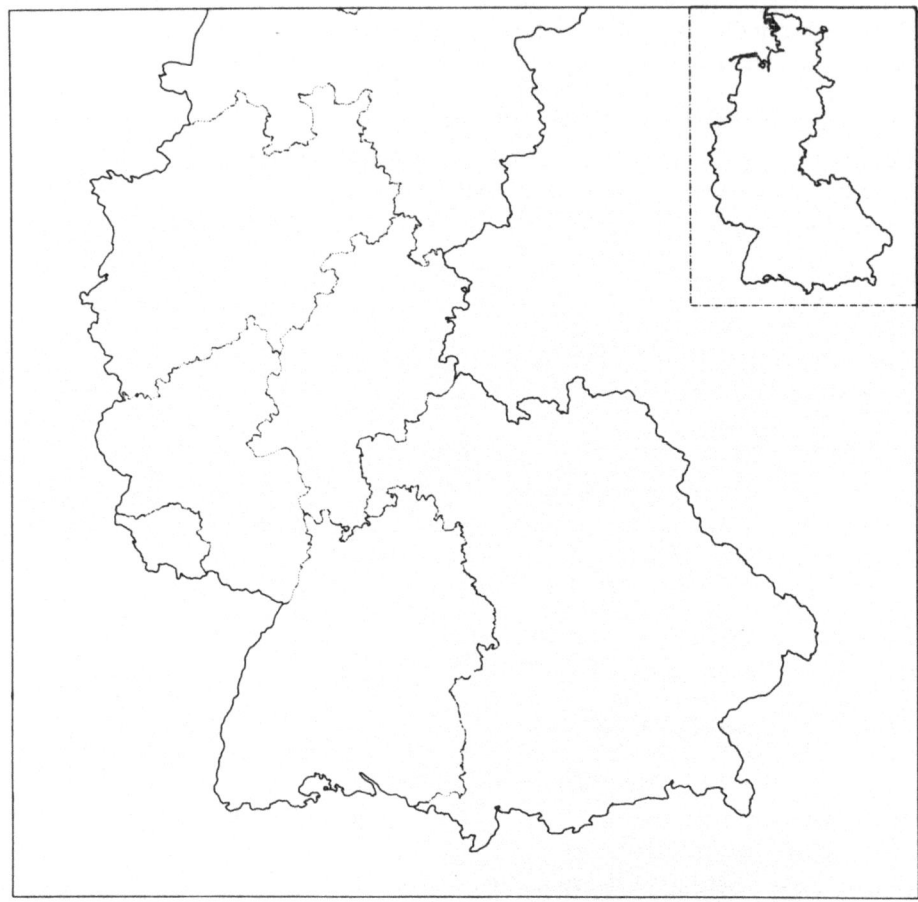

Figure 5.4 Global and zoomed view within one display space

{Set viewport input priority as vip0 < vip1 < vip2}

L100 SET_VIEWPORT_INPUT_PRIORITY (0, 1, LOWER);
L110 SET_VIEWPORT_INPUT_PRIORITY (1, 2, LOWER);

—————————————————————— *Fortran* ——————————————————————

```
    C    *** Draw zoomed part of map onto full display
L20         CALL GSWN (1, 300.0, 6300.0, 300.0, 6300.0)
L30         CALL GSVP (1, 0.0, 1.0, 0.0, 1.0)
L40         CALL GSELNT (1)
L50         CALL DRFILE (FRG)
    C    *** see Example 6.1

    C    *** Draw global view of map onto small viewport
L60         CALL GSWN (2, 0.0, 7000.0, 0.0, 9000.0)
L70         CALL GSVP (2, 0.72, 1.0, 0.64, 1.0)
```

L80   CALL GSELN (2)
L90   CALL DRFILE (FRG)
     C   *** see Example 6.1

     C   *** Set viewport input priority as vip0 < vip1 < vip2
L100   CALL GSVPIP (0, 1, LOWER)
L110   CALL GSVPIP (1, 2, LOWER)

5.7   Exercises

Exercise 5.1   Setting of transformations

Assume WC coordinates in the range $0 < x < 7$, $0 < y < 11$ and a display surface
of size $0.21\,\text{m} \times 0.296\,\text{m}$. Solve the following problems:

1. Ensure that all data are displayed on the display surface.
2. Ensure that the display surface is used optimally.

What is the minimum set of transformation setting functions needed in both
cases? What are the effective values of normalization transformation and workstation transformation which will be applied to the coordinate data?

Exercise 5.2   Uniform scaling

Solve Exercise 5.1 with the restriction that only transformations with equal
scaling in x and y are allowed.

Exercise 5.3   Prescribed scaling

Assume that the WC data in Exercise 5.1 are measured in inches. Generate
a drawing in true scale.

Exercise 5.4   Clipping

Example 5.5 shows clipping in conjunction with the normalization transformation. The same effect can be achieved with the workstation transformation.
Rewrite Example 5.5 so that lines L90-120 remain unchanged and the two
pictures in Figure 5.3 are generated by two different workstation transformations.

Exercise 5.5   Shielding

If arbitrary transformations are applied to the zoomed part in Figure 5.4, Example 5.6, the zoomed drawing may penetrate into the small rectangle containing
the global view. Although both normalization transformations defined in Example 5.6 may generate output within the small rectangle, the setting of the viewport input priority decides that in any case normalization transformation 2

will be used for LOCATOR input within the small rectangle. This may be confusing for casual users. It would be more convenient to suppress any output from normalization transformation 1 which would appear within the viewport of normalization transformation 2.

The blanking out of a drawing within a given rectangle ("shielding") is not supported as a standard GKS facility. However, by use of three normalization transformations, it can be achieved that the global view and the zoomed view in Figure 5.4 do not interfere with each other. Write a program.

6   OUTPUT PRIMITIVES

6.1   Introduction

The graphical output which is generated by GKS consists of two groups of basic elements:
— output primitives;
— output primitive attributes.

The *output primitives* are abstractions of the basic actions that a graphical device can perform. GKS provides the following six output primitives:

POLYLINE: GKS generates a set of connected lines defined by a point sequence.

POLYMARKER: GKS generates symbols of one type centred at given positions.

TEXT: GKS generates a character string at a given position.

FILL AREA: GKS generates a polygon which may be hollow or filled with a uniform colour, a pattern, or a hatch style.

CELL ARRAY: GKS generates an array of pixels with individual colours.

GENERALIZED DRAWING PRIMITIVE (GDP): GKS addresses the special geometrical output capabilities of a workstation, such as the drawing of spline curves, circular arcs, and elliptic arcs. The objects are characterized by an identifier, a set of points and additional data. GKS applies all transformations to these points but leaves the interpretation to the workstation.

The definition of the primitives contains information about their geometrical shape. More geometrical details and information about the appearance of the primitives can be added to the primitives' definition through using *output primitive attributes*. In GKS, attributes can be defined and bound to the primitives in different ways. For a better understanding, these different schemes are explained in this section. The meaning of attributes is explained in the context of the respective primitive in the subsequent sections.

Table 6.1 Geometric attributes in GKS

TEXT:	CHARACTER HEIGHT
	CHARACTER UP VECTOR
	TEXT PATH
	TEXT ALIGNMENT
FILL AREA:	PATTERN SIZE
	PATTERN REFERENCE POINT

GKS distinguishes geometric from non-geometric attributes. *Geometric attributes* affect the shape and size of a primitive. They are treated in the same way as the coordinates in the parameter list of a primitive. They are defined in world coordinates (e.g., CHARACTER HEIGHT gives the height of characters within the WC system) or are applied to the primitive in WC (e.g., TEXT PATH 'left' gives the writing direction in WC which is not necessarily the same on the display surface). They are subject to all transformations. Therefore, when transformations are set differently this will yield different results. For example, if a segment is dynamically scaled by setting the segment transformation, this will affect the geometric attributes and, for example, scale the character height. The default character height 0.01 is 1/100 of the default window (unit square) and, if used with the default transformations, will generate characters with the size of 1/100 of the display space. After setting the window to (0.0, 0.0, 100.0, 100.0), illegible characters of 1/10000 of the display space will be generated until the character height is reset accordingly. Table 6.1 lists all geometric attributes in GKS.

Non-geometric attributes control aspects of a primitive which cannot be transformed, like COLOUR, or which should not be transformed, like LINEWIDTH and MARKER SIZE. LINEWIDTH was excluded from the set of geometric attributes because most common devices have no transformable LINEWIDTH and it thus seemed unreasonable to make such a facility a requirement within the standard. MARKER SIZE is not transformable as markers designate points, which have no size. However, independent of transformations, different linewidths and marker sizes, if available, can be selected by using a linewidth and marker size scale factor. CHARACTER SPACING and CHARACTER EXPANSION FACTOR affect the geometry. As they are defined relative to CHARACTER HEIGHT, they change according to CHARACTER HEIGHT without needing a transformation. They can be considered part of the definition of a specific text font rather than being independently transformable geometric attributes.

An attribute may be bound *immediately* (i.e., at the time when primitives are defined) to the primitive, or the binding can be *delayed* until display time. Figure 6.1 shows the different points in the transformation pipeline where attributes are bound. This figure also illustrates the binding of segment attributes. Segment attributes are discussed in detail in Chapter 7.

An attribute can be specified *directly* by giving the attribute value, or *indirectly* or *indexed* by providing an index which points to the respective attribute.

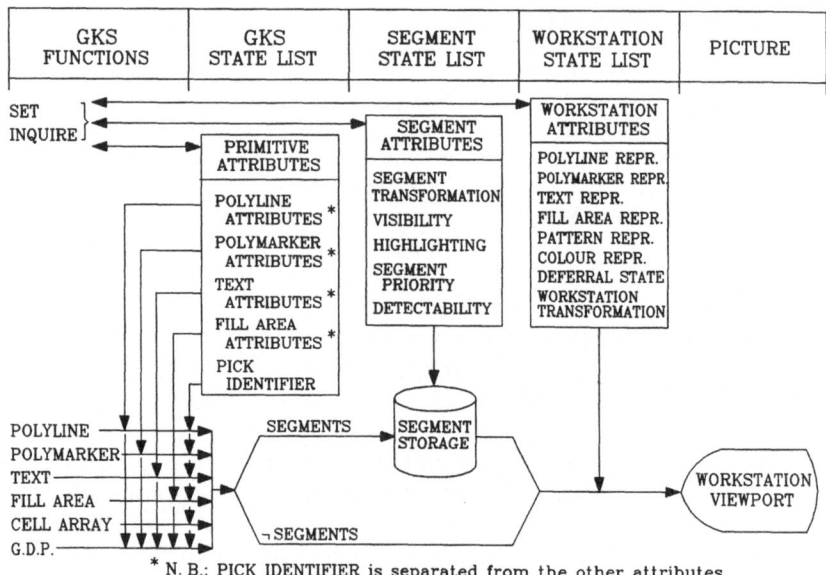

* N. B.: PICK IDENTIFIER is separated from the other attributes
for the same primitive in this figure only.

Figure 6.1 Binding of attributes

In GKS, geometric attributes are always specified directly. On the other hand, colour is an attribute which cannot be specified directly but only by using an index pointing to a colour table. The following sequence is necessary for generating red polylines:

SET_POLYLINE_COLOUR_INDEX (1)
SET_COLOUR_REPRESENTATION (workstation, 1, 1.0, 0.0, 0.0)
POLYLINE (N, POINTS1)

Furthermore, there are attributes which can be used in both fashions, either directly or indirectly (indexed). Table 6.5 contains a list of these attributes.

The indexed attributes can be divided into two sets: those kept in static tables provided by the implementation and those contained in adjustable workstation tables.

Table 6.2 lists all the static tables provided by the implementation. The value ranges are defined by the implementor. He has to provide a minimal set of entries, as specified in the description of the individual attribute functions below. He may provide more entries than are necessary for some workstations. However, if the same entry is present at different workstations, it must refer to the same capability.

Only entries with negative indices can be used freely by an implementor. Entries with positive indices are reserved for standardized values. In addition to the values specified within the standard, new values can be submitted for registration by the International Register of Graphical Items which is maintained by the Registration Authority within the International Organization for

Table 6.2 Indices pointing to the static workstation tables provided by the implementation

LINETYPE	→ linetype table (minimal length 4)
MARKER TYPE	→ marker type table (minimal length 5)
TEXT FONT AND PRECISION	→ text font and precision table (minimal requirement depends on level)
FILL AREA STYLE INDEX	→ hatch table (minimal length 3) (if FILL AREA INTERIOR STYLE = hatch and hatching supported at the workstation)

Standardization (ISO). The register ensures that new line styles, marker symbols, etc. can be introduced and that a unique index is used for this value in all implementations supporting the additional value.

The adjustable workstation tables include the:
— polyline bundle table,
— polymarker bundle table,
— text bundle table,
— fill area bundle table,
— pattern table,
— colour table.

Table 6.3 lists all indices pointing to these tables and all aspects of the indices which can be set in the respective bundle table. Indexing may occur in several stages. For example, the fill area index points to a bundle containing a fill area style index. This index may point to a pattern array. The pattern array contains colour indices pointing to the colour table.

The primary purpose of the workstation tables is to enable the specific capabilities of each workstation type to be used when one picture is being displayed at different workstations. This can be achieved by setting the tables immediately after opening the workstation. In addition, GKS allows the workstation tables to be reset at any time. This adds a powerful dynamic functionality to GKS and means, for example, that the dynamic capabilities of colour tables of raster displays can be addressed via this mechanism.

Attributes may be *static* or *dynamic*. The value of a static attribute is bound to a primitive when the primitives are generated. This specific value cannot be changed during the whole lifetime of the primitive. The attribute itself can be redefined so that primitives subsequently generated are given another value. Character height is a static attribute. Therefore, the sequence

SET_CHARACTER_HEIGHT (1.0)
TEXT (P, 'First text')
SET_CHARACTER_HEIGHT (2.0)
TEXT (Q, 'Second text')

generates two text strings of different size.

Table 6.3 Indices pointing to adjustable workstation tables

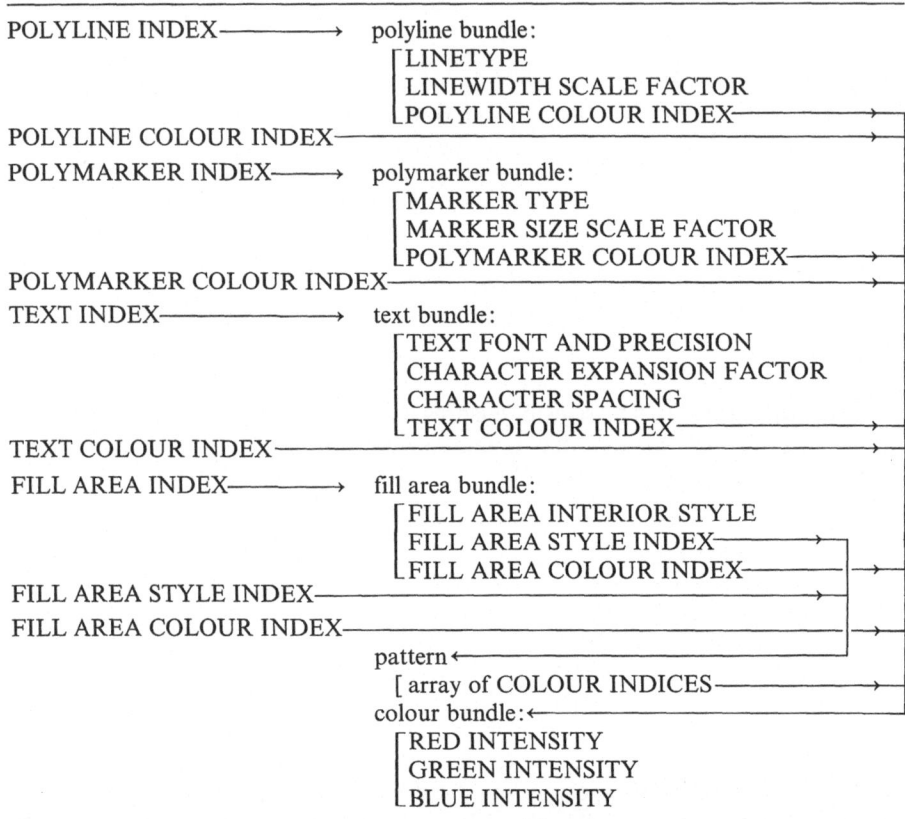

N.B. The FILL AREA STYLE INDEX points to the pattern table only if FILL AREA
   INTERIOR STYLE = pattern.

The value of a dynamic attribute is taken from a workstation table. Each time a primitive is regenerated, the present value is bound to the primitive. All attributes contained in adjustable workstation tables (cf. right-hand column in Table 6.3) are dynamic attributes. If a dynamic attribute is changed, this change affects primitives generated previously and subsequently. As changing the attributes for previously generated primitives requires the storage of graphical information, this effect is only guaranteed for primitives within segments.

The dynamic capabilities of workstation tables apply to any workstation, independent of whether they are well supported or not by that workstation. It is conceivable that some workstation, e.g., plotter workstations, will not behave well dynamically. However, it is not assumed that each workstation will react immediately when an entry in a bundle table is reset. According to its capabilities, the workstation may react immediately (which may also affect primitives outside segments) or it may use the segment storage to regenerate the display in order to achieve the desired effect. The latter case is called 'implicit regeneration' and this may be deferred arbitrarily by setting the deferral state appropriately (cf. Section 4.6). Whether a workstation is capable of performing dynamic changes immediately or not is described in the workstation state list by the entry 'dynamic modification accepted'.

Dynamic attributes are referred to via indices. The index itself may be a static or a dynamic attribute. Colour is a typical dynamic attribute. The sequence

SET_POLYLINE_COLOUR_INDEX(1)
SET_COLOUR_REPRESENTATION (workstation, 1, 1.0, 0.0, 0.0)
POLYLINE (N, POINTS1)
SET_COLOUR_REPRESENTATION (workstation, 1, 0.0, 1.0, 0.0)
POLYLINE (N, POINTS2)

at first generates a red polyline. By redefining the colour representation, this polyline becomes green. The second polyline generated is green.

Attributes can be *global* or *workstation-dependent*. In the case of global attributes, one attribute value is valid for all workstations. Workstation-dependent attributes can be set individually for each workstation.

Global attributes serve to specify the desired attributes without referring to available capabilities. Another appropriate attribute will be taken if an attribute is not supported at a workstation.

Workstation-dependent attributes will be used to exploit specific features of an individual workstation. Therefore, workstation-dependent attributes are restricted to the values valid for that workstation. An error is generated when other values are used.

However, the default error reaction will probably replace an erroneous value by a valid value as in the case of global attributes.

Geometric attributes are global attributes as the geometry of a picture is not allowed to vary between workstations. Other attributes controlling the appearance of primitives may be workstation-dependent. For example, a map generated on a storage tube will use different linetypes to distinguish classes of lines. The same map generated on a plotter will use different colours for the same purpose. This is achieved by indexed attributes. A global index is bound to the primitive which points to workstation-specific tables containing the workstation-dependent aspects of that index. Table 6.4 gives an overview of global and workstation-dependent attributes.

Attributes may be set *individually* or *bundled*. In the first case, a separate function exists for each attribute so that one individual attribute can be set without affecting another one. In the second case, a whole bundle of aspects is defined with one function call. In GKS, all global attributes are set individually. The workstation-dependent attributes are set bundled. These attributes are stored in bundle tables, whereby each entry describes several aspects. For example, the POLYLINE bundle table describes the aspects LINETYPE, LINEWIDTH SCALE FACTOR, and POLYLINE COLOUR INDEX. The whole bundle of aspects is defined with one function call, i.e., LINETYPE cannot be specified without specifying the two other aspects.

In GKS, one attribute usually applies exactly to one primitive class. The setting of the attributes of one primitive, therefore, cannot have side effects on the appearance of another primitive. Only the PICK IDENTIFIER attribute and the colour table are used by all primitives.

The PICK IDENTIFIER attribute does not describe visual aspects of a primitive but is used to identify single primitives or sets of primitives within segments. It is discussed in more detail in Chapter 7.3.

Only one colour table exists at each workstation which is used by all primitives displayed at that workstation. However, the COLOUR INDEX which gives reference to the colour table is specific for each primitive class.

Table 6.4 gives a survey of output primitive attributes. The left-hand column lists all the global attributes. They are static attributes and their values are set individually and are bound immediately. The right-hand column lists all workstation-dependent attributes which are pointed to by indices. The aspects of a specific index are set bundled and are stored in adjustable workstation tables. The binding of the value is delayed and, therefore, redefinition of a table entry is possible and will cause a retroactive change of the appearance of all related primitives.

As shown in Table 6.4, some attributes occur twice, both within a bundle at a workstation and as individual attributes. This richness has been introduced to serve the needs of small single workstation graphics systems where the cost of workstation tables could present a serious problem and direct attributes are sufficient. The flexibility provided by table driven, workstation-dependent attributes takes effect primarily in multi-workstation systems or when graphical output is manipulated dynamically.

If an attribute could be defined both INDIVIDUALLY and BUNDLED conflicts would occur. To avoid this, it must be decided beforehand in which

Table 6.4 Synopsis of the attributes of GKS output primitives

global, static, immediate binding	workstation-dependent, dynamic, delayed binding
For all primitives: PICK IDENTIFIER	
	colour: ⌈RED INTENSITY ∣GREEN INTENSITY ⌊BLUE INTENSITY
POLYLINE: POLYLINE INDEX LINETYPE LINEWIDTH SCALE FACTOR POLYLINE COLOUR INDEX	polyline bundle: ↔⌈LINETYPE ↔∣LINEWIDTH SCALE FACTOR ↔⌊POLYLINE COLOUR INDEX
POLYMARKER: POLYMARKER INDEX MARKER TYPE MARKER SIZE SCALE FACTOR POLYMARKER COLOUR INDEX	polymarker bundle: ↔⌈MARKER TYPE ↔∣MARKER TYPE SCALE FACTOR ↔⌊POLYMARKER COLOUR INDEX

Table 6.4 (continued)

global, static, immediate binding	workstation-dependent, dynamic, delayed binding

TEXT:
CHARACTER HEIGHT
CHARACTER UP VECTOR
TEXT PATH
TEXT ALIGNMENT
TEXT INDEX   text bundle:
TEXT FONT AND PRECISION   ↔⌈TEXT FONT AND PRECISION
CHARACTER EXPANSION FACTOR   ↔⎹CHARACTER EXPANSION FACTOR
CHARACTER SPACING   ↔⎹CHARACTER SPACING
TEXT COLOUR INDEX   ↔⌊TEXT COLOUR INDEX

FILL AREA:
FILL AREA INDEX   fill area bundle:
FILL AREA INTERIOR STYLE   ↔⌈FILL AREA INTERIOR STYLE
FILL AREA STYLE INDEX   ↔⎹FILL AREA STYLE INDEX
FILL AREA COLOUR INDEX   ↔⌊FILL AREA COLOUR INDEX
PATTERN SIZE
PATTERN REFERENCE POINT

pattern:
[array of COLOUR INDICES

CELL ARRAY:
(array of COLOUR INDICES)
(specified in the primitive's definition
rather than as a separate attribute)

GENERALIZED DRAWING PRIMITIVE (GDP):
No attributes of its own, may adopt attributes
from zero or more of the above primitives

Legend: ↔ indicates the presence of an additional global attribute, the ASPECT
SOURCE FLAG (ASF), which for each of the respective attributes indicates,
whether the global attribute on the left-hand side or the workstation-dependent attribute in the bundle on the right-hand side applies to this primitive.

way an attribute is to be used. This is done by a list of aspect source flags
(ASF) which, for each attribute, can have the value INDIVIDUAL or
BUNDLED, there by indicating which way the attribute is to be used.

By default, all the ASFs will either have the value BUNDLED or INDIVID-
UAL, depending on the implementation. This reflects the feeling that the two
different concepts should best be kept apart. However, the application program
may redefine the ASFs according to its needs. It may use some attributes
BUNDLED and others INDIVIDUALLY, e.g., the polyline LINETPYE as

Table 6.5 Attributes to be used either INDIVIDUALLY or BUNDLED

POLYLINE:	LINETYPE
	LINEWIDTH SCALE FACTOR
	POLYLINE COLOUR INDEX
POLYMARKER:	MARKER TYPE
	MARKER SIZE SCALE FACTOR
	POLYMARKER COLOUR INDEX
TEXT:	TEXT FONT AND PRECISION
	CHARACTER EXPANSION FACTOR
	CHARACTER SPACING
	TEXT COLOUR INDEX
FILL AREA:	FILL AREA INTERIOR STYLE
	FILL AREA STYLE INDEX
	FILL AREA COLOUR INDEX

a workstation-dependent attribute and the POLYLINE COLOUR INDEX as a global attribute. The assignment can be changed dynamically. This has no retroactive effect but only affects primitives generated later on. However, it is not considered to be good programming style if one manipulates the ASFs. It is, therefore, recommended either to make all the ASFs the same or, at least, to fix each ASF at the beginning of a session and never to change it afterwards. Table 6.5 lists all attributes which can be used either BUNDLED or INDIVIDUALLY.

With regard to attributes, CELL ARRAY and GDP occupy a special position. Both have no attributes of their own other than PICK IDENTIFIER. CELL ARRAY is defined by an array of colour indices which specify the colour attributes of the primitive. These colour indices are treated like the colour attributes of other primitives. GDP may use the most appropriate attributes from one or more of the other primitives or none at all. For each specific GDP function, the implementor may take another decision. The selection of attributes, however, must be documented with the description of the GDP function. For example, an interpolating curve, implemented as a specific GDP function, is sure to use polyline attributes. A solid circle, on the other hand, may use polyline attributes for the boundary and fill area attributes for the interior.

In the following sections, all output primitives, output primitive attributes, and workstation-specific aspects of a primitive are discussed in detail. Colour table, pick identifier, and aspect source flags are described in Section 6.8.

6.2 POLYLINE Primitive

POLYLINE generates a sequence of straight lines which connects a sequence of points given in the primitive's definition. The points are specified by absolute world coordinates. Relative coordinates are not supported by GKS. In addition, the elementary primitives MOVETO and LINETO, used in many graphics packages for positioning a pen and drawing one straight line, are not present in GKS. The reasons for this decision were conceptual difficulties stemming from the concept of the so-called 'current position'. To draw one straight line, an array of two points must be given in the primitive's definition. This is the minimum number of points needed for a meaningful definition.

POLYLINE only allows a series of straight lines with vertices to be drawn. If a non-linear curve is needed, it can be approximated either by a POLYLINE, consisting of many short straight lines, or by the interpolation capabilities of a workstation, which if present, can be addressed via an appropriate GDP (cf. Section 6.7).

POLYLINE WSAC,SGOP   L0a

Parameters:

Input	number of points		(2..n)	I
Input	coordinates of points	WC		n × P

Effect:

A sequence of connected straight lines is generated, starting from the first point and ending at the last point. The current values of the polyline attributes, as given by the GKS state list (see Section 3.4), are bound to the primitive.

Errors:

5	GKS not in proper state: GKS should be either in the state WSAC or in the state SGOP
100	Number of points is invalid

———————————————— *FORTRAN Interface* ————————————————

CALL GPL (N,PX,PY)

Parameters:

Input	N number of points		(2..n)	INTEGER
Input	PX(N),PY(N) coordinates of points	WC		2 × n × REAL

6.2.1   Global POLYLINE Attributes

Output generated by POLYLINE can be drawn by using values of LINETYPE, LINEWIDTH, and POLYLINE COLOUR INDEX. The current setting of the ASF (cf. Section 3.8.2) decides individually for each of these attributes whether the current setting of the attribute in the GKS state list or the POLYLINE INDEX is bound to the primitive. In the latter case, the POLYLINE INDEX will be replaced at the time of display by values taken from a workstation-dependent table.

By default, all attributes will be initialised to select the most common way of drawing lines in that environment. The default POLYLINE INDEX 1 will point to an entry in the polyline bundle table which describes the most natural way of drawing lines at each workstation.

If lines are to look different from each other, the application program can draw them with different POLYLINE INDICES. The first entries in each poly-

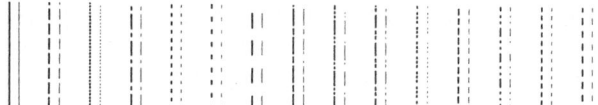

Figure 6.2 Different linetypes shown with two linewidths

line bundle table will be predefined by the implementor so that they address the most common ways of drawing lines at that workstation, for example, by using different pens on a plotter, different linetypes on a storage tube, or different colours on a colour raster display. At the very least, POLYLINE INDICES 1 to 4 have to be predefined by any implementation of GKS. Specific workstation aspects can be selected by calling SET POLYLINE REPRESENTATION (cf. Section 6.2.2).

The direct selection of the polyline attributes LINETYPE, LINEWIDTH, and POLYLINE COLOUR INDEX is reasonable in environments with only one workstation or workstations with homogeneous capabilities. If a workstation cannot provide a specified feature, it will be replaced by some available feature selected by the implementor of GKS.

LINETYPE allows the selection of a specific dash-dotting from a list defined when GKS is implemented. Linetypes 1 to 4 are solid, dashed, dotted and dashed-dotted respectively. These must be available at every output workstation and their described effects cannot be avoided. Linetypes smaller than 0 may be available but they are implementation-dependent. The linetype specifies a sequence of line segments and gaps which are repeated when drawing a POLYLINE. For some applications, it is of great importance whether this sequence is restarted or continued at the start of POLYLINE, at the start of a clipped piece of POLYLINE, or at each vertex of a POLYLINE. Nevertheless, GKS leaves it to the implementor as to how to implement the linetypes. If a specific way of restarting is needed, it should be implemented as an additional linetype.

LINEWIDTH SCALE FACTOR allows the specification of the linewidth. This is calculated by multiplying the linewidth scale factor by a nominal linewidth. This value is mapped by the workstation to the nearest linewidth available at the workstation. The nominal linewidth and the capabilities of a workstation generating different linewidths can be determined from the workstation description table. Linewidth is not affected by GKS transformations.

POLYLINE COLOUR INDEX selects a colour from the workstation's colour table (cf. Section 6.8).

SET LINETYPE   GKOP, WSOP, WSAC, SGOP   L0a
Parameters:
   Input   linetype $(-n..-1, 1..n)$ I
Effect:
   The 'current linetype' entry in the GKS state list is set equal to the value specified
   by the parameter. When the 'current linetype ASF' entry in the GKS state list is

INDIVIDUAL, POLYLINE output primitives subsequently generated will be displayed with this linetype. When the 'current linetype ASF' entry in the GKS state list is BUNDLED, this function will not affect the display of such POLYLINE output primitives until the 'current linetype ASF' is reset.

Linetype values produce linetypes as indicated:

< 0 implementation-dependent

1. solid line
2. dashed line
3. dotted line
4. dashed-dotted line

≥ 5 reserved for registration or future standardization

If the specified linetype is not available on a workstation, linetype 1 is used.

Errors:

8   GKS not in proper state: GKS should be in one of the states GKOP, WSOP, WSAC or SGOP

63   Linetype is equal to zero

──────────────── *FORTRAN Interface* ────────────────

CALL GSLN (LTYPE)

Parameters:

Input   LTYPE   linetype $(-n..-1,1..n)$ INTEGER

───

SET LINEWIDTH SCALE FACTOR   GKOP,WSOP,WSAC,SGOP   L0a

Parameters:

Input   linewidth scale factor ≥ 0 R

Effect:

The 'current linewidth scale factor' entry in the GKS state list is set equal to the value specified by the parameter. When the 'current linewidth scale factor ASF' entry in the GKS state list is INDIVIDUAL, POLYLINE output primitives subsequently generated will be displayed with this linewidth scale factor. When the 'current linewidth scale factor ASF' entry in the GKS state list is BUNDLED, this function will not affect the display of POLYLINE output primitives subsequently created until the 'current linewidth scale factor ASF' is reset.

The linewidth scale factor is multiplied by the nominal linewidth at a workstation; the result is mapped by the workstation to the nearest available linewidth.

Errors:

8   GKS not in proper state: GKS should be in one of the states GKOP, WSOP, WSAC or SGOP

65   Linewidth scale factor is less than zero

──────────────── *FORTRAN Interface* ────────────────

CALL GSLWSC (LWIDTH)

Parameters:

Input   LWIDTH linewidth scale factor ≥ 0 REAL

───

SET POLYLINE COLOUR INDEX   GKOP,WSOP,WSAC,SGOP   L0a

Parameters:

Input   colour index $(0..n)$ I

Effect:

The 'current polyline colour index' entry in the GKS state list is set equal to the value specified by the parameter. When the 'current polyline colour index ASF' entry in the GKS state list is INDIVIDUAL, POLYLINE output primitives subsequently generated will be displayed with this polyline colour index. When the 'current polyline colour index ASF' entry in the GKS state list is BUNDLED, this function will not affect the display of POLYLINE output primitives subsequently created until the 'current polyline colour index ASF' is reset.

The colour index is a pointer to the colour tables at the workstations. If the specified colour index is not present in a workstation colour table, a workstation-dependent colour index is used at that workstation.

Errors:

8	GKS not in proper state: GKS should be in one of the states GKOP, WSOP, WSAC or SGOP
92	Colour index is less than zero

—————————————— *FORTRAN Interface* ——————————————

CALL GSPLCI (COLI)

Parameters:

Input   COLI   colour index   (0..n)   INTEGER

SET POLYLINE INDEX	GKOP, WSOP, WSAC, SGOP L0a

Parameters:

Input   polyline index   (1..n)   I

Effect:

The 'current polyline index' entry in the GKS state list is set equal to the value specified by the parameter. This value is used for creating subsequent POLYLINE output primitives.

Errors:

8	GKS not in proper state: GKS should be in one of the states GKOP, WSOP, WSAC or SGOP
60	Polyline index is invalid

—————————————— *FORTRAN Interface* ——————————————

CALL GSPLI (INDEX)

Parameters:

Input   INDEX   polyline index   (1..n)   INTEGER

6.2.2   Workstation-Dependent POLYLINE Attributes

The GKS function SET POLYLINE REPRESENTATION allows the selection of polyline aspects LINETYPE, LINEWIDTH SCALE FACTOR, and POLYLINE COLOUR INDEX, for each workstation individually. These values are accessed via a POLYLINE INDEX, if the respective aspect source flag is BUNDLED.

The capabilities of each workstation with respect to these attributes can be determined from the workstation description table. If capabilities are requested which are not supported at that workstation, GKS will generate an error message. This contrasts with the treatment of global attributes. Here, an attribute which is not supported at a particular workstation is mapped automatically to an appropriate valid value.

SET POLYLINE REPRESENTATION   WSOP,WSAC,SGOP   L1a

Parameters:

Input	workstation identifier		N
Input	polyline index	$(1..n)$	I
Input	linetype	$(-n..-1,1..n)$	I
Input	linewidth scale factor	≥ 0	R
Input	polyline colour index	$(0..n)$	I

Effect:

In the polyline bundle table of the workstation state list, the given polyline index is associated with the specified parameters.

Linetype values produce linetypes as indicated:

    < 0 implementation-dependent
1. solid line
2. dashed line
3. dotted line
4. dashed-dotted line

≥ 5 reserved for registration or future standardization

If the specified linetype is not available, linetype 1 is used.

Linewidth scale factor: a scale factor multiplied by the nominal linewidth. The result is mapped by the workstation to the nearest available linewidth.

Polyline colour index: pointer to the colour table at the workstation.

The polyline bundle table in the workstation state list has predefined entries taken from the workstation description table; at least one should be predefined for every workstation of category OUTPUT and OUTIN. Any table entry (including the predefined entries) may be redefined by this function.

When polylines are displayed, the polyline index refers to an entry in the polyline bundle table. If POLYLINES are displayed with a polyline index which is not present in the polyline bundle table, polyline index 1 will be used. The setting of the corresponding ASFs determines which aspects in the entry are used (cf. Section 6.8.2).

Errors:

7	GKS not in proper state: GKS should be in one of the states WSOP, WSAC or SGOP
20	Specified workstation identifier is invalid
25	Specified workstation is not open
33	Specified workstation is of category MI
35	Specified workstation is of category INPUT
36	Specified workstation is Workstation-Independent Segment Storage
60	Polyline index is invalid
63	Linetype is equal to zero
64	Specified linetype is not supported on this workstation
65	Linewidth scale factor is less than zero
86	Colour index is invalid

—————————————————— *FORTRAN Interface* ——————————————————

CALL GSPLR (WKID,PLI,LTYPE,LWIDTH,COLI)
Parameters:

Input	WKID	workstation identifier		INTEGER
Input	PLI	polyline index	(1..n)	INTEGER
Input	LTYPE	linetype	(−n..−1,1..n)	INTEGER
Input	LWIDTH	linewidth scale factor	≥0	REAL
Input	COLI	polyline colour index	(0..n)	INTEGER

6.3   POLYMARKER Primitive

POLYMARKER is a means of identifying points on the display surface. A marker symbol is drawn, centred at each position specified in the definition of the POLYMARKER. Figure 6.3 shows three sets of points connected by polylines in different linetypes and polymarkers with different marker types.

It should be noted that the marker facility is quite separate from a symbol facility, which allows the drawing of several instances of a subpicture. For such purposes the INSERT SEGMENT function (cf. Section 7.7) has been introduced. A symbol containing a subpicture should be properly transformed. With the POLYMARKER primitive only the positions are transformed. The size and the orientation of a marker symbol will not be affected. In Figures 6.3 and 6.4, it is shown how different normalization transformations affect the position but not the size of markers.

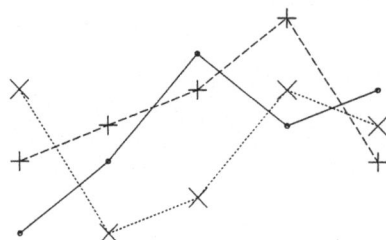

Figure 6.3 Example of a POLYLINE plus POLYMARKER output

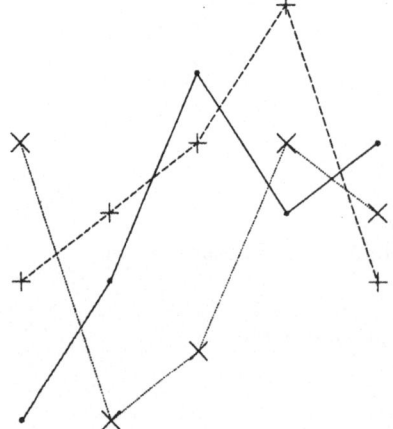

Figure 6.4
Marker not affected by transformation

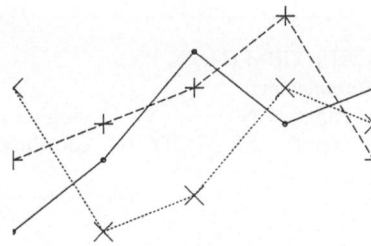

Figure 6.5a Clipping of POLYMARKER,
points inside clipping rectangle

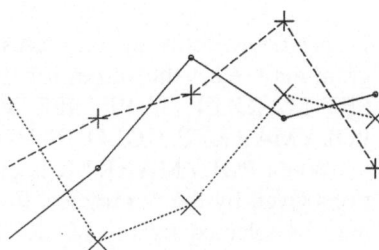

Figure 6.5b Clipping of POLYMARKER,
some points outside clipping rectangle

The size may be addressed, however, by using the POLYMARKER SCALE FACTOR attribute (cf. Figure 6.6). This attribute allows different sizes of a marker symbol to be selected relative to a nominal size measured in device coordinates.

This approach to markers also has consequences for the clipping algorithm. A marker symbol is drawn if, and only if, its position is inside the clipping rectangle. If its position is inside but parts of the marker are outside, the implementation can choose whether to clip properly or not. If the position is outside and parts of the marker extend into the inside, no part of the marker may be drawn. Figure 6.5a shows the same output as Figure 6.3 with the leftmost and rightmost points lying on the boundary of the clipping rectangle. The markers are clipped exactly. In Figure 6.5b the clipping rectangle is slightly shifted by a quarter of the marker size to the right. The markers in the left-hand margin are omitted totally and the markers in the right-hand margin are clipped properly.

POLYMARKER   WSAC,SGOP   L0a

Parameters:

Input	number of points	(1..n)	I
Input	coordinates of points	WC	n × P

Effect:

A sequence of markers is generated to identify all the given positions. The current values of the polymarker attributes, as given by the GKS state list (cf. Section 3.4), are bound to the primitive.

N.B.:

A marker is visible if and only if the marker position is within the clipping rectangle.

Errors:

5	GKS not in proper state: GKS should be either in the state WSAC or in the state SGOP
100	Number of points is invalid

―――――――――――――― *FORTRAN Interface* ――――――――――

CALL GPM (N,PX,PY)
Parameters:
  Input   N   number of points   (1..n)   INTEGER
  Input   PX(N),PY(N)   coordinates of points   WC   2 × n × REAL

6.3.1   Global Polymarker Attributes

If specific symbols, symbol sizes, and colours are desired, the application pro·
gram may select the values for the polymarker attributes by the GKS function:
SET MARKER TYPE, SET MARKER SIZE SCALE FACTOR, and SET
POLYMARKER COLOUR INDEX.

When POLYMARKER is called the same symbol is drawn at all the posi·
tions given by the parameter. For each POLYMARKER call different symbol:
may be selected by the MARKER TYPE attribute from an implementation·
provided table. GKS requires the implementation of the five symbols . + * o ×
which must be realized with recognizable shapes at any output workstation
Further symbols can be added by an implementor to serve the needs of hi:
clientele.

The application program may ask GKS to draw markers with specified
MARKER SIZES. Marker type 1 is always displayed as the smallest displayable
dot and, therefore, is not affected by the size attribute. The size is specified
as a factor which is applied to a workstation-specific nominal marker size and
it is not affected by GKS transformations. As nominal sizes may vary from
workstation to workstation the same scale factor may lead to different marker
sizes.

It is not compulsory for a workstation to support different marker sizes
An implementor may implement any number of marker sizes according to hi:
particular needs. A different decision may be taken for each workstation. I:
a desired marker size is not present at a workstation, GKS will select the neares·
available marker size.

For colour devices, the colour of a marker can be selected by a colour
index specific to POLYMARKER primitives.

If the above attributes are selected on a workstation basis, a POLY·
MARKER INDEX can be used, which points to workstation tables containing
a trio of values for the above attributes for each index value. At the very
least POLYMARKER INDICES 1 to 5 can be used immediately, as they are
predefined, by any implementation.

Whether global or workstation-dependent attributes are applied is decided
by the current (at primitive generation time) setting of the aspect source flag:
(cf. Section 3.8.2).

Figure 6.6
The minimal set of markers in two siz

SET MARKER TYPE   GKOP, WSOP, WSAC, SGOP   L0a

Parameters:

Input   marker type $(-n..-1, 1..n)$ I

Effect:

The 'current marker type' entry in the GKS state list is set equal to the value specified
by the parameter. When the 'current marker type ASF' entry in the GKS state list
is INDIVIDUAL, subsequently generated POLYMARKER output primitives will be
displayed with this marker type. When the 'current marker type ASF' entry in the
GKS state list is BUNDLED, this function will not affect the display of subsequently
created POLYMARKER output primitives until the 'current marker type ASF' is
reset.

Marker type values produce centred symbols as indicated:

<0 implementation-dependent

 1 .

 2 +

 3 *

 4 o

 5 ×

≥ 6 reserved for registration or future standardization

Marker type 1 is always displayed as the smallest displayable dot. If the specified
marker type is not available, marker type 3 (*) is used on that workstation.

Errors:

8   GKS not in proper state: GKS should be in one of the states GKOP, WSOP,
        WSAC or SGOP

69   Marker type is equal to zero

──────────────────── *FORTRAN Interface* ────────────────────

CALL GSMK (MTYPE)

Input   MTYPE   marker type $(-n..-1, 1..n)$ INTEGER

SET MARKER SIZE SCALE FACTOR   GKOP, WSOP, WSAC, SGOP   L0a

Parameters:

Input   marker size scale factor ≥ 0 R

Effect:

The 'current marker size scale factor' entry in the GKS state list is set equal to
the value specified by the parameter. When the 'current marker size scale factor ASF'
entry in the GKS state list is INDIVIDUAL, subsequently generated POLYMARKER
output primitives will be displayed with this marker size scale factor. When the 'current
marker size scale factor ASF' entry in the GKS state list is BUNDLED, this function
will not affect the display of subsequently created POLYMARKER output primitives
until the 'current marker size scale factor ASF' is reset.

The marker size scale factor is applied to the nominal marker size at a workstation;
the result is mapped by the workstation to the nearest available marker size.

Errors:

8   GKS not in proper state: GKS should be in one of the states GKOP, WSOP,
        WSAC or SGOP

71   Marker size scale factor is less than zero

——————————————— *FORTRAN Interface* ———————————————

CALL GSMKSC (MSZSF)
Parameters:
Input   MSZSF   marker size scale factor   ≥0   REAL

SET POLYMARKER COLOUR INDEX GKOP,WSOP,WSAC,SGOP   L0a
Parameters:
Input   polymarker colour index   (0..n)   I
Effect:
The 'current polymarker colour index' entry in the GKS state list is set equal to the value specified by the parameter. When the 'current polymarker colour index ASF' entry in the GKS state list is INDIVIDUAL, subsequently generated POLY-MARKER output primitives will be displayed with this polymarker colour index. When the 'current polymarker colour index ASF' entry in the GKS state list is BUNDLED, this function will not affect the display of subsequently created POLY-MARKER output primitives until the 'current polymarker colour index ASF' is re-set.
The colour index points to the colour tables of the workstations. If the specified colour index is not present in a workstation colour table, a workstation-dependent colour index is used at that workstation.
Errors:
8   GKS not in proper state: GKS should be in one of the states GKOP, WSOP, WSAC or SGOP
92   Colour index is less than zero

——————————————— *FORTRAN Interface* ———————————————

CALL GSPMCI (COLI)
Parameters:
Input   COLI   polymarker colour index   (0..n)   INTEGER

SET POLYMARKER INDEX   GKOP,WSOP,WSAC,SGOP   L0a
Parameters:
Input   polymarker index   (1..n)   I
Effect:
The 'current polymarker index' entry in the GKS state list is set equal to the value specified by the parameter. This value is used for creating subsequent POLYMARKER output primitives.
Errors:
8   GKS not in proper state: GKS should be in one of the states GKOP, WSOP, WSAC or SGOP
66   Polymarker index is invalid

——————————————— *FORTRAN Interface* ———————————————

CALL GSPMI (INDEX)
Parameters:
Input   INDEX   polymarker index   (1..n)   INTEGER

6.3.2   Workstation-Dependent POLYMARKER Attributes

The GKS function SET POLYMARKER REPRESENTATION allows the polymarker attributes, MARKER TYPE, MARKER WIDTH SCALE FACTOR, and POLYMARKER COLOUR INDEX to be selected for each workstation individually. These values are accessed by using a POLYMARKER INDEX if the respective aspect source flag is BUNDLED.

The capabilities of each workstation with respect to the attributes can be determined from the workstation description table. If capabilities are requested which are not supported at that workstation, GKS will generate an error message. This contrasts with the treatment of the global attributes. Here, an attribute which is not supported at a particular workstation is mapped automatically to an appropriate valid value.

SET POLYMARKER REPRESENTATION   WSOP, WSAC, SGOP   L1a

Parameters:

Input	workstation identifier		N
Input	polymarker index	$(1..n)$	I
Input	marker type	$(-n..-1, 1..n)$	I
Input	marker size scale factor	≥ 0	R
Input	polymarker colour index	$(0..n)$	I

Effect:

In the polymarker bundle table of the workstation state list, the given polymarker index is associated with the specified parameters.

Marker type: marker type values produce centred symbols as indicated:

<0 implementation-dependent

  1 .

  2 +

  3 *

  4 o

  5 ×

≥ 6 reserved for registration or future standardization

Marker type 1 is always displayed as the smallest displayable dot.

Marker scale factor: a scale factor applied to the nominal marker size. The result is mapped by the workstation to the nearest available marker size.

Polymarker colour index: a pointer to the colour table at the workstation.

The polymarker bundle table in the workstation state list has predefined entries taken from the workstation description table; at least one should be predefined for every workstation category OUTPUT and OUTIN. Any table entry (including the predefined entries) may be redefined with this function.

When POLYMARKERS are displayed, the polymarker index refers to an entry in the polymarker bundle table. If POLYMARKERS are displayed with a polymarker index which is not present in the polymarker bundle table, polymarker index 1 will be used. The setting of the corresponding ASFs determines which aspects in the entry are used (cf. Section 6.8.2).

Errors:

  7   GKS not in proper state: GKS should be in one of the states WSOP, WSAC or SGOP

20	Specified workstation identifier is invalid
25	Specified workstation is not open
33	Specified workstation is of category MI
35	Specified workstation is of category INPUT
36	Specified workstation is Workstation-Independent Segment Storage
66	Polymarker index is invalid
69	Marker type is equal to zero
70	Specified marker type is not supported on this workstation
71	Marker size scale factor is less than zero
86	Colour index is invalid

―――――――――――――― *FORTRAN Interface* ――――――――――――――

CALL GSPMR (WKID, PMI, MTYPE, MSZSF, COLI)
Parameters:

Input	WKID	workstation identifier		INTEGER
Input	PMI	polymarker index	$(1..n)$	INTEGER
Input	MTYPE	marker type	$(-n..-1, 1..n)$	INTEGER
Input	MSZSF	marker size scale factor	≥ 0	REAL
Input	COLI	polymarker colour index	$(0..n)$	INTEGER

6.4 TEXT Primitive

Pictures usually contain inscriptions which give additional textual information. The TEXT primitive conveniently allows the generation of character strings on the display space. The application program specifies the character codes, and GKS automatically translates this code into geometrical data describing the shape of the individual characters. GKS, at the very least, provides a character set used in data processing which is the well known ASCII-character set. This set has been standardized in the ISO 646 standard.

As well as the character string, a starting position in world coordinates also has to be specified. This allows the proper positioning of characters relative to other graphical primitives. The geometry of each individual character is maintained by GKS. GKS provides geometrical text attributes which allow precise control of the overall size, shape and orientation of characters and character strings. Other attributes allow the selection of a specific font and the manipulation of font characteristics such as spacing and aspect ratio. Text geometry is defined in world coordinates and the shape of a character will be transformed in the same way as other primitives. For reasons of efficiency this strict rule may be relaxed by a text precision attribute. More details about text attributes are given in the subsequent sections.

――

TEXT   WSAC, SGOP   L0a
Parameters:

Input	starting point	WC	P
Input	character string		S

Effect:
  A character string is generated. The current values of the text attributes, as given by the GKS state list (cf. Section 3.4), are bound to the primitive. The text position is given in WC and transformed by the current normalization transformation.

N.B.:
TEXT is clipped in a way which depends on the text precision.
Errors:

5	GKS not in proper state: GKS should be either in the state WSAC or in the state SGOP
101	Invalid code in string

———————————— *FORTRAN Interface* ————————————

CALL GTX (X0,Y0,CHARS)
Parameters:

Input	X0,Y0	starting point	WC	2 × REAL
Input	CHARS	string of characters (ISO 646)		CHARACTER*(*)

6.4.1   TEXT Attributes for Beginners

GKS provides a variety of text attributes which allow a powerful control of the appearance of text on the display surface. To understand all the effects which can be achieved by these attributes, a thorough knowledge of some typographical terms is necessary and this will be given in the subsequent sections. However, the text attributes have been structured in such a way that a standard user will not have to deal with all these technical details. Therefore, in this section, a short description of those concepts is given which are of importance for most users, i.e. the text attributes CHARACTER HEIGHT, CHARACTER UP VECTOR, TEXT COLOUR INDEX, and TEXT INDEX. This section should be read by a novice. The subsequent sections deal with advanced features of text generation and are aimed at the experienced user or the implementor of GKS.

By setting CHARACTER HEIGHT, the size of characters can be determined. CHARACTER HEIGHT specifies the height of a capital letter and it also controls character width and spacing, as these values are specified relative to CHARACTER HEIGHT. This means that, by doubling the character height, character width and spacing are also implicitly doubled (cf. Figure 6.7).

The height value is specified in world coordinates and, therefore, is influenced by transformations. For example, if the current normalization transformation is reset, subsequently generated text primitives may show a different character size on the display surface (cf. Figure 6.9). Segment transformations and workstation transformations influence text primitives in a similar way.

The default value of CHARACTER HEIGHT is 0.01 which in conjunction with the default window and viewport (unit square) will specify a character size just about large enough to be read. With a window of [0,100] × [0,100], illegible characters will be generated. It is therefore recommended that CHARACTER HEIGHT be explicitly set for each normalization transformation used for TEXT output.

By default, strings are written along a horizontal baseline starting at the position specified by the first parameter of the TEXT primitive. The baseline may be rotated to allow strings to be written in other directions. For this purpose, a CHARACTER UP VECTOR must be set which specifies the vertical

HEIGHT_1

HEIGHT_2

HEIGHT_3

Figure 6.7 TEXT with different CHARACTER HEIGHT values

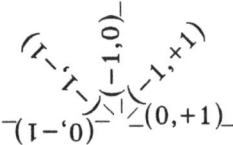

Figure 6.8 TEXT with different CHARACTER UP VECTOR values

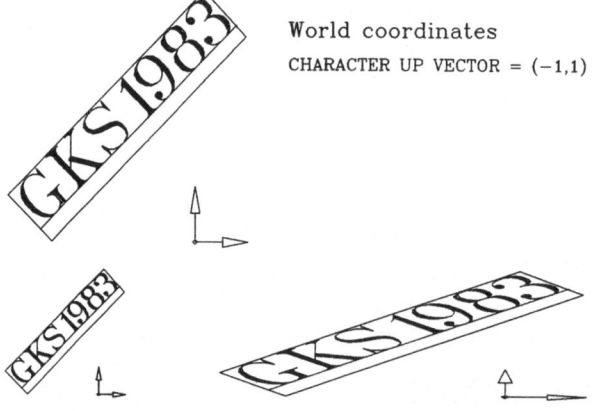

World coordinates

CHARACTER UP VECTOR = $(-1,1)$

After a normalization transformation which scales x and y equally.

After a normalization transformation which scales x by a factor of 3 compared with y.

Figure 6.9 Text with different normalization transformations

orientation of characters (cf. Figure 6.8). The baseline is perpendicular to this vector.

CHARACTER UP VECTOR and baseline are defined in the world coordinate system and undergo all transformations. However, as they define angles only, many transformations will have no effect, i.e., the angles will be the same in the world coordinate system and on the display surface. It is obvious that a segment transformation specifying a rotation will rotate TEXT primitives accordingly. It is less evident that a transformation performing different scaling in the x- and y-direction (this is possible for the normalization and segment transformations) may affect the angles and may even shear characters (cf. Figure 6.9). However, this can only happen if the CHARACTER UP VECTOR is not parallel to one of the axes. These latter effects may be irritating for the novice and for applications where a text is regarded more in terms of device coordinates rather than world coordinates. However, the definition of text in world coordinates ensures that the text behaves like other output primitives. For example, if text is surrounded by a rectangle, both should be transformed in the same way.

For colour devices, the colour of text can be selected by a TEXT COLOUR INDEX specific for TEXT primitives.

Some text attributes can be selected on a workstation basis. A TEXT INDEX can be used which points to text bundles in tables at the individual workstations. See Section 6.4.6 for details about which attributes can be selected workstation-dependently.

6.4.2 Character Body

This section explains how the size and shape of the individual characters are determined in world coordinates. At the beginning, the terminology used for the description of character fonts is explained in detail.

Fonts are defined with respect to certain horizontal and vertical lines. *Topline* and *bottomline* delimit characters in a vertical direction whereas *leftline* and *rightline* do so in a horizontal direction. All four lines define a rectangle, parallel to the axes of a 2 D Cartesian font coordinate system, which is called the *character body*. It is assumed that the characters lie within their character body, with the exception of the kerned characters (cf. characters j and f in Figure 6.10) which may exceed the side limits of the character body. The character body includes some space around the character, so that characters written with their bodies touching horizontally should appear well-spaced, and characters with their bodies touching vertically should avoid any clashing of the ascender/descender.

The distance between the topline and the bottomline will be the same for all the characters. The distance from the leftline to the rightline, however, may vary, allowing narrow characters like i or l to occupy less space than broad ones, such as M and W. Fonts with character-dependent width of the character box are called *proportionally spaced fonts* in contrast to *monospaced fonts*.

Baseline and *capline* must lie within the vertical space of the character body and, usually, will limit the extent of a capital letter. *Halfline* and *centreline* bisect the character body vertically and horizontally, respectively. The exact positions of these lines are specified by the font designer who, for example, may use aesthetical criteria to find the best position rather than choosing the geometric mean.

The size of the character body is affected by the CHARACTER HEIGHT and CHARACTER EXPANSION FACTOR attributes.

CHARACTER HEIGHT specifies the nominal height of a capital letter character, i.e., the distance from baseline to capline, in world coordinates. The character body is scaled uniformly in the x- and y-direction to achieve the desired CHARACTER HEIGHT. Therefore, the width/height ratio remains unchanged (cf. Figure 6.7).

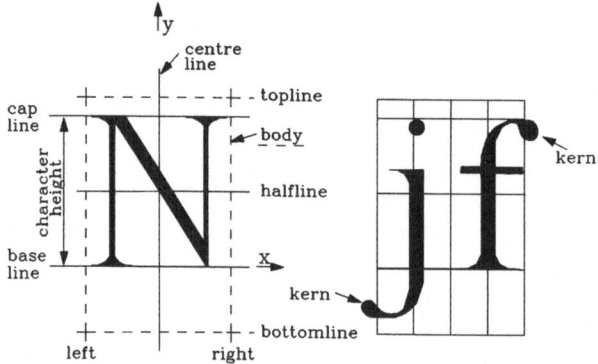

Figure 6.10 Font geometry

CHARACTER EXPANSION FACTOR allows the manipulation of the width/height ratio of the character body. The width of the character body is scaled by the specified factor. A factor of 1/2 narrows the body to half the width, whereas a factor of 2 doubles the width.

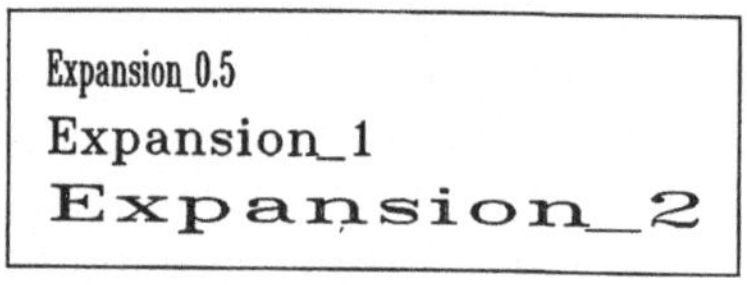

Expansion_0.5
Expansion_1
Expansion_2

Figure 6.11 Text with different CHARACTER EXPANSION FACTOR values

The attributes CHARACTER HEIGHT and CHARACTER EXPANSION FACTOR, in conjunction with the font geometry as determined by the font designer, completely define the shape and size of the character body for each character in world coordinates.

6.4.3   Text Extent Rectangle

This section deals with the building up of a character string. The purpose of the character body and the horizontal and vertical lines related to the character body is to allow the characters to be positioned precisely and in a well-defined manner with respect to their neighbouring characters. Generally, when drawing a string of characters, character bodies are placed adjacent to their neighbours, unless additional spacing is demanded by the CHARACTER SPACING attribute (see below).

The side of the character body, where the next character body is placed, is selected by the text attribute TEXT PATH, which has four values: RIGHT, LEFT, UP, DOWN. RIGHT is the usual writing direction. LEFT specifies that a 'string' is written backwards, i.e., 'gnirts'. UP and DOWN allow strings to be written in a vertical sequence; with UP the first character is at the bottom and with DOWN it is at the top of the string. The inter-character alignment is trivial for horizontally written text as all characters use the same baseline, capline, etc. For vertically written text, however, problems occur with proportionally spaced fonts. Note that vertically written text characters are aligned along the centre line.

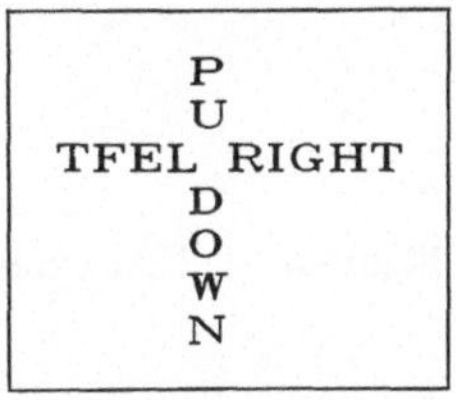

```
        P
        U
TFEL  RIGHT
        D
        O
        W
        N
```

Figure 6.12 TEXT with different TEXT PATH values

The character body already includes some standard amount of space around each character. The CHARACTER SPACING value specifies how much additional space is to be inserted between two adjacent character bodies. If the value of CHARACTER SPACING is zero, the character bodies are arranged one after the other along the TEXT PATH. A positive value of CHARACTER SPACING will insert additional space between character bodies. A negative value of CHARACTER SPACING will cause adjacent character bodies to overlap. CHARACTER SPACING is specified as a fraction of the font-nominal character height, i.e., a value of 1 will insert a space as long as the distance between the baseline and capline, a value of -1 will backspace by the same distance. It should be noted that this extra spacing applies for all writing directions as specified by TEXT PATH.

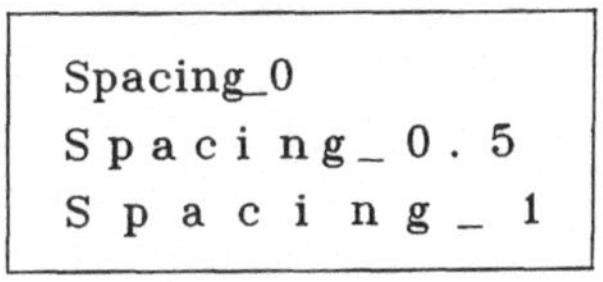

```
Spacing_0
S p a c i n g _ 0 . 5
S  p  a  c  i  n  g _  1
```

Figure 6.13 TEXT with different CHARACTER SPACING values

TEXT PATH and CHARACTER SPACING, in conjunction with the character body geometry as defined in the previous section, completely define the geometry of a string. The rectangle which encloses all the characters of a string is called a *text extent rectangle*. It is formed by:
— the topline of the top-most character,
— the bottomline of the bottom character,
— the leftline of the left-most character,
— the rightline of the right-most character.
For the text extent rectangle lines are defined in a similar way as for the character body (cf. Figure 6.10). However, depending on the TEXT PATH value, some of the lines are not as meaningful as they are for single characters.

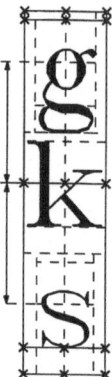

Figure 6.14 Text extent rectangle

For horizontally written text, bottomline, baseline, halfline, capline, and topline of the text extent rectangle coincide with the respective lines of each character body. The leftline coincides with the leftline of the left-most character, the rightline with the rightline of the right-most character, and the centreline lies in the middle of both.

For vertically written text, bottomline and baseline of the text extent rectangle coincide with the respective lines of the bottom character, capline and topline coincide with the respective lines of the top-most character, and halfline lies in the middle of the halflines of the bottom and top-most characters. Rightline, centreline and leftline coincide with the respective lines of all character bodies for monospaced fonts and with the respective lines of the widest character for proportionally spaced fonts.

These lines are introduced to allow the text extent rectangle to be precisely positioned relative to the starting position given when the TEXT primitive is called. The TEXT ALIGNMENT attribute has two components, a horizontal component with the three values LEFT, CENTRE, RIGHT and a vertical component with the five values TOP, CAP, HALF, BASE, BOTTOM which refer to the respective lines within the text extent rectangle (cf. Figure 6.14). The text string is positioned so that the starting point given in the parameter list of TEXT is at the point where the selected vertical and horizontal lines intersect.

In order to relieve the normal user from having to set attributes explicitly which are of no specific importance to him, GKS should provide default values which satisfy the most common needs. However, as the natural alignment depends on the value of the TEXT PATH attribute, it is impossible to give one default value for all TEXT PATH values. For example, TEXT PATH value RIGHT will usually be combined with alignment to leftline and LEFT with alignment to rightline. This problem has been solved by introducing an additional value for horizontal and vertical alignment called NORMAL. By specifying this value, the programmer indicates that the most natural alignment for the current TEXT PATH value should be chosen. In detail, the following alignment values will be taken:

TEXT PATH value:	RIGHT	LEFT	UP	DOWN
Horizontal alignment NORMAL:	LEFT	RIGHT	CENTRE	CENTRE
Vertical alignment NORMAL:	BASE	BASE	BASE	TOP

When the text extent rectangle together with its enclosed characters has been positioned in world coordinate space, it will be rotated so that the CHARACTER UP VECTOR is parallel to the direction of the vertical lines, e.g., the leftline, and points from the bottomline to the topline. See Figure 6.8 for an illustration of this effect.

The horizontal lines, e.g., the baseline, are perpendicular to this direction. Note for implementors: The perpendicular relation between vertical and horizontal font lines only holds in a world coordinate system. Therefore, when characters are sent to a workstation, it is generally not sufficient to send a transformed CHARACTER UP VECTOR with the text primitive but also a transformed baseline vector is needed.

The attributes presented in the above sections provide a detailed means of specifying the text extent rectangle in the world coordinate system. Nevertheless, it is not possible for the application program to determine for every case the effective size of the text extent rectangle. This difficulty arises because the effect of the above attributes depends on the geometry of a specific font which is not readily available especially for proportionally spaced fonts. Their effect, furthermore, depends on the text precision (cf. Section 6.4.4) which allows the text attributes which are too expensive for a workstation to be ignored. Some of the text attributes can be chosen globally or on a workstation basis. Therefore, character body and text extent rectangle, although defined in world coordinates, are workstation-dependent.

In some cases, a precise knowledge of the size of the text extent rectangle may be needed. In order to make control of the aggregated effects of workstation-dependent and workstation-independent attributes easier for the application programmer, GKS provides an INQUIRE TEXT EXTENT function (cf. Section 10.2.4) which delivers information about the text rectangle for any given text string on a workstation basis. Furthermore, it supplies a concatenation point which permits the proper concatenation of strings at one specific workstation.

6.4.4   Text Font and Precision

The TEXT FONT attribute can be used to select a particular font. Every workstation must support at least one font which is able to create a graphical representation of the characters defined in ISO 646 Standard (ASCII-character set). This is to be font number 1. The fonts available for a workstation should be documented in the implementation manual.

The generation of text may be expensive for workstations with inadequate hardware. The TEXT PRECISION attribute is a means of indicating that a poorer realization of the text primitives should be made for reasons of efficiency. The TEXT PRECISION value is used to select the 'closeness' of the text representation in relation to that defined by the above text attributes and the transformation/clipping currently applicable. The TEXT PRECISION has the following possible values:

STRING: The TEXT character string is generated in the requested text font and is positioned by aligning the TEXT output primitive to the given TEXT starting position. CHARACTER HEIGHT and CHARACTER EXPANSION FACTOR are evaluated as closely as is reasonable, given the capabilities of the workstation. CHARACTER UP VECTOR, TEXT PATH, TEXT ALIGNMENT, and CHARACTER SPACING need not be used. Clipping is done in an implementation- and workstation-dependent way.

CHAR: Individual characters of the TEXT character string in the requested text font are positioned relative to each other according to the TEXT PATH, CHARACTER EXPANSION FACTOR, and CHARACTER SPACING. The direction of writing is defined by the CHARACTER UP VECTOR and TEXT PATH. The position of the resulting text extent rectangle is determined by the TEXT ALIGNMENT and the text starting position. For the representation of each individual character, the attributes CHARACTER HEIGHT, the upwards direction of the CHARACTER UP VECTOR, and CHARACTER EXPANSION FACTOR are evaluated as closely as possible, in a workstation-dependent way. Clipping is done on a character body basis.

STROKE: The TEXT character string in the requested text font is displayed at the starting position of the text by applying all the text attributes. The character string is transformed and clipped exactly at the clipping rectangle. It should be recognized that STROKE precision does not necessarily mean vector strokes; as long as the representation adheres to the rules governing STROKE precision, the font may be realized in any form, for example by raster fonts.

Figure 6.15 shows the different behaviour of TEXT for TEXT PRECISION values STRING, CHAR, and STROKE. The string 'TEXT DEMONSTRATION' is written with all these three values; in Figure 6.15a, the string is clipped around the clipping rectangle; in Figure 6.15b, clipping is switched off and only clipping at the workstation window occurs.

A GKS output level 0 implementation must support TEXT PRECISION values STRING and CHAR. Above output level 0, all three values must be supported as defined below. A workstation may use a higher precision than the one requested, i.e., if STROKE precision is supported for a particular font, this implies that both STRING and CHAR precision are available for that font.

Even when using STRING precision, the CHARACTER HEIGHT should be set. The use of CHARACTER HEIGHT is optional for STRING precision and the default value of CHARACTER HEIGHT will not always produce legible characters depending on the current normalization transformation.

TEXT FONT AND PRECISION are binding for workstations. This means that for any GKS level supporting a STROKE precision font, every workstation in this particular installation has to support at least one STROKE precision

Figure 6.15 TEXT with different TEXT
PRECISION values   a   b

TEXT font. This is to be font number 1, and should contain the character
set defined by ISO 646. This implies that, for STROKE precision TEXT, some
sort of software character generator will be required for those implementations
with inadequate hardware. Not all workstations need to support all fonts, but
for those that do the same font number should be used to select that font
on all workstations in this particular installation.

6.4.5   Setting Global Text Attributes

The previous sections gave an introduction to the semantics of text attributes.
The following Figures 6.16a, b illustrate, with a series of examples, the interde-
pendence between the different text attributes.

Most of the attributes can only be used as global attributes. The attributes
TEXT FONT AND PRECISION, CHARACTER EXPANSION FACTOR,
CHARACTER SPACING, and TEXT COLOUR INDEX can also be selected
on a workstation basis. In this case a TEXT INDEX can be used which points
to workstation tables containing, for each index value, a bundle of values for
these attributes.

The decision whether global or workstation-dependent attributes are applied
is made by referring to the current (at primitive generation time) setting of
the aspect source flags (cf. Section 6.8.2).

In the following, a description of all functions which set the global text
attributes will be given. The initial values of these attributes are compiled in
Table 6.6.

Table 6.6 Initial values of the global text attributes

CHARACTER HEIGHT	WC	0.01 (i.e. 1% of the height of the default window)
CHARACTER UP VECTOR	WC	(0,1)
TEXT COLOUR INDEX		1
TEXT INDEX		1
TEXT PATH		RIGHT
TEXT ALIGNMENT		(NORMAL;NORMAL)
TEXT FONT AND PRECISION		(1;STRING)
CHARACTER EXPANSION FACTOR		1
CHARACTER SPACING		0

SET CHARACTER HEIGHT   GKOP, WSOP, WSAC, SGOP   L0 a

Parameters:

| Input | character height | WC | >0 | R |

Effect:

The 'current character height' entry in the GKS state list is set to the value specified by the parameter. This value is used for creating subsequent TEXT output primitives.

Errors:

| 8 | GKS not in proper state: GKS should be in one of the states GKOP, WSOP, WSAC or SGOP |
| 78 | Character height is less than or equal to zero |

———————————————— *FORTRAN Interface* ————————————————

CALL GSCHH (CHH)

Parameters:

| Input | CHH | character height | WC | >0 | REAL |

SET CHARACTER UP VECTOR   GKOP, WSOP, WSAC, SGOP   L0 a

Parameters:

| Input | character up vector | WC | | $2 \times R$ |

Effect:

The 'current character up vector' entry in the GKS state list is set to the value specified by the parameter. This value is used for creating subsequent TEXT output primitives.

Errors:

| 8 | GKS not in proper state: GKS should be in one of the states GKOP, WSOP, WSAC or SGOP |
| 79 | Length of character up vector is zero |

———————————————— *FORTRAN Interface* ————————————————

CALL GSCHUP (CHUX, CHUY)

Parameters:

| Input | CHUX, CHUY | character up vector | WC | | $2 \times$ REAL |

SET TEXT COLOUR INDEX   GKOP, WSOP, WSAC, SGOP   L0 a

Parameters:

| Input | text colour index | | (0..n) | I |

Effect:

The 'current text colour index' entry in the GKS state list is set equal to the value specified by the parameter. When the 'current text colour index ASF' entry in the GKS state list is INDIVIDUAL, subsequently generated TEXT output primitives will be displayed with this text colour index. When the 'current text colour index ASF' entry in the GKS state list is BUNDLED, this function will not affect the display of subsequently created TEXT output primitives until the 'current text colour index ASF' is reset.

The colour index is a pointer to the colour tables at the workstations. If the specified colour index is not present in a workstation colour table, a workstation dependent colour index is used at that workstation.

Errors:

| 8 | GKS not in proper state: GKS should be in one of the states GKOP, WSOP, WSAC or SGOP |
| 92 | Colour index is less than zero |

Examples are illustrated with STROKE precision,
a character expansion factor of 1 and a zero
character spacing.

character height

CHARACTER HEIGHT = 1, CHARACTER UP VECTOR = (0,1),
TEXT PATH = RIGHT, TEXT ALIGNMENT = (NORMAL,NORMAL)

CHARACTER HEIGHT = 0.5, CHARACTER UP VECTOR = (0,1)
TEXT PATH = RIGHT, TEXT ALIGNMENT = (NORMAL,NORMAL)

CHARACTER HEIGHT = 1, CHARACTER UP VECTOR = (0,1),
TEXT PATH = RIGHT, TEXT ALIGNMENT = (RIGHT,TOP)

CHARACTER HEIGHT = 1
CHARACTER UP VECTOR = (0,1)
TEXT PATH = DOWN
TEXT ALIGNMENT = (NORMAL,NORMAL)

CHARACTER HEIGHT = 1
CHARACTER UP VECTOR = (−1,0)
TEXT PATH = RIGHT
TEXT ALIGNMENT = (NORMAL,NORMAL)

X   text position
------ baseline or centreline
— — — text extent rectangle
       (indicated for PATH = DOWN)
N.B.: capline = topline in these
       examples

Figure 6.16a Examples of the effect of
text attributes

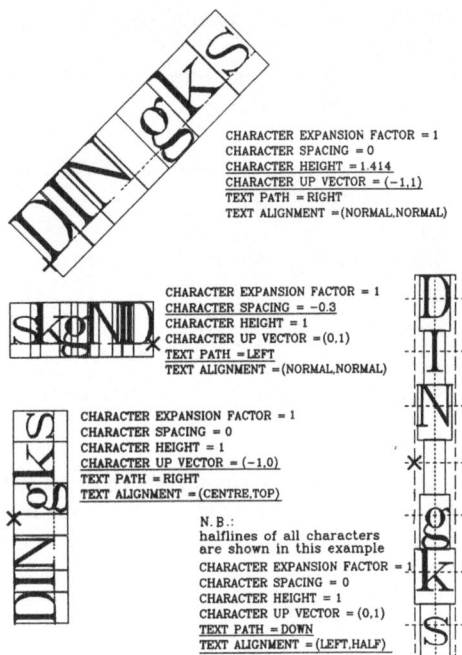

CHARACTER EXPANSION FACTOR = 1
CHARACTER SPACING = 0
CHARACTER HEIGHT = 1.414
CHARACTER UP VECTOR = (−1,1)
TEXT PATH = RIGHT
TEXT ALIGNMENT = (NORMAL,NORMAL)

CHARACTER EXPANSION FACTOR = 1
CHARACTER SPACING = −0.3
CHARACTER HEIGHT = 1
CHARACTER UP VECTOR = (0,1)
TEXT PATH = LEFT
TEXT ALIGNMENT = (NORMAL,NORMAL)

CHARACTER EXPANSION FACTOR = 1
CHARACTER SPACING = 0
CHARACTER HEIGHT = 1
CHARACTER UP VECTOR = (−1,0)
TEXT PATH = RIGHT
TEXT ALIGNMENT = (CENTRE,TOP)

N.B.:
halflines of all characters
are shown in this example
CHARACTER EXPANSION FACTOR = 1
CHARACTER SPACING = 0
CHARACTER HEIGHT = 1
CHARACTER UP VECTOR = (0,1)
TEXT PATH = DOWN
TEXT ALIGNMENT = (LEFT,HALF)

Figure 6.16b Examples of the effect of
text attributes (continued)

—————————————————— *FORTRAN Interface* ——————————————————

CALL GSTXCI (COLI)
Parameters:
Input   COLI   colour index   (0..n)   INTEGER

SET TEXT INDEX   GKOP, WSOP, WSAC, SGOP   L0a
Parameters:
Input   text index   (1..n)   I
Effect:
The 'current text index' entry in the GKS state list is set equal to the value specified
by the parameter. This value is used for creating subsequent TEXT output primitives.
Errors:
    8   GKS not in proper state: GKS should be in one of the states GKOP, WSOP,
             WSAC or SGOP
    72   Text index is invalid

—————————————————— *FORTRAN Interface* ——————————————————

CALL GSTXI (INDEX)
Parameters:
Input   INDEX   text index   (1..n)   INTEGER

SET TEXT PATH   GKOP, WSOP, WSAC, SGOP   L0a
Parameters:
Input   text path   (RIGHT, LEFT, UP, DOWN)   E
Effect:
The 'current text path' entry in the GKS state list is set equal to the value specified
by the parameter. This value is used for creating subsequent TEXT output primitives.
Errors:
    8   GKS not in proper state: GKS should be in one of the states GKOP, WSOP,
             WSAC or SGOP

—————————————————— *FORTRAN Interface* ——————————————————

CALL GSTXP (TXP)
Parameters:
Input   TXP   text path   (0 = right, 1 = left, 2 = up, 3 = down)   INTEGER

SET TEXT ALIGNMENT   GKOP, WSOP, WSAC, SGOP   L0a
Parameters:
Input   text alignment   (NORMAL, LEFT, CENTRE, RIGHT;
                                NORMAL, TOP, CAP, HALF, BASE, BOTTOM)   2 × E
Effect:
The 'current text alignment' entry in the GKS state list is set equal to the value
specified by the parameter. This value is used for creating subsequent TEXT output
primitives. Text alignment has two components: horizontal and vertical.
Errors:
    8   GKS not in proper state: GKS should be in one of the states GKOP, WSOP,
             WSAC or SGOP

─────────────── *FORTRAN Interface* ───────────────

CALL GSTXAL (TXALH, TXALV)

Parameters:

Input	TXALH	text alignment horizontal

              (0 = normal, 1 = left, 2 = centre, 3 = right)   INTEGER

Input	TXALV	text alignment vertical

              (0 = normal, 1 = top, 2 = cap, 3 = half, 4 = base, 5 = bottom)   INTEGER

SET TEXT FONT AND PRECISION   GKOP, WSOP, WSAC, SGOP   L0a

Parameters:

Input   text font and precision

              $(-n.. -1, 1..n;$ STRING, CHAR, STROKE)   (I; E)

Effect:

The 'current text font and precision' entry in the GKS state list is set equal to the value specified by the parameter. When the 'current text font and precision ASF' entry in the GKS state list is INDIVIDUAL, subsequently generated TEXT output primitives will be displayed with this text font and precision. When the 'current text font and precision ASF' entry in the GKS state list is BUNDLED, this function will not affect the display of subsequently created TEXT output primitives until the 'current text font and precision ASF' is reset.

Text font and precision is a single text aspect; a particular text font can be available at some, but not necessarily all, precisions. Text font 1 contains a graphical representation of the characters defined in ISO 646. Text fonts greater than 1 are reserved for registration or future standardization. Text fonts less than 0 are implementation-dependent. The text precision value determines the exactitude with which the other text aspects are used. The values of text precision, in order of increasing exactitude, are STRING, CHAR, and STROKE.

If the specified text font is not available at a workstation, the value (1; STRING) is used at that workstation.

Errors:

8	GKS not in proper state: GKS should be in one of the states GKOP, WSOP, WSAC or SGOP
75	Text font is equal to zero

─────────────── *FORTRAN Interface* ───────────────

CALL GSTXFP (FONT, PREC)

Parameters:

Input	FONT	text font	$(-n.. -1, 1..n)$	INTEGER
Input	PREC	text precision	(0 = string, 1 = char, 2 = stroke)	INTEGER

SET CHARACTER EXPANSION FACTOR
                                         GKOP, WSOP, WSAC, SGOP   L0a

Parameters:

Input   character expansion factor   > 0   R

Effect:

The 'current character expansion factor' entry in the GKS state list is set equal to the value specified by the parameter.

When the 'current character expansion factor ASF' entry in the GKS state list is INDIVIDUAL, subsequently generated TEXT output primitives will be displayed with this character expansion factor. When the 'current character expansion factor ASF' entry in the GKS state list is BUNDLED, this function will not affect the display of subsequently created TEXT output primitives until the 'current character expansion factor ASF' is reset.

Errors:

8   GKS not in proper state: GKS should be in one of the states GKOP, WSOP, WSAC or SGOP

77   Character expansion factor is less than or equal to zero

———————————————— *FORTRAN Interface* ————————————————

CALL GSCHXP (CHXP)

Parameters:

Input   CHXP   character expansion factor   >0   REAL

———

SET CHARACTER SPACING   GKOP, WSOP, WSAC, SGOP   L0a

Parameters:

Input   character spacing   R

Effect:

The 'current character spacing' entry in the GKS state list is set equal to the value specified by the parameter.

When the 'current character spacing ASF' entry in the GKS state list is INDIVIDUAL, subsequently generated TEXT ouput primitives will be displayed with this character spacing. When the 'current character spacing ASF' entry in the GKS state list is BUNDLED, this function will not affect the display of subsequently created TEXT output primitives until the 'current character spacing ASF' is reset.

Errors:

8   GKS not in proper state: GKS should be in one of the states GKOP, WSOP, WSAC or SGOP

———————————————— *FORTRAN Interface* ————————————————

CALL GSCHSP (CHSP)

Parameters:

Input   CHSP   character spacing   REAL

6.4.6   Workstation-Dependent TEXT Attributes

The GKS function SET TEXT REPRESENTATION allows the selection of text attributes TEXT FONT AND PRECISION, CHARACTER EXPANSION FACTOR, CHARACTER SPACING, and TEXT COLOUR INDEX for each workstation as a bundle. These values are accessed via TEXT INDEX if the respective aspect source flag is BUNDLED.

The capabilities of each workstation with respect to these attributes can be determined from the workstation description table. If capabilities are requested which are not supported at the workstation, GKS will generate an error message. This contrasts with the treatment of the global attributes. Here, an attribute which is not supported at a particular workstation is mapped automatically to an appropriate valid value.

SET TEXT REPRESENTATION   WSP,WSAC,SGOP   L0a

Parameters:

Input	workstation identifier		N
Input	text index	(1..n)	I
Input	text font and precision		
		(−n.. −1,1..n; STRING,CHAR,STROKE)	(I;E)
Input	character expansion factor	>0	R
Input	character spacing		R
Input	text colour index	(0..n)	I

Effect:

In the text bundle table of the workstation state list, the given text index is associated with the specified parameters.

Text font and precision: gives the text font to be used and determines the exactitude with which the other text attributes are used. Text font 1 contains a graphical representation of the characters defined in ISO 646. Text fonts greater than 1 are reserved for registration or future standardization. Text fonts less than 0 are implementation-dependent.

Character expansion factor: specifies the deviation of the width to height ratio of the characters from the ratio indicated by the font designer.

Character spacing: specifies how much additional space is to be inserted between two adjacent character bodies. Character spacing is specified as a fraction of the font-nominal character height.

Text colour index: a pointer to the colour table of the workstation.

The text bundle table in the workstation state list has predefined entries taken from the workstation description table; at least one should be predefined for every workstation of category OUTPUT and OUTIN. Any table entry (including the predefined entries) may be redefined by using this function.

When TEXT is displayed the TEXT index refers to an entry in the text bundle table. If TEXT is displayed with a text index which is not present in the text bundle table, text index 1 will be used. Which aspects in the entry are used depends upon the setting of the corresponding ASFs (cf. Section 6.8.2).

Errors:

7	GKS not in proper state: GKS should be in one of the states WSOP, WSAC or SGOP
20	Specified workstation identifier is invalid
25	Specified workstation is not open
33	Specified workstation is of category MI
35	Specified workstation is of category INPUT
36	Specified workstation is Workstation-Independent Segment Storage
72	Text index is invalid
75	Text font is equal to zero
76	Requested text font is not supported for the required precision on this workstation
77	Character expansion factor is less than or equal to zero
93	Colour index is invalid

──────────── *FORTRAN Interface* ────────────

CALL GSTXR (WKID,TXI,FONT,PREC,CHXP,CHSP,COLI)

Parameters:

Input	WKID	workstation identifier		INTEGER
Input	TXI	text index	$(1..n)$	INTEGER
Input	FONT	text font	$(-n.. -1,1..n)$	INTEGER
Input	PREC	text precision	$(0 =$ string, $1 =$ char, $2 =$ stroke$)$	INTEGER
Input	CHXP	character expansion factor	> 0	REAL
Input	CHSP	character spacing		REAL
Input	COLI	colour index	$(0..n)$	INTEGER

6.5   FILL AREA Primitive

FILL AREA is used to display areas. It generates a closed polygon which is filled with a uniform colour, a pattern, or a hatch style. Workstations having difficulties with such techniques must at least draw a hollow polygon.

The FILL AREA primitive has gained increasingly in importance with the advent of colour raster displays where the main primitive is the display of solid areas. Areas have been of interest before but other devices did not provide adequate capabilities. Black and white raster displays can easily display solid areas but there are no colours available to distinguish between different areas. This difficulty has been overcome by providing a set of characteristic patterns with which the areas can be filled. Vector devices use hatching for displaying areas, for example, in cartography and in business graphics. However, the hatching algorithm is computationally expensive so that interactive vector devices usually abandon hatching for efficiency reasons.

The different methods of area display have been combined into one FILL AREA primitive. By using workstation-specific aspects, this primitive allows one to address the appropriate technique at each workstation.

Areas are defined by their bounding polygon. The polygon given in the parameter list is closed by connecting the last point with the first one. There are no restrictions concerning the shape of the polygon; it may define convex and nonconvex areas and may cross itself. Figure 6.17 shows how the interior of the polygon is defined in such cases. However, insular structures, i.e., areas with holes which require several separate polygons to be defined, have been excluded from GKS. Such structures were regarded as being outside the scope of a kernel system and, therefore, must be handled on top of GKS.

FILL AREA is clipped precisely around the clipping rectangle. Therefore, clipping may change the boundaries of the area and even generate multiple subareas from one area (cf. Figure 6.18).

A problem which does exist for all primitives but which has special relevance for FILL AREA is the treatment of overlapping primitives. In the case of line primitives, overlapping occurs only at points of intersection and, usually, is ignored. With FILL AREA, large portions of the display can be overlapped and a decision has be be taken as to which primitive is to be displayed and which primitive is to be partially suppressed.

For this reason, GKS has introduced a segment priority which, at least at the segment level, allows one to specify which primitives should be preferred (cf. Section 7.6 for details).

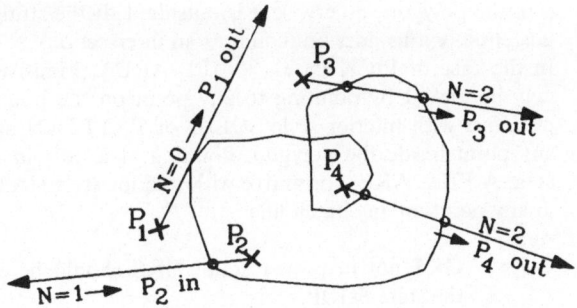

P_i :   points to be tested

N: intersection count

Figure 6.17 Testing whether P lies inside a polygon

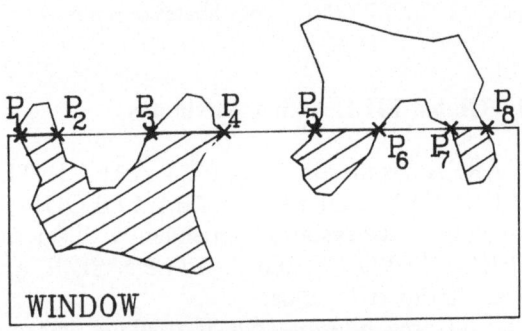

WINDOW

⬜ resulting AREAs after clipping at the WINDOW

× P_i points added to polygon

Figure 6.18 Examples of FILL AREA clipping

FILL AREA   WSAC,SGOP   L0a

Parameters:

Input	number of points		(3..n)	I
Input	coordinates of points	WC		$n \times P$

Effect:

A FILL AREA primitive is generated. The current values of the fill area attributes, as given by the GKS state list (cf. Section 3.4), are bound to the primitive. The polygon, defined by the points, is filled according to the fill area interior style currently selected. When using HOLLOW style the boundary of this polygon is drawn. It is not drawn when using any other interior styles.

If parts of the area are clipped, the resulting new boundaries generated become part of the area boundaries. Multiple subareas may be generated (cf. Figure 6.18).

The interior of a polygon is defined in the following way (cf. Figure 6.17): For a given point, create a straight line starting at that point and going to infinity. If the number of intersections between the straight line and the polygon is odd, the point is in the polygon; otherwise it is outside it. If the straight line passes a polygon vertex tangentially, this does not count as an intersection.

In the case of PICK input, a FILL AREA primitive with interior style HOLLOW may be picked by pointing to any point on the bounding polygon. A FILL AREA primitive with interior style SOLID or PATTERN may be identified by pointing at any point inside the polygon. Pointing at a hole in the area does not identify that area. A FILL AREA primitive with interior style HATCH may be picked by pointing to any point on any hatch line.

Errors:

5	GKS not in proper state: GKS should be either in the state WSAC or in the state SGOP
100	Number of points is invalid

———————————————— *FORTRAN Interface* ————————————————

CALL GFA (N,PX,PY)
Parameter:

Input	N	number of points		INTEGER
Input	PX(N),PY(N)	coordinates of points	WC	2 × n × REAL

6.5.1   Global FILL AREA Attributes

FILL AREA has the attributes FILL AREA INTERIOR STYLE, FILL AREA STYLE INDEX, and FILL AREA COLOUR INDEX which can either be set globally or workstation-dependently. Two further attributes, PATTERN REFERENCE POINT and PATTERN SIZE, are relevant only for a specific fill area interior style value.

The fill area interior style is used to determine the style to be used for filling the area. It has the following values:

SOLID: The interior of the polygon is filled with the colour specified by the fill area colour index. This style is usually used on colour raster displays.

PATTERN: The interior of the polygon is filled with a pattern specified by the fill area style index. In this context, the style index points to an adjustable pattern table and is therefore, sometimes referred to as the pattern index. Patterns are widely used on black-and-white raster devices as they are the only means of distinguishing different areas. Colour raster devices may use patterns for generating textures.

HATCH: The interior of the polygon is hatched using the colour specified by the fill area colour index. In this context, the style index points to an implementation-provided hatch table containing different hatch styles and is, therefore, sometimes referred to as the hatch index. Hatching is a technique primarily used with plotters.

HOLLOW: There is no filling of the area, but the bounding polyline is drawn, using the fill area colour index. Linetype and linewidth are implementation-dependent. This style is often used with vector refresh displays which have a limited number of displayable vectors.

Figure 6.19 Example of a map with hatching

Fill area attributes on a colour raster display are shown in Figure C2 (page 618), a map with solid area filling is shown in Figure C4 (page 619), hatching on a flatbed plotter is illustrated in Figure C8 (page 621). Figure 6.19 shows hatching in black and white.

In the case of fill area interior style PATTERN, two global attributes, PATTERN REFERENCE POINT and PATTERN SIZE, define the geometry of the pattern rectangle. The pattern rectangle is parallel to the axes in WC space. Its extent in the x- and y-directions is given by the PATTERN SIZE values SX, SY > 0. PATTERN REFERENCE POINT defines the location of one corner point. As the pattern is replicated, it is immaterial which one is taken. The style index points to a pattern table on the workstation. The pattern can be set by SET PATTERN REPRESENTATION (cf. Section 6.5.2). Each entry contains an array of COLOUR INDICES.

The pattern rectangle is divided into a regular grid of cells according to the dimensions DX, DY of the colour index array. Each cell is assigned a colour index from the colour index array so that array fields (1,1), (1,DY), (DX,1), and (DX,DY) correspond to the upper left, lower left, upper right, and lower right corner of the pattern rectangle (cf. Figure 6.20). The pattern rectangle is repeated in all directions parallel to its sides until the interior of the polygon is covered completely. Then the cells are transformed and mapped to the pixels of the workstation. The pixels of a workstation are assigned colour indices by point sampling the transformed cells at the pixel's centrepoint. If a pixel's centrepoint lies inside the transformed polygon, it is assigned the colour index of the transformed cell the centrepoint lies in. Otherwise, the pixel is not touched. This scheme compares exactly with the scheme described for

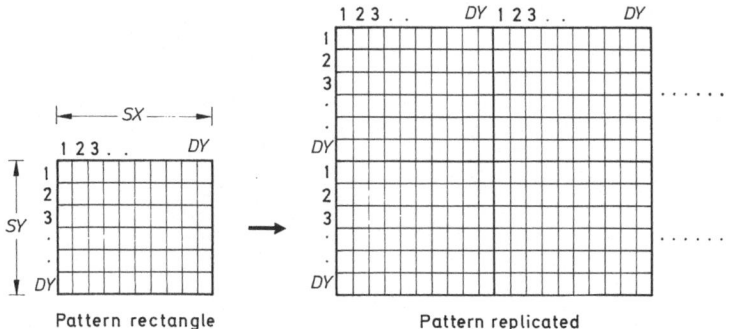

Pattern rectangle   Pattern replicated

Figure 6.20 Definition of patterns

CELL ARRAY (cf. Section 6.6), the only difference being that CELL ARRAY is limited by the cell array rectangle whereas FILL AREA is limited by the polygon.

Transformation of patterns is necessary if one wants to get a realistic view of transformed picture parts. If the pattern is not transformed, a viewer has the impression of looking through a moving outline onto a wall with a stationary wallpaper pattern.

Workstations are not required to perform all types of area display. The workstation description table indicates the capabilities supported by a specific workstation type. In the case of a workstation which is able to display areas with patterns but cannot transform the patterns, it is then appropriate to generate non-transformable patterns to fill a polygon.

For interior style HATCH, the style index selects the desired hatch pattern. Each workstation must support at least one hatch style. If a workstation has no hatching capacity, using this hatch style will produce the same effect as HOLLOW. The hatch patterns cannot be set by the application program. It is only possible to make a choice between hatch patterns provided by the implementor of GKS. Whether hatching is affected by transformations or not is workstation-dependent.

Although not stated explicitly in the standard, it seems to be good practice to make the hatch styles depend on the PATTERN REFERENCE POINT and PATTERN SIZE. The PATTERN REFERENCE POINT can be used to align hatching. This enables the hatching of independent areas to be aligned with each other and solves the problem of hatch lines coinciding with the area boundary.

PATTERN SIZE can be used to control the distance between hatch lines. The implementation of such hatch styles has to be documented in the implementation documentation.

If a workstation is not capable of producing the interior styles SOLID, PATTERN or HATCH, the minimal action required is the interior style HOLLOW.

The representation of FILL AREA at the workstation can be controlled by the current FILL AREA INDEX, which is a pointer to the fill area bundle table.

SET FILL AREA INTERIOR STYLE   GKOP, WSOP, WSAC, SGOP   L0a

Parameters:

Input   fill area interior style   (HOLLOW, SOLID, PATTERN, HATCH)   E

Effect:

The 'current fill area interior style' entry in the GKS state list is set equal to the value specified by the parameter. When the 'current fill area interior style ASF' entry in the GKS state list is INDIVIDUAL, subsequently generated FILL AREA output primitives will be displayed with this fill area interior style. When the 'current fill area interior style ASF' entry in the GKS state list is BUNDLED, this function will not affect the display of subsequently created FILL AREA output primitives until the 'current fill area interior style ASF' is reset.

The fill area interior style is used to determine in what style the area is to be filled. If the requested interior style is not available at a workstation, HOLLOW will be used on that workstation.

Errors:

8   GKS not in proper state: GKS should be in one of the states GKOP, WSOP, WSAC or SGOP

———————————————— *FORTRAN Interface* ————————————————

CALL GSFAIS (INTS)

Parameters:

Input   INTS   interior style

(0 = hollow, 1 = solid, 2 = pattern, 3 = hatch)   INTEGER

SET FILL AREA STYLE INDEX   GKOP, WSOP, WSAC, SGOP   L0a

Parameters:

Input   fill area style index $(-n.. -1, 1..n)$ I

Effect:

The 'current fill area style index' entry in the GKS state list is set equal to the value specified by the parameter. When the 'current fill area style index ASF' entry in the GKS state list is INDIVIDUAL, subsequently generated FILL AREA output primitives will be displayed with this fill area style index. When the 'current fill area style index ASF' entry in the GKS state list is BUNDLED, this function will not affect the display of subsequently created FILL AREA output primitives until the 'current fill area style index ASF' is reset.

In the case of interior styles HOLLOW and SOLID, the style index value is unused. For interior style PATTERN, the style index value is greater than 0 and points to the pattern tables of the workstations. For interior style HATCH, the style index value is non-zero and determines which of a number of workstation-dependent hatch styles is used: hatch styles greater than 0 are reserved for registration or future standardization; hatch styles less than 0 are workstation-dependent.

If the requested style index is not available at a particular workstation, style index 1 is used at that workstation. If style index 1 is not present at that workstation, the result is workstation-dependent.

Errors:

8   GKS not in proper state: GKS should be in one of the states GKOP, WSOP, WSAC or SGOP

84   Style (pattern or hatch) index is equal to zero

——————————————— *FORTRAN Interface* ———————————————

CALL GSFASI (STYLI)
Parameters:
Input   STYLI   fill area style index $(-n..1,1..n)$ INTEGER

SET FILL AREA COLOUR INDEX   GKOP,WSOP,WSAC,SGOP   L0a
Parameters:
Input   fill area colour index $(0..n)$ I
Effect:
The 'current fill area colour index' entry in the GKS state list is set equal to the value specified by the parameter. When the 'current fill area colour index ASF' entry in the GKS state list is INDIVIDUAL, subsequently generated FILL AREA output primitives will be displayed with this fill area colour index. When the 'current fill area colour index ASF' entry in the GKS state list is BUNDLED, this function will not affect the display of subsequently created FILL AREA output primitives until the 'current fill area colour index ASF' is reset.
The colour index is a pointer to the colour tables of the workstations. If the specified colour index is not present in a workstation colour table, a workstation-dependent colour index is used at that workstation.
Errors:
   8   GKS not in proper state: GKS should be in one of the states GKOP, WSOP, WSAC or SGOP
   92   Colour index is less than zero

——————————————— *FORTRAN Interface* ———————————————

CALL GSFACI (COLI)
Parameters:
Input   COLI   colour index $(0..n)$ INTEGER

SET FILL AREA INDEX   GKOP,WSOP,WSAC,SGOP   L0a
Parameters:
Input   fill area index $(1..n)$ I
Effect:
The 'current fill area index' entry in the GKS state list is set equal to the value specified by the parameter. This value is used for creating subsequent FILL AREA output primitives.
Errors:
   8   GKS not in proper state: GKS should be in one of the states GKOP, WSOP, WSAC or SGOP
   80   Fill area index is invalid

——————————————— *FORTRAN Interface* ———————————————

CALL GSFAI (INDEX)
Parameters:
Input   INDEX   fill area index $(1..n)$ INTEGER

SET PATTERN SIZE   GKOP,WSOP,WSAC,SGOP   L0a
Parameters:
Input   pattern size   WC   SX,SY>0 $2 \times R$

Effect:
The 'current pattern size' entry in the GKS state list is set equal to the value specified by the parameter. When the currently selected (either via the fill area bundle or individually, depending on the corresponding ASF) fill area interior style is PATTERN, this value is used, where possible, in conjunction with the 'current pattern reference point' entry in the GKS state list to display the FILL AREA output primitives.

Errors:

8	GKS not in proper state: GKS should be in one of the states GKOP, WSOP, WSAC or SGOP
81	Pattern size value is not positive

——————————————————— *FORTRAN Interface* ———————————————————

CALL GSPA (SX,SY)
Parameters:
Input   SX,SY   pattern size   WC   SX,SY>0   2×REAL

SET PATTERN REFERENCE POINT   GKOP,WSOP,WSAC,SGOP   L0a
Parameters:
Input   reference point   WC   P
Effect:
The 'current pattern reference point' entry in the GKS state list is set equal to the value specified by the parameter. When the currently selected (either via the fill area bundle or individually, depending on the corresponding ASF) fill area interior style is PATTERN, this value is used, where possible, in conjunction with the 'current pattern size' entry in the GKS state list to display the FILL AREA output primitives.

Errors:

8	GKS not in proper state: GKS should be in one of the states GKOP, WSOP, WSAC or SGOP

——————————————————— *FORTRAN Interface* ———————————————————

CALL GSPARF (RFX,RFY)
Parameters:
Input   RFX,RFY   pattern reference point   WC   2×REAL

6.5.2   Workstation-Dependent FILL AREA Attributes

The GKS function SET FILL AREA REPRESENTATION allows the selection of the fill area attributes FILL AREA INTERIOR STYLE, FILL AREA STYLE INDEX, and FILL AREA COLOUR INDEX for each individual workstation. These values are accessed via a FILL AREA INDEX if the respective aspect source flag is BUNDLED.

The capabilities of each workstation with respect to these attributes can be determined from the workstation description table. If capabilities are requested which, however, are not supported at a workstation, GKS will generate an error message. This contrasts with the treatment of the global attributes where a specified attribute which is not supported at a particular workstation is mapped automatically to an appropriate valid value.

If a workstation supports interior style PATTERN, there then is a pattern table at that workstation which describes the patterns to be used for area filling. For GKS output levels 1 and 2, at least 10 entries must be present which can be redefined via the function SET PATTERN REPRESENTATION. The application program has to specify a colour index array which defines the pattern unit which is to be repeated until it covers any given area. The location and the size of this pattern unit is determined by the global attributes PATTERN REFERENCE POINT and PATTERN SIZE introduced in the previous section.

SET FILL AREA REPRESENTATION   WSOP, WSAC, SGOP   L1a
Parameters:

Input	workstation identifier		N
Input	fill area index	$(1..n)$	I
Input	fill area interior style	(HOLLOW, SOLID, PATTERN, HATCH)	E
Input	fill area style index	$(-n..-1, 1..n)$	I
Input	fill area colour index	$(0..n)$	I

Effect:

In the fill area bundle table of the workstation state list, the given fill area index is associated with the specified parameters.

Fill area interior style: is used to determine which style the area should be filled with.

Fill area style index: In the case of the interior styles HOLLOW and SOLID, this value is unused. For style PATTERN, it is a pointer to the pattern table of the workstation. For style HATCH, its value determines which of a number of workstation-dependent hatch styles is used: hatch styles greater than 0 are reserved for registration or future standardization; hatch styles less than 0 are workstation-dependent.

Fill area colour index: Pointer to the colour table of the workstation.

The fill area bundle table in the workstation state list has predefined entries taken from the workstation description table; at least one should be predefined for every workstation of category OUTPUT and OUTIN. Any table entry (including the predefined entries) may be redefined by using this function.

When fill area is displayed, the current fill area index refers to an entry in the fill area bundle table. If FILL AREAS are displayed with a fill area index which is not present in the fill area bundle table, fill area index 1 is used. Which aspects in the entry are used depends upon the setting of the corresponding ASFs (cf. Section 6.8.2).

Errors:

7	GKS not in proper state: GKS should be in one of the states WSOP, WSAC or SGOP
20	Specified workstation identifier is invalid
25	Specified workstation is not open
33	Specified workstation is of category MI
35	Specified workstation is of category INPUT
36	Specified workstation is Workstation-Independent Segment Storage
80	Fill area index is invalid
83	Specified fill area interior style is not supported on this workstation
85	Specified pattern index is invalid
86	Specified hatch style is not supported on this workstation
93	Colour index is invalid

———————————————— *FORTRAN Interface* ————————————————

CALL GSFAR (WKID,FAI,INTS,STYLI,COLI)

Parameters:

Input	WKID	workstation identifier		INTEGER
Input	FAI	fill area index	(1..n)	INTEGER
Input	INTS	fill area interior style		
		(0 = hollow, 1 = solid, 2 = pattern, 3 = hatch)		INTEGER
Input	STYLI	fill area style index	(−n.. −1,1..n)	INTEGER
Input	COLI	fill area colour index	(0..n)	INTEGER

SET PATTERN REPRESENTATION	WSOP,WSAC,SGOP L1a

Parameters:

Input	workstation identifier		N
Input	pattern index	(1..n)	I
Input	dimensions of pattern array DX,DY	(1..n)	2 × I
Input	pattern array	(0..n)	n × n × I

Effect:

In the pattern table of the workstation state list, the given pattern index is associated with the specified parameters. A grid of DX × DY cells (DX horizontal, DY vertical) is specified. The colour is given individually for each cell by a colour index, which is a pointer to the colour table of the workstation.

If the workstation supports interior style PATTERN, the pattern table in the workstation state list has predefined entries taken from the workstation description table. Any table entry (including the predefined entries) may be redefined with this function. When a fill area is displayed, if the currently selected (either via the fill area bundle or individually, depending upon the corresponding ASF) interior style is PATTERN, the currently selected style index refers to an entry in the pattern table. If fill areas are displayed with a pattern index which is not present in the pattern table, pattern index 1 will be used. If pattern index 1 is not present, the result is workstation-dependent.

Errors:

7	GKS not in proper state: GKS should be in one of the states WSOP, WSAC or SGOP
20	Specified workstation identifier is invalid
25	Specified workstation is not open
33	Specified workstation is of category MI
35	Specified workstation is of category INPUT
36	Specified workstation is Workstation-Independent Segment Storage
85	Specified pattern index is invalid
90	Interior style PATTERN is not supported on this workstation
91	Dimensions of colour array are invalid
93	Colour index is invalid

———————————————— *FORTRAN Interface* ————————————————

CALL GSPAR (WKID,PAI,DIMX,DIMY,ISC,ISR,DX,DY,COLIA)

Input	WKID	workstation identifier		INTEGER
Input	PAI	pattern index	(1..n)	INTEGER
Input	DIMX,DIMY	dimensions of COLIA	(1..n)	2 × INTEGER
Input	ISC,ISR	indices to start column, start row	(1..n)	2 × INTEGER
Input	DX,DY	number of columns, rows used	(1..n)	2 × INTEGER
Input	COLIA	colour index array	(0..n)	
	(DIMX,DIMY)			n × n × INTEGER

6.6   CELL ARRAY Primitive

The output primitive CELL ARRAY is used to pass raster images to GKS. The raster image is defined by a colour index matrix, and its size and position are determined by a rectangle in WC. All workstations must accept this primitive. However, it is not intended that workstations with inadequate capabilities should have to simulate colour raster displays. The minimum reaction expected is to draw the boundaries of the cell rectangle.

Whereas the FILL AREA primitive introduced in the previous section allows only one colour or one pattern to be specified for the whole area, CELL ARRAY allows areas to be specified with varying colours where the dimensions of the colour array determine the resolution. Therefore, this primitive is well-suited to displaying photographic images with some random colour distribution or surfaces with continuously varying colours (cf. Figure C3 on page 619).

Given the close relationship between the CELL ARRAY primitive and the hardware of raster devices, one might expect that the matrix specified in the primitive's definition would be immediately mapped onto the pixels of the raster device. However, in order to maintain consistency with other GKS primitives, the CELL ARRAY primitive is defined in WC space and has to be transformed like all other GKS primitives. Otherwise, it could not be used together with other primitives. However, this does not imply that transformation of CELL ARRAY is the usual case. If an application requires pixels only at a specific workstation to be addressed immediately, it will set transformations in such a way that each cell of CELL ARRAY corresponds exactly to one pixel on the display surface.

The cell rectangle is parallel to the world coordinate axes. Its extent is specified by two diagonal points $P = (PX, PY)$ and $Q = (QX, QY)$. The cell rectangle is divided into a regular grid with congruent rectangular cells so that the number of cell rows and columns corresponds to the dimensions DX, DY of the colour index array. Each cell is assigned a colour index from the colour index array so that the array fields $(1,1)$, $(1,DY)$, $(DX,1)$, and (DX,DY) correspond to the cells adjacent to the points P, (PX,QY), (QX,PY), and Q, respectively (cf. Figure 6.21).

The grid defined in WC is subject to all transformations potentially rotating the grid and transforming the rectangular cells into parallelograms and to clipping. Then the colour index of a pixel on a workstation is set by point sampling the transformed cells at the pixel's centrepoint. If a pixel's centrepoint lies inside a transformed cell, it is assigned the corresponding colour index. Otherwise, the pixel is not touched.

The simple point sampling approach of GKS has some disadvantages compared to area sampling or filtering. Transformed CELL ARRAYS may show unexpected distortions due to the rounding of transformed cells to the pixels available on the workstation. However, it is the responsibility of the application program to avoid such effects by carefully selecting transformations or by choosing an appropriate resolution of the CELL ARRAY.

CELL ARRAY has no attributes other than PICK IDENTIFIER. The colours are specified by using a matrix of colour indices in the definition of

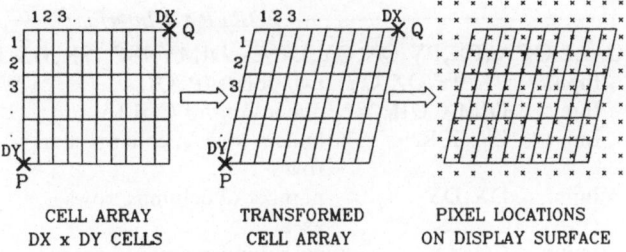

CELL ARRAY DX x DY CELLS	TRANSFORMED CELL ARRAY	PIXEL LOCATIONS ON DISPLAY SURFACE

Cells are mapped on display surface.
If display location is within cell then
cell colour is assigned to pixel.

Figure 6.21   Mapping of CELL ARRAY

a cell array rather than as separate attributes. However, these colour indices are handled just the same as the colour indices used as attributes for other primitives.

CELL ARRAY   WSAC, SGOP   L0a
Parameters:

Input cell rectangle (P,Q)	WC	$2 \times P$
Input dimensions of colour index array DX,DY	(1..n)	$2 \times I$
Input colour index array	(0..n)	$n \times n \times I$

Effect:

A CELL ARRAY primitive is generated using the cell rectangle corners, the dimensions of the colour index array and the colour index array.

A rectangle, which is taken to be aligned with the world coordinates axes, is defined by the points P and Q. This rectangle is conceptually divided into a grid in DX × DY cells. Each cell has a width of $|PX - QX|/DX$ and a height of $|PY - QY|/DY$, where (PX,PY) are the coordinates of the corner point P and (QX,QY) are the coordinates of the corner point Q. The colour of each cell is specified by the index of the corresponding element of the colour index array. If an index value is not present in the colour index table then a workstation-dependent index value is used.

The rectangular grid defined by P, Q, DX and DY is subject to all transformations which potentially transform the rectangular cells into parallelograms. If part of a transformed cell is outside the window, the transformed cell is partially clipped. Mapping the transformed cells onto the cells of a raster display is performed according to the following rules (cf. Figure 6.21):

a) If the centrepoint of a raster display pixel lies inside the parallelogram defined by the transformed rectangle, its colour is set.

b) The raster display pixel will be assigned the colour of the cell which contains the pixel's centrepoint. Thus, the pixel colour is selected by using point sampling on the transformed rectangle at the pixel centrepoint rather than area sampling or filtering.

The minimal simulation required is to draw the transformed boundaries of the cell rectangle, using implementation-dependent colour, linewidth and linetype.

Errors:

5   GKS not in proper state: GKS should be either in the state WSAC or in the state SGOP

91   Dimensions of colour array are invalid

———————————————— *FORTRAN Interface* ————————————————

CALL GCA (PX,PY,QX,QY,DIMX,DIMY,ISC,ISR,DX,DY COLIA)

Input	PX,PY,QX,QY	two points (P, Q)	WC	$4 \times$ REAL
Input	DIMX,DIMY	dimensions of COLIA	(1..n)	$2 \times$ INTEGER
Input	ISC,ISR	indices to start column, start row	(1..n)	$2 \times$ INTEGER
Input	DX,DY	number of columns, rows used	(1..n)	$2 \times$ INTEGER
Input	COLIA (DIMX,DIMY)	colour index array	(0..n)	$n \times n \times$ INTEGER

6.7   GENERALIZED DRAWING PRIMITIVE (GDP)

GENERALIZED DRAWING PRIMITIVE (GDP) is a standard way of providing additional non-standard output primitives. The purpose of GDP is to use the special capabilities of a workstation such as circle generation and spline interpolation.

The implementation documentation will specify which GDPs are available at a workstation and what parameters are needed to address them. The set of GDPs implemented at a workstation may be empty.

A specific GDP is selected by a GDP identifier. Geometric data is passed to the workstation via a list of points; non-geometric data is collected in a GDP data record.

Although GDP is a means of introducing non-standard primitives, it is assumed that the GKS design concepts are nevertheless adhered to. This implies that transformation and clipping of the geometric shape of a GDP is done correctly. For this purpose, GKS transforms the points before delivering them to the workstation. The clipping rectangle is sent to the workstation anyhow which enables the workstation to clip properly. There may be workstation facilities which cannot fulfill these requirements under all circumstances. For example, a circle interpolator may be unable to clip or to generate an ellipse which is required for non-uniform scaling of a circle. In such cases, the workstation will report error 105, thus indicating that the GDP has been handled incompletely or incorrectly.

An implementor of a GDP has to pay attention to the fact that, in some cases, the transformation of the points by GKS is not sufficient to ensure proper transformation of the shape of the GDP. For example, if a circle is defined by its centre and one peripheral point, a non-uniform transformation will still yield two points which define a circle rather than an ellipse. To ensure that proper transformation and proper error reporting takes place, a better definition ought to be selected (e.g., the centre and two appropriate peripheral points in the above case). Otherwise, knowledge about such specific GDPs must be included in the GKS nucleus to make proper handling possible.

It is not necessary that a GDP be supported. If a workstation does not support a specific GDP function, an error message is generated. At least a module generating the appropriate error messages must be implemented within

GKS. A good implementation should also provide an appropriate default action. This could be, for example, generating a POLYLINE with the geometric data of the GDP.

As a variety of GDPs can be defined by the implementor, no specific attributes are assigned to GDP except the PICK IDENTIFIER. However, if a specific GDP has features common to one or more of the other output primitives, the implementor may use the corresponding primitive attributes. Further accompanying information may be specified in a data record in the primitive's parameter list. This must be described in the implementation documentation.

GDP is not only a means of satisfying the exotic requirements of some users but it also provides some widely used primitives which have not yet found sufficient support to be included in the standard as primitives in their own right. However, it can be anticipated that the most common GDPs are good candidates for inclusion when new primitives are next reviewed for the GKS standard. For example, some kind of circle or conic arc will probably be included. In the meantime, the most common GDPs can be registered in the ISO International Register of Graphical Items, which is maintained by the Registration Authority. After approval by the ISO Working Group on Computer Graphics, currently known as ISO/TC97/SC21/WG2, the GDP identifier will be assigned by the Registration Authority. To avoid naming conflicts with implementation-specific GDPs, for all programming languages where the GDP identifier is represented by an integer, the same rule applies for GDP identifiers as it does for line styles, marker types, etc.: Negative values are free for implementors to use, whereas positive values are reserved for registration or future standardization.

GENERALIZED DRAWING PRIMITIVE (GDP)   WSAC,SGOP   L0a
Parameters:

Input	number of points		$(0..n)$	I
Input	points	WC		$n \times P$
Input	GDP identifier			N
Input	GDP data record			D

Effect:
A Generalized Drawing Primitive (GDP) of the type indicated by the GDP identifier is generated on the basis of the given points and the GDP data record. The current values of the entries in the GKS state list for the sets of polyline, polymarker, text, or fill area attributes are bound to the primitive. When the GDP generates output at a workstation, zero or more of the sets of attributes are used. These are the sets of attributes most appropriate for the specific GDP function and they are selected for the GDP as part of the definition of the GDP. (They are defined in the workstation description table.)

N.B.:
The parameters are transmitted to the workstation and interpreted in a workstation-specific way. In this way special capabilities of the workstation can be addressed. Even if error 104 or 105 occurs, the GDP is displayed on all active workstations capable of doing so. For example, some of the primitives anticipated at present are:
a) circle: points given are centre, peripheral point;
b) circular arc: points given are centre, start point, end point to be connected counter-clockwise in world coordinates;

c) ellipse: points given are 2 focal points, peripheral point;
d) elliptic arc: points given are 2 focal points, start point, end point to be connected counter-clockwise in world coordinates;
e) interpolating curve (for example, spline): points given are interpolated.

The recommended bundle to use for the above GDP examples would be the polyline attributes.

Errors:

5	GKS not in proper state: GKS should be either in the state WSAC or in the state SGOP
100	Number of points is invalid.
102	Generalized drawing primitive identifier is invalid
103	Content of generalized drawing primitive data record is invalid
104	At least one active workstation is not able to generate the specified generalized drawing primitive
105	At least one active workstation is not able to generate the specified generalized drawing primitive given the current transformations and clipping rectangle

——————————————— *FORTRAN Interface* ———————————————

CALL GGDP (N,PX,PY,PRIMID,LDR,DATREC)

Parameters:

Input	N	number of points	(0..n)	INTEGER
Input	PX(N),PY(N)	coordinates of points	WC	$2 \times n \times$ REAL
Input	PRIMID	GDP identifier	(-n..-1,1..n)	INTEGER
Input	LDR	length of data record	(0..n)	INTEGER
Input	DATREC (LDR)	data record		$n \times$ CHARACTER $*80$

N.B.:

GDP identifiers less than 0 can be used arbitrarily by any implementation. GDP identifiers greater than 0 are reserved for registration or future standardization.

6.8 Attribute Setting Functions Which Concern All Primitives

6.8.1 Setting the Colour Table

Colour is an attribute of all primitives. It may be specified as a global attribute, as a workstation-dependent attribute or in the pattern or CELL ARRAY definition (cf. Table 6.4). In any one of these cases, it is not possible to specify a colour directly. A COLOUR INDEX which points to a colour table located at each workstation must be used.

For each COLOUR INDEX value, the colour table contains an entry which specifies colour in terms of red/green/blue intensities in the range [0,1]. This colour table is modelled according to the colour table present in many colour raster devices. The colour table can be reset at any time so as to allow dynamic colour changes which are a powerful feature of colour raster devices.

However, not all devices have such a comfortable colour manipulation facility. If a dynamic colour table is not available on the device, a colour table must be kept in the driver and a regeneration of the picture must be initiated if a dynamic change of colour has been requested.

Some workstations are not capable of displaying colours but can generate one colour in different intensities (monochrome devices). In this case, the colour specified is mapped to an intensity in a workstation-dependent way, e.g.,

$$\text{intensity} = 0.5 \times (M + m)$$

where $M = \max(\text{red}, \text{green}, \text{blue})$, $m = \min(\text{red}, \text{green}, \text{blue})$.

If colours or intensities are not available at a workstation, the requested values are mapped to the nearest available value.

The colour table is set individually for each workstation so as to allow the application program to address the specific colour capabilities of each workstation. The colour table must contain at least two entries. Entry 0 corresponds to the background colour. Entry 1 is the default foreground colour. This corresponds exactly to the capabilities of black and white devices.

The workstation's colour table will be predefined according to the available capabilities so that a number of well-distinguishable colours are associated with different entries in the colour table. If a specific colour is required, it can be selected, if available, by SET COLOUR REPRESENTATION.

SET COLOUR REPRESENTATION   WSOP, WSAC, SGOP   L0a
Parameters:

Input	workstation identifier		N
Input	colour index	(0..n)	I
Input	colour (red/green/blue intensities)	[0,1]	$3 \times R$

Effect:

In the colour table of the workstation state list, the given colour index is associated with the specified colour. The colour is mapped by the workstation to the nearest one available.

The colour table in the workstation state list has predefined entries taken from the workstation description table; at the very least indices 0 and 1 should be predefined for every workstation of category OUTPUT or OUTIN. Any table entry (including the predefined entries) may be redefined by using this function.

When output primitives are displayed, the colour index refers to an entry in the colour table. If output primitives are displayed with a colour index that is not present in the colour table, a workstation-dependent colour index will be used. The background colour is defined by colour index 0.

N.B.:

On monochrome devices, the intensity is computed from the colour values in a workstation-dependent way.

Errors:

7	GKS not in proper state: GKS should be in one of the states WSOP, WSAC or SGOP
20	Specified workstation identifier is invalid
25	Specified workstation is not open
33	Specified workstation is of category MI
35	Specified workstation is of category INPUT
36	Specified workstation is Workstation-Independent Segment Storage
93	Colour index is invalid
96	Colour is outside range [0,1]

──────────────── *FORTRAN Interface* ────────────────

CALL GSCR (WKID, CI, CR, CG, CB)
Parameters:

Input	WKID	workstation identifier		INTEGER
Input	CI	colour index	(0..n)	INTEGER
Input	CR, CG, CB	red, green, blue	[0,1]	3 × REAL

6.8.2 Setting the Aspect Source Flags

Some output primitive attributes can be set INDIVIDUALLY or BUNDLED. In Table 6.4 on page 178 all these attributes are listed. The individual attributes are bound directly and, therefore, cannot be manipulated. The bundled attributes are addressed by bundle indices pointing to bundle tables which are set workstation-dependently. The binding is delayed so that the bundle entries can be set dynamically.

The function SET ASPECT SOURCE FLAGS sets a flag for each of these attributes indicating in which way the attribute is to be applied. Any combination of bundled and individual attributes is admissible, even for attributes belonging to one bundle. For example, the setting

linetype ASF = INDIVIDUAL
linewidth ASF = INDIVIDUAL
polyline colour index ASF = BUNDLED

specifies that the linetype and linewidth of a POLYLINE should be taken from the current setting of the respective attributes in the GKS state list. The values are bound directly to each POLYLINE primitive. The colour is derived from the respective entry in the polyline bundle table. The latter value may be different for each workstation and may be changed dynamically.

The ASFs have been introduced for efficiency reasons. The powerful facility whereby attributes are addressed via bundle tables involves some overhead. There are, however, applications which are content with limited attribute capabilities (e.g., if only one type of workstation is used), or which need more, different attributes than can reasonably be stored in workstation tables. Such applications will be satisfied with having their attributes set directly. They should not be forced to pay for the overhead for capabilities which they cannot use.

Being able to manipulate a specific attribute in two totally different ways can be very confusing. It is therefore recommended that the function SET ASPECT SOURCE FLAGS be used with care. This would mean, for example, having all attributes either bundled or individual, or setting the ASFs only once after opening GKS according to individual requirements. The application program may redefine the ASFs at any time; however, this will affect only the primitives subsequently generated.

The default setting of the ASFs reflects the principle that bundled and individual attributes are two concepts which should best be left apart. An implementor may choose to have all defaults for the ASFs either BUNDLED or INDIVIDUAL according to the needs of his users, but he may not provide a mixed set of defaults.

SET ASPECT SOURCE FLAGS	GKOP, WSOP, WSAC, SGOP L0a

Parameters:

Input	list of aspect source flags	(BUNDLED, INDIVIDUAL)	13 × E

Effect:

The aspect source flags (ASFs) in the GKS state list are set equal to the values indicated by the parameter. The elements of the list of ASFs are arranged in the following order:

1   linetype ASF
2   linewidth scale factor ASF
3   polyline colour index ASF
4   marker type ASF
5   marker size scale factor ASF
6   polymarker colour index ASF
7   text font and precision ASF
8   character expansion factor ASF
9   character spacing ASF
10   text colour index ASF
11   fill area interior style ASF
12   fill area style index ASF
13   fill area colour index ASF

Errors:

8   GKS not in proper state: GKS should be in one of the states GKOP, WSOP, WSAC or SGOP

――――――――――――― *FORTRAN Interface* ―――――――――――――

CALL GSASF (LASF)

Input	LASF(13)	list of aspect source flags		
			(0 = bundled, 1 = individual)	13 × INTEGER

6.8.3   Setting the Pick Identifier

The pick identifier is relevant only if a PICK input device and the segment storage are available. The reader of this section should be familiar with both concepts (cf. Chapters 7 and 8).

The pick identifier is different from other primitive attributes in the sense that it does not affect the graphical output but is stored for use with the PICK input device. It has been introduced for applications which use their own data structure for manipulation purposes but which still want to use the PICK input device causing a minimum of expense for the segment mechanism. The pick identifier makes identification of primitives within a segment possible and, thus, establishes a second level of naming. However, GKS provides no function to access and manipulate primitives with a given pick identifier. Therefore, the use of pick identifiers is not as restricted as is the use of segment names. The same pick identifier may be assigned to non-contiguous groups of primitives within a segment. The pick identifier may be set outside segments but this setting becomes relevant only when GKS enters the state SGOP. See Example 7.3 for the use of the pick identifier.

SET PICK IDENTIFIER   GKOP, WSOP, WSAC, SGOP   L1b

Parameters:

Input   pick identifier   N

Effect:

The 'current pick identifier' entry in the GKS state list is set equal to the value specified by the parameter.

Errors:

8   GKS not in proper state: GKS should be in one of the states GKOP, WSOP, WSAC or SGOP

97   Pick identifier is invalid

———————————————— *FORTRAN Interface* ————————————————

CALL GSPKID (PCID)

Input   PCID   pick identifier   INTEGER

6.8.4   Clipping Rectangle

The clipping associated with the normalization transformation is postponed until primitives are displayed at a workstation. Different normalization transformations can be applied to different primitives. Therefore, the clipping rectangle has to be associated with the primitives like an attribute in order to allow proper clipping at the workstation. The current setting of the clipping rectangle attribute is recorded in the GKS state list. Usually, it will coincide with the viewport of the current normalization transformation. Its value can be reset also by INTERPRET ITEM, when an item containing a clipping rectangle is read from a metafile. See Chapter 5.4 for more details about clipping.

The clipping rectangle differs from the other attributes because when a primitive is processed by the function INSERT SEGMENT, the clipping rectangle which may be bound to it is replaced by the current clipping rectangle.

6.9   Examples

Example 6.1   Plotting coordinate data in a file by POLYLINE

Assume that coordinate data describing polylines is stored in a file. The procedure DRAW_FILE reads in one data record after the other and generates a polyline with each of them. Such a procedure was used for the generation of Figures 5.1—5.4.

———————————————————— *Pascal* ————————————————————

                                        {Read data from FILE and draw polylines}

```
L10   procedure DRAW_FILE (var input_file: text);
L20   var xarray, yarray: array [1..1000] of real;          {Declarations}
L30       i, length: integer;
```

```
L50  begin
L60    reset (input_file);
L60    while not eof (input_file) do
L70    begin
L80      read (input_file, length);
L90      if (length > 0) then
L100     begin
L110       for i := 1 to length do read (input_file, xarray[i], yarray[i]);
L120       POLYLINE (length, xarray, yarray);
L130     end;
L140   end;
L150 end {DRAW_FILE};
```

─────────────────────── *Fortran* ───────────────────────

```
     C                           *** Read data from FILE and draw polylines
L10          SUBROUTINE DRFILE (FILE)

     C                                                    *** Declarations
L20          REAL XARRAY (1000), YARRAY (1000)
L30          INTEGER FILE, LENGTH, I

L110  110    READ (FILE, 160, END = 150)
          +  LENGTH, (XARRAY (I), YARRAY (I), I = 1, LENGTH)
L120         CALL GPL (LENGTH, XARRAY, YARRAY)
L130         GOTO 110

L150  150    RETURN
L160  160    FORMAT (I10/(2F12.2))
L170         END
```

Example 6.2   Use of direct POLYLINE attributes

A map containing borders, rivers and roads is to be drawn. The different sorts of lines can be distinguished by different line attributes. The map is drawn at workstation 'display' with attributes: border lines = solid, rivers = dashed, roads = dotted, and then is drawn on workstation 'plotter' with attributes: border lines = red, rivers = blue, roads = black. It is assumed that there are predefined colour table entries at the plotter workstation:
1 = black; 2 = red; 3 = green; 4 = blue.

─────────────────────── *Pascal* ───────────────────────

```
                        {Setting of transformations see Example 5.4, L10—50}
L40  ACTIVATE_WORKSTATION (display);          {Generate picture on display}

L60  SET_LINETYPE (1);                 {Set linetype and draw line data in files}
L70  DRAW_FILE (borderlines);
L80  SET_LINETYPE (2);
```

L90 DRAW_FILE(rivers);
L100 SET_LINETYPE (3);
L110 DRAW_FILE(roads);

L120 DEACTIVATE_WORKSTATION (display);

{Generate picture on plotter using different colours}
L130 ACTIVATE_WORKSTATION (plotter);
{Setting of workstation transformation see Example 5.4, L140—150}
L160 SET_POLYLINE_COLOUR_INDEX (2);   {Set colour index and}
L170 DRAW_FILE(borderlines);   {draw line data in files}
L180 SET_POLYLINE_COLOUR_INDEX (4);
L190 DRAW_FILE(rivers);
L200 SET_POLYLINE_COLOUR_INDEX (1);
L210 DRAW_FILE(roads);

L220 DEACTIVATE_WORKSTATION (plotter);

Fortran

```
        C       *** Setting of transformations see Example 5.4, L10—50
        C       *** Generate picture on display using different linetypes
L40             CALL GACWK (DISPL)
        C       *** Set linetype and draw line data in files 21, 22, 23
L60             CALL GSLN (1)
L70             CALL DRFILE (21)
L80             CALL GSLN (2)
L90             CALL DRFILE (22)
L100            CALL GSLN (3)
L110            CALL DRFILE (23)
L120            CALL GDAWK (DISPL)

        C       *** Generate picture on plotter using different colours
L130            CALL GACWK (PLOTTR)
        C       *** Setting of workstation transformation see Example 5.4, L140—150
        C       *** Set colour index and draw line data in files 21, 22, 23
L160            CALL GSPLCI (2)
L170            CALL DRFILE (21)
L180            CALL GSPLCI (4)
L190            CALL DRFILE (22)
L200            CALL GSPLCI (1)
L210            CALL DRFILE (23)

L220            CALL GDAWK (PLOTTR)
```

Example 6.3   Use of indexed POLYLINE attributes

The same task as in Example 6.2 is performed with the use of a polyline index. As the polyline representation is defined separately for each workstation, the picture can be generated simultaneously at both workstations which eliminates every second call for DRAW_FILE.

Indexed attributes can also be used for dynamic attribute change at the same workstation (cf. Example 7.1).

─────────────────── *Pascal* ───────────────────

{Initialising of POLYLINE INDEX REPRESENTATION}
{Using different linetypes for workstation display}

L10 SET_POLYLINE_REPRESENTATION (display, 1, 1, 1.0, 1);
L20 SET_POLYLINE_REPRESENTATION (display, 2, 2, 1.0, 1);
L30 SET_POLYLINE_REPRESENTATION (display, 3, 3, 1.0, 1);

{Using different colours for workstation plotter}

L40 SET_POLYLINE_REPRESENTATION (plotter, 1, 1, 1.0, 2);
L50 SET_POLYLINE_REPRESENTATION (plotter, 2, 1, 1.0, 4);
L60 SET_POLYLINE_REPRESENTATION (plotter, 3, 1, 1.0, 1);
L70 SET_COLOUR_REPRESENTATION (plotter, 1, 1.0, 1.0, 1.0);   {black}
L80 SET_COLOUR_REPRESENTATION (plotter, 2, 1.0, 0.0, 0.0);   {red}
L90 SET_COLOUR_REPRESENTATION (plotter, 4, 0.0, 0.0, 1.0);   {blue}

{Setting of transformations see Example 5.4, L10−50, L140−150}

L100 ACTIVATE_WORKSTATION (display);
L110 ACTIVATE_WORKSTATION (plotter);

L120 SET_POLYLINE_INDEX (1);   {Draw line data in data sets}
L130 DRAW_FILE (borderlines);
L140 SET_POLYLINE_INDEX (2);
L150 DRAW_FILE (rivers);
L160 SET_POLYLINE_INDEX (3);
L170 DRAW_FILE (roads);

L180 DEACTIVATE_WORKSTATION (display);
L190 DEACTIVATE_WORKSTATION (plotter);

─────────────────── *Fortran* ───────────────────

```
        C              *** Initialising of POLYLINE INDEX REPRESENTATION
        C                    *** Using different linetypes for workstation display
L10            CALL GSPLR (DISPL, 1, 1, 1.0, 1)
L20            CALL GSPLR (DISPL, 2, 2, 1.0, 1)
L30            CALL GSPLR (DISPL, 3, 3, 1.0, 1)
        C                        *** Using different colours for workstation plotter
L40            CALL GSPLR (PLOTTR, 1, 1, 1.0, 2)
L50            CALL GSPLR (PLOTTR, 2, 1, 1.0, 4)
L60            CALL GSPLR (PLOTTR, 3, 1, 1.0, 1)
        C                    *** Set colour table entries 1 = black, 2 = red, 4 = blue
L70            CALL GSCR (PLOTTR, 1, 1.0, 1.0, 1.0)
L80            CALL GSCR (PLOTTR, 2, 1.0, 0.0, 0.0)
L90            CALL GSCR (PLOTTR, 4, 0.0, 0.0, 1.0)

        C          *** Setting of transformations see Example 5.4, L10−50, L150−160
L100           CALL GACWK (DISPL)
L110           CALL GACWK (PLOTTR)
```

```
        C       *** Draw line data in files 21, 22, 23
L120            CALL GSPLI (1)
L130            CALL DRFILE (21)
L140            CALL GSPLI (2)
L150            CALL DRFILE (22)
L160            CALL GSPLI (3)
L170            CALL DRFILE (23)

L180            CALL GDAWK (DISPL)
L190            CALL GDAWK (PLOTTR)
```

Example 6.4   Drawing a chart with three histograms

Three different sets of values (e.g., returns of three companies over several years) are given in the arrays *yarray1*, *yarray2*, and *yarray3*. The array *xarray* contains the dates of the years. A POLYLINE, connecting the returns values, is drawn for each company, and the vertices of the POLYLINE are marked by marker symbols.

For a sample of output see Figure 6.3 on page 186.

——————————————————— *Pascal* ———————————————————

```
L10   SET_MARKER_TYPE(1);   {Choose different marker type for each set of points}
L20   POLYMARKER (length,xarray,yarray1);       {Draw symbol at given positions}
L30   SET_LINETYPE(1);              {Choose different linetypes for each set of points}
L40   POLYLINE (length,xarray,yarray1);                {Connect given positions}

      {repeat the above statements with marker type 2 and 3
      and linetype 2 and 3 for yarray2 and yarray3}
```

——————————————————— *Fortran* ———————————————————

```
        C       *** Choose different marker type for each set of points
L10             CALL GSMK (1)
        C       *** Draw symbol at given positions
L20             CALL GPM (LENGTH,XARRAY,YARRAY1)
        C       *** Choose different linetypes for each set of points
L30             CALL GSLN (1)
        C       *** Draw POLYLINE to connect given positions
L40             CALL GPL (LENGTH,XARRAY,YARRAY1)
        C
        C       *** Repeat the above statements with marker type 2 and 3
        C       *** and linetype 2 and 3 for YARRAY2 and YARRAY3
```

Example 6.5   Effect of transformation and clipping on POLYMARKER

This example illustrates the generation of Figures 6.3—6.5 (pages 186—187) which show the effect of clipping and transformations on POLYMARKER. Figure 6.5 shows a very comfortable clipping. An implementor has some freedom to implement less comfortable clipping.

The picture to be clipped has been defined in Example 6.4. Data is assumed to be in the range $1 \le x \le 5$, $1 \le y \le 5$.

─────────────────────── *Pascal* ───────────────────────

L10   SET_WINDOW (1, 1.0, 5.0, 1.0, 5.0);
L20   SET_VIEWPORT (1, 0.1, 0.5, 0.1, 0.5);
L30   SET_CLIPPING_INDICATOR (NOCLIP);
    {Insert Example 6.4;   Figure 6.3 generated}

L40   SET_VIEWPORT (1, 0.1, 0.5, 0.1, 0.9);
    {Insert Example 6.4;   Figure 6.4 generated}

L50   SET_VIEWPORT (1, 0.1, 0.5, 0.1, 0.5);
L60   SET_CLIPPING_INDICATOR (CLIP);
    {Insert Example 6.4;   Figure 6.5a generated}

L70   SET_WINDOW (1, 1.05, 5.05, 1.0, 5.0);
    {Insert Example 6.4;   Figure 6.5b generated}

─────────────────────── *Fortran* ───────────────────────

L01   INTEGER CLIP,NOCLIP
L02   DATA CLIP/1/, NOCLIP/0/

L10   CALL GSWN (1, 1.0, 5.0, 1.0, 5.0)
L20   CALL GSVP (1, 0.1, 0.5, 0.1, 0.5)

L30   CALL GSCLIP (NOCLIP)
    C   *** Insert Example 6.4;   Figure 6.3 generated

L40   CALL GSVP (1, 0.1, 0.5, 0.1, 0.9)
    C   *** Insert Example 6.4;   Figure 6.4 generated

L50   CALL GSVP (1, 0.5, 0.1, 0.5)
L60   CALL GSCLIP (CLIP)
    C   *** Insert Example 6.4;   Figure 6.5a generated

L70   CALL GSWN (1, 1.05, 5.05, 1.0, 5.0)
    C   *** Insert Example 6.4;   Figure 6.5b generated

Example 6.6   Setting the TEXT attributes

This example illustrates some typical settings for different TEXT attributes. The TEXT attributes are set directly. Generated figures are shown on pages 194—197.

─────────────────────── *Pascal* ───────────────────────

L10   SET_WINDOW (1, 0.0, 20.0, 0.0, 20.0);
             {Set workstation viewport on plotter to 20 cm × 20 cm}
L20   SET_WORKSTATION_VIEWPORT (1, 0.0, 0.2, 0.0, 0.2);

L30 SET_CHARACTER_HEIGHT (0.9);   {Vary CHARACTER HEIGHT}
L40 TEXT (1.0, 1.0, 'HEIGHT_3');
L50 SET_CHARACTER_HEIGHT (0.6);
L60 TEXT (1.0, 2.2, 'HEIGHT_2');
L70 SET_CHARACTER_HEIGHT (0.3);
L80 TEXT (1.0, 3.1, 'HEIGHT_1');   {generates Figure 6.7}

          {Vary CHARACTER UP VECTOR, character baseline is rotated accordingly}
L90   SET_CHARACTER_UP_VECTOR (0.0, −1.0);
L100 TEXT (10.0, 10.0, '_(0, −1)_');
L110 SET_CHARACTER_UP_VECTOR (−1.0, −1.0);
L120 TEXT (10.0, 10.0, '_(−1, −1)');
L130 SET_CHARACTER_UP_VECTOR (−1.0, 0.0);
L140 TEXT (10.0, 10.0, '_(−1,0)_');
L150 SET_CHARACTER_UP_VECTOR (−1.0, 1.0);
L160 TEXT (10.0, 10.0, '_(−1, +1)');
L170 SET_CHARACTER_UP_VECTOR (0.0, 1.0);
L180 TEXT (10.0, 10.0, '_(0, +1)_');   {generates Figure 6.8}

                              {vary CHARACTER EXPANSION FACTOR}
L190 SET_CHARACTER_EXPANSION_VECTOR (2.0);
L200 TEXT (10.0, 1.0, 'EXPANSION_2');
L210 SET_CHARACTER_EXPANSION_VECTOR (0.5);
L220 TEXT (10.0, 2.4, 'EXPANSION_0.5');
L230 SET_CHARACTER_EXPANSION_VECTOR (1.0);
L240 TEXT (10.0, 1.7, 'EXPANSION_1');   {generates Figure 6.11}

L250 SET_TEXT_PATH (UP); {TEXT PATH selects one from four writing directions}
L260 TEXT (15.0, 10.5, 'UP');   {without rotating the individual characters}
L270 SET_TEXT_PATH (DOWN);
L280 TEXT (15.0, 9.8, 'DOWN');
L290 SET_TEXT_PATH (LEFT);
L300 TEXT (14.8, 10.0, 'LEFT');
L310 SET_TEXT_PATH (RIGHT);
L320 TEXT (15.2, 10.0, 'RIGHT');   {generates Figure 6.12}

                         {CHARACTER SPACING sets additional spacing}
L330 SET_CHARACTER_SPACING (1.0);
L340 TEXT (1.0, 5.0, 'SPACING_1');
L350 SET_CHARACTER_SPACING (0.5);
L360 TEXT (1.0, 5.7, 'SPACING_0.5');
L370 SET_CHARACTER_SPACING (0.0);
L380 TEXT (1.0, 6.4, 'SPACING_0');   {generates Figure 6.13}

─────────────────────────── *Fortran* ───────────────────────────

L10   CALL GSWN (1, 0.0, 20.0, 0.0, 20.0)
      C   *** Set workstation viewport on plotter to 20 cm × 20 cm
L20   CALL GSWKVP (1, 0.0, 0.2, 0.0, 0.2)
      C   *** Vary CHARACTER HEIGHT
L30   CALL GSCHH (0.9)
L40   CALL GTX (1.0, 1.0, 'HEIGHT_3')
L50   CALL GSCHH (0.6)
L60   CALL GTX (1.0, 2.2, 'HEIGHT_2')

```
L70          CALL GSCHH (0.3)
L80          CALL GTX (1.0, 3.1, 'HEIGHT_1')
     C                                              *** generates Figure 6.7

     C                              *** Vary CHARACTER UP VECTOR,
     C                              *** character baseline is rotated accordingly
L90          CALL GSCHUP (0.0, -1.0)
L100         CALL GTX (10.0, 10.0, '_(0, -1)_')
L110         CALL GSCHUP (-1.0, -1.0)
L120         CALL GTX (10.0, 10.0, '_(-1, -1)')
L130         CALL GSCHUP (-1.0, 0.0)
L140         CALL GTX (10.0, 10.0, '_(-1,0)_')
L150         CALL GSCHUP (-1.0, 1.0)
L160         CALL GTX (10.0, 10.0, '_(-1, +1)')
L170         CALL GSCHUP (0.0, 1.0)
L180         CALL GTX (10.0, 10.0, '_(0, +1)_')
     C                                              *** generates Figure 6.8

     C                              *** vary CHARACTER EXPANSION FACTOR
L190         CALL GSCHXP (2.0)
L200         CALL GTX (10.0, 1.0, 'EXPANSION_2')
L210         CALL GSCHXP (0.5)
L220         CALL GTX (10.0, 2.4, 'EXPANSION_0.5')
L230         CALL GSCHXP (1.0)
L240         CALL GTX (10.0, 1.7, 'EXPANSION_1')
                                                    *** generates Figure 6.11
     C                      *** TEXT PATH selects one from four writing directions
     C                      *** without rotating the individual characters
L250         CALL GSTXP (2)
L260         CALL GTX (15.0, 10.5, 'UP')
L270         CALL GSTXP (3)
L280         CALL GTX (15.0, 9.8, 'DOWN')
L290         CALL GSTXP (1)
L300         CALL GTX (14.8, 10.0, 'LEFT')
L310         CALL GSTXP (0)
L320         CALL GTX (15.2, 10.0, 'RIGHT')
     C                                              *** generates Figure 6.12

     C                      *** CHARACTER SPACING sets additional spacing
L330         CALL GSCHSP (1.0)
L340         CALL GTX (1.0, 5.0, 'SPACING_1')
L350         CALL GSCHSP (0.5)
L360         CALL GTX (1.0, 5.7, 'SPACING_0.5')
L370         CALL GSCHSP (0.0)
L380         CALL GTX (1.0, 6.4, 'SPACING_0')
     C                                              *** generates Figure 6.13
```

Example 6.7   Generating digits on a clock using TEXT_ALIGNMENT

Example 7.4 in the next chapter describes the generation of a clock. This example shows how the digits on the clock face can be drawn. Digits are written horizontally. Text alignment is used to put the centre of the digits in position on corresponding radial lines at a distance of 0.85 from the centre of the clock face. Character height for digits is 0.036. The clock time (hours) is transformed to an angle (radians) by adhering to the following rules: 3 o'clock corresponds to angle 0 (angle: = hours-3); a time interval of 12 hours corresponds to angle twopi; radians are measured counter-clockwise (angle: = -twopi*(hours-3)/12).

—————————————————— *Pascal* ——————————————————

```
L10    procedure CLOCK_FACE_DIGITS;                {Draw digits on clock face}
L20    const twopi = 6.2831852;
L25    type char2 = array [1..2] of char;
L30    var i, j, length: integer;
L40      init_x, init_y: real;
L50      digit: array [1..9] of char;
L52      digit2: array [10..12] of char2;
```

{Initialising of the arrays 'digit' and 'digit2' with the character strings '1',...,'12'
is omitted}

```
L60    begin
L70      SET_CHARACTER_HEIGHT (0.036);
                                                {select high text precision}
L80      SET_TEXT_FONT_AND_PRECISION (1, STROKE);
L90      SET_TEXT_ALIGNMENT (CENTRE, HALF);        {text centred to position}
L100     for i: = 1 to 12 do
L110     begin
       {Compute centrepoint of string on clock; − twopi*(i − 3)/12 gives angle in radians}
L120       init_x: = 0.85 * cos(− twopi*(i − 3)/12);
L130       init_y: = 0.85 * sin(− twopi*(i − 3)/12);
L140       if i < 10 then TEXT (init_x, init_y, digit[i])
L141             else TEXT (init_x, init_y, digit2[i]);
L150     end;
L160   end {CLOCK_FACE_DIGITS};
```

—————————————————— *Fortran* ——————————————————

```
L10            SUBROUTINE DIGITS
L20            INTEGER I, CENTRE, HALF, STROKE, FIRST
L30            REAL TWOPI, XI, YI
L35            CHARACTER*2 DIGIT
L40            DATA TWOPI/6.2831852/, CENTRE/2/, HALF/3/, STROKE/2/

L70            CALL GSCHH (0.036)
L80            CALL GSTXEP (1, STROKE)
L90            CALL GSTXAL (CENTRE, HALF)

L100           DO 1 I = 1, 12
       C       *** Compute centre of string on clock;
       C       *** − TWOPI*(I − 3)/12.0 gives angle in radians
L120           XI = 0.85*COS(− TWOPI*(I − 3)/12.0)
L130           YI = 0.85*SIN(− TWOPI*(I − 3)/12.0)

L135           WRITE (UNIT = DIGIT, FMT = '(I2)') I
L136           FIRST = 2
L137           IF (I.GT.9) FIRST = 1
```

L140		CALL GTX (XI,YI, DIGIT (FIRST:2))
L150	1	CONTINUE
L160		RETURN
L161		END

6.10   Exercises

Exercise 6.1   Text in given DC size and orientation

Text geometry is always specified in WC to ensure that character strings can be fully transformed. However, there are valid applications where the geometry of a character string ought to be defined in DC. This could be, for example, when a temperature/time diagram is drawn and an inscription is to be written at a certain temperature/time position. Assume that no segment transformation applies and that the workstation transformation of workstation 'plot' is not changed.

a) Assume that the normalization transformation performs uniform scaling. Design procedures SET CHARACTER HEIGHT DC and SET CHARACTER UP VECTOR DC which accept DC values and which call SET CHARACTER HEIGHT and SET CHARACTER UP VECTOR with appropriate WC values of character height and character up vector so that on workstation 'plot' characters are generated with the specified height and orientation in DC.

b) Assume an arbitrary normalization transformation with non-uniform scaling and restrict CHARACTER UP VECTOR to being parallel to the axes. Write a procedure SET CHARACTER HEIGHT DC for this constellation. Do we need a procedure SET CHARACTER UP VECTOR DC?

c) Consider the general case of an arbitrary normalization transformation and an arbitrary CHARACTER UP VECTOR. Design procedures SET CHARACTER HEIGHT DC and SET CHARACTER UP VECTOR DC which accept DC values and which ensure that the specified character height and the baseline orientation as specified implicitly by the character up vector are achieved in DC.

d) Consider all text attributes and discuss the effect which may occur to text under the assumptions of part c).

Exercise 6.2   Line formatting of text without hyphenation

The functionality provided with the TEXT primitive allows high-quality text to be generated. A common function provided with text systems is the capability of line formatting with justification.

Given a routine GET WORD which reads one word at a time from a text file and given a fixed line length, write a program which reads the text file sequentially, puts as many words as possible (without hyphenation) into each line and positions each word so that the interword gaps in each line are the same size and that the first word is aligned to the left-hand margin and the last word aligned to the right-hand margin.

Note that the size of the text extent rectangle can be determined by the function INQUIRE TEXT EXTENT (cf. Section 10.2.4). Can this line formatting be done for several workstations simultaneously? Can the metafile be used for this purpose?

Exercise 6.3   Generating an RGB colour cube

Write a program which generates an RGB colour cube as shown in Figure C5 on page 620. Calculate a colour index array which can be passed to CELL ARRAY and set the colour table accordingly. Assume that the colour table can store a maximum of 256 colours. What is a reasonable size for the colour index array?

Exercise 6.4   Temperature flow

When heating up an object, the temperature will increase differently in different parts of the object. For control purposes, an image of the object showing the temperature is to be generated

a) Select a sequence of 16 RGB values which represent well the colour transitions occurring when an object is heated up: black, blue, red, yellow, white (avoid green).
b) Given an array of 500×500 temperature values in the range $[0, 2000]$, calculate a colour index array to be passed to CELL ARRAY showing the temperature distribution within the object.
c) Even if only one array of measurements at a specific time is available, the temperature flow can be well demonstrated by merely manipulating the mapping of temperatures to colours. Let T range over all the temperatures. For each value of T map the temperature interval $[T, T + 100]$ on the full range of the above 16 RGB values, making all points with a temperature $t < T$ black, and making all points with a temperature $t > T + 100$ white. This reassignment of colours can be done in the colour table only. Write a program.
d) Making the above assumptions, give reasonable estimates for the size of the colour table needed for b) and c).

Exercise 6.5   Building up of polygons for FILL AREA

If FILL AREA is generated in a style different from HOLLOW, the bounding polygon is not drawn. It should be noted that it is not good practice to generate a boundary by simply combining the two functions
— FILL AREA (n, points);
— POLYLINE (n, points).

A line separating two areas occurs in the boundary of both areas and would be drawn twice.

Assume that the boundary network is cut at all points of intersection into small polylines. These polylines are numbered and stored in a file. A second file contains a description of each area consisting of a list of signed line numbers.

By concatenating the lines in the sequence as specified by the list, the bounding polygon is constructed. The sign of the line number indicates whether the polyline must be traversed forwards ($+$) or backwards ($-$).

Write a program which reads the description of each area, then collects all line pieces from a direct access storage device, and forms the bounding polygon for each area. Then generate a picture where the interior of each area is filled using colour index 1 and the polygons are drawn using colour index 2.

7   SEGMENTS

7.1   Introduction

A picture consists of output primitives. After having generated the corresponding graphical output on a display surface, the primitives are no longer accessible. However, there are many applications where it is desirable to have access to previously generated output primitives, e.g., when
— editing a picture and then redrawing the modified picture,
— sending a picture edited at one workstation to a second one to make a hard copy,
— one has several instances of one subpicture (symbol) within one picture.

To enable such picture manipulations, a picture must be structured, the structure elements must be named, a description of the picture must be stored, and a set of manipulation functions must be provided.

A kernel system like GKS cannot satisfy all possible requests for picture structuring and manipulation. The GKS segment storage, however, provides some basic tools for picture structuring and manipulation which will be appropriate for many applications.

7.2   How Are Segments Generated?

When calling the GKS function CREATE SEGMENT, GKS enters the state SGOP (Segment Open) in which all output primitives and all related primitive attributes are recorded in a record called segment. The segment is closed by CLOSE SEGMENT which puts GKS back into the state WSAC (At Least One Workstation Active). The segment currently being created in state SGOP is called the open segment. Each time GKS enters state SGOP, exactly one segment is created. It is identified by a unique segment name and is assigned an individual set of segment attributes. More segments may, of course, be generated by reentering the state SGOP. Example 7.1 on page 259 shows how several segments are created.

GKS supports only one level of segmentation. The brackets CREATE SEG-MENT and CLOSE SEGMENT delimit a contiguous group of primitives from the stream of output primitives. Segments cannot contain references to other segments nor can segments be nested (i.e., call CREATE SEGMENT while another segment is open) which would allow the definition of segment hierarchies.

The PICK IDENTIFIER (cf. Section 6.8.3) is a primitive attribute which allows the naming of primitives inside segments, thus establishing a second level of naming (cf. Example 7.3). However, the PICK IDENTIFIER can be used only with the PICK input device and offers no further manipulation possibilities.

It is not allowed to re-open an existing segment and add more primitives to it. Although such a feature would be useful for some applications, it has not been included for reasons of simplicity. As some primitive attributes are set modally, confusion may occur as to which attribute setting is effective, the one at segment closing time or the current one. The INSERT SEGMENT function, however, offers the functionality needed to create such an additional facility on top of GKS (cf. Exercise 7.3).

Output primitives are displayed at all workstations which are active at primitive generation time. Similarly, segments are assigned to all active workstations. To ensure proper assignment, the activation and deactivation of any workstation in state SGOP is not allowed.

Conceptually, one instance of each segment is stored at each active workstation. This does not preclude a specific way of implementing the segment storage but serves as a model for describing the effects of segment manipulations. The manipulation of segment attributes affects all instances of a segment, even at those workstations not currently active. Thus, segment manipulations may cause visible effects on an inactive workstation. This however, does not contradict the rule that graphical output is generated only for active workstations, as no new primitives are being accepted by that workstation. It is merely existing primitives which are being manipulated.

All primitives are affected by the workstation transformation and by the workstation specific tables which define the interpretation of the bundle index stored as a primitive attribute in the segment. These are the only aspects in which the appearance of a segment may differ at different workstations.

Primitives outside segments are displayed only once at a workstation. They are retained until the workstation performs an implicit regeneration (cf. Section 4.6) or an explicit one. Primitives within segments are retained until the segment is deleted.

7.3   What Is Stored in a Segment?

A segment contains all the output primitives generated in the time between CREATE SEGMENT and CLOSE SEGMENT being called. For each of these primitives, all the corresponding primitive attributes must be stored, irrespective of the time or GKS state in which they were set.

Segments may be transformed by a segment transformation. In contrast to the other GKS transformations, this transformation is a general affine transformation which includes rotation and shearing as well as translation and scaling. As a consequence, rectangles such as character body, pattern rectangle and cell rectangle may be sheared. In order that primitives may be properly transformed, additional information has to be stored so that sheared rectangles may be reconstructed.

As the clipping associated with the normalization transformation is delayed until a primitive is actually displaced, the clipping rectangles must also be stored.

Table 7.1 lists all the items which may be stored in a segment. Of course, the implementor will store the attributes in the segment only if necessary and when needed. This could be the first time a primitive occurs or, e.g., each time an attribute changes. Furthermore, depending on the setting of the aspect source flags, either the direct attributes or the ⟨output primitive⟩ INDEX might be omitted.

After generation of a segment the application program no longer has access to the data contained in it. It is not possible to inquire about, to modify, or to extend the contents of a segment. However, there are functions which allow the manipulation of the segment as a whole. The aspects of a segment which can be changed are described by the segment attributes which are stored in the segment state list.

7.4   When Are Primitives Taken from the Transformation Pipeline?

There are different locations on the transformation pipeline where primitives can be taken from it to be stored in segments. At the beginning of the pipeline, a full definition of the primitives and attributes is available and can be manipulated. However, if primitives have not been pre-processed before being stored in segment storage, the efficiency of the pictures generated will be poor. At the end of the pipeline, all transformations, clipping and attribute binding have been done so that pictures can be generated efficiently from this data structure. However, only very limited segment manipulations are now possible. GKS has chosen a solution in between these two extremes.

In GKS, the transformation pipeline is split into two parts. In the first part a workstation-independent picture is defined and in the second part it is adapted to the workstation coordinate system. Similarly, the binding of the workstation-dependent aspects of the primitive attributes is split into two stages, whereby in the first stage a symbolic attribute (an index) is bound to the primitive and in the second stage the aspects are assigned to the symbolic attributes. In this way, GKS has introduced an 'abstract viewing surface' in the middle of the pipeline on which a workstation-independent representation of a picture is defined. This is the point where the data which describe segments are removed from the pipeline and where they are later put back.

Therefore, the segment storage contains primitives which have passed through the normalization transformation. Global attributes have been bound

Table 7.1 Contents of a segment

A segment contains an arbitrary sequence of the following items:
 CLIPPING RECTANGLE
 PICK IDENTIFIER
 ASPECT SOURCE FLAGS
 LINETYPE
 LINEWIDTH SCALE FACTOR
 POLYLINE COLOUR INDEX
 POLYLINE INDEX
 POLYLINE

 CLIPPING RECTANGLE
 PICK IDENTIFIER
 ASPECT SOURCE FLAGS
 MARKER TYPE
 MARKER SIZE SCALE FACTOR
 POLYMARKER COLOUR INDEX
 POLYMARKER INDEX
 POLYMARKER

 CLIPPING RECTANGLE
 PICK IDENTIFIER
 ASPECT SOURCE FLAGS
 CHARACTER HEIGHT
 CHARACTER UP AND BASELINE VECTOR
 TEXT PATH
 TEXT ALIGNMENT
 TEXT FONT AND PRECISION
 CHARACTER EXPANSION FACTOR
 CHARACTER SPACING
 TEXT COLOUR INDEX
 TEXT INDEX
 TEXT

 CLIPPING RECTANGLE
 PICK IDENTIFIER
 ASPECT SOURCE FLAGS
 FILL AREA INTERIOR STYLE
 FILL AREA STYLE INDEX
 FILL AREA COLOUR INDEX
 FILL AREA INDEX
 PATTERN RECTANGLE
 FILL AREA

 CLIPPING RECTANGLE
 PICK IDENTIFIER
 CELL ARRAY

 CLIPPING RECTANGLE
 PICK IDENTIFIER
 optional (implementation-dependent): any of the above attributes
 GDP

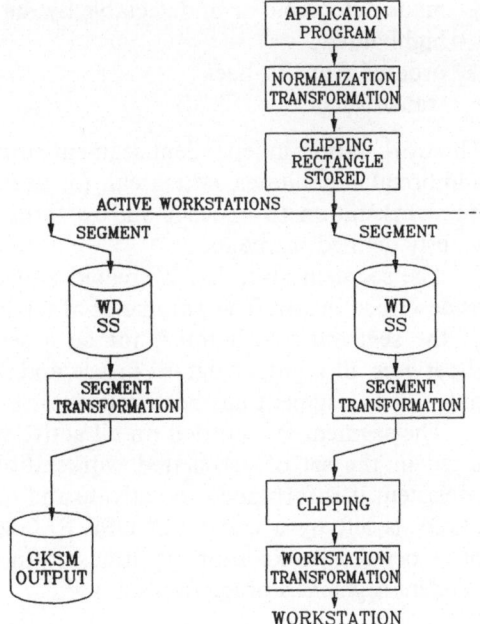

Figure 7.1 Data flow
to and from the segment storage

to the primitives. The effect of both these operations cannot be changed. The clipping rectangles are stored enabling segment transformations to be performed before clipping. Clipping rectangles also cannot be manipulated except by using the INSERT SEGMENT function which just discards all stored clipping rectangles. On the other hand, workstation transformation and workstation attributes are related to the second part of the transformation pipeline which takes effect after segment storage. They can be reset at any time and will have retroactive effects on all the primitives stored in segments and displayed at the respective workstation.

7.5   Segment Creation and Deletion

CREATE SEGMENT puts GKS into the state SGOP in which all output primitives are collected to form a segment. This happens independently of the display process, so that primitives inside and outside of segments are still sent immediately to the display surface for display except if the deferral state specifies otherwise (cf. Section 4.6).

For each segment, GKS creates a segment state list (cf. Table 7.2) which describes the state of a segment, i.e., all aspects of a segment which may be manipulated. A segment may be:
— renamed;
— deleted;
— made visible or invisible;

— made detectable or undetectable by the PICK input device;
— highlighted;
— ordered front-to-back;
— transformed.

The workstation-independent segment storage described in Section 7.7 provides additional capabilities, which can for example be used to copy segments from one workstation to another and to form new segments with the help of previously defined segments.

The segment state list is created and initialised by CREATE SEGMENT as described below. The parameter of CREATE SEGMENT specifies the name of the segment which must not be a segment name currently in use. GKS supervises all segment names in use and allows the re-use of a segment name only after a segment has been deleted or renamed.

The segment is recorded on all active workstations. These workstations are listed in the set of associated workstations. To ensure that this set remains consistent it is forbidden to activate and deactivate workstations until the state SGOP is left by a call to CLOSE SEGMENT. The manipulation of the set of associated workstations is discussed in the context of the workstation-independent segment storage in Section 7.7.

Table 7.2 Segment state list

segment name	N	
set of associated workstations	$n \times N$	active work-stations at create time
segment transformation matrix	$2 \times 3 \times R$	1,0,0
(the elements $M13$ and $M23$ are in NDC coordinates and the other elements are unitless)		0,1,0
visibility (VISIBLE, INVISIBLE)	E	VISIBLE
highlighting (NORMAL, HIGHLIGHTED)	E	NORMAL
segment priority [0,1]	R	0
detectability (UNDETECTABLE, DETECTABLE)	E	UNDETECTABLE

N.B.: The notation is explained in Section 3.2.

The segment attributes are initialised as shown in Table 7.2. These attributes may be changed by the functions described in Section 7.6.

There is only one segment state list for each segment, i.e., the entries are valid for all the workstations where the segment is stored.

CREATE SEGMENT   WSAC   L1a
Parameters:
Input   segment name   N
Effect:
   GKS is put into the operating state SGOP = "Segment open". The segment state list is drawn up and initialised as indicated in Table 7.2. The segment name is recorded as the 'name of the open segment' in the GKS state list (cf. Section 3.3). All subsequent output primitives until the next CLOSE SEGMENT will be collected into this segment.

The segment name is entered in the 'set of stored segments for this workstation' in the workstation state list (cf. Section 4.3) for every active workstation. All active workstations are included in the 'set of associated workstations' of the segment state list of the newly opened segment. The segment name is entered into the 'set of segment names in use' in the GKS state list. Primitive attributes are not affected.

Errors:

3	GKS not in proper state: GKS should be in the state WSAC
120	Specified segment name is invalid
121	Specified segment name is already in use

――――――――――――――― *FORTRAN Interface* ―――――――――――――――

CALL GCRSG (SGNA)

Parameters:

Input	SGNA	segment name	INTEGER

CLOSE SEGMENT puts GKS back into the state WSAC (At Least One Workstation Active). The definition of the segment is thus complete. It is not possible to add any more primitives to the segment, to modify or to delete primitives stored in the segment. Only manipulations of the whole segment by using the segment attributes are possible.

―――

CLOSE SEGMENT   SGOP   L1a

Parameters: none

Effect:

GKS is put into the operating state WSAC = "At least one workstation active". Primitives may no longer be added to the previously open segment. The 'name of the open segment' in the GKS state list (cf. Section 3.2) cannot be inquired into.

Errors:

4	GKS not in proper state: GKS should be in the state SGOP

――――――――――――――――――― *FORTRAN Interface* ――――――――――――――――――

CALL GCLSG

Parameters: none

RENAME SEGMENT allows a new name to be assigned to an existing segment or to the open segment. The new name must, of course, not be one in use. Subsequently the old name is available for re-use.

―――

RENAME SEGMENT   WSOP, WSAC, SGOP   L1a

Parameters:

Input	old segment name		N
Input	new segment name		N

Effect:

Each occurrence of an old segment name in the 'set of stored segments for this workstation' in a workstation state list (cf. Section 4.3) and in the 'set of segment names in use' in the GKS state list is replaced by a new segment name. If the old segment name is the name of the open segment, the 'name of the open segment' in the GKS state list is set to the new segment name.

N.B.:
The old segment name may be re-used by the application program.
Errors:

7	GKS not in proper state: GKS should be in one of the states WSOP, WSAC or SGOP
120	Specified segment name is invalid
121	Specified segment name is already in use
122	Specified segment does not exist

—————————————————— *FORTRAN Interface* ——————————————————

CALL GRENSG (OLD,NEW)
Parameters:

Input	OLD	old segment name	INTEGER
Input	NEW	new segment name	INTEGER

DELETE SEGMENT deletes the specified segment from the display surfaces of all workstations and from the segment storage. Such a deletion cannot be reversed. If segments are to be temporarily deleted from the display surface, the function SET VISIBILITY may be used. The open segment cannot be deleted. After deletion, the segment name is available for re-use.

DELETE SEGMENT   WSOP,WSAC,SGOP   L1a
Parameters:

Input   segment name   N

Effect:
The segment and the entry in the 'set of stored segments for this workstation' in each workstation state list (cf. Section 4.3) which contains the segment name are deleted. The segment name is removed from the 'set of segment names in use' in the GKS state list. The segment's state list is cancelled.
N.B.:
The segment name may be re-used by the application program.
Errors:

7	GKS not in proper state: GKS should be in one of the states WSOP, WSAC or SGOP
120	Specified segment name is invalid
122	Specified segment does not exist
125	Specified segment is open

—————————————————— *FORTRAN Interface* ——————————————————

CALL GDSG (SGNA)
Parameters:

Input	SGNA	segment name	INTEGER

DELETE SEGMENT FROM WORKSTATION only deletes the segment from one specific workstation's display space and segment storage. If the segment is only present at this workstation, the effect is equivalent to DELETE SEGMENT. In some sense, DELETE SEGMENT FROM WORKSTATION can be regarded as a counterpart to ASSOCIATE SEGMENT WITH WORK-STATION (cf. Section 7.7).

DELETE SEGMENT FROM WORKSTATION   WSOP,WSAC,SGOP   L1a

Parameters:

Input	workstation identifier	N
Input	segment name	N

Effect:

The segment is deleted from the specified workstation. The segment name is removed from the 'set of stored segments for this workstation' in the workstation state list (cf. Section 4.3). The workstation identifier is removed from the 'set of associated workstations' in the segment state list. If the 'set of associated workstations' becomes empty, the segment is deleted, i.e. the DELETE SEGMENT function is performed.

Errors:

7	GKS not in proper state: GKS should be in one of the states WSOP, WSAC or SGOP
20	Specified workstation identifier is invalid
25	Specified workstation is not open
33	Specified workstation is of category MI
35	Specified workstation is of category INPUT
120	Specified segment name is invalid
123	Specified segment does not exist on specified workstation
125	Specified segment is open

———————————————— *FORTRAN Interface* ————————————————

CALL GDSGWK (WKID,SGNA)

Parameters:

Input	WKID	workstation identifier	INTEGER
Input	SGNA	segment name	INTEGER

CLEAR WORKSTATION (cf. Section 4.4) clears the display surface of one specified workstation and deletes all segments from its segment storage. This allows a new picture to be generated on a fresh display surface.

Usually, the new picture will not start from scratch but will use the pictorial information stored in the segment storage again. REDRAW ALL SEGMENTS ON WORKSTATION clears the display surface in the same way as CLEAR WORKSTATION. Then all segments stored for the specified workstation are redrawn. This is an efficient way of generating a sequence of pictures whose background remains constant while parts of the foreground can be changed. The parts of the picture which are constant can be stored in segments and will be regenerated automatically for each picture by REDRAW ALL SEG-MENTS ON WORKSTATION. Only the parts that change have to be generated by the application program directly (cf. Example 7.2).

REDRAW ALL SEGMENTS ON WORKSTATION
WSOP,WSAC,SGOP   L1a

Parameters:

Input	workstation identifier	N

Effect:

All of the following actions are executed in the given sequence:

a) All deferred actions for the specified workstation are executed (without intermediate clearing of the display surface).

b) The display surface is cleared only if the 'display surface empty' entry in the workstation state list is NOTEMPTY. The entry is set to EMPTY.

c) If the 'workstation transformation update state' entry in the workstation state list is PENDING, the 'current workstation window' and 'current workstation viewport' entries in the workstation state list are assigned the values of the 'requested workstation window' and 'requested workstation viewport' entries; the 'workstation transformation update state' entry is set to NOTPENDING.

d) All visible segments stored at this workstation (i.e. contained in the 'set of stored segments for this workstation' in the workstation state list) are redisplayed. This action usually causes the 'display surface empty' entry in the workstation state list to be set to NOTEMPTY.

e) The 'new frame action necessary at update' entry in the workstation state list is set to NO.

Errors:

7	GKS not in proper state: GKS should be in one of the states WSOP, WSAC or SGOP
20	Specified workstation identifier is invalid
25	Specified workstation is not open
33	Specified workstation is of category MI
35	Specified workstation is of category INPUT
36	Specified workstation is Workstation-Independent Segment Storage

———————————————— *FORTRAN Interface* ————————————————

CALL GRSGWK (WKID)
Parameters:
Input   WKID   workstation identifier   INTEGER

7.6   Manipulation of the Segment Attributes

In the following section, the functions for manipulating the segment attributes are described. The segment attributes include visibility, detectability, highlighting, segment priority, and segment transformation.

Visibility can assume one of two values: VISIBLE and INVISIBLE. In the former case, the primitives in the segment are stored and displayed. In the latter case, primitives are only stored and can be made visible later on. The default setting is VISIBLE. If a segment's visibility attribute changes from VISIBLE to INVISIBLE, the segment is erased from all display surfaces. At some workstations, this may lead to an implicit regeneration of the whole display. If a segment's visibility attribute changes to VISIBLE, this segment will be drawn at all workstations which were active while it was being generated (not which are currently active!).

The visibility attribute is useful for complex pictures where the display space is overloaded with graphical output. By setting the VISIBILITY attribute, those parts of the picture currently not of interest can be temporarily removed from the display surface.

The setting of the visibility attribute only affects the segment's state list and the display surface. The data structure in the segment storage is not affected.

This attribute can be reset arbitrarily. This is an important difference to the DELETE SEGMENT or DELETE SEGMENT FROM WORKSTATION functions.

SET VISIBILITY   WSOP,WSAC,SGOP   L1a
Parameters:
  Input   segment name   N
  Input   visibility   (VISIBLE,INVISIBLE)   E
Effect:
  The 'visibility' entry in the segment state list of the named segment is set equal to the value specified by the parameter.
Errors:
  7   GKS not in proper state: GKS should be in one of the states WSOP, WSAC or SGOP
  120   Specified segment name is invalid
  122   Specified segment does not exist

──────────────────── *FORTRAN Interface* ────────────────────

CALL GSVIS (SGNA,VIS)
Parameters:
  Input   SGNA   segment name   INTEGER
  Input   VIS   visibility   (0 = invisible, 1 = visible)   INTEGER

Detectability is used to select those segments which should be identifiable by the PICK input device. Therefore, it is supported only in those GKS levels where segments and input devices are present. This attribute can assume one of two values: DETECTABLE and UNDETECTABLE. The default setting is UNDETECTABLE so that an explicit action by the application program is necessary to make a segment available for the PICK input device. Detectability is subordinate to the visibility. Invisible segments are treated as undetectable, regardless of the setting of the detectability attribute.

There are several reasons why this attribute was introduced:
— to facilitate the identification of objects in complicated drawings;
— to avoid unwanted identifications;
— to optimize the performance of the PICK input device.

The detectability attribute restricts the sphere of the PICK input device to those objects the application program is interested in and is ready to work with. The display may show a lot of accompanying information which is helpful for decision making. By making such accompanying information undetectable, identification is not impeded, even if the manipulated structure is overlapped by accompanying data. Furthermore, if the PICK input device is simulated by searching the entire segment storage for the segment lying closest to the picked position, the performance may be improved considerably.

An example of the use of detectability is a map showing roads, railways, rivers, and towns. These four classes of objects may overlap or lie very closely, side by side. Even if the operator is editing one class of objects only, it is very helpful for him to see the entire map, as it improves his orientation on the map and the context may be important for his editing task.

SET DETECTABILITY   WSOP, WSAC, SGOP   L1b

Parameters:

Input	segment name		N
Input	detectability	(UNDETECTABLE, DETECTABLE)	E

Effect:

The 'detectability' entry in the segment state list of the named segment is set equal to the value specified by the parameter. If the segment is marked as DETECTABLE and VISIBLE, the primitives in it are available for PICK input. DETECTABLE but INVISIBLE segments cannot be picked.

Errors:

7   GKS not in proper state: GKS should be in one of the states WSOP, WSAC or SGOP

120   Specified segment name is invalid

122   Specified segment does not exist

———————————————— *FORTRAN Interface* ————————————————

CALL GSDTEC (SGNA, DET)

Parameters:

Input	SGNA	segment name	INTEGER
Input	DET	detectability (0 = undetectable, 1 = detectable)	INTEGER

The highlighting attribute is used to emphasize a segment and to draw the attention of an operator to a specific part of the display. A standard application is the echo of the segment picked by the PICK input device. The highlighting attribute can assume the values HIGHLIGHTED and NORMAL. The default setting is NORMAL. The highlighting is subordinate to the visibility attribute. Invisible segments are not highlighted, regardless of how the highlighting attribute is set.

The way a segment is highlighted depends on the capabilities of the respective workstation. Some devices can increase the intensity and use this technique to emphasize a segment. Others use blinking or they repeatedly draw the segment.

SET HIGHLIGHTING   WSOP, WSAC, SGOP   L1a

Parameters:

Input	segment name		N
Input	highlighting	(NORMAL, HIGHLIGHTED)	E

Effect:

The 'highlighting' entry in the segment state list of the named segment is set equal to the value specified by the parameter. If the segment is marked as HIGHLIGHTED and VISIBLE, the primitives in it are highlighted in an implementation-dependent manner.

Errors:

7   GKS not in proper state: GKS should be in one of the states WSOP, WSAC or SGOP

120   Specified segment name is invalid

122   Specified segment does not exist

———————————— *FORTRAN Interface* ————————————

CALL GSHLIT (SGNA,HIL)

Parameters:

Input	SGNA	segment name		INTEGER
Input	HIL	highlighting	(0 = normal, 1 = highlighted)	INTEGER

The segment priority decides in the case of segments which visibly overlap, which segment should be given preference. This preference has an effect on the display of primitives and for the PICK input device. The segment priority lies in the interval [0,1] and the default value is 0, which is the lowest priority.

If output primitives overlap, the visible effect on the display surface depends on the device. For many devices, for example, plotter and vector devices, the effect is beyond the control of the graphics system or is very difficult to control. As long as only lines are drawn, the overlapping may be neglected.

However, there are devices today which are gaining more and more importance and where the effect of overlapping primitives is fully under the control of the graphics software. This is the case for raster devices where the picture is converted into a raster image and stored in a frame buffer from which it is repeatedly displayed on a display surface. The overlapping takes place in the frame buffer and an implementor has to make a decision as to what to do. The segment priority is intended to address these capabilities. It is not intended that such capabilities should be simulated on vector devices.

Segment priority only applies to segments as a whole. If primitives within one segment overlap, the effect is not defined by GKS and, therefore, is implementation-dependent.

SET SEGMENT PRIORITY   WSOP, WSAC, SGOP   L1a

Parameters:

Input	segment name		N
Input	segment priority	[0,1]	R

Effect:

The 'segment priority' entry in the segment state list of the named segment is set equal to the value specified by the parameter. Segment priority affects the display of segments and PICK input if segments overlap, in which case GKS gives precedence to segments with higher priority. If segments with the same priority overlap, the result is implementation-dependent.

N.B.:

The use of segment priority applies only to workstations where the entry 'number of segment priorities supported' in the workstation description table is greater than 1 or equal to 0 (indicating an infinite number of priorities supported).

If 'number of segment priorities supported' is greater than 1, the range [0,1] for segment priority is mapped to the range 1 to 'number of segment priorities supported' for a specific workstation before being used by a device driver. If 'number of segment priorities supported' is equal to 0, the implementation will allow all values of segment priority to be differentiated.

This feature is intended to address appropriate hardware capabilities only. It cannot be used to force software checking of interference between segments on non-raster displays.

The segment priority is also used for picking segments. When overlapping or intersecting segments are picked, the segment with higher priority is delivered as a result of the PICK input primitive. All workstations having PICK input should provide this mechanism.

Errors:

7	GKS not in proper state: GKS should be in one of the states WSOP, WSAC or SGOP
120	Specified segment name is invalid
122	Specified segment does not exist
126	Segment priority is outside the range $[0, 1]$

―――――――――――――――― *FORTRAN Interface* ――――――――――――――――

CALL GSSGP (SGNA, PRIOR)
Parameters:

Input	SGNA	segment name		INTEGER
Input	PRIOR	segment priority	$[0, 1]$	REAL

A segment transformation is a mapping from NDC onto NDC comprising of translation, non-uniform scaling and rotation components. The segment transformation is specified by a 2×3 transformation matrix consisting of a 2×2 scaling and rotation portion and a 2×1 translation portion. Utility functions (cf. Section 7.9) are available to the application program for setting up the transformation matrix. A fixed point for scaling and rotation, and a shift vector in either WC or NDC may be specified. In the former case, the WC values of the shift vector are first transformed by using the current normalization transformation.

The segment transformation takes place after the normalization transformation but before any clipping. The primitives of the transformed segment are clipped around the clipping rectangle which is stored with the primitives. It should be noted that the clipping rectangle itself is not transformed.

A segment transformation, specified by the SET SEGMENT TRANSFORMATION function, does not actually take place in the segment storage but is only saved in the segment state list. Every time the segment is redrawn, this segment transformation will be applied before clipping. Successive SET SEGMENT TRANSFORMATION function calls for the same segment are not accumulated; in fact each succeeding transformation matrix replaces its predecessor. By calling SET SEGMENT TRANSFORMATION with an identity transformation matrix, the original segment can be obtained without any loss of information.

It should be noted that LOCATOR input data is not affected by any segment transformation.

―――

SET SEGMENT TRANSFORMATION	WSOP, WSAC, SGOP	L1a
Parameters:		
Input segment name		N
Input transformation matrix		$2 \times 3 \times R$

Effect:

The 'segment transformation matrix' in the segment state list is set equal to the value specified by the parameter. When a segment is displayed, the coordinates of its primitives will be transformed by applying the following matrix multiplication to them:

$$\begin{bmatrix} x' \\ y' \end{bmatrix} = \begin{bmatrix} M11 & M12 & M13 \\ M21 & M22 & M23 \end{bmatrix} \times \begin{bmatrix} x \\ y \\ 1 \end{bmatrix}$$

The original coordinates are (x,y), the transformed coordinates are (x',y'), both in NDC. The values M13 and M23 of the transformation matrix are in NDC coordinates, the other values are unitless. In the case of geometric attributes which are vectors (for example, CHARACTER UP VECTOR), the values M13 and M23 are ignored.

This function can be used to transform a segment stored on a workstation. The transformation applies to all workstations where the specified segment is stored, even if they are not all active.

The segment transformation (conceptually) takes place in NDC space. The segment transformation will be stored in the segment state list and will not affect the contents of the segment. The segment transformation is not cumulative, i.e., it always applies to the segment which was originally created.

N.B.:

Applying the same segment transformation twice to a segment will give identical results. The identity transformation will show the segment in its original geometrical appearance.

Errors:

7	GKS not in proper state: GKS should be in one of the states WSOP, WSAC or SGOP
120	Specified segment name is invalid
122	Specified segment does not exist

———————————————— *FORTRAN Interface* ————————————————

CALL GSSGT (SGNA,M)

Parameters:

Input	SGNA	segment name	INTEGER
Input	M(2,3)	transformation matrix	$2 \times 3 \times$ REAL

7.7 The Workstation-Independent Segment Storage (WISS)

In the preceding sections, it was assumed that each segment had a unique definition and that there was one instance of this conceptual segment on each associated workstation. This model was chosen to make it clearer that a segment is related to all workstations activated at segment generation time. However, GKS does not presume anything about the implementation of a segment storage. An implementor may implement the segment storage in different ways as long as the functional requirements are met.

All functions mentioned in the previous sections only manipulate segments at workstations for which they were created. This functionality can be realized by decentralized segment storages as well as with one central segment storage, and by segments stored in workstation-dependent as well as in workstation-independent format. If efficiency is required it is better to have a local storage of segments because there will be no delay due to transmission. Furthermore, data will be stored in a workstation-dependent format which also improves performance.

Such a local *workstation-dependent segment storage (WDSS)* is good for local manipulations. However, there are other requirements which cannot be met by a WDSS. If a segment is generated and edited at one workstation and then is to be sent to another workstation, a workstation-independent representation of the segment is required. This is also true if a segment storage is used as a symbol facility containing subpictures from which a picture is to be constructed. As some overhead is involved with the workstation-independent representation, GKS has introduced a special workstation called *workstation-independent segment storage (WISS)*. The WISS is only a conceptual scheme which need not necessarily be realized by using a physical workstation. The WISS is a means of identifying those segments which must be stored in such a manner that the following functions can be provided:
— sending copies of segments to another workstation for immediate output;
— sending copies of segments as an entity into the segment storage of a workstation which was not active during segment generation;
— symbol facility which enables pictures to be constructed from previously defined segments.

Being a conceptual scheme, there is only one WISS workstation in GKS.

COPY SEGMENT TO WORKSTATION creates a copy of a segment stored in the WISS. The primitives and their geometric attributes are transformed by the segment transformation. The transformed data, together with the other attributes and the associated clipping rectangles, is inserted into the viewing pipeline at the same place where the information previously left it. Then it is sent down the pathway to the workstation specified when the function was called. No segment can be open when this function is invoked.

The main purpose of this function is to send a copy of a picture generated and edited at an interactive workstation to a hard copy workstation so that the final result of an interactive session can be saved.

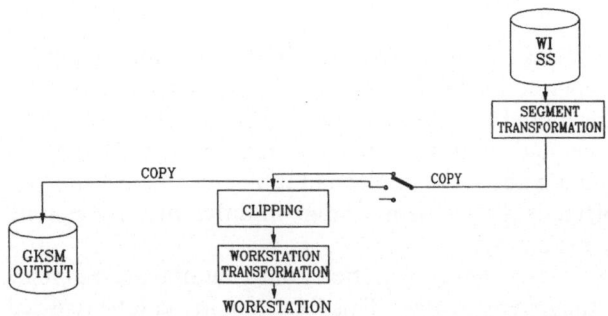

Figure 7.2 Data flow for COPY SEGMENT TO WORKSTATION

COPY SEGMENT TO WORKSTATION   WSOP, WSAC   L2a

Parameters:

Input	workstation identifier	N
Input	segment name	N

Effect:

The primitives in the segment are sent to the specified workstation after segment transformation and clipping. They are not stored in a segment.

N.B.:

The specified segment must be present in the workstation-independent segment storage. The specified workstation must not be workstation-independent segment storage. All primitives keep the values of the primitive attributes (for example, polyline index, text path, pick identifier) which are assigned to them when they are created, for their whole lifetime. In particular, when segments are copied, the values of the primitive attributes within the copied segments remain unchanged.

Errors:

6	GKS not in proper state: GKS should be either in the state WSOP or in the state WSAC
20	Specified workstation identifier is invalid
25	Specified workstation is not open
27	Workstation-Independent Segment Storage is not open
33	Specified workstation is of category MI
35	Specified workstation is of category INPUT
36	Specified workstation is Workstation-Independent Segment Storage
120	Specified segment name is invalid
124	Specified segment does not exist on Workstation-Independent segment Storage

———————————————— *FORTRAN Interface* ————————————————

CALL GCSGWK (WKID,SGNA)

Parameters:

Input	WKID	workstation identifier	INTEGER
Input	SGNA	segment name	INTEGER

ASSOCIATE SEGMENT WITH WORKSTATION sends the segment to the specified workstation. With the use of this function the same situation is achieved as if the workstation had been active when the segment was created.

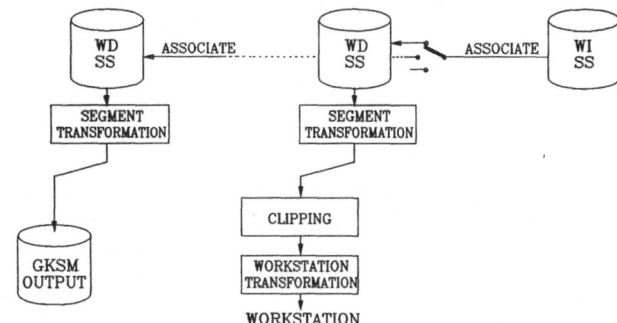

Figure 7.3 Data flow for ASSOCIATE SEGMENT WITH WORKSTATION

Only segments contained in the WISS may be sent to other workstations. This function merely manipulates the entry 'set of associated workstations' in the segment state list of the specified segment. Whereas ASSOCIATE SEGMENT WITH WORKSTATION adds one new element to the 'set of associated workstations', the function DELETE SEGMENT FROM WORKSTATION (cf. Section 7.5) can be used to remove one element. This function cannot be invoked when a segment is open.

ASSOCIATE SEGMENT WITH WORKSTATION   WSOP, WSAC   L2a

Parameters:

Input   workstation identifier   N
Input   segment name   N

Effect:

The segment is sent to the specified workstation in the same way as if the workstation were active when the segment was created. The segment name is added to the 'set of stored segments' in the workstation state list (cf. Section 4.3). The workstation identifier is included in the 'set of associated workstations' in the segment state list (cf. Section 7.5).

N.B.:

The specified segment must be present in the workstation-independent segment storage. If the segment is already associated with the specified workstation, this function has no effect.

Errors:

6	GKS not in proper state: GKS should be either in the state WSOP or in the state WSAC
20	Specified workstation identifier is invalid
25	Specified workstation is not open
27	Workstation-Independent Segment Storage is not open
33	Specified workstation is of category MI
35	Specified workstation is of category INPUT
120	Specified segment name is invalid
124	Specified segment does not exist on Workstation-Independent Segment Storage

——————————— *FORTRAN Interface* ———————————

CALL GASGWK (WKID, SGNA)

Parameters:

Input   WKID   workstation identifier   INTEGER
Input   SGNA   segment name   INTEGER

INSERT SEGMENT copies the primitives contained in a segment from the WISS, applies the segment transformation followed by the insert transformation and then inserts them into the viewing pipeline at the point before data is distributed to the workstations. Thus, inserted information may re-enter the WISS if the WISS is active and a segment is open. The primitives retain all their attributes except the clipping rectangle. The old clipping rectangles are discarded. Each primitive processed is assigned the current clipping rectangle

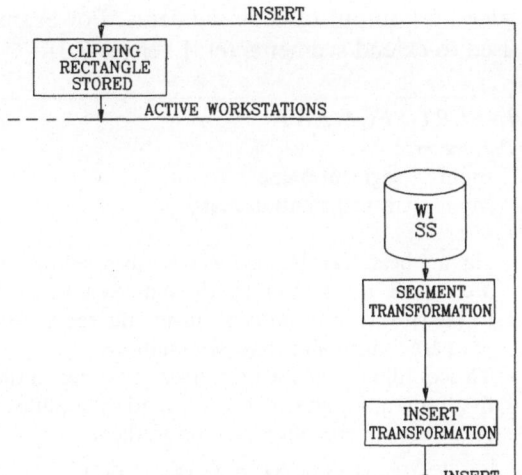

Figure 7.4 Data flow
for INSERT SEGMENT

which is the viewport of the currently selected normalization transformation
if the clipping indicator is on, and is $[0,1] \times [0,1]$ if the clipping indicator is
off. In other words, clipping rectangles are assigned to inserted primitives in
the same manner as currently generated primitives.

Calling INSERT SEGMENT has no effect on the output primitives passing
through the pipeline before or after the call. For example, the attributes bound
to the inserted primitives do not affect the current setting of attributes which
are applied to freshly generated primitives. The INSERT SEGMENT function
can be used when a segment is open. It should be noted that the open segment
itself cannot be inserted to avoid recursive copying.

The insert transformation is specified in the same way as the segment transformation. For consistency, both transformations, the segment transformation
and the insert transformation, will be applied. However, in practice, at most
one of them will be different from identity. The main advantage of the insert
transformation is that it provides the possibility of copying one segment several
times at different places and in different sizes. The same effect could be achieved
by setting the segment transformation before inserting the segment. However,
a separate insert transformation has been included in order to simplify the
user interface and to avoid annoying effects which might occur at workstations
which have no adequate capabilities for dynamically changing the segment transformation.

Example 7.7 shows the use of the insert transformation for generating 60
minute markers from two sample markers.

It is not allowed to re-open an existing segment and add more primitives.
A major difference between COPY SEGMENT TO WORKSTATION and
INSERT SEGMENT is that output from INSERT SEGMENT may be sent
to another segment whereas COPY SEGMENT TO WORKSTATION only

generates output outside segments. For example, INSERT SEGMENT can be used to extend segments (cf. Exercise 7.3).

INSERT SEGMENT   WSAC, SGOP   L2a

Parameters:

Input   segment name   N
Input   transformation matrix $2 \times 3 \times R$

Effect:

Having been transformed as described below, the primitives contained in the segment are copied and sent either (in state SGOP) to the open segment or (in state WSAC) to the stream of primitives outside the segments. In both cases the transformed primitives are sent to all active workstations.

The coordinates of the primitives contained in the inserted segment will be transformed firstly by any segment transformation specified for it, and secondly by applying the following matrix multiplication to them.

$$\begin{bmatrix} x' \\ y' \end{bmatrix} = \begin{bmatrix} M11 & M12 & M13 \\ M21 & M22 & M23 \end{bmatrix} \times \begin{bmatrix} x \\ y \\ 1 \end{bmatrix}$$

The original coordinates are (x,y), the transformed coordinates are (x',y'), both in NDC. The values $M13$ and $M23$ of the transformation matrix are NDC coordinates, the other values are unitless. For geometric attributes which are vectors (for example, CHARACTER UP VECTOR), the values $M13$ and $M23$ are ignored.

The insert transformation (conceptually) takes place in NDC space. Apart from the segment transformation, attributes associated with the inserted segment are ignored.

All clipping rectangles in the inserted segment are ignored. Each primitive processed is assigned a new clipping rectangle which is the viewport of the currently selected normalization transformation if the clipping indicator is ON, and is $[0,1] \times [0,1]$ if the clipping indicator if OFF. All primitives processed by a single call of INSERT SEGMENT receive the same clipping rectangle.

N.B.:

The specified segment must be in workstation-independent segment storage and not be the open segment. All primitives retain the values of the primitive attributes (e.g., polyline index, text path, pick identifier) which are assigned to them when they are created for their whole lifetime. In particular, when segments are inserted, the values of the primitive attributes within the inserted segments remain unchanged. The values of primitive attributes used to generate subsequent primitives with the segment into which the insertion takes place are unaffected by this insertion.

Errors:

5   GKS not in proper state: GKS should be either in the state WSAC or in the state SGOP
27   Workstation-Independent Segment Storage is not open
120   Specified segment name is invalid
124   Specified segment does not exist on Workstation-Independent Segment Storage
125   Specified segment is open

――――――――――――――― *FORTRAN Interface* ―――――――――――――――

CALL GINSG (SGNA,M)

Parameters:

Input   SGNA   segment name   INTEGER
Input   M(2,3)   transformation matrix $2 \times 3 \times REAL$

7.8   Different Levels of Segmentation

The segment mechanism of GKS provides some powerful features which must be paid for in terms of implementation costs and performance. However, these segmentation capabilities are not satisfactory for all applications. There may be applications which do not need a segment storage at all. For example, batch plotting programs generating complex maps from a consistent cartographical data basis do not need interactive capabilities and efficiency is very important. There may also be applications which have requirements not met by the GKS segment storage. These applications have to build their own comfortable data structure outside GKS and would prefer to avoid paying the overhead for a second data structure within GKS.

When the level structure of GKS was defined, these requirements were considered. GKS thus provides three segmentation levels:
0. no segmentation at all,
1. basic segmentation. This includes all functions which can be implemented only by workstation-dependent segment storages (WDSS).
2. full segmentation. This includes those functions which use the workstation-independent segment storage (WISS).

To ensure there is compatibility between level 0 and 1, output primitives in GKS may be generated outside and inside of segments, even in those levels supporting segmentation. Therefore, a programmer may optimize his program by storing in the segments only those primitives to be re-used later on, and generating outside the segments all primitives to be displayed only once.

7.9   Utility Functions

The GKS functions SET SEGMENT TRANSFORMATION and INSERT SEGMENT allow a segment to be transformed. The transformation is defined by a 2×3 transformation matrix. This matrix is a compact means of specifying the full range of affine transformation capabilities but it is not suitable for a programmer. Therefore, GKS includes two utility functions which accept definitions of transformations in terms of shift, scaling, rotation and generate the respective transformation matrix to be passed to SET SEGMENT TRANS-FORMATION and INSERT SEGMENT. For scaling and rotation a fixed point must be specified relative to which scaling is performed or which serves as the centrepoint for rotation. The fixed point and shift vector can be specified either in world coordinates, which is the usual coordinate system for GKS users, or in normalized coordinates, which reflects the fact that segment transformations take place in NDC exclusively.

The order in which the single transformation operations take place is firstly to scale, and then rotate and shift. It should be noted that a different order generally yields different results. The first utility function EVALUATE TRANS-FORMATION MATRIX directly generates a matrix from the single operations specified in the parameter list. The second function ACCUMULATE TRANS-

FORMATION MATRIX allows any number of shift, scale, rotate operations to be accumulated in any order and multiplicity in one transformation matrix. This function requires an input matrix which probably will have been initialised by EVALUATE TRANSFORMATION MATRIX.

EVALUATE TRANSFORMATION MATRIX
GKOP, WSOP, WSAC, SGOP   L1a

Parameters:

Input	fixed point	WC/NDC	P
Input	shift vector	WC/NDC	P
Input	rotation angle in radians (positive if anti-clockwise)		R
Input	scale factors		$2 \times$ R
Input	coordinate switch	(WC, NDC)	E
Output	segment transformation matrix		$2 \times 3 \times$ R

Effect:

The transformation defined by fixed point, shift vector, rotation angle, and scale factors is evaluated and the result is put in the output segment transformation matrix (for use by INSERT SEGMENT and SET SEGMENT TRANSFORMATION). The coordinate switch determines whether the shift vector and fixed point are given in WC or NDC. If WC are used, the shift vector and the fixed point are transformed by the current normalization transformation. The order of transformation is: scale, rotate (both relative to the specified fixed point), and shift. The elements $M13$ and $M23$ of the resulting 2×3 transformation matrix are in NDC, the other elements are unitless.

Errors:

8   GKS not in proper state: GKS should be in one of the states GKOP, WSOP, WSAC or SGOP

─────────────────────── *FORTRAN Interface* ───────────────────────

CALL GEVTM (X0, Y0, DX, DY, PHI, FX, FY, SW, MOUT)

Parameters:

Input	X0, Y0	fixed point	WC/NDC	$2 \times$ REAL
Input	DX, DY	shift vector	WC/NDC	$2 \times$ REAL
Input	PHI	rotation angle in radians		REAL
Input	FX, FY	scale factors		$2 \times$ REAL
Input	SW	coordinate switch	(0 = WC, 1 = NDC)	INTEGER
Output	MOUT(2,3)	segment transformation matrix		$2 \times 3 \times$ REAL

ACCUMULATE TRANSFORMATION MATRIX
GKOP, WSOP, WSAC, SGOP   L1a

Parameters:

Input	segment transformation matrix		$2 \times 3 \times$ R
Input	fixed point	WC/NDC	P
Input	shift vector	WC/NDC	P
Input	rotation angle in radians (positive if anti-clockwise)		R
Input	scale factors		$2 \times$ R
Input	coordinate switch	(WC, NDC)	E
Output	segment transformation matrix		$2 \times 3 \times$ R

Effect:

The transformation defined by fixed point, shift vector, rotation angle, and scale factors is composed with the input segment transformation matrix and the result is returned in the output segment transformation matrix (for use by INSERT SEGMENT and SET SEGMENT TRANSFORMATION). The coordinate switch determines whether the shift vector and fixed point are given in WC or NDC. If WC are used, the shift vector and the fixed point are transformed by the current normalization transformation. The order of transformation is: specified input matrix, scale, rotate (both relative to the specified fixed point), and shift. The elements $M13$ and $M23$ of the 2×3 input matrix and the resulting 2×3 transformation matrix are in NDC, the other elements are unitless.

Errors:

8	GKS not in proper state: GKS should be in one of the states GKOP, WSOP, WSAC or SGOP

———————————— *FORTRAN Interface* ————————————

CALL GACTM (MIN, X0, Y0, DX, DY, PHI, FX, FY, SW, MOUT)

Parameters:

Input	MIN(2,3)	segment transformation matrix		$2 \times 3 \times$ REAL
Input	X0, Y0	fixed point	WC/NDC	$2 \times$ REAL
Input	DX, DY	shift vector	WC/NDC	$2 \times$ REAL
Input	PHI	rotation angle in radians		REAL
Input	FX, FY	scale factors		$2 \times$ REAL
Input	SW	coordinate switch	(0 = WC, 1 = NDC)	INTEGER
Output	MOUT(2,3)	segment transformation matrix		$2 \times 3 \times$ REAL

7.10   Examples

Example 7.1   Zooming where content of picture depends on scale

The primary purpose of zooming is to make details present in the picture recognizable by changing the scale. Figure 5.2 on page 157 demonstrates a simple zoom.

The segment mechanism, however, makes a more powerful zoom capability possible. In this example, a map is drawn showing political boundaries at different levels (national, state, county). According to these levels, boundaries are stored in different segments. After this initialisation stage, the map can be zoomed in on. Depending on the scale, a particular level of boundaries can be made visible or can be suppressed (cf. Figure 7.5). It is assumed that the operator, when selecting the region to be zoomed in on, has the possibility of setting a switch 'interrupt'.

———————————————— *Pascal* ————————————————

```
L10   ACTIVATE_WORKSTATION(display);                    {select workstation}

L20   CREATE_SEGMENT (seg1);        {Segment 1 contains national boundaries}
L30      DRAW_FILE (borders_1);
L40   CLOSE_SEGMENT;                                        {See Figure 7.5a}
```

L50 CREATE_SEGMENT (seg2);   {Segment 2 contains state boundaries}
L60   SET_VISIBILITY (2, INVISIBLE);
L70   DRAW_FILE (borders_2);
L80 CLOSE_SEGMENT;
L90 CREATE_SEGMENT (seg3);   {Segment 3 contains county boundaries}
L100   SET_VISIBILITY (3, INVISIBLE);
L110   DRAW_FILE (borders_3);
L120 CLOSE_SEGMENT;

L130 repeat
              ,{Select interactively region to be zoomed; statements are omitted here.}
L150   SET_WORKSTATION_WINDOW (display, xmin, xmax, ymin, ymax);
L160   **if** xmax − xmin < 0.5 **then** SET_VISIBILITY (seg2, VISIBLE) {See Figure 7.5b}
L170   **else** SET_VISIBILITY (seg2, INVISIBLE);
L180   **if** xmax − xmin < 0.25 **then** SET_VISIBILITY (seg3, VISIBLE) {See Figure 7.5c}
L190   **else** SET_VISIBILITY (seg3, INVISIBLE);
L200 until interrupt;

───────────────────────── *Fortran* ─────────────────────────

```
         C       *** select workstation
L10              CALL GACWK (DISPL)
         C       *** Segment 1 contains national boundaries
L20              CALL GCRSG (SEG1)
L30              CALL DRFILE (21)
L40              CALL GCLSG
         C       *** See Figure 7.5a


         C       *** Segment 2 contains state boundaries
L50              CALL GCRSG (SEG2)
L60              CALL GSVIS (SEG2, INVIS)
L70              CALL DRFILE (22)
L80              CALL GCLSG


         C       *** Segment 3 contains county boundaries
L90              CALL GCRSG (SEG3)
L100             CALL GSVIS (SEG3, INVIS)
L110             CALL DRFILE (23)
L120             CALL GCLSG
L130    130      CONTINUE
         C       *** Select interactively region to be zoomed;
         C       *** statements are omitted here.
L150             CALL GSWKWN (DISPL, XMIN, XMAX, YMIN, YMAX)
L160             IF (XMAX − XMIN .LT. 0.5) CALL GSVIS (SEG2, VISIBL)
L170             IF (XMAX − XMIN .GE. 0.5) CALL GSVIS (SEG2, INVIS)
         C       *** See Figure 7.5b
L180             IF (XMAX − XMIN .LT. 0.25) CALL GSVIS (SEG3, VISIBL)
L190             IF (XMAX − XMIN .GE. 0.25) CALL GSVIS (SEG3, INVIS)
         C       *** See Figure 7.5c
L200             IF (.NOT. INTRPT) GOTO 130
```

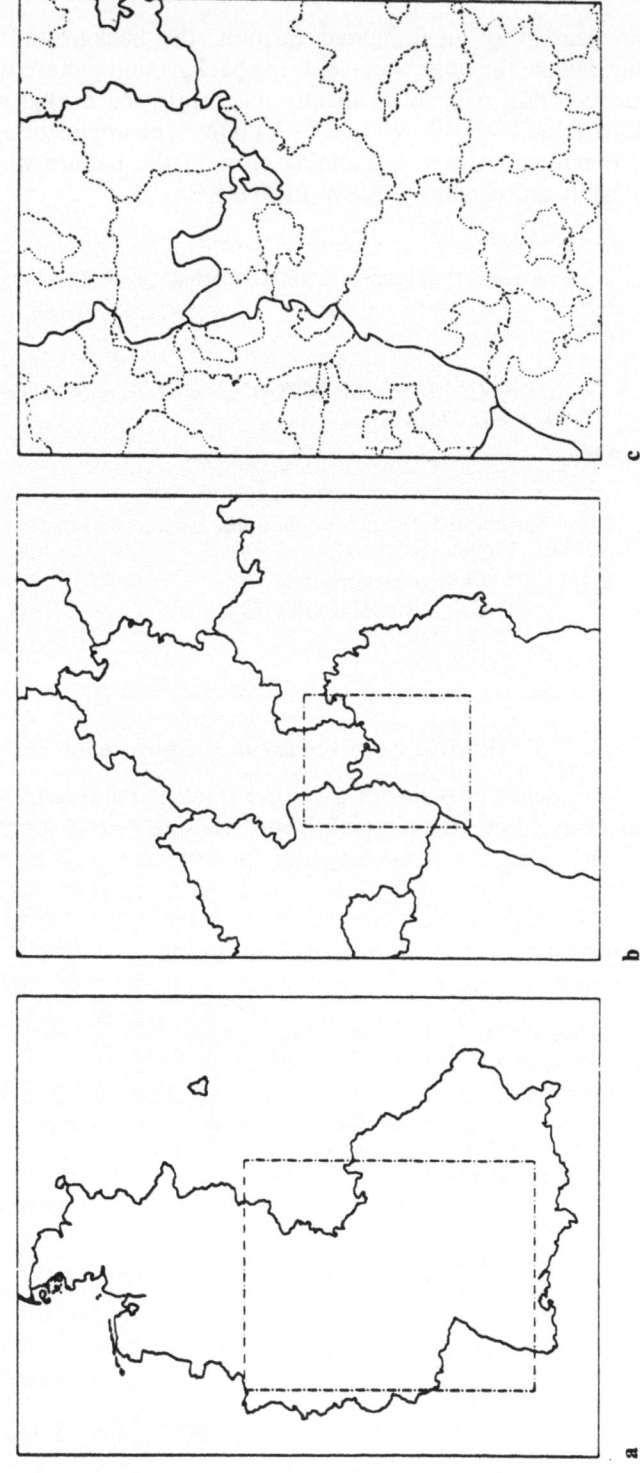

Figure 7.5 Zooming with details added to the picture depending on scale

Example 7.2   Generating a sequence of pictures with invariant background

When generating an animated cartoon, the background often remains unchanged while the objects move. If the background picture is generated by using segments, GKS will automatically regenerate the background by REDRAW ALL SEGMENTS ON WORKSTATION. The application program can focus on the generation of the changing parts in the picture which is assumed will be done by a procedure DRAW_PICTURE.

Pascal

```
L10        {Assume that segments containing background picture have been generated}
L20   for i: = 1 to max do
L30   begin
                                                              {Draw background}
L40      REDRAW_ALL_SEGMENTS_ON_WORKSTATION (plot);
L50      DRAW_PICTURE(i);                                    {draw i-th picture}
L60   end;
```

Fortran

```
L10   C     Assume that segments containing background picture have been generated
L20           DO 60 I = 1, MAX
      C       *** Draw background
L40           CALL GRSGWK (PLOT)
L50           CALL DRPICT (I)
L60    60     CONTINUE
```

Example 7.3   Illustration of the use of the pick identifier

The pick identifier provides a second level of naming on top of the segment mechanism. However, the pick identifier is an output primitive attribute and, therefore, is governed by the rules for attributes rather than by the naming conventions for segments. This example demonstrates that the pick identifier can be assigned to non-contiguous groups of primitives and that its value is not affected by a segment opening and closing.

Pascal

```
L10   SET_PICK_IDENTIFIER (pi1);      {pick identifier = pi1, no effect on primitives}
L20   CREATE_SEGMENT (seg1);
L30   Output primitives;
                {pick identifier pi1 associated to these primitives in segment storage}
L40   SET_PICK_IDENTIFIER (pi2);
L50   Output primitives;
                {pick identifier pi2 associated to these primitives in segment storage}
L60   SET_PICK_IDENTIFIER (pi1);
L70   Output primitives;
                {pick identifier pi1 associated to these primitives in segment storage}
L80   SET_PICK_IDENTIFIER (pi3);
L90   Output primitives;
                {pick identifier pi3 associated to these primitives in segment storage}
L100  CLOSE_SEGMENT;
L110  Output primitives;              {pick identifier = pi3, no effect on primitives}
```

—————————————— *Fortran* ——————————————

L10	CALL GSPKID (1)
C	*** pick identifier = 1, no effect on primitives
L20	CALL GCRSG (SEG1)
L30	Output primitives
C	*** pick identifier 1 associated to these primitives in segment storage
L40	CALL GSPKID (2)
L50	Output primitives
C	*** pick identifier 2 associated to these primitives in segment storage
L60	CALL GSPKID (1)
L70	Output primitives
C	*** pick identifier 1 associated to these primitives in segment storage
L80	CALL GSPKID (3)
L90	Output primitives
C	*** pick identifier 3 associated to these primitives in segment storage
L100	CALL GCLSG
L110	Output primitives
C	*** pick identifier = 3, no effect on primitives

Example 7.4   Clock with dynamic hands realized by CREATE, DELETE, RENAME

Three segments (seg1, seg2, seg3) are created which contain the hour, minute, and second hands of a clock. Every second, a new segment (temp) is created for each hand which shows the updated position. The old segment is deleted and the new segment is given the original name.

Procedure HAND contains the description of a standard hand pointing upwards towards 12 on the clock face. This hand is transformed so that it takes on different sizes for the hour, minute, and second hands. Furthermore, the hand is rotated to point to the correct position on the clock face. The rotation angle corresponds to the clock time in the following way: 12 hours correspond to angle twopi (angle: = twopi * hours/12); 60 minutes correspond to angle twopi (angle: = twopi * minutes/60); 60 seconds correspond to angle twopi (angle: = twopi * seconds/60); radians are measured counter-clockwise (angle: = − angle). The hour hand does not jump from one hour to the next but is moved slightly every minute with 60 minutes corresponding to one hour (angle: = − twopi * (hours + minutes/60.0)/12).

—————————————— *Pascal* ——————————————

L630 procedure HAND (segment: **name**; angle, width, length: **real**)
    {Creates segment 'segment' containing a clock hand with width 'width' and length
                     'length' at angle 'angle'. $0 \leq$ angle ≤ 1, clockwise}

L640 const twopi = 6.2831852;
L650 var hand_x, hand_y: **real**;
L660   x, y, xx, yy: **array** [1 .. 5] **of real**;
L670 begin
                     {x, y describe hand with length 1 pointing upwards}
L680   x[1]: = 0.00; x[2]: = width; x[3]: = 0.0; x[4]: = − width; x[5]: = 0.00;
L690   y[1]: = 0.01; y[2]: = 0.15; y[3]: = 1.0; y[4]: = 0.15; y[5]: = 0.01;
                     {Compute complex number which is to be multiplied with x, y}

```
L700    hand_x:=cos(−angle∗twopi)∗length; {to achieve proper scaling and rotation}
L710    hand_y:=sin(−angle∗twopi)∗length;

L720    for i:=1 to 5 do
L730    begin
L740      xx[i]:=x[i]∗hand_x−y[i]∗hand_y;
L750      yy[i]:=x[i]∗hand_y+y[i]∗hand_x;
L760    end;
L770    CREATE_SEGMENT (segment);
L780    POLYLINE (5,xx,yy);                              {Generating hand}
L790    CLOSE_SEGMENT;
L800  end {HAND};

L510  procedure HHAND (segment: name; hours,minutes: integer)
L520  begin HAND (segment, (hours+minutes/60.0)/12.0, 0.05, 0.6);
L540  end {HHAND};                                       {Draws hour hand}

L550  procedure MHAND (segment: name; minutes: integer)
L560  begin HAND (segment, minutes/60.0, 0.03, 0.8);     {Draws minute hand}
L580  end {MHAND};

L590  procedure SHAND (segment: name; seconds: integer)
L600  begin HAND (segment, seconds/60.0, 0.01, 0.95);    {Draws second hand}
L620  end {SHAND};

L10   procedure CLOCK1;
                    {Generating real time clock using CREATE, DELETE, RENAME}
L20   const error_file=..... ;
L30     memory_limit=..... ;
L40     display=..... ;
L50     connection=..... ;
L60     type=..... ;
L70   var stop: boolean;
L80     hours,minutes,seconds,hours1,minutes1,seconds1: integer;
L90     seg1,seg2,seg3,temp,digits: name;
                          {Names must be initialised to distinct values}
L100  begin                                              {Initialisation}
L110    OPEN_GKS (error_file,memory_limit);
L120    OPEN_WORKSTATION (display,connection,type);
L130    ACTIVATE_WORKSTATION (display);
                      {Set and select normalization transformation 1}
L140    SET_WINDOW (1, −1.0,+1.0, −1.0,+1.0);
L150    SELECT_NORMALIZATION_TRANSFORMATION (1);

L160    MINUTE_MARKERS;              {Draws minute markers, see Example 7.7}
L170    CREATE_SEGMENT (digits);
L171    CLOCK_FACE_DIGITS;           {Generates digits, see Example 6.7}
L172    CLOSE_SEGMENT;
L180    TIME (hours,minutes,seconds); {Assume that TIME delivers clock time}
L190    HHAND (seg1, hours, minutes);             {Generate hands}
L200    MHAND (seg2, minutes);
L210    SHAND (seg3, seconds);
```

```
L220    while (not stop) do                                    {Loop forever}
                                          {Wait for 1 second very useful here}
                              {Examine some input device here which sets 'stop'}
L230    begin                                    {Updating of real time clock}
L240       TIME (hours1,minutes1,seconds1);                       {Get real time}

L250    if not ((hours=hours1) and (minutes=minutes1)) then
L260    begin                              {Redraw hour hand once a minute}
L270       HHAND (temp, hours1, minutes1);
L280       DELETE_SEGMENT (seg1);
L290       RENAME_SEGMENT (temp,seg1);
L300       hours:=hours1;
L310    end;
L320    if not (minutes=minutes1) then
L330    begin                              {Redraw minute hand once a minute}
L340       MHAND (temp, minutes1);
L350       DELETE_SEGMENT (seg2);
L360       RENAME_SEGMENT (temp,seg2);
L370       minutes:=minutes1;
L380    end;
L390    if not (seconds=seconds1) then
L400    begin                              {Redraw second hand once a second}
L410       SHAND (temp,seconds1);
L420       DELETE_SEGMENT (seg3);
L430       RENAME_SEGMENT (temp,seg3);
L440       seconds:=seconds1;
L450    end;
L460   end;
L470 DEACTIVATE_WORKSTATION (display);
L480 CLOSE_WORKSTATION (display);
L490 CLOSE_GKS;
L500 end {CLOCK1};
```

─────────────────────────── *Fortran* ───────────────────────────

```
L10             PROGRAM CLOCK1
       C        *** Generating real time clock using CREATE,DELETE,RENAME
L70             LOGICAL STOP
L80             INTEGER HOUR,MIN,SEC,HOUR1,MIN1,SEC1
L81             INTEGER ERRFIL,DISP,CONID,TYPE
L82             DATA ERRFIL/9/,DISP/1/,CONID/0/,TYPE/3/

L110            CALL GOPKS (ERRFIL, BUFA)
L120            CALL GOPWK (DISP,CONID,TYPE)
L130            CALL GACWK (DISP)
       C        *** Set and select normalization transformation 1
L140            CALL GSWN (1, −1.0, 1.0, −1.0, 1.0)
L150            CALL GSELNT (1)
       C *** Generate clock digits and minute markers (see Examples 7.7 and 6.7)
L160            CALL MINMAR
L170            CALL GCRSG (80)
L171            CALL DIGITS
```

```
L172                CALL GCLSG
L180                CALL TIME (HOUR,MIN,SEC)
      C             *** Assume that TIME delivers real time
L190                CALL HHAND (100, HOUR, MIN)
L200                CALL MHAND (200, MIN)
L210                CALL SHAND (300, SEC)

      C             *** Loop forever
L220     1          CONTINUE
      C             *** Examine some input device here which sets STOP
L221                IF (STOP) GOTO 9
      C             *** Updating of real time clock
      C             *** Wait for 1 sec very useful here
L240                CALL TIME (HOUR1,MIN1,SEC1)
      C             *** Redraw hour hand once a minute
L250                IF (HOUR.EQ.HOUR1 .AND. MIN.EQ.MIN1) GOTO 2
L270                CALL HHAND (101, HOUR1, MIN1)
L280                CALL GDSG (100)
L290                CALL GRENSG (101,100)
L300                HOUR=HOUR1
      C             *** Redraw minute hand once a minute
L320                IF (MIN.EQ.MIN1) GOTO 2
L340                CALL MHAND (201, MIN1)
L350                CALL GDSG (200)
L360                CALL GRENSG (201,200)
L370                MIN=MIN1
      C             *** Redraw second hand once a second
L390     2          IF (SEC.EQ.SEC1) GOTO 1
L410                CALL SHAND (301, SEC1)
L420                CALL GDSG (300)
L430                CALL GRENSG (301,300)
L440                SEC=SEC1
L450                GOTO 1

L470     9          CALL GDAWK (DISP)
L480                CALL GCLWK (DISP)
L490                CALL GCLKS
L500                STOP
L501                END

      C             *** Draw hour hand
L510                SUBROUTINE HHAND (SEGNR, HOUR, MIN)
L511                INTEGER SEGNR,HOUR,MIN
L530                CALL HAND (SEGNR,(HOUR+MIN/60.0)/12.0, 0.05, 0.6)
L540                RETURN
L541                END

      C             *** Draw minute hand
L550                SUBROUTINE MHAND (SEGNR, MIN)
L551                INTEGER SEGNR,MIN
L570                CALL HAND (SEGNR, MIN/60.0, 0.03, 0.8)
L580                RETURN
L581                END
```

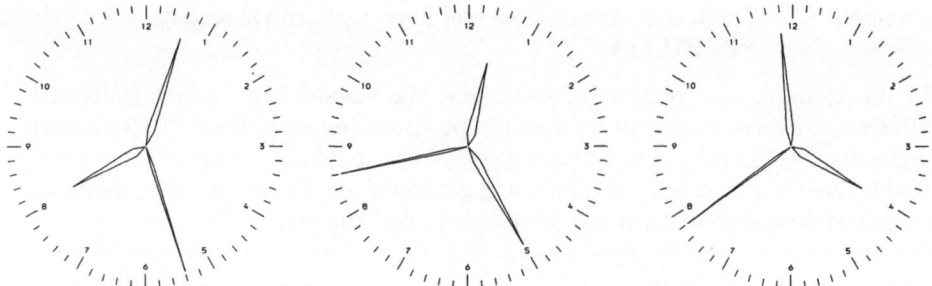

Figure 7.6 Clock at 8:03:27, 12:25:43, 15:59:39

```
           C        *** Draw second hand
L590                SUBROUTINE SHAND (SEGNR, SEC)
L591                INTEGER SEGNR, SEC
L610                CALL HAND (SEGNR, SEC/60.0, 0.01, 0.95)
L620                RETURN
L621                END


L630                SUBROUTINE HAND (SEGNR, ANGLE, WIDTH, LENGTH)
           C *** Creates segment SEGNR containing a clock hand with width WIDTH
           C *** and length LENGTH at angle ANGLE (0 ≤ ANGLE ≤ 1, clockwise).
L640                INTEGER SEGNR
L641                REAL X(5), Y(5), XX(5), YY(5), XR, YR,
                  +   ANGLE, WIDTH, LENGTH, TWOPI
L650                DATA X/5*0.0/, Y/0.01, 0.15, 1.0, 0.15, 0.01/, TWOPI/6.2831852/
           C        *** X, Y describe hand with length 1 pointing upwards
           C        *** Setting width of clock hand
L660                X(2) = WIDTH
L670                X(4) = −WIDTH
           C        *** Compute complex number (XR, YR) which is to be multiplied with
           C        *** hand (X, Y) to give proper length and angle
L700                XR = COS(−ANGLE*TWOPI)*LENGTH
L710                YR = SIN(−ANGLE*TWOPI)*LENGTH

           C        *** Compute hand rotated by ANGLE and scaled by LENGTH
L720                DO 10 I = 1,5
L740                XX(I) = X(I)*XR − Y(I)*YR
L750                YY(I) = X(I)*YR + Y(I)*XR
L760       10       CONTINUE
L770                CALL GCRSG (SEGNR)
           C        *** Generate hand
L780                CALL GPL (5, XX, YY)
L790                CALL GCLSG
L800                RETURN
L801                END
```

Example 7.5   Clock with dynamic second hand realized via setting VISIBILITY

In this example, for reasons of efficiency, the second hand is not generated afresh every second, but all 60 possible positions are predefined in 60 distinct segments and the current position is displayed by making the respective segment visible. As hour and minute hands are generated only every minute, they can be generated afresh without any great loss in performance.

———————————————————— *Pascal* ————————————————————

```
L10    procedure CLOCK2;                    {Same as Example 7.4 except:}
L11    var seg: array[1..60] of name;
                                            {Names must be initialised to distinct values}


.....
                                            {Replace line L210 by:}
L210   for i:=0 to 59 do
L211   begin                                {Generate all possible second hands}
L212     SHAND (seg[i], i);
L213     SET_VISIBILITY (seg[i], INVISIBLE);
L214   end;
L215   SET_VISIBILITY (seg[seconds], VISIBLE);


.....
                                            {Replace lines L410—430 by:}
L410     SET_VISIBILITY (seg[seconds1], VISIBLE);
L420     SET_VISIBILITY (seg[seconds], INVISIBLE);
.....
```

———————————————————— *Fortran* ————————————————————

```
L10            PROGRAM CLOCK2
.....
       C       *** Same as Example 7.4 except:
       C       *** Replace line L210 by:
       C       *** Generate all possible second hands
L210           DO 10 I=0,59
L211           CALL SHAND (I, I)
L212           CALL GSVIS (I, 0)
L213    10     CONTINUE
L214           CALL GSVIS (SEC, 1)
.....
       C       *** Replace lines L410—430 by:
       C       *** Make second hand visible
L410           CALL GSVIS (SEC1, 1)
L420           CALL GSVIS (SEC, 0)
.....
```

Example 7.6   Clock with dynamic hands realized by using SET SEGMENT TRANSFORMATION

The immediate way of generating a clock with dynamic hands is to use the segment transformation attribute. Only three segments, one for each hand, have to be maintained. The positions are updated merely by setting the appropriate transformation value.

———————————————————— *Pascal* ————————————————————

L10   **procedure** CLOCK 3;   {Same as Example 7.4 except:}

·····

                                                                   {Add line L 92}

L92   **var** transf: **array** [1..2, 1..3] **of real**;

·····

                                                                   {Replace lines L270—290 by:}

L270   angle: = − twopi ∗ (hours1 + minutes1/60.0)/12.0;
L280   EVALUATE_TRANSFORMATION_MATRIX
           (0.0,0.0,0.0,0.0,angle,1.0,1.0,0.0, transf);
L290   SET_SEGMENT_TRANSFORMATION (seg1, transf);

·····

                                                                   {Replace lines L340—360 by:}

L340   angle: = − twopi ∗ minutes1/60.0;
L350   EVALUATE_TRANSFORMATION_MATRIX
           (0.0,0.0,0.0,0.0,angle,1.0,1.0,0.0,transf);
L360   SET_SEGMENT_TRANSFORMATION (seg2, transf);

·····

                                                                   {Replace lines L410—430 by:}

L410   angle: = − twopi ∗ seconds1/60.0;
L420   EVALUATE_TRANSFORMATION_MATRIX
           (0.0,0.0,0.0,0.0,angle,1.0,1.0,0.0,transf);
L430   SET_SEGMENT_TRANSFORMATION (seg3, transf);

·····

———————————————————— *Fortran* ————————————————————

L10   PROGRAM CLOCK 3
        C   *** Same as Example 7.4 except:

·····

        C   *** Add line L 92
L92   REAL TRANSF (2,3)

·····

        C   *** Replace lines L270—290 by:
L270   ANGLE = − TWOPI ∗ (HOUR + MIN/60.0)/12.0
L280   CALL GEVTM (0.0,0.0,0.0,0.0,ANGLE,1.0,1.0,0,TRANSF)
L290   CALL GSSGT (100,TRANSF)

·····

        C   *** Replace lines L340—360 by:
L340   ANGLE = − TWOPI ∗ MIN/60.
L350   CALL GEVTM (0.0,0.0,0.0,0.0,ANGLE,1.0,1.0, 0,TRANSF)
L360   CALL GSSGT (200,TRANSF)

·····

        C   *** Replace lines L410—430 by:
L410   ANGLE = − TWOPI ∗ SEC/60.
L420   CALL GEVTM (0.0, 0.0, 0.0, 0.0, ANGLE, 1.0, 1.0, 0, TRANSF)
L430   CALL GSSGT (300,TRANSF)

·····

Example 7.7   Generating minute markers on a clock using INSERT SEGMENT

Whereas Example 7.4 explains the generation of clock hands, this example shows how the INSERT SEGMENT function can be applied to place copies of the one minute marker and one hour marker respectively at all the 60 positions around a clock face. At first, the minute and hour markers are generated in two distinct temporary segments stored in the workstation-independent segment storage (WISS). These segments are copied by using appropriate transformations several times into a third segment which finally contains the description of all the markers on the clock face.

──────────────────── *Pascal* ────────────────────

```
L10    procedure MINUTE_MARKERS;          {Drawing of minute markers on clock}

L20    const twopi = 6.2831852;
L30        wiss = 'WISS';
L40        connection = '.....';
L50        type = 'WISS';
L60        display = '.....';
L70    var x, y: array [1..2] of real;
L80        transf: array [1..2, 1..3] of real;
L90        angle: real;
L100       i: integer;
L110       minute, hour, markers: name;      {Names must be initialised to distinct values}
L120   begin
L130       DEACTIVATE_WORKSTATION (display);
L140       OPEN_WORKSTATION (wiss);                          {Activate WISS}
L150       ACTIVATE_WORKSTATION (wiss);

L160       x[1]: = 0.95;
L170       x[2]: = 1.0;
L180       y[1]: = 0.0;
L190       y[2]: = 0.0;
L200       CREATE_SEGMENT (minute);                 {Create one minute marker}
L210           POLYLINE (2, X, Y);
L220       CLOSE_SEGMENT;

L230       x[1]: = 0.9;
L240       CREATE_SEGMENT (hour);                    {Create one hour marker}
L250           POLYLINE (2, X, Y);
L260       CLOSE_SEGMENT;

L270       DEACTIVATE_WORKSTATION (wiss);
                                        {No more segments recorded in WISS}
L280       ACTIVATE_WORKSTATION (display);            {Activate output device}

           {Create segment with minute markers by inserting segments hour and minute
                                        under appropriate rotation}
L290       CREATE_SEGMENT (markers);
L300           for i = 1 to 60 do
L310           begin
L320           angle: = twopi * i/60.0;                {Angle corresponding to i}
```

L330		EVALUATE_TRANSFORMATION_MATRIX
		(0.0, 0.0, 0.0, 0.0, angle, 1.0, 1.0, 0.0, transf);
L340		**if** i **div** 5 * 5 = i **do** INSERT_SEGMENT (hour, transf)
L350		**else** INSERT_SEGMENT (minute, transf);
L360		**end**;
L370		CLOSE_SEGMENT;
L380		DELETE_SEGMENT (minute);
L390		DELETE_SEGMENT (hour);
L400		CLOSE_WORKSTATION (wiss);
L410		**end** {MINUTE_MARKERS};

──────────────── *Fortran* ────────────────

L10		SUBROUTINE MINMAR
	C	*** Drawing of minute markers on clock
L20		REAL X(2), Y(2), TRANSF(2,3), ANGLE, TWOPI
L30		INTEGER WISS, CONID, TYPE, DISP
L40		DATA X/0.95,1.0/, Y/0.0,0.0/, TWOPI/6.2831852/
L50		DATA WISS/7/, CONID/0/, TYPE/0/, DISP/1/
	C	*** Activate WISS
L130		CALL GDAWK (DISP)
L140		CALL GOPWK (WISS, CONID, TYPE)
L150		CALL GACWK (WISS)
	C	*** Create one minute marker
L200		CALL GCRSG (71)
L210		CALL GPL (2, X, Y)
L220		CALL GCLSG
	C	*** Create one hour marker
L230		X(1) = 0.9
L240		CALL GCRSG (72)
L250		CALL GPL (2, X, Y)
L260		CALL GCLSG
	C	*** No more segments recorded in WISS
L270		CALL GDAWK (WISS)
L280		CALL GACWK (DISP)
	C	*** Create segment with minute markers
	C	*** by inserting segments 71, 72 under appropriate rotation
L290		CALL GCRSG (70)
L300		DO 1 I = 1,60
	C	*** angle corresponding to I
L320		ANGLE = TWOPI * I/60.0
L330		CALL GEVTM (0.0, 0.0, 0.0, 0.0, ANGLE, 1.0, 1.0, 0, TRANSF)
L340		IF (I/5 * 5 .EQ. I) CALL GINSG (72, TRANSF)
L350		IF (I/5 * 5 .NE. I) CALL GINSG (71, TRANSF)
L360	1	CONTINUE
L370		CALL GCLSG
L380		CALL GDSG (71)
L390		CALL GDSG (72)
L400		CALL GCLWK (WISS)
L410		RETURN
L420		END

7.11   Exercises

Exercise 7.1   Dynamic change of indexed attributes

In Example 6.3 indexed POLYLINE attributes were used in the generation of a map. Rewrite this program so that data is generated in segments and the local segment storage of workstation 'display' can be used to dynamically change the linetype attribute.

— Is workstation 'plotter' affected by the dynamic manipulations on workstation 'display'?
— Has workstation 'plotter' to pay for the additional capabilities of workstation 'display'?

Exercise 7.2   Use of the WISS

In Exercise 7.1 both workstations are active at the same time. For a novice, it may be difficult to imagine what happens at a passive workstation while interactive manipulations of a common picture take place at an interactive workstation. To simplify such situations, the WISS can be used.
— Rewrite Exercise 7.1 so that the interactive manipulations only take place on workstation 'display' and WISS, and the final picture is then copied to the plotter by COPY SEGMENT.
— Can the same be done with ASSOCIATE SEGMENT WITH WORKSTATION or INSERT SEGMENT? Explain the differences.

Exercise 7.3   Append primitives to an existing segment

An existing segment cannot be reopened to add more primitives to it. However, it is possible to create a second segment, to send a copy of the first segment to the second one and then to add primitives as required. Then the first segment can be deleted and the second be renamed with the name of the first segment. Write a program which
— generates segment 'segment1' containing a TEXT primitive using CHARACTER HEIGHT 1;
— generates segment 'segment2' containing a TEXT primitive using CHARACTER HEIGHT 2;
— replaces segment 'segment1' by a segment containing all primitives of the old segment 'segment1' and an additional TEXT primitive using CHARACTER HEIGHT 1.

Which of the functions COPY SEGMENT, ASSOCIATE SEGMENT WITH WORKSTATION and INSERT SEGMENT must be used to copy 'segment1'? Does the copying of segment 'segment1' influence the current setting of CHARACTER HEIGHT?

Exercise 7.4   Compare INSERT SEGMENT with COPY SEGMENT TO WORKSTATION

Example 7.7 shows how minute markers are generated by INSERT SEGMENT. Write a program which generates the minute markers from segments 'minute' and 'hour' with the help of TRANSFORM SEGMENT and COPY SEGMENT TO WORKSTATION. Can your program also be used for a dynamic clock? (What may happen after the first clock update?)

Exercise 7.5   Segment transformations

In Example 7.7, two separate segments 'minute' and 'hour' are used to generate minute markers. However, segment 'hour' can be obtained from segment 'minute' by applying a segment transformation to it. Rewrite Example 7.7 so that all minute markers are generated by inserting segment 'minute' only.

8   INPUT

Computer graphics input is a rather complex area and accordingly the GKS input concept has to consider many application and implementation details. In many cases, the reader of this book will only need to know some aspects. Therefore, we want to provide some information as to how to study this chapter.

— All readers should study the following Sections 8.1 and 8.2 very carefully. They contain detailed information about logical input data which form the basis for providing the application programs with input.

— If one is dealing with simple input applications it is then appropriate to skip to Section 8.5. There, the REQUEST input functions and some sample programs are presented which are sufficient for many applications. Using these functions and studying the examples, the reader will often notice the need to INITIALISE functions. The necessary details about them can be found in Section 8.3.

— In the case of more sophisticated interactive applications, sample and event input is used. To understand this the Sections 8.6 and 8.7 should be read, where SAMPLE and EVENT input and the concept of input queuing are described. Section 8.4 may also be of value as it describes how to set the operating modes of logical devices.

— If the reader requires more details about applications of input functions, he should read Section 8.8. This contains examples of flexible bindings of logical input devices to physical input devices.

— Finally, Chapter V.2 describes the mapping from the logical input level to the physical equipment and the concept of measure/trigger devices from an implementation's point of view.

8.1   Introduction to Logical Input Devices

An application program obtains graphical input from an operator who controls logical input devices which deliver logical input values to the program.

The application program has available a range of logical input devices and, thus, a range of associated logical data types. If, for instance, a position is required in an application program, a LOCATOR device has to be selected (instead of a physical cursor device, for example), or if a character string is required, the logical device STRING has to be used (instead of a physical keyboard, for example). Whereas the application program can control the available logical input devices, the mapping of logical to physical devices is done by the implementation.

8.1.1   Identification

Each logical input device is identified by:
— a workstation identifier,
— an input class,
— and a device number.

The workstation identifier is a name for selecting the workstation; it is a parameter of the input functions. The input class specifies which one of the six logical device types is addressed (see below). For every class a specific set of input functions is present in GKS. The device number selects one of several logical input devices of the same class at the same workstation. It is an integer parameter of the input functions.

Logical input devices are connected to input or output/input workstations. To use such a logical device, the corresponding workstation must be open. The logical input device is implemented with respect to the physical device or devices present at the workstation.

8.1.2   Logical Input Classes and Values

GKS provides six logical input classes: LOCATOR, STROKE, VALUATOR, CHOICE, PICK, and STRING. Each input class determines the type of logical input value that the logical input device delivers. The six input classes and the logical input values they provide are:

LOCATOR: a position in world coordinates (a pair of REAL values) and a normalization transformation number;

STROKE: a sequence of positions in world coordinates and a normalization transformation number;

VALUATOR: a REAL number;

CHOICE: a non-negative INTEGER value which represents a selection from a number of choices and a choice status (NONE, OK, NOCHOICE)

PICK: a PICK status (NONE, OK, NOPICK), a segment name and a pick identifier. Primitives outside segments cannot be picked;

STRING: a string of CHARACTERS.

8.1.3   Operating Modes

Each logical input device can be operated in three modes, called operating modes. At any time, it is in one, and only one, of the modes set by invoking a function in the group SET ⟨input class⟩ MODE. The three operating modes are REQUEST, SAMPLE and EVENT. Input from devices is obtained in different ways depending on the mode:

REQUEST: When an input function is called in REQUEST MODE an attempt is then made to read a logical input value from a specified logical input device, which must be in REQUEST mode. GKS waits until the input is entered or a break action is performed by the operator. The break action depends on the logical input device and on the implementation. If a break occurs, the logical input value is not valid.

SAMPLE: When an input function is called in SAMPLE MODE it causes GKS to return the current logical input value of a specified logical input device, without waiting for the operator to act. The device must be put in SAMPLE MODE.

EVENT: GKS maintains one input queue containing temporally ordered event reports. An event report contains the identification of a logical input device and a logical input value from that device. Event reports are generated asynchronously, by operator action only, from input devices in EVENT mode.
The application program can remove the oldest event report from the queue, and examine its contents. It can also flush all event reports from a specified logical input device from the queue.

It should be noted that in contrast to other systems, STROKE, CHOICE, PICK, and STRING devices also can be in sample mode and that any LOCATOR and VALUATOR devices can generate events. The operating modes are independent of physical device characteristics: all logical input devices provide all three operating modes. This is made possible by the concept of measure/trigger devices which is explained in the following sections and in Chapter V.2.

8.1.4   Logical Input Device Model

A logical input device contains a measure, a trigger, an initial value, a prompt/ echo type, an echo area and a data record containing details about the echo type. A logical input device's measure and trigger are parts of the implementation of the workstation which contains the logical input device. The initial value, echo type, echo area, and data record can all be supplied by the application program.

Interaction
A specific logical input device is said to be taking part in an interaction while it is in SAMPLE or EVENT mode, but, when it is in REQUEST mode, only

while a REQUEST function for that device is being executed. Many devices at many workstations may be taking part in interactions simultaneously.

Measure

The measure of a logical input device is a value determined by one or more physical input devices together with a "measure mapping" from physical to logical values. More than one measure can be simultaneously determined by a single physical device. A separate measure mapping is taken for each measure. A measure can be seen as the state of an independent, active process (a measure process). Each state corresponds exactly to a logical input value.

The current state of the measure process (i.e. the device's measure) is available to GKS as a logical input value. The measure process exists as long as an interaction with the logical input device is taking place. Under other conditions, this process does not exist.

When a measure process comes into existence, the data in the workstation state list entry for the logical input device is examined. The initial value is checked for validity, according to input class dependent rules explained in Section 8.3. If the check is successful, the initial value is then used as the current state of the process; otherwise a value dependent on the logical input device is used. This value is echoed on the display surface and this, together with a prompt, indicates when the creation of the measure process is complete.

Prompt/Echo

Prompting information is output which indicates to the operator that the device is ready for use. Echoing indicates the current state of the measure process. While the measure process is still going on, an echo is sent to the operator only if the prompt/echo switch is ON. The prompt/echo technique for a device may be selected by calling the appropriate INITIALISE function. For example, the crosshair of a LOCATOR device is a specific echo; its appearance when the LOCATOR is initialised may be seen at the same time as prompting. However, prompting could also be implemented independently from echoing as a message to the operator such as "please enter a position".

Trigger

The trigger of a logical input device is a physical input device or a set of them together with a "trigger mapping". The operator can use a trigger to indicate which moments in time are significant. At such moments, a message is sent to the measure process of the corresponding device (devices). The effect of this depends on the logical device's mode in the following way:
— In REQUEST mode, the measure process returns its data value to the application program, and then terminates.
— In SAMPLE mode, trigger messages are always ignored. The application program may obtain the data value from the measure process whenever it pleases.
— In EVENT mode, the measure process attempts to add an event record to the input queue; if more than one logical device refers to the same trigger,

all corresponding measure values are added to the queue as a "group of simultaneous event reports" when the trigger fires.

A single operator action (for example, pressing a button or a lightpen tip switch) causes not more than one trigger to fire. Several logical input devices can refer to the same trigger.

A trigger can be seen as an independent, active process (a trigger process) that sends a message to one or more recipients when it fires. A logical input device is a recipient of its trigger if there is a pending REQUEST for it or if it is in EVENT mode.

Acknowledgement

When a trigger fires, GKS provides the operator with an acknowledgement which varies according to the implementation of the logical input device. The acknowledgement cannot be controlled by a GKS function.

8.1.5 Setting the Logical Input Device Mode

Initially, a logical input device is in REQUEST mode, which implies that its measure process does not exist and its identifier is not on its trigger's list of recipients.

The mode of a logical input device may be changed by invoking the appropriate SET ⟨input class⟩ MODE function. After a SET ⟨input class⟩ MODE invocation with parameter REQUEST no measure or trigger process exists for the specified device. After a SET ⟨input class⟩ MODE invocation with parameter SAMPLE, a newly initialised measure process exists for the specified device, but the device is not on its trigger's list of recipients. After a SET ⟨input class⟩ MODE invocation with parameter EVENT, a newly initialised measure process exists for the specified device, and the device is on its trigger's list of recipients.

— While a device is in REQUEST mode, a logical input value may be obtained by invoking the appropriate REQUEST ⟨device class⟩ function. The effects of doing so are described in Section 8.5.
— While a logical input device is in SAMPLE mode, a logical input value can be obtained by invoking the appropriate SAMPLE ⟨device class⟩ function. The effect of doing so will set the logical input value to the current state of the measure process without waiting for a trigger to fire.
— While a logical input device is in EVENT mode, logical input values are added as event records to the event queue, and may be obtained in sequence by invoking AWAIT EVENT, and then the appropriate GET ⟨device class⟩ function.

The following Example 8.1 describes how a logical LOCATOR device operates in the three operating modes. The LOCATOR may be implemented, for example, by using a tablet with a pointing device and a button attached to it.

Example 8.1   Use of a LOCATOR device in all operating modes

──────────────── *Pascal* ────────────────

```
                                           {LOCATOR in REQUEST mode}
L10   REQUEST_LOCATOR (display,lc1,status,tnr,pos);
                                           {LOCATOR in SAMPLE mode}
L20   SET_LOCATOR_MODE (display,lc1,sample,echo);
L30   SAMPLE_LOCATOR (display,lc1,tnr,pos);
                                           {LOCATOR in EVENT mode}
L40   SET_LOCATOR_MODE (display,lc1,event,echo);
L50   AWAIT_EVENT (timeout,workstation,input_class,device_number);
L60   if (input_class=locator) then
L70      GET LOCATOR (tnr,pos):
L80   SET_LOCATOR_MODE (display,lc1,request,echo);    {DISABLE LOCATOR}
```

──────────────── *Fortran* ────────────────

```
      C                            *** LOCATOR in REQUEST mode
L10          CALL GRQLC (DISP,LC1,STATUS,TNR,PX,PY)
      C                            *** LOCATOR in SAMPLE mode
L20          CALL GSLCM (DISP,LC1,GSAMPL,GECHO)
L30          CALL GSMLC (DISP,LC1,TNR,PX,PY)
      C                            *** LOCATOR in EVENT mode
L40          CALL GSLCM (DISP,LC1,GEVENT,GECHO)
L50          CALL GWAIT (TOUT,WK,CLASS,DEVNB)
L60          IF (CLASS=GLOCAT) CALL GGTLC (NTR,PX,PY)
      C                 *** disable LOCATOR (put into REQUEST mode)
L80          CALL GSLCM (DISP,LC1,GREQU,GECHO)
```

8.2   Details About Logical Input Devices

8.2.1   LOCATOR and STROKE Devices

The input value delivered by a device of class LOCATOR is a pair consisting of a position in world coordinates, P, and the number of a normalization transformation, N.

Similarly, devices of class STROKE return values in the form $(P1,...Pm,n)$, where $P1...Pm$ are positions in world coordinates, and n is the number of a normalization transformation, N.

In both cases, the positions (P, or $P1...Pm$) lie within the window specified by N, and their images under N lie within the workstation window, but outside all the viewports of transformations with a higher priority than N.

The position(s) or the normalization transformation returned by a device can change as a result of calls to SET WINDOW, SET VIEWPORT or SET VIEWPORT INPUT PRIORITY, and in the case of STROKE devices, the normalization transformation may change when new points are added to the stroke. In any case, however, the above condition for the positions and the transformation must be maintained.

This condition implies that no normalization transformation with a priority less than that of transformation 0 can appear in the state of a LOCATOR or STROKE measure process (please note that, at the default setting of the viewport input priorities, that of normalization transformation 0 is the highest).

The LOCATOR and STROKE positions are transformed from device coordinates (DC) to world coordinates (WC) by applying the following algorithm:
— When a physical locator returns a value, the workstation transforms it back to normalized device coordinates (NDC) using the inverse of the current workstation transformation.
    It should be noted that LOCATOR and STROKE input can be obtained only from positions within the part of the current workstation viewport into which the current workstation window is mapped. (If workstation window and workstation viewport both have the same aspect ratio, then the complete workstation viewport can be used for LOCATOR and STROKE input.) This ensures that LOCATOR and STROKE positions are in NDC space.
— In NDC space, from all the normalization transformations in whose viewports the NDC position lies, the normalization transformation with the highest priority is selected. (Each normalization transformation has an associated viewport input priority which is used to arrange the normalization transformations into order of priority).
— The inverse of the selected transformation is used to calculate a world coordinate value.
— Both the world coordinate value and the index of the selected transformation are stored as the current measure value of the logical device.

To ensure that the NDC position lies within at least one viewport, there is a default transformation which cannot be changed. It has number zero and both its window and its viewport are set to the unit square $[0,1] \times [0,1]$. The world coordinates returned are in effect NDC coordinates in two cases:
— If no normalization transformation is defined with a higher viewport input priority than that of transformation number 0. Transformation zero is initialised with the highest priority;
— If the LOCATOR/STROKE positions, which have been transformed to NDC space, lie outside any application-defined viewport.

Figure 8.1 depicts an application of LOCATOR input. Here it is assumed that the application program defines two window/viewport transformations: T1 maps window 1 to viewport 1, and T2 maps window 2 to viewport 2 which lies within viewport 1. There is the default transformation T0 which performs the unit transformation window 0 = viewport 0 = NDC space = $[0,1] \times [0,1]$. Furthermore, this application uses a default workstation transformation, which maps the NDC space onto the largest rectangle that fits on the display surface while preserving the aspect ratio.

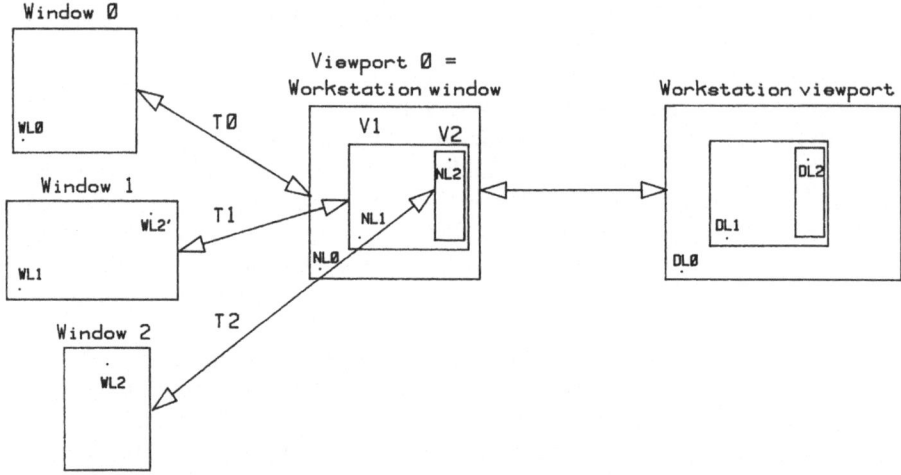

Figure 8.1 LOCATOR/STROKE input transformations

Let us further assume two application cases, c1 and c2: in the first case, viewport 2 has a higher priority than viewport 1 and this in turn has a higher priority than viewport 0. In case c2 viewport 2 has a lower priority than viewport 1 but a higher one than viewport 0. Thus, the lists of normalization transformations are placed in order of increasing viewport input priority as shown:
— case c1: T0, T1, T2
— case c2: T0, T2, T1.

Figure 8.1 demonstrates the following transformation cases:
1. Using a physical LOCATOR device, position DL0 is entered; it is transformed back to the NDC position, NL0; NL0 only lies within the default viewport (outside any application-defined viewport) and, thus, the measure value is the tuple (NL0=WL0, T0).
2. DL1 is entered and transformed to NL1; this lies within the two viewports V0 and V1. Since we assumed V1 to be of higher priority than V0, NL1 is transformed back using T1 and, therefore, the measure value is (WL1, T1).
3. DL2 is entered and transformed to NL2; this lies within all three viewports; in the first case (c1), NL2 is transformed back to WL2 by applying T2. In case c2, T1 is used to transform NL2 back to WL2.

Obviously the viewport input priority can be used to "hide" world coordinate systems below other ones. Changing the viewport input priority can be performed dynamically using the function SET VIEWPORT INPUT PRIORITY as a means of navigating LOCATOR/STROKE input transformations within coordinate systems.

8.2.2 VALUATOR

GKS also has a VALUATOR class, which returns a real number in a range specified by the application. For each valuator device, a low, a high, and an initial value are given. Additionally, the resolution of the valuator device may be adjusted if the device is suitably implemented.

8.2.3 CHOICE

The CHOICE class is intended to provide a "menu" or a "function key" capability. It returns a status value and an integer value which indicates which alternative has been selected. The status of "no choice" may be returned if, for example, the device is in a state where no buttons are pressed down or an alternative which does not exist is selected (for example, by marking outside the menu box). The number of choice alternatives defines the maximum integer value that can be returned. The choice device class represents a powerful input facility in that it provides potentially complex application-controlled prompting techniques, such as displaying a menu consisting of strings or of graphical symbols.

Choice input usually occurs when an operator presses a button (the numeric identification of the button determines the value) or combinations of buttons (the value is derived from the combinations of buttons pressed).

8.2.4 PICK

The PICK device class returns a PICK status, a segment name, and a pick identifier; the PICK status indicates OK (a valid PICK input has occurred), or NOPICK. NOPICK would occur, for example, if the light pen was not pointing at any detectable segment. If the PICK status is OK, the segment name and pick identifier must obey the following rules:
— The segment exists and has VISIBILITY and DETECTABILITY on.
— The segment is present at the workstation containing the PICK device.
— The pick identifier is the pick identifier attribute of at least one output primitive in the segment, satisfying the following condition: part of the primitive is within the clipping rectangle which was in effect on the workstation when it arrived there. This rectangle is either the workstation window, if the clipping indicator in the GKS state list is set to off, or the intersection of the workstation window and the primitive's normalization clipping rectangle, if the clipping indicator is set to on. Furthermore, the primitive must not be completely overlapped by primitives in a segment with a higher priority.

The PICK initial value is tested according to the above rules whenever the PICK measure process is initiated. If the rules are not satisfied, the process state is set to NOPICK.

N.B.:

For certain workstations, the third rule, when the PICK measure process is initiated, may be computationally very expensive. In such cases, only the first two rules need be adhered to.

N.B.:

The PICK measure is defined by using the properties of output primitives and segments. PICK devices can exist only at an output/input workstation.

8.2.5 STRING

The GKS STRING device class returns a character string, which may also be empty (null string). The operator is prompted by the initial string, and a cursor at an application-specified position within it. Replacement of characters starts at the cursor position, and can extend the string up to an application-specified maximum length.

8.3 Initialising Logical Input Devices

For each input class, there is an initialisation function which can only be called if the respective logical device is in REQUEST mode. The functions provide the following information to a device via the workstation state list. If the initialisation function is not called for a device, default values apply as defined in the workstation description table by the workstation implementor.

Initial Values

Initial values appropriate to the device class can be defined. If they violate the rules defined in Section 8.2, an error occurs and the workstation state list remains unchanged. Initial values are used to start the display of prompts and echoes and to set initial measure values. Each time a device is activated (a REQUEST function is invoked or the device is set into sample or event mode), the initial values are taken from the internal workstation state list.

The "initial values" feature aims to make input tools easier to handle. The application program may adjust the input device to some "expected" value and the operator then only needs to confirm this adjustment if he is in agreement with it. If not he may change it to the desired value starting from an initial value, which may be situated nearby. Obviously, the calculation of initial values is highly application-specific. Experience has shown, for example, that for locator input it is often convenient to initialise the locator device, before each activation, to that position which was last entered via this device; thus the operator may continue entering coordinates where he had left off.

Prompt/Echo Types

For each input device class, GKS defines a number of prompt/echo types. An implementation-dependent prompt/echo type (type 1) is required for all logical input devices. Further prompt/echo types appropriate to each class may be provided by an implementation, thereby following the definition of the INITIALISE functions; additional prompt/echo types are device-dependent. The echo appearance may be switched on and off using the SET ⟨device⟩ MODE functions.

Echo Area

For some prompt/echo types, an echo area is of importance. It may be used to control where the echo and the prompt appear, as with menus on a screen, prompt messages on a scroll area, display of digital values, or echo of STRING input devices. The echo area is defined in device coordinates in the form (left/right/bottom/top).

Data Record

Depending on the device class, the device implementation, and the selected prompt/echo type, the data record of the INITIALISE function may contain both certain required values and other additional information. Some input classes have compulsory control values in the data record and some prompt/echo types in an input class have them as well. These values occupy well-defined places in the data record. In any data record used to initialise an input device, any compulsory values for an input class must appear first followed by any compulsory values for the prompt/echo type.

The items required by each class in the data record are:
>   for STROKE: input buffer size in number of points;
>   for VALUATOR: low value and high value;
>   for STRING: input buffer size and initial cursor position.

The prompt/echo types which have compulsory values are types 3 and 4 for STROKE and types 2,3,4 and 5 for CHOICE. These values and other optional values are listed with the INITIALISE functions in the following section.

   It should be noted that the FORTRAN language binding has a special subroutine which packs data values into a data record. In this way, the number of parameters which represent the data type "data record" in FORTRAN is minimized. Applications of this mapping function are shown in the Sections 8.5, 8.6, and 8.7, together with applications of the INITIALISE functions.

   This function is defined as follows:

PACK DATA RECORD	GKOP, WSOP, WSAC, SGOP L0a

———————————— *FORTRAN Interface* ————————————

CALL GPREC (IL, IA, RL, RA, LSTR, STR, MLDR, ERRIND, LDR, DATR)

Parameters:

Input	IL	length of integer array	(1..n)	INTEGER
Input	IA(IL)	integer array		n × INTEGER
Input	RL	length of real array	(1..n)	INTEGER
Input	RA(RL)	real array		nxREAL
Input	LSTR	number of characters in string	(0..n)	INTEGER
Input	STR	string array		CHARACTER*(*)
Input	MLDR	maximal length of data record	(1..n)	INTEGER
Output	ERRIND	error indicator (zero if no error)		INTEGER
Output	LDR	actual length of data record	(0..n)	INTEGER
Output	DATR(MLDR)	data record		n × CHARACTER*80

Initialise functions

INITIALISE LOCATOR   WSOP, WSAC, SGOP   L0b
Parameters:

Input	workstation identifier		N
Input	locator device number	(1..n)	I
Input	initial locator position	WC	P
Input	initial normalization transformation number	(0..n)	I
Input	prompt/echo type	(−n..−1,1..n)	I
Input	echo area XMIN < XMAX, YMIN < YMAX	DC	4 × R
Input	data record		D

Effect:

The initial locator position, initial normalization transformation number, prompt/echo type, echo area and data record are stored in the workstation state list entry for the specified LOCATOR device.

For some LOCATOR prompt/echo types, two positions are required. One of the positions, which remains fixed during the input operation, is the initial locator position. The other position is the current locator position which varies dynamically as the operator uses the LOCATOR.

The prompt/echo area is required for prompt/echo type 6 only; other (implementation-dependent) techniques may also use it.

Prompt/echo type:

1: Implementation Standard.

This designates the current position of the LOCATOR using an implementation-defined technique. Normally, hardware-provided facilities are used for this type; e.g., the display of position registers at some tablets and digitizers, or some of the prompt/echo types explained below.

2: Crosshair.

A crosshair is displayed, i.e., the current position of the LOCATOR is designated, using a vertical line and a horizontal line spanning the display surface or the workstation viewport intersecting at the current locator position. This technique should be used if applications request positions which are horizontally or vertically dependent on other — possibly already generated — parts of the picture. Examples are flow chart construction, electrical layout design, etc.

3: Tracking Cross.

This designates the current position of the LOCATOR using a tracking cross symbol. This echo is mainly useful for applications which need quick and less precise freehand drawings, e.g., architectural drafting systems.

4: Rubber Band.

This designates the current position of the LOCATOR using a rubber band line connecting the initial LOCATOR position given by this function and the current locator position. A rubber band line may be used to determine intersections and local dependencies of picture components.

5: Rectangle.

This designates the current position of the LOCATOR using a rectangle. The diagonal of the rectangle is the line connecting the initial LOCATOR position given by this function and the current locator position. The rectangle combines some of the advantages of the rubber band and crosshair echoes. It helps to indicate local geometrical dependencies, mainly in horizontal and vertical directions. It may be used to determine parts of the picture overlapping or "contained conditions" of components.

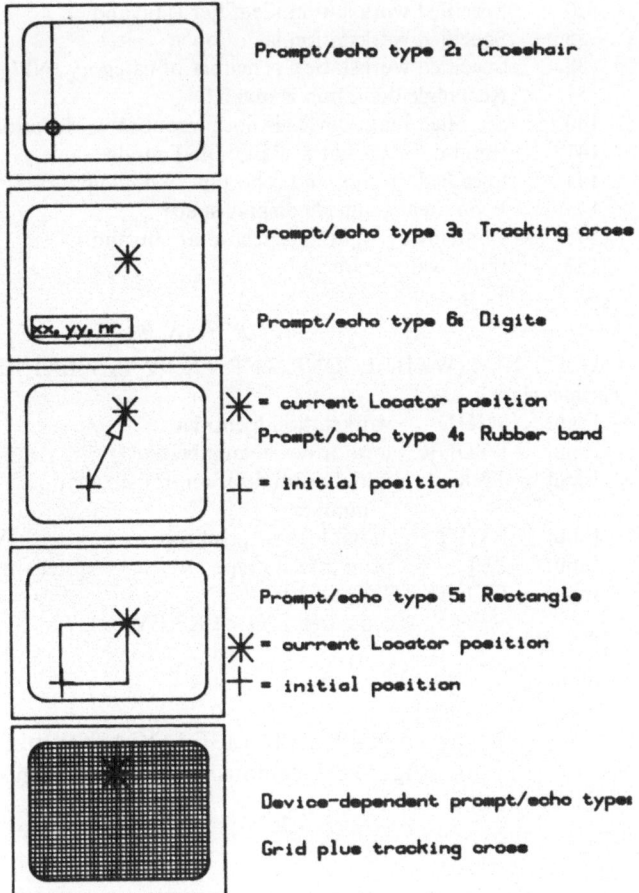

Figure 8.2 LOCATOR device prompts and echoes

6: Digits.

They give a digital representation of the current LOCATOR position in LOCATOR device-dependent coordinates within the echo area. This echo is mainly intended for precise determination of coordinates.

>6: Reserved for future registration.

<0: Device-Dependent.

Prompting and echoing is LOCATOR device-dependent. An example of a specific LOCATOR implementation is the input of discrete positions as points on a grid. The step width of the grid may be adjusted according to an entry in the locator data record. Each time the LOCATOR device is activated (requested, or put into sample or event mode), the grid is displayed. A cursor may be implemented so that it moves only from grid point to grid point or so that it moves arbitrarily, and the nearest grid point is used to calculate world coordinate positions.

Errors:

7 GKS not in proper state: GKS should be in one of the states WSOP, WSAC or SGOP

20	Specified workstation identifier is invalid	
25	Specified workstation is not open	
38	Specified workstation is neither of category INPUT nor of category OUTIN	
51	Rectangle definition is invalid	
140	Specified input device is not present at workstation	
141	Input device is not in REQUEST mode	
144	Specified prompt and echo type is not supported on this workstation	
145	Echo area is outside display space	
146	Contents of input data record are invalid	
152	Initial value is invalid	

─────────────────── *FORTRAN Interface* ───────────────────

CALL GINLC (WKID, LCDNR, TNR, PX, PY, PET, EX1, EX2, EY1, EY2, IL, CA)

Parameters:

Input	WKID	workstation identifier	$(1..n)$	INTEGER
Input	LCDNR	locator device number	$(1..n)$	INTEGER
Input	TNR	initial normalization transformation number	$(0..n)$	INTEGER
Input	PX, PY	initial locator position	WC	$2 \times$ REAL
Input	PET	prompt/echo type	$(-n..-1, 1..n)$	INTEGER
Input	EX1, EX2, EY1, EY2	echo area $EX1 < EX2, EY1 < EY2$	DC	$4 \times$ REAL
Input	IL, CA (IL) data record		$n \times$ CHARACTER $*80$	

An application of the INITIALISE LOCATOR function is shown in Section 8.5 on page 300. Figure 8.2 demonstrates some prompt/echo types of the LOCATOR device.

───

INITIALISE STROKE   WSOP, WSAC, SGOP   L0b

Parameters:

Input	workstation identifier		N
Input	stroke device number	$(1..n)$	I
Input	number of points in initial stroke	$(0..n)$	I
Input	points in initial stroke	WC	$n \times$ P
Input	initial normalization transformation number	$(0..n)$	I
Input	prompt/echo type	$(-n..-1, 1..n)$	I
Input	echo area XMIN < XMAX, YMIN < YMAX	DC	$4 \times$ R
Input	stroke data record		D

Effect:

The initial stroke, initial normalization transformation number, prompt/echo type, echo area and stroke data record are stored in the workstation state list entry for the specified STROKE device.

For all prompt/echo types, the first entry in the stroke data record must be the input buffer size which is an integer in the range $(0..n)$. This is compared with an implementation-defined 'maximum input buffer size for stroke devices' (contained in the workstation description table). If the requested buffer size is larger, the 'maximum input buffer size for stroke devices' is substituted in the stored data record. If the initial stroke is longer than the buffer size, an error is issued.

When a stroke measure process comes into existence, it obtains a buffer with the current input buffer size. A copy of the initial stroke is sent into the buffer, and the editing position is placed at the initial buffer editing position within it. Replacement of points begins at this initial position.

Prompt/echo types:

1: Implementation Standard.

This displays the current STROKE using an implementation-defined technique; normally, hardware-provided facilities are used for this type: e.g., the display of position registers at some tablets and digitizers, or some of the prompt/echo types explained below.

2: Digits.

They display a digital representation of the current STROKE position within the echo area.

3: Marker.

This displays a marker at each point of the current STROKE.

4: Line.

This displays a line joining successive points of the current STROKE.

>4: Reserved for future registration.

<0: Device-Dependent.

Prompting and echoing is STROKE device-dependent.

If the operator enters more points than fit in the current input buffer size, the additional points are lost. It is anticipated that the operator would be informed of this. It is anticipated that stroke data record entries for variables such as intervals in X, Y and time may be provided to limit the number of points delivered.

N.B.:

For all prompt/echo types, the stroke data record may contain an initial buffer editing position, which may range from 1 to the length of initial stroke plus 1.

Errors:

7	GKS not in proper state: GKS should be in one of the states WSOP, WSAC or SGOP
20	Specified workstation identifier is invalid
25	Specified workstation is not open
38	Specified workstation is neither of category INPUT nor of category OUTIN
51	Rectangle definition is invalid
140	Specified input device is not present on workstation
141	Input device is not in REQUEST mode
144	Specified prompt and echo type is not supported on this workstation
145	Echo area is outside display space
146	Contents of input data record are invalid
152	Initial value is invalid
153	Number of points in the initial stroke is greater than the buffer size

———————————————— *FORTRAN Interface* ————————————————

CALL GINSK (WKID,SKDNR,TNR,IN,IPX,IPY,PET,EX1,EX2,EY1,EY2,
BUFLEN,INIPOS,IL,CA)

Parameters:

Input	WKID	workstation identifier	(1..n)	INTEGER
Input	SKDNR	stroke device number	(1..n)	INTEGER
Input	TNR	initial normalization transformation number	(0..n)	INTEGER
Input	IN	number of points in initial stroke	(1..n)	INTEGER

Input	IPX, IPY	initial stroke positions	WC	$n \times$ REAL
Input	PET	prompt/echo type	$(-n.. -1, 1..n)$	INTEGER
Input	EX1, EX2, EY1, EY2			
		echo area EX1 < EX2, EY1 < EY2		
			DC	$4 \times$ REAL
Input	BUFLEN	buffer length for stroke	$(1..n)$	INTEGER
Input	INIPOS	editing position		INTEGER
Input	IL, CA (IL)	data record		$n \times$ CHARACTER $*80$

INITIALISE VALUATOR   WSOP, WSAC, SGOP   L0b

Parameters:

Input	workstation identifier		N
Input	valuator device number	$(1..n)$	I
Input	initial value		R
Input	prompt/echo type	$(-n.. -1, 1..n)$	I
Input	echo area XMIN < XMAX, YMIN < YMAX	DC	$4 \times$ R
Input	data record		D

Effect:

The initial value, prompt/echo type, echo area, and data record are stored in the workstation state list entry for the specified VALUATOR device.

For all VALUATOR prompt/echo types, the data record must include a low value and a high value, thus specifying the range. The values issued from the device will be scaled linearly to the specified range.

The data record may also contain a resolution value which determines the desired precision of the valuator. The implementation of the device may support this technique; if it does not, the resolution value is ignored.

Prompt/echo types:

1: Implementation Standard.

This designates the current VALUATOR value using an implementation-defined technique, e.g., it uses hardware-provided facilities like potentiometer devices, etc.

2: Dial.

This displays a graphical representation of the current VALUATOR value within the echo area (for example, a dial or a pointer).

A lot of sophisticated techniques exist to adjust a desired value, both quickly and precisely. Most of them use different modes of operation enabling values to change at different speeds. The slowest mode can be used for precise adjustments.

Common input devices are lightpens, control panels, function keyboards, potentiometers, track balls, etc.

3: Digits.

These display a digital representation of the current VALUATOR value within the echo area.

This simple technique allows the use of alphanumeric keyboards in addition to the input devices supported by prompt/echo type 2.

>3: Reserved for future registration.

<0: Device-Dependent.

Prompting and echoing is VALUATOR device-dependent.

Errors:

7	GKS not in proper state: GKS should be in one of the states WSOP, WSAC or SGOP
20	Specified workstation identifier is invalid
25	Specified workstation is not open

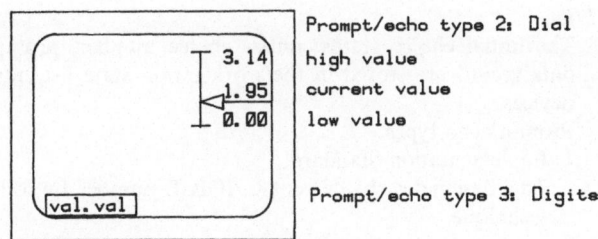

Figure 8.3 Valuator device prompts and echoes

38	Specified workstation is neither of category INPUT nor of category OUTIN
51	Rectangle definition is invalid
140	Specified input device is not present on workstation
141	Input device is not in REQUEST mode
144	Specified prompt and echo type is not supported on this workstation
145	Echo area is outside display space
146	Contents of input data record are invalid
152	Initial value is invalid

———————————————— *FORTRAN Interface* ————————————————

CALL GINVL (WKID, VLDNR, VAL, PET, EX1, EX2, EY1, EY2, LOVAL,
HIVAL, IL, CA)

Parameters:

Input	WKID	workstation identifier	$(1..n)$	INTEGER
Input	VLDNR	valuator device number	$(1..n)$	INTEGER
Input	VAL	initial valuator value		REAL
Input	PET	prompt/echo type	$(-n..-1, 1..n)$	INTEGER
Input	EX1, EX2, EY1, EY2			
		echo area $EX1 < EX2, EY1 < EY2$		
			DC	$4 \times$ REAL
Input	LOVAL, HIVAL			
		low value, high value		$2 \times$ REAL
Input	IL, CA (IL)	data record		$n \times$ CHARACTER*80

An application of the INITIALISE VALUATOR function is shown in Section 8.5 on page 304. Figure 8.3 demonstrates some prompt/echo types of the VALUATOR device.

INITIALISE CHOICE		WSOP, WSAC, SGOP	L0b
Parameters:			
Input	workstation identifier		N
Input	choice device number	$(1..n)$	I
Input	initial choice status	(OK, NOCHOICE)	E
Input	initial choice number	$(0..n)$	I
Input	prompt/echo type	$(-n..-1, 1..n)$	I
Input	echo area $XMIN < XMAX, YMIN < YMAX$	DC	$4 \times$ R
Input	data record		D

Effect:
The initial choice status, initial choice number, prompt/echo type, echo area, and data record are stored in the workstation state list entry for the specified CHOICE device.

Prompt/echo types:

1: Implementation Standard.

This designates the current CHOICE number by using an implementation-defined technique.

2: Lamps.

The physical input devices that are most commonly used to implement a CHOICE logical input device normally have a built-in prompting capability, e.g., lamps which can be switched on and off. This prompt/echo type allows the application program to invoke this prompting capability. If the value of the i-th element of 'prompt array' in the data record is OFF, prompting of the i-th alternative of the specified choice input device is turned off. An ON value indicates that prompting for that alternative is turned on.

This prompt/echo type may especially be used for skilled and frequent operators who neither need nor want explicit dialogue guidance.

3: String Menu.

This allows the operator to indicate a CHOICE number by selecting, using an appropriate technique, one of a set of CHOICE strings. The CHOICE strings are contained in the data record and are displayed within the echo area. The logical input value is the number of the string selected.

This means that text strings may be displayed as screen command menus. Using a lightpen or a positioning device such as a track ball or thumb wheels, the operator may identify the desired alternative. Example 8.4 demonstrates an application of this prompt/echo type.

4: String Commands.

They allow the operator to indicate a CHOICE number by selecting, via an alphanumeric keyboard, one of a set of CHOICE strings. The CHOICE strings are contained in the data record and may be displayed in the echo area as a prompt. The string typed in by the operator is echoed in the echo area. The logical input value is the number of the string that has been typed in by the operator.

This prompt/echo type allows the proper use of alphanumeric keyboards, the largest used input device. The alternative commands may be displayed in the echo area, if the operator needs such help-facilities.

5: Symbol Menu.

The segment named by the data record is interpreted while INITIALISE CHOICE is being executed for later use as a prompt in the specified CHOICE device. It will be displayed within the echo area by mapping the unit square $[0,1] \times [0,1]$ of NDC space onto the echo area. The pick identifiers in the segment are mapped to CHOICE numbers in a CHOICE device-dependent fashion. Picking these primitives selects the corresponding CHOICE value. When the interpretation is complete, no logical connection exists between the specified segment and the specified CHOICE device.

This most powerful choice facility allows the graphical representation of menu alternatives which may be defined by the application program. Groups of graphical primitives contained in a segment and separated by primitive identifiers form the single alternatives.

> 5: Reserved for future registration.

< 0: Device-Dependent.

Prompting and echoing is CHOICE device-dependent.

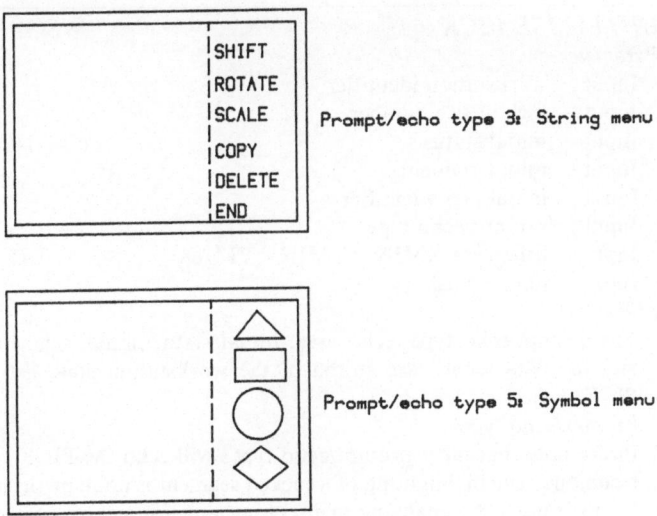

Figure 8.4 Choice device prompts and echoes

Errors:

7	GKS not in proper state: GKS should be in one of the states WSOP, WSAC or SGOP
20	Specified workstation identifier is invalid
25	Specified workstation is not open
38	Specified workstation is neither of category INPUT nor of category OUTIN
51	Rectangle definition is invalid
140	Specified input device is not present on workstation
141	Input device is not in REQUEST mode
144	Specified prompt and echo type is not supported on this workstation
145	Echo area is outside display space
146	Contents of input data record are invalid
152	Initial value is invalid

——————————— *FORTRAN Interface* ———————————

CALL GINCH (WKID, CHDNR, ISTAT, NR, PET, EX1, EX2, EY1, EY2, IL, CA)

Parameters:

Input	WKID	workstation identifier	$(1..n)$	INTEGER
Input	CHDNR	choice device number	$(1..n)$	INTEGER
Input	ISTAT	initial choice status	$(0 = ok, 1 = no\ choice)$	INTEGER
Input	NR	initial choice number	$(0..n)$	INTEGER
Input	PET	prompt/echo type	$(-n..-1, 1..n)$	INTEGER
Input	EX1, EX2, EY1, EY2			
		echo area $EX1 < EX2, EY1 < EY2$		
			DC	$4 \times$ REAL
Input	IL, CA (IL) data record			$n \times$ CHARACTER $*80$

An application of the INITIALISE CHOICE function is given in Section 8.5 on page 305. Figure 8.4 demonstrates some prompt/echo types of the CHOICE device.

INITIALISE PICK   WSOP, WSAC, SGOP   L1b

Parameters:

Input	workstation identifier		N
Input	pick device number	(1..n)	I
Input	initial status	(OK, NOPICK)	E
Input	initial segment		N
Input	initial pick identifier		N
Input	prompt/echo type	(−n..−1,1..n)	I
Input	echo area XMIN < YMIN < YMAX	DC	4 × R
Input	data record		D

Effect:

The prompt/echo type, echo area, initial status, initial segment, initial pick identifier and the data record are stored in the workstation state list entry for the specified PICK device.

Prompt/echo types:

Please note that most prompt/echo types will echo the PICK device by a highlighting technique. The highlighting of a picked segment is done by primitives blinking, increasing their intensity, changing their colour, etc., for a short period of time.

Typical input devices suitable for PICK input are a lightpen and positioning devices such as the cursor of a digitizer or tablet, a mouse, a track ball, thumb wheels, or function keyboards.

1: Implementation Standard.

This uses an implementation-defined technique that at least highlights the "picked" primitive for a short period of time.

2: Pick Identifier Group.

This echoes the contiguous group of primitives with the same pick identifier as the "picked" primitive, or all primitives of the segment with the same pick identifier as the "picked" primitive.

3: Segment.

This echoes the whole segment containing the "picked" primitive.

> 3: Reserved for future registration.

< 0: Device-Dependent.

Prompting and echoing is PICK device-dependent.

Errors:

7	GKS not in proper state: GKS should be in one of the states WSOP, WSAC or SGOP
20	Specified workstation identifier is invalid
25	Specified workstation is not open
37	Specified workstation is not of category OUTIN
51	Rectangle definition is invalid
140	Specified input device is not present on workstation
141	Input device is not in REQUEST mode
144	Specified prompt and echo type is not supported on this workstation
145	Echo area is outside display space
146	Contents of input data record are invalid
152	Initial value is invalid

———————————— *FORTRAN Interface* ————————————

CALL GINPK (WKID,PCDNR,STAT,SGNA,PCID,PET,EX1,EX2,EY1,EY2,IL,CA)

Parameters:

Input	WKID	workstation identifier	(1..n)	INTEGER
Input	PCDNR	pick device number	(1..n)	INTEGER

Input	STAT	initial status	(0 = ok, 1 = nopick)	INTEGER
Input	SGNA	initial segment name	(1..n)	INTEGER
Input	PCID	initial pick identifier	(1..n)	INTEGER
Input	PET	prompt/echo type	(−n..−1,1..n)	INTEGER
Input	EX1, EX2, EY1, EY2			
		echo area EX1 < EX2, EY1 < EY2		
			DC	4 × REAL
Input	IL, CA (IL) data record			n × CHARACTER * 80

INITIALISE STRING   WSOP, WSAC, SGOP   L0b

Parameters:

Input	workstation identifier		N
Input	string device number	(1..n)	I
Input	initial string		S
Input	prompt/echo type	(−n..−1,1..n)	I
Input	echo area XMIN < XMAX, YMIN < YMAX	DC	4 × R
Input	data record		D

Effect:

The initial string, prompt/echo type, echo area and data record are stored in the workstation state list entry for the specified STRING device.

For all prompt/echo types, the data record must contain an input buffer size, which is compared with an implementation-defined "maximum input buffer size for string devices" (contained in the workstation description table). If the requested buffer size is larger, the "maximum input buffer size for string devices" is substituted in the record. If the initial string is longer than the buffer size, an error is issued.

For all prompt/echo types, the data record must contain an initial cursor position, which may range from 1 to the length of initial string plus 1.

When a STRING measure process comes into existence, it obtains a buffer with the current input buffer size. The initial string is copied into the buffer, and the cursor is placed at the initial cursor position within it. Replacement of characters begins at this cursor position.

Using specific buttons, the cursor may be moved within the string without changing characters. As well as this, certain buttons may be used to "insert" a character (extending the string), or to "remove" a character (contracting the string).

Prompt/echo types:

1: Implementation Standard.

   This displays the current STRING value within the echo area.

>1: Reserved for future registration.

<0: Device-Dependent.

   Prompting and echoing is STRING device-dependent.

N.B.:

If the operator enters a number of characters greater than the current input buffer size, the additional characters are lost.

Errors:

7	GKS not in proper state: GKS should be in one of the states WSOP, WSAC or SGOP
20	Specified workstation identifier is invalid
25	Specified workstation is not open
38	Specified workstation is neither of category INPUT nor of category OUTIN
51	Rectangle definition is invalid
140	Specified input device is not present on workstation

141   Input device is not in REQUEST mode
144   Specified prompt and echo type is not supported on this workstation
145   Echo area is outside display space
146   Contents of input data record are invalid
152   Initial value is invalid
154   Length of the initial string is greater than the buffer size

———————————————————— *FORTRAN Interface* ————————————————————

CALL GINST (WKID,STDNR, LSTR, STR,PET,EX1,EX2,EY1,EY2,BUFLEN, INIPOS,IL,CA)

Parameters:

Input	WKID	workstation identifier	(1..n)	INTEGER
Input	STDNR	string device number	(1..n)	INTEGER
Input	LSTR	length of the initial string	(≥ 0)	INTEGER

The number of characters actually used is the minimum of LSTR and the length of STR.

Input	STR	initial string		CHARACTER*(*)
Input	PET	prompt/echo type	$(-n..-1,1..n)$	INTEGER
Input	EX1,EX2,EY1,EY2			
		echo area EX1 < EX2,EY1 < EY2		
			DC	4 × REAL
Input	BUFLEN	buffer length of string	(1..n)	INTEGER
Input	INIPOS	initial cursor position	(1..n)	INTEGER
Input	IL,CA(IL)	data record		n × CHARACTER*80

An application of the INITIALISE STRING function is shown in Section 8.5 on page 309.

8.4   Changing the Input Device Mode

All GKS logical input devices can operate in each of the three modes REQUEST, SAMPLE, and EVENT. Devices are initialised to REQUEST mode when the corresponding workstation is opened. SET ⟨device class⟩ MODE functions are provided to control the operating modes and the echo switch. At any time when the workstation is open, a device can be put into one of the three modes.

The effect of setting a device into REQUEST mode is to stop any current interaction with this device. Such interaction always occurs when the device is in SAMPLE or EVENT mode. Any existing prompting or echoing output is deleted from the screen. The measure process is terminated. The device's identifier is removed from its trigger's list of recipients. If the list becomes empty, the trigger process is terminated.

A REQUEST function can only be issued if the logical input device it addresses is in REQUEST mode. The operating scheme and the effect of the REQUEST functions are described in Section 8.5.

If a device is put into SAMPLE or EVENT mode, the following actions are performed:

— The current interaction with the specified device is stopped (this is the case if the device is already in SAMPLE or EVENT mode).
— The measure process of the specified device is initiated; prompting and echoing are started if the echo switch is on, using the initial values from the workstation state list.
— If the device is put into EVENT mode, its measure identification is added to its trigger's list of recipients.

SET LOCATOR MODE   WSOP,WSAC,SGOP   L0b

Parameters:

Input	workstation identifier		N
Input	locator device number	(1..n)	I
Input	operating mode	(REQUEST,SAMPLE,EVENT)	E
Input	echo switch	ECHO,NOECHO)	E

Effect:

The given LOCATOR device is put into the specified operating mode and its echoing state is set to ECHO or NOECHO. Depending on the specified operating mode, an interaction with the given device may begin or end. The input device state defined by 'operating mode' and 'echo switch' is stored in the workstation state list for the given LOCATOR device.

Errors:

7	GKS not in proper state: GKS should be in one of the states WSOP, WSAC or SGOP
20	Specified workstation identifier is invalid
25	Specified workstation is not open
38	Specified workstation is neither of category INPUT nor of category OUTIN
140	Specified input device is not present on workstation
143	EVENT/SAMPLE input mode is not available at this level of GKS

——————————————— *FORTRAN Interface* ———————————————

CALL GSLCM (WKID,LCDNR,MODE,ESW)

Parameters:

Input	WKID	workstation identifier	(1..n)	INTEGER
Input	LCDNR	locator device number	(1..n)	INTEGER
Input	MODE	mode (0=REQUEST,1=SAMPLE,2=EVENT)		INTEGER
Input	ESW	echo switch	(0=OFF,1=ON)	INTEGER

SET STROKE MODE   WSOP,WSAC,SGOP   L0b

Parameters:

Input	workstation identifier		N
Input	stroke device number	(1..n)	I
Input	operating mode	(REQUEST,SAMPLE,EVENT)	E
Input	echo switch	ECHO,NOECHO)	E

Effect:

The given STROKE device is put into the specified operating mode and its echoing state is set to ECHO or NOECHO. Depending on the specified operating mode, an interaction with the given device may begin or end. The input device state defined by 'operating mode' and 'echo switch' is stored in the workstation state list for the given STROKE device.

Errors:

7	GKS not in proper state: GKS should be in one of the states WSOP, WSAC or SGOP
20	Specified workstation identifier is invalid
25	Specified workstation is not open
38	Specified workstation is neither of category INPUT nor of category OUTIN
140	Specified input device is not present on workstation
143	EVENT/SAMPLE input mode is not available at this level of GKS

———————————————— *FORTRAN Interface* ————————————————

CALL GSSKM (WKID,SKDNR,MODE,ESW)

Parameters:

Input	WKID	workstation identifier	(1..n)	INTEGER
Input	SKDNR	stroke device number	(1..n)	INTEGER
Input	MODE	mode (0=REQUEST,1=SAMPLE,2=EVENT)		INTEGER
Input	ESW	echo switch	(0=OFF,1=ON)	INTEGER

SET VALUATOR MODE WSOP,WSAC,SGOP L0b

Parameters:

Input	workstation identifier		N
Input	valuator device number	(1..n)	I
Input	operating mode	(REQUEST,SAMPLE,EVENT)	E
Input	echo switch	(ECHO,NOECHO)	E

Effect:

The given VALUATOR device is put into the specified operating mode and its echoing state is set to ECHO or NOECHO. Depending on the specified operating mode, an interaction with the given device may begin or end. The input device state defined by "operating mode" and "echo switch" is stored in the workstation state list for the given VALUATOR device.

Errors:

7	GKS not in proper state: GKS should be in one of the states WSOP, WSAC or SGOP
20	Specified workstation identifier is invalid
25	Specified workstation is not open
38	Specified workstation is neither of category INPUT nor of category OUTIN
140	Specified input device is not present on workstation
143	EVENT/SAMPLE input mode is not available at this level of GKS

———————————————— *FORTRAN Interface* ————————————————

CALL GSVLM (WKID,VLDNR,MODE,ESW)

Parameters:

Input	WKID	workstation identifier	(1..n)	INTEGER
Input	VLDNR	valuator device number	(1..n)	INTEGER
Input	MODE	mode (0=REQUEST,1=SAMPLE,2=EVENT)		INTEGER
Input	ESW	echo switch	(0=OFF,1=ON)	INTEGER

SET CHOICE MODE WSOP,WSAC,SGOP L0b

Parameters:

Input	workstation identifier		N
Input	choice device number	(1..n)	I
Input	operating mode	(REQUEST,SAMPLE,EVENT)	E
Input	echo switch	(ECHO,NOECHO)	E

Effect:

The given CHOICE device is put into the specified operating mode and its echoing state is set to ECHO or NOECHO. Depending on the specified operating mode, an interaction with the given device may begin or end. The input device state defined by "operating mode" and "echo switch" is stored in the workstation state list for the given CHOICE device.

Errors:

7	GKS not in proper state: GKS should be in one of the states WSOP, WSAC or SGOP
20	Specified workstation identifier is invalid
25	Specified workstation is not open
38	Specified workstation is neither of category INPUT nor of category OUTIN
140	Specified input device is not present on workstation
143	EVENT/SAMPLE input mode is not available at this level of GKS

———————————— *FORTRAN Interface* ————————————

CALL GSCHM (WKID,CHDNR,MODE,ESW)

Parameters:

Input	WKID	workstation identifier	(1..n)	INTEGER
Input	CHDNR	choice device number	(1..n)	INTEGER
Input	MODE	mode (0=REQUEST,1=SAMPLE,2=EVENT)		INTEGER
Input	ESW	echo switch	(0=OFF,1=ON)	INTEGER

SET PICK MODE   WSOP,WSAC,SGOP   L0b

Parameters:

Input	workstation identifier		N
Input	pick device number	(1..n)	I
Input	operating mode	(REQUEST,SAMPLE,EVENT)	E
Input	echo switch	(ECHO,NOECHO)	E

Effect:

The given PICK device is put into the specified operating mode and its echoing state is set to ECHO or NOECHO. Depending on the specified operating mode, an interaction with the given device may begin or end. The input device state defined by "operating mode" and "echo switch" is stored in the workstation state list for the given PICK device.

Errors:

7	GKS not in proper state: GKS should be in one of the states WSOP, WSAC or SGOP
20	Specified workstation identifier is invalid
25	Specified workstation is not open
37	Specified workstation is not of category OUTIN
140	Specified input device is not present on workstation
143	EVENT/SAMPLE input mode is not available at this level of GKS

———————————— *FORTRAN Interface* ————————————

CALL GSPKM (WKID,PCDNR,MODE,ESW)

Parameters:

Input	WKID	workstation identifier	(1..n)	INTEGER
Input	PCDNR	pick device number	(1..n)	INTEGER
Input	MODE	mode (0=REQUEST,1=SAMPLE,2=EVENT)		INTEGER
Input	ESW	echo switch	(0=OFF,1=ON)	INTEGER

SET STRING MODE   WSOP,WSAC,SGOP   L0b
Parameters:
  Input   workstation identifier   N
  Input   string device number   (1..n)   I
  Input   operating mode   (REQUEST,SAMPLE,EVENT)   E
  Input   echo switch   (ECHO,NOECHO)   E
Effect:
The given STRING device put into the specified operating mode and its echoing
state is set to ECHO or NOECHO. Depending on the specified operating mode, an
interaction with the given device may begin or end. The input device state defined
by "operating mode" and "echo switch" is stored in the workstation state list for
the given STRING device.
Errors:
  7   GKS not in proper state: GKS should be in one of the states WSOP, WSAC
         or SGOP
  20   Specified workstation identifier is invalid
  25   Specified workstation is not open
  38   Specified workstation is neither of category INPUT nor of category OUTIN
  140   Specified input device is not present on workstation
  143   EVENT/SAMPLE input mode is not available at this level of GKS

———————————————— *FORTRAN Interface* ————————————————

CALL GSSTM (WKID,STDNR,MODE,ESW)
Parameters:
  Input   WKID   workstation identifier   (1..n)   INTEGER
  Input   STDNR   string device number   (1..n)   INTEGER
  Input   MODE   mode   (0=REQUEST,1=SAMPLE,2=EVENT)   INTEGER
  Input   ESW   echo switch   (0=OFF,1=ON)   INTEGER

8.5 Request Input

When a REQUEST function is specifically invoked, an attempt is then made
to read a logical input value from a specified logical input device which must
be in REQUEST mode. GKS waits until the input is entered by the operator
or a break action is performed. If a break occurs, the logical input value then
becomes invalid.

In order to support a wide range of interactive graphics applications with
simple input facilities, GKS defines three levels which contain the REQUEST
input feature but not SAMPLE and EVENT input: L0b, L1b, and L2b. All
REQUEST functions operate in a uniform scheme:
— After being invoked, a measure process is created for the specified device.
  Its value is set to the initial value from the workstation state list.
— The device's identifier is added to its trigger's list of recipients. If this list
  was previously empty, the trigger process is started.
— The operator is prompted for input, indicating both the logical value to
  be entered and the physical devices to be used; for example, a tracking

cross is displayed at the initial LOCATOR position. Additionally, a message may be issued such as "USE TABLET TO ENTER A POSITION", but normally the assignment of a specific LOCATOR device to the physical device(s) is made known by the documentation which accompanies the system.

— If the echo switch of the specified device is on, echoing is performed by the measure process, starting with the initial values; in the above example, the appearance of the tracking cross represents prompting and initial echoing at the same time.

— GKS is suspended, while the operator is adjusting a desired input value; the operator receives an immediate echo (if the echo switch is ON); e.g., the tracking cross moves according to the movement of a pen on the tablet.

— The operator terminates the adjusting loop by pressing a button (or more generally, by causing a trigger device to fire). This either indicates that the adjusted value should be entered into the system, or that a break should be made without entering any value. The operator's action should be acknowledged. This could be a short highlighting of the tracking cross symbol, to confirm the system's acceptance of the input value.

— The particular request function returns the value of the logical device or, in a separate STATUS parameter, an indication that the break facility was invoked. The measure process is terminated and the device's identifier is removed from its trigger's list of recipients. If the list becomes empty, the trigger process is also terminated.

REQUEST LOCATOR   WSOP,WSAC,SGOP   L0b

Parameters:

Input	workstation identifier		N
Input	locator device number	(1..n)	I
Output	status	(OK,NONE)	E
Output	normalization transformation number	(0..n)	I
Output	locator position	WC	P

Effect:

GKS performs a REQUEST on the specified LOCATOR device. If the break facility is invoked by the operator the status NONE will be returned; otherwise, OK is returned together with the logical input value entered by the operator. This value consists of a LOCATOR position in world coordinates and the normalization transformation number which was used in the conversion to world coordinates. The locator position is within the window of the normalization transformation.

Errors:

7	GKS not in proper state: GKS should be in one of the states WSOP, WSAC or SGOP
20	Specified workstation identifier is invalid
25	Specified workstation is not open
38	Specified workstation is neither of category INPUT nor of category OUTIN
140	Specified input device is not present on workstation
141	Input device is not in REQUEST mode

───────────────────────── *FORTRAN Interface* ─────────────────────────

CALL GRQLC (WKID,LCDNR,STATUS,TNR,PX,PY)
Parameter:

Input	WKID	workstation identifier	(1..n)	INTEGER
Input	LCDNR	locator device number	(1..n)	INTEGER
Output	STATUS	status	(0 = NONE,1 = OK)	INTEGER
Output	TNR	normalization transformation number	(0..n)	INTEGER
Output	PX,PY	LOCATOR position	WC	2 × REAL

Example 8.2   Generating triangles using REQUEST and INITIALISE LOCATOR

The following part of a program generates a triangle: its vertices are entered by an operator. Three positions are requested using the REQUEST LOCATOR function. The logical device with number 1 is used and it is connected to the workstation 'DISPLAY'. The workstation has to have been opened previously. The coordinates are collected and the POLYLINE function is invoked to display the triangle (cf. Figure 8.5).

───────────────────────── *Pascal* ─────────────────────────

```
......
L10   for I: = 1 to 3 do begin
L20     REQUEST_LOCATOR (display,lc1,status,tnr,p[i]);
L30   end {end because of coming extensions};
L40   p[4]: = p[1];
L50   POLYLINE (4,p);
.....
L999  999 end;
```

If the operator does not want to enter data when the REQUEST function is pending, he should invoke the "break facility". Normally, this is implemented by a special "break" button. The REQUEST function does not then return a locator position but sets the STATUS parameter to "NONE". The application program uses this information to do some exception handling, such as terminating the loop of triangle generation and continuing with other parts of the program:

───────────────────────── *Pascal* ─────────────────────────

```
L25   if status = 'none' then begin
L26     EXCEPTION_HANDLING;
L27     goto 999;
L28   end;
```

It might occur that locator positions are returned in a different coordinate system than the one at present active for output (cf. also Section 8.2.1). In order to apply the appropriate normalization transformation, the transformation TNR, as delivered by the REQUEST function, is selected as the current one:

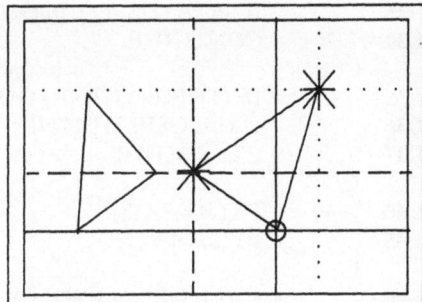

Figure 8.5
Generating triangles using crosshair echo

───────── *Pascal* ─────────

L35 if tnr < > current_tnr **then begin**
L36   SELECT_NORMALIZATION_TRANSFORMATION (tnr);
L37   current_tnr:=tnr:
L38 **end**;

In a further extension of this program, we would like to provide different echoes to give the operator more convenient guidance. It is often a good idea to supply the last position entered by the operator (or a starting position before the first activation) as the initial position for each new REQUEST call. The following four instructions realize the desired effect:

───────── *Pascal* ─────────

L5   p[0]:=(0,0);   {origin in the window of normalization}
                                               {transformation 0}

L6   tnr:=0;
                          {current normalization transformation assumed to be 0}

L7   current_tnr:=0;
L8   p_e_type:=2;   {use crosshair echo}
·····
L15 INITIALISE_LOCATOR
         (display,lc1,p[i-1],tnr,p_e_type,echo_area,empty);

───────── *Fortran* ─────────

·····
         C   *** set origin in the window belonging to transformation 0
L5   PX(1)=0.
L6   PY(1)=0.
L7   TNR=0
L8   CTNR=0
L9   PET=2
L10   DO 30 I=2,4
L15   CALL GINLC (DISP,LC1,TNR,PX(I-1),PY(I-1),
                PET,EX1,EX2,EY1,EY2,1,EMPTD)
L20   CALL GRQLC (DISP,LC1,STATUS,TNR,PX(I),PY(I))

```
L25          IF (STATUS .EQ. 0) GOTO 990
L30    30    CONTINUE
   C                    *** select normalization transformation tnr if not yet done
L35          IF (TNR.EQ.CTNR) GOTO 40
L36          CALL GSELNT (TNR)
L37          CTNR = TNR
   C                                                      *** complete triangle
L40    40    PX(5) = PX(2)
L45          PY(5) = PY(2)
   C                                                      *** draw triangle
L50          CALL GPL (4,PX(2),PY(2))
L60          GOTO 998
L990   990   CONTINUE
   C                                                      *** exception handling
.....
L998   998   STOP
L999         END
```

The INITIALISE LOCATOR function is explained in detail in Section 8.3.1. Here we want to briefly describe two prompt/echo types. They are shown in Figure 8.5.

Prompt/echo type 2: Crosshair

In the above example, the prompt is displayed in the form of a crosshair at the initial position. A vertical and a horizontal line spanning the screen intersect at this position. Both lines vary dynamically as the operator uses the input device, which could be a tracking ball, a pair of thumb wheels, a pen on a tablet or digitizer, or a lightpen on a screen. They always intersect at the current LOCATOR position. This makes it possible to construct new triangles with regard to the location of the other triangles which have already been created.

Prompt/echo type 4: Rubber Band

A rubber band line is displayed. It starts and is fixed at the initial position (in our example at the last entered position). As the operator uses the input device, it dynamically connects the current locator position with the initial position, thus demonstrating the intersections with the triangles which have been already generated.

REQUEST STROKE		WSOP,WSAC,SGOP	L0b
Parameters:			
Input	workstation identifier		N
Input	stroke device number	(1..n)	I
Output	status	(OK,NONE)	E
Output	normalization transformation number	(0..n)	I
Output	number of points	(0..n)	I
Output	points in stroke	WC	n × P

Effect:
GKS performs a REQUEST on the specified STROKE device. If the break facility is invoked by the operator, the status NONE will be returned; otherwise, OK is returned

together with the logical input value which is the current measure of the STROKE device. This consists of a sequence of not more than 'input buffer size' (in the stroke data record) points in world coordinates, and the normalization transformation number used in the conversion to world coordinates. The points in the stroke all lie within the window of the normalization transformation.

N.B.:

If an operator enters more points than the stroke input buffer size (in the workstation state list) allows, the additional points are lost. It is anticipated that the operator would be informed of this.

Errors:

7	GKS not in proper state: GKS should be in one of the states WSOP, WSAC or SGOP
20	Specified workstation identifier is invalid
25	Specified workstation is not open
38	Specified workstation is neither of category INPUT nor of category OUTIN
140	Specified input device is not present on workstation
141	Input device is not in REQUEST mode

———————————————— *FORTRAN Interface* ————————————————

CALL GRQSK (WKID,SKDNR,MNB,STATUS,TNR,NB,PX,PY)

Parameters:

Input	WKID	workstation identifier	$(1..n)$	INTEGER
Input	SKDNR	stroke device number	$(1..n)$	INTEGER
Input	MNB	maximum number of points	$(1..n)$	INTEGER
Output	STATUS	status	$(0=\text{NONE},1=\text{OK})$	INTEGER
Output	TNR	normalization transformation number	$(0..n)$	INTEGER
Output	NB	number of points	$(0..n)$	INTEGER
Output	PX(MNB),PY(MNB)			
		STROKE positions	WC	$n \times 2 \times$ REAL

REQUEST VALUATOR WSOP,WSAC,SGOP L0b

Parameters:

Input	workstation identifier		N
Input	valuator device number	$(1..n)$	I
Output	status	(OK,NONE)	E
Output	value		R

Effect:

GKS performs a REQUEST on the specified VALUATOR device. If the break facility is invoked by the operator, the status NONE will be returned; otherwise, OK is returned together with the logical input value entered by the operator. The value delivered is in the range specified in the workstation state list entry for this device. The application program may define the range using the INITIALISE VALUATOR function (cf. Section 8.3).

Errors:

7	GKS not in proper state: GKS should be in one of the states WSOP, WSAC or SGOP
20	Specified workstation identifier is invalid
25	Specified workstation is not open
38	Specified workstation is neither of category INPUT nor of category OUTIN
140	Specified input device is not present on workstation
141	Input device is not in REQUEST mode

──────────────── *FORTRAN Interface* ────────────────

CALL GRQVL (WKID,VLDNR,STATUS,VAL)
Parameters:

Input	WKID	workstation identifier	(1..n)	INTEGER
Input	VLDNR	valuator device number	(1..n)	INTEGER
Output	STATUS	status	(0=NONE,1=OK)	INTEGER
Output	VAL	value		REAL

Example 8.3   Adjusting picture size using REQUEST and INITIALISE VALUATOR

This part of a program adjusts the size of a picture to be drawn interactively. It prompts the operator to enter the desired x-scale by using the MESSAGE function, REQUESTS a real value from the operator and sets the workstation viewport to the size defined by the real value. It should be noted that in this first version of the example, the range of the real values is completely implementation-dependent.

──────────────── *Pascal* ────────────────

```
L10   MESSAGE (display, 'enter picture scale in x-direction');
L20   REQUEST_VALUATOR (display,vl1,status,val);
L30   SET_WORKSTATION VIEWPORT (display,0,val,0,val);
```

To prevent real values being entered which are too large or negative, the range of the values should be defined beforehand. The data record of the INITIALISE VALUATOR function is assigned the range 0 as low value, and the maximum display surface size as high value; the latter may be determined from the workstation description table. Using these values, a VALUATOR device prompting is displayed when the REQUEST function is invoked, indicating the range of possible values. An example is shown below.

──────────────── *Pascal* ────────────────

```
L5   maxdisplaysizex:= .... ;
L6   data:=(0,maxdisplaysizex);
L7   INITIALISE_VALUATOR (display,vl1,maxdisplaysizex,1,echo_area,data);
```

If the operator does not want to enter a precise value but would rather use a default adjustment instead, he may press the "break" button. The following statement ensures that in this case the program behaves correctly and adjusts the picture scale to the maximum size.

──────────────── *Pascal* ────────────────

```
L25   if (status = 'none') then val:=maxdisplaysizex;
```

──────────────── *Fortran* ────────────────

```
      C                          *** set maximum display size and data record
L5            MAXDX = ....
L9            CALL GINVL (DISP,VL1,MAXDX,1,EX1,EX2,EY1,EY2,0.,
              MAXDX,1,EMPTD)
```

```
        C                                 *** prompt operator for input, request value
L10              CALL GMSG (DISP,34HENTER PICTURE SCALE IN X-DIREC-
                 TION)
L20              CALL GRQVL (DISP,VL1,STATUS,VAL)
        C                                 *** if break occurs, set maximum length
L25              IF (STATUS .EQ. 0) VAL=MAXDX
        C                                 *** set workstation viewport
L30              CALL GSWKVP (DISP,0.0,VAL,0.0,VAL)
.....
```

REQUEST CHOICE   WSOP,WSAC,SGOP   L0b

Parameters:

Input	workstation identifier		N
Input	choice device number	(1..n)	I
Output	status	(OK,NOCHOICE,NONE)	E
Output	choice number	(1..n)	I

Effect:

GKS performs a REQUEST on the specified CHOICE device. If the break facility is invoked by the operator, the status NONE will be returned; otherwise, OK is returned together with the logical input value which is the current measure of the CHOICE device.

Errors:

7	GKS not in proper state: GKS should be in one of the states WSOP, WSAC or SGOP
20	Specified workstation identifier is invalid
25	Specified workstation is not open
38	Specified workstation is neither of category INPUT nor of category OUTIN
140	Specified input device is not present at workstation
141	Input device is not in REQUEST mode

———————————————— *FORTRAN Interface* ————————————————

CALL GRQCH (WKID,CHDNR,STATUS,CHNR)

Parameters:

Input	WKID	workstation identifier	(1..n)	INTEGER
Input	CHDNR	choice device number	(1..n)	INTEGER
Output	STATUS	status	(0=NONE,1=OK,2=NOCHOICE)	INTEGER
Output	CHNR	choice number	(1..n)	INTEGER

Example 8.4   Command control using REQUEST and INITIALISE CHOICE

This part of the program demonstrates command control in an interactive system. The alternative commands contained in a menu are assigned to a data record. The logical CHOICE device is initialised to display the single commands as identifiable distinct buttons within the echo area, defined by the area limits EX1 to EX2 and EY1 to EY2. The echo area coordinates must be specified in device coordinates.

―――――――――――――― *Pascal* ――――――――――――――

L5   echo_area:={right part of a rectangular screen};
L10 data:='GENERATE,TRANSFORM,COPY,DELETE';
L20 INITIALISE_CHOICE (display,ch1,1,3,echo_area,data);   {string menu echo}
L30 **repeat**
L40 REQUEST_CHOICE (display,ch1,status,nb);
L50 **if** (status='ok') **then begin**
L60   **case** nb **of**
L70   1: PROCEDURE_GENERATE_OBJECTS;   {extension of Example 8.5.1}
L80   2: PROCEDURE_TRANSFORM_OBJECTS;
L100   3: PROCEDURE_COPY_OBJECTS;
L110   4: PROCEDURE_DELETE: {see Example 8.5.4}
L120:   **end**;
L130 end;
L140 until (status='none');

―――――――――――――― *Fortran* ――――――――――――――

```
         C                    *** assign right part of a rectangular screen as echo area
L5              EX1= ...
L6              EX2= ...
L7              EY1= ...
L8              EY2= ...
         C                                        *** define menu string in data record
L10             CALL GPREC (1,EMPTI,1,EMPTR,30,30HGENERATE,
                TRANSFORM,COPY,DELETE,MDL,ERRIND,IL,CA)
L20      20     CALL GINCH (DISP,CH1,1,3,EX1,EX2,EY1,EY2,IL,CA)
L30             CALL GRQCH (DISP,CH1,STATUS,NB)
L40             IF (STATUS .EQ. 0) GOTO 130
L60             GOTO (70,80,100,110),NB
L70      70     CALL {PROCEDURE_GENERATE_OBJECTS}
         C                                        *** extension of Example 8.2
L75             GOTO 20
L80      80     CALL {PROCEDURE_TRANSFORM_OBJECTS}
L90             GOTO 20
L100     100    CALL {PROCEDURE_COPY_OBJECTS}
L105            GOTO 20
L110     110    CALL {PROCEDURE_DELETE_OBJECTS}
         C                                        *** see Example 8.5
L120            GOTO 20
L130     130    CONTINUE
.....
```

―――――――――――――――――――――――――――――――――――――

REQUEST PICK   WSOP,WSAC,SGOP L1b
Parameters:

Input	workstation identifier		N
Input	pick device number	(1..n)	I
Output	status	(OK,NOPICK,NONE)	E
Output	segment name		N
Output	pick identifier		N

Effect:
GKS performs a REQUEST on the specified PICK device. If the break facility is
invoked by the operator, the status NONE will be returned. If the measure of the

PICK device indicates no pick, status NOPICK will be returned; otherwise, OK is returned together with a segment name and a pick identifier which are set according to the current measure of the PICK device. The pick identifier is associated with the primitive within the segment that was picked.

Errors:

7	GKS not in proper state: GKS should be in one of the states WSOP, WSAC or SGOP
20	Specified workstation identifier is invalid
25	Specified workstation is not open
37	Specified workstation is not of category OUTIN
140	Specified input device is not present at workstation
141	Input device is not in REQUEST mode

——————————————— *FORTRAN Interface* ———————————————

CALL GRQPK (WKID,PCDNR,STATUS,SGNA,PCID)

Parameters:

Input	WKID	workstation identifier	(1..n)	INTEGER
Input	PCDNR	pick device number	(1..n)	INTEGER
Output	STATUS	status (0=NONE,1=OK,2=NOPICK)		INTEGER
Output	SGNA	segment name		INTEGER
Output	PCID	pick identifier		INTEGER

Example 8.5   Segment deletion using the REQUEST PICK function

The following program realizes the deletion of a set of segments. It is aimed at applications which, on average, delete several segments in a sequence without forcing the operator to enter the "deletion" command each time anew. Furthermore, it provides user control over segments picked by mistake. If the operator recognizes that the segment just picked must not be deleted, he may identify it a second time. The operator is given feedback in the form of highlighting the currently picked segment. The operator terminates the loop by using the "break" facility.

——————————————— *Pascal* ———————————————

```
L10    twice:=true;
L20    repeat if twice then REQUEST_PICK (display,pc1,status1,segment1,pickid);
L30       if status1=ok then
L40       begin twice:=false;
L50         SET_HIGHLIGHTING (segment1,highlighted);
L60         REQUEST_PICK (display,pc1,status2,segment2,pickid);
L70         if status2=ok then
L80         begin twice:=segment1=segment2;
L90           if twice
L100          then SET_HIGHLIGHTING (segment1,normal)
L110          else begin DELETE_SEGMENT (segment1);
L120             status1:=status2;
L130             segment1:=segment2
L140          end
L150        end
L160     end
L170   until (status1=none) or (status2=none);
L180 if not twice then DELETE_SEGMENT (segment1);
```

─────────────────────── *Fortran* ───────────────────────

```
L10                TWICE = .TRUE.
L20        20       IF (TWICE) CALL GRQPK (DISP,PC1,STAT1,SEG1,PCID)
L30                IF (STAT1 .EQ. 1) THEN
L40                  TWICE = .FALSE.
L50                  CALL GSHLIT (SEG1,1)
L60                  CALL GRQPK (DISP,PC1,STAT2,SEG2,PCID)
L70                  IF (STAT2 .EQ. 1) THEN
L80                    TWICE = SEG1 .EQ. SEG2
L90                    IF (.NOT. TWICE) THEN
L100                     CALL GDSG (SEG1)
L110                     STAT1 = STAT2
L120                     SEG1 = SEG2
L130                    ENDIF
L140                  ELSEIF CALL GSHLIT (SEG1,0)
L150                  ENDIF
L160               ENDIF
L170               IF (STAT1 .EQ. 1 .AND. STAT2 .EQ. 1) GOTO 20
L180               IF (.NOT. TWICE) CALL GDSG (SEG1)
```

REQUEST STRING   WSOP,WSAC,SGOP   L0b

Parameters:

Input	workstation identifier		N
Input	string device number	(1..n)	I
Output	status	(OK,NONE)	E
Output	character string		S

Effect:

GKS performs a REQUEST on the specified STRING device. If the break facility is invoked by the operator, the status NONE will be returned; otherwise, OK is returned together with the logical input value which is the current measure of the STRING device.

N.B.:

The length of the returned string is less than or equal to the buffer size specified in the workstation state list entry (for this device) in the data record.

Errors:

7	GKS not in proper state: GKS should be in one of the states WSOP, WSAC or SGOP
20	Specified workstation identifier is invalid
25	Specified workstation is not open
38	Specified workstation is neither of category INPUT nor of category OUTIN
140	Specified input device is not present on workstation
141	Input device is not in REQUEST mode

─────────────────────── *FORTRAN Interface* ───────────────────────

CALL GRQST (WKID,STDNR,STATUS,L,STR)

Parameters:

Input	WKID	workstation identifier	(1..n)	INTEGER
Input	STDNR	string device number	(1..n)	INTEGER
Output	STATUS	status	(0=NONE,1=OK)	INTEGER
Output	L	length of string	(in character)	INTEGER
Output	STR	character string		CHARACTER*(*)

Example 8.6   Form editing using REQUEST and INITIALISE STRING

This program is used to fill in forms, starting with given default text strings for the single compartments on the form. The reference text is read in from an external file. The text string is used as the initial string for the STRING device and the field position is used for calculating a text box which defines the string echo area. Character replacement starts at the end of the actual string and may extend it up to the maximum permissible length. Of course, the operator may reset the cursor position to the previous characters, or, depending on the application, the initial cursor position may be set to 1:

L30 D=(MAXSTLENGTH,1);

After the string is edited and reentered, it is stored in a second external form file.

────────────────────── *Pascal* ──────────────────────

```
L10   repeat
L20      READ (position,max_st_length,act_st_length,string);
L30      d:=(max_st_length, act_st_length+1);
L35      with echoarea do begin
L40         ex1:=position.x;
L50         ey1:=position.y;
L60         ex2:=ex1+max_st_length*characterwidth;
L70         ey2:=ey1+characterheight;
L75      end;
L80      INITIALISE_STRING (display,st1,string,1,echoarea,d);
L90      REQUEST_STRING (display,st1,status,string);
L100     act_st_length:=length (string);
L110     write (position,max_st_length,act_st_length,string);
L120  until (end of file);
```

────────────────────── *Fortran* ──────────────────────

```
      C                   *** start loop of reading the given text with starting position,
      C                   *** maximum length, and actual length
L10      10   READ(INFIL,121,EOF=990)
                  PX,PY,MAXLST,ACTLST,(STR(I),I=1,ACTLST)
L30           EX1=PX
L40           EY1=PY
L50           EX2=EX1+MAXSTL*CHARWI
L60           EY2=EY1+CHARHE
L70           CALL GINST (DISP,ST1,ACTLST,STR,1,EX1,EX2,EY1,
                  EY2,MAXLST,ACTLST+1,1,EMPTD)
L80           CALL GRQST (DISP,ST1,STATUS,ACTLST,STR)
L90           WRITE (OUTFIL,122)
                  PX,PY,MAXLST,ACTLST,(STR(I),I=+1,ACTLST)
L100          GOTO 10
L121    121   FORMAT (2F8.3,2I3,80A1)
L122    122   FORMAT (1H,2F8.3,2I3,80A1)
.....
L990    990   STOP
L999          END
```

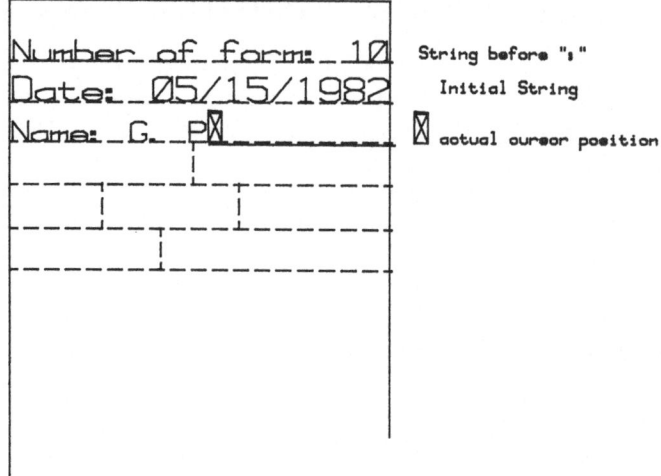

Figure 8.6   Form editing

8.6   Sample Input Functions

When SAMPLE input functions are activated, this causes GKS to return the current logical input value of a specified logical input device without waiting for an operator action. The logical input device must be in SAMPLE mode.

Typical applications of SAMPLE input can be characterized as ones which directly couple program operations to certain input device states which can be adjusted dynamically by an operator. Not the operator but the program performance determines the significant moments in time when input data is transferred to the application. This is all in contrast to what happens with REQUEST and EVENT input.

SAMPLE input may, for example, be used to perform dynamic picture changes via segment transformations, to zoom in on and window complete pictures on workstations, to change attribute table entries and also to control other, non-graphic parts of application programs.

The following parts of this chapter describe the SAMPLE input functions and demonstrate SAMPLE input applications.

SAMPLE LOCATOR		WSOP,WSAC,SGOP	L0c
Parameters:			
Input workstation identifier			N
Input locator device number		(1..n)	I
Output normalization transformation number		(0..n)	I
Output locator position	WC		P

Effect:

The logical input value, which is the current measure of the specified LOCATOR device, is returned. The measure consists of a LOCATOR position in world coordinates and the normalization transformation number which was used in the conversion to world coordinates. The LOCATOR position is within the window of the normalization transformation.

Errors:

7	GKS not in proper state: GKS should be in one of the states WSOP, WSAC or SGOP
20	Specified workstation identifier is invalid
25	Specified workstation is not open
38	Specified workstation is neither of category INPUT nor of category OUTIN
140	Specified input device is not present on workstation
142	Input device is not in SAMPLE mode

──────────────── *FORTRAN Interface* ────────────────

CALL GSMLC (WKID,LCDNR,TNR,PX,PY)

Parameters:

Input	WKID	workstation identifier	(1..n)	INTEGER
Input	LCDNR	locator device number	(1..n)	INTEGER
Output	TNR	normalization transformation number	(0..n)	INTEGER
Output	PX,PY	LOCATOR position	WC	2 × REAL

Example 8.7 Moving objects with the SAMPLE LOCATOR function

This part of a program moves an object (a group of segments) depending on the present state of a LOCATOR device. We assume that the group of segments has been determined by other program parts, for example, as in Example 8.5.

Transformations are performed on a NDC level, i.e., in the unit square $[0,1] \times [0,1]$. To ensure that the LOCATOR device delivers NDC coordinates, transformation number zero (the unity transformation) is given the highest priority.

This program is incomplete in that it never stops. Complete control may be gained as shown in Example 8.5.

──────────────── *Pascal* ────────────────

```
.....
      {get list of normalization transformation numbers. The first one has}
      {highest priority. Give transformation zero highest priority}
L10   INQUIRE_LIST_OF_NORMALIZATION_TRANSFORMATION_NUMBERS
      (error,length,transformation_numbers);
L20   SET_VIEWPORT_INPUT_PRIORITY (0,transformation_number[1],higher);
                    {select transformation 0, set initial transformation matrix}
L30   SELECT_NORMALIZATION_TRANSFORMATION (0);
L40   EVALUATE_TRANSFORMATION_MATRIX ((0,0),(0,0),0,(1,1),ndc,m);
                    {enable LOCATOR and get reference point for relative shifts}
L50   SET_LOCATOR_MODE (display,lc1,sample,echo),
L60   SAMPLE_LOCATOR (display,lc1,status,tnr,p);         {loop of transformations}
L70   repeat
L80     SAMPLE_LOCATOR (display,lc1,status,tnr,q);
L90     ACCUMULATE_TRANSFORMATION_MATRIX
          (m,(0,0),q − p,0,(1,1),ndc,m);
```

L100 p:=q;
L110 **for** i:=1 **to** numb_seg **do**
L120   SET_SEGMENT_TRANSFORMATION (segments[i],m);
L130 **until** (stop);
.....

──────────────────── *Fortran* ────────────────────

.....
```
       C                      *** get normalization transformation number one; this has
       C                      *** highest priority. Give transformation zero highest priority
L10            CALL GQENTN (1,ERRIND,ACTL,TNRL)
L20            CALL GSVPIP (0,TNRL,GHIGHR)
       C                      *** select transformation 0, set initial transformation matrix
L30            CALL GSELNT (0)
L40            CALL GEVTM (0.0,0.0,0.0,0.0,0.0,1.0,1.0,NDC,M)
       C                      *** enable LOCATOR and get reference point for relative shifts
L50            CALL GSLCM (DISP,LC1,GSAMPL,GECHO)
L60            CALL GSMLC (DISP,LC1,TNR,PX,PY)
       C                                           *** loop of transformations
L70       70   CONTINUE
L80            CALL GSMLC (DISP,LC1,TNR,QX,QY)
L90            CALL GACTM (M,0.0,0.0,PX-QX,PY-QY,0.0,1.0,1.0,NDC,M)
L100           PX=QX
L105           PY=QY
       C                      *** transform group of segments (stored in segl(1..nbseg))
L110           DO 120 I=1,NBSEG
L120     120   CALL GSSGT (SEGL(I),M)
L130           IF (.NOT.STOP)GOTO 70
...
L990     990   CONTINUE
L998           STOP
```

──

SAMPLE STROKE   WSOP,WSAC,SGOP   L0c

Parameters:

Input	workstation identifier		N
Input	stroke device number	(1..n)	I
Output	normalization transformation number	(0..n)	I
Output	number of points	(0..n)	I
Output	points in stroke	WC	$n \times P$

Effect:

The logical input value, which is the current measure of the specified STROKE device, is returned. The measure consists of a sequence of points in world coordinates and the normalization transformation number used in the conversion to world coordinates. The points in the stroke all lie within the window of the normalization transformation.

N.B.:

If an operator enters more points than the stroke input buffer size (in the workstation state list) allows, the additional points are lost. It is anticipated that the operator would be informed of this.

Errors:

7   GKS not in proper state: GKS should be in one of the states WSOP, WSAC or SGOP

20   Specified workstation identifier is invalid
25   Specified workstation is not open
38   Specified workstation is neither of category INPUT nor of category OUTIN
140   Specified input device is not present on workstation
142   Input device is not in SAMPLE mode

———————————————— *FORTRAN Interface* ————————————————

CALL GSMSK (WKID,SKDNR,MNB,TNR,NB,PX,PY)

Parameters:

Input	WKID	workstation identifier	(1..n)	INTEGER
Input	SKDNR	stroke device number	(1..n)	INTEGER
Input	MNB	maximum number of points	(1..n)	INTEGER
Output	TNR	normalization transformation number	(0..n)	INTEGER
Output	NB	number of points in stroke	(0..n)	INTEGER
Output	PX(MNB),PY(MNB)			
		STROKE positions	WC	$n \times 2 \times$ REAL

SAMPLE VALUATOR   WSOP,WSAC,SGOP   L0c

Parameters:

Input	workstation identifier		N
Input	valuator device number	(1..n)	I
Output	value		R

Effect:

The logical input value, which is the current measure of the specified VALUATOR device, is returned. The value delivered is in the range specified in the workstation state list entry (for this device) in the data record.

Errors:

7   GKS not in proper state: GKS should be in one of the states WSOP, WSAC or SGOP

20   Specified workstation identifier is invalid
25   Specified workstation is not open
38   Specified workstation is neither of category INPUT nor of category OUTIN
140   Specified input device is not present on workstation
142   Input device is not in SAMPLE mode

———————————————— *FORTRAN Interface* ————————————————

CALL GSMVL (WKID,VLDNR,VAL)

Parameters:

Input	WKID	workstation identifier	(1..n)	INTEGER
Input	VLDNR	valuator device number	(1..n)	INTEGER
Output	VAL	value		REAL

Example 8.8   Rotation of objects using the SAMPLE VALUATOR function

This part of a program rotates an object (a group of segments) dynamically, depending on the present state of a VALUATOR device. The rotation is relative to a fixed point. Transformation takes place in NDC space.

Let us assume that the group of segments has been determined by other parts of the program, e.g., as in Example 8.5.

―――――――――――――――――― *Pascal* ――――――――――――――――――

.....
```
                          {set fixed point and initial segment transformation matrix}
L10   fixp:=(.5,.5);
L20   EVALUATE_TRANSFORMATION_MATRIX (fixp,(0.0),0,(1,1),ndc,m);
                          {initialise valuator to range [−1 : +1], initial value 0}
L30   datarecord:=(−1,+1);
L40   INITIALISE_VALUATOR (display,vl1,0,1,echo_area,datarecord);
                          {put VALUATOR into SAMPLE mode, switch echo off}
L50   SET_VALUATOR_MODE (display,vl1,sample,noecho);
                          {loop of rotation}
L60   repeat
L70      SAMPLE_VALUATOR (display,vl1,val);
L80      accumulate_transformation_matrix
            (m,fixp,(0,0),val,(1,1),m);
                          {transform group of segments}
L90      for i:=1 to numb_seg do
L100        SET_SEGMENT_TRANSFORMATION (segments[i],m);
L110     until (stop);
.....
```

―――――――――――――――――― *Fortran* ――――――――――――――――――

.....
```
      C                       *** set fixed point and initial segment transformation matrix
L10           FX=0.5
L15           FY=0.5
L20           CALL GEVTM (FX,FY,0.0,0.0,0.0,1.0,1.0,NDC,M)
      C                   *** initialise valuator to range [−1 : +1], initial value 0
L40           CALL GINVL (DISP,VL1,0.0,1,EX1,EX2,EY1,EY2,−1.,1.,1,EMPTD)
      C                   *** put VALUATOR into SAMPLE mode, switch echo off
L50           CALL GSVLM (DISP,VL1,GSAMPL,GNECHO)
      C                                       *** loop of rotation
L60      10   CONTINUE
L70           CALL GSMVL (DISP,VL1,VAL)
L80           CALL GACTM (M,FX,FY,0.0,0.0,VAL,1.0,1.0,NDC,M)
      C                   *** transform group of segments (stored in segl(1..nbseg))
L90           DO 100 I=1,NBSEG
L100    100   CALL GSSGT (SEGL(I),M)
L110          IF (.NOT.STOP) GOTO 10
.....
L990    990   CONTINUE
L998          STOP
```

SAMPLE CHOICE		WSOP,WSAC,SGOP L0c
Parameters:		
Input workstation identifier		N
Input choice device number	(1..n)	I
Output choice status	(OK,NOCHOICE)	E
Output choice number	(1..n)	I

Effect:
The logical input value, which is the current measure of the specified CHOICE device, is returned.

Errors:

7	GKS not in proper state: GKS should be in one of the states WSOP, WSAC or SGOP
20	Specified workstation identifier is invalid
25	Specified workstation is not open
38	Specified workstation is neither of category INPUT nor of category OUTIN
140	Specified input device is not present on workstation
142	Input device is not in SAMPLE mode

―――――――――――――――― *FORTRAN Interface* ――――――――――――――――

CALL GSMCH (WKID,CHDNR,STATUS,CHNR)

Parameters:

Input	WKID	workstation identifier	(1..n)	INTEGER
Input	CHDNR	choice device number	(1..n)	INTEGER
Output	STATUS	choice status	(0=ok,1=nochoice)	INTEGER
Output	CHNR	choice number	(1..n)	INTEGER

Example 8.9   Scaling objects using the SAMPLE CHOICE function

The following program part demonstrates a SAMPLE CHOICE application. As long as specific buttons are pressed, the application program performs certain actions which depend on the present CHOICE number. In this example, an object is dynamically reduced (or, respectively, expanded) in size, depending on whether button 1 or button 2 is pressed down.

A CHOICE device is put into SAMPLE mode. In SAMPLE mode, the state of the CHOICE device always indicates whether any buttons are depressed at that moment (then the CHOICE number is greater than 0), and which button (or combination of buttons) is actually depressed.

A typical implementation might use a function keyboard with at least two buttons. These are mapped to the CHOICE numbers 1 to 4:

The operator interface looks like the following:
— no buttons are pressed: CHOICE number = 1; nothing happens;
— button 1 is pressed: CHOICE number = 2; reduce object in size dynamically;
— button 2 is pressed: CHOICE number = 3; expand object dynamically;
— both buttons are pressed: CHOICE number = 4; stop program.

―――――――――――――――――――― *Pascal* ――――――――――――――――――――

```
.....
                                           {select transformation 0}
L10   SELECT_NORMALIZATION_TRANSFORMATION (0);
                      {set fixed point and initial segment transformation matrix}
L20   fixp:=(.5,.5);
L30   EVALUATE_TRANSFORMATION_MATRIX (fixp,(0.0),0,(1,1),ndc,m);
                      {put CHOICE into SAMPLE mode; no echo, since direct feedback}
L40   SET_CHOICE_MODE (display,ch1,sample,noecho);
                                           {loop of transformations}
```

L50   **repeat**
L60   SAMPLE_CHOICE (display,ch1,status,chnb);
L70   **case** chnb **of**
L80   1: **goto** 170;
L90   2: (reduce object in size);
L100   ACCUMULATE_TRANSFORMATION_MATRIX
              $(m,fixp,(0,0),0,(1-delta\_x,1-delta\_y),m)$;
L110   3: {expand object};
L120   ACCUMULATE_TRANSFORMATION_MATRIX
              $(m,fixp,(0,0),val,(1+delta\_x,1+delta\_y),m)$;
L130   4: **goto** 170;
L140   **end** {end case};
L150   **for** i:=1 **to** numb_seg **do**
L160   SET_SEGMENT_TRANSFORMATION (segments[i],m);
L170   170 **until** (chnb=4);
.....

──────────────── *Fortran* ────────────────

.....
```
        C                                           *** select transformation 0
L10             CALL GSELNT (0)
        C                    *** set fixed point and initial segment transformation matrix
L20             FX=0.5
L25             FY=0.5
L30             CALL GEVTM (FX,FY,0.0,0.0,0.0,1.0,1.0,NDC,M)
        C                        *** put CHOICE into SAMPLE mode, no echo needed
L40             CALL GSCHM (DISP,CH1,GSAMPL,GNECHO)
        C                                           *** loop of transformations
L50      50     CONTINUE
L60             CALL GSMCH (DISP,CH1,STATUS,CHNB)
L65             CHNB=CHNB
L70             GOTO (170,90,110,170), CHNB
L90      90     CONTINUE
        C                                           *** reduce object in size
L100            CALL GACTM (M,FX,FY,0.0,0.0,0.0,1.0-DX,1.0-DY,M)
L105            GOTO 150
L110    110     CONTINUE
        C                                           *** expand object
L120            CALL GACTM (M,FX,FY,0.0,0.0,0.0,1.0+DX,1.0+DY,M)
        C                    *** transform group of segments (stored in segl(1..nbseg))
L150    150     DO 160 I=1,NBSEG
L160    160     CALL GSSGT (SEGL(I),M)
L170    170     IF (CHNB .NE. 3) GOTO 50
.....
L990    990     CONTINUE
L998            STOP
```

──

SAMPLE PICK   WSOP,WSAC,SGOP   L1c
Parameters:
   Input   workstation identifier   N
   Input   pick device number   (1..n)   I

Output status   (OK,NOPICK)   E
Output segment name   N
Output pick identifier   N

Effect:

If the current measure of the specified PICK device is indicating no pick, status NO-PICK will be returned; otherwise, OK will be returned together with the segment name and the pick identifier associated with the primitive within the segment that was picked.

Errors:

7	GKS not in proper state: GKS should be in one of the states WSOP, WSAC or SGOP
20	Specified workstation identifier is invalid
25	Specified workstation is not open
37	Specified workstation is not of category OUTIN
140	Specified input device is not present on workstation
142	Input device is not in SAMPLE mode

───────────────────── *FORTRAN Interface* ─────────────────────

CALL GSMPK (WKID,PCDNR,STAT,SGNA,PCID)

Parameters:

Input	WKID	workstation identifier	(1..n)	INTEGER
Input	PCDNR	pick device number	(1..n)	INTEGER
Output	STAT	status	(0=OK,1=NOPICK)	INTEGER
Output	SGNA	segment name		INTEGER
Output	PCID	pick identifier		INTEGER

Example 8.10   Identifying segments via the SAMPLE PICK function

A PICK input device is put into SAMPLE mode. Then, by moving a suitable physical device (e.g. a lightpen) over the screen, the PICK device state is changed. The logical PICK device always contains the segment name and pick identifier which belong to the primitive which the physical input device currently indicates.

Certain physical devices can only change the PICK device state when an internal trigger is set. In such implementations, a lightpen switch, for example, is considered to be an internal trigger. It is therefore used to change the logical PICK device measure in SAMPLE mode.

The present example demonstrates the following application:

— the operator identifies primitives on the screen by moving a suitable input device, e.g., a lightpen or a cursor, over the display surface;

— the state of the logical PICK device changes, and it always indicates the segment name and the pick identifier to which the currently identified primitive belongs. The segment may be echoed, e.g., highlighted, as long as the input device points at one of its primitives.

— the application program reads the current PICK device state via the SAMPLE PICK function;

— the application program checks whether the delivered segment fulfills certain application-specific rules (e.g., belongs to a specific object), and, if it does, feedback is generated (e.g., the segment is permanently highlighted), the

segment name is put into a segment list for further use, and it is set to "non-detectable" in order not to detect it a second time;
— the loop is terminated when the specified CHOICE device (which is also in SAMPLE mode) changes its value from zero to one.

——————————————————— *Pascal* ———————————————————

```
.....
L10   SET_PICK_MODE (display,pc1,sample,echo);
L20   SET_CHOICE_MODE (display,ch1,sample,echo);
L30   index:=1;
L40   repeat
L50     SAMPLE_CHOICE (display,ch1,status,chnb);
L60     if (chnb=1) then
L70       SAMPLE_PICK (display,pc1,status,segment_name;pick_id);
L80       CHECK_RULES (segment_name,admissible);
L90       if (admissible) then
L100        segment_list[index]:=segment_name;
L110        index:=index+1;
L120        SET_DETECTABILITY (segment_name,undetectable);
L130        SET HIGHLIGHTING (segment_name,highlighted);
L140      end;
L150    end;
L160  until (chnb=1);
.....
```

——————————————————— *Fortran* ———————————————————

```
.....
      C                     *** set PICK and CHOICE devices into SAMPLE mode
L10           CALL GSPKM (DISP,PC1,GSAMPL,GECHO)
L20           CALL GSCHM (DISP,CH1,GSAMPL,GECHO)
L30           INDEX=1
      C                             *** start segment gathering loop
L40    40     CONTINUE
L50           CALL GSMCH (DISP,CH1,STATUS,CHNB)
L60           IF (CHNB .EQ. 2) GOTO 999
L70           CALL GSMPK (DISP,PC1,STATUS,SEGN,PCID)
L80           CALL CHECK_RULES (SEGN,ADMISS)
L90           IF (.NOT. ADMISS) GOTO 40
L100          SEGL(INDEX)=SEGN
L110          INDEX=INDEX+1
L120          CALL GSDTEC (SEGN,GUNDET)
L130          CALL GSHLIT (SEGN,GHILIT)
L160          GOTO 40
.....
L990   999    STOP
L999          END
```

SAMPLE STRING		WSOP,WSAC,SGOP	L0c
Parameters:			
Input	workstation identifier		N
Input	string device number	(1..n)	I
Output	character string		S

Effect:
   The logical input value, which is the current measure of the specified STRING device, is returned. The length of the returned string is less than or equal to the buffer size specified in the workstation state list entry (for this device) in the data record.

Errors:

7	GKS not in proper state: GKS should be in one of the states WSOP, WSAC or SGOP
20	Specified workstation identifier is invalid
25	Specified workstation is not open
38	Specified workstation is neither of category INPUT nor of category OUTIN
140	Specified input device is not present on workstation
142	Input device is not in SAMPLE mode

———————————— *FORTRAN Interface* ————————————

CALL GSMST (WKID,STDNR,LC,STR)
Parameters:

Input	WKID	workstation identifier	(1..n)	INTEGER
Input	STDNR	string device number	(1..n)	INTEGER
Output	LC	actual length of string in characters	(0..n)	INTEGER
Output	STR	string		CHARACTER*(*)

8.7 Event Input

8.7.1 Input Queue and Current Event Report

The input queue contains zero or more event reports. Event reports contain device identifier/logical input value pairs resulting from trigger firings. Event reports can be added to the input queue when logical input devices in EVENT mode are triggered by the operator. Events can be removed from the input queue by calling AWAIT EVENT, FLUSH DEVICE EVENTS and CLOSE WORKSTATION. The input queue can overflow, in which case it must be emptied before any further event reports can be added.

   When a trigger which is part of one or more logical input devices in EVENT mode fires, the resulting event reports are entered into the queue and labelled as a group of simultaneous event reports. An event report for each device is added to the input queue if and only if there is room for the whole group of simultaneous event reports.

   The way in which reports in a group of simultaneous event reports are ordered is undefined.

   If there is not enough room in the queue for all event reports when a trigger fires, input queue overflow has occurred. Input queue overflow is not reported to the application program immediately. It is reported via the error mechanism when the next GKS function that can remove event reports from the input queue is called, i.e. AWAIT EVENT, FLUSH DEVICE EVENTS, and CLOSE WORKSTATION. In the time between the detection of input queue overflow and the next call of AWAIT EVENT with an empty input queue, no events are generated by trigger firings. (This allows the application program to determine how many events were in the queue when overflow occurred by calling AWAIT EVENT with timeout zero.)

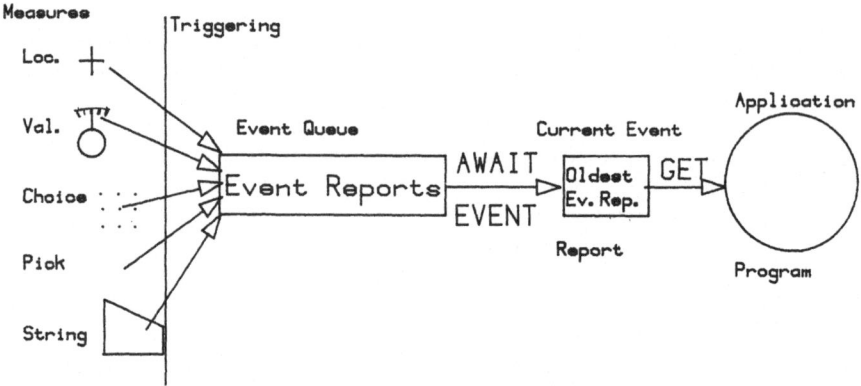

Figure 8.7 Model of event input

When the "input queue overflow" error is reported, the trigger which caused the overflow is noted. This is done by identifying any one logical input device which uses that trigger and which was in EVENT mode at the time the overflow was detected, and putting such an identification into the error state list.

If the queue is not empty, AWAIT EVENT removes the first event report after copying the logical input value into the current event report in the GKS state list. The workstation identifier and device number are returned to the application program directly by AWAIT EVENT. If the queue is empty, AWAIT EVENT suspends execution until an event report is in the queue or until the specified timeout period has elapsed.

The application program may obtain the contents of the current event report by calling the appropriate GET ⟨input class⟩ function.

If, after having removed the event report, there still remain other reports in the queue from the same group of simultaneous events as the removed report, the "more simultaneous events" flag in the GKS state list is set to MORE. Otherwise, it is set to NOMORE.

FLUSH DEVICE EVENTS removes all the event reports for a specific device from the input queue. CLOSE WORKSTATION removes from the input queue all the event reports for all logical devices at that workstation.

If the "more simultaneous events" flag has the value MORE, when either FLUSH DEVICE EVENTS or CLOSE WORKSTATION is invoked, and they remove all the remaining reports in the group of simultaneous event reports at the head of the queue, then the flag is set to NOMORE.

8.7.2   Functions to Await and Delete Event Queue Entries

AWAIT EVENT	WSOP,WSAC,SGOP L0c
Parameters:	
Input timeout (seconds)	R
Output workstation identifier	N

Output input class   (NONE,LOCATOR,STROKE,   E
                                VALUATOR,CHOICE,PICK,STRING)
Output logical input device number   (1..n)   I

Effect:

If the input queue is empty, GKS is put into a waiting state until an input event is written into the queue or the time specified in the timeout parameter has elapsed. If a timeout occurs and there is still no entry in the queue, a NONE value is returned for input class.

If there is at least one entry in the queue, the oldest event report is moved from the event queue to the current event report in the GKS state list. The workstation identifier, the input class, and the logical input device number are returned and the corresponding values are made available for subsequent interrogation by the GET ⟨device class⟩ functions.

N.B.:

The operation is performed even if error 147 (input queue has overflowed) has occurred. Note that a timeout of zero causes an immediate inspection of the queue, and a NONE value for input class is returned if the queue is empty. Note also that some operating systems may not provide a reliable timeout facility. In this case, a timeout different from zero may never cause a timeout at all. Repeated calls of the AWAIT EVENT function overwrite event reports which have already been stored in the current event report as a result of previous calls of AWAIT EVENT (cf. also Example 8.7.1).

Errors:

7   GKS not in proper state: GKS should be in one of the states WSOP, WSAC or SGOP

147   Input queue has overflowed

151   Timeout is invalid

———————————————— *FORTRAN Interface* ————————————————

CALL GWAIT (TOUT,WKID,INCL,INDNR)

Parameters:

Input	TOUT	time out (in seconds)		REAL
Input	WKID	workstation identifier	(1..n)	INTEGER
Output	INCL	input class		INTEGER
		(0=NONE,1=LOCATOR,2=STROKE,		INTEGER
		3=VALUATOR,4=CHOICE,5=PICK,6=STRING)		
Output	INDNR	logical input device number	(1..n)	INTEGER

Example 8.11   Waiting for specific input data via AWAIT EVENT

This part of a program awaits a logical input of a specific data type (INPUT_ CLASS), from a specific input device (WK_ID, INPUT_DEVICE). All other input data which might have been stored in the event queue is ignored and deleted.

———————————————————— *Pascal* ————————————————————

```
.....
L10    timeout:=28800;                              {8 hour working day}
L20    repeat
L30       AWAIT_EVENT (timeout,wkid,class,dev);
L40       if (class=none) then goto 999;
```

L50   **until** (wkid = wk_id **and** class = input_class **and**
          dev = input_device)

> {at this stage, the current event report contains an}
> {entry of the desired type.}

.....
L999 999 **end**;

─────────────────────────────── *Fortran* ───────────────────────────────

.....
    C   *** set time out = 8 hours
```
L10              TOUT = 28800.
L20      20      CONTINUE
L30              CALL GWAIT (TOUT,WKID,INCL,INDV)
L40              IF (INCL.EQ.0) GOTO 999
L50              IF (WKID.NE.SWKID .OR. INCL.NE.SINCL.OR.
                    INDV.NE.SINDV)GOTO 20
      C                    *** at this stage, the current event report contains an
      C                    *** entry of the desired type
.....
L999     999     STOP
L1000            END
```

───

FLUSH DEVICE EVENTS   WSOP,WSAC,SGOP   L0c
Parameters:
Input   workstation identifier   N
Input   input class   (LOCATOR,STROKE,   E
                                        VALUATOR,CHOICE,PICK,STRING)
Input   logical input device number   (1..n)   I
All entries in the input queue from the specified logical input device are removed.
The operation is performed even if error 147 has occurred.

Errors:
7	GKS not in proper state: GKS should be in one of the states WSOP, WSAC or SGOP
20	Specified workstation identifier is invalid
25	Specified workstation is not open
38	Specified workstation is neither of category INPUT nor of category OUTIN
140	Specified input device is not present on workstation
147	Input queue has overflowed

─────────────────────────── *FORTRAN Interface* ───────────────────────────

CALL GFLUSH (WKID,INCL,INDNR)
Parameters:
Input   WKID   workstation identifier   (1..n)   INTEGER
Input   INCL   input class
                              (0 = NONE,1 = LOCATOR,2 = STROKE,   INTEGER
                              3 = VALUATOR,4 = CHOICE,5 = PICK,6 = STRING)
Input   INDNR   logical input device number   (1..n)   INTEGER

Example 8.12   FLUSH DEVICE EVENTS

The following examples show how to delete specific event reports from the event queue. The following cases can be disinguished:
— All event reports of a specific input class (INPUT_CLASS), which have come from a specific workstation (WKID), are deleted from the event queue.

—————————————————————— *Pascal* ——————————————————————

```
.....
                      {get workstation type and number of input devices connected}
                                          {to this type of workstation}
L10   INQUIRE_WORKSTATION_CONNECTION_AND_TYPE
         (wkid,error,con_id,wk_type);
L20   INQUIRE_NUMBER_OF_AVAILABLE_LOGICAL_INPUT_DEVICES
         (wk_type,error,numb[loc],numb[sto],numb[val],
         numb[cho],numb[pic],numb[str]);
L30   if (numb[input_class] < > 0) then begin
L40     for i:=1 to numb[input_class] do
L50     FLUSH_DEVICE_EVENTS (wkid,input_class,i);
L60   end:
```

— All entries of a specific input class are deleted from the input queue. It should be noted that there can be several input devices of the same input class on one or several workstations. Then the following instructions need to be added:

—————————————————————— *Pascal* ——————————————————————

```
.....
L3    INQUIRE_SET_OF_OPEN_WORKSTATIONS
         (error,numb_wk,set_wk);
L5    for i:=1 to numb_wk begin
L7    wkid:=set_wk[j];
.....
L55   end
```

— Finally, all entries in the event queue are deleted; this is done by adding the following two instructions:

—————————————————————— *Pascal* ——————————————————————

```
.....
L25   for input_class:=1 to 6 begin
.....
L52   end;
```

The last case, (flush event queue), reads when completed:

───────────────────────── *Pascal* ─────────────────────────

.....
L3   INQUIRE_SET_OF_OPEN_WORKSTATIONS
         (error,numb_wk,set_wk);
                                              {delete for all open workstations}
L5   **for** j: = 1 **to** numb_wk **do begin**
L7   wkid: = set_wk[j],
                              {get workstation type and number of input devices connected}
                                              {to this type of workstation}
L10   INQUIRE_WORKSTATION_CONNECTION_AND_TYPE
              (wkid,error,con_id,wk_type);
L20   INQUIRE_NUMBER_OF_AVAILABLE_LOGICAL_INPUT_DEVICES
              (wk_type,error,numb[loc],numb[sto],numb[val],
              numb[cho],numb[pic],numb[str]);
                                              {delete for all input classes}
L25   **for** input_class: = 1 **to** 6 **begin**
L30   **if** (numb[input_class] < > 0) **then**
                                              {delete for all input devices}
L40   **for** i: = 1 **to** numb[input_class] **do**
L50   FLUSH_DEVICE_EVENTS (wkid,input_class,i);
L52   **end**;
L55   **end**;
L60 **end**;

───────────────────────── *Fortran* ─────────────────────────

(Gather list of open workstations (due to some cryptic FORTRAN interface design decisions))
L2   DO 10 J = 1, MAXL
L3   10   CALL GQOPWK (J,ERR,NWK,SETWK(J))
         C   *** delete for all open workstations
L5   DO 60 J = 1,NWK
L7   WKID = SETWK(J)
         C   *** get workstation type and number of input devices connected
         C   *** to this type of workstation
L10   CALL GQWKC (WKID,ERR,CONID,WKTYPE)
L20   CALL GQLI
                   +(WKTYPE,ERR,NDV(1),NDV(2),
                    NDV(3),NDV(4),NDV(5),NDV(6))
         C   *** delete for all input classes
L25   DO 55 CLASS = 1,6
L30   IF (NDV(CLASS).EQ.0) GOTO 200
L35   N = NDV(CLASS)
         C   *** delete for all input devices
L40   DO 52 I = 1,N
L52   52   CALL GFLUSH (WKID,CLASS,I)
L55   55   CONTINUE
L60   60   CONTINUE
.....

8.7.3   Get Input Functions

GET LOCATOR   WSOP,WSAC,SGOP   L0c

Parameters:

Output   normalization transformation number $(0..n)$ I
Output   locator position   WC   P

Effect:

The LOCATOR logical input value in the current event report is returned. This consists of a LOCATOR position in world coordinates and the normalization transformation number which was used in the conversion to world coordinates.

Errors:

7   GKS not in proper state: GKS should be in one of the states WSOP, WSAC or SGOP

150   No input value of the correct class in the current event report

---

———————————————— *FORTRAN Interface* ————————————————

CALL GGTLC (TNR,PX,PY)

Parameters:

Output   TNR   normalization transformation number $(0..n)$ INTEGER
Output   PX,PY   locator position   WC $2 \times$ REAL

Example 8.13   Asynchronous input and processing of curves

This program part demonstrates an application made up of the following steps:
— the operator enters a series of positions into the GKS event queue;
— they are read from the GKS event queue using the AWAIT EVENT and the GET LOCATOR functions and then they are gathered into an application program data record;
— when a series is completed, a resulting curve is calculated and displayed.

While the curve is processed, the operator may continue entering positions into the GKS event queue where they are buffered. Each series of coordinates is terminated by a special alternative of a CHOICE device.

A typical implementation may use a cursor device (tablet) with at least one button, and a button device with at least two buttons. The two devices might be physically connected as in the case of a cursor on a tablet with three buttons attached.

The LOCATOR is implemented using the positioning facility as the measure value and the button as the trigger. The CHOICE device is realized either by the two buttons of a keyboard or by the two remaining buttons of the cursor.

Further methods for mapping logical to physical devices are shown in Section 8.8; more flexible implementation structures are given in detail in Chapter V.2.

The operator interface is as follows:
— the cursor is moved, no buttons are pressed: an echo indicates the current value of the LOCATOR device;

— button 1 (the button attached to the LOCATOR device) is pressed: the present state of the LOCATOR device is put into the event queue as a LOCATOR event report;
— button 2 (button 1 of the CHOICE device) is pressed: a CHOICE event report with choice number 1 is generated and put into the event queue. When this event report is read by the application program, it is used to terminate the present series of positions, and to start further processing of them;
— button 3 (button 2 of the CHOICE device) is pressed: a CHOICE event report with choice number 2 is put into the event queue; when it is read, the program terminates.

───────────────────────── *Pascal* ─────────────────────────

```
.....
L10          SET_LOCATOR_MODE (display,lc1,event,echo);
L20          SET_CHOICE_MODE (display,chi,event,noecho);
L30          index:=1;
L40          timeout:=28800;
L50          chnb:=0;
L60          repeat
L70            AWAIT_EVENT (timeout,wkid,class,device);
L80            case class of
L90              none: goto 999;
L100             locator: begin
L110               GET_LOCATOR (tnr,points(index));
L120               index:=index+1;
L130             end;
L140             choice: begin
L150               GET_CHOICE (status,chnb);
L160               if (chnb=1) then begin
L170                 CALCULATE_CURVE (points,curve);
L180                 POLYLINE (curve);
L190               end;
L200             end;
L210           end;
L220         until (chnb=2);
.....
L1000        999 END;
```

───────────────────────── *Fortran* ─────────────────────────

```
.....
      C              *** set LOCATOR and CHOICE devices into EVENT mode
L10          CALL GSLCM (DISP,LC1,GEVENT,GECHO)
L20          CALL GSCHM (DISP,CH1,GEVENT,GNECHO)
L30          INDEX=1
L40          TOUT=28800
L50          CHNB=0
L60     60   CONTINUE
```

```
       C                           *** await event of type LOCATOR or CHOICE
L70                CALL GWAIT (TOUT,WKID,CLASS,DEV)
L75                CLASS=CLASS+1
       C                           *** case NONE,LOCATOR,STROKE,VALUATOR,CHOICE,PICK,
       C                           ***                                    and STRING
L80                GOTO (999,100,999,999,140,999,999),CLASS
       C                                               *** case LOCATOR
L100      100      CONTINUE
L110               CALL GTLC (TNR,P(INDEX))
L120               INDEX=INDEX+1
L130               GOTO 60
       C                                               *** case CHOICE
L140      140      CONTINUE
L150               CALL GTCH (STATUS,CHNB)
L160               IF (CHNB .EQ. 2) GOTO 999
       C                           *** case CHOICE number 1: process curve
L170               CALL CALCULATE_CURVE (INDEX−1,P,LEN,CURVE)
L180               CALL GPL (LEN,CURVE)
L220               IF (CHNB .NE. 2) GOTO 60
....
L999      999      STOP
L1000             END
```

GET STROKE   WSOP,WSAC,SGOP   L0c

Parameters:

Output	normalization transformation number	(0..n)	I
Output	number of points	(0..n)	I
Output	points in stroke	WC	n × P

Effect:

The STROKE logical input value from the current event report is returned. This consists of a sequence of points in world coordinates and the normalization transformation number used in the conversion to world coordinates. The normalization transformation number is determined (when the event was queued).

N.B.:

The number of points in the stroke is less than or equal to the stroke buffer size specified in the workstation state list for this device.

Errors:

7	GKS not in proper state: GKS should be in one of the states WSOP, WSAC or SGOP
150	No input value of the correct class is in the current event report

———————————— *FORTRAN Interface* ————————————

CALL GGTSK (MNB,TNR,NB,PX,PY)

Parameters:

Input	MNB	maximum number of points	(1..n)	INTEGER
Output	TNR	normalization transformation number	(0..n)	INTEGER
Output	NB	number of points in stroke	(0..n)	INTEGER
Output	PX(MNB),PY(MNB)		WC	n × 2 × REAL
		STROKE positions		

GET VALUATOR   WSOP,WSAC,SGOP   L0c

Parameters:

Output   value   R

Effect:

The VALUATOR logical input value in the current event report is returned. The value delivered is in the range specified in the workstation state list entry (for the device) in the data record.

Errors:

7   GKS not in proper state: GKS should be in one of the states WSOP, WSAC or SGOP

150   No input value of the correct class is in the current event report

─────────────────────── *FORTRAN Interface* ───────────────────────

CALL GGTVL (VAL)

Parameters:

Output   VAL   value   REAL

GET CHOICE   WSOP,WSAC,SGOP   L0c

Parameters:

Output   choice status   (OK,NOCHOICE)   E
Output   choice number   (1..n)   I

Effect:

The CHOICE logical input value in the current event report is returned.

Errors:

7   GKS not in proper state: GKS should be in one of the states WSOP, WSAC or SGOP

150   No input value of the correct class is in the current event report

─────────────────────── *FORTRAN Interface* ───────────────────────

CALL GGTCH (STATUS,CHNR)

Parameters:

Output   STATUS   choice status   (0=ok,1=nochoice)   INTEGER
Output   CHNR   choice number   (1..n)   INTEGER

GET PICK   WSOP,WSAC,SGOP   L1c

Parameters:

Output   status   (OK,NOPICK)   I
Output   segment name   N
Output   pick identifier   N

Effect:

The PICK logical input value in the current event report is returned. This consists of a PICK status, a segment name and the pick identifier associated with the primitive within the segment that was picked.

Errors:

7   GKS not in proper state: GKS should be in one of the states WSOP, WSAC or SGOP

150   No input value of the correct class is in the current event report

──────────────── *FORTRAN Interface* ────────────────

CALL GGTPK (STAT,SGNA,PCID)
Parameters:

Output	STAT	status	(0 = OK,1 = NOPICK)		INTEGER
Output	SGNA	segment name		(1..n)	INTEGER
Output	PCID	pick identifier		(1..n)	INTEGER

Example 8.14   Identifying segment for sending a copy to a plotter

This example makes it possible to identify segments interactively and put their names into the event queue where the application program reads them.

For each segment identified at an interactive workstation a copy is sent to a plotter workstation. Since the process of copying lasts considerably longer than that of identifying the segments, it is useful to have an event report queuing facility, so that the operator can enter data without waiting for certain program states.

This part of the program ends when the operator does not enter a PICK input for more than 10 seconds after the last copied segment has been sent to the plotter, or if the operator generates data other than PICK input data.

──────────────────── *Pascal* ────────────────────

```
.....
L10   OPEN_WORKSTATION (plotter,connection,plottertype);
L20   SET_PICK_MODE (display,pc1,event,echo);
L30   repeat
L40     AWAIT_EVENT (10,wkid,class,device),
L50     if (class = pick) then begin
L60       GET_PICK (status,segment_name,pick_id);
L70       if (status = ok) then begin
L80         SET_HIGHLIGHTING (segment_name,highlighted);
L90         SET_DETECTABILITY (segment_name,undetectable);
L100        COPY_SEGMENT_TO_WORKSTATION
                (plotter,segment_name);
L110      end;
L120    end;
L130  until (class < > pick)
                            {disable pick device (put into request mode)}
L140  SET_PICK_MODE (display,pc1,request,echo);
L150  CLOSE_WORKSTATION (plotter);
.....
```

──────────────────── *Fortran* ────────────────────

```
.....
      C                 *** open plotter workstation and set pick device into event mode
L10             CALL GOPWK (PLOT,CONID,PLTYP)
L20             CALL GSPKM (DISP,PC1,GEVENT,GECHO)
L30      30     CONTINUE
      C                 *** await pick event input (all other input leads to termination)
L40             CALL GWAIT (10.0,WKID,CLASS,DEVICE)
L50             IF(CLASS .NE. GPICK) GOTO 140
```

```
L60            CALL GTPK (STATUS,SEGN,PCID)
L70            IF (STATUS .EQ. GNPICK) GOTO 140
      C                    *** highlight segment, make it undetectable, and copy it to
      C                                                    *** plotter workstation
L80            CALL GSHLIT (SEGN,GHILIT)
L90            CALL GSDTEC (SEGN,GUNDET)
L100           CALL GCSGWK (PLOT,SEGN)
L130           IF (CLASS .EQ. GPICK) GOTO 30
      C                            *** disable pick device (put it into request mode)
L140    140    CALL GSPKM (DISP,PC1,GREQU,GECHO)
L150           CALL GCLWK (PLOT)
.....
L998           STOP
L999           END
```

GET STRING   WSOP,WSAC,SGOP   L0c

Parameters:

Output   character string   S

Effect:

The STRING logical input value in the current event report is returned. The length of the returned string is less than or equal to the buffer size specified in the workstation state list entry (for this device) in the data record at the time the event was queued.

Errors:

7   GKS not in proper state: GKS should be in one of the states WSOP, WSAC or SGOP

150   No input value of the correct class is in the current event report

――――――――――――――――― *FORTRAN Interface* ―――――――――――――――――

CALL GGTST (LC,STR)

Parameters:

Output   LC   length of returned string   (0..n)   INTEGER
Output   STR   string   CHARACTER*(*)

8.8   A Compound Example of Using the GKS Input Functions

An interactive process reads segments from the long term storage (the GKSM) and displays them on the display surface (instructions L10 to L170). It allows the operator to pick one of the segments (instructions L180 to L340), to place and transform it on the screen (instructions L360 to L880), and to print it on a plotter as part of the picture he constructs (instruction L850). He can do this until he presses an 'end of picture' key (instruction L880). The program is then properly terminated (instructions L890 to L970).

The segments might be symbols in a flowchart. They appear at the top or bottom or at the side of the screen and are then used to compose the flow-chart.

The logical input devices used in this example are:
— PICK device PC1 in event mode;
— LOCATOR device LC1 in event and sample mode;
— VALUATOR device VL1 in sample mode;
— CHOICE device CH1 with at least 6 alternatives (0 to 5) in event mode.

This program is written in such a way that its correct performance is independent of the particular physical input devices used in a given installation. All logical input devices could be implemented on distinct physical input devices in the following way:
— the PICK device on a lightpen with a tip switch;
— the LOCATOR device on a track ball or thumb wheels, etc. with one button connected;
— the VALUATOR device on a potentiometer or via simulations using a light-pen, a position device, a function keyboard, etc.;
— and the CHOICE device on function or alphanumeric keyboards or screen menus.

It is also possible that several logical input devices can be realized on the same physical input device. An extreme example of this is given when all logical devices are implemented on a three-button puck of a tablet. This means that the operator only has to deal with one physical input device and the appropriate echoes which indicate the respective logical values.

The PICK and the LOCATOR devices are both mapped to the pointing device. In the case of the PICK device, the pointing device's position is used to calculate a segment name, which in turn is the measure value for the PICK device; for the LOCATOR device, its position can be used directly (after appropriate transformations are applied) as the LOCATOR device measure value.

If both devices are simultaneously in EVENT mode, then one operator action, namely pressing one of the three buttons, puts two event reports into the queue, i.e., the identified segment and the identified position. This is caused by the instructions L180 to L340 in the program. The position which identifies the segment is used at the same time as a segment reference point.

The VALUATOR device is implemented by using the puck position; the CHOICE device uses the three puck buttons. Following the instructions L360 to L650, the CHOICE device is set into EVENT mode, and either no device, or the LOCATOR or the VALUATOR device, is in SAMPLE mode; the VALUATOR device delivers values either in the range 0 to 10 (for scaling), or in the range 0 to 3.14 (for rotation). Whichever one is selected depends on the last CHOICE alternative entered by the operator:
— Button 1 was pressed: the segment is shifted by moving the pointing device on the tablet. The LOCATOR is in SAMPLE mode.
— Button 2 was pressed: the segment is scaled by moving the pointing device. The VALUATOR is in SAMPLE mode (range 0 to 10).
— Buttons 1 and 2 were pressed: the segment is rotated by moving the pointing device. The VALUATOR is again in SAMPLE mode. The range goes from 0 to 3.14.

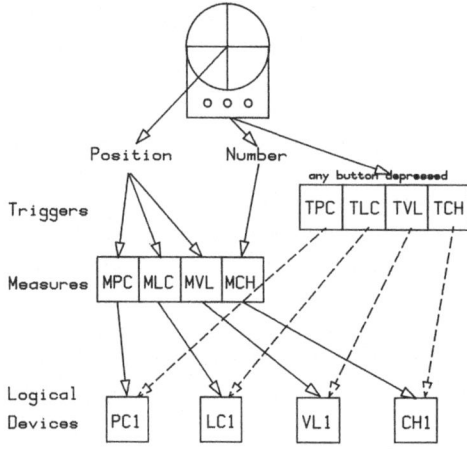

Triggers

Measures

Logical
Devices

Figure 8.8 Mapping of logical input
devices to a data tablet puck

— Button 3 was pressed: the segment is copied to the plotter. PICK and LO-
CATOR devices are put into EVENT mode, VALUATOR and CHOICE
devices are disabled. Pointing at a segment and pressing one of the buttons
starts the loop again.

If buttons 1 and 3 are pressed, then the program is terminated.

Example 8.15   A compound input program

———————————————————— *Pascal* ————————————————————

```
L10   OPEN_GKS (error_file, buffer_size);
L20   OPEN_WORKSTATION (display,dddis,refresh);          {display workstation}
L30   OPEN_WORKSTATION (plotter,ddplt,plottyp);          {plotter workstation}
L40   OPEN_WORKSTATION (gksm_in,file1,gksm_input);          {metafile input}
                                        {device-independent segment storage}
L50   OPEN_WORKSTATION (segstore,ddseg,wiss);
L60   INQUIRE_MAXIMUM_DISPLAY_SURFACE_SIZE
        (refresh,error,units,msize);
L70   dx:=msize.x/20;                              {size of an echo area}
L80   dy:=msize.y/20;
                  {the contents of the metafile are displayed on the display}
                  {segments, if present, are stored on segment storage}
L90   ACTIVATE_WORKSTATION (display);                 {output on display}
L100  ACTIVATE_WORKSTATION (segstore);                    {output on DIS}
L110  repeat                                        {reading the GKSM}
L120  GET_ITEM_TYPE_FROM_GKSM (gksm_in,item_type,item_length);
L130    READ_ITEM_FROM_GKSM (gksm_in,array_length,array);
L140    INTERPRET_ITEM (item_type,item_length,array);
L150  until (item_type=eoftype);
L160  CLOSE_WORKSTATION (gksm_in)                    {metafile released}
L170  DEACTIVATE_WORKSTATION (segstore);        {no more output on WISS}
                  {By now the picture contained in the metafile is visible on the display.}
                  {The segments contained in this data can be used for}
                  {creating a new picture which will be output on a plotter}
```

L 180 repeat   {each loop transition handles one segment}
                              {A segment is identified and provided with a reference point}
                                   {set pick PC1 and locator LC1 both in EVENT mode}
L 190   SET_PICK_MODE (display,pc1,event,echo);
L 200   SET_LOCATOR_MODE (display,lc1,event,echo);
L 210   **for** i: = 1 **to** 2 **do**
L 220   **begin**
                              {read one pick and one locator event in arbitrary sequence}
L 230   timeout = 8_hours;   {standard working day}
                                         {wait for pick and locator input}
L 240   AWAIT_EVENT (timeout,wkid,class,dev);
L 250   **if** (class = pick) **then**
L 260   **begin**   {SEGNAME received}
L 270   GET_PICK (status,segname,pickid);
L 280   SET_PICK_MODE (display,pc1,request,echo);   {disable pick}
L 290   **end else**
L 300   **begin**   {segment reference point POINT1 received}
L 310   GET_LOCATOR (tnr1,point1);
L 320   SET_LOCATOR_MODE (display,lc1,request,echo);
L 330   **end**;   {disable locator}
L 340   **end**;
L 350   SELECT_NORMALIZATION_TRANSFORMATION (tnr1);
                              {subsequent points are expected to be in viewport of}
                                      {normalization transformation TNR1.}
                              {This would be zero, since no transformations have}
                                              {been set up explicitly}
                                      {set choice CH1 in EVENT mode}
L 360   SET_CHOICE_MODE (display,ch1,event,echo);
                              {inquire initial segment transformation matrix}
L 370   INQUIRE_SEGMENT_ATTRIBUTES
             (segname,error,m,vis,high,prior,detec);
             chnb: = 0;   {wait for first CHOICE alternative}
L 380   **repeat**   {each loop transition for one transformation}
                                       {step or a program control change}
L 390   timeout: = 0;
L 400   AWAIT_EVENT (timeout,wkid,class,dev);
L 410   **if** (class = choice) **then**   {change of program control}
L 420   **begin**
                              {disable locator and valuator to initialize them anew}
L 430   SET_VALUATOR_MODE (display,vl1,request,echo);
L 440   SET_LOCATOR_MODE (display,lc1,request,echo);
L 450   GET_CHOICE (stat,chnb);
L 460   **case** chnb **of**
L 470   1: **begin**   {switch to shift}
L 480   echo_area: = (0, msize.x,0,msize.y);
                              {LC1 has initial value = segment refpoint and crosshairs}
L 490   INITIALISE_LOCATOR
             (display,lc1,refp,tnr1,2,echo_area,emptd);
L 500   SET_LOCATOR_MODE (display,lc1,sample,echo);
L 510   SAMPLE_LOCATOR (display,lc1,tnr1,point1);
L 520   **end**;   {start point}

```
L530   2: begin                                      {switch to scaling}
L540      data_record:=(0,10)
L550      echo_area:=(msize.x−dx,msize.x,msize.y−dy,msize.y);
L560      INITIALISE_VALUATOR
          (display,vl1,1,1,echo_area,data_record);
L570      SET_VALUATOR_MODE (display,vl1,sample,echo);
L580      end;
L590   3: begin                                      {switch to rotation}
L600      data_record:=(0,3.14)
L610      echo_area:=
          (msize.x−2∗dx,msize.x−dx,msize.y−dy,msize.y);
L620      INITIALISE_VALUATOR
          (display,vl1,1,1,echo_area,data_record);
L630      end;                                        {end case}
L640   end;                                           {end if}
L650   end;
L660   case chnb of
L670   1: begin                                       {shift}
L680      SAMPLE_LOCATOR (display,lc1,tnr2,point2);
                                                      {target point}
L690      if (tnr2 < > tnr1) goto 890;
                              {segment is shifted by POINT2−POINT1}
L700      d:=point2−point1;
L710      ACCUMULATE_TRANSFORMATION_MATRIX
             (m,refp,d,0,(1,1),wc,m);
L720      SET_SEGMENT_TRANSFORMATION (segname,m);
L730      end;
L740   2: begin                                       {scale}
L750      SAMPLE_VALUATOR (display,vl1,val);          {scale factor}
                        {segment is scaled by VAL in x and y direction.}
L760      ACCUMULATE_TRANSFORMATION_MATRIX
          (m,refp,(0,0),0,(val,val),wc,m);
L770
L775      SET_SEGMENT_TRANSFORMATION (segname,m);
L780      end;
L790   3: begin                                       {rotate}
L800      SAMPLE_VALUATOR (display,vl1,val);          {angle}
                        {segment is rotated by ANGLE (relative to REFP)}
L810      ACCUMULATE_TRANSFORMATION_MATRIX
          (m,refp,(0,0),val,(0,0),wc,m);
L820
L830      SET_SEGMENT_TRANSFORMATION (segname,m);
L840      end;
L850   4: begin              {copy segment to plotter, disable choice device}
L852      COPY_SEGMENT_TO_WORKSTATION (plotter,segname); '
L854      SET_CHOICE_MODE (display,ch1,request,echo);
L856   end
L860      end                                          {end case}
L870      until chnb=4 or chnb=5;           {end of transformation loop}
L880      until chnb=5;                  {end of segment handling loop}
L890 890:
```

{disable input devices}

L900 SET_LOCATOR_MODE (display,lc1,request,echo);
L910 SET_VALUATOR_MODE (display,vl1,request,echo);
L920 SET_CHOICE_MODE (display,ch1,request,echo);

{deactivate and close workstations, close GKS}

L930 DEACTIVATE_WORKSTATION (display);
L940 CLOSE_WORKSTATION (plotter);
L950 CLOSE_WORKSTATION (display);
L960 CLOSE_WORKSTATION (segstore);
L970 CLOSE_GKS;

───────────────────── *Fortran* ─────────────────────

```
L10            CALL GOPKS (ERRFIL,MEMORY)
       C              *** Open display, plotter, metafile input, and segment storage
L20            CALL GOPWK (DISP,DDDIS,REFR)
L30            CALL GOPWK (PLOT,DDPLT,PLTYP)
L40            CALL GOPWK (GKSMIN,FILE1,GMI)
L50            CALL GOPWK (SEGS,DDSEG,GWISS)
       C                  *** Compute echo areas as part of the display surface
L60            CALL GQMDS (REFR,ERR,UNIT,SZLX,SZLY,SZRX,SZRY)
L70            DX = SZLX / 20.
L80            DY = SZLY / 20.
       C              *** The contents of the metafile are displayed on the display.
       C              *** Segments, if present, are stored on segment storage.
       C              *** Activate display and segment storage workstations
L90            CALL GACWK (DISP)
L100           CALL GACWK (SEGS)
L110    110    CONTINUE
L120           CALL GGTITM (GKSMIN,TYPE,LENGTH)
L130           CALL GRDITM (GKSMIN,MAXL,ARLEN,AR)
L140           CALL GIITM (TYPE,ARLEN,AR)
L150           IF (TYPE .NE. EOFTYP) GOTO 110
       C                  *** Close metafile and deactivate segment storage
L160           CALL GCLWK (GKSMIN)
L170           CALL GDAWK (SEGS)
       C              *** By now the picture contained in the metafile is visible on
       C              *** the display. The segments contained in this data can be used
       C              *** for creating a new picture which will be output on a plotter
       C                  *** Each loop transition handles one segment
L180    180    CONTINUE
       C              *** A segment is identified and provided with a reference point.
       C                  *** Set pick PC1 and locator LC1 both in EVENT mode
L190           CALL GSPKM (DISP,PC1,GEVENT,GECHO)
L200           CALL GSLCM (DISP,LC1,GEVENT,GECHO)
L210           DO 330 I = 1,2
       C              *** Read one pick and one locator event in arbitrary sequence
L230           TOUT = 28800.
       C                  *** Wait for pick and locator input
L240           CALL GWAIT (TOUT,WKID,CLASS,DEV)
L250           IF (CLASS .NE. GPICK) GOTO 290
L270           CALL GGTPK (STAT,SEGN,PCID)
       C                                          *** Disable pick
```

```
L280          CALL GSPKM (DISP,PC1,GREQU,GECHO)
L290    290   IF (CLASS .NE. GLOCAT) GOTO 330
L310          CALL GGTLC (TNR1,RX,RY)
        C                                          *** Disable locator
L320          CALL GSLCM (DISP,LC1,GREQU,GECHO)
L330    330   CONTINUE
L350          CALL GSELNT (TNR1)
        C                        *** Subsequent points are expected to be in viewport of
        C                *** normalization transformation TNR1. This would be zero, since
        C                        *** no transformations have been set up explicitly
        C                                *** Set choice CH1 in EVENT mode
L360          CALL GSCHM (DISP,CH1,GEVENT,GECHO)
        C                        *** Inquire initial segment transformation matrix
L370          CALL GQSGA (SEGN,ERR,M,VIS,HIGH,PRIOR,DET)
        C                        *** Wait for first CHOICE alternative
L375          CHNB=0
        C                *** Each loop transition causes one transformation step
        C                        *** or a change of program control
L380    380   CONTINUE
L390          TOUT=0
L400          CALL GWAIT (TOUT,WKID,CLASS,DEV)
L410          IF (CLASS .NE. GCHOIC) GOTO 640
L410    C                               *** Change of program control
        C                *** Disable locator and valuator to initialize them anew
L430          CALL GSVLM (DISP,VL1,GREQU,GECHO)
L440          CALL GSLCM (DISP,LC1,GREQU,GECHO)
L450          CALL GGTCH (STAT,CHNB)
L455          CHNB=CHNB
L460          GOTO (640,470,530,590,640,640),CHNB
L470    470   CONTINUE
        C                        *** Switch to shift, set echo area for LOCATOR device
L480          EX1=0.
L481          EY1=SZLX
L482          EX2=0.
L483          EY2=SZLY
        C                *** LC1 has initial value=segment refpoint and crosshairs echo
L490          CALL GINLC
                (DISP,LC1,TNR1,RX,RY,2,EX1,EX2,EY1,EY2,1,EMPTD)
        C                *** Set locator LC1 into sample mode and sample starting point
L500          CALL GSLCM (DISP,LC1,GSAMPL,GECHO)
L510          CALL GSMLC (DISP,LC1,TNR1,PX1,PY1)
L520          GOTO 640
L530    530   CONTINUE
        C                                *** Switch to scaling
        C                *** Pack data record with initial values: range 0 to 10
        C                        *** Set echo area for VALUATOR device
L550          EX1=SZLX-DX
L551          EX2=SZLX
L552          EY1=SZLY-DY
L553          EY2=SZLY
        C                        *** Initialise valuator and put it into sample mode
L560          CALL GINVL (DISP,VL1,1,1,EX1,EX2,EY1,EY2,0.,10.,1,EMPTD)
L570          CALL GSVLM (DISP,VL1,GSAMPL,GECHO)
```

```
L580              GOTO 640
L590       590    CONTINUE
     C                                          *** Switch to rotation
     C                               *** Set echo area for VALUATOR device
L610              EX1 = SZLX − 2*DX
L611              EX2 = SZLX − DX
L612              EY1 = SZLY − DY
L613              EY2 = SZLY
L620              CALL GINVL (DISP,VL1,1,1,EX1,EX2,EY1,EY2,0.,3.14,1,EMPTD)
L640       640    CONTINUE
L660              GOTO (870,670,740,790,850,870),CHNB
L670       670    CONTINUE
     C                               *** Shift segment; sample target point
L680              CALL GSMLC (DISP,LC1,TNR2,PX2,PY2)
L690              IF (TNR2 .NE. TNR1) GOTO 890
     C                               *** Segment is shifted by POINT2 − POINT1
L700              DX = PX2 − PX1
L701              DY = PY2 − PY1
L710              CALL GACTM (M,RX1,RY1,DX,DY,0.0,1.0,1.0,GWC,M)
L720              CALL GSSGT (SEGN,M)
L730              GOTO 870
L740       740    CONTINUE
     C                               *** Scale segment; sample scale factor
L750              CALL GSMVL (DISP,VL1,VAL)
L760              CALL GACTM (M,RX,RY,0.0,0.0,0.0,VAL,VAL,GWC,M)
L775              CALL GSSGT (SEGN,M)
L780              GOTO 880
L790       790    CONTINUE
     C                               *** Rotate segment; sample angle
L800              CALL GSMVL (DISP,VL1,VAL)
L810              CALL GACTM (M,RX,RY,0.0,0.0,VAL,0.0,0.0,GWC,M)
L830              CALL GSSGT (SEGN.M)
L840              GOTO 870
L850       850    CONTINUE
     C                               *** Copy segment to plotter, disable CHOICE device
L852              CALL GCSGWK (PLOT,SEGN)
L854              CALL GSCHM (DISP,CH1,GREQU,GECHO)
     C                               *** End of transformation loop if CHNB = 4 or CHNB = 5
L870       870    IF (CHNB .NE. 4 .AND. CHNB .NE. 5) GOTO 380
     C                               *** End of segment handling loop if CHNB = 5
L880              IF (CHNB .NE. 5) GOTO 180
L890       890    CONTINUE
     C                               *** Disable input devices
L990              CALL GSLCM (DISP,LC1,GREQU,GECHO)
L910              CALL GSVLM (DISP,VL1,GREQU,GECHO)
L920              CALL GSCHM (DISP,CH1,GREQU,GECHO)
     C                               *** Deactivate and close workstations, close GKS
L930              CALL GDAWK (DISP)
L940              CALL GCLWK (PLOT)
L950              CALL GCLWK (DISP)
L960              CALL GCLWK (SEGS)
L970              CALL GCLKS
```

8.9   Exercises

Exercise 8.1   Interactive construction of polygons

Develop a program which allows the user to construct polygons interactively. Use the REQUEST LOCATOR function to do this. Program the same application using the REQUEST STROKE function.

Exercise 8.2   Using rubber band echo

Extend the program in Exercise 8.1: use rubber band echo and provide a useful operator feedback for the positions of the current polygon which have already been entered. This feedback output should disappear when the polygon is finally displayed.

Exercise 8.3   Interactive construction of FILL AREA primitives

Write a program which allows the user to generate FILL AREA primitives with different attributes: colour and interior style (hollow, solid, pattern, and hatch) should be adjustable.
— Decide which logical input devices are needed and are suitable for entering the specific data.
— Develop a control structure which minimizes operator actions assuming that several FILL AREA primitives will be constructed, and that attributes do not change for a series of FILL AREA primitives.

Exercise 8.4   Graphical symbols for choice input

Program an example using the prompt/echo type 5 of the CHOICE input device (an application-specified segment is used to represent a screen menu). The screen menu should contain graphic representations for four alternatives, namely a symbol for a triangle, a rectangle, a circle, and a rhombus.

Exercise 8.5   Simple picture construction

Extend the program in Exercise 8.4. By identifying one of the buttons using the REQUEST CHOICE function, an operator may construct a picture which is composed of the above four symbols. The operator should be able to position these symbols anywhere on the screen and the program should automatically connect the symbol which is currently being processed with the last symbol generated at predefined connection points. Facilities for modifying parts of the picture already generated need not be provided.

Exercise 8.6   Adding inscriptions

Extend the program in Exercise 8.3. Add a facility to inscribe the FILL AREA picture components, by additionally using the REQUEST STRING function. The text attributes colour and character height should be interactively adjustable.

Exercise 8.7   Sampling curve positions

A LOCATOR is to be put into SAMPLE mode so that polygons can be constructed by sampling the positions. When accepting positions from the input device to the application program, the following two constraints should be observed:
— a position can only be accepted if there is a certain distance to the last point (DELTA_X, DELTA_Y);
— a certain time slice (DELTA_T) has to have elapsed before the next point can be sampled.

Exercise 8.8   Using rubber band echo for curve input

Extend the program in Exercise 8.7 by adding proper feedback. Rubber band echo should be provided. When a point is accepted by the application program, its position on the screen is fixed as the next starting position for the rubber band echo. The connecting line between the last two points must be displayed as feedback. All such connecting lines disappear when the final polygon is generated.

Exercise 8.9   Dynamic zoom of pictures

Write a program which adjusts the scale of a picture on a workstation display surface according to the value of the VALUATOR device in SAMPLE mode. This should be performed both on the workstation viewport level (pure scaling), and on the workstation window level (dynamic windowing). The constraints laid down by GKS have to be obeyed, i.e. the workstation viewport must be within the display surface; the workstation window must be within the NDC space.

Exercise 8.10   Recognizing text command input

A STRING device is put into SAMPLE mode; an operator tries to enter text commands which he does not exactly know or which can be recognized uniquely by the system before being typed in completely.

Write a program which samples the currently typed in string, tries to recognize a possible command and, if it succeeds, gives the operator a suitable message.

Exercise 8.11   Handling the GKS event queue

Delete all entries in the GKS event queue which have originated from all the input devices of a specific workstation, without closing the workstation.

Exercise 8.12   Guiding an operator when event queue has overflowed

While an AWAIT EVENT function was being called, an "event queue has overflowed" error has been reported. Write a program which processes all event reports and which tells the operator where to restart input after the queue has been eventually emptied.

Exercise 8.13   Entering curves from a digitizer

Develop a digitizing application, where points are entered by a LOCATOR device (pen or puck of a digitizer with at least two buttons). The points entered have different meanings to the application program depending on which button (combination of buttons) is pressed to enter the point. The single CHOICE alternatives which are logically connected to each point entered, should mean the following.

— choice number=1: draw line from last point to this one;
— choice number=2: display a marker symbol at this position; no connection line between the last point and this one should be drawn;
— choice number=3: this point is the last one of a series; a new series will start;
— choice number=4: this point is the last one of a series; process it and terminate the program.

Program several alternatives for solving this problem and discuss their impacts. The alternatives are:
— LOCATOR in REQUEST or EVENT mode, CHOICE in SAMPLE mode;
— LOCATOR in SAMPLE mode; CHOICE in REQUEST or EVENT mode;
— both LOCATOR and CHOICE devices in REQUEST mode;
— both LOCATOR and CHOICE devices in SAMPLE mode;
— both LOCATOR and CHOICE devices in EVENT mode.

9   ERROR HANDLING

9.1   Strategy

For each GKS function, a finite number of error situations is specified, any of which will cause the ERROR HANDLING procedure to be called. Every GKS implementation must support this error checking. The ERROR HANDLING procedure provides an interface between GKS and the application program.

Figure 9.1 demonstrates the structural organization of the error handling components:
— The application programs call GKS functions.
— If the GKS functions detect error situations, they perform as described in Section 9.4 and call the ERROR HANDLING procedure.

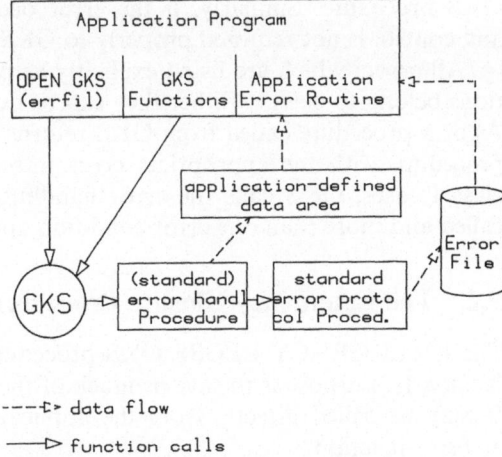

---⊏▷ data flow

─────▷ function calls

Figure 9.1 Organization of error handling

— The ERROR HANDLING procedure is either provided as a standard facility or supplied by the application program. If provided by the application program, it may interpret the information about the error (supplied by GKS via parameters and INQUIRY functions) and may store data in a data area. The ERROR HANDLING procedure provided by GKS merely calls the ERROR LOGGING procedure.
— The ERROR LOGGING procedure writes the error message and the function identification on the error file and returns to the ERROR HANDLING procedure which in turn returns to the GKS function which called it.
— The application program may inspect the contents of the data area and the error file after it has regained control from GKS. It may react to the reported error.

The GKS error handling strategy is based on the following classification of errors:
I   errors resulting in a precisely defined reaction;
II   errors resulting in an attempt to save the results of previous operations;
III   errors which cause unpredictable results including the loss of information.

GKS recognizes several situations in which errors are detected:
A error detected in GKS procedures;
B error detected outside GKS (driver procedures and operating system procedures called by GKS, and application programs).

If errors are detected outside GKS (situation B), either the application program can regain control over the execution or program execution will be terminated abnormally. In the latter case, results are unpredictable (case III) and at worst, all the graphical information produced so far may be lost. If, however, the application program gains control, it may attempt to close GKS properly or at least attempt an emergency closure by calling the EMERGENCY CLOSE

GKS procedure. Similarly, if the error occurs in procedures called by GKS and control is not returned properly to GKS, the effects are unpredictable.

All errors which are listed explicitly as part of the definition of GKS functions belong to class I. Either they can be detected within GKS itself (situation A) or a procedure called from GKS returns control to the corresponding GKS procedure with the appropriate error information (situation B). In all these class I cases, GKS calls the error handling procedure. If a GKS function is called and more than one error condition applies, at least one error is reported.

9.2   The Emergency Closure Procedure

The EMERGENCY CLOSE GKS procedure is an implementation-dependent facility. Its purpose is to save as much of the graphical information as possible. It may be called directly from the application program or by GKS itself as an error reaction.

The principal way in which the graphical information is saved by the EMERGENCY CLOSE GKS procedure is by properly closing the workstations which are active or open when the error condition occurs. Metafile output workstations, for example, are deactivated, suitable "END records" are written to the files, and they are properly released. Similar things may happen if certain workstations produce intermediate graphical files (e.g., the buffers of microfilm and plotter workstations). Implementations of the emergency closure procedure should take care that such files are properly closed so that pictures may be subsequently produced from them.

The definition of the emergency closure procedure is as follows:

EMERGENCY CLOSE GKS   GKCL,GKOP,WSOP,WSAC,SGOP   L0a
Parameters: none
Effect:
  GKS is emergency closed. The following actions are performed (if possible):
    — CLOSE SEGMENT (if open);
    — UPDATE for all open workstations;
    — DEACTIVATE all active workstations;
    — CLOSE all open workstations;
    — CLOSE GKS.
N.B.:
  This function may be called even if the error state is ON.

———————————— *FORTRAN Interface* ————————————

CALL GECLKS
Parameters: none

9.3   The ERROR HANDLING and ERROR LOGGING Procedures

The application program may either provide its own error handling procedure or may use the standard ERROR HANDLING procedure provided as part of GKS. The error handling procedure is called by GKS in any of the error situations listed in Section 9.6. The following information is passed to it:

— the identification of the error condition (error number as listed in Section 9.6);
— the identification of the GKS function called by the application program which called the ERROR HANDLING procedure (procedure names as defined in the GKS document or in a language binding);
— the error file.

The ERROR HANDLING procedure provided by GKS just calls the ERROR LOGGING procedure using the same set of parameters. The latter does the following:
a) prints an error message and GKS function identification on the error file;
b) returns to the calling procedure.

The definition of the ERROR HANDLING procedure is as follows:

ERROR HANDLING   GKCL,GKOP,WSOP,WSAC,SGOP   L0a

Parameters:

Input	error number as listed in Section 9.6	I
Input	identification of the GKS procedure called by the application program which caused the error detection	N
Input	error file	N

N.B.:
The last parameter has been defined in OPEN GKS.

Effect:
The ERROR HANDLING procedure is called by GKS in any of the error situations listed in Section 9.6. The standard procedure just calls the ERROR LOGGING procedure with the same parameters.

N.B.:
The ERROR HANDLING procedure may be replaced by an application-program-supplied procedure to allow a specific reaction to some error situations. Any application-program-supplied error handling procedure should at least have the effect of the standard error handling procedure.

———————————————— *FORTRAN Interface* ————————————————

CALL GERHND (ERRNR,FCTID,ERRFIL)

Parameters:

Input	ERRNR	error number	(1..n)	INTEGER
Input	FCTID	function identification	(1..n)	INTEGER
Input	ERRFIL	error message file		INTEGER

An application-supplied error handling procedure which replaces the standard one may define a common area that can be accessed both by the error handling routine and the application program. Examples are given below. It has access to the GKS state table information via the GKS inquiry functions. The actual GKS state corresponds to the GKS operating state, prior to the GKS function call which caused the error. The ERROR HANDLING procedure, however, can only call the GKS INQUIRY functions, the ERROR LOGGING procedure and the EMERGENCY CLOSE GKS procedure, and no modification of GKS states is possible during error handling. This is achieved by setting the error state to ON, prior to calling the ERROR HANDLING procedure from GKS, and resetting the error state to OFF afterwards. An inquiry function cannot generate an error; if one is called in an erroneous situation, it reports the error condition in a specific output parameter.

The definition of the ERROR LOGGING procedure is as follows:

ERROR LOGGING   GKCL,GKOP,WSOP,WSAC,SGOP   L0a
Parameters:
   Input   error number as listed in Section 9.6   I
   Input   identification of the GKS procedure called by the   N
           application program which caused the error detection
   Input   error file   N
N.B.:
The last parameter has been defined in OPEN GKS.
Effect:
  The ERROR LOGGING procedure prints an error message and GKS function identification on the error file and returns to the calling procedure.

——————————————— *FORTRAN Interface* ———————————————
CALL GERLOG (ERRNR,FCTID,ERRFIL)
Parameters:
   Input   ERRNR   error number   (1..n)   INTEGER
   Input   FCTID   function identification   (1..n)   INTEGER
   Input   ERRFIL error message file   INTEGER

An example of an error handling procedure supplied by an application program follows:

Example 9.1   Error handling (special treatment)

——————————————————— *Pascal* ———————————————————
```
L10   PROCEDURE ERROR HANDLING (error_number,function_ident,error_file)
                                        {call ERROR LOGGING procedure}
L20   ERROR_LOGGING (error_number, function_ident, error_file)
          {interpret GKS FUNCTION IDENTIFICATION and ERROR NUMBER}
                              {to select case of special treatment via procedure ST}
L30   special_treatment = ST (function_ident, error_number);
L40   if special_treatment then begin
                    {gather more relevant information about the error environment}
                                                      {using inquiry functions};
L50   INQUIRE .....;
L60   INQUIRE .....;
                    {store information in application-program-provided global area};
L70   global_variable_a:=;
L80   global_variable_b:=;
L90   end {end if};
L100  end {return to calling GKS procedure};
```

——————————————— *Fortran* ———————————————

```
L10               SUBROUTINE GERHND (ERRNB,FCTID,ERRFIL)
L11               INTEGER ERRNB,FCTID,ERRFIL
        C               *** common data area for communication with application program
L12               COMMON /GKCERR/ COMA,COMB
        C                               *** call ERROR LOGGING procedure
L20               CALL GERLOG (ERRNB,FCTID,ERRFIL)
        C                   *** interpret GKS function identification and error number to
        C                               *** select a special case of treatment
L30               IF (.NOT. ST (FCTID,ERRNR)) RETURN
        C               *** gather more relevant information about the error environment
        C                               *** using the GKS inquiry functions
L50               CALL GQ.........
L60               CALL GQ.........
        C                       *** store information in application program provided
        C                               *** COMMON AREA variables
L70               COMA = .......
L80               COMB = .......
L90               RETURN
L100              END
```

9.4   Error Detection Within GKS Procedures

All GKS procedures perform the following actions after an error condition
has been detected:
— set error state to ON;
— call error handling procedure with parameters as described above;
— reset error state to OFF;
— perform built-in error reaction (normally, a function causing an error has
  no effect; in some cases this requires some clean-up operations).

All GKS procedures must check on entry (in the following order):
— that GKS is in the correct state;
— that the values of input parameters are valid.

At the very least the first error detected must be reported.

9.5   Reaction of Application Programs to Error Detections

An application program is notified of an error detection by entries in the error
communication area. Usually, the application program has to deal with higher,
application-specific error handling procedures to process erroneous situations
which might occur.

Within the application program, error checking procedures should be provided at all places where errors are anticipated or where possible errors might

cause damage to future processing. This may range from checking error states after each call of a GKS function (or a group of those) in highly interactive applications, to merely checking if an error has taken place at the end of a program. The latter case might be supported by Example 9.1. Some typical error situations and reactions are listed in the following Section 9.6.

9.6   List of GKS Error Numbers and Messages

GKS recognizes several types of error situations. A classification of them is given in this chapter. One specific type of error, the invalid parameters, deserve a particular mention. This type of error occurs if data lies outside a given range. Examples of this are:
— Negative or zero integer numbers are used, when only positive numbers are allowed, such as those restricting polyline indices to the integer range 1 to n. These restrictions are listed with the parameter definitions of the GKS function specifications.
— Language-dependent restrictions are violated. Enumeration types in FORTRAN, for example, are mapped to a range of integer values starting with 0.

Thus, when determining parameter values, the language binding rules have to be taken into account. With each FORTRAN GKS function in this textbook, these additional rules are listed.

9.6.1   States

In every implementation of each GKS function, the first error to be checked is whether or not the function has been applied in the correct state. If an operating state error has occurred it first has to be reported. All other errors which might follow might be meaningless. For each GKS function, the appropriate operating states are listed together with the function name. If this error occurs, the program should be aborted and carefully corrected.
    Some examples of situations which cause errors are:
— The first call to GKS is not OPEN GKS (errors 2 to 8, especially 2 and 8).
— It was forgotten to OPEN a WORKSTATION before accessing attached input devices and workstation states such as attributes (errors 6 and 7).
— The program has failed to ACTIVATE a WORKSTATION before producing output and generating segments (errors 3,5,7).
— A segment is not OPEN when CLOSE SEGMENT is called (error 4).
— An attempt is made to re-OPEN GKS when GKS is open (error 1).

Errors:
1	GKS not in proper state: GKS should be in the state GKCL
2	GKS not in proper state: GKS should be in the state GKOP
3	GKS not in proper state: GKS should be in the state WSAC
4	GKS not in proper state: GKS should be in the state SGOP

5   GKS not in proper state: GKS should be either in the state WSAC or in the state SGOP
6   GKS not in proper state: GKS should be either in the state WSOP or in the state WSAC
7   GKS not in proper state: GKS should be in one of the states WSOP, WSAC or SGOP
8   GKS not in proper state: GKS should be in one of the states GKOP, WSOP, WSAC or SGOP

9.6.2 Workstations

A variety of errors can be produced by erroneously addressing workstations. As well as the error of having invalid names for workstation identifiers (error 20), for connection identifiers (error 21), and for workstation types (error 22), a desired workstation type may not be available in an installation (error 23) or cannot be opened (error 26). The latter case might, for example, occur when the workstation is assigned to another user (GKS program).

The remaining errors are caused in most cases by trying to gain access to workstation states either when the workstation is not in a suitable operating state (open, not open, active, not active), or if the workstation is not the suitable type. An example of the latter case is the definition of workstation attributes or workstation transformations for segment storage and metafile input workstations.

In most cases, workstation errors occur for three reasons:
— Workstations are not available.
— A wrong workstation identifier is used (editing mistake).
— A series of GKS functions is applied to all open or all active workstations without inspecting and distinguishing between their types.

Errors:
20   Specified workstation identifier is invalid
21   Specified connection identifier is invalid
22   Specified workstation type is invalid
23   Specified workstation type does not exist
24   Specified workstation is open
25   Specified workstation is not open
26   Specified workstation cannot be opened
27   Workstation-Independent Segment Storage is not open
28   Workstation-Independent Segment Storage is already open
29   Specified workstation is active
30   Specified workstation is not active
31   Specified workstation is of category MO
32   Specified workstation is not of category MO
33   Specified workstation is of category MI
34   Specified workstation is not of category MI
35   Specified workstation is of category INPUT
36   Specified workstation is Workstation-Independent Segment Storage
37   Specified workstation is not of category OUTIN
38   Specified workstation is neither of category INPUT nor of category OUTIN
39   Specified workstation is neither of category OUTPUT nor of category OUTIN

40	Specified workstation has no pixel store readback capability
41	Specified workstation type is not able to generate the specified generalized drawing primitive
42	Maximum number of simultaneously open workstations would be exceeded
43	Maximum number of simultaneously active workstations would be exceeded

9.6.3 Transformations

Most of the transformation errors occur because specific boundaries are violated:
— The viewport and the workstation window have to be within NDC space (errors 52 and 53).
— The workstation viewport has to be within the maximum display surface size (error 54) which can be determined by the function INQUIRE MAXIMUM DISPLAY SURFACE SIZE.
— The order of the parameters is wrong (XMIN,XMAX,YMIN,YMAX) (error 51).

Errors:

50	Transformation number is invalid
51	Rectangle definition is invalid
52	Viewport is not within the Normalized Device Coordinate unit square
53	Workstation window is not within the Normalized Device Coordinate unit square
54	Workstation viewport is not within the display space

9.6.4 Output Attributes

Apart from when data restrictions are violated (polyline, polymarker, text, fill area, and pattern indices have to be in the range 1 to n) other errors usually occur when inquire functions are called for non-existing attribute representations.

Errors:

60	Polyline index is invalid
61	A representation for the specified polyline index has not been defined on this workstation
62	A representation for the specified polyline index has not been predefined on this workstation
63	Linetype is equal to zero
64	Specified linetype is not supported on this workstation
65	Linewidth scale factor is less than zero
66	Polymarker index is invalid
67	A representation for the specified polymarker index has not been defined on this workstation
68	A representation for the specified polymarker index has not been predefined on this workstation
69	Marker type is equal to zero
70	Specified marker type is not supported on this workstation
71	Marker size scale factor is less than zero
72	Text index is invalid
73	A representation for the specified text index has not been defined on this workstation

74	A representation for the specified text index has not been predefined on this workstation
75	Text font is equal to zero
76	Requested text font is not supported for the required precision on this workstation
77	Character expansion factor is less than or equal to zero
78	Character height is less than or equal to zero
79	Length of character up vector is zero
80	Fill area index is invalid
81	A representation for the specified fill area index has not been defined on this workstation
82	A representation for the specified fill area index has not been predefined on this workstation
83	Specified fill area interior style is not supported on this workstation
84	Style (pattern or hatch) index is equal to zero
85	Specified pattern index is invalid
86	Specified hatch style is not supported on this workstation
87	Pattern size value is not positive
88	A representation for the specified pattern index has not been defined on this workstation
89	A representation for the specified pattern index has not been predefined on this workstation
90	Interior style PATTERN is not supported on this workstation
91	Dimensions of colour array are invalid
92	Colour index is less than zero
93	Colour index is invalid
94	A representation for the specified colour index has not been defined on this workstation
95	A representation for the specified colour index has not been predefined on this workstation
96	Colour is outside range [0,1]
97	Pick identifier is invalid

9.6.5 Output Primitives

Errors:

100	Number of points is invalid
101	Invalid code in string
102	Generalized drawing primitive identifier is invalid
103	Content of generalized drawing primitive data record is invalid
104	At least one active workstation is not able to generate the specified generalized drawing primitive
105	At least one active workstation is not able to generate the specified generalized drawing primitive under the current transformations and clipping rectangle

9.6.6 Segments

Errors:

120	Specified segment name is invalid
121	Specified segment name is already in use
122	Specified segment does not exist
123	Specified segment does not exist on specified workstation

124   Specified segment does not exist on Workstation-Independent Segment Storage
125   Specified segment is open
126   Segment priority is outside the range [0,1]

9.6.7 Input

Errors:
140   Specified input device is not present on workstation
141   Input device is not in REQUEST mode
142   Input device is not in SAMPLE mode
143   EVENT SAMPLE input mode is not available at this level of GKS
144   Specified prompt and echo type is not supported on this workstation
145   Echo area is outside display space
146   Contents of input data record are invalid
147   Input queue has overflowed
148   Input queue has not overflowed since GKS was opened or the last INQUIRE INPUT QUEUE OVERFLOW was invoked
149   Input queue has overflowed, but associated workstation has been closed
150   No input value of the correct class is in the current event report
151   Timeout is invalid
152   Initial value is invalid
153   Number of points in the initial stroke is greater than the buffer size
154   Length of the initial string is greater than the buffer size

9.6.8 Metafiles

Errors:
160   Item type is not allowed for user items
161   Item length is invalid
162   No record is left in GKS metafile input
163   Metafile item is invalid
164   Item type is not a valid GKS item
165   Content of item data record is invalid for the specified item type
166   Maximum item data record length is invalid
167   User item cannot be interpreted
168   Specified function is not supported at this level of GKS

9.6.9 Escape

Errors:
180   Specified escape function is not supported
181   Specified escape function identification is invalid
182   Contents of escape data record are invalid

9.6.10 Miscellaneous Errors

Errors:
200   Specified error file is invalid

9.6.11   System Errors

The detections of the following errors depend on the particular GKS implementation, the operating system, the linkage editor, the run-time support system, etc. They are likely to cause an emergency closure of GKS as in many cases unpredictable results may have already been produced by the time these errors have been detected. GKS functions may already have changed states and performed operations which cannot be reverted.

Error 306 is usually reported during linkage editor time in the form of references to non-existing library elements. Erroneously bound programs cannot or should not be executed, except when it is ensured that the non-existing functions are not called during program execution.

Errors 300 and 301 report internal storage overflow. These errors can only be dealt with properly if programs react immediately after their occurrence. A reaction, for example, might be:
— to close the open segment;
— to delete it (since its contents are unsafe);
— to swap other existing segments to metafiles or to plot and delete them;
— and possibly, to increase the storage space.

Errors 302 to 308 usually lead to abnormal program termination; if control is returned to GKS properly, it could either try to send or receive data repeatedly, or stop the program by calling the emergency closure procedure.

Typical situations producing I/O errors arise when devices and communication lines do not work properly, are not connected, are interrupted, etc.

Errors:

300	Storage overflow has occurred in GKS
301	Storage overflow has occurred in segment storage
302	Input/Output error has occurred while reading
303	Input/Output error has occurred while writing
304	Input/Output error has occurred while sending data to a workstation
305	Input/Output error has occurred while receiving data from a workstation
306	Input/Output error has occurred during program library management
307	Input/Output error has occurred while reading workstation description table
308	Arithmetic error has occurred

9.6.12   Reserved Errors

Unused error numbers less than 2000 are reserved for future standardization. Error numbers 2000—3999 are reserved for language bindings.

Error numbers greater than or equal to 4000 are reserved for registration or future standardization.

9.6.13   Implementation-Dependent Errors

Implementation-dependent errors are given negative numbers. They have to be listed in the documentation of each implementation.

9.7 Exercises

Exercise 9.1 Emergency closing GKS

Design an EMERGENCY CLOSE GKS procedure as defined in Section 9.2 using GKS functions. Care should be taken that the GKS functions are only called if necessary in accordance with the current GKS states, e.g., only active workstations should be deactivated.

Exercise 9.2 Reaction to operating state errors

Write an extension to the error handling procedure of Example 9.1 and design a corresponding error reaction of the application program. Assume that the application program calls a POLYLINE function, and error 5 occurs. Program the following actions:
— Within the error handling procedure, record the current operating state in an error communication area.
— Within the application program, check when the POLYLINE function is returned whether an error has occurred. Using the INQUIRY functions, correct the GKS state in such a way that the POLYLINE function can be applied.

Exercise 9.3 Reaction to segment storage overflow

Write a program which creates segments and which can cope with error 301 (storage overflow has occurred in segment storage). It should ensure that the finally produced graphical information is consistent (no output is lost). Use a metafile workstation for your application program.

10 INQUIRY FUNCTIONS

10.1 State Lists and Inquiry Functions

Inquiry functions allow the application program to get information about the current state of GKS. As explained in Chapter 3, the complete state of GKS is stored in a number of state lists and description tables. Every value present in one of the lists can be retrieved by the application program by using an inquiry function. Hence, the inquiry functions can be divided into the following eight groups:
— an inquiry function for the operating state;
— inquiry functions for the GKS state list;
— inquiry functions for the workstation state lists;
— inquiry functions for the segment state lists;

— inquiry functions for the GKS error state list;
— inquiry functions for the pixel memory of raster type workstations;
— inquiry functions for the GKS description table;
— inquiry functions for the workstation description table.

10.1.1 Error Reports in Inquiry Functions

Since inquiry functions are the only functions that can be called by an error recovery routine, a recursion might occur if the inquiry routine itself tried to report an error (cf. Chapter 9). In order to avoid this 'error in the error recovery' situation, the inquiry functions do not report errors by using the normal GKS error handling method, but instead they return an additional parameter 'error indicator'. The error indicator has the value zero if no error has been detected by the inquiry function. If an error is to be reported the error number is returned in the error indicator and the values of the other output parameters are implementation-dependent.

10.1.2 Inquiry Functions for the Settable State Lists

The first five groups of inquiry functions generally return values that previously have been set by the application program itself. It could be asked why then such functions are needed, since the application program itself could keep track of the values it has set. One advantage in using inquiry functions is given in the following example. If an application layer is to be constructed on top of GKS, it will probably consist of a set of subroutines that themselves call GKS functions. If such an application subroutine changes the state of GKS, it might wish to reset it to the previous state before returning control to its caller. This can be easily done by inquiring about the GKS state after the subroutine is entered, saving the values, and resetting the state to the values before returning (cf. Example 10.1, page 394).

The group of inquiry functions for the workstation state list can also be used in another way. In many cases the workstations are not able to realize the parameters of the functions which change the workstation state in exactly the way they are passed to them, e.g., the SET POLYLINE REPRESENTATION function contains the parameters 'linetype', 'linewidth scale factor', and 'colour index'. The workstation will use a linetype and linewidth which are as close as possible to the ones desired, and use colour index 1 if the desired colour index is outside the permitted range at the workstation. Thus, there will be a difference between the SET values and the REALIZED values at a workstation. In order to be able to retrieve both types of values, most of the inquiry functions for the workstation state list have an input parameter of enumeration type 'type of returned value'. It can be set either to SET or to REALIZED. The inquiry function will return the workstation state list values either as those SET by the application program or as those REALIZED by the workstation (cf. Example 10.2, page 397).

10.1.3   Inquiry Functions for the Workstation Description Table

The GKS description table and the workstation description table cannot be changed by the application program, as they are set up by the implementation. The GKS description table contains information about the GKS implementation, e.g., GKS level, available workstation types, and number of normalization transformations. The workstation description table contains a set of values describing the capabilities of every workstation type present in the implementation. Therefore, the description tables are the most important source of information for an application program that wants to test its graphical environment. If application programs based on GKS are to be portable for a wide range of GKS implementations and graphics devices, they will have to make extensive use of the inquiry functions for the description tables. They will also find out whether the GKS implementation and the workstations have sufficient capabilities for the application to be realized, and adjust their behaviour accordingly (cf. Example 10.3, page 399).

10.1.4   Inquiry Functions for the Error State List and Pixel Memories

The only inquiry function for the GKS error state list is INQUIRE INPUT QUEUE OVERFLOW. It identifies the input device that caused the queue to overflow. Inquiry functions for the pixel memory of a raster type workstation return the colour indices of one or more pixels from the pixel memory of that workstation. Since there is a GKS rule that inquiry functions can only return values from one of the GKS state lists, the pixel memories of raster type workstations have to be considered as part of the GKS state. Normally, the state of a workstation pixel memory has been set by a number of GKS output functions (e.g., CLEAR WORKSTATION, SET xxx INDEX, SET xxx REPRESENTATION, SET COLOUR REPRESENTATION, POLYLINE, FILL AREA, CELL ARRAY, ...). However, the pixel memory could also be filled by a process not under the control of GKS or by an ESCAPE function call. For example, the memory of a raster type workstation could be filled with a picture obtained by scanning a photograph. The pixel inquiry functions could be used to read the colour or intensity information into the GKS application program (see Example 10.4, page 400). Of course, not all workstations (not even all raster type workstations) will be able to deliver the colour values of pixels. In such a case the pixel inquiry functions will return in the error indicator parameter, error number 40 ("Specified workstation has no pixel store readback capability").

10.2   Description of the Inquiry Functions

This section presents all inquiry functions from the GKS document and the FORTRAN interface for them.

In order to reduce the amount of space needed for representing the inquiry functions the 'effect' is in most cases reduced to the following short form:

Effect:
The inquired values are returned. Possible error numbers:

This form replaces the following sentences that are part of the effect of almost all of the inquiry functions:

Effect:
If the inquired information is available, the error indicator is returned as 0 and values are returned in the output parameters. If the inquired information is not available, the values returned in the output parameters are implementation-dependent and the error indicator is set to one of the following error numbers to indicate the reason for non-availability:

Also, since none of the inquiry functions can raise an error, the phrase "Errors: none" has been omitted from the function definitions.

The error numbers that can be returned in the error indicator parameter by an inquiry function are listed; however, the error message text has been omitted. The message texts corresponding to the error numbers are listed in Chapter 9.6 on page 346).

10.2.1   Inquiry Function for Operating State

INQUIRE OPERATING STATE VALUE
                        GKCL,GKOP,WSOP,WSAC,SGOP   L0a
Parameters:
Output   operating state value (GKCL,GKOP,WSOP,WSAC,SGOP)   E
Effect:
The operating state of GKS is returned.

———————————————— *FORTRAN Interface* ————————————————
CALL GQOPS (OPSTA)
Parameters:
Output   OPSTA   operating state value
                        (0=GKCL,1=GKOP,2=WSOP,3=WSAC,4=SGOP)   INTEGER

10.2.2   Inquiry Functions for GKS Description Table

INQUIRE LEVEL OF GKS   GKOP,WSOP,WSAC,SGOP   L0a
Parameters:
Output   error indicator   I
Output   level of GKS   (0a,0b,0c,1a,1b,1c,2a,2b,2c)   E
Effect:
The inquired values are returned. Possible error numbers: 8.

––––––––––––––––––––––––––– *FORTRAN Interface* –––––––––––––––––––––––––––

CALL GQLVKS (ERRIND,LEVEL)
Parameters:

Output	ERRIND	error indicator	INTEGER
Output	LEVEL	level of GKS	INTEGER

(0=L0a, 1=L0b, 2=L0c, 3=L1a, 4=L1b,
5=L1c, 6=L2a, 7=L2b, 8=L2c)

INQUIRE LIST OF AVAILABLE WORKSTATION TYPES
GKOP,WSOP,WSAC,SGOP   L0a

Parameters:

Output	error indicator	I
Output	number of available workstation types	(1..n)	I
Output	list of available workstation types	n×N

Effect:
The inquired values are returned. Possible error numbers: 8.

––––––––––––––––––––––––––– *FORTRAN Interface* –––––––––––––––––––––––––––

CALL GQEWK (N,ERRIND,NUMBER,WKTYPL)
Parameters:

Input	N	list element requested		INTEGER
Output	ERRIND	error indicator		INTEGER
Output	NUMBER	number of workstation types	(1..n)	INTEGER
Output	WKTYPL	nth element of available workstation types		INTEGER

INQUIRE WORKSTATION MAXIMUM NUMBERS
GKOP,WSOP,WSAC,SGOP   L1a

Parameters:

Output	error indicator	I
Output	maximum number of simultaneously open workstations	(1..n)	I
Output	maximum number of simultaneously active workstations	(1..n)	I
Output	maximum number of workstations associated with segment	(1..n)	I

Effect:
The inquired values are returned. Possible error numbers: 8.

––––––––––––––––––––––––––– *FORTRAN Interface* –––––––––––––––––––––––––––

CALL GQWKM (ERRIND,MXOPWK,MXACWK,MXWKAS)

Output	ERRIND	error indicator		INTEGER
Output	MXOPWK	max. number of simult. open workst.	(1..n)	INTEGER
Output	MXACWK	max. number of simult. active workst.	(1..n)	INTEGER
Output	MXWKAS	max. number of workst. associated with segment	(1..n)	INTEGER

INQUIRE MAXIMUM NORMALIZATION TRANSFORMATION NUMBER

INQUIRE MAXIMUM NORMALIZATION TRANSFORMATION
NUMBER   GKOP,WSOP,WSAC,SGOP   L0a

Parameters:

Output   error indicator   I
Output   maximum normalization transformation number   (1..n)   I

Effect:

The inquired values are returned. Possible error numbers: 8.

────────────────────── *FORTRAN Interface* ──────────────────────

CALL GQMNTN (ERRIND,MAXTNR)

Parameters:

Output   ERRIND   error indicator   INTEGER
Output   MAXTNR   max. norm. transformation number   (1..n)   INTEGER

10.2.3   Inquiry Functions for GKS State List

INQUIRE SET OF OPEN WORKSTATIONS
                                            GKOP,WSOP,WSAC,SGOP   L0a

Parameters:

Output   error indicator   I
Output   number of open workstations   (0..n)   I
Output   set of open workstations   n × N

Effect:

The inquired values are returned. At GKS level 0a, there is a maximum of one workstation in the set. Possible error numbers: 8.

────────────────────── *FORTRAN Interface* ──────────────────────

CALL GQOPWK (N,ERRIND,OL,WKIDL)

Parameters:

Input   N   set member requested   INTEGER
Output   ERRIND   error indicator   INTEGER
Output   OL   number of open workstations   (0..n)   INTEGER
Output   WKIDL   n th member of set open workstations   INTEGER

INQUIRE SET OF ACTIVE WORKSTATIONS
                                            GKOP,WSOP,WSAC,SGOP   L1a

Parameters:

Output   error indicator   I
Output   number of active workstations   (0..n)   I
Output   set of active workstations   n × N

Effect:

The inquired values are returned. Possible error numbers: 8.

──────────────── *FORTRAN Interface* ────────────────

CALL GQACWK (N,ERRIND,OL,WKIDL)
Parameters:

Input	N	set member requested		INTEGER
Output	ERRIND	error indicator		INTEGER
Output	OL	number of active workstations	(0..n)	INTEGER
Output	WKIDL	nth member of set of active workstations		INTEGER

INQUIRE CURRENT PRIMITIVE ATTRIBUTE VALUES
GKOP,WSOP,WSAC,SGOP   L0a

Parameters:

Output	error indicator			I
Output	current polyline index		(1..n)	I
Output	current polymarker index		(1..n)	I
Output	current text index		(1..n)	I
Output	current character height	WC	>0	R
Output	current character up vector	WC		2×R
Output	current character width	WC	>0	R
Output	current character base vector	WC		2×R
Output	current text path	(RIGHT,LEFT,UP,DOWN)		E
Output	current text alignment			
	(NORMAL,LEFT,CENTRE,RIGHT;			
	NORMAL,TOP,CAP,HALF,BASE,BOTTOM)			2×E
Output	current fill area index		(1..n)	I
Output	current pattern width vector	WC		2×R
Output	current pattern height vector	WC		2×R
Output	current pattern reference point	WC		P

Effect:
The inquired values are returned. Possible error numbers: 8.

──────────────── *FORTRAN Interface* ────────────────

CALL GQPLI (ERRIND,POLYLI)
Parameters:

Output	ERRIND	error indicator		INTEGER
Output	POLYLI	current polyline index	(1..n)	INTEGER

CALL GQPMI (ERRIND,POLYMI)
Parameters:

Output	ERRIND	error indicator		INTEGER
Output	POLYMI	current polymarker index	(1..n)	INTEGER

CALL GQTXI (ERRIND,TEXTI)
Parameters:

Output	ERRIND	error indicator		INTEGER
Output	TEXTI	current text index	(1..n)	INTEGER

CALL GQCHH (ERRIND,CHARHI)
Parameters:

Output	ERRIND	error indicator			INTEGER
Output	CHARHI	current character height	WC	>0	REAL

CALL GQCHUP (ERRIND,CHRUPX,CHRUPY)
Parameters:

Output	ERRIND	error indicator		INTEGER
Output	CHRUPX,CHRUPY	current character up		
		vector	WC	2 × REAL

CALL GQCHW (ERRIND,CHRWI)
Parameters:

Output	ERRIND	error indicator			INTEGER
Output	CHRWI	current character width	WC	>0	REAL

CALL GQCHB (ERRIND,CNRBX,CHRBY)
Parameters:

Output	ERRIND	error indicator		INTEGER
Output	CHRBX,CHRBY	current character base		
		vector	WC	2 × REAL

CALL GQTXP (ERRIND,TXPATH)
Parameters:

Output	ERRIND	error indicator	INTEGER
Output	TXPATH	current character path	INTEGER
		(0 = right, 1 = left, 2 = up, 3 = down)	

CALL GQTXAL (ERRIND,TXALH,TXALV)
Parameters:

Output	ERRIND	error indicator	INTEGER
Output	TXALH	current horizontal alignment	INTEGER
		(0 = normal, 1 = left, 2 = centre, 3 = right)	
Output	TXALV	current vertical alignment	INTEGER
		(0 = normal, 1 = top, 2 = cap, 3 = half, 4 = base, 5 = bottom)	

CALL GQFAI (ERRIND,FILLAI)
Parameters:

Output	ERRIND	error indicator		INTEGER
Output	FILLAI	current fill area index	(1..n)	INTEGER

CALL GQPA (ERRIND,PWX,PWY,PHX,PHY)
Parameters:

Output	ERRIND	error indicator		INTEGER
Output	PWX,PWY	current pattern width		
		vector	WC	REAL
Output	PHX,PHY	current pattern height		
		vector	WC	REAL

CALL GQPARF (ERRIND,REFPNX,REFPNY)
Parameters:

Output	ERRIND	error indicator	INTEGER
Output	REFPNX,REFPNY	current pattern reference point WC	REAL

INQUIRE CURRENT PICK IDENTIFIER VALUE

GKOP,WSOP,WSAC,SGOP   L1b

Parameters:

Output	error indicator	I
Output	current pick identifier	N

Effect:

The inquired values are returned. Possible error numbers: 8.

─────────────────────────── *FORTRAN Interface* ───────────────────────────

CALL GQPKID (ERRIND,PCID)

Parameters:

Output	ERRIND	error indicator	INTEGER
Output	PCID	pick identifier	INTEGER

───

INQUIRE CURRENT INDIVIDUAL ATTRIBUTE VALUES
GKOP,WSOP,WSAC,SGOP   L0a

Parameters:

Output	error indicator		I
Output	linetype	$(-n..-1,1..n)$	I
Output	linewidth scale factor		R
Output	polyline colour index	$(0..n)$	I
Output	marker type	$(-n..-1,1..n)$	I
Output	marker size scale factor		R
Output	polymarker colour index	$(0..n)$	I
Output	text font and precision	$(1..n;$ STRING,CHAR,STROKE)	(I;E)
Output	character expansion factor	>0	R
Output	character spacing		R
Output	text colour index	$(0..n)$	I
Output	fill area interior style		
		(HOLLOW,SOLID,PATTERN,HATCH)	E
Output	fill area style index	$(-n..-1,1..n)$	I
Output	fill area colour index	$(0..n)$	I
Output	list of aspect source flags	(BUNDLED,INDIVIDUAL)	$13 \times$ E

Effect:

The inquired values are returned. Possible error numbers: 8.

─────────────────────────── *FORTRAN Interface* ───────────────────────────

CALL GQLN (ERRIND,LNTYPE)

Parameters:

Output	ERRIND	error indicator		INTEGER
Output	LNTYPE	line type	$(-n..-1,1..n)$	INTEGER

CALL GQLWSC (ERRIND,LNWDSF)

Parameters:

Output	ERRIND	error indicator		INTEGER
Output	LNWDSF	linewidth scale factor		REAL

CALL GQPLCI (ERRIND,PLCOLI)

Parameters:

Output	ERRIND	error indicator		INTEGER
Output	PLCOLI	polyline colour index	$(0..n)$	INTEGER

CALL GQMK (ERRIND,MKTYPE)

Parameters:

Output	ERRIND	error indicator		INTEGER
Output	MKTYPE	marker type	$(-n..-1,1..n)$	INTEGER

CALL GQMKSC (ERRIND,MKSZSF)

Parameters:

Output	ERRIND	error indicator		INTEGER
Output	MKSZSF	marker size scale factor		REAL

CALL GQPMCI (ERRIND,PMCOLI)
Parameters:
Output	ERRIND	error indicator		INTEGER
Output	PMCOLI	polymarker colour index	(0..n)	INTEGER

CALL GQTXFP (ERRIND,TXFONT,TXPREC)
Parameters:
Output	ERRIND	error indicator	(1..n)	INTEGER
Output	TXFONT	text font		INTEGER
Output	TXPREC	text precision (0=string, 1=char, 2=stroke)		INTEGER

CALL GQCHXP (ERRIND,CHARXP)
Parameters:
Output	ERRIND	error indicator		INTEGER
Output	CHARXP	character expansion factor	>0	REAL

CALL GQCHSP (ERRIND,CHARSP)
Parameters:
Output	ERRIND	error indicator		INTEGER
Output	CHARSP	character spacing		REAL

CALL GQTXCI (ERRIND,TXCOLI)
Parameters:
Output	ERRIND	error indicator		INTEGER
Output	TXCOLI	text colour index	(0..n)	INTEGER

CALL GQFAIS (ERRIND,FAINTS)
Parameters:
Output	ERRIND	error indicator		INTEGER
Output	FAINTS	fill area interior style		
		(0=hollow, 1=solid, 2=pattern, 3=hatch)		INTEGER

CALL GQFASI (ERRIND,FASI)
Parameters:
Output	ERRIND	error indicator		INTEGER
Output	FASI	fill area style index	(−n..−1,1..n)	INTEGER

CALL GQFACI (ERRIND,FACOLI)
Parameters:
Output	ERRIND	error indicator		INTEGER
Output	FACOLI	fill area colour index	(0..n)	INTEGER

CALL GQASF (ERRIND,LASP)
Parameters:
Output	ERRIND	error indicator		INTEGER
Output	LASP(13)	list of aspect source flags		
		(0=bundled, 1=individual)		INTEGER

INQUIRE CURRENT NORMALIZATION TRANSFORMATION NUMBER
GKOP,WSOP,WSAC,SGOP   L0a

Parameters:
Output	error indicator		I
Output	current normalization transformation number	(0..n)	I

Effect:
The inquired values are returned. Possible error numbers: 8.

─────────────────── *FORTRAN Interface* ───────────────────

CALL GQCNTN (ERRIND,CTNR)

Parameters:

Output	ERRIND	error indicator		INTEGER
Output	CTNR	current norm. transf. number	(0..n)	INTEGER

INQUIRE LIST OF NORMALIZATION TRANSFORMATION
NUMBERS   GKOP,WSOP,WSAC,SGOP   L0a

Parameters:

Output	error indicator	I
Output	list of transformation numbers	$n \times I$

Effect:

The inquired values are returned. The list of transformation numbers is ordered by viewport input priority, starting with the highest priority. Possible error numbers: 8.

─────────────────── *FORTRAN Interface* ───────────────────

CALL GQENTN (N,ERRIND,OL,NPRIO)

Parameters:

Input	N	list element requested	INTEGER
Output	ERRIND	error indicator	INTEGER
Output	OL	length of list	INTEGER
Output	NPRIO	nth element of list of transformation numbers, ordered by viewport input priority in decreasing order	INTEGER

INQUIRE NORMALIZATION TRANSFORMATION
GKOP,WSOP,WSAC,SGOP   L0a

Parameters:

Input	normalization transformation number		I
Output	error indicator		I
Output	window limits	WC	$4 \times R$
Output	viewport limits	NDC	$4 \times R$

Effect:

The inquired values are returned. Possible error numbers: 8, 50.

─────────────────── *FORTRAN Interface* ───────────────────

CALL GQNT (NTNR,ERRIND,WINDOW,VIEWPT)

Parameters:

Input	NTNR	transformation number		INTEGER
Output	ERRIND	error indicator		INTEGER
Output	WINDOW(4)	window limits in world coordinates	WC	REAL
Output	VIEWPT(4)	viewport limits in normalized device coordinates	NDC	REAL

INQUIRE CLIPPING   GKOP,WSOP,WSAC,SGOP   L0a

Parameters:

Output	error indicator		I
Output	clipping indicator	(CLIP,NOCLIP)	E
Output	clipping rectangle	NDC	$4 \times R$

Effect:

The inquired values are returned. Possible error numbers: 8.

─────────────── *FORTRAN Interface* ───────────────

CALL GQCLIP (ERRIND,CLIP,CLRECT)

Parameters:

Output	ERRIND	error indicator		INTEGER
Output	CLIP	clipping indicator	(0 = noclip, 1 = clip)	INTEGER
Output	CLRECT(4)	clipping rectangle	WC	REAL

INQUIRE SET OF SEGMENT NAMES IN USE
WSOP,WSAC,SGOP   L1a

Parameters:

Output	error indicator		I
Output	number of segment names	(0..n)	I
Output	set of segment names in use		n × N

Effect:

The inquired values are returned. Possible error numbers: 7.

─────────────── *FORTRAN Interface* ───────────────

CALL GQSGUS (N,ERRIND,OL,SEGNAM)

Parameters:

Input	N	set member requested		INTEGER
Output	ERRIND	error indicator		INTEGER
Output	OL	number of segment names	(0..n)	INTEGER
Output	SEGNAM	nth member of set of segment names in use		INTEGER

INQUIRE NAME OF OPEN SEGMENT
SGOP   L1a

Parameters:

Output	error indicator	I
Output	name of open segment	N

Effect:

The inquired values are returned. Possible error numbers: 4.

─────────────── *FORTRAN Interface* ───────────────

CALL GQOPSG (ERRIND,SEGNAM)

Parameters:

Output	ERRIND	error indicator	INTEGER
Output	SEGNAM	name of open segment	INTEGER

INQUIRE MORE SIMULTANEOUS EVENTS   WSOP,WSAC,SGOP   L0c

Parameters:

Output	error indicator		I
Output	more simultaneous events	(NOMORE,MORE)	E

Effect:

The inquired values are returned. Possible error numbers: 7.

─────────────── *FORTRAN Interface* ───────────────

CALL GQSIM (ERRIND,FLAG)

Parameters:

Output	ERRIND	error indicator		INTEGER
Output	FLAG	more simultaneous events	(0 = nomore, 1 = more)	INTEGER

10.2.4   Inquiry Functions for Workstation State List

INQUIRE WORKSTATION CONNECTION AND TYPE

WSOP,WSAC,SGOP   L0a

Parameters:

Input	workstation identifier		N
Output	error indicator		I
Output	connection identifier		N
Output	workstation type		N

Effect:

The inquired values are returned. Possible error numbers: 7, 20, 25.

------------------------ *FORTRAN Interface* ------------------------

CALL GQWKC (WKID,ERRIND,CONID,WTYPE)

Parameters:

Input	WKID	workstation identifier	INTEGER
Output	ERRIND	error indicator	INTEGER
Output	CONID	connection identifier	INTEGER
Output	WTYPE	workstation type	INTEGER

INQUIRE WORKSTATION STATE   WSOP,WSAC,SGOP   L0a

Parameters:

Input	workstation identifier		N
Output	error indicator		I
Output	workstation state	(INACTIVE,ACTIVE)	E

Effect:

The inquired values are returned. Possible error numbers: 7, 20, 25, 33, 35.

------------------------ *FORTRAN Interface* ------------------------

CALL GQWKS (WKID,ERRIND,STATE)

Parameters:

Input	WKID	workstation identifier		INTEGER
Output	ERRIND	error indicator		INTEGER
Output	STATE	workstation state	(0 = inactive, 1 = active)	INTEGER

INQUIRE WORKSTATION DEFERRAL AND UPDATE STATES

WSOP,WSAC,SGOP   L0a

Parameters:

Input	workstation identifier		N
Output	error indicator		I
Output	deferral mode	(ASAP,BNIL,BNIG,ASTI)	E
Output	implicit regeneration mode	(SUPPRESSED,ALLOWED)	E
Output	display surface empty	(EMPTY,NOTEMPTY)	E
Output	new frame action necessary at update	(NO,YES)	E

Effect:

The inquired values are returned. Possible error numbers: 7, 20, 25, 33, 35, 36.

―――――――――――― *FORTRAN Interface* ――――――――――――

CALL GQWKDU (WKID,ERRIND,DEFMOD,REGMOD,EMPTY,NFRAME)

Parameters:

Input	WKID	workstation identifier	INTEGER
Output	ERRIND	error indicator	INTEGER
Output	DEFMOD	deferral mode	
		(0=asap, 1=bnil, 2=bnig, 3=asti)	INTEGER
Output	REGMOD	implicit regeneration mode	
		(0=suppressed, 1=allowed)	INTEGER
Output	EMPTY	display surface empty	
		(0=empty, 1=notempty)	INTEGER
Output	NFRAME	new frame action necessary at update	
		(0=no, 1=yes)	INTEGER

INQUIRE LIST OF POLYLINE INDICES   WSOP,WSAC,SGOP   L1a

Parameters:

Input	workstation identifier		N
Output	error indicator		I
Output	number of polyline bundle table entries	(5..n)	I
Output	list of defined polyline indices	(1..n)	n × I

Effect:

The inquired values are returned. Possible error numbers: 7, 20, 25, 33, 35, 36.

―――――――――――― *FORTRAN Interface* ――――――――――――

CALL GQEPLI (WKID,N,ERRIND,OL,PLIND)

Parameters:

Input	WKID	workstation identifier		INTEGER
Input	N	list element requested		INTEGER
Output	ERRIND	error indicator		INTEGER
Output	OL	number of polyline bundle table entries	(5..n)	INTEGER
Output	PLIND	nth element of list of defined polyline indices	(1..n)	INTEGER

INQUIRE POLYLINE REPRESENTATION   WSOP,WSAC,SGOP   L1a

Parameters:

Input	workstation identifier		N
Input	polyline index	(1..n)	I
Input	type of returned values	(SET,REALIZED)	E
Output	error indicator		I
Output	linetype	(−n..−1,1..n)	I
Output	linewidth scale factor		R
Output	polyline colour index	(0..n)	I

Effect:

The inquired values are returned. Possible error numbers: 7, 20, 25, 33, 35, 36, 60, 61.

———————————————— *FORTRAN Interface* ————————————————

CALL GQPLR (WKID,PLI,TYPE,ERRIND,LNTYPE,LWIDTH,COLI)
Parameters:

Input	WKID	workstation identifier		INTEGER
Input	PLI	polyline index	(1..n)	INTEGER
Input	TYPE	type of returned values	(0 = set, 1 = realized)	INTEGER
Output	ERRIND	error indicator		INTEGER
Output	LNTYPE	linetype	(−n..−1,1..n)	INTEGER
Output	LWIDTH	linewidth scale factor		REAL
Output	COLI	colour index	(0..n)	INTEGER

INQUIRE LIST OF POLYMARKER INDICES   WSOP,WSAC,SGOP   L1a
Parameters:

Input	workstation identifier		N
Output	error indicator		I
Output	number of polymarker bundle table entries	(5..n)	I
Output	list of defined polymarker indices	(1..n)	n × I

Effect:

The inquired values are returned. Possible error numbers: 7, 20, 33, 35, 36.

———————————————— *FORTRAN Interface* ————————————————

CALL GQEPMI (WKID,N,ERRIND,OL,PMIND)
Parameters:

Input	WKID	workstation identifier		INTEGER
Input	N	list element requested		INTEGER
Output	ERRIND	error indicator		INTEGER
Output	OL	number of polymarker bundle table entries	(5..n)	INTEGER
Output	PMIND	nth element of list of defined polymarker indices	(1..n)	INTEGER

INQUIRE POLYMARKER REPRESENTATION WSOP,WSAC,SGOP   L1a
Parameters:

Input	workstation identifier		N
Input	polymarker index	(1..n)	I
Input	type of returned values	(SET,REALIZED)	E
Output	error indicator		I
Output	marker type	(−n..−1,1..n)	I
Output	marker size scale factor		R
Output	polyline colour index	(0..n)	I

Effect:

The inquired values are returned. Possible error numbers: 7, 20, 25, 33, 35, 36, 66, 67.

———————————————— *FORTRAN Interface* ————————————————

CALL GQPMR (WKID,PMI,TYPE,ERRIND,MKTYPE,MKSSCF,COLI)
Parameters:

Input	WKID	workstation identifier		INTEGER
Input	PMI	polymarker index	(1..n)	INTEGER
Input	TYPE	type of returned values	(0 = set, 1 = realized)	INTEGER
Output	ERRIND	error indicator		INTEGER

Output	MKTYPE	marker type	$(-n..-1, 1..n)$	INTEGER
Output	MKSSCF	marker size scale factor		REAL
Output	COLI	colour index	$(0..n)$	INTEGER

INQUIRE LIST OF TEXT INDICES   WSOP,WSAC,SGOP   L1a
Parameters:

Input	workstation identifier		N
Output	error indicator		I
Output	number of text bundle table entries	$(6..n)$	I
Output	list of defined text indices	$(1..n)$	$n \times I$

Effect:
The inquired values are returned. Possible error numbers: 7, 20, 25, 33, 35, 36.

──────────────── *FORTRAN Interface* ────────────────

CALL GQETXI (WKID,N,ERRIND,OL,TXIND)
Parameters:

Input	WKID	workstation identifier		INTEGER
Input	N	list element requested		INTEGER
Output	ERRIND	error indicator		INTEGER
Output	OL	number of text bundle table entries	$(6..n)$	INTEGER
Output	TXIND	nth element of list of defined text indices	$(1..n)$	INTEGER

INQUIRE TEXT REPRESENTATION   WSOP,WSAC,SGOP   L1a
Parameters:

Input	workstation identifier		I
Input	text index	$(1..n)$	I
Input	type of returned values	(SET,REALIZED)	E
Output	error indicator		I
Output	text font and precision	$(-n..-1, 1..n;$ STRING,CHAR,STROKE)	(I;E)
Output	character expansion factor	>0	R
Output	character spacing		R
Output	text colour index	$(0..n)$	I

Effect:
The inquired values are returned. Possible error numbers: 7, 20, 25, 33, 35, 36, 72, 73.

──────────────── *FORTRAN Interface* ────────────────

CALL GQTXR
 (WKID,TXI,TYPE,ERRIND,FONT,PREC,CHARXP,CHARSP,COLI)
Parameters:

Input	WKID	workstation identifier		INTEGER
Input	TXI	text index	$(1..n)$	INTEGER
Input	TYPE	type of returned values	(0 = set, 1 = realized)	INTEGER
Output	ERRIND	error indicator		INTEGER
Output	FONT	text font	$(-n..-1, 1..n)$	INTEGER
Output	PREC	text precision	(0 = string, 1 = char, 2 = stroke)	INTEGER
Output	CHARXP	character expansion factor	>0	REAL
Output	CHARSP	character spacing		REAL
Output	COLI	text colour index	$(0..n)$	INTEGER

INQUIRE TEXT EXTENT   WSOP,WSAC,SGOP   L0a

Parameters:

Input	workstation identifier		N
Input	text position	WC	P
Input	character string		S
Output	error indicator		I
Output	concatenation point	WC	P
Output	text extent parallelogram	WC	$4 \times P$

Effect:

The inquired values are returned. The extent of the specified character string is computed using the text font and precision, character expansion factor and character spacing currently selected (either via the bundle or individually, depending upon the corresponding aspect source flag settings) and the current text attributes (CHARACTER HEIGHT, CHARACTER UP VECTOR, TEXT PATH, TEXT ALIGNMENT). The concatenation point can be used as the origin of a subsequent TEXT output primitive for the concatenation of character strings. For LEFT and RIGHT text path directions, the offset of the concatenation point from the text position is the character string width plus one additional CHARACTER SPACING along the text path direction. For UP and DOWN text paths, it is the character string height plus one additional CHARACTER SPACING along the text path. The text extent parallelogram points define the parallelogram which completely encloses the character bodies of the string (see Figure 10.1). For UP and DOWN text paths, the widest character body available in the font has to be enclosed. The text extent points are given in counterclockwise order. Possible error numbers: 7, 20, 25, 39, 101.

———————————————— *FORTRAN Interface* ————————————————

CALL GQTXX (WKID,PX,PY,STR,ERRIND,CPX,CPY,TXEXPX,TXEXPY)

Parameters:

Input	WKID	workstation identifier		INTEGER
Input	PX,PY	text position	WC	$2 \times$ REAL
Input	STR	character string		CHARACTER*(*)
Output	ERRIND	error indicator		INTEGER
Output	CPX,CPY	concatenation point	WC	$2 \times$ REAL
Output	TXEXPX(4),TXEXPY(4)			
		text extent parallelogram	WC	REAL

INQUIRE LIST OF FILL AREA INDICES   WSOP,WSAC,SGOP   L1a

Parameters:

Input	workstation identifier		N
Output	error indicator		I
Output	number of fill area bundle table entries	(5..n)	I
Output	list of defined fill area indices	(1..n)	$n \times I$

Effect:

The inquired values are returned. Possible error numbers: 7, 20, 25, 33, 35, 36.

———————————————— *FORTRAN Interface* ————————————————

CALL GQEFAI (WKID,N,ERRIND,OL,FAIND)

Parameters:

Input	WKID	workstation identifier		INTEGER
Input	N	list element requested		INTEGER

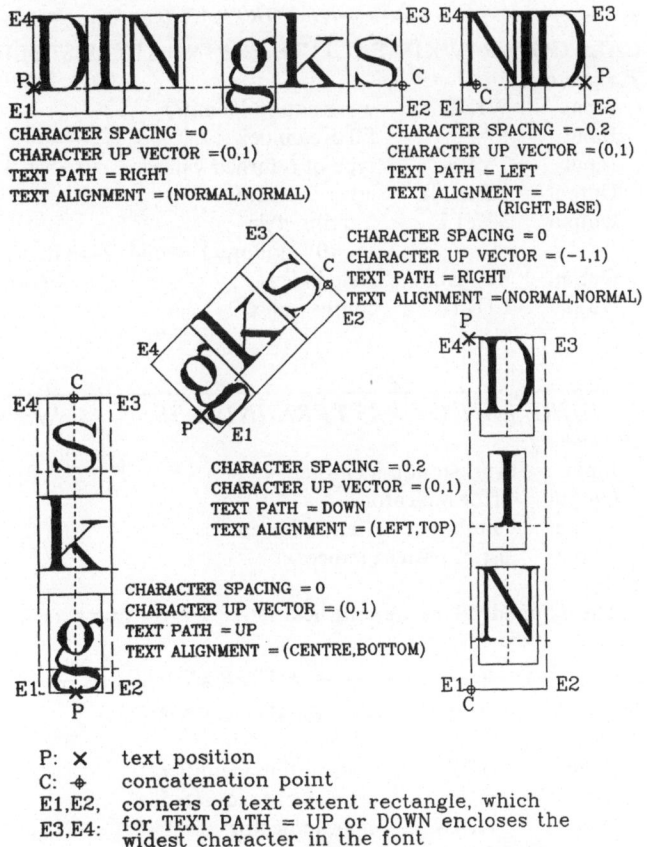

P: ✗   text position
C: ✦   concatenation point
E1,E2,   corners of text extent rectangle, which
E3,E4:   for TEXT PATH = UP or DOWN encloses the
          widest character in the font

Fig. 10.1 Examples of INQUIRE TEXT EXTENT

Output	ERRIND	error indicator		INTEGER
Output	OL	number of fill area bundle table entries	(5..n)	INTEGER
Output	FAIND	nth element of list of defined fill area indices	(1..n)	INTEGER

INQUIRE FILL AREA REPRESENTATION   WSOP,WSAC,SGOP   L1a

Parameters:

Input	workstation identifier		N
Input	fill area index	(1..n)	I
Input	type of returned values	(SET,REALIZED)	E
Output	error indicator		I
Output	interior style	(HOLLOW,SOLID,PATTERN,HATCH)	E
Output	fill area style index	(−n..−1,1..n)	I
Output	fill area colour index	(0..n)	I

Effect:

The inquired values are returned. Possible error numbers: 7, 20, 25, 33, 35, 36, 80, 81.

——————————————— *FORTRAN Interface* ———————————————

CALL GQFAR (WKID,FAI,TYPE,ERRIND,STYLE,STYLID,COLI)
Parameters:

Input	WKID	workstation identifier		INTEGER
Input	FAI	fill area index	(1..n)	INTEGER
Input	TYPE	type of returned values	(0 = set, 1 = realized)	INTEGER
Output	ERRIND	error indicator		INTEGER
Output	STYLE	interior style		
		(0 = hollow, 1 = solid, 2 = pattern, 3 = hatch)		INTEGER
Output	STYLID	style index	(−n..−1,1..n)	INTEGER
Output	COLI	colour index	(0..n)	INTEGER

INQUIRE LIST OF PATTERN INDICES   WSOP,WSAC,SGOP   L1a
Parameters:

Input	workstation identifier		N
Output	error indicator		I
Output	number of pattern table entries	(0..n)	I
Output	list of pattern indices	(1..n)	n × 1

Effect:
The inquired values are returned. Possible error numbers: 7, 20, 25, 33, 35, 36.

——————————————— *FORTRAN Interface* ———————————————

CALL GQEPAI (WKID,N,ERRIND,OL,PAIND)
Parameters:

Input	WKID	workstation identifier		INTEGER
Input	N	list element requested		INTEGER
Output	ERRIND	error indicator		INTEGER
Output	OL	number of pattern table entries	(0..n)	INTEGER
Output	PAIND	nth element of list of pattern indices	(1..n)	INTEGER

INQUIRE PATTERN REPRESENTATION   WSOP,WSAC,SGOP   L1a
Parameters:

Input	workstation identifier		N
Input	pattern index	(1..n)	I
Input	type of returned values	(SET,REALIZED)	E
Output	error indicator		I
Output	pattern array dimensions I,m	(1..n)	2 × I
Output	pattern array	(0..n)	1 × m × I

Effect:
The inquired values are returned. Possible error numbers: 7, 20, 25, 33, 35, 36, 85, 90, 91.

——————————————— *FORTRAN Interface* ———————————————

CALL GQPAR (WKID,PAI,TYPE,NMX,MMX,ERRIND,N,M,PARRAY)
Parameters:

Input	WKID	workstation identifier		INTEGER
Input	PAI	pattern index	(1..n)	INTEGER

Input	TYPE	type of returned values	(0=set, 1=realized)	INTEGER
Input	NMX,MMX	maximum pattern array dimensions		INTEGER
Output	ERRIND	error indicator		INTEGER
Output	N,M	pattern array dimensions	(1..n)	INTEGER
Output	PARRAY(NMX,MMX)			
		pattern array	(0..n)	INTEGER

INQUIRE LIST OF COLOUR INDICES   WSOP,WSAC,SGOP   L0a

Parameters:

Input	workstation identifier		N
Output	error indicator		I
Output	number of colour table entries	(2..n)	I
Output	list of colour indices	(0..n)	n × I

Effect:

The inquired values are returned. Possible error numbers: 7, 20, 25, 33, 35, 36.

———————————————— *FORTRAN Interface* ————————————————

CALL GQECI (WKID,N,ERRIND,OL,COLIND)

Parameters:

Input	WKID	workstation identifier		INTEGER
Input	N	list element requested		INTEGER
Output	ERRIND	error indicator		INTEGER
Output	OL	number of colour table entries	(2..n)	INTEGER
Output	COLIND	nth element of list of colour indices	(0..n)	INTEGER

INQUIRE COLOUR REPRESENTATION   WSOP,WSAC,SGOP   L0a

Parameters:

Input	workstation identifier		N
Input	colour index	(0..n)	I
Input	type of returned values	(SET,REALIZED)	E
Output	error indicator		I
Output	colour (red/green/blue intensities)	[0,1]	3 × R

Effect:

The inquired values are returned. Possible error numbers: 7, 20, 25, 33, 35, 36, 93, 94.

———————————————— *FORTRAN Interface* ————————————————

CALL GQCR (WKID,COLI,TYPE,ERRIND,RED,GREEN,BLUE)

Parameters:

Input	WKID	workstation identifier		INTEGER
Input	COLI	colour index	(0..n)	INTEGER
Input	TYPE	type of returned values	(0=set, 1=realized)	INTEGER
Output	ERRIND	error indicator		INTEGER
Output	RED,GREEN,BLUE			
		red/green/blue intensities	[0,1]	REAL

INQUIRE WORKSTATION TRANSFORMATION

WSOP,WSAC,SGOP   L0a

Parameters:

Input	workstation identifier		N
Output	error indicator		I
Output	workstation transformation update state		
	(NOTPENDING,PENDING)		E
Output	requested workstation window	NDC	4 × R
Output	current workstation window	NDC	4 × R
Output	requested workstation viewport	DC	4 × R
Output	current workstation viewport	DC	4 × R

Effect:

The inquired values are returned. The workstation transformation update state is PENDING if a workstation transformation change has been requested but not yet provided. Possible error numbers: 7, 20, 25, 33, 36.

────────────────── *FORTRAN Interface* ──────────────────

CALL GQWKT (WKID,ERRIND,TUS,RWINDO,CWINDO,RVIEWP,CVIEWP)

Parameters:

Input	WKID	workstation identifier		INTEGER
Output	ERRIND	error indicator		INTEGER
Output	TUS	workstation transformation update state		
		(0 = notpending, 1 = pending)		INTEGER
Output	RWINDO(4)	requested workstation window	NDC	REAL
Output	CWINDO(4)	current workstation window	NDC	REAL
Output	RVIEWP(4)	requested workstation viewport	DC	REAL
Output	CVIEWP(4)	current workstation viewport	DC	REAL

INQUIRE SET OF SEGMENT NAMES ON WORKSTATION

WSOP,WSAC,SGOP   L1a

Parameters:

Input	workstation identifier		N
Output	error indicator		I
Output	number of segment names	(0..n)	I
Output	set of stored segments for this workstation		n × N

Effect:

The inquired values are returned. Possible error numbers: 7, 20, 25, 33, 35.

────────────────── *FORTRAN Interface* ──────────────────

CALL GQSGWK (WKID,N,ERRIND,OL,SEGNAM)

Parameters:

Input	WKID	workstation identifier		INTEGER
input	N	set member requested		INTEGER
Output	ERRIND	error indicator		INTEGER
Output	OL	number of segment names	(0..n)	INTEGER
Output	SEGNAM	nth set member of list of stored		
		segments for this workstation		INTEGER

INQUIRE LOCATOR DEVICE STATE   WSOP,WSAC,SGOP   L0b

Parameters:

Input	workstation identifier		N
Input	locator device number	(1..n)	I
Input	type of returned values	(SET,REALIZED)	E
Output	error indicator		I
Output	operating mode	(REQUEST,SAMPLE,EVENT)	E
Output	echo switch	(NOECHO,ECHO)	E
Output	initial normalization transformation number	(0..n)	I
Output	initial locator position	WC	P
Output	prompt/echo type	(−n..−1,1..n)	I
Output	echo area	DC	4×R
Output	locator data record		D

Effect:
The inquired values are returned. Possible error numbers: 7, 20, 25, 38, 140.

─────────────────────── *FORTRAN Interface* ───────────────────────

CALL GQLCS(WKID,LCDNR,TYPE,ILI,ERRIND,MODE,ESW,ITNR,ILPX,
ILPY,PET,EAREA,IL,IA)

Parameters:

Input	WKID	workstation identifier		INTEGER
Input	LCDNR	locator device number	(1..n)	INTEGER
Input	TYPE	type of returned values	(0=set, 1=realized)	INTEGER
Input	ILI	dimension of data record		INTEGER
Output	ERRIND	error indicator		INTEGER
Output	MODE	mode	(0=request, 1=sample, 2=event)	INTEGER
Output	ESW	echo switch	(0=noecho, 1=echo)	INTEGER
Output	ITNR	init. norm. transformation number	(0..n)	INTEGER
Output	ILPX,ILPY	initial locator position	WC	2×REAL
Output	PET	prompt/echo type	(−n..−1,1..n)	INTEGER
Output	EAREA(4)	echo area	DC	REAL
Output	IL	number of array elements used in data record		INTEGER
Output	IA(ILI)	data record		CHARACTER*80

INQUIRE STROKE DEVICE STATE   WSOP,WSAC,SGOP   L0b

Parameters:

Input	workstation identifier		N
Input	stroke device number	(1..n)	I
Input	type of returned values	(SET,REALIZED)	E
Output	error indicator		I
Output	operating mode	(REQUEST,SAMPLE,EVENT)	E
Output	echo switch	(ECHO,NOECHO)	E
Output	initial normalization transformation number	(0..n)	I
Output	initial number of points	(0..n)	I
Output	initial points in stroke	WC	n×P
Output	prompt/echo type	(−n..−1,1..n)	I
Output	echo area	DC	4×R
Output	stroke data record		D

Effect:
The inquired values are returned. Possible error numbers: 7, 20, 25, 38, 140.

───────────────── *FORTRAN Interface* ─────────────────

CALL GQSKS(WKID,SKDNR,TYPE,N,ILI,ERRIND,MODE,ESW,INTR,
NP,PX,PY,PET,EAREA,BUFLEN,IL,IA)

Parameters:

Input	WKID	workstation identifier		INTEGER
Input	SKDNR	stroke device number	(1..n)	INTEGER
Input	TYPE	type of returned values	(0=set, 1=realized)	INTEGER
Input	N	maximum number of points		INTEGER
Input	ILI	dimension of stroke data record		INTEGER
Output	ERRIND	error indicator		INTEGER
Output	MODE	mode (0=request, 1=sample, 2=event)		INTEGER
Output	ESW	echo switch (0=noecho, 1=echo)		INTEGER
Output	ITNR	init. norm. transformation number	(0..n)	INTEGER
Output	NP	number of points	(0..n)	INTEGER
Output	PX,PY	initial points in stroke	WC	$n \times 2 \times$ REAL
Output	PET	prompt/echo type	(-n..-1,1..n)	INTEGER
Output	EAREA(4)	echo area	DC	REAL
Output	BUFLEN	buffer length for STROKE		INTEGER
Output	IL	number of array elements used in data record		INTEGER
Output	IA(ILI)	data record		CHARACTER*80

INQUIRE VALUATOR DEVICE STATE   WSOP,WSAC,SGOP   L0b

Parameters:

Input	workstation identifier		N
Input	valuator device number	(1..n)	I
Output	error indicator		I
Output	operating mode	(REQUEST,SAMPLE,EVENT)	E
Output	echo switch	(ECHO,NOECHO)	E
Output	initial value		R
Output	prompt/echo type	(1..n)	I
Output	echo area	DC	$4 \times$ R
Output	valuator data record		D

Effect:

The inquired values are returned. Possible error numbers: 7, 20, 25, 38, 140.

───────────────── *FORTRAN Interface* ─────────────────

CALL GQVLS (WKID,VLDNR,ILI,ERRIND,MODE,ESW,IVAL,PET,EAREA,
LOVAL,HIVAL,IL,IA)

Parameters:

Input	WKID	workstation identifier		INTEGER
Input	VLDNR	valuator device number	(1..n)	INTEGER
Input	ILI	dimension of data record		INTEGER
Output	ERRIND	error indicator		INTEGER
Output	MODE	mode (0=request, 1=sample, 2=event)		INTEGER
Output	ESW	echo switch (0=noecho, 1=echo)		INTEGER
Output	IVAL	initial value		REAL
Output	PET	prompt/echo type	(1..n)	INTEGER
Output	EAREA(4)	echo area	DC	REAL
Output	LOVAL, HIVAL	minimal and maximal value		$2 \times$ REAL
Output	IL	number of array elements used in data record		INTEGER
Output	IA(ILI)	data record		CHARACTER*80

INQUIRE CHOICE DEVICE STATE   WSOP,WSAC,SGOP   L0b

Parameters:

Input	workstation identifier		N
Input	choice device number	(1..n)	I
Output	error indicator		I
Output	operating mode	(REQUEST,SAMPLE,EVENT)	E
Output	echo switch	(ECHO,NOECHO)	E
Output	initial states	(OK,NOCHOICE)	E
Output	initial choice number	(1..n)	I
Output	prompt/echo type	(−n..−1,1..n)	I
Output	echo area	DC	4 × R
Output	choice data record		D

Effect:

The inquired values are returned. Possible error numbers: 7, 20, 25, 38, 140.

———————————————— *FORTRAN Interface* ————————————————

CALL GQCHS (WKID,CHDNR,ILI,ERRIND,MODE,ESW,ISTAT,ICHNR,PET,
EAREA,IL,IA)

Parameters:

Input	WKID	workstation identifier		INTEGER
Input	CHDNR	choice device number	(1..n)	INTEGER
Input	ILI	dimension of data record		INTEGER
Output	ERRIND	error indicator		INTEGER
Output	MODE	mode	(0 = request, 1 = sample, 2 = event)	INTEGER
Output	ESW	echo switch	(0 = noecho, 1 = echo)	INTEGER
Output	ISTAT	initial status	(0 = ok, 1 = nochoice)	INTEGER
Output	ICHNR	initial choice number	(1..n)	INTEGER
Output	PET	prompt/echo type	(−n..−1,1..n)	INTEGER
Output	EAREA(4)	echo area	DC	REAL
Output	IL	number of array elements used in data record		INTEGER
Output	IA(ILI)	data record		CHARACTER*80

INQUIRE PICK DEVICE STATE   WSOP,WSAC,SGOP   L1b

Parameters:

Input	workstation identifier		N
Input	pick device number	(1..n)	I
Input	type of returned values	(SET,REALIZED)	I
Output	error indicator		I
Output	operating mode	(REQUEST,SAMPLE,EVENT)	E
Output	echo switch	(ECHO,NOECHO)	E
Output	initial status	(NONE,OK,NOPICK)	E
Output	initial segment		N
Output	initial pick identifier		N
Output	prompt/echo type	(−n..−1,1..n)	I
Output	echo area	DC	4 × R
Output	pick data record		D

Effect:

The inquired values are returned. Possible error numbers: 7, 20, 25, 37, 140.

——————————————— *FORTRAN Interface* ———————————————

CALL GQPKS (WKID,PCDNR,TYPE,ILI,ERRIND,MODE,ESW,ISTAT,
ISGNA,IPCID,PET,EAREA,IL,IA)

Parameters:

Input	WKID	workstation identifier		INTEGER
Input	PCDNR	pick device number	(1..n)	INTEGER
Input	TYPE	type of returned values	(0 = set, 1 = realized)	INTEGER
Input	ILI	dimension of data record		INTEGER
Output	ERRIND	error indicator		INTEGER
Output	MODE	mode	(0 = request, 1 = sample, 2 = event)	INTEGER
Output	ESW	echo switch	(0 = noecho, 1 = echo)	INTEGER
Output	ISTAT	initial status	(0 = none, 1 = ok, 2 = nopick)	INTEGER
Output	ISGNA	initial segment		INTEGER
Output	IPCID	initial pick identifier		INTEGER
Output	PET	prompt/echo type	(−n.. −1,1..n)	INTEGER
Output	EAREA(4)	echo area	DC	REAL
Output	IL	number of array elements used in data record		INTEGER
Output	IA(ILI)	data record		CHARACTER*80

INQUIRE STRING DEVICE STATE   WSOP,WSAC,SGOP   L0b

Parameters:

Input	workstation identifier		N
Input	string device number	(1..n)	I
Output	error indicator		I
Output	operating mode	(REQUEST,SAMPLE,EVENT)	E
Output	echo switch	(ECHO,NOECHO)	E
Output	initial string		S
Output	prompt/echo type	(−n.. −1,1..n)	I
Output	echo area	DC	4 × R
Output	string data record		D

Effect:

The inquired values are returned. Possible error numbers: 7, 20, 25, 38, 140.

——————————————— *FORTRAN Interface* ———————————————

CALL GQSTS (WKID,STDNR,ILI,ERRIND,MODE,ESW,LISTR,ISTR,
PET,EAREA,BUFLEN,INIPOS,IL,IA)

Parameters:

Input	WKID	workstation identifier		INTEGER
Input	STDNR	string device number	(1..n)	INTEGER
Input	ILI	dimension of string data record		INTEGER
Output	ERRIND	error indicator		INTEGER
Output	MODE	mode	(0 = request, 1 = sample, 2 = event)	INTEGER
Output	ESW	echo switch	(0 = noecho, 1 = echo)	INTEGER
Output	LISTR	character count (ISTR)		INTEGER
Output	ISTR	initial string		CHARACTER*(*)
Output	PET	prompt/echo type	(−n.. −1,1..n)	INTEGER
Output	EAREA(4)	echo area	DC	REAL
Output	BUFLEN	buffer length of string		INTEGER
Output	INIPOS	initial cursor position		INTEGER
Output	IL	number of array elements used in data record		INTEGER
Output	IA(ILI)	data record		CHARACTER*80

10.2.5   Inquiry Functions for Workstation Description Table

INQUIRE WORKSTATION CATEGORY GKOP,WSOP,WSAC,SGOP   L0a

Parameters:

Input	workstation type	N
Output	error indicator	I
Output	workstation category	
	(OUTPUT,INPUT,OUTIN,WISS,MO,MI)	E

Effect:

The inquired values are returned. Possible error numbers: 8, 22, 23.

─────────────────── *FORTRAN Interface* ───────────────────

CALL GQWKCA (WTYPE,ERRIND,WKCAT)

Parameters:

Input	WTYPE	workstation type	INTEGER
Output	ERRIND	error indicator	INTEGER
Output	WKCAT	workstation category	
		(0 = output, 1 = input, 2 = outin, 3 = wiss, 4 = mo, 5 = mi)	INTEGER

INQUIRE WORKSTATION CLASSIFICATION

GKOP,WSOP,WSAC,SGOP   L0a

Parameters:

Input	workstation type	N
Output	error indicator	I
Output	vector/raster/other type (VECTOR,RASTER,OTHER)	E

Effect:

The inquired values are returned. Possible error numbers: 8, 22, 23, 39.

─────────────────── *FORTRAN Interface* ───────────────────

CALL GQWKCL (WTYPE,ERRIND,VRTYPE)

Parameters:

Input	WTYPE	workstation type	INTEGER
Output	ERRIND	error indicator	INTEGER
Output	VRTYPE	vector/raster/other type	
		(0 = vector, 1 = raster, 2 = other)	INTEGER

INQUIRE DISPLAY SPACE SIZE   GKOP,WSOP,WSAC,SGOP   L0a

Parameters:

Input	workstation type		N
Output	error indicator		I
Output	device coordinate units	(METRES,OTHER)	E
Output	maximum display surface size	DC >0	$2 \times R$
Output	maximum display surface size in raster units	(1..n)	$2 \times I$

Effect:

The inquired values are returned. Possible error numbers: 8, 22, 23, 31, 33, 36.

———————————— *FORTRAN Interface* ————————————
CALL GQDSP (WTYPE,ERRIND,DCUNIT,RX,RY,LX,LY)
Parameters:

Input	WTYPE	workstation type	INTEGER
Output	ERRIND	error indicator	INTEGER
Output	DCUNIT	device coordinate units (0=metres, 1=other)	INTEGER
Output	RX,RY	maximum display surface size DC >0	REAL
Output	LX,LY	maximum display surface size (raster units)	INTEGER

INQUIRE POLYLINE FACILITIES   GKOP,WSOP,WSAC,SGOP   L0a
Parameters:

Input	workstation type		N
Output	error indicator		I
Output	number of available linetypes	$(4..n)$	I
Output	list of available linetypes	$(-n..-1,1..n)$	$n \times I$
Output	number of available linewidths	$(0..n)$	I
Output	normal linewidth	DC >0	R
Output	range of linewidths (minimum,maximum)	DC >0	$2 \times R$
Output	number of predefined polyline indices	$(5..n)$	I

Effect:
The inquired values are returned. If the number of linewidths is returned as 0, the workstation supports a continuous range of linewidths. Possible error numbers: 8, 22, 23, 39.

———————————— *FORTRAN Interface* ————————————
CALL GQPLF (WTYPE,N,ERRIND,NLT,LT,NLW,NOMLW,RLWMIN,
RLWMAX,NPPLI)
Parameters:

Input	WTYPE	workstation type		INTEGER
Input	N	list element requested		INTEGER
Output	ERRIND	error indicator		INTEGER
Output	NLT	number of available linetypes	$(4..n)$	INTEGER
Output	LT	nth element of list of available		
		linetypes	$(-n..-1,1..n)$	INTEGER
Output	NLW	number of available linewidths	$(0..n)$	INTEGER
Output	NOMLW	nominal linewidth	DC >0	REAL
Output	RLWMIN,RWLMAX			
		range of linewidths	DC >0	REAL
Output	NPPLI	number of predefined polyline indices	$(5..n)$	INTEGER

INQUIRE PREDEFINED POLYLINE REPRESENTATION
GKOP,WSOP,WSAC,SGOP   L0a
Parameters:

Input	workstation type		N
Input	predefined polyline index	$(1..n)$	I
Output	error indicator		I
Output	linetype	$(-n..-1,1..n)$	I
Output	linewidth scale factor		R
Output	polyline colour index	$(0..n)$	I

Effect:
The inquired values are returned. Possible error numbers: 8, 22, 23, 39, 60, 62.

———————————— *FORTRAN Interface* ————————————
CALL GQPPLR (WTYPE,PLI,ERRIND,LNTYPE,LWIDTH,COLI)
Parameters:

Input	WTYPE	workstation type		INTEGER
Input	PLI	predefined polyline index	(1..n)	INTEGER
Output	ERRIND	error indicator		INTEGER
Output	LNTYPE	linetype	(−n..−1,1..n)	INTEGER
Output	LWIDTH	linewidth scale factor		REAL
Output	COLI	colour index	(0..n)	INTEGER

INQUIRE POLYMARKER FACILITIES GKOP,WSOP,WSAC,SGOP L0a
Parameters:

Input	workstation type		N
Output	error indicator		I
Output	number of available marker types	(5..n)	I
Output	list of available marker types	(−n..−1,1..n)	n × I
Output	number of available marker sizes	(0..n)	I
Output	nominal marker size	DC >0	R
Output	range of marker sizes (minimum,maximum)	DC >0	2 × R
Output	number of predefined polymarker indices	(5..n)	I

Effect:
The inquired values are returned. If the number of marker sizes is returned as 0, the workstation supports a continuous range of marker sizes. Possible error numbers: 8, 22, 23, 39.

———————————— *FORTRAN Interface* ————————————
CALL GQPMF (WTYPE,N,ERRIND,NMT,MT,NMS,NOMMS,RMSMIN,
RMSMAX,NPPMI)
Parameters:

Input	WTYPE	workstation type		INTEGER
Input	N	list element requested		INTEGER
Output	ERRIND	error indicator		INTEGER
Output	NMT	number of available marker types	(5..n)	INTEGER
Output	MT	nth element of list of available marker types	(−n..−1,1..n)	INTEGER
Output	NMS	number of available marker sizes	(0..n)	INTEGER
Output	NOMMS	nominal marker size	DC >0	REAL
Output	RMSMIN,RMSMAX	range of marker sizes	DC >0	REAL
Output	NPPMI	number of predefined polymarker indices	(5..n)	INTEGER

INQUIRE PREDEFINED POLYMARKER REPRESENTATION
GKOP,WSOP,WSAC,SGOP L0a
Parameters:

Input	workstation type		N
Input	predefined polymarker index	(1..n)	I
Output	error indicator		I
Output	marker type	(−n..−1,1..n)	I
Output	marker size scale factor		R
Output	polymarker colour index	(0..n)	I

Effect:
The inquired values are returned. Possible error numbers: 8, 22, 23, 39, 66, 67.

─────────────────── *FORTRAN Interface* ───────────────────

CALL GQPPMR (WTYPE,PMI,ERRIND,MKTYPE,MKSSCF,COLI)

Parameters:

Input	WTYPE	workstation type		INTEGER
Input	PMI	predefined polymarker index	$(1..n)$	INTEGER
Output	ERRIND	error indicator		INTEGER
Output	MKTYPE	marker type	$(-n..-1,1..n)$	INTEGER
Output	MKSSCF	marker size scale factor		REAL
Output	COLI	colour index	$(0..n)$	INTEGER

INQUIRE TEXT FACILITIES   GKOP,WSOP,WSAC,SGOP   L0a

Parameters:

Input	workstation type		N
Output	error indicator		I
Output	number of font and precision pairs	$(1..n)$	I
Output	list of font and precision pairs		
	$(-n..-1,1..n;\text{STRING,CHAR,STROKE})$		$n \times (\text{I;E})$
Output	number of available character heights	$(0..n)$	I
Output	minimum character height	>0	R
Output	maximum character height	>0	R
Output	number of available character expansion factors	$(0..n)$	I
Output	minimum character expansion factor	>0	R
Output	maximum character expansion factor	>0	R
Output	number of predefined text indices	$(2..n)$	I

Effect:

The inquired values are returned. If the number of character heights is returned as 0, the workstation supports a continuous range of character heights. Possible error numbers: 8, 22, 23, 39.

─────────────────── *FORTRAN Interface* ───────────────────

CALL GQTXF (WTYPE,N,ERRIND,NFPP,FONT,PREC,NCHH,MINCHH,
MAXCHH,NCHE,MINCHE,MAXCHE,NPTXI)

Parameters:

Input	WTYPE	workstation type		INTEGER
Input	N	list element requested		INTEGER
Output	ERRIND	error indicator		INTEGER
Output	NFPP	number of text font/precision pairs	$(1..n)$	INTEGER
Output	FONT	nth element of list of available text fonts	$(-n..-1,1..n)$	INTEGER
Output	PREC	nth element of list of available text precisions	$(0=\text{string}, 1=\text{char}, 2=\text{stroke})$	INTEGER
Output	NCHH	number of available character heights	$(0..n)$	INTEGER
Output	MINCHH,MAXCHH	range of character heights	>0	$2 \times$ REAL
Output	NCHE	number of available character expansion factors	$(0..n)$	INTEGER
Output	MINCHE,MAXCHE	range of character expansion factors		$2 \times$ REAL
Output	NPTXI	number of predefined text indices	$(2..n)$	INTEGER

INQUIRE PREDEFINED TEXT REPRESENTATION
GKOP,WSOP,WSAC,SGOP   L0a

Parameters:

Input	workstation type		N
Input	predefined text index	(1..n)	I
Output	error indicator		I
Output	text font and precision	(1..n;STRING,CHAR,STROKE)	(I;E)
Output	character expansion factor	>0	R
Output	character spacing		R
Output	text colour index	(0..n)	I

Effect:

The inquired values are returned. Possible error numbers: 8, 22, 23, 39, 72, 74.

——————————— *FORTRAN Interface* ———————————

CALL GQPTXR (WTYPE,PTXI,ERRIND,FONT,PREC,CHARXP,CHARSP,COLI)

Parameters:

Input	WTYPE	workstation type		INTEGER
Input	PTXI	predefined text index	(1..n)	INTEGER
Output	ERRIND	error indicator		INTEGER
Output	FONT	text font	(1..n)	INTEGER
Output	PREC	text precision (0=string, 1=char, 2=stroke)		INTEGER
Output	CHARXP	character expansion factor	>0	REAL
Output	CHARSP	character spacing		REAL
Output	COLI	colour index	(0..n)	INTEGER

INQUIRE FILL AREA FACILITIES   GKOP,WSOP,WSAC,SGOP   L0a

Parameters:

Input	workstation type		N
Output	error indicator		I
Output	number of available fill area interior styles	(1..n)	I
Output	list of available fill area interior styles		
	(HOLLOW,SOLID,PATTERN,HATCH)		n×E
Output	number of available hatch styles	(1..n)	I
Output	list of available hatch styles	(−n..−1,1..n)	n×I
Output	number of predefined fill area indices	(5..n)	I

Effect:

The inquired values are returned. Possible error numbers: 8, 22, 23, 39.

——————————— *FORTRAN Interface* ———————————

CALL GQFAF (WTYPE,NI,NH,ERRIND,NIS,IS,NHS,HS,NPFAI)

Parameters:

Input	WTYPE	workstation type		INTEGER
Input	NI	list element of IS requested		INTEGER
Input	NH	list element of HS requested		INTEGER
Output	ERRIND	error indicator		INTEGER
Output	NIS	number of fill area interior styles	(1..n)	INTEGER
Output	IS	NIth element of list of fill area interior styles		
		(0=hollow, 1=solid, 2=pattern, 3=hatch)		INTEGER
Output	NHS	number of fill area hatch styles	(1..n)	INTEGER
Output	HS	NHth element of list of fill area hatch		
		styles	(−n..−1,1..n)	INTEGER
Output	NPFAI	number of predefined fill area indices	(5..n)	INTEGER

INQUIRE PREDEFINED FILL AREA REPRESENTATION
GKOP,WSOP,WSAC,SGOP   L0a

Parameters:

Input	workstation type		N
Input	predefined fill area index	(1..n)	I
Output	error indicator		I
Output	fill area interior style		
	(HOLLOW,SOLID,PATTERN,HATCH)		E
Output	fill area style index	(−n..−1,1..n)	I
Output	fill area colour index	(0..n)	I

Effect:

The inquired values are returned. Possible error numbers: 8, 22, 23, 39, 80, 82.

———————————————— *FORTRAN Interface* ————————————————

CALL GQPFAR (WTYPE,PFAI,ERRIND,STYLE,STYLID,COLI)

Parameters:

Input	WTYPE	workstation type		INTEGER
Input	PFAI	predefined fill area index	(1..n)	INTEGER
Output	ERRIND	error indicator		INTEGER
Output	STYLE	interior style		
		(0 = hollow, 1 = solid, 2 = pattern, 3 = hatch)		INTEGER
Output	STYLID	style index	(−n..−1,1..n)	INTEGER
Output	COLI	colour index	(0..n)	INTEGER

INQUIRE PATTERN FACILITIES   GKOP,WSOP,WSAC,SGOP   L0a

Parameters:

Input	workstation type		N
Output	error indicator		I
Output	number of predefined pattern indices	(0..n)	I

Effect:

The inquired values are returned. Possible error numbers: 8, 22, 23, 39.

———————————————— *FORTRAN Interface* ————————————————

CALL GQPAF (WTYPE,ERRIND,NPPAI)

Parameters:

Input	WTYPE	workstation type		INTEGER
Output	ERRIND	error indicator		INTEGER
Output	NPPAI	number of predef. pattern indices	(0..n)	INTEGER

INQUIRE PREDEFINED PATTERN REPRESENTATION
GKOP,WSOP,WSAC,SGOP   L0a

Parameters:

Input	workstation type		N
Input	predefined pattern index	(1..n)	I
Output	error indicator		I
Output	pattern array dimensions l,m	(1..n)	$2 \times I$
Output	pattern array	(0..n)	$l \times m \times I$

Effect:

The inquired values are returned. Possible error numbers: 8, 22, 23, 39, 85, 89, 90.

―――――――――――――― *FORTRAN Interface* ――――――――――――――

CALL GQPPAR (WTYPE,PPAI,NMX,MMX,ERRIND,N,M,PARRAY)

Parameters:

Input	WTYPE	workstation type		INTEGER
Input	PPAI	predefined pattern index	(1..n)	INTEGER
Input	NMX,MMX	maximum pattern array dimensions		INTEGER
Output	ERRIND	error indicator		INTEGER
Output	N,M	pattern array dimensions	(1..n)	INTEGER
Output	PARRAY(NMX,MMX)			
		pattern array	(0..n)	INTEGER

INQUIRE COLOUR FACILITIES GKOP,WSOP,WSAC,SGOP L0a

Parameters:

Input	workstation type		N
Output	error indicator		I
Output	number of colours or intensities	(0,2..n)	I
Output	colour available	(MONOCHROME,COLOUR)	E
Output	number of predefined colour indices	(2..n)	I

Effect:

The inquired values are returned. Possible error numbers: 8, 22, 23, 39.

―――――――――――――― *FORTRAN Interface* ――――――――――――――

CALL GQCF (WTYPE,ERRIND,NCOLI,COLA,NPCI)

Parameters:

Input	WTYPE	workstation type		INTEGER
Output	ERRIND	error indicator		INTEGER
Output	NCOLI	number of colours or intensities	(0,2..n)	INTEGER
Output	COLA	colour available (0=monochrome, 1=colour)		INTEGER
Output	NPCI	number of predef. colour indices	(2..n)	INTEGER

INQUIRE PREDEFINED COLOUR REPRESENTATION
GKOP,WSOP,WSAC,SGOP L0a

Parameters:

Input	workstation type		N
Input	predefined colour index	(0..n)	I
Output	error indicator		I
Output	colour (red green/blue intensities)	[0,1]	$3 \times R$

Effect:

The inquired values are returned. Possible error numbers: 8, 22, 23, 39, 93, 95.

―――――――――――――― *FORTRAN Interface* ――――――――――――――

CALL GQPCR (WTYPE,PCI,ERRIND,RED,GREEN,BLUE)

Parameters:

Input	WTYPE	workstation type		INTEGER
Input	PCI	predefined colour index	(0..n)	INTEGER
Output	ERRIND	error indicator		INTEGER
Output	RED,GREEN,BLUE			
		colour (RGB values)	[0,1]	REAL

INQUIRE LIST OF AVAILABLE GENERALIZED DRAWING
PRIMITIVES   GKOP,WSOP,WSAC,SGOP   L0a
Parameters:

Input	workstation type		N
Output	error indicator		I
Output	number of available generalized drawing primitives	(0..n)	I
Output	list of GDP identifiers		n × N

Effect:

The inquired values are returned. Possible error numbers: 8, 22, 23, 39.

———————————————— *FORTRAN Interface* ————————————————

CALL GQEGDP (WTYPE,N,ERRIND,NGDP,GDPL)
Parameters:

Input	WTYPE	workstation type		INTEGER
Input	N	list element requested		INTEGER
Output	ERRIND	error indicator		INTEGER
Output	NGDP	number of available generalized drawing primitives	(0..n)	INTEGER
Output	GDPL	n th element of list of GDP identifiers		INTEGER

INQUIRE GENERALIZED DRAWING PRIMITIVE
GKOP,WSOP,WSAC,SGOP   L0a
Parameters:

Input	workstation type		N
Input	GDP identifier		N
Output	error indicator		I
Output	number of sets of attributes used	(0..n)	I
Output	list of sets of attributes used		
	(POLYLINE,POLYMARKER,TEXT,FILL AREA)		n × E

Effect:

The inquired values are returned. Possible error numbers: 8, 22, 23, 39, 39, 41.

———————————————— *FORTRAN Interface* ————————————————

CALL GQGDP(WTYPE,GDP,ERRIND,MB,BUNTAB)
Parameters:

Input	WTYPE	workstation type		INTEGER
Input	GDP	GDP identifier		INTEGER
Output	ERRIND	error indicator		INTEGER
Output	MB	number of sets of attributes used	(0..4)	INTEGER
Output	BUNTAB(4)	list of bundle tables used		
		(0 = polyline, 1 = polymarker, 2 = text, 3 = fill area)		INTEGER

INQUIRE NUMBER OF SEGMENT PRIORITIES SUPPORTED
GKOP,WSOP,WSAC,SGOP   L1a
Parameters:

Input	workstation type		N
Output	error indicator		I
Output	number of segment priorities supported	(0..n)	I

Effect:

The inquired values are returned. If a value of 0 is returned, the workstation supports an infinite number of segment priorities. Possible error numbers: 8, 22, 23, 39.

─────────────── *FORTRAN Interface* ───────────────

CALL GQSGP (WTYPE,ERRIND,NSG)
Parameters:

Input	WTYPE	workstation type		INTEGER
Output	ERRIND	error indicator		INTEGER
Output	NSG	number of segment priorities		
		supported	(0..n)	INTEGER

INQUIRE MAXIMUM LENGTH OF WORKSTATION STATE TABLES
GKOP,WSOP,WSAC,SGOP L1a

Parameters:

Input	workstation type		N
Output	error indicator		I
Output	maximum number of polyline table entries	(5..n)	I
Output	maximum number of polymarker bundle table entries	(5..n)	I
Output	maximum number of text bundle table entries	(2..n)	I
Output	maximum number of fill area bundle table entries	(5..n)	I
Output	maximum number of pattern indices	(0..n)	I
Output	maximum number of colour indices	(2..n)	I

Effect:
The inquired values are returned. Possible error numbers: 8, 22, 23, 39.

─────────────── *FORTRAN Interface* ───────────────

CALL GQLWK (WTYPE,ERRIND,MPLBTE,MPMBTE,MTXBTE,MFABTE,
MPAI,MCOLI)
Parameters:

Input	WTYPE	workstation type		INTEGER
Output	ERRIND	error indicator		INTEGER
Output	MPLBTE	length of polyline bundle table	(5..n)	INTEGER
Output	MPMBTE	length of polymarker bundle table	(5..n)	INTEGER
Output	MTXBTE	length of text bundle table	(2..n)	INTEGER
Output	MFABTE	length of fill area bundle table	(5..n)	INTEGER
Output	MPAI	maximum number of pattern indices	(0..n)	INTEGER
Output	MCOLI	maximum number of colour indices	(2..n)	INTEGER

INQUIRE DYNAMIC MODIFICATION OF WORKSTATION
ATTRIBUTES   GKOP,WSOP,WSAC,SGOP L1a

Parameters:

Input	workstation type		N
Output	error indicator		I
Output	polyline bundle representation changeable	(IRG,IMM)	E
Output	polymarker bundle representation changeable	(IRG,IMM)	E
Output	text bundle representation changeable	(IRG,IMM)	E
Output	fill area bundle representation changeable	(IRG,IMM)	E
Output	pattern representation changeable	(IRG,IMM)	E
Output	colour representation changeable	(IRG,IMM)	E
Output	workstation transformation changeable	(IRG,IMM)	E

Effect:
The inquired values are returned. IRG means that implicit regeneration is necessary; IMM means the action is performed immediately. Possible error numbers: 8, 22, 23, 39.

──────────────── *FORTRAN Interface* ────────────────

CALL GQDWKA (WTYPE,ERRIND,PLBUN,PMBUN,TXBUN,FABUN,PAREP,
COLREP,WKTR)

Parameters:

Input	WTYPE	workstation type		INTEGER
Output	ERRIND	error indicator		INTEGER
Output	PLBUN	polyline bundle representation changeable		
			(0=irg, 1=imm)	INTEGER
Output	PMBUN	polymarker bundle represent changeable		
			(0=irg, 1=imm)	INTEGER
Output	TXBUN	text bundle representation changeable		
			(0=irg, 1=imm)	INTEGER
Output	FABUN	fill area bundle represent changeable		
			(0=irg, 1=imm)	INTEGER
Output	PAREP	pattern representation changeable		
			(0=irg, 1=imm)	INTEGER
Output	COLREP	colour representation changeable		
			(0=irg, 1=imm)	INTEGER
Output	WKTR	workstation transformation changeable		
			(0=irg, 1=imm)	INTEGER

INQUIRE DYNAMIC MODIFICATION OF SEGMENT ATTRIBUTES
GKOP,WSOP,WSAC,SGOP   L1a

Parameters:

Input	workstation type		N
Output	error indicator		I
Output	segment transformation changeable	(IRG,IMM)	E
Output	visibility changeable from 'visible' to 'invisible'	(IRG,IMM)	E
Output	visibility changeable from 'invisible' to 'visible'	(IRG,IMM)	E
Output	highlighting changeable	(IRG,IMM)	E
Output	segment priority changeable	(IRG,IMM)	E
Output	adding primitives to the open segment	(IRG,IMM)	E
Output	segment deletion immediately visible	(IRG,IMM)	E

Effect:

The inquired values are returned. IRG means that implicit regeneration is necessary; IMM means the action is performed immediately. Possible error numbers: 8, 22, 23, 39.

──────────────── *FORTRAN Interface* ────────────────

CALL GQDSGA (WTYPE,ERRIND,SGTR,VONOFF,VOFFON,HIGH,SGPR,
ADD,SGDEL)

Parameters:

Input	WTYPE	workstation type		INTEGER
Output	ERRIND	error indicator		INTEGER
Output	SGTR	segment transformation changeable		
			(0=irg, 1=imm)	INTEGER
Output	VONOFF	visibility changeable from on to off		
			(0=irg, 1=imm)	INTEGER
Output	VOFFON	visibility changeable from off to on		
			(0=irg, 1=imm)	INTEGER
Output	HIGH	highlighting changeable	(0=irg, 1=imm)	INTEGER

Output	SGPR	segment priority changeable (0 = irg, 1 = imm)	INTEGER
Output	ADD	adding primitives to the open segment	
		(0 = irg, 1 = imm)	INTEGER
Output	SGDEL	segment deletion immediately visible	
		(0 = irg, 1 = imm)	INTEGER

INQUIRE DEFAULT DEFERRAL STATE VALUES
GKOP,WSOP,WSAC,SGOP   L1a

Parameters:

Input	workstation type	N
Output	error indicator	I
Output	default value for deferral mode (ASAP,BNIL,BNIG,ASTI)	E
Output	default value for implicit regeneration mode	
	(SUPPRESSED,ALLOWED)	E

Effect:
The inquired values are returned. Possible error numbers: 8, 22, 23, 39.

———————————— *FORTRAN Interface* ————————————

CALL GQDDS (WTYPE,ERRIND,DEFMOD,REGMOD)

Parameters:

Input	WTYPE	workstation type	INTEGER
Output	ERRIND	error indicator	INTEGER
Output	DEFMOD	default value for deferral mode	
		(0 = asap, 1 = bnil, 2 = bnig, 3 = asti)	INTEGER
Output	REGMOD	default value for implicit regeneration mode	
		(0 = suppressed, 1 = allowed)	INTEGER

INQUIRE NUMBER OF AVAILABLE LOGICAL INPUT DEVICES
GKOP,WSOP,WSAC,SGOP   L0b

Parameters:

Input	workstation type		N
Output	error indicator		I
Output	number of locator devices	(0..n)	I
Output	number of stroke devices	(0..n)	I
Output	number of valuator devices	(0..n)	I
Output	number of choice devices	(0..n)	I
Output	number of pick devices	(0..n)	I
Output	number of string devices	(0..n)	I

Effect:
The inquired values are returned. Possible error numbers: 8, 22, 23, 38.

———————————— *FORTRAN Interface* ————————————

CALL GQLI (WTYPE,ERRIND,NLCD,NSKD,NVLD,NCHD,NPCD,NSTD)

Parameters:

Input	WTYPE	workstation type		INTEGER
Output	ERRIND	error indicator		INTEGER
Output	NLCD	number of locator devices	(0..n)	INTEGER
Output	NSKD	number of stroke devices	(0..n)	INTEGER
Output	NVLD	number of valuator devices	(0..n)	INTEGER
Output	NCHD	number of choice devices	(0..n)	INTEGER
Output	NPCD	number of pick devices	(0..n)	INTEGER
Output	NSTD	number of string devices	(0..n)	INTEGER

INQUIRE DEFAULT LOCATOR DEVICE DATA
GKOP,WSOP,WSAC,SGOP   L0b

Parameters:

Input	workstation type		N
Input	logical input device number	(1..n)	I
Output	error indicator		I
Output	default initial locator position for locators	WC	P
Output	number of available prompt/echo types	(1..n)	I
Output	list of available prompt/echo types	(−n..−1,1..n)	n×I
Output	default echo area	DC	4×R
Output	default locator data record		D

Effect:

The inquired values are returned. Possible error numbers: 8, 22, 23, 38, 140.

———————————— *FORTRAN Interface* ————————————

CALL GQDLC (WTYPE,IDCNR,N,JL,ERRIND,DPX,DPY,OL,PETL,EAREA,
DL,LDAT)

Parameters:

Input	WTYPE	workstation type		INTEGER
Input	IDCNR	logical input device number	(1..n)	INTEGER
Input	N	list element requested		INTEGER
Input	JL	dimension of array LDAT		INTEGER
Output	ERRIND	error indicator		INTEGER
Output	DPX,DPY	default init. locator position	WC	2×REAL
Output	OL	number of av. prompt/echo types	(1..n)	INTEGER
Output	PETL	nth element of list of available prompt/echo types	(−n..−1,1..n)	INTEGER
Output	EAREA(4)	default echo area	DC	REAL
Output	DL	number of array elements used in locator data record		INTEGER
Output	LDAT(JL)	default locator data record		CHARACTER*80

INQUIRE DEFAULT STROKE DEVICE DATA
GKOP,WSOP,WSAC,SGOP   L0b

Parameters:

Input	workstation type		N
Input	logical input device number	(1..n)	I
Output	error indicator		I
Output	maximum input buffer size	(64..n)	I
Output	number of available prompt/echo types	(1..n)	I
Output	list of available prompt/echo types	(−n..−1,1..n)	n×I
Output	default echo area	DC	4×R
Output	default stroke data record		D

Effect:

The inquired values are returned. Possible error numbers: 8, 22, 23, 38, 140.

———————————— *FORTRAN Interface* ————————————

CALL GQDSK (WTYPE,IDCNR,N,JL,ERRIND,BUFSIZ,OL,PETL,EAREA,
BUFLEN,DL,SDAT)

Parameters:

Input	WTYPE	workstation type		INTEGER
Input	IDCNR	logical input device number	(1..n)	INTEGER

Input	N	list element requested		INTEGER
Input	JL	dimension of array SDAT		INTEGER
Output	ERRIND	error indicator		INTEGER
Output	BUFSIZ	maximum input buffer size	(64..n)	INTEGER
Output	OL	number of av. prompt/echo types	(1..n)	INTEGER
Output	PETL	nth element of list of available prompt/echo types	(−n..−1,1..n)	INTEGER
Output	EAREA(4)	default echo area	DC	REAL
Output	BUFLEN	buffer length for stroke		INTEGER
Output	DL	number of array elements used in stroke data record		INTEGER
Output	SDAT(JL)	default stroke data record		INTEGER

INQUIRE DEFAULT VALUATOR DEVICE DATA
GKOP,WSOP,WSAC,SGOP   L0b

Parameters:

Input	workstation type		N
Input	logical input device number	(1..n)	I
Output	error indicator		I
Output	default initial value		R
Output	number of available prompt/echo types	(1..n)	I
Output	list of available prompt/echo types	(−n..−1,1..n)	n × I
Output	default echo area	DC	4 × R
Output	default valuator data record		D

Effect:

The inquired values are returned. Possible error numbers: 8, 22, 23, 38, 140.

———————————— *FORTRAN Interface* ————————————

CALL GQDVL (WTYPE,IDCNR,N,JL,ERRIND,VALUE,OL,PETL,EAREA,
LOVAL,HIVAL,DL,VDAT)

Parameters:

Input	WTYPE	workstation type		INTEGER
Input	IDCNR	logical input device number	(1..n)	INTEGER
Input	N	list element requested		INTEGER
Input	JL	dimension of array VDAT		INTEGER
Output	ERRIND	error indicator		INTEGER
Output	VALUE	default initial value		REAL
Output	OL	number of av. prompt/echo types	(1..n)	INTEGER
Output	PETL	nth element of list of available prompt/echo types	(−n..−1,1..n)	INTEGER
Output	EAREA(4)	default echo area	DC	REAL
Output	LOVAL,HIVAL	minimal and maximal value		2 × REAL
Output	DL	number of array elements used in valuator data record		INTEGER
Output	VDAT(JL)	default valuator data record		CHARACTER*80

INQUIRE DEFAULT CHOICE DEVICE DATA
GKOP,WSOP,WSAC,SGOP   L0b

Parameters:

Input	workstation type		N
Input	logical input device number	(1..n)	I

Output	error indicator		I
Output	maximum number of choice alternatives		I
Output	number of available prompt/echo types	(1..n)	I
Output	list of available prompt/echo types	(1..n)	n × I
Output	default echo area	DC	4 × R
Output	default choice data record		D

Effect:

The inquired values are returned. Possible error numbers: 8, 22, 23, 38, 140.

———————————————— *FORTRAN Interface* ————————————————

CALL GQDCH (WTYPE,IDCNR,N,JL,ERRIND,NUMBER,OL,PETL,EAREA, DL,CDAT)

Parameters:

Input	WTYPE	workstation type		INTEGER
Input	IDCNR	logical input device number	(1..n)	INTEGER
Input	N	list element requested		INTEGER
Input	JL	dimension of array CDAT		INTEGER
Output	ERRIND	error indicator		INTEGER
Output	NUMBER	maximum number of choice alternatives		INTEGER
Output	OL	number of av. prompt/echo types	(1..n)	INTEGER
Output	PETL	nth element of list of available prompt/echo types	(1..n)	INTEGER
Output	EAREA(4)	default echo area	DC	REAL
Output	DL	number of array elements used in choice data record		INTEGER
Output	CDAT(JL)	default choice data record		CHARACTER*80

INQUIRE DEFAULT PICK DEVICE DATA
GKOP,WSOP,WSAC,SGOP   L0b

Parameters:

Input	workstation type		N
Input	logical input device number	(1..n)	I
Output	error indicator		I
Output	number of available prompt/echo types	(1..n)	I
Output	list of available prompt/echo types	(−n..−1,1..n)	n × I
Output	default echo area	DC	4 × R
Output	default pick data record		D

Effect:

The inquired values are returned. Possible error numbers: 8, 22, 23, 38, 140.

———————————————— *FORTRAN Interface* ————————————————

CALL GQDPK (WTYPE,IDCNR,N,JL,ERRIND,OL,PETL,EAREA,DL,PDAT)

Parameters:

Input	WTYPE	workstation type		INTEGER
Input	IDCNR	logical input device number	(1..n)	INTEGER
Input	N	list element requested		INTEGER
Input	JL	dimension of array PDAT		INTEGER
Output	ERRIND	error indicator		INTEGER
Output	OL	number of av. prompt/echo types	(1..n)	INTEGER
Output	PETL	nth element of list of available prompt/echo types	(−n..−1,1..n)	INTEGER

Output	EAREA(4)	default echo area	DC	REAL
Output	DL	number of array elements used in pick data record		INTEGER
Output	PDAT(JL)	default pick data record		CHARACTER*80

INQUIRE DEFAULT STRING DEVICE DATA
GKOP,WSOP,WSAC,SGOP   L0b

Parameters:

Input	workstation type		N
Input	logical input device number	(1..n)	I
Output	error indicator		I
Output	maximum string buffer size	(72..n)	I
Output	number of available prompt/echo types	(1..n)	I
Output	list of available prompt echo types	(−n..−1,1..n)	n × I
Output	default echo area	DC	4 × R
Output	default string data record		D

Effect:
The inquired values are returned. Possible error numbers: 8, 22, 23, 38, 140.

───────────────────── *FORTRAN Interface* ─────────────────────

CALL GQDST (WTYPE,IDCNR,N,JL,ERRIND,MAXBUF,OL,PETL,EAREA,
BUFLEN,DL,TDAT)

Parameters:

Input	WTYPE	workstation type		INTEGER
Input	IDCNR	logical input device number	(1..n)	INTEGER
Input	N	list element requested		INTEGER
Input	JL	dimension of array TDAT		INTEGER
Output	ERRIND	error indicator		INTEGER
Output	MAXBUF	maximum string buffer size	(72..n)	INTEGER
Output	OL	number of av. prompt/echo types	(1..n)	INTEGER
Output	PETL	nth element of list of available prompt/echo types	(−n..−1,1..n)	INTEGER
Output	EAREA(4)	default echo area	DC	REAL
Output	BUFLEN	buffer length of string		INTEGER
Output	DL	number of array elements used in data record		INTEGER
Output	TDA(JL)	default string data record		CHARACTER*80

10.2.6 Inquiry Functions for Segment State List

INQUIRE SET OF ASSOCIATED WORKSTATIONS
WSOP,WSAC,SGOP   L1a

Parameters:

Input	segment name		N
Output	error indicator		I
Output	number of associated workstations	(1..n)	I
Output	set of associated workstation identifiers		n × N

Effect:
The inquired values are returned. Possible error numbers: 7, 120, 122.

─────────────── *FORTRAN Interface* ───────────────

CALL GQASWK (SGNA,N,ERRIND,OL,WKIDL)

Parameters:

Input	SGNA	segment name	INTEGER
Input	N	set member requested	INTEGER
Output	ERRIND	error indicator	INTEGER
Output	OL	number of associated workstations (1..n)	INTEGER
Output	WKIDL	nth element of set of associated workstation identifiers	INTEGER

INQUIRE SEGMENT ATTRIBUTES   WSOP,WSAC,SGOP   L1a

Parameters:

Input	segment name		N
Output	error indicator		I
Output	segment transformation matrix		$2 \times 3 \times R$
Output	visibility	(INVISIBLE,VISIBLE)	E
Output	highlighting	(NORMAL,HIGHLIGHTED)	E
Output	segment priority	[0,1]	R
Output	detectability	(UNDECTABLE,DETECTABLE)	E

Effect:

The inquired values are returned. Possible error numbers: 7, 120, 122.

─────────────── *FORTRAN Interface* ───────────────

CALL GQSGA (SGNA,ERRIND,SEGTM,VIS,HIGH,SGPR,DET)

Parameters:

Input	SGNA	segment name	INTEGER
Output	ERRIND	error indicator	INTEGER
Output	SEGTM(6)	segment transformation matrix	REAL
Output	VIS	visibility (0 = invisible, 1 = visible)	INTEGER
Output	HIGH	highlighting (0 = normal, 1 = highlighted)	INTEGER
Output	SGPR	segment priority [0,1]	REAL
Output	DET	detectability (0 = undetectable, 1 = detectable)	INTEGER

10.2.7   Pixel Inquiries

INQUIRE PIXEL ARRAY DIMENSIONS   WSOP,WSAC,SGOP   L0a

Parameters:

Input	workstation identifier		N
Input	2 points P,Q	WC	$2 \times P$
Output	error indicator		I
Output	dimensions of pixel array	(1..n)	$2 \times I$

Effect:

The inquired values are returned. The points P,Q define a rectangle. By transforming P and Q using the current normalization and workstation transformations, the rectangle is mapped onto the display surface. The number of columns and the number of rows of pixels whose positions lie within the rectangle are returned. For this calculation no clipping is applied. Possible error numbers: 7, 20, 25, 39.

―――――――――――― *FORTRAN Interface* ――――――――――――

CALL GQPXAD (WKID,PX,PY,QX,QY,ERRIND,N,M)

Parameters:

Input	WKID	workstation identifier		INTEGER
Input	PX,PY,QX,QY			
		upper left and lower right corner	WC	4 × REAL
Output	ERRIND	error indicator		INTEGER
Output	N,M	dimensions of pixel array	(1..n)	INTEGER

INQUIRE PIXEL ARRAY   WSOP,WSAC,SGOP   L0a

Parameters:

Input	workstation identifier		N
Input	point P	WC	P
Input	dimensions of colour index array l,m	(1..n)	2 × I
Output	error indicator		I
Output	presence of invalid values	(ABSENT,PRESENT)	E
Output	colour index array	(-1..n)	l × m × I

Effect:

The inquired values are returned. The point P is transformed by the current normalization and workstation transformations and mapped onto the closest pixel of the display surface. This pixel is the upper left pixel of the index array returned. If a colour index cannot be ascertained (for example, if the point P was transformed so that the position of a pixel is not on the display surface), the value -1 (i.e. invalid) is assigned and will be returned. In this case, the parameter 'presence of invalid values' will be set to PRESENT. Possible error numbers: 7, 20, 25, 39, 40, 91.

―――――――――――― *FORTRAN Interface* ――――――――――――

CALL GQPXA (WKID,PX,PY,DIMX,DIMY,ISC,ISR,DX,DY,ERRIND,
    INVVAL,COL)

Parameters:

Input	WKID	workstation identifier		INTEGER
Input	PX,PY	upper left corner	WC	2 × REAL
Input	DIMX,DIMY	dimensions of COL		2 × INTEGER
Input	ISC,ISR	start column, start row		2 × INTEGER
Input	DX,DY	size of requested pixel array		2 × INTEGER
Output	ERRIND	error indicator		INTEGER
Output	INVVAL	presence of invalid values		
			(0 = absent, 1 = present)	INTEGER
Output	COL(DIMX,DIMY)			
		colour index array	(-1..n)	INTEGER

INQUIRE PIXEL   WSOP,WSAC,SGOP   L0a

Parameters:

Input	workstation identifier		N
Input	point P	WC	P
Output	error indicator		I
Output	colour index	(-1..n)	I

Effect:

The inquired values are returned. By transforming P using the current normalization and workstation transformations, it is mapped onto a pixel of the display surface. The colour index of this pixel is returned. If a colour index cannot be ascertained, the value -1 (i.e. invalid) is returned. Possible error numbers: 7, 20, 25, 39, 40.

———————————————————— *FORTRAN Interface* ————————————————————

CALL GQPX (WKID,PX,PY,ERRIND,COLI)

Parameters:

Input	WKID	workstation identifier		INTEGER
Input	PX,PY	point	WC	REAL
Output	ERRIND	error indicator		INTEGER
Output	COLI	colour index	(-1..n)	INTEGER

10.2.8   Inquiry Function for GKS Error State List

INQUIRE INPUT QUEUE OVERFLOW   WSOP,WSAC,SGOP   L0c

Parameters:

Output	error indicator		I
Output	workstation identifier		N
Output	input class	(LOCATOR,STROKE,VALUATOR, CHOICE,PICK,STRING)	E
Output	input device number	(1..n)	I

Effect:

The inquired values are returned. If the input queue has overflowed, the error indicator is returned as 0 and the identification of the logical input device that caused the overflow is returned. The entry is removed from the error state list. Possible error numbers: 7, 148, 149.

———————————————————— *FORTRAN Interface* ————————————————————

CALL GQIQOV (ERRIND,WKID,ICL,IDN)

Parameters:

Output	ERRIND	errror indicator		INTEGER
Output	WKID	workstation identifier		INTEGER
Output	ICL	input class	(1=locator, 2=stroke, 3=valuator, 4=choice, 5=pick, 6=string)	INTEGER
Output	IDN	input device number	(1..n)	INTEGER

10.3   Examples

Example 10.1   Inquiring into the GKS state list

GKS state list variables are determined and saved. Later they are reset to the saved values. It is necessary to save and restore state list values in those cases where an application subroutine changes these values. The values are saved upon entry to the subroutine and restored before returning to the calling program.

———————————— *Pascal* ————————————

{Saving values: save normalization transformations}
L10 INQUIRE_CURRENT_NORMALIZATION_TRANSFORMATION_
NUMBER (err_ind,cnum):
L20 INQUIRE_LIST_OF_NORMALIZATION_TRANSFORMATION_NUMBERS
(err_ind,nums);
L30 **for** i:=1 **to** length(nums) **do**
L40 **begin**
L50 INQUIRE_NORMALIZATION_TRANSFORMATION
(nums[i], err_ind, windows[i], viewports[i]);
L60 **end**;
{save primitive attributes}
L70 INQUIRE_CURRENT_PRIMITIVE_ATTRIBUTE_VALUES
(err_ind,ipolyl,ipolym,itext,ch_height,ch_w,ch_base,ch_up,tx_path,
tx_align,ifill,p_width,p_height,p_refp);
L80 INQUIRE_CURRENT_INDIVIDUAL_ATTRIBUTE_VALUES
(err_ind,ltype,lwidth,icpolyl,mtype,msize,icpolym,
txfonp,ch_exp,ch_sp,ictext,style,isfill,icfill,asf);
L95 INQUIRE_CURRENT_PICK_IDENTIFIER_VALUE (err_ind, ipick)

{Resetting the values: reset normalization transformations}
L100 **for** i:= **to** length(nums) **do**
L110 **begin**
L120 SET_WINDOW (nums[i], windows[i]);
L130 SET_VIEWPORT (nums[i],viewports[i]);
L140 **end**;
{order transformations by viewport input priority}
L150 **for** i:=2 **to** length(nums) **do**
L160 **begin**
L170 SET_VIEWPORT_INPUT_PRIORITY (nums[i],nums[i−1], lower);
L180 **end**;
{reset current transformation}
L190 SELECT_NORMALIZATION_TRANSFORMATION (cnum);
{reset bundle indices}
L200 SET_POLYLINE_INDEX (ipolyl);
L210 SET_POLYMARKER_INDEX (ipolym);
L220 SET_TEXT_INDEX (itext);
L230 SET_FILL_AREA_INDEX (ifill);
{reset POLYLINE attribute}
L240 SET_LINETYPE (ltype);
L250 SET_LINEWIDTH_SCALE_FACTOR (lwidth);
L260 SET_POLYLINE_COLOUR_INDEX (icpolyl);
{reset POLYMARKER attribute}
L270 SET_MARKER_TYPE (mtype);
L280 SET_MARKER_SIZE_SCALE_FACTOR (msize);
L290 SET_POLYMARKER_COLOUR_INDEX (icpolym);
{reset TEXT attributes}
L300 SET_CHARACTER_HEIGHT (ch_height);
L310 SET_CHARACTER_UP_VECTOR (ch_up);
L320 SET_TEXT_PATH (tx_path);
L330 SET_TEXT_ALIGNMENT (tx_align);
L340 SET_TEXT_FONT_AND_PRECISION (txfonp);

L350 SET_CHARACTER_EXPANSION_FACTOR (ch_exp);
L360 SET_CHARACTER_SPACING (ch_sp);
L370 SET_TEXT_COLOUR_INDEX (ictext);

{reset FILL AREA attributes}

L380 SET_PATTERN_SIZE (p_width [1], p_height [2]);
L390 SET_PATTERN_REFERENCE_POINT (p_refp);
L400 SET_FILL_AREA_INTERIOR_STYLE (style);
L410 SET_FILL_AREA_STYLE_INDEX (isfill);
L420 SET_FILL_AREA_COLOUR_INDEX (icfill);

{reset aspect source flags}

L430 SET_ASPECT_SOURCE_FLAGS (asf);

{reset PICK identifier}

L440 SET_PICK_IDENTIFIER (ipick)

───────────────────────── *Fortran* ─────────────────────────

```
        C        *** save normalization transformation
L10              CALL GQCNTN(ERRIND,CNUM)
L20              CALL GQENTN(1,ERRIND,LENGTH,NUMS(1))
L30              DO 60 I=1,LENGTH
L31                 CALL GQENTN(I,ERRIND,LENGTH,NUMS(I))
L50                 CALL GQNT(NUMS(I),ERRIND,WINDO(I,1),VIEWP(I,1))
L60      60      CONTINUE
        C        *** save primitive attributes
L61              CALL GQPLI (ERRIND,IPOLYL)
L62              CALL GQPMI (ERRIND,IPOLYM)
L63              CALL GQTXI (ERRIND,ITEXT)
L64              CALL GQCHH (ERRIND,CHHEIG)
L67              CALL GQCHUP (ERRIND,CHUPX,CHUPY)
L68              CALL GQTXP (ERRIND,TXPATH)
L69              CALL GQTXAL (ERRIND,TXALH,TXALV)
L70              CALL GQFAI (ERRIND,IFILL)
L71              CALL GQPA (ERRIND,PWX,PWY,PHX,PHY)
L72              CALL GQPARF (ERRIND,PREFX,PREFY)
L73              CALL GQPKID (ERRIND,IPICK)
L80              CALL GQLNA (ERRIND,LTYPE)
L81              CALL GQLWSC (ERRIND,LWIDTH)
L82              CALL GQPLCI (ERRIND,ICPL)
L83              CALL GQMK (ERRIND,MTYPE)
L84              CALL GQMKSC (ERRIND,MSIZE)
L85              CALL GQPMCI (ERRIND,ICPM)
L86              CALL GQTXFP (ERRIND,TXFONT,TXPREC)
L87              CALL GQCHXP (ERRIND,CHEXP)
L88              CALL GQCHSP (ERRIND,CHSP)
L89              CALL GQTXCI (ERRIND,ICTEXT)
L90              CALL GQFAIS (ERRIND,STYLE)
L91              CALL GQFASI (ERRIND,ISFILL)
L92              CALL GQFACI (ERRIND,ICFILL)
L93              CALL GQASF (ERRIND,ASF)
L95              CALL GQPKID (ERRIND,IPICK)
```

Resetting the values:
```
        C        *** reset normalization transformations
L100             DO 140 I=1,LENGTH
```

L120		CALL GSWN(NUMS(I),WINDO(I,1),WINDO(I,2),WINDO(I,3),
	+	WINDO(I,4))
L130		CALL GSVP(NUMS(I),VIEWP(I,1),VIEWP(I,2),VIEWP(I,3),
	+	VIEWP(I,4))
L140	140	CONTINUE
L150		DO 180 I=2,LENGTH
L170		CALL GSVPIP(NUMS(I),NUMS(I−1),LOWER)
L180	180	CONTINUE
	C	*** reset current transformation
L190		CALL GSELNT(CNUM)
	C	*** reset bundle indices
L200		CALL GSPLI(IPOLYL)
L210		CALL GSPMI(IPOLYM)
L220		CALL GSTXI(ITEXT)
L230		CALL GSFAI(IFILL)
	C	*** reset POLYLINE attributes
L240		CALL GSLN(LTYPE)
L250		CALL GSLWSC(LWIDTH)
L260		CALL GSPLCI(ICPL)
	C	*** reset POLYMARKER attributes
L270		CALL GSMK(MTYPE)
L280		CALL GSMKSC(MSIZE)
L290		CALL GSPMCI(ICPM)
	C	*** reset TEXT attributes
L300		CALL GSCHH(CHHEIG)
L320		CALL GSCHUP(CHUPX,CHUPY)
L320		CALL GSTXP(CHPATH)
L330		CALL GSTXAL(TXALH,TXALV)
L340		CALL GSTXFP(TXFONT,TXPREC)
L350		CALL GSCHXP(CHEXP)
L360		CALL GSCHSP(CHSP)
L370		CALL GSTXCI(ICTEXT)
	C	*** reset FILL AREA attributes
L380		CALL GSPA(PWX,PHY)
L390		CALL GSPARF(PREFX,PREFY)
L400		CALL GSFAIS(STYLE)
L410		CALL GSFASI(ISFILL)
L420		CALL GSFACI(ICFILL)
	C	*** reset aspect source flags
L430		CALL GSASF(ASF)
	C	*** reset PICK identifier
L440		CALL GSPKID(IPICK)

Example 10.2   Inquiring into a colour table

The colour table of an output type workstation is inspected. The colour indices whose values are closest to pure red and pure green are to be found. "Close" means in this context that the distance between two colour values is calculated as the sum of the differences between their corresponding RGB values. For example, the colour value of green is (0,1,0) and hence the distance between a given colour (R,G,B) and green is given by $R+(1-G)+B$. The colour index which points to the entry in the colour table for which this sum has the minimum value, is the colour "closest to green". The colour values realised by the workstation will be tested. The distances between the tested colours and red or green, respectively, are stored in the variables DIFRED and DIFGRN. The indices closest to red and green are stored in the variables INDRED and INDGRN.

─────────────────────────── *Pascal* ───────────────────────────

```
                                        {get list of colour indices}
L10   INQUIRE_LIST_OF_COLOUR_INDICES (wsid,err_ind,number,list);
                                 {initialise differences to maximal value}
                                 {(colour values R,G,B are in the range 0..1)}
L20   difred:=3; difgrn:=3;

                                        {initialise indices to −1}
L30   indred:=−1; indgrn:=−1;
L40   for i:=1 to number do              {inspect all colour table entries}
L41   begin
                                        {inquire colour table}
L50      INQUIRE_COLOUR_REPRESENTATION
         (wsid,list[i],realized,err_ind,colour);
                                        {test if colour is closer to red}
L60      if (1−colour.red)+colour.green+colour.blue<difred
         then do
L70      begin
L80        difred:=(1−colour.red)+colour.green+colour.blue;
L90        indred:=list[i];
L100     end;
                                        {test if colour is closer to green}
L110     if colour.red+(1−colour.green)+colour.blue<difgrn
         then do
L120     begin
L130       difgrn:=colour.red+(1−colour.green)+colour.blue;
L140       indgrn:=list[i];
L150     end;
L160  end;
                                 {if indred or indgrn are not equal to −1}
                {they contain colour indices closest to red or green, respectively}
```

─────────────────────────── *Fortran* ───────────────────────────

```
      C        *** get number of colour indices
L10            CALL GQECI(WSID,1,ERRIND,NUMBER,LIST(1))
      C        *** initialize differences to maximal values possible
L20            DIFRED=3.0
L21            DIFGRN=3.0
      C        *** initialize indices to −1
L30            INDRED=−1
L31            INDGRN=−1
L40            DO 160 I=1,NUMBER
      C           *** get colour index
L45               CALL GQCI(WSID,I,ERRIND,NUMBER,LIST(I))
      C           *** test inquire colour table
L50               CALL GQCR(WSID,LIST(I),REALIZED,ERRIND,RED,
                  GREEN,BLUE)
```

```
        C              *** test if colour is closer to red
L60                    IF ((1.0−RED)+GREEN+BLUE.GE.DIFRED) GOTO 110
L80                    DIFRED=(1.0−RED)+GREEN+BLUE
L90                    INDRED=LIST(I)
        C              *** test if colour is closer to green
L110    110           IF (RED+(1.0−GREEN)+BLUE.GE.DIFGRN) GOTO 160
L130                   DIFGRN=RED+(1.0−GREEN)+BLUE
L140                   INDGRN=LIST(I)
L160    160           CONTINUE
```

Example 10.3   Inquiring into the workstation description table

The workstation description table of a workstation type WSTYPE is inspected. The following GKS function calls determine:
— whether or not colour is available;
— if colour is available, the number of colour table entries.

Then the POLYLINE and FILL AREA bundles will be set up according to the inquired values.

─────────────────── *Pascal* ───────────────────

```
                                              {test if colour available}
L10     INQUIRE_COLOUR_FACILITIES
            (wstype,err_ind,icolours,cavail,nindex);
L20     if cavail=colour then do
L30     begin
L50        if nindex> =3 then do
L60        begin              {set first three polyline bundles to colours red, green, blue}
L70          SET_POLYLINE_REPRESENTATION (wsid,1,1,1.0,1);
L80          SET_POLYLINE_REPRESENTATION (wsid,2,1,1.0,2);
L90          SET_POLYLINE_REPRESENTATION (wsid,3,1,1.0,3);
L100         SET_COLOUR_REPRESENTATION (wsid,1,1.0,0.0,0.0);            {red}
L110         SET_COLOUR_REPRESENTATION (wsid,2,0.0,1.0,0.0);            {green}
L120         SET_COLOUR_REPRESENTATION (wsid,3,0.0,0.0,1.0);            {blue}
L130       end;
L140    end;
L150    else do
L160    begin                       {set first three polyline bundles to three linetypes}
L170      SET_POLYLINE_REPRESENTATION (wsid,1,1,1.0,1);
L180      SET_POLYLINE_REPRESENTATION (wsid,2,2,1.0,1);
L190      SET_POLYLINE_REPRESENTATION (wsid,3,3,1.0,1);
L200    end;
```

─────────────────── *Fortran* ───────────────────

```
        C              *** test if colour available
L10                    CALL GQCF(WSTYPE,ERRIND,ICOLS,CAVAIL,NINDEX)
L20                    IF (CAVAIL.NE.COLOUR) GOTO 170
L50                    IF (NINDEX.LT.3) GOTO 200
        C              *** set first three polyline bundles to colours
        C              *** red, green, blue
L70                    CALL GSPLR(WSID,1,1,1.0,1)
L80                    CALL GSPLR(WSID,2,1,1.0,2)
```

L90		CAL GSPLR(WSID,3,1,1.0,3)
L100		CALL GSCR(WSID,1,1.0,0.0,0.0)
L110		CALL GSCR(WSID,2,0.0,1.0,0.0)
L120		CALL GSCR(WSID,3,0.0,0.0,1.0)
L130		GOTO 200
	C	*** set first three polyline bundles
	C	*** to three linetypes
L170	170	CALL GSPLR(WSID,1,1,1.0,1)
L180		CALL GSPLR(WSID,2,2,1.0,1)
L190		CALL GSPLR(WSID,3,3,1.0,1)
L200	200	CONTINUE

Example 10.4   Pixel inquiry

The pixel memory of a workstation is inspected by using pixel inquiry functions. It is assumed in this example that an ESCAPE function is used to fill the pixel memory and the colour table of a workstation with values obtained from outside GKS (e.g., from an external file set up by a scanner). Then the pixel inquiries are used to find a pixel with a given colour (yellow in the example, yellow has RGB values (1,1,0)). All yellow pixels will then be set to the background colour by using the CELL ARRAY output primitive function. The background colour index in GKS is always zero. The window and the viewport of the normalization transformation are both set to the workstation window. In this way it is ensured that the pixel array sent to the workstation will overlay the pixel array read in.

─────────────────── *Pascal* ───────────────────

```
                                              {get workstation window cww}
L10   INQUIRE_WORKSTATION_TRANSFORMATION
          (wsid,err_ind,ws,rww,cww,rwv,cwv);
                             {set window and viewport to workstation window cww}
L20   SET_WINDOW (1,cww);
L30   SET_VIEWPORT (1,cww);
L35   SELECT NORMALISATION TRANSFORMATION (1);
                  {get dimensions n,m of pixel array covering the whole workstation}
                  {window. Points p,q are set to window corners.}
L40   p[1]:=cww[1]; p[2]:=cww[4];
L50   q[1]:=cww[2]; q[2]:=cww[3];
L60   INQUIRE_PIXEL_ARRAY_DIMENSIONS (wsid,p,q,err_ind,n,m);
                        {start traversing picture at upper left corner with pixel array of}
                        {dimensions 5 x 5 until lower right corner is reached}
L70   pp[2]:=p[2];                       {y-value of upper left corner of 5 x 5 pixel array}
L80   repeat
L90     pp[1]:=p[1];                     {x-value of upper left corner 5 x 5 pixel array}
L100    repeat
                                                            {lower right corner}
L110      qq[1]:=pp[1]+5*(cww[2]-cww[1])/n;
L120      qq[2]:=pp[2]-5*(cww[4]-cww[3])/m;
L130      changed:=false;
```

```
                                              {inquire 5 × 5 pixel array}
L140        INQUIRE_PIXEL_ARRAY (sid,pp,5,5,err_ind,pres,cind);
                                              {look for yellow pixels}
L150        for i:=1 to 5 do
L160          for j:=1 to 5 do
L170          begin
L180            INQUIRE_COLOUR_REPRESENTATION (wsid,cind[i,j],
L190            vtype,err_ind,red,green,blue);
                                              {if yellow set colour index to 0}
L200          if red>0.95 & green>0.95 & blue<0.05 then do
L210          begin
L220            cind[i,j]:=0;
L230            changed:=true
L240          end
L250          end;
                 {if indices changed send changed pixel array back to workstation}
L260        if changed then do
L270          CELL_ARRAY (pp,qq,5,5,cind);
                                              {increment x of upper left corner}
L280        pp[1]:=pp[1]+5*(cww[2]-cww[1])/n;
L290      until qq[1]>=q[1];
                                              {increment y of upper left corner}
L300      pp[2]:=pp[2]:=-5*(cww[4]-cww[3])/m;
L310    until qq[2]<=q[2];
```

——————————————————————————— *Fortran* ———————————————————————————

```
        C          *** get workstation window
L10               CALL GQWKT(WSID,ERRIND,WS,RWINDO,CWINDO,
            +     RVIEW,CVIEW)
        C          *** set window and viewport to workstation window
L20               CALLGSWN(1,CWINDO(1),CWINDO(2),CWINDO(3),CWINDO(4))
L30               CALL GSVP(1,CWINDO(1),CWINDO(2),CWINDO(3),CWINDO(4))
L35               CALL GSELNT(1)
        C          *** get dimensions N,M of pixel array covering the
        C          *** whole workstation window. Points P,Q are set to
        C          *** window corners.
L40               PX=CWINDO(1)
L41               PY=CWINDO(4)
L50               QX=CWINDO(2)
L51               QY=CWINDO(3)
L60               CALL GQPXAD(WSID,PX,PY,QX,QY,ERRIND,N,M)
        C          *** start traversing picture at upper left corner with
        C          *** pixel array of dimension 5 × 5 until lower right
        C          *** corner is reached
        C          *** y-value of upper left corner 5 × 5 pixel array
L70               PPY=PY
        C          *** repeat until ymax is reached
L80        80     CONTINUE
        C          *** x-value of upper left corner of 5 × 5 pixel array
L90               PPX=PX
        C          *** repeat until xmax is reached
```

```
L100     100        CONTINUE
         C                  *** calculate lower right corner of 5 x 5 array
L110                QQX=PPX+5*(CWINDO(2)-CWINDO(1))/N
L120                QQY=PPY-5*(CWINDO(4)-CWINDO(3))/M
L130                CHANGED=.FALSE.
         C                  *** inquire 5 x 5 pixel array
L140                CALL GQPXA(WSID,QQX,QQY,5,5,ERRIND,PRES,CIND)
         C                  *** look for yellow pixels
L150                DO 250 I=1,5
L160                   DO 240 J=1,5
L180                      CALL GQCR(WSID,CIND(I,J),
L190            +            VTYPE,ERRIND,RED,GREEN,BLUE)
         C                  *** if yellow set colour index to 0
L200                      IF (RED.LE.0.95.OR. GREEN.LE.0.95.OR.
L201            +            BLUE.GE.0.05) GOTO 240
L220                      CIND(I,J)=0
L230                      CHANGED=.TRUE.
L240     240           CONTINUE
L250     250        CONTINUE
         C                  *** if indices changed send changed pixel array
         C                  *** array back to workstation
L260                IF (CHANGED) THEN
L270            +      CALL GCA(PPX,PPY,QQX,QQY,5,5,CIND)
         C                  *** increment x of upper left corner
L280                PPX=PPX+5.0*(CWINDO(2)-CWINDO(1))/N
L290                IF (QQX.LT.QX) GOTO 100
         C                  *** increment y of upper left corner
L300                PPY=PPY-5.0*(CWINDO(4)-CWINDO(3))/M
L310             IF (QQY.GT.QY) GOTO 80
```

10.4   Exercises

Exercise 10.1   Saving workstation state list values

Extend the program parts in Example 10.1 in such a way that not only GKS
state list values but also workstation state list values of a workstation given
by its workstation identifier are saved and restored. Design, realize and test
two general purpose subroutines for saving and restoring state list values.

Exercise 10.2   Searching for lines in raster picture

Imagine a pixel memory has been filled by an ESCAPE function as in Example 10.4. The picture consists of a number of irregular line segments, each one
pixel wide, with different colours. Change Example 10.4 in such a way that
the lines of a given colour index c1 are followed and all the pixels are set
to colour index c2 (c2 $\neq$ c1).

Exercise 10.3   Searching for lines in raster picture

Change the program resulting from Exercise 10.2 in such a way that not the lines of a given colour index, but rather those of a given colour bandwidth (Rmin..Rmax,Gmin..Gmax,Bmin..Bmax) are followed and set to colour index c2.

11   METAFILE INTERFACE

11.1   Overview

Graphics metafiles are a facility for the long-term storage of pictures. GKS provides an interface to graphics metafiles. One metafile format, the GKS Metafile (GKSM), is described in an appendix to the GKS standard. Whereas the GKS workstation-independent segment storage is available for the storage of segments only during a GKS application, i.e. between OPEN GKS and CLOSE GKS, the metafile is retained for an unlimited time. The most important applications for the metafile are:
— storage of graphical data from one GKS application to the next one;
— storage of graphical data for archiving purposes;
— transport of graphical data to a different installation;
— transmission of graphical data to a different graphics system;
— saving the state of a GKS application for continuation of the session or run at a later time;
— device-independent storage of graphical data for deferred transmission to an output device;
— storage of non-graphical, application-defined data which is logically connected to the graphics data.

GKS provides functions for routeing data to the metafile for long-term storage. When the metafile is addressed in this way, it is called a *GKSM output* workstation. However, GKS also provides functions for reading the metafile back into the system, and displaying the graphical contents at an output workstation, or storing segments contained in the metafile in the workstation-dependent segment storage. In this case, the metafile is used as a *GKSM input* workstation.

When generating output on the GKSM, GKS functions will cause units of data to be written on a file. These units are called GKSM *items*. In most cases, a GKS function will cause one item to be recorded on the metafile. When reading a metafile, one item at a time will be retrieved from the metafile. The different item types are identified by an item number.

While the contents and the format of the metafile, as described in Appendix E of the GKS document, are not part of the international standard, the functional interface to the metafile has been integrated into the GKS standard. As soon as an international graphics metafile standard is established, the GKS metafile interface will be used for GKS communication with the ISO standard metafile, called "Computer Graphics Metafile" [ISO85c]. An appendix of that standard describes its relationship to the GKS metafile interface. However, the GKS metafile format defined in Appendix E is suitable for all GKS applications, and this format will be used in this chapter when specific questions relating to the format are dealt with. The contents and the format of the GKS metafile are described in detail in Chapter V.6.

11.2   The Metafile Workstation

In order to use the metafile in a consistent and easy-to-use fashion, it is addressed in GKS in the same way as a workstation. Two workstation types for metafiles are defined in an implementation: the GKSM output and GKSM input workstation.

The following workstation control functions are used to control GKSM output workstations:

GKS name	FORTRAN name
OPEN WORKSTATION	GOPWK
CLOSE WORKSTATION	GCLWK
ACTIVATE WORKSTATION	GACWK
DEACTIVATE WORKSTATION	GDAWK
SET DEFERRAL STATE	GSDFS
CLEAR WORKSTATION	GCLRWK
UPDATE WORKSTATION	GUWK
REDRAW ALL SEGMENTS ON WORKSTATION	GRSGWK
MESSAGE	GMSG
ESCAPE	GESC

Any number of GKSM output workstations can be open or active at the same time (unless restricted by the implementation). As with other workstations, output will be sent to a GKSM output workstation only as long as it is active. CLEAR WORKSTATION, UPDATE WORKSTATION, REDRAW ALL SEGMENTS and MESSAGE are valid only as long as the workstation is open or active. Not only output, but also control and segment functions will be recorded on the metafile as they are called turning the GKSM output workstation into an *audit trail* for output related GKS functions.

In the case of GKSM input workstations, only the workstation control functions OPEN WORKSTATION and CLOSE WORKSTATION are valid. Any number of GKSM input workstations can be open at one time (unless restricted by the implementation). Input can be obtained from the metafile, using the GKSM input functions, only when the GKSM input workstation is open. All other control functions will cause error number 33 ("Specified workstation is of category GKSM input") to be generated.

The GKSM output workstation and the GKSM input workstation only have a very limited workstation description table. Since the characteristics of these workstations are completely specified by the workstation interface of the GKS standard, they cannot vary from one installation to the other.

Conceptionally the GKSM output workstation is a output type workstation which is equipped with everything. It is capable of both VECTOR and RASTER output, the device coordinate units are METRES, and the display area size is undefined (limited by the NDC range). The deferral mode can be considered to be ASAP (all output effects visible immediately) and implicit regeneration will not occur. The function SET DEFERRAL STATE is valid for a GKSM output workstation; however, it will not create any output on the GKSM, but will set the deferral state of the metafile workstation itself.

11.3 GKSM Output

Output is generated on a GKSM output workstation only as long as it is active, i.e., GKS is in one of the operating states WSAC or SGOP. Figure 11.1 shows the data flow from the application program to the GKSM. (The complete GKS data flow diagram is shown in Figure I.9.2 on page 31).

Three main paths for user data going from the application program to the metafile can be identified in this figure: non-graphical user data, passed directly to the metafile, and graphical output data which is either contained in segments or not.

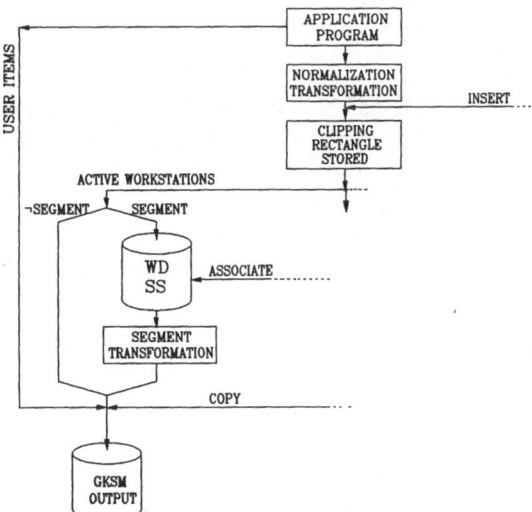

Figure 11.1 Data flow from the application program to the GKS metafile

11.3.1 Non-graphical Data

The user data is passed to the GKSM by a GKS function only applicable to GKSM output workstations. In all other cases error 32 ("Specified workstation is not of category GKSM output") will be generated.

WRITE ITEM TO GKSM   WSAC,SGOP   L0a
Parameters:
  Input   workstation identifier   N
  Input   item type   I
  Input   item data record length   (0..n)   I
  Input   item data record   D
Effect:
  A record containing non-graphical data provided by the application program is written
  to the GKSM. The parameters 'item data record' and 'item data record length' define
  the data to be output whilst 'item type' specifies its type.
N.B.:
  This function will be used only to transfer non-graphical information to the GKSM.
  Graphical data will be sent automatically after GKSM output has been activated.
Errors:
  5   GKS not in proper state: GKS should be either in the state WSAC or in
          the state SGOP
  20   Specified workstation identifier is invalid
  30   Specified workstation is not active
  32   Specified workstation is not of category MO
  160   Item type is not allowed for user items
  161   Item length is invalid

———————————————— *FORTRAN Interface* ————————————————

CALL GWITM (WKID,TYPE,NCHS,LINT,ITEM)
Parameters:
  Input   WKID   workstation identifier   INTEGER
  Input   TYPE   item type   INTEGER
  Input   NCHS   number of significant characters in ITEM   INTEGER
  Input   LINT   item dimension   (1..n)   INTEGER
  Input   ITEM(LINT)   item data record   CHARACTER*80

The WRITE ITEM TO GKSM function will pass non-graphical data to the metafile. Item types >100 are reserved for this purpose. The purpose of this function is to allow user data related to the graphics data to be stored on the same file so that it is convenient to archive and process by the application program. It is recommended that the 'item' should contain a key in its first part identifying the kind of user data stored. In this way, unknown user data items can be identified if the metafile is processed by a different application program or a different system.

11.3.2 Graphical GKSM Output

Output is passed to the GKSM after the normalization transformation has been applied to all geometrical parameters. If clipping is on, the viewport of the selected normalization transformation is stored as a clipping rectangle on the metafile along with the output primitives. The following control functions are recorded on the metafile:

GKS name	FORTRAN name	item created
OPEN WORKSTATION	GOPWK	file header
CLOSE WORKSTATION	GCLWK	end item
CLEAR WORKSTATION	GCLRWK	item no 1
REDRAW ALL SEGMENTS ON WORKSTATION	GRSGWK	item no 2
UPDATE WORKSTATION	GUWK	item no 3
SET DEFERRAL STATE	GSDS	item no 4
MESSAGE	GMSG	item no 5
ESCAPE	GESC	item no 6

The transformation functions:

SET VIEWPORT	GSVP	
SELECT NORMALIZATION TRANSFORMATION	GSELNT	
SET CLIPPING INDICATOR	GSCLIP	

cause a clipping rectangle to be stored on the metafile (item no 61) if the clipping rectangle is changed by one of these functions. This can occur by selecting a normalization transformation with a different viewport while clipping is on, or by changing the viewport of the currently selected normalization transformation while clipping is on. If clipping is turned off, the clipping rectangle on the metafile is set to the NDC range. This is also the default clipping rectangle.

The parameters of the following output primitive functions and attribute setting functions will be recorded on the GKSM:

GKS name	FORTRAN name	item created
POLYLINE	GPL	item no 11
POLYMARKER	GPM	item no 12
TEXT	GTX	item no 13
FILL AREA	GFA	item no 14
CELL ARRAY	GCA	item no 15
GENERALIZED DRAWING PRIMITIVE	GGDP	item no 16
SET POLYLINE INDEX	GSPLI	item no 21
SET LINETYPE	GSLN	item no 22
SET LINEWIDTH SCALE FACTOR	GSLWSC	item no 23
SET POLYLINE COLOUR INDEX	GSPLCI	item no 24
SET POLYMARKER INDEX	GSPMI	item no 25
SET MARKER TYPE	GSMK	item no 26
SET MARKER SIZE SCALE FACTOR	GSMKSC	item no 27
SET POLYMARKER COLOUR INDEX	GSPMCI	item no 28
SET TEXT INDEX	GSTXI	item no 29
SET TEXT FONT AND PRECISION	GSTXFP	item no 30
SET CHARACTER EXPANSION FACTOR	GSCHXP	item no 31
SET CHARACTER SPACING	GSCHSP	item no 32
SET TEXT COLOUR INDEX	GSTXCI	item no 33

SET CHARACTER HEIGHT	GSCHH	item no 34
SET CHARACTER UP VECTOR	GSCHUP	item no 34
SET TEXT PATH	GSTXP	item no 35
SET TEXT ALIGNMENT	GSTXAL	item no 36
SET FILL AREA INDEX	GSFAI	item no 37
SET FILL AREA INTERIOR STYLE	GSFAIS	item no 38
SET FILL AREA STYLE INDEX	GSFASI	item no 39
SET FILL AREA COLOUR INDEX	GSFACI	item no 40
SET PATTERN SIZE	GSPA	item no 41
SET PATTERN REFERENCE POINT	GSPARF	item no 42
SET ASPECT SOURCE FLAGS	GSASF	item no 43
SET PICK IDENTIFIER	GSPKID	item no 44

Since the NDC values of the character up vector, the pattern size and the pattern reference point may change when the functions SET WINDOW, SET VIEWPORT or SELECT NORMALISATION TRANSFORMATION are called, these functions will also send items no. 34, 41 and 42 to the metafile.

The following workstation attribute functions are recorded if the addressed workstation is the GKSM output workstation:

GKS name	FORTRAN name	item created
SET POLYLINE REPRESENTATION	GSPLR	item no 51
SET POLYMARKER REPRESENTATION	GSPMR	item no 52
SET TEXT REPRESENTATION	GSPMR	item no 53
SET FILL AREA REPRESENTATION	GSFAR	item no 54
SET PATTERN REPRESENTATION	GSPAR	item no 55
SET COLOUR REPRESENTATION	GSCR	item no 56
SET WORKSTATION WINDOW	GSWKWN	item no 71
SET WORKSTATION VIEWPORT	GSWKVP	item no 72

11.3.3 Segment Functions

Some segment functions are simply recorded on the metafile. As can be seen from Figure 11.1, other functions are evaluated before they are recorded there. All segment functions related to the workstation-dependent segment storage (present in GKS output level 1) are recorded on the metafile, whereas the segment functions which make use of the workstation-independent segment storage (present only in output level 2) are evaluated. Their recorded segment functions are:

GKS name	FORTRAN name	item created
CREATE SEGMENT	GCRSG	item no 81
CLOSE SEGMENT	GCLSG	item no 82
RENAME SEGMENT	GRENSG	item no 83
DELETE SEGMENT	GDSG	item no 84

DELETE SEGMENT FROM WORKSTATION (GKSM)	GDSGWK	item no 84
SET SEGMENT TRANSFORMATION	GSSGT	item no 91
SET VISIBILITY	GSVIS	item no 92
SET HIGHLIGHTING	GSHLIT	item no 93
SET SEGMENT PRIORITY	GSSGP	item no 94
SET DETECTABILITY	GSDTEC	item no 95

The DELETE SEGMENT FROM WORKSTATION function will cause item no 84 to be written to the GKSM only if the workstation addressed by the function is the GKSM output workstation. The evaluated segment functions are:

ASSOCIATE SEGMENT WITH WORKSTATION (GKSM)	GASGWK
COPY SEGMENT TO WORKSTATION (GKSM)	GCSGWK
INSERT SEGMENT	GINSG

When the ASSOCIATE SEGMENT WITH WORKSTATION function is used in connection with a GKSM output workstation, it causes all those functions to be recorded on the metafile which have called to build the segment. The effect is the same as if the GKSM output workstation had been active at the time the segment was created, i.e., between CREATE SEGMENT and CLOSE SEGMENT. Thus, the sequence of recorded items will comprise CREATE SEGMENT (item no 81), output primitives, clipping, attribute functions, segment attribute functions, and CLOSE SEGMENT (item no 82).

The COPY SEGMENT TO WORKSTATION function will record the output contained in a segment and send it to the metafile. Only output primitive functions, clipping, and attribute functions will be recorded. Just like other workstations, COPY SEGMENT TO WORKSTATION uses the clipping rectangle which was in effect when the primitives in the segment were created.

INSERT SEGMENT behaves in much the same way as COPY, except for the way clipping is dealt with and the additional INSERT transformation. INSERT will apply the INSERT transformation to the geometrical information contained in the segment, then use the clipping that is in effect when INSERT takes place, and then will send the clipping rectangle and the transformed contents of the segment to the GKSM. If a segment is open when INSERT happens, the inserted output primitives and their attributes will be collected in the open segment (all output type workstations are treated in this way).

Table 11.1 summarizes the GKS functions which cause items to be written to the GKS metafile.

Example 11.1   GKSM output

All existing segments are copied from the workstation-independent segment storage to the GKSM. The segment structure will be recorded on the GKSM. A procedure SAVPIC is used to copy the segments. Both the workstation-independent segment storage and the output metafile have to be OPEN when the procedure is called. The GKSM will be activated and deactivated within the procedure.

Table 11.1 GKS functions causing items to be recorded on the GKSM

GKS functions which apply to GKSM output	FORTRAN name	GKSM item or effect
OPEN WORKSTATION (GKSM-OUT,...)	GOPWK	—(file header) 1
CLOSE WORKSTATION (GKSM-OUT)	GCLWK	0 (end item)
ACTIVATE WORKSTATION (GKSM-OUT	GACWK	enable output
DEACTIVATE WORKSTATION (GKSM-OUT)	GDAWK	disable output
CLEAR WORKSTATION (GKSM-OUT,...)	GCLRWK	1
REDRAW ALL SEGMENTS ON WORKSTATION (GKSM-OUT)	GRSGWK	2
UPDATE WORKSTATION (GKSM-OUT,...)	GUWK	3
SET DEFERRAL STATE (GKSM-OUT,...)	GSDS	4
MESSAGE (GKSM-OUT),...	GMSG	5 (message)
ESCAPE	GESC	6
POLYLINE	GPL	11 (output
POLYMARKER	GPM	12 primitives)
TEXT	GTX	13
FILL AREA	GFA	14
CELL ARRAY	GCA	15
GENERALIZED DRAWING PRIMITIVE	GGDP	16
SET POLYLINE INDEX	GSPLI	21 (attributes
SET LINETYPE	GSLN	22 for output
SET LINEWIDTH SCALE FACTOR	GSLWSC	23 primitives)
SET POLYLINE COLOUR INDEX	GSPLCI	24
SET POLYMARKER INDEX	GSPMI	25
SET MARKER TYPE	GSMK	26
SET MARKER SIZE SCALE FACTOR	GSMKSC	27
SET POLYMARKER COLOUR INDEX	GSPMCI	28
SET TEXT INDEX	GSTXI	29
SET TEXT FONT AND PRECISION	GSTXFP	30
SET CHARACTER EXPANSION FACTOR	GSCHXP	31
SET CHARACTER SPACING	GSCHSP	32
SET TEXT COLOUR INDEX	GSTXCI	33
SET CHARACTER HEIGHT	GSCHH	34
SET CHARACTER UP VECTOR	GSCHUP	34
SET TEXT PATH	GSTXP	35
SET TEXT ALIGNMENT	GSTXAL	36
SET FILL AREA INDEX	GSFAI	37
SET FILL AREA INTERIOR STYLE	GSFAIS	38
SET FILL AREA STYLE INDEX	GSFASI	39
SET FILL AREA COLOUR INDEX	GSFACI	40
SET PATTERN SIZE	GSPA	41
SET PATTERN REFERENCE POINT	GSPARF	42
SET ASPECT SOURCE FLAGS	GSASF	43
SET PICK IDENTIFIER	GSPKID	44
The following functions, if applied to the workstation GKSM Output:		

Table 11.1 (continued)

GKS functions which apply to GKSM output	FORTRAN name	GKSM item or effect
SET POLYLINE REPRESENTATION	GSPLR	51 (workstation
SET POLYMARKER REPRESENTATION	GSPMR	52 attributes)
SET TEXT REPRESENTATION	GSTXR	53
SET FILL AREA REPRESENTATION	GSFAR	54
SET PATTERN REPRESENTATION	GSPAR	55
SET COLOUR REPRESENTATION	GSCR	56
SET WORKSTATION WINDOW .	GSWKWN	71
SET WORKSTATION VIEWPORT	GSWKVP	72
SET WINDOW of current normalization transformation	GSWN	34, 41, 42
SET VIEWPORT of current normalization transformation	GSVP	61 (clipping rect-angle), 34, 41, 42
SELECT NORMALIZATION TRANSFORMATION	GSELNT	61, 34, 41, 42
SET CLIPPING INDICATOR	GSCLIP	61
CREATE SEGMENT	GCRSG	81 (segment
CLOSE SEGMENT	GCLSG	82 mani-
RENAME SEGMENT	GRENSG	83 pulation)
DELETE SEGMENT	GDSG	84
DELETE SEGMENT FROM WORKSTATION (GKSM-OUT)	GDSGWK	84
ASSOCIATE SEGMENT WITH WORKSTATION (GKSM-OUT)	GASGWK	81, 91-95, (21-44, 11-16, 61), 82
COPY SEGMENT TO WORKSTATION	GCSGWK	(21-44, 11-16, 61)
INSERT SEGMENT	GINSG	(21-44, 11-16, 61)
SET SEGMENT TRANSFORMATION	GSSGT	91 (segment
SET VISIBILITY	GSVIS	92 attributes)
SET HIGHLIGHTING	GSHLIT	93
SET SEGMENT PRIORITY	GSSGP	94
SET DETECTABILITY	GSDTEC	95
WRITE ITEM TO GKSM	GWITM	>100

———————————————— *Pascal* ————————————————

```
L10   procedure SAVPIC(gksm_out:string);
                                            {gksm_out is GKSM identifier}
L20   var  i,ierror,nsegs: integer;
L30      segnames: array[1..250] of integer;
L31   begin
                                            {route output to GKSM output}
L40   ACTIVATE_WORKSTATION (gksm_out);
                                            {get all segments' names}
L50   INQUIRE_SET_OF_SEGMENT_NAMES_IN_USE
         (ierror,nsegs,segnames);
```

L60   **for** i: = 1 **to** nsegs **do** {for all segments copy the segment and its contents}
L70   ASSOCIATE_SEGMENT_WITH_WORKSTATION
                (gksm_out,segnames[i]);
L80   **end**;
L90   DEACTIVATE_WORKSTATION (gksm_out);

If, in this example, the segment structure is not to be recorded on the metafile, the ASSOCIATE SEGMENT function has to be replaced by the COPY SEGMENT function. In this case, the metafile will contain an unstructured picture.

--- *Fortran* ---

```
L10            SUBROUTINE SAVPIC (GKSMID)
     C                              ***copies all segments to GKSM via GKSMID
L20            INTEGER NSEGS,GKSMID,IERROR,I
L30            INTEGER SEGNAM(250)
     C                              ***ACTIVATE, INQUIRE segments
L40            CALL GACWK(GKSMID)
L50            CALL GQSGUS(1,IERROR,NSEGS,SEGNAM)
     C                    ***test if error or too many segments for array SEGNAM
L51            IF (IERROR) 52,52,55
L52      52    WRITE(6,1000) IERROR
L53    1000    FORMAT('ERROR NO',I3, 'IN SAVPIC')
L54            RETURN
L55      55    IF (NSEGS.LE.250) GOTO 60
L56            WRITE(6,2000) NSEGS
L57    2000    FORMAT('NO OF SEGMENTS IN SAVPIC=',I3,'>250')
L58            NSEGS=250
     C                              ***send segments to GKSM
L60      60    DO 71 I=1,NSEGS
L61            CALL GQSGUS(I,IERROR,NSEGS,SEGNAM(I))
L70            CALL GASGWK(GKSMID,SEGNAM(I))
L71      71    CONTINUE
     C                              ***DEACTIVATE metafile
L80            CALL GDAWK(GKSMID)
L81            RETURN
L90            END
```

11.4   GKSM Input

Data can be retrieved from a GKS metafile by special GKS functions valid only in connection with an open GKSM input workstation. These functions cause the data in the metafile to be passed to the application program in a data record. Then the data record can be passed back to GKS for interpretation. The interpretation of a GKSM item will normally have the same effect as the function which caused the GKSM item to be recorded. The interpretation of primitive attributes, clipping rectangle or clipping indicator causes appro-

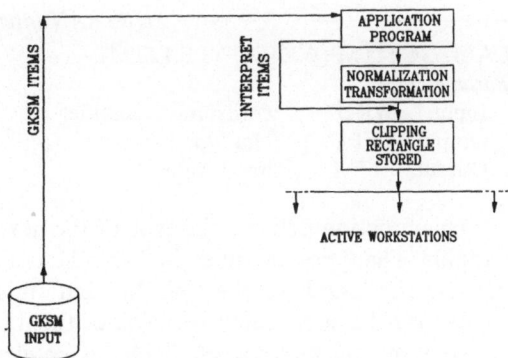

Figure 11.2 Data flow for GKSM input

priate changes to the GKS state list. The data flow from the GKSM to the application program is shown in Figure 11.2.

When output primitives are interpreted, they are not subject to any normalization transformation. The current primitive attributes from the GKS state list are bound to them. The interpretation of geometric attributes will use the currently selected normalization transformation to convert the values back into world coordinates. These values will be entered in the GKS state list. The interpretation of the character vectors will not only set the 'current character up vector' and the 'current character base vector' in the GKS state list, but also the 'current character height' and the 'current character width'. These values are derived from the lengths of the transformed character vectors. The interpretation of the clipping rectangle item sets both the 'clipping rectangle' entry in the GKS state list to its respective values and also the 'clipping indicator' entry to CLIP.

After the GKSM input workstation has been opened, the following functions can be used to retrieve data from the metafile:

GET ITEM TYPE FROM GKSM   WSAC,SGOP,SGOP   L0a

Parameters:

Input	workstation identifier		N
Output	item type		I
Output	item data record length	(0..n)	I

Effect:

GKS inspects the type of the next record and its length in the GKSM and returns type and length back to the application program.

Errors:

7	GKS not proper state: GKS should be in one of the states WSOP, WSAC or SGOP
20	Specified workstation identifier is invalid
25	Specified workstation is not open
34	Specified workstation is not of category MI
162	No record is left in GKS metafile input
163	Metafile item is invalid

———————————————— *FORTRAN Interface* ————————————————

CALL GGTITM (WKID,TYPE,LITM)

Parameters:

Input	WKID	workstation identifier		INTEGER
Output	TYPE	item type		INTEGER
Output	LITM	item length	(0..n)	INTEGER

This function delivers the type of the next item on the metafile in an integer variable. The types are given in Table 11.1. Together with the type, the function delivers the length of the GKSM item; this is the length of the data record needed for the subsequent retrieval of the item. In FORTRAN, the item length is given by the number of 80 character elements needed for the item. After the GET ITEM TYPE function has been called, the item itself can be retrieved from the GKSM by the READ ITEM function:

READ ITEM FROM GKSM		WSAC,SGOP L0a

Parameters:

Input	workstation identifier		N
Input	maximum length of item data record	(0..n)	I
Output	item data record		D

Effect:

GKS returns the next item on the GKSM back to the application program. If its data record length is greater than the maximum length specified, excess parts of the item are lost.

N.B.:

By specifying 'maximum item data record length'=0, the next item can be skipped without reading.

Errors:

7	GKS not in proper state: GKS should be in one of the states WSOP, WSAC or SGOP
20	Specified workstation identifier is invalid
25	Specified workstation is not open
34	Specified workstation is not of category MI
162	No record is left in GKS metafile input
163	Metafile item is invalid
165	Content of item data record is invalid for the specified item type
166	Maximum item data record length is invalid

———————————————— *FORTRAN Interface* ————————————————

CALL GRDITM (WKID,ITMAX,LMAX,ITEM)

Parameters:

Input	WKID	workstation identifier		INTEGER
Input	ITMAX	maximum item data record length		INTEGER
Input	LMAX	dimension of item data record	(0..n)	INTEGER
Output	ITEM(LMAX)	item data record		CHARACTER*80

If the application program wishes to ignore (skip) an item on the metafile, this can be done by specifying an item data record length of zero. After the application program has recognized the item type and has retrieved the item itself in a data record (CHARACTER*80 array in FORTRAN), it can choose to perform any calculations it wishes. In particular, user records can be dealt with exclusively by the application program. However, if the format of the GKSM is known to the application program, it could also extract the information from the graphical GKSM items and inspect or modify them. Normally though, the graphical GKSM items will be passed back to GKS for interpretation. The GKS function used for this purpose is the INTERPRET ITEM function:

INTERPRET ITEM   GKOP,WSOP,WSAC,SGOP   L0a

Parameters:

Input	item type		I
Input	item data record length	(0..n)	I
Input	item data record		D

Effect:

The item is interpreted. The effect normally will be the same as if the function which generated the GKSM item were invoked again. Functions used to control the output workstation while creating the metafile are applied to all active workstations. Attribute items, referring to attributes stored in the GKS state list, will not change the GKS state list. However, they will be used for interpreting subsequent primitive items on the metafile.

N.B.:

Apart from errors noted below, other GKS errors may occur as a result of interpreting the item.

Errors:

7	GKS not in proper state: GKS should be in one of the states WSOP, WSAC or SGOP
161	Item length is invalid
163	Metafile item is invalid
164	Item type is not a valid GKS item
165	Content of item data record is invalid for the specified item type
167	User item cannot be interpreted

――――――――――――――― *FORTRAN Interface* ―――――――――――――――

CALL GIITM (TYPE,LITM,ITEM)

Parameters:

Input	TYPE	item type		INTEGER
Input	LITM	item data record dimension	(0..n)	INTEGER
Input	ITEM(LITM)	item data record		CHARACTER*80

Table 11.2 lists the functions which are internally called by GKSM items. There is a one-to-one correspondence between metafile items and GKS functions. However, three special cases should be noted:

— Output primitives are not transformed by the currently selected normalization transformation. Since the coordinates of the items stored on the metafile are already in NDC units, they do not need to be normalized again during interpretation. Thus, the normalization transformation which was in effect when the GKSM was written in is applied to them. These functions are marked "(b)" in Table 11.2.

Table 11.2   GKS functions called for interpretation of GKSM items

metafile item	resulting GKS functions by INTERPRET ITEM	
— (file header)	interpretation parameters set	
0 (end item)	condition for error 'no record left in GKSM input' set	
1	CLEAR WORKSTATION	(a)
2	REDRAW ALL SEGMENTS ON WORKST.	(a)
3	UPDATE	(a)
4	SET DEFERRAL STATE	(a)
5 (message)	MESSAGE	(a)
6	ESCAPE	
11 (output	POLYLINE	(b)
12 primitives)	POLYMARKER	(b)
13	TEXT	(b)
14	FILL AREA	(b)
15	CELL ARRAY	(b)
16	GENERALIZED DRAWING PRIMITIVE	(b)
21 (attributes	SET POLYLINE INDEX	
22 for output	SET LINETYPE	
23 primitives)	SET LINEWIDTH SCALE FACTOR	
24	SET POLYLINE COLOUR INDEX	
25	SET POLYMARKER INDEX	
26	SET MARKER TYPE	
27	SET MARKER SIZE SCALE FACTOR	
28	SET POLYMARKER COLOUR INDEX	
29	SET TEXT INDEX	
30	SET TEXT FONT AND PRECISION	
31	SET CHARACTER EXPANSION FACTOR	
32	SET CHARACTER SPACING	
33	SET TEXT COLOUR INDEX	
34	(SET CHARACTER HEIGHT and	(c)
	SET CHARACTER UP VECTOR)	(c)
35	SET TEXT PATH	
36	SET TEXT ALIGNMENT	
37	SET FILL AREA INDEX	
38	SET FILL AREA INTERIOR STYLE	
39	SET FILL AREA STYLE INDEX	
40	SET FILL AREA COLOUR INDEX	
41	(SET PATTERN SIZE)	(c)
42	SET PATTERN REFERENCE POINT	
43	SET ASPECT SOURCE FLAGS	
44	SET PICK IDENTIFIER	
51 (workstation	SET POLYLINE REPRESENTATION	(a)
52 attributes)	SET POLYMARKER REPRESENTATION	(a)
53	SET TEXT REPRESENTATION	(a)

Table 11.2 (continued)

metafile item	resulting GKS functions by INTERPRET ITEM	
54	SET FILL AREA REPRESENTATION	(a)
55	SET PATTERN REPRESENTATION	(a)
56	SET COLOUR REPRESENTATION	(a)
61 (clipping rectangle)	(SET VIEWPORT)	(c)
71 (workstation	SET WORKSTATION WINDOW	(a)
72 transformation)	SET WORKSTATION VIEWPORT	(a)
81 (segment	CREATE SEGMENT	
82 mani-	CLOSE SEGMENT	
83 pulation)	RENAME SEGMENT	
84	DELETE SEGMENT	
91 (segment	SET SEGMENT TRANSFORMATION	
92 attributes)	SET VISIBILITY	
93	SET HIGHLIGHTING	
94	SET SEGMENT PRIORITY	
95	SET DETECTABILITY	

— All items containing workstation attribute settings cause the corresponding attribute setting function to be executed for all active workstations. In this way, attribute bundles, the deferral state, and the workstation transformation can be stored on the metafile. During interpretation, the items are used to set the workstation attributes of the workstations on which the metafile contents are displayed. These functions are marked "(a)" in Table 11.2.

— Character height and width, character up and character base vector, clipping rectangle, and pattern size correspond to GKS state list entries rather than to GKS functions. These items are marked "(c)". The GKS functions listed are the ones which change the respective GKS state list entries.

Normally, the application program will pass the graphical items obtained by the READ ITEM function to the INTERPRET ITEM function without touching them. No GKS rule will be violated, however, if the items are modified, e.g. if the attribute values are changed or if transformations are applied to the coordinates of the primitives. The application program can even generate GKSM items by itself without reading them from any GKSM input workstation. In these cases, the application program makes use of information which is not contained in the GKS standard, but defined by the implementation. It is, therefore, a good idea for implementors to use the GKSM format in Appendix E of the GKS document, at least until the CGM metafile extension standard is defined.

Example 11.2   GKSM input

The GETPIC procedure will read a GKSM and display it at an output workstation. Only output primitive items, attribute items and segment items will be
interpreted. If a new picture starts (CLEAR WORKSTATION item), the program will wait for a CHOICE obtained by the REQUEST CHOICE input
function before continuing to process the metafile. The output workstation
must be OPEN but INACTIVE when the procedure is called. The input metafile
workstation is opened and closed by the procedure itself.

———————————————————— *Pascal* ————————————————————

```
L10    procedure GETPIC(gk_file:file of char,display:string);
                                          {read GKSM from file gk_file and}
                                          {display it on workstation display}
L20    const gksm_in='GKSM_IN';           {name for GKSM input workstation}
L30    var type,length,ch_no: integer;
L40      item: string[1..1000];                    {string to hold GKSM item}
L50      none: string[1..1];
L60    begin
                                                      {Open metafile input}
                                          {assume ws-type 1 = GKSM input}
L70      OPEN_WORKSTATION (gksm_in,gk_file,1);
                                                   {display output on display}
L80      ACTIVATE_WORKSTATION (display);
L90      repeat                              {until end of GKSM input}
                                          {get type and length of item}
L100       GET_ITEM_TYPE_FROM_GKSM (gksm_in,type,length);
L110       if type=1 then                     {CLEAR WORKSTATION item}
L120       begin
                                          {wait for any CHOICE or break}
L130         REQUEST_CHOICE (display,1,status,ch_no);
                                                          {skip item}
L140         READ_ITEM_FROM_GKSM (gksm_in,0,none);
L150       end;
L160       else if type> =11 and type< =95 then
L170       begin                 {output primitive, attribute or segment item}
                                          {READ and INTERPRET item}
L180         READ_ITEM_FROM_GKSM (gksm_in,length,item);
L190         INTERPRET_ITEM (type,length,item);
L200       end;
L210       else
                                                          {skip item}
L220         READ_ITEM_FROM_GKSM (gksm_in,0,none);
L230     until type=0;                                      {end record}
                                          {DEACTIVATE output workstation}
L240     DEACTIVATE_WORKSTATION (display);
                                                   {CLOSE input metafile}
L250     CLOSE_WORKSTATION (gksm_in);
L260 end;
```

─────────────────────────────── *Fortran* ───────────────────────────────

```
L10            SUBROUTINE GETPIC(FILNO,DISID)
     C                        *** reads GKSM via file no FILNO and displays it on
     C                                    *** workstation with identifier DISID
L30            INTEGER STATUS,CHNO,LENGTH,FILNO,GKSMID,
               DISID,TYPE
L40            CHARACTER*80 ITEM(250)
L20            GKSMID=777
     C                                        *** OPEN input metafile
L70            CALL GOPWK(GKSMID,FILNO,1)
     C                                        *** ACTIVATE display
L80            CALL GACWK(DISID)
     C                                        *** DO UNTIL end record
L90      90    CONTINUE
L100           CALL GGTITM(GKSMID,TYPE,LENGTH)
     C                                        *** test if item too long
L101              IF (LENGTH.LE.250) GOTO 110
L102                 WRITE (6,2000) LENGTH
L103     2000        FORMAT('ITEM LENGTH IN GETPIC=',I4,'>250')
L104                 GOTO 220
     C                                    *** CLEAR WORKSTATION item?
L110     110   IF (TYPE.NE.1) GOTO 160
     C                                        *** wait for CHOICE
L130              CALL GRQCH (DISID,1,STATUS,CHNO)
L131              GOTO 220
     C                            *** output, attribute or segment item?
L160     160   IF (TYPE.LT.11.OR.TYPE.GT.95) GOTO 210
     C                                    *** READ and INTERPRET item
L180              CALL GRDITM(GKSMID,250,LENGTH,ITEM)
L190              CALL GIITM(TYPE,LENGTH,ITEM)
L191              GOTO 230
L210     210   CONTINUE
     C                                            *** skip item
L220     220   CALL GRDITM(GKSMID,0,LENGTH,ITEM)
L230     230   IF (TYPE.NE.0) GOTO 90
     C                                        *** DEACTIVATE display
L240           CALL GDAWK(DISID)
     C                                        *** CLOSE input metafile
L250           CALL GCLWK(GKSMID)
L251           RETURN
L260           END
```

11.5 Program Examples

The following two examples demonstrate how the state of a GKS session can be saved and restored. In Example 11.3, a subroutine SAVEGK is used to save the current state of an interactive GKS session on an output metafile. In Example 11.4, the subroutine RESTGK restores the state of the session

from the metafile. The two examples make use of the subroutines SAVPIC and GETPIC in the Examples 11.1 and 11.2 (pages 411 and 418). It is assumed that the workstation-independent segment storage was active during the session which is to be saved, and that one workstation was used for output and input (its reference is the workstation identifier DISID). When saving and restoring the state of the session two sets of information have to be considered:
— the workstation state of the interactive workstation;
— the segments currently in existence and the primitives and attributes contained therein.

In the subroutine SAVEGK the workstation state is determined and then sent to the GKSM output workstation. Then all the segments together with the primitives and attributes inside them are sent to the GKSM output workstation by calling subroutine SAVPIC. The subroutine RESTGK calls GETPIC which uses the READ and INTERPRET functions to restore the workstation state of the display workstation and to recreate segments. The GKS state list values will be restored to the values present at saving time.

Example 11.3   Save state

———————————————————— *Pascal* ————————————————————

```
L10   procedure SAVEGK (disid:string;mfile:file of char);
                              {disid is the workstation identifier of the interactive}
                              {workstation, mfile the metafile}
L20   const gksm_out='GKSM_OUT';
L30   type dmode=(ASAP,BNIL,BNIG,ASTI);
L31      imode=(SUPPRESSED,ALLOWED);
L32      nframe=(YES,NO);
L33      surf=(EMPTY,NOTEMPTY);
L34      ustate=(PENDING,NOTPENDING);
L35      vtype=(SET,REALIZED);
L40   var err_ind,nind,i,ltype,cind:integer;
L41      lwidth:real;
L42      dm:dmode;
L43      im:imode;
L44      nf:nframe;
L45      em:surf;
L46      us:ustate;
L50      list: array[1..250] of integer;
L60      rww,cww,rwv,cwv:array[1..4] of real;
L70   begin
                              {OPEN metafile output, assume output metafile has type 2}
L80   OPEN_WORKSTATION (gksm_out,mfile,2);
L90   ACTIVATE_WORKSTATION (gksm_out);    {output routed to GKSM output}
                              {get deferral mode and implicit regeneration mode}
L100  INQUIRE_WORKSTATION_DEFERRAL_AND_UPDATE_STATES
         (disid,err_ind,dm,im,em,nf);
L110  SET_DEFERRAL_STATE (gksm_out,dm,im);        {send the modes to metafile}
```

```
                                                {get workstation transformation}
L120  INQUIRE_WORKSTATION_TRANSFORMATION
          (disid,us,rww,cww,rwv,cwv);
                                    {send current transformation to the metafile}
L130  SET_WORKSTATION_WINDOW (gksm_out,cww);
L140  SET_WORKSTATION_VIEWPORT (gksm_out,cwv);
                                                      {get polyline indices}
L150  INQUIRE_LIST_OF_POLYLINE_INDICES (disid,err_ind,nind,list);
L160  for i: = 1 to nind do                          {for all POLYLINE indices}
L161  begin
                                                     {get polyline bundle}
L170     INQUIRE_POLYLINE_REPRESENTATION
             (disid,list[i],set,err_ind,ltype,lwidth,cind);
                                                  {send bundle to metafile}
L180     SET_POLYLINE_REPRESENTATION
             (gksm_out,list[i], ltype,lwidth,cind);
L190  end;
                               {repeat lines L150 through L190 for POLYMARKER,
                                            TEXT, FILL AREA bundles}
                               {and for PATTERN and COLOUR tables}
L200  DEACTIVATE_WORKSTATION (gksm_out);
L210  SAVPIC (gksm_out);                    {now call SAVPIC to save segments}
L220  CLOSE_WORKSTATION (gksm_out);              {CLOSE output metafile}
L230  CLOSE_WORKSTATION (disid);            {CLOSE interactive workstation}
L240  end;
```

——————————————————— *Fortran* ———————————————————

```
L10          SUBROUTINE SAVEGK (DISID,MFILE)
      C                      ***stores state of workstation DISID on the MFILE
L20          INTEGER GKSMID
L21          DATA GKSMID/777/
L40          INTEGER MFILE,DISID,I,ERRIND,NIND,LTYPE,CIND
L41          INTEGER D,M,IM,EM,NF,US
L50          INTEGER LIST(250)
L60          REAL RWINDO(4),CWINDO(4),RVIEWP(4),CVIEWP(4)
      C                              *** OPEN and ACTIVATE output metafile
L80          CALL GOPWK(GKSMID,MFILE,2)
L90          CALL GACWK(GKSMID)
      C                         *** get workstation state and send it to GKSM
L100         CALL GQWKDU(DISID,ERRIND,DM,IM,EM,NF)
L110         CALL GSDS(GKSMID,DM,IM)
      C                         *** get and send workstation transformation
L120         CALL GQWKT(DISID,ERRIND,US,RWINDO,CWINDO,
           +   RVIEWP,CVIEWP)
L130         CALL GSWKWN(GKSMID,CWINDO(1),CWINDO(2),
           +   CWINDO(3),CWINDO(4))
L140         CALL GSWKVP(GKSMID,CVIEWP(1),CVIEWP(2),
           +   CVIEWP(3),CVIEWP(4))
      C                                      *** get polyline indices
L150         CALL GQEPLI(DISID,1,ERRIND,NIND,LIST)
```

```
L160               DO 190 I=1,NIND
      C                                    *** get and send all POLYLINE bundles
L165               CALL GQPLI(DISID,I,ERRIND,NIND,LIST(I))
L170               CALL GQPLR(DISID,LIST(I),0,ERRIND,LTYPE,
          +          LWIDTH,CIND)
L180               CALL GSPLR(GKSMID,LIST(I),LTYPE,LWIDTH,CIND)
L190      190      CONTINUE
      C        .
      C        .               *** repeat lines L150 through L190 for POLYMARKER,
      C        .                            *** TEXT, FILL AREA bundles
      C        .                    *** and for PATTERN and COLOUR tables
      C        .
      C        .                                   *** DEACTIVATE metafile
L200               CALL GDAWK(GKSMID)
      C                                        *** call SAVPIC to save segments
L210               CALL SAVPIC(GKSMID)
      C                                              *** CLOSE metafile
L220               CALL GCLWK(GKSMID)
      C                                        *** CLOSE output workstation
L230               CALL GCLWK(DISID)
L231               RETURN
L240               END
```

Example 11.4   Restore state

―――――――――――――――― *Pascal* ――――――――――――――――

```
L10   procedure RESTGK (disid:string;dfile,mfile:file of char);
                          {disid is the workstation identifier and dfile the file}
                          {identifier for the interactive workstation. mfile is the}
                          {file identifier for the metafile}
L20   begin
                                    {OPEN the interactive workstation}
                                    {assume it has type 5}
L30   OPEN_WORKSTATION (disid,dfile,5);
                                    {now call GETPIC to restore state}
L40   GETPIC (mfile,disid);
                                    {ACTIVATE interactive workstation}
L50   ACTIVATE_WORKSTATION (disid);
L60   end;
```

―――――――――――――――― *Fortran* ――――――――――――――――

```
L10               SUBROUTINE RESTGK (DISID, MFILE)
      C           *** restores the state of workstation DISID from
      C           *** metafile. DISID: workstation identifier
      C           *** DFILE: file number of interactive workstation
      C           *** MFILE: file number of input metafile
L11               INTEGER MFILE,DISID,DFILE
      C                                        *** OPEN interactive workstation
L30               CALL GOPWK(DISID,DFILE,5)
      C                                        *** call GETPIC to restore state
```

L40	CALL GETPIC(MFILE,DISID)	
C		*** ACTIVATE interactive workstation
L50	CALL GACWK(DISID)	
L51	RETURN	
L60	END	

Example 11.5   User item

In this example a user item is used to store the current normalization transformation on the metafile. When reading the metafile back into GKS, these values can be used to restore the values in the GKS state list. In this way, Examples 11.3 and 11.4 could be extended. Appropriate program parts would have to be inserted after line L210 in Example 11.2 and before line L200 in Example 11.3.

──────────────── *Pascal* ────────────────

{Definitions and declarations:}

L10	**type** trans = **record** key :**string** [1 .. 8]; trans_no :**integer**;
L11	window,viewport: **array** [1 .. 4] **of real**;
L12	**end**;
L20	**var** ct :trans;

{Storing the normalization transformation:}
{insert before line L200 in example 11.3, page 421}
{get normalization transformation}

L30	INQUIRE_CURRENT_NORMALIZATION_TRANSFORMATION_
	NUMBER (err_ind,ct.trans_no);
L40	INQUIRE_NORMALIZATION_TRANSFORMATION
	(ct.trans_no,err_ind,ct.window,ct.viewport);

{use the string variable as key for identifying the user item}

L50	ct.key = 'NORMTRAN';

{send user item to GKSM, item type = 177, length = 44
(implementation-dependent)}

L60	WRITE_ITEM_TO_GKSM (gksm_out,177,44,ct);

{Retrieving the user item from the metafile:}
{insert after line L200 in example 11.2, page 418}

L30	**else if** type = 177 **then**	{user item type 177}
L40	**begin**	
L50	READ_ITEM_FROM_GKSM (gksm_in,44,ct);	{read item into record}
L60	**if** ct.key = 'NORMTRAN' **then**	{test correct key}
L70	**begin**	
L80	SET_WINDOW (ct.trans_no,ct.window);	

{set WINDOW and VIEWPORT}

L90	SET_VIEWPORT (ct.trans_no,ct.viewport);	
L100	SELECT_NORMALIZATION_TRANSFORMATION (ct.trans_no);	

{select transformation}

L110	**end**;
L120	**end**;

──────────────── *Fortran* ────────────────

L10	REAL WIN(4),VIEW(4)
L11	INTEGER NO
L13	CHARACTER*80 CT(2)

```
        C        *** Storing the normalization transformation:
        C        *** insert before line L200 in example 11.3, page 422
        C                                        *** get normalization transformation
L30              CALL GQNTN(ERRIND,NO)
L40              CALL GQNT(NO,ERRIND,WIN,VIEW)
        C                                        *** store key and transformation in record
L50              WRITE(CT(1),'(A8,I4,4E14.7)')'NORMTRAN',NO,WIN
L51              WRITE(CT(2),'(4E14.7)')VIEW
        C        *** send user item to GKSM, item type=177, length=2×80 characters
L60              CALL GWITM(GKSM_OUT,177,2,80,CT)


        C        *** Retrieving the user item from the metafile:
        C        *** insert after line L210 in example 11.2, page 419
        C                                                  *** user item 177?
L30              IF (TYPE.NE.177) GOTO 220
        C                                        *** read item into array CT
L50               CALL GRDITM(GKSMID,2,LENGTH,CT)
        C                                        *** test correct length and key
L60              IF (LENGTH.NE.2) GOTO 220
L61              READ(CT(1),'(8X,I4,4E14.7)')NO,WIN
L62              READ(CT(2),'(4E14.7)')VIEW
L63              IF (CT(1)(1:8).NE.'NORMTRAN') GOTO 220
        C                                        *** set WINDOW and VIEWPORT
L80              CALL GSWN(NO,WIN)
L90              CALL GSVP(NO,VIEW)
L100             CALL GSELNT(NO)
L120     220     CONTINUE
```

11.6   Exercises

Exercise 11.1   Display metafile

Design, realize and test a procedure that reads an input metafile given by a file identifier and displays its contents at an output workstation given by its workstation identifier. All items referring to capabilities not present in GKS level 0a are to be discarded.

Exercise 11.2   Backup copy on metafile

Design, realize and test two procedures for using the metafile as a backup copy of the pictures created at an output workstation. One procedure is to be called after OPEN GKS, the other one before CLOSE GKS. Which deferral state would you choose for the GKSM output workstation and why?

Exercise 11.3   Concatenate metafiles

Design, realize and test a procedure for concatenating two input metafiles and copying them onto one output metafile. All three metafiles are identified by their file identifier. The metafiles may contain user items.

PART IV

GKS-3D

Part IV introduces a set of functions for generating and manipulating three-dimensional (3D) graphics. These functions are part of GKS-3D, a compatible extension of GKS for 3D graphics. GKS-3D has been defined subsequent to GKS standardization and is on the way to reaching the status of an International Standard.

Chapter 1 traces the history of 3D standardization. Chapter 2 gives an overview of GKS-3D. The subsequent Chapters 3—10 are organized like the respective chapters in Part III. They give a detailed introduction to concepts and new functions of GKS-3D. These chapters can serve as a basic reference for the application programmer writing 3D application programs with GKS-3D. Chapter 11 describes how the 2D functions of GKS were embedded into the 3D environment of GKS-3D and points out some of the problems which must be carefully considered by a programmer when mixing 2D and 3D functions. Chapter 12 gives a preview of the next emerging graphics standard, the Programmer's Hierarchical Interactive Graphics Standard (PHIGS), which extends GKS towards more comfortable data structuring and manipulation facilities.

As the process of standardization has not yet been finished at the time of printing, there may be minor differences between this description and the final version of the GKS-3D standard.

1 HISTORY

The real world is three-dimensional. As a consequence, a system drawing images of real world objects on a display surface has to support 3D graphics. When standardization efforts in the field of Computer Graphics began in the years 1974—1977, the primary goal was a standard for 3D graphics. It seemed pointless spending time and effort on 2D graphics when a 3D standard could cover both and a 2D standard could be easily derived from it.

However, an overwhelming majority of applications dealt exclusively with 2D graphics. It seemed unfair to put the burden of 3D overhead on all these applications thus affecting seriously the efficiency of the graphics system. Furthermore, 2D graphics presented enough problems so that it seemed unwise to tackle them together with all the unresolved problems of 3D graphics. Examples of such 3D problems are: how to handle solid objects and non-planar surfaces, how to specify the projection transformation, how to handle 3D coordinate input, how to provide hidden line/hidden surface elimination.

It followed that two major developments evolved which represented the two different positions: on the one hand the *Core Proposal* from the Graphics Standards Planning Committee (GSPC), formed by the Association for Computing Machinery's Special Interest Group on Computer Graphics (ACM—SIGGRAPH), which aimed at providing a comprehensive standard for 3D graphics, and on the other hand the Graphical Kernel System (GKS) from the West German standardization organization, DIN, which preferred a step-by-step approach and started with the definition of a 2D standard.

The GSPC effort resulted in two important reports [GSPC77, GSPC79] which described in detail the functionality of a possible 3D standard, the Core. These papers had a considerable influence on the graphics scene as they represented in condensed form the state of the art of computer graphics. However, the Core proposal failed to pass the standardization committees as it did not meet all the needs of its possible users and it left open some controversial problems. For example, raster graphics was addressed only in an appendix and not integrated into the rest of the document and the segment storage was designed to contain 2D rather than 3D data which reduced its usefulness drastically. Also, some concepts which had been pushed forward by the GKS proposal such as workstations, pens, and a two-stage transformation pipeline and had found widespread acceptance were missing in the Core document. No language bindings had been specified.

The GKS proposal for 2D graphics was drawn up in three years, then underwent a thorough review period of another three years and, finally, passed the voting procedures in the national and international standardization committees.

When technical work on GKS was finished in 1983, resources were available to tackle new projects. One major activity which started at that time was a 3D extension to GKS. As a sound basis for 2D graphics had been established in GKS, it seemed worthwhile to add 3D functionality to it [KANS85a, 85b].

By this time, two papers by the Norwegian [BO82] and West German [EKP84, Chapter IV.9] standards groups were available. They described how 3D functionality could be added to GKS simply by providing a 3D counterpart for each function which has a geometric parameter. The major difference between both papers was the design of the transformation pipeline and the way in which the projection function (viewing) was introduced. These papers were more a kind of feasibility study which showed what a 3D extension to GKS could look like rather than fully elaborated and reviewed proposals.

At a meeting in Gananoque, Canada, in 1983, the working group ISO TC97/ SC5/WG2 *Computer Graphics* of the International Organization for Standardization established the scope and purpose [ISO83] of a 3D extension of GKS which was named GKS-3D. The Dutch standardization committee NNI took on the task of creating a document which was submitted for formal review and reached the status of a draft international standard [ISO86] in 1986.

2   OVERVIEW OF GKS-3D

2.1   Scope and Purpose

The scope of GKS-3D is deliberately restricted to the functionality which is present in many current 3D systems. It excludes areas where it seems difficult to reach common agreement (e.g., defining primitives for solid objects and curved surfaces), while including all 3D features which are needed in today's 3D graphics applications. [ISO83] lists the following capabilities:

— Definition and display of 3D graphical primitives;
— Mechanisms to control viewing transformations and associated parameters;
— Mechanisms to control the appearance of primitives, including optional support for hidden line and/or hidden surface removal but excluding light sources, shading, and shadow computation;
— Mechanisms to obtain 3D input.

GKS-3D is designed in a way which guarantees full compatibility with GKS. This is expressed in the goals of GKS-3D, which are:

— Existing 2D GKS applications should run without any modification to systems incorporating these extensions.
— Where appropriate, 3D functions should be generalizations of existing 2D functions.
— The interaction between 2D and 3D functions should be precisely defined and not be implementation-dependent.
— No changes should be made to existing 2D functions.
— Additional functions should be added solely to provide 3D functionality.

2.2 Functionality of GKS-3D

GKS-3D is an extension of GKS for 3D graphics. It enables the display of 3D output primitives which are direct extensions of the GKS output primitives in a 3D coordinate system. It provides mechanisms to transform these primitives, including a facility for specifying the projection onto a 2D display surface. The display of primitives is controlled by the same set of attributes as in GKS with the addition of a few new attributes specific for 3D. Hidden line/hidden surface removal is an optional facility within GKS-3D.

GKS-3D is a purely three-dimensional system with a 3D transformation pipeline. All coordinate spaces with the possible exception of device coordinates are three-dimensional. The transformation pipeline is modelled according to the GKS transformation pipeline with the addition of a projection transformation introduced primarily for the purposes of 2D display surfaces (see Figure 5.1).

GKS-3D is a *lean* extension of GKS. This implies that GKS-3D contains all functions of GKS plus some more functions to provide 3D functionality. The set of GKS-3D functions can roughly be grouped into the following classes:

1. GKS functions which do not refer to geometry. An example is the GKS functions OPEN WORKSTATION and CLOSE WORKSTATION which are used for the allocation and deallocation of workstations within GKS-3D as within GKS. These functions are fully described in Part III of this book.

Table 2.1 New functions in GKS-3D which have no counterpart in GKS

FILL AREA SET 3: A generalization of FILL AREA which supports areas with holes and includes the edges.

SET EDGE FLAG: Determines whether edges of FILL AREA SET 3 are to be drawn or not.

SET EDGE TYPE, SET EDGE WIDTH SCALE FACTOR, SET EDGE COLOUR INDEX: Set attributes similar to POLYLINE attributes for edges.

SET EDGE INDEX, SET EDGE REPRESENTATION: Allow indirect setting of edge attributes edge flag, edge type, edge width scale factor, and edge colour index.

SET ASPECT SOURCE FLAGS 3: Sets aspect source flags for the edge attributes.

SET VIEW INDEX: Selects a bundle index for the viewing transformation.

SET VIEW REPRESENTATION: Defines the viewing transformation to be associated with a specific view index at a workstation.

SET VIEW TRANSFORMATION INPUT PRIORITY: Sets the input priority for a view transformation at a workstation for coordinate input.

EVALUATE VIEW ORIENTATION MATRIX: Utility function which sets the view orientation matrix parameter of SET VIEW REPRESENTATION.

EVALUATE VIEW MAPPING MATRIX: Utility function which sets the view mapping matrix parameter of SET VIEW REPRESENTATION.

SET HLHSR IDENTIFIER: Primitive attribute for use by a hidden line/hidden surface algorithm. The semantics is implementation-dependent.

SET HLHSR MODE: Workstation attribute for use by a hidden line/hidden surface algorithm. The semantics is implementation-dependent.

Some INQUIRY functions

---

2. GKS functions which take 2D coordinates as arguments. These functions have to be interpreted in the 3D environment of GKS-3D. This is mostly achieved by adding 0 as a default z-coordinate to the x- and y-values. An example of this is the GKS output primitives of GKS which, according to this scheme, are generated within the $z=0$ plane of WC3. These functions are listed in the left-hand column of Table 11.1.

3. Counterparts to the functions of the last group, with the 2D parameters replaced by 3D parameters. These functions allow the full WC3 space to be addressed. Typical examples are the 3D output primitives POLYLINE 3 and POLYMARKER 3. These functions are listed in the right-hand column of Table 11.1, and are fully described in the subsequent chapters.

4. New functions which relate to the output primitive FILL AREA SET 3 and the viewing transformation. These functions are listed in Table 2.1 and are fully described in the subsequent chapters.

2.3 Levels

The functionality of GKS-3D is divided into nine levels which, analogous to the GKS levels, are a combination of the three output and three input levels (see Section III.2.2). Each GKS-3D level contains the functions of the respective GKS level and any 3D counterparts of these functions. The new functions listed in Table 2.1 belong to level 0a with the exception of SET EDGE REPRE-SENTATION, SET HLHSR IDENTIFIER and SET HLHSR MODE which are available in level 1a only. SET EDGE REPRESENTATION is handled just like other functions which set attribute bundles (e.g., SET POLYLINE REPRESENTATION). Hidden line/hidden surface removal requires the storage of the picture data and, therefore, is available only with the segment storage.

From a formal point of view, both the GKS levels and the GKS-3D levels can be put into one level structure where the two axes of GKS level structure, input and output, are supplemented by a third axis, dimensionality, which has the two values 2D and 3D. This emphasizes the fact that GKS-3D is a fully compatible extension of GKS. All functions present in a specific level of GKS are also present in the respective level of GKS-3D and have the same effect.

However, the presence of 3D functions affects the 2D functions and expands their functionality. For example, the 3D viewing transformation allows 2D output primitives to be viewed from behind which is impossible in a mere 2D environment. This is due to the fact that GKS-3D has only one transformation pipeline which, of course, is 3D. 2D functions containing geometrical data are not kept properly apart but are considered to be a shorter version of a corresponding 3D function. The 2D function is immediately expanded into a 3D function before going through the pipeline and is always interpreted in a 3D environment. Looked at in this way, it is more accurate to keep the 2D and 3D environments apart and to have two separate systems with nine levels in each of them.

As well as the functions, the minimal requirements for table lengths, attribute ranges, etc. may vary between levels. Table 2.2 gives the additional requirements for view and edge bundle tables.

Table 2.2 Minimal support required at each level (Extension of Table III.2.2)

CAPABILITY	Level								
	0a	0b	0c	1a	1b	1c	2a	2b	2c
HLHSR identifiers	1	1	1	1	1	1	1	1	1
Predefined view transformations*	2	2	2	6	6	6	6	6	6
Settable view transformations	1	1	1	5	5	5	5	5	5
Predefined edge bundles	5	5	5	5	5	5	5	5	5
Settable edge bundles	-	-	-	20	20	20	20	20	20

*   The view transformation with index 0 is always defined, cannot be changed, and is set to the default values.

3   STATE LISTS

The extension of GKS to 3D has an effect on the state lists. All entries containing geometrical data have to be changed to accept a third coordinate. New primitives and new attributes give rise to new entries. The GKS state list, the workstation state list, the workstation description table and the segment state list are all affected by these changes. Tables 3.1, 4.1, 4.2 and 7.1 list all changes which must be made to produce the respective lists or tables in GKS-3D. The operating state, the GKS description table, and the error state list remain unchanged.

In the lists and tables and in the description of the individual functions, the notation 'P3' is used to indicate a 3D point. The coordinate systems are indicated by the abbreviations WC3, NDC3, VRC, NPC, or DC3 (cf. Chapter 5 for details).

The GKS-3D state list contains new entries for the two global attributes view index (to select a viewing transformation) and HLHSR identifier (to control hidden line/hidden surface removal), and also for the edge attributes of FILL AREA SET 3. The 'window'/'viewport' entries of the normalization transformation and the 'clipping rectangle' are described in the form of boxes rather than rectangles. The 'current pattern reference point' of the GKS state list is replaced by 'current pattern reference points 3' containing three points spanning the pattern plane. The LOCATOR and STROKE entries in the event queue and the current event report have been extended to contain the view index and 3D coordinate values.

Table 3.1   Changes to the GKS state list (Table III.3.7)

Add the following entries:

current view index	(0..n)	I	0
current HLHSR identifier	(0..n)	I	0
current edge index	(1..n)	I	1
current edge flag	(OFF,ON)	E	OFF
current edge type	$(-n..-1,1..n)$	I	1
current edge width scale factor	≥ 0	R	0
current edge colour index	(0..n)	I	1
current edge flag ASF	(BUNDLED,INDIVIDUAL)	E	note 1
current edge type ASF	(BUNDLED,INDIVIDUAL)	E	note 1
current edge width scale			
factor ASF	(BUNDLED,INDIVIDUAL)	E	note 1
current edge colour index ASF	(BUNDLED,INDIVIDUAL)	E	note 1

Change the entries 'window' and 'viewport' in the list of normalization transformations and the entry 'clipping rectangle' to:

window	WC3	$6 \times R$	$0, 1, 0, 1, -1, 0$
viewport	NDC3	$6 \times R$	$0, 1, 0, 1, -1, 0$
clipping volume	NDC3	$6 \times R$	$0, 1, 0, 1, -1, 0$

Replace the entry 'current pattern reference point' by:

current pattern reference point	WC3	P3	$(0, 0, 0),$
current pattern reference vectors	WC3	$2 \times P3$	$(1, 0, 0),$
			$(0, 1, 0)$

Replace the entries for LOCATOR and STROKE in the current event report and in each event report in the input queue by:

if LOCATOR

normalization transformation number	(0..n)	I
view index	(0..n)	I
position	WC3	P3

if STROKE

normalization transformation number	(0..n)	I
view index	(0..n)	I
number of points	(0..n)	I
points in stroke	WC3	$n \times P3$

4   WORKSTATIONS

Workstations are grouped together in workstation types according to characteristics and capabilities. Each workstation type is characterized by a GKS-3D workstation description table which is an extension of the GKS workstation description table. Changes are listed in Table 4.1.

Table 4.1   Changes in the workstation description table (Table III.4.1)

Replace the entries which exist for all workstations of categories OUTPUT, INPUT, OUT-IN by:

Entries which exist for categories OUTPUT, INPUT, OUTIN

device coordinate units		(METRES,OTHER)	E	i.d
maximum display space size				
in length units	DC3	>0, >0, ≥0	$3 \times R$	i.d
in raster units		>0	$3 \times I$	i.d
maximum number of view bundle table entries		(2..n)	I	i.d
number of predefined view bundle table entries		(1..n)	I	i.d
for every entry:				
orientation matrix			$4 \times 4 \times R$	i.d
view mapping matrix			$4 \times 4 \times R$	i.d
projection viewport limits		NPC	$6 \times R$	i.d
window clipping indicator		(CLIP,NOCLIP)	E	i.d
back clipping indicator		(CLIP,NOCLIP)	E	i.d
front clipping indicator		(CLIP,NOCLIP)	E	i.d

Add the following entries to the set of entries which exist for all workstations of categories OUTPUT, OUTIN:

number of available HLHSR modes	(1..n)	I	i.d
list of available HLHSR modes	(0..n)	$n \times I$	i.d
number of available HLHSR identifiers	(1..n)	I	i.d
list of available HLHSR identifiers	(0..n)	$n \times I$	i.d

Insert after FILL AREA:

FILL AREA SET

number of available edge types		(4..n)	I	i.d
list of available edge types		(−n..−1,1..n)	$n \times I$	i.d
number of available edge widths		(0..n)	I	i.d
(a value of 0 implies that a continuous				
range of edge widths is supported)				
nominal edge width	DC3	>0	R	i.d
minimum edge width	DC3	>0	R	i.d
maximum edge width	DC3	>0	R	i.d
number of predefined edge indices (bundles)		(5..n)	I	i.d
table of predefined edge bundles				
for every entry:				
edge flag		(OFF,ON)	E	i.d
edge type		(−n..−1,1..n)	I	i.d
edge width scale factor		≥0	R	i.d
edge colour index		(0..n)	I	i.d
(within range of predefined colour indices)				
maximum number of edge bundle table entries		(5..n)	I	i.d

Replace the entry 'list of sets of attributes used' for GDP by:

list of sets of attributes used	(POLYLINE,POLYMARKER, TEXT,FILL AREA,EDGE)	$n \times E$	i.d

Table 4.1 (continued)

Add the following entries to the section concerning dynamic capabilities:
dynamic modification accepted for:

viewing transformation	(IRG,IMM)	E	i.d
edge bundle representation	(IRG,IMM)	E	i.d
HLHSR mode	(IRG,IMM)	E	i.d

Replace the entry 'default initial position' for LOCATOR by:

default initial position	WC3	P3	i.d

Replace the entry 'default echo area' for all input devices by:

default echo volume	DC3	$6 \times R$	i.d

The entry 'maximum display surface' has been changed to 'maximum display space' which describes the width, height and depth of the display space. Width and height must be greater than zero as in GKS. Depth may be greater than or equal to zero. The depth value will usually refer to the physical extent of the display space of the workstation. It will be greater than zero for true 3D devices such as sculpturing devices or systems which use a vibrating mirror to produce a virtual 3D image and will be zero for workstations which use viewing transformation and hidden line/hidden surface removal to generate a 2D picture of 3D objects on a 2D display surface.

However, there are situations where the implementor can choose freely whether a 2D display surface is assigned a zero or a positive depth value. High performance workstations usually provide local viewing transformation capabilities which can be controlled directly by using dials. When these capabilities are not put under the control of GKS-3D, the workstation appears to GKS-3D as a workstation with a true 3D display and, therefore, the display volume will be assigned a positive depth value. When these capabilities are used to perform GKS-3D viewing, the workstation appears to GKS-3D as a 2D workstation and the depth of the display volume will be set to zero. Local viewing capabilities may be used for both purposes, e.g., by using the setting of the GKS viewing transformation as an initial value for the dials. In any case, it is the responsibility of the implementor to ensure that input and output are transformed as described in this document.

New entries have been provided which describe the capabilities of a workstation with respect to viewing and hidden line/hidden surface removal. At least one HLHSR mode must be implemented which may indicate that no hidden line/hidden surface removal is performed. At least two viewing transformations must be available, i.e. the viewing transformation 0 which is an identity transformation and cannot be changed and another settable viewing transformation. There are also new entries provided for FILL AREA SET 3 which describe the edge attributes. The enumeration type for 'sets of attributes used' for GDP 3 has been extended to contain the edge attributes also. The list of dynamic capabilities has been extended for the above attributes.

The description of LOCATOR has been changed to include a 3D default initial position. Whether true 3D input devices are available or whether a 3D point is generated by a 2D input device, together with a more or less sophisticated method of selecting a third coordinate, cannot be deduced from this table. The implementor should describe in the implementation description what capabilities are present for a certain input device. For all input devices the entry 'default echo rectangle' is replaced by 'default echo volume'.

The workstation state list contains new entries for the state of the hidden line/hidden surface removal mode, for the new edge attributes of FILL AREA SET 3, and for the viewing transformation bundle table. The workstation transformation entries have been extended to contain boxes rather than rectangles. The LOCATOR and STROKE entries have been changed to suit the needs of 3D coordinate input.

Table 4.2   Changes in the workstation state list (Table III.4.2)

Add the following entries to the set of entries which exist for all workstations of categories OUTPUT, OUTIN:			
requested HLHSR mode	(0..n)	I	0
current HLHSR mode	(0..n)	I	0
HLHSR update state	(NOTPENDING,PENDING)	E	NOTPENDING
Insert after FILL AREA:			

FILL AREA SET			
number of edge bundle entries	(5..n)	I	w.d.t
table of defined edge bundles			
for every entry:			
edge index	(1..n)	I	w.d.t
edge flag	(OFF,ON)	E	w.d.t
edge type	$(-n..-1,1..n)$	I	w.d.t
edge width scale factor	≥ 0	R	w.d.t
edge colour index	(0..n)	I	w.d.t
Add new entries for the viewing transformation:			

VIEWING TRANSFORMATION			
number of view bundle table entries	(1..n)	I	w.d.t
table of defined view bundles for every entry:			
view index	(0..n)	I	0
viewing transformation			
update state	(NOTPENDING,PENDING)	E	NOTPENDING
current view orientation matrix	$4 \times 4 \times$ R		$1, 0, 0, 0$
			$0, 1, 0, 0$
			$0, 0, 1, 0$
			$0, 0, 0, 1$
current view mapping matrix	$4 \times 4 \times$ R		$1, 0, 0, 0$
			$0, 1, 0, 0$
			$0, 0, 1, 0$
			$0, 0, 0, 1$
current view clipping limits	NPC	$6 \times$ R	$0, 1, 0, 1, -1, 0$
current window clipping indicator	(CLIP,NOCLIP)	E	CLIP
current back clipping indicator	(CLIP,NOCLIP)	E	CLIP
current front clipping indicator	(CLIP,NOCLIP)	E	CLIP

Table 4.2 (continued)

requested view orientation matrix		$4 \times 4 \times R$	$1, 0, 0, 0$
			$0, 1, 0, 0$
			$0, 0, 1, 0$
			$0, 0, 0, 1$
requested view mapping matrix		$4 \times 4 \times R$	$1, 0, 0, 0$
			$0, 1, 0, 0$
			$0, 0, 1, 0$
			$0, 0, 0, 1$
requested view clipping limits	NPC	$6 \times R$	$0, 1, 0, 1, -1, 0$
requested window clipping indicator	(CLIP,NOCLIP)	E	CLIP
requested back clipping indicator	(CLIP,NOCLIP)	E	CLIP
requested front clipping indicator	(CLIP,NOCLIP)	E	CLIP

Replace the entries for the workstation transformation by:

WORKSTATION TRANSFORMATION			
requested workstation window limits	NPC	$6 \times R$	$0, 1, 0, 1, -1, 0$
requested workstation viewport limits	DC3	$6 \times R$	$0, 1x, 0, ly, 0, lz$
current workstation window limits	NPC	$6 \times R$	$0, 1, 0, 1, -1, 0$
current workstation viewport limits	DC3	$6 \times R$	$0, lx, 0, ly, 0, lz$

where lx, ly, lz are the maximum display volume size in length units from w.d.t

workstation transformation update state	(NOTPENDING,PENDING)	E	NOTPENDING

Replace the entry 'initial position' for LOCATOR by:

view index	(0..n)	I	0
initial position	WC3	P3	w.d.t

Replace the entry 'initial points in stroke' for STROKE by:

view index	(0..n)	I	0
initial points in stroke	WC3	$n \times P3$	empty

Replace the entry 'echo area' for all input devices by:

echo volume	DC3	$6 \times R$	w.d.t

The workstation control in GKS-3D is basically not dependent on dimensionality and remains unchanged, with one exception. Changing the viewing transformation or the HLHSR mode, both of which are not present in GKS, can be deferred. Such a deferral is stopped as described in Section III.4.6 by the functions:

CLEAR WORKSTATION
UPDATE WORKSTATION
REDRAW ALL SEGMENTS ON WORKSTATION

The description of the effect of these functions has to be extended to include additional possibilities for deferred actions:

Effect:

— ....

— If the 'viewing transformation update state' entry in the workstation state list is PENDING, the current entries of the viewing transformations in the workstation state list are assigned the value of the corresponding requested entries; the 'viewing transformation update state' is set to NOTPENDING.

— If the 'HLHSR update state' entry in the workstation state list is PENDING, the 'current HLHSR mode' entry in the workstation state list is assigned the value of the 'requested HLHSR mode' entry; the 'HLHSR update state' is set to NOT-PENDING.

5   TRANSFORMATIONS

GKS-3D adopts all coordinate systems and transformations present in the 2D transformation pipeline of GKS and extends them to 3D. This set of 3D coordinate systems and transformations would be sufficient if only 3D devices had to be considered. However, in practice, true 3D devices are rare. To do 3D graphics on 2D display surfaces, a projection function with hidden line/hidden surface removal is needed. For this reason, a workstation-dependent viewing function has been introduced into GKS-3D. It is applied immediately before the workstation transformation.

It has been proposed to expand the workstation transformation so that it would include the projection functionality. However, this would change the concept of the workstation transformation so fundamentally that it would be difficult to regard it as a direct counterpart of the 2D workstation transformation. Furthermore, there is a need to have different projections on the same display surface, e.g., for displaying different aspects of an object. GKS allows only one workstation transformation at a time. Changing the workstation transformation leads to an implicit regeneration.

5.1   Coordinate Systems

GKS-3D uses 3D extensions of the coordinate systems of GKS: 3D world coordinates (WC3), 3D normalized device coordinates (NDC3), and 3D device coordinates (DC3). These coordinate systems serve the same purposes as their 2D counterparts do.

For viewing purposes, two new 3D coordinate systems have been introduced called viewing reference coordinates (VRC) and normalized projection coordinates (NPC). The VRC system is a reference system which allows the convenient specification of viewing parameters (cf. EVALUATE VIEW MAPPING MATRIX in Section 5.3). The NPC system contains the result of the viewing transformation (cf. Figure 5.1). This is convenient for performing the view clipping and hidden line/hidden surface removal.

Although NDC3 and NPC conceptually extend to infinity, only the unit cube $[0, 1] \times [0, 1] \times [-1, 0]$ can be fully used by the transformations.

The z-interval $[-1, 0]$ has been chosen rather than $[0, 1]$ to have the $z = 0$ plane in front under the default viewing direction.

All coordinate systems in GKS-3D are *right-handed* systems. Right-handedness in an x-, y-, z-coordinate system means that thumb, forefinger and middle

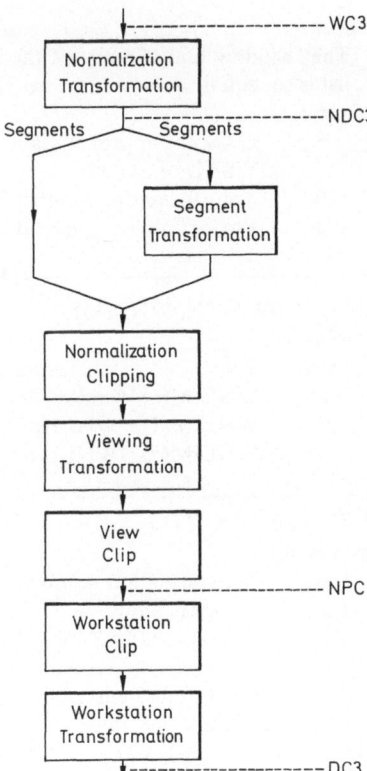

Figure 5.1   Transformation pipeline of GKS-3D

finger of the right hand can be aligned with the coordinate axes in a way that the fingers point into the direction of the positive x-, y-, z-axes, respectively.

Output primitives are defined in WC3. A 3D normalization transformation maps WC3 onto NDC3. Segment transformations transform the NDC3 space and they may also be applied to primitives within segments. The subsequent transformations are workstation-specific. A viewing transformation maps NDC3 onto NPC. It applies to all primitives on a workstation with the same view index. Finally, a workstation transformation is applied to all primitives on a workstation which maps NPC onto DC3.

5.2   Normalization Transformation

The 3D normalization transformation is defined by a 3D window and a 3D viewport which are boxes aligned to the axes of the world coordinate system and the normalized device coordinate system, respectively. The functionality of this transformation includes, as in 2D, translation and scaling.

SET WINDOW 3		GKOP,WSOP,WSAC,SGOP	L0a

Parameters:

Input	transformation number		(1..n)	I
Input	window limits		WC3	$6 \times R$
	XMIN < XMAX, YMIN < YMAX, ZMIN ≤ ZMAX			

Effect:
The 'window limits' entry of the normalization transformation in the GKS-3D state list is set equal to the values specified by the parameters.

Errors:

8	GKS not in proper state: GKS should be in one of the states GKOP, WSOP, WSAC or SGOP
50	Transformation number is invalid
406	Box definition is invalid

———————————— *FORTRAN Interface* ————————————

CALL GSW3 (TN, WNLIM)

Parameters:

Input	TN	transformation number	(1..n)	INTEGER
Input	WNLIM(6)	window limits	WC3	6 × REAL
	WNLIM(1) < WNLIM(2), WNLIM(3) < WNLIM(4),			
	WNLIM(5) ≤ WNLIM(6)			

SET VIEWPORT 3   GKOP,WSOP,WSAC,SGOP   L0a

Parameters:

Input	transformation number	(1..n)	I
Input	viewport limits	NDC3	6 × R
	XMIN < XMAX, YMIN < YMAX, ZMIN ≤ ZMAX		

Effect:
The 'viewport limits' entry of the normalization transformation in the GKS-3D state list is set equal to the values specified by the parameters.

Errors:

8	GKS not in proper state: GKS should be in one of the states GKOP, WSOP, WSAC or SGOP
50	Transformation number is invalid
406	Box definition is invalid
407	Viewport is not within NDC3 unit box

———————————— *FORTRAN Interface* ————————————

CALL GSV3 (TN, VPLIM)

Parameters:

Input	TN	transformation number	(1..n)	INTEGER
Input	VPLIM(6)	viewport limits	NDC3	6 × REAL
	VPLIM(1) < VPLIM(2), VPLIM(3) < VPLIM(4), VPLIM(5) ≤ VPLIM(6)			

5.3 Viewing Transformation

The viewing transformation maps NDC3 onto a 3D coordinate system called NPC. The viewing transformation does all the mathematics necessary to generate a 2D projection of 3D data. However, the third coordinate is not at this point discarded but in fact retained for two reasons. Firstly, the result of the viewing transformation is well suited for hidden line/hidden surface removal. All points which will superimpose each other on a 2D display surface receive the same x- and y-values and the z-value decides which point is in front of the other. Secondly, 3D devices can also use this transformation for selecting a

specific orientation. Some 3D devices can be looked at only from certain directions and it is therefore very useful for selecting the proper face to be the
front side. It should be noted, that the workstation transformation cannot be
used for this purpose as it does not provide rotation.

The viewing transformation is included in GKS-3D as a workstation-dependent primitive attribute. It is selected via a VIEW INDEX which points to
a workstation-specific table containing a description of the viewing transformation. This scheme compares well with the selection of POLYLINE attributes
via POLYLINE INDEX.

Different primitives may have different VIEW INDICES and, hence, may
be processed by different viewing transformations at the same workstation.
As the VIEW INDEX points to workstation-dependent view tables, the same
primitive may be transformed by different viewing transformations on different
workstations. If different views of the same primitives are to be displayed on
one workstation, the respective primitives must be generated twice with different
view indices or they must be copied by the INSERT SEGMENT 3 function
which removes all view indices and replaces them by the current view index.

SET VIEW INDEX   GKOP,WSOP,WSAC,SGOP   L0a
Parameters:
  Input   view index   (0..n)   I
Effect:
  The 'current view index' entry of the GKS-3D state list is set equal to the value
  specified by the parameter. This value is bound to each subsequent output primitive.
Errors:
  8   GKS not in proper state: GKS should be in one of the states GKOP,
           WSOP,WSAC or SGOP

———————————————————— *FORTRAN Interface* ————————————————————

CALL GSVWI (VWIX)
Parameters:
  Input   VWIX   view index   (1..n)   INTEGER

The view index points to a workstation-dependent view table which contains
the parameters of the viewing transformation. Each viewing transformation
is specified by two 4×4 matrices, i.e., the orientation matrix and the view
mapping matrix. The orientation matrix defines the orientation of the viewing
system and the view mapping matrix specifies projection parameters. It is obvious that the viewing transformation could be fully specified by only one 4×4
matrix which is the product of the two single matrices. There are however
two reasons for the redundant specification: Firstly, the orientation matrix establishes an intermediate VRC coordinate system which is very useful for the
specification of the projection parameters. Secondly, current devices often support only some subset of the functionality required for a full transformation.
By splitting the transformation into two parts, it becomes feasible to use as
much as possible of the capabilities of the device.

Using two matrices to define the viewing transformation gives the experienced user total freedom. However, in more usual cases, where only a parallel

or perspective projection is needed, this matrix approach is very inconvenient. Therefore, GKS-3D provides two utility functions, EVALUATE VIEW ORIENTATION MATRIX and EVALUATE VIEW MAPPING MATRIX, the parameters of which may be specified in terms of a simple camera model and which generate the matrices needed for SET VIEW REPRESENTATION. The intention of having two steps of viewing becomes more obvious in the description of these utility functions below.

In addition to the mapping, a clipping volume in NPC space can be specified. Clipping around this volume can be switched on and off. There are three clip indicators which allow individual clip control for front, back and sides.

SET VIEW REPRESENTATION   WSOP,WSAC,SGOP   L0a

Parameters:

Input	workstation identifier		N
Input	view index	(1..n)	I
Input	orientation matrix		$4 \times 4 \times R$
Input	view mapping matrix		$4 \times 4 \times R$
Input	view clipping limits	NPC	$6 \times R$
	XMIN < XMAX, YMIN < YMAX, ZMIN $\leq$ ZMAX		
Input	window clipping indicator	(CLIP,NOCLIP)	E
Input	back clipping indicator	(CLIP,NOCLIP)	E
Input	front clipping indicator	(CLIP,NOCLIP)	E

Effect:

In the view bundle table of the specified workstation, the given view index is associated with the specified parameters. Each view index has two sets of entries containing the requested and the current values of the viewing parameters. The requested values are set immediately; the setting of the current values may be postponed depending on the state of the workstation, the 'dynamic modification accepted for viewing transformation' entry, and the deferral state. If postponed, the 'viewing transformation update state' is set to PENDING. Otherwise, the current values are set and the 'viewing transformation update state' is set to NOTPENDING.

Errors:

7	GKS not in proper state: GKS should be in one of the states WSOP, WSAC or SGOP
20	Specified workstation identifier is invalid
25	Specified workstation is not open
33	Specified workstation is of category MI
36	Specified workstation is Workstation-Independent Segment Storage
406	Box definition is invalid
408	Specified view index is invalid
413	View clipping limits are not within NPC range

--- *FORTRAN Interface* ---

CALL GSVWR
 (WKID,VWIX,ORMAT,VWMAT,VWCLPL,WNCLIP,BKCLIP,FRCLIP)
Parameters:

Input	WKID	workstation identifer		INTEGER
Input	VWIX	view index	(1..n)	INTEGER
Input	ORMAT(4,4)	orientation matrix		$4 \times 4 \times REAL$

Input	VWMAT(4,4)	view mapping matrix		$4 \times 4 \times$ REAL
Input	VWCLPL(6)	view clipping limits	NPC	$6 \times$ REAL

VWCLPL(1) < VWCLPL(2), VWCLPL(3) < VWCLPL(4),
VWCLPL(5) ≤ VWCLPL(6)

Input	WNCLIP	window clipping indicator		
			(0 = noclip, 1 = clip)	INTEGER
Input	BKCLIP	back clipping indicator	(0 = noclip, 1 = clip)	INTEGER
Input	FRCLIP	front clipping indicator	(0 = noclip, 1 = clip)	INTEGER

The entries in the view table are set by default to perform an identity transformation and clip around the unit cube $[0, 1] \times [0, 1] \times [-1, 0]$ in NPC space. An entry 0 exists which cannot be reset and which will always retain this default setting. Viewing transformation 0 plays a similar role as normalization transformation 0. By default, transformation 0 is active. It is needed for a consistent transformation of coordinate input if all other transformation cannot be applied. It is also of importance in providing compatibility between 2D and 3D as this identity transformation does not affect 2D primitives. The default parameters are as follows:

orientation matrix	1 0 0 0
	0 1 0 0
	0 0 1 0
	0 0 0 1
view mapping matrix	1 0 0 0
	0 1 0 0
	0 0 1 0
	0 0 0 1
view clipping limits	(0, 1, 0, 1, -1, 0)
window clipping indicator	CLIP
back clipping indicator	CLIP
front clipping indicator	CLIP

The orientation matrix and the view mapping matrix will usually be generated by the utility functions EVALUATE VIEW ORIENTATION MATRIX and EVALUATE VIEW MAPPING MATRIX. These functions use a camera model of the viewing transformation.

The underlying model is as follows: An observer is located at a position called the projection reference point or eye point. He is looking at a view plane where the image will be generated. The mapping is performed by projectors which emanate from the eye point (projection reference point) and are passing through the view plane to the object (cf. Figure 5.2).

The scene can be limited at the sides by a view window on the view plane. The projectors passing through the view window form an unlimited pyramid. Furthermore, the scene can be limited in the viewing direction by two clipping planes which somehow simulate the depth of focus of a camera. Everything beyond a back clipping plane and in front of a front clipping plane can be

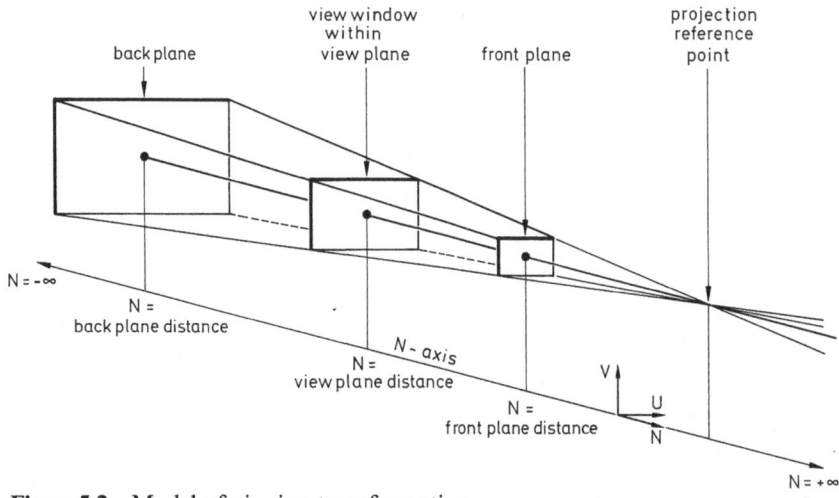

Figure 5.2   Model of viewing transformation

eliminated. The two clipping planes are parallel to the view plane and cut a frustum out of the pyramid. This frustum is now called the viewing volume.

The above scenario describes a perspective projection which represents a model of the common human way of looking at things. A parallel projection can be regarded as a perspective projection where the observer is located at infinite distance $(N = +\infty)$. This implies that in the case of parallel projection the position of the projection reference point is ignored and only the direction from it to the centre of the view window is used to define the direction of the parallel projectors. The viewing volume will be a parallelepiped in this case.

To arrive at a good definition of the viewing volume using three planes, a view window, and a projection reference point proves difficult. This is especially true when an observer looks from an arbitrary oblique direction rather than along one of the axes. In this case, the viewing volume is not aligned to any axis. Therefore, the user may choose an arbitrary coordinate system called the VRC system which is convenient for the viewing geometry and provides a simpler way of defining the viewing volume parameters. Let U, V, N designate the axes of the VRC system. The N-axis serves as the *principal axis* of the viewing system which usually will designate the viewing direction. All clipping and view planes are aligned perpendicular to the N-axis so that their positions can simply be specified by their N-values which are called front plane distance, back plane distance and view plane distance, respectively. The view window lies on the view plane and is specified in terms of UV coordinates. The projection reference point may not lie on the view plane and, in the case of a perspective projection, in between front and back plane; the preferred position will be in some distance in front of the view plane, with the same UV coordinates as the centre of the view window.

To understand the sequence of N-values for these viewing parameters, one should be aware that the VRC coordinate system is right-handed. If the positive U-axis points to the right and the positive V-axis points upwards, the positive N-axis points to the observer. Hence, the observer is looking from positive infinity to negative infinity. The front plane limits the viewing volume in the direction of positive infinity, and the back plane in the direction of negative infinity. A typical set of parameters specifying a viewing volume is:

back plane distance	$N = -1$
view plane distance	$N = -1/2$
view window limits	UMIN$=0$, UMAX$=1$, VMIN$=0$, VMAX$=1$
front plane distance	$N = 0$
projection reference point	$N = 10$
	U $=$ (UMIN $+$ UMAX)/2
	V $=$ (VMIN $+$ VMAX)/2

The above description has concentrated on how to get meaningful viewing parameters. GKS-3D, however, accepts all parameter values which are mathematically feasible. Moving the projection reference point from the centre of the view plane gives oblique projections which corresponds to an observer looking from the side onto the projection plane. If the projection reference point is moved close to an object, this increases the perspective distortion. A user should remain close to the above parameter values unless he understands what he is doing.

The utility function EVALUATE VIEW ORIENTATION MATRIX specifies the VRC system with the axes U, V, N. EVALUATE VIEW ORIENTATION MATRIX takes as parameters the origin of the VRC system, the upward direction (V-axis) and the direction from origin to the observer (N-axis). These parameters may be specified as WC3 or NDC3 values. The resulting 4×4 output matrix then has to be passed on to the SET VIEW REPRESENTATION function in order to achieve the desired effect.

EVALUATE VIEW ORIENTATION MATRIX
GKOP,WSOP,WSAC,SGOP   L0a

Parameters:

Input	view reference point	WC3 or NDC3	P3
Input	view up vector	WC3 or NDC3	P3
Input	view plane normal	WC3 or NDC3	P3
Input	coordinate switch	(WC3,NDC3)	E
Output	orientation matrix		$4 \times 4 \times R$

Effect:

If the coordinate switch is set to WC, the three view parameters are specified in WC3 and are transformed by the current normalization transformation to NDC3. Otherwise, the three view parameters are given in NDC3.

The view reference point, view up vector, and view plane normal vector specify the VRC system of the viewing transformation. An orientation matrix is compiled which performs the respective mapping from NDC3 to VRC. This matrix can be used as a parameter for the SET VIEW REPRESENTATION function.

Errors:

8   GKS not in proper state: GKS should be in one of the states GKOP, WSOP, WSAC or SGOP
400   View up vector and view plane normal are collinear
401   View plane normal is a null vector
402   View up vector is a null vector

———————————————————— *FORTRAN Interface* ————————————————————

CALL GEVORM (VRFPX,VRFPY,VRFPZ,VUPX,VUPY,VUPZ,
VPNX,VPNY,VPNZ,CSW,VWMAT)
Parameters:

Input	VRFPX,VRFPY,VRFPZ			
		view reference point	WC3 or NDC3	$3 \times$ REAL
Input	VUPX,VUPY,VUPZ			
		view up vector	WC3 or NDC3	$3 \times$ REAL
Input	VPNX,VPNY,VPNZ			
		view plane normal	WC3 or NDC3	$3 \times$ REAL
Input	CSW	coordinate switch	(0 = WC3, 1 = NDC3)	INTEGER
Output	VWMAT(4,4)	orientation matrix		$4 \times 4 \times$ REAL

The utility function EVALUATE VIEW MAPPING MATRIX specifies the projection parameters within the VRC system with the axes U, V, N. EVALUATE VIEW MAPPING MATRIX takes as parameters the projection type, the projection reference point in VRC, the view window by UV limits and the N-values of the view plane, front plane, and back plane. The resulting 4×4 output matrix then has to be passed on to the SET VIEW REPRESENTATION function in order to achieve the desired effect.

——

EVALUATE VIEW MAPPING MATRIX GKOP,WSOP,WSAC,SGOP   L0a
Parameters:

Input	projection type	(PARALLEL,PERSPECTIVE)	E
Input	projection reference point	VRC	P3
Input	view window limits	VRC	$4 \times$ R
	UMIN < UMAX, VMIN < VMAX		
Input	view plane distance	VRC	R
Input	back plane distance	VRC	R
Input	front plane distance	VRC	R
Input	projection viewport limits	NPC	$6 \times$ R
	XMIN < XMAX, YMIN < YMAX, ZMIN $\leq$ ZMAX		
Output	view mapping matrix		$4 \times 4 \times$ R

Effect:

A viewing volume is defined by projection reference point, view window limits, view plane distance, back plane distance, front plane distance It is a frustum for projection type PERSPECTIVE and a parallelepiped for projection type PARALLEL. The mapping of the viewing volume onto the projection viewport is evaluated and stored in the view mapping matrix. This matrix can be used as a parameter for the SET VIEW REPRESENTATION function.

Errors:

8   GKS not in proper state: GKS should be in one of the states GKOP, WSOP, WSAC or SGOP
403   Projection viewport limits are not within NPC range
404   Projection reference point is between the front and back clipping planes
405   Projection reference point is positioned in the view plane
406   Box definition is invalid

──────────────── *FORTRAN Interface* ────────────────

CALL GEVVWM (PJTYPE,PJRX,PJRY,PJRZ,VWWNL,VPLD,BPLD,
FPLD,PRVPLM,VWMAT)

Parameters:

Input	PJTYPE	projection type (0=parallel, 1=perspective)		INTEGER
Input	PJRX,PJRY,PJRZ			
		projection reference point	VRC	3×REAL
Input	VWWNL(4)	view window limits	VRC	4×REAL
	VWWNL(1)<VWWNL(2), VWWNL(3)<VWWNL(4)			
Input	VPLD	view plane distance	VRC	REAL
Input	BPLD	back plane distance	VRC	REAL
Input	FPLD	front plane distance	VRC	REAL
Input	PRVPLM(6)	projection viewport limits	NPC	6×REAL
	PRVPLM(1)<PRVPLM(2), PRVPLM(3)<PRVPLM(4),			
	PRVPLM(5)≤PRVPLM(6)			
Output	VWMAT(4,4)	view mapping matrix		4×4 REAL

A novice will not need all the possibilities provided by the viewing transformation. On the contrary, it will be difficult to find a way of setting the parameters which will give some meaningful output. The following provides some general rules on how the parameters can be selected.

The VRC system should be defined relative to the object to be viewed. The view reference point could be at the lower left-hand corner of the reverse side of the object. The view up vector gives the upward orientation and the view plane normal points from the object to the observer.

Within the VRC, the viewing volume should be close to the unit cube. With the coordinate switch set to NDC, this can be achieved by setting both the view plane distance and the back plane distance to -1 and the front plane distance to 0, thus locating the planes at coordinates $N = -1$ and $N = 0$ respectively along a line normal to the view plane. A view window of $[0, 1] \times [0, 1]$ will ensure that the unit cube $[0, 1] \times [0, 1] \times [-1, 0]$ of NDC3 is contained in the viewing volume. The projection reference point could be at $(0.5, 0.5, n)$ with say $2 < n < \infty$ where n controls the degree of perspective distortion. The projection viewport could be the unit cube $[0, 1] \times [0, 1] \times [-1, 0]$. The clipping indicators should be set to CLIP. NOCLIP is advisable if a certain parameter setting does not generate any output at all and the error is being searched for.

One feature of the camera model should be pointed out. In contrast to a camera or the human eye, the distance from the object to the projection reference point does not affect the size of the image but only the distortion between the front and the back. Scaling of the image is determined by the sizes of the viewing volume (view window) and the projection viewport.

5.4   Hidden Line/Hidden Surface Removal (HLHSR)

When looking at 3D objects, only the front side is visible and back sides do not appear. This effect is trivial in the real world but not readily achieved in computer graphics. Without any precautions, a 3D scene would be generated as shown in Figure 5.3 on the left-hand side, where it is very difficult to recognize the displayed objects. Having removed invisible faces (Figure 5.3, right side), the content of the 3D scene is much easier to understand. The suppression of invisible parts which obscure an image is therefore an essential part of 3D graphics. The corresponding techniques are called hidden line removal if the image is composed of lines, or hidden surface removal if solid surfaces can be displayed (Figure C3).

There are many different approaches to solving the problem of hidden line/ hidden surface removal (HLHSR). Efficiency is a crucial point for most algorithms. Approaches vary for different device types. Vector devices usually represent solid objects by using a wire frame model. A considerable amount of computing is needed to recognize lines or line pieces belonging to back faces and to remove them. For raster devices with frame buffer and graphics primarily consisting of solid areas, hidden surface removal is easier. Primitives have to be put into order according to their z-value and hidden surface removal will happen automatically, as primitives being processed later will overwrite primitives generated previously in the frame buffer. If the frame buffer can also store a z-value for each pixel, even the sorting of primitives can be avoided as the decision as to which pixel covers the other can be made by comparing the z-values of the stored and the new pixel.

GKS-3D provides two functions for the control of hidden line/hidden surface removal algorithms. As only primitives stored in segments are considered for hidden line/hidden surface removal, these functions belong to Level 1 a.

SET HLHSR MODE allows the control of hidden line/hidden surface removal on a workstation basis. It applies primarily to workstations which have one or more HLHSR algorithms but can support only one algorithm at

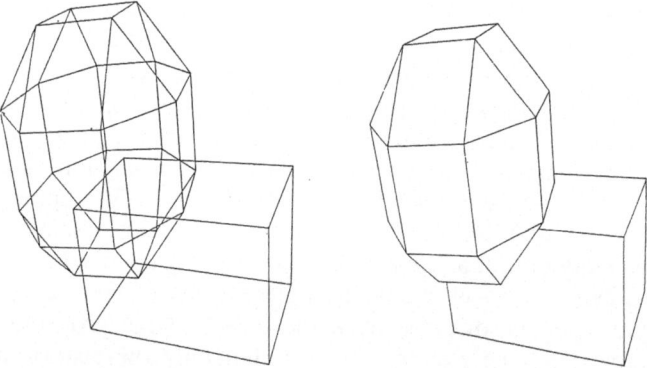

Figure 5.3   Wire frame representation of 3D object with and without hidden line/hidden surface removal

a time. The HLHSR MODE selects one of these algorithms. HLHSR MODE 0 selects the cheapest method for that workstation. Currently, the cheapest method will often be to apply no algorithm. This attribute allows an application program to select the cheapest method during interactive work and to switch to a comfortable method for the final result.

SET HLHSR IDENTIFIER allows the control of hidden line/hidden surface removal on a primitive basis. It enables primitives to be grouped together for processing by the hidden line/hidden surface algorithm. Such groups may be processed by different algorithms. Efficiency can be increased if primitives which do not affect each other with respect to HLHSR can be put into separate groups. One example could be to assign the same HLHSR IDENTIFIER to primitives which are transformed by one viewing transformation.

The above description lists several possible interpretations of the two HLHSR attributes but does not prescribe a specific one. The standards committee felt that the area of hidden line/hidden surface removal is not yet ready for a full standardization. Therefore, two HLHSR attributes have been introduced which allow control on two different levels and which are sufficient for the control of many algorithms currently available. The use and the interpretation of the two attributes is deliberately left to the implementor. This should give total freedom for any future development in the area of HLHSR.

An implementor is even allowed to ignore these attributes totally and to provide no HLHSR algorithm. Although such an implementation would formally conform to the standard, it would be useless for almost all applications. It is expected that a workable implementation will provide some kind of hidden line/hidden surface removal. The implementor will give details about these algorithms in the implementation documentation.

If a primitive is sent to a display surface, hidden line/hidden surface removal may result in an implicit regeneration. As HLHSR algorithms tend to be expensive, deferral is very important to avoid superfluous implicit regenerations and to balance the update state of the current image with the overall performance.

The HLHSR identifier is set by the function SET HLHSR IDENTIFIER. It is a global attribute which can be interpreted differently at different workstations.

SET HLHSR IDENTIFIER   GKOP,WSOP,WSAC,SGOP   L1a
Parameters:
  Input   HLHSR identifier   (0..n)   I
Effect:
  The 'current HLHSR identifier' entry in the GKS-3D state list is set equal to the specified value. This value is bound to each primitive generated subsequently in state 'Segment Open'. It supplies HLHSR information for use by a HLHSR module on a workstation. If the requested HLHSR identifier cannot be interpreted at a workstation, the workstation will use another identifier.
Errors:
  8   GKS not in proper state: GKS should be in one of the states GKOP, WSOP, WSAC or SGOP
  428   Specified HLHSR identifier is invalid

─────────────────────────── *FORTRAN Interface* ───────────────────────────
CALL GSHRID (HID)
Parameters:
  Input   HID   HLHSR identifier   (0..n)   INTEGER

The HLHSR MODE is set by the function SET HLHSR MODE. A possible application for this function may be switching HLHSR on and off at a workstation.

───
SET HLHSR MODE   WSOP,WSAC,SGOP   L1a
Parameters:
  Input   workstation identifier   N
  Input   HLHSR mode   (0..n)   I
Effect:
The 'requested HLHSR mode' entry in the workstation state list of the specified workstation is set equal to the specified value.
If the 'dynamic modification accepted for HLHSR mode' entry in the workstation description table is equal to IMM, or if the 'display surface empty' entry in the workstation state list is equal to EMPTY, then the 'current HLHSR mode' entry in the workstation state list is set to the value specified by the parameter and the 'HLHSR update state' entry in the workstation state list is set to NOTPENDING. Otherwise, the 'HLHSR update state' entry in the workstation state list is set to PENDING and the 'current HLHSR mode' entry is not changed.
Errors:
  7   GKS not in proper state: GKS should be in one of the states WSOP, WSAC or SGOP
  20   Specified workstation identifier is invalid
  25   Specified workstation is not open
  33   Specified workstation is of category MI
  35   Specified workstation is of category INPUT
  36   Specified workstation is Workstation-Independent Segment Storage
  427   Specified HLHSR mode is not supported on this workstation
─────────────────────────── *FORTRAN Interface* ───────────────────────────
CALL GSHRM (WKID, HM)
Parameters:
  Input   WKID   workstation identifier   INTEGER
  Input   HM   HLHSR mode   (0..n)   INTEGER

Although the implementation details of HLHSR have deliberately been left open, nevertheless, some rules have been formulated which must be considered in this area: Primitives in segments with segment attribute INVISIBLE must not obscure other primitives. Primitives outside segments cannot be considered for hidden line/hidden surface removal. Primitives removed by hidden line/hidden surface removal cannot be detected by a PICK input device.

5.5 Workstation Transformation

The 3D workstation transformation is defined by a 3D workstation window and a 3D workstation viewport which are boxes aligned to the axes in the

NPC and DC3 system, respectively. The functionality comprises, as in the case of 2D, translation and scaling. The same scale factor applies to the x- and y-axes which, if necessary, can be enforced by reducing the workstation viewport as in the case of 2D. The z-extent of the workstation window will be mapped on the full z-extent of the workstation viewport. This reflects the fact that 2D display surfaces are the usual equipment where the z-axis plays a special role.

The DC3 are related to the display space of a workstation in the following way: The origin is at the bottom left-hand corner, furthest from the observer of the display space; x, y, and z increase to the right, upwards and towards the observer, respectively. DC3 units are metres where applicable.

SET WORKSTATION WINDOW 3   WSOP, WSAC, SGOP   L0a

Parameters:

Input	workstation identifier		N
Input	workstation window limits	NPC	$6 \times R$
	XMIN < XMAX, YMIN < YMAX, ZMIN ≤ ZMAX		

Effect:
The 'requested workstation window limits' entry in the workstation state list of the specified workstation is set equal to the specified value.

If the 'dynamic modification accepted for workstation transformation' entry in the workstation description table is equal to IMM, or if the 'display surface empty' entry in the workstation state list is equal to EMPTY, then the 'current workstation window limits' entry in the workstation state list is set to the value specified by the parameter and the 'workstation transformation update state' entry in the workstation state list is set to NOTPENDING. Otherwise, the 'workstation transformation update state' entry in the workstation state list is set to PENDING and the 'current workstation window limits' entry is not changed.

Errors:

7	GKS not in proper state: GKS should be in one of the states WSOP, WSAC or SGOP
20	Specified workstation identifier is invalid
25	Specified workstation is not open
33	Specified workstation is of category MI
36	Specified workstation is Workstation-Independent Segment Storage
406	Box definition is invalid
411	Workstation window limits are not within NPC unit cube

———————————————— *FORTRAN Interface* ————————————————

CALL GSWKW3 (WKID, WKWN)

Parameters:

Input	WKID	workstation identifier		INTEGER
Input	WKWN(6)	workstation window limits	NPC	$6 \times REAL$
	WKWN(1) < WKWN(2), WKWN(3) < WKWN(4),			
	WKWN(5) ≤ WKWN(6)			

SET WORKSTATION VIEWPORT 3   WSOP, WSAC, SGOP   L0a

Parameters:

Input	workstation identifier		N
Input	workstation viewport limits	DC3	$6 \times R$
	XMIN < XMAX, YMIN < YMAX, ZMIN ≤ ZMAX		

Effect:

The 'requested workstation viewport limits' entry in the workstation state list of the specified workstation is set equal to the specified value.

If the 'dynamic modification accepted for workstation transformation' entry in the workstation description table is equal to IMM, or if the 'display surface empty' entry in the workstation state list is equal to EMPTY, then the 'current workstation viewport limits' entry in the workstation state list is set to the value specified by the parameter and the 'workstation transformation update state' entry in the workstation state list is set to NOTPENDING. Otherwise, the 'workstation transformation update state' entry in the workstation state list is set to PENDING and the 'current workstation viewport limits' entry is not changed.

Errors:

7	GKS not in proper state: GKS should be in one of the states WSOP, WSAC or SGOP
20	Specified workstation identifier is invalid
25	Specified workstation is not open
33	Specified workstation is of category MI
36	Specified workstation is Workstation Independent-Segment Storage
54	Workstation viewport is not within the display space
406	Box definition is invalid

———————————————— *FORTRAN Interface* ————————————————

CALL GSWKV3 (WKID, WKVP)

Parameters:

Input	WKID	workstation identifier		INTEGER
Output	WKVP(6)	workstation viewport limits	DC3	6 × REAL
		WKVP(1) < WKVP(2), WKVP(3) < WKVP(4),		
		WKVP(5) ≤ WKVP(6)		

5.6   Transformation of LOCATOR 3 and STROKE 3 Input

Graphical output is defined in world coordinates and transformed to device coordinates for display. Coordinate input is generated in device coordinates and transformed back to world coordinates for symmetry reasons. This means that the inverses of a workstation transformation, a viewing transformation, and a normalization transformation are applied to the coordinate values.

The workstation transformation can be identified immediately because only one workstation transformation is defined at the workstation where input is generated. However, different normalization and viewing transformations are defined simultaneously and one of them has to be selected to transform the input values. The normalization transformation is selected according to the priority scheme as described in Section III.5.5. A similar mechanism has been introduced for the viewing transformation.

Firstly, the view clipping limits of all viewing transformations at a workstation are compared with the LOCATOR 3 value or all STROKE 3 values.

At least the view clipping limits of viewing transformation 0 will contain the input value or values. If there is more than one viewing transformation, a viewing transformation input priority will arbitrate.

The viewing transformation input priority puts the viewing transformations into a relative order and compares well with the viewport input priority for normalization transformations. However, as the viewing transformation is workstation-dependent, the priority must be set individually for each workstation rather than globally.

SET VIEW TRANSFORMATION INPUT PRIORITY
WSOP,WSAC,SGOP   L0a

Parameters:

Input	workstation identifier		N
Input	view index	$(0..n)$	I
Input	reference view index	$(0..n)$	I
Input	relative priority	(HIGHER,LOWER)	E

Effect:

At the specified workstation, the viewing transformation input priority of the specified viewing transformation is set to the next higher or lower priority relative to the reference viewing transformation. If both indices are the same, the function has no effect.

Errors:

7	GKS not in proper state: GKS should be in one of the states WSOP, WSAC or SGOP
20	Specified workstation identifier is invalid
25	Specified workstation is not open
33	Specified workstation is of category MI
36	Specified workstation is Workstation-Independent Segment Storage
408	Specified view index is invalid

FORTRAN Interface

CALL GSVTIP (WKID,VWIX,RFVWIX,RELPRI)

Parameters:

Input	WKID	workstation identifier		INTEGER
Input	VWIX	view index	$(0..n)$	INTEGER
Input	RFVWIX	reference view index	$(0..n)$	INTEGER
Input	RELPRI	relative priority	$(0=$higher, $1=$lower$)$	INTEGER

6 OUTPUT PRIMITIVES

6.1 Introduction

3D output primitives are generally defined as 3D counterparts of the 2D output primitives of GKS. They differ, however, in that positions can be specified in 3D space. The new 3D output primitives are as follows:

POLYLINE 3
   defines a set of straight lines passing through a sequence of points in 3D space;
POLYMARKER 3
   allows a marker symbol to be positioned at each point in a set of positions in 3D space;
TEXT 3
   defines a planar text, i.e., the text lies within a plane which, however, can be positioned and oriented arbitrarily in 3D space;
FILL AREA 3
   defines a planar area which can be positioned and oriented arbitrarily in 3D space;
CELL ARRAY 3
   defines a planar cell array which can be positioned and oriented arbitrarily in 3D space;
GENERALIZED DRAWING PRIMITIVE 3 (GDP3)
   transfers 3D data to a workstation for addressing non-standard 3D output capabilities.

Although the FILL AREA primitive is a truly high-level primitive compared to the other ones, it was felt that many applications still needed more functionality. Areas with holes are difficult and clumsy to handle. The edge of a FILL AREA has to be drawn by a separate POLYLINE which is inconvenient for interactive applications dealing with areas as one entity. It was felt that future revisions of GKS should contain a FILL AREA SET primitive which would support edge control and areas with holes. In anticipation of such an extension, a new 3D primitive has been added which has no counterpart in GKS:

FILL AREA SET 3
   defines a planar area which can be positioned and oriented arbitrarily in 3D space; in addition to the capabilities of FILL AREA, this primitive allows the specification of areas with holes.

For reasons of consistency, a corresponding 2D primitive FILL AREA SET has also been included in GKS-3D.

   GKS-3D contains primitives for zero-dimensional (POLYMARKER 3), one-dimensional (POLYLINE 3), and two-dimensional objects (TEXT 3, FILL AREA 3, FILL AREA SET 3, CELL ARRAY 3), but no primitives for the definition of curved surfaces and solid objects which truly constitute 3D graphics. This exclusion does not underestimate the importance of advanced-level 3D primitives but merely reflects the fact that such primitives are at present not well developed enough for standardization.

Whereas POLYLINE 3 and POLYMARKER 3 take full advantage of the new third dimension, TEXT 3, FILL AREA 3, FILL AREA SET 3, and CELL ARRAY 3 essentially remain flat primitives in the sense that each single primitive lies within one plane. This plane, however, can be positioned arbitrarily in WC3 for each primitive. TEXT 3 specifies the plane by using the text reference point and two direction vectors. The plane for FILL AREA 3 and FILL AREA SET 3 is determined implicitly by the boundary points. CELL ARRAY 3 specifies a plane by taking the three corner points of the cell parallelogram.

Depending on the viewing direction, this plane can be looked at from both sides. In the case of a solid FILL AREA 3 there are no differences between the sides. However, in the cases of TEXT 3, FILL AREA 3 with interior style HATCH and PATTERN and CELL ARRAY 3, it is necessary to identify an observe side, where the primitive is generated, and a reverse side, where the primitive appears mirrored. TEXT 3 defines a local coordinate system where the origin is the text reference point and the x- and y-directions are given by the text direction vectors for TEXT 3. Text is generated within this 2D system as described for TEXT. For the pattern and cell parallelogram, three corner points are given which determine how the cells are arranged.

The appearance of the 3D output primitives is controlled by attributes which are mostly taken directly from GKS. Many output primitive attributes are not affected by dimensionality and have the same effect in GKS and GKS-3D. The PATTERN REFERENCE POINT is expanded to PATTERN REFERENCE POINT AND VECTORS which, by a reference point and x- and y-direction vectors, defines a pattern plane similar to the text plane. All the other geometric attributes (CHARACTER HEIGHT, CHARACTER UP VECTOR, TEXT PATH, TEXT ALIGNMENT, and PATTERN SIZE) are interpreted in GKS-3D on the text plane or pattern plane and, thus, remain in a 2D environment. Due to this, it was possible to avoid introducing new 3D attributes for concepts which are now well established in GKS.

As well as PATTERN REFERENCE POINT AND VECTORS, the new attributes in GKS-3D are EDGE FLAG, EDGE TYPE, EDGE WIDTH SCALE FACTOR, and EDGE COLOUR INDEX, which have been introduced to control the edges of FILL AREA SET 3. Such a means of control does not exist for FILL AREA and FILL AREA 3. The edge attributes can be set globally or by using an EDGE INDEX which points to an EDGE REPRESENTATION in the workstation state list. The ASPECT SOURCE FLAGS for the four new attributes can be set by SET ASPECT SOURCE FLAGS 3.

Two new attributes, VIEW INDEX and HLHSR IDENTIFIER, apply to all output primitives. They specify the viewing transformation and control the hidden line/hidden surface module which is to be applied for each primitive. These attributes are introduced in Sections 5.3 and 5.4.

The new attributes are listed in Table 6.1. Details of primitives and attributes are given in the subsequent chapters. It is assumed that the reader is familiar with the GKS output primitives and attributes as introduced in Chapter III.6.

Table 6.1 Synopsis of GKS-3D attributes not present in GKS (cf. Table III.6.4 for other attributes)

global, static, immediate binding	workstation-dependent, dynamic, delayed binding

For all primitives:

VIEW INDEX
HLHSR IDENTIFIER

FILL AREA 3 and FILL AREA SET 3:
'pattern reference point' attribute superseded by:
PATTERN REFERENCE POINT AND VECTORS

FILL AREA SET 3:

EDGE INDEX	text bundle:
EDGE FLAG	↔EDGE FLAG
EDGE TYPE	↔EDGE TYPE
EDGE WIDTH SCALE FACTOR	↔EDGE WIDTH SCALE FACTOR
EDGE COLOUR INDEX	↔EDGE COLOUR INDEX

6.2   POLYLINE 3 Primitive

POLYLINE 3 accepts a list of 3D points and generates a sequence of connected straight lines passing through the given vertices. The minimum number of points is 2 in which case just one straight line is drawn from the first to the second point.

The POLYLINE attributes LINETYPE, LINEWIDTH SCALE FACTOR, and POLYLINE COLOUR INDEX apply also for POLYLINE 3. Values can be specified globally or via a POLYLINE INDEX pointing to a polyline representation in the workstation state list.

POLYLINE 3   WSAC,SGOP   L0a
Parameters:

Input	number of points		$(2..n)$	I
Input	points	WC3		$n \times P3$

Effect:
A sequence of points connected with straight lines is generated, starting from the first point and ending at the last point. The current values of the polyline attributes, as given by the GKS-3D state list, are bound to the primitive.

Errors:

   5   GKS not in proper state: GKS should be either in the state WSAC or in the state SGOP

100   Number of points is invalid

————————————————— *FORTRAN Interface* —————————————————

CALL GPL3 (NP,XA,YA,ZA)
Parameters:

Input	NP	number of points	$(2..n)$	INTEGER
Input	XA(NP),YA(NP),ZA(NP)			
		points	WC3	$3 \times n \times REAL$

6.3   POLYMARKER 3 Primitive

POLYMARKER 3 accepts a list of 3D points and generates a marker symbol at each of the given locations. This allows a visual representation of arbitrary point sets in 3D space. It should be remembered that the points are the true content of the POLYMARKER primitive, whereas the marker symbols are only a means to make these points visible. Therefore, only the points are properly transformed, whereas the marker symbols need not be subject to any GKS transformation. Consequently, a 3D marker displayed on a 2D display surface will show its front side as defined in the 2D case whether it has been rotated by a segment or viewing transformation or not. However, this should not prevent the implementation of three-dimensional transformable markers on appropriate workstations. For example, workstations which can performing depth cueing can change the marker size to achieve a depth cueing effect for markers as well.

The POLYMARKER attributes MARKER TYPE, MARKER SIZE SCALE FACTOR, and POLYMARKER COLOUR INDEX apply to POLYMARKER 3 as well. Values can be specified globally or by using a POLYMARKER INDEX which points to a polymarker representation in the workstation state list.

POLYMARKER 3   WSAC,SGOP   L0a

Parameters:

Input	number of points		(1..n)	I
Input	points	WC3		n × P3

Effect:

A sequence of markers is generated to identify all the given positions. The current values of the polymarker attributes, as given by the GKS-3D state list, are bound to the primitive.

Errors:

5	GKS not in proper state: GKS should be either in the state WSAC or in the state SGOP
100	Number of points is invalid

———————————————— *FORTRAN Interface* ————————————————

CALL GPM3 (NP,XA,YA,ZA)

Parameters:

Input	NP	number of points	(1..n)	INTEGER
Input	XA(NP),YA(NP),ZA(NP)			
		points	WC3	3 × n × REAL

6.4   TEXT 3 Primitive

TEXT 3 generates a text string at a given text position within a text plane in 3D space. The text plane is defined by the text position P and two text direction vectors D_1 and D_2. A local coordinate system is established in the following way: P designates the origin, the vector D_1 defines the direction of the positive x-axis, and the vector D_2 defines the direction of the positive y-axis, if necessary, after having been forced to be orthogonal to the x-axis (cf. Figure 6.1).

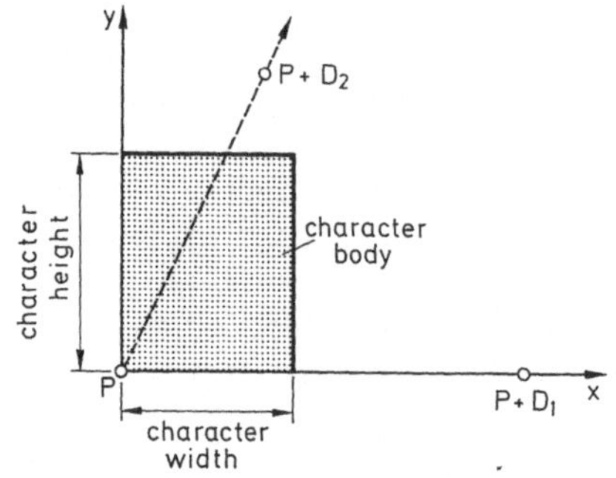

Figure 6.1 Definition of text plane and character body

Having established the text plane, an obverse side of the plane must be identified onto which text is to be generated. The obverse side is the side where the positive x-axis points to the right and the positive y-axis points upwards after a possible rotation within the text plane has taken place. If looked at from the reverse side, a text will be mirrored (cf. Figure 6.2). This will be true at least for STROKE precision text.

	TEXT PATH	
	RIGHT	LEFT
obverse	+GKS-3D	D3-SKG+
reverse	ᗡƐ-ƧꓘᎮ+	+ᎮꓘƧ-Ɛᗡ

Figure 6.2 Text looked at from the reverse with text path RIGHT and LEFT

The geometrical text attributes CHARACTER HEIGHT, CHARACTER UP VECTOR, TEXT PATH, and TEXT ALIGNMENT are interpreted within the coordinate system on the text plane. The CHARACTER UP VECTOR defines the orientation of a character body on the text plane, as described in III.6.4.2. The size of the character body is determined by the text attributes CHARACTER HEIGHT and CHARACTER EXPANSION FACTOR. The character body is bound to the TEXT primitive as a rectangle in WC3.

The TEXT attributes TEXT FONT AND PRECISION, CHARACTER EXPANSION FACTOR, CHARACTER SPACING, and TEXT COLOUR INDEX also apply for TEXT 3. Values can be specified globally or via a TEXT INDEX which points to a text representation in the workstation state list.

TEXT 3 WSAC,SGOP L0a

Parameters:

Input	text position	WC3	P3
Input	text direction vectors	WC3	2×P3
Input	character string		S

Effect:

A character string is generated in a plane defined by the text position and the text direction vectors. The current values of the text attributes, as given by the GKS-3D state list, are bound to the primitive. The geometric attributes are interpreted in the specified plane.

Errors:

5   GKS not in proper state: GKS should be either in the state WSAC or in the state SGOP

101   Invalid code in string

430   Text direction vectors are collinear

———————————————— *FORTRAN Interface* ————————————————

CALL GTX3 (TPX,TPY,TPZ,TDX,TDY,TDZ,STR)

Parameters:

Input	TPX, TPY, TPZ			
		text position	WC3	$3 \times$ REAL
Input	TDX(2),TDY(2),TDZ(2)			
		text direction vectors	WC3	$2 \times 3 \times$ REAL
Input	STR	character string		CHARACTER*(*)

6.5   FILL AREA 3 Primitive

FILL AREA 3 generates a planar area whose boundary is specified by a list of points. Planar means that the area has to lie within one plane in WC3. Curved surfaces are not covered by this primitive. The plane is determined implicitly by the boundary points. If, however, the boundary points do not belong to one plane (e.g., as a consequence of round-off errors or wrong data), the best-fitting plane will be selected according to some implementation-dependent algorithm.

The FILL AREA attributes FILL AREA INTERIOR STYLE, FILL AREA STYLE INDEX, and FILL AREA COLOUR INDEX also apply to FILL AREA 3. Values can be specified globally or via a FILL AREA INDEX which points to a fill area representation in the workstation state list.

In the case of interior style PATTERN, a pattern parallelogram can be specified in the following way (see Figure 6.3). The SET PATTERN REFERENCE POINT AND VECTORS function allows one pattern reference point R and two direction vectors D_1, D_2 to be specified. The points R, $R+D_1$, $R+D_2$ in WC3 are moved onto the FILL AREA 3 plane by projecting them along a line normal to the fill area plane. To avoid undesired distortions it is recommended one choose direction vectors parallel to the FILL AREA 3 plane. Let S_1, S_2, S_3 designate the projected points. Then S_1 defines the lower left-hand corner of the pattern parallelogram, i.e., S_1 serves as PATTERN REFERENCE POINT. $\overline{S_1 S_2}$ defines the lower side and $\overline{S_1 S_3}$ the left-hand side of the pattern parallelogram. The lengths SX, SY of the sides is given by the GKS attribute PATTERN SIZE. The parallelogram is subdivided into cells of equal size, according to the dimensions DX, DY of the pattern array, and each of these cells is assigned the respective colour index as specified by

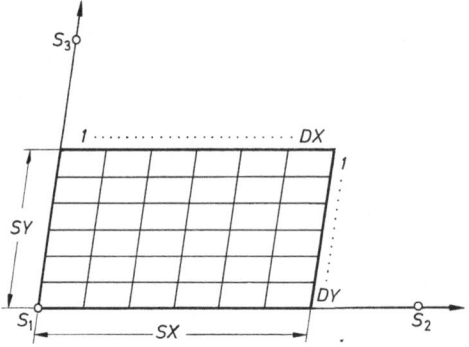

Figure 6.3 Definition of the pattern parallelogram

SET FILL AREA STYLE INDEX and SET PATTERN REPRESENTA-TION. The element (1,DY) of the pattern array is associated with the cell adjacent to S_1. This pattern is then replicated to cover the whole area of FILL AREA 3.

The obverse side of the fill area plane is that side where the positive x-axis points to the right and the positive y-axis points upwards after a possible rotation within the fill area plane has taken place. If looked at from the reverse side, a pattern will be mirrored.

The boundary is not part of FILL AREA 3. If the boundary is to be drawn, a separate call to POLYLINE 3 has to be issued except in the case of interior style HOLLOW where only the boundary is drawn, using the current fill area colour index and an implementation-dependent linetype and linewidth.

FILL AREA 3   WSAC,SGOP   L0a

Parameters:

Input	number of points	(3..n)	I
Input	points	WC3	n × P3

Effect:

A FILL AREA 3 primitive is generated. The current values of the FILL AREA attributes, as given by the GKS-3D state list, are bound to the primitive. It is assumed that the points defining FILL AREA 3 are lying in a plane. Otherwise, a FILL AREA 3 primitive will still be generated but its exact form is implementation-dependent. No error message will be generated. See the definition of FILL AREA in Section III.6.5 for further details of clipping and picking.

Errors:

    5   GKS not in proper state: GKS should be either in the state WSAC or in the state SGOP

  100   Number of points is invalid

————————————————— *FORTRAN Interface* —————————————————

CALL GFA3 (NP,XA,YA,ZA)

Parameters:

Input	NP	number of points	(3..n)	INTEGER
Input	XA(NP),YA(NP),ZA(NP)			
		points	WC3	3 × n × REAL

SET PATTERN REFERENCE POINT AND VECTORS

		GKOP,WSOP,WSAC,SGOP	L0a
Input	pattern reference point	WC3	P3
Input	pattern reference vectors	WC3	$2 \times P3$

Effect:

The 'current pattern reference point' and 'current pattern reference vectors' entries in the GKS-3D state list are set to the values specified by the parameters. When the currently selected fill area interior style is PATTERN, these values are used to determine a pattern parallelogram for FILL AREA 3 or FILL AREA SET 3.

Errors:

8	GKS-3D not in proper state: GKS-3D should be in one of the states GKOP, WSOP, WSAC or SGOP WSOP, WSAC or SGOP
426	Pattern reference vectors are collinear

———————————————— *FORTRAN Interface* ————————————————

CALL GSPRPV (PRPX,PRPY,PRPZ,PRVX,PRVY,PRVZ)

Input	PRPX,PRPY,PRPZ		
	pattern reference point	WC3	$3 \times REAL$
Input	PRVX(2),PRVY(2),PRVZ(2)		
	pattern reference vectors	WC3	$3 \times 2 \times REAL$

6.6   FILL AREA SET 3 Primitive

FILL AREA is a very flexible and powerful primitive for the generation of areas. However, it does not cover all the required needs. The major drawback is the lack of an adequate method for handling areas with holes in them (cf. Figure 6.4). Using FILL AREA to do this involves calling FILL AREA several times, i.e., first a FILL AREA with the outer boundary and lower segment priority and then with the inner boundaries and a higher segment priority. Another technique is to introduce subsidiary lines which connect the outer and inner boundaries. Both ways are undesirable as they use extraneous concepts for achieving the required effect.

A second drawback is that FILL AREA only deals with the interior of an area but not with its boundary (with the exception of interior style HOLLOW). The boundary has to be drawn with a separate POLYLINE primitive. Different segment priorities must be assigned to the interior and boundary

Figure 6.4   Example of
FILL AREA SET 3

to prevent the boundary being covered by the interior. This complication could be avoided if both the interior and boundary could be specified with one primitive call.

The most direct solution would be to extend the functionality of FILL AREA. This can only be done in a future revision of the GKS standard. In anticipation of such a future extension of GKS, however, GKS-3D has already introduced such a function: FILL AREA SET and its 3D counterpart FILL AREA SET 3. FILL AREA SET is only a shorthand notation of FILL AREA SET 3 as described in Table 11.1.

FILL AREA SET 3 accepts a list of point lists, one for each closed boundary. All the points defined in one call of FILL AREA SET 3 have to lie within one plane, i.e., FILL AREA SET 3 is planar like FILL AREA 3. The plane is determined implicitly by the boundary points. If the boundary points do not belong to one plane (e.g., as a consequence of round-off errors or wrong data), the best-fitting plane will be selected according to some implementation-dependent algorithm.

The definition of the interior is identical to that in 2D: A line is drawn within the FILL AREA SET 3 plane from the point which is to be tested to infinity. If the number of intersections this line makes with all the boundaries is odd, the point lies within the interior; otherwise, it is outside it. This implies that the intersection of two polygons does not belong to the area, i.e., a hole is generated. If polygons are lying apart, each of them defines a separate area.

FILL AREA SET 3   WSAC,SGOP   L0a
Parameters:
  Input   list of point lists   WC3   L3
Effect:
  A FILL AREA SET 3 primitive is generated. The current values of the FILL AREA SET attributes, as given by the GKS-3D state list, are bound to the primitive. It is assumed that the points defining FILL AREA SET 3 are lying in a plane. Otherwise, a FILL AREA SET 3 primitive will still be generated but its exact form is implementation-dependent. No error message will be generated. Look at the definition of FILL AREA in Section III.6.5 for further details of the definition of the interior and clipping.
  If the edge flag is ON, edges of a FILL AREA SET are drawn and clipped as if they were polylines with aspects given by the edge attributes. The polylines are drawn with a higher priority than the interiors of the corresponding areas.
  PICK input of a FILL AREA SET primitive can be achieved in the following ways: For interior style SOLID and PATTERN, it may be picked at any point in the interior but not by pointing to a point in a hole. For interior style HATCH, it may be picked at any point of the hatch lines. In both cases, it may be picked also at any point along the boundary if the edge flag is ON. For interior style HOLLOW, it may be picked by pointing at any point on the boundary independent of the setting of the edge flag.
Errors:
  5   GKS not in proper state: GKS should be either in the state WSAC or in the state SGOP
  431   List of point lists is invalid

———————————— *FORTRAN Interface* ————————————

CALL GFAS3 (NPL,IA,XA,YA,ZA)

Parameters:

Input	NPL	number of point lists	(1..n)	INTEGER
Input	IA(NPL)	starting indices for point lists	(4..n)	n × INTEGER
		(the index range is 1 to IA(1)−1 for list 1		
		and IA(*l*−1) to IA(*l*)−1 for list *l*≥2;		
		IA(1)≥4 and IA(*l*)−IA(*l*−1)≥4 for *l*≥2)		
Input	XA(NP),YA(NP),ZA(NP)			
		points	WC3	3 × n × REAL
		with NP=IA(NPL)−1		

As FILL AREA SET 3 is regarded an extension of FILL AREA 3 rather than a new primitive, it uses all FILL AREA 3 attributes. These attributes give full control of the appearance of the interior of areas.

In the case of interior style HOLLOW, only the boundary is drawn with an implementation-dependent line style and line width and with the colour currently selected via the fill area colour index. For other interior styles, the boundaries may be drawn or not according to the setting of the EDGE FLAG attribute. If the EDGE FLAG has the value ON, the boundaries will be generated like POLYLINES with a separate set of polyline attributes, specified as edge attributes EDGE TYPE, EDGE WIDTH SCALE FACTOR, and EDGE COLOUR INDEX. These attributes are similar to the polyline attributes LINETYPE, LINEWIDTH SCALE FACTOR, and POLYLINE COLOUR INDEX.

Areas defined by one FILL AREA SET 3 call have the same attributes. Values of the edge attributes can be specified globally or by using an EDGE INDEX which points to an edge representation in the workstation state list. As we know from Section III.6.8.2, aspect source flags are used to indicate where an attribute value is to be taken from. A function SET ASPECT SOURCE FLAGS 3 is provided which sets the aspect source flags for the four edge attributes.

SET EDGE FLAG   GKOP,WSOP,WSAC,SGOP   L0a

Parameters:

Input	edge flag	(OFF, ON)	E

Effect:

The 'current edge flag' entry in the GKS-3D state list is set equal to the specified value. This value is used for the display of subsequent FILL AREA SET 3 output primitives created when the 'current edge flag ASF' entry in the GKS-3D state list is INDIVIDUAL. This value does not affect the display of subsequent FILL AREA SET 3 output primitives created when the mentioned ASF entry in the GKS-3D state list is BUNDLED.

Errors:

8   GKS not in proper state: GKS should be in one of the states GKOP, WSOP, WSAC or SGOP

———————————— *FORTRAN Interface* ————————————

CALL GSEDFG (EDFLAG)

Parameters:

Input	EDFLAG	edge flag	(0=off, 1=on) INTEGER

SET EDGE TYPE   GKOP,WSOP,WSAC,SGOP   L0a
Parameters:
Input   edge type $(-n..-1,1..n)$ I
Effect:
The 'current edge type' entry in the GKS-3D state list is set equal to the specified
value. This value is used for the display of subsequent FILL AREA SET 3 output
primitives created when the 'current edge type ASF' entry in the GKS-3D state list
is INDIVIDUAL. This value does not affect the display of subsequent FILL AREA
SET 3 output primitives created when the mentioned ASF entry in the GKS-3D state
list is BUNDLED.
The edge type attribute adopts the same values as the linetype attribute. If the specified
edge type is not available at a workstation, edge type 1 is used at that workstation.
Errors:
   8   GKS not in proper state: GKS should be in one of the states GKOP, WSOP,
         WSAC or SGOP
 423   Edge type is equal zero

───────────────────────── *FORTRAN Interface* ─────────────────────────
CALL GSEDT (EDTYPE)
Parameters:
Input   EDTYPE   edge type $(-n..-1,1..n)$ INTEGER

SET EDGE WIDTH SCALE FACTOR   GKOP,WSOP,WSAC,SGOP   L0a
Parameters:
Input   edge width scale factor ≥ 0 R
Effect:
The 'current edge width scale factor' entry in the GKS-3D state list is set equal
to the specified value. This value is used for the display of subsequent FILL AREA
SET 3 output primitives created when the 'current edge width scale factor ASF' entry
in the GKS-3D state list is INDIVIDUAL. This value does not affect the display
of subsequent FILL AREA SET 3 output primitives created when the mentioned
ASF entry in the GKS-3D state list is BUNDLED.
The edge width scale factor is applied to the nominal edge width at a workstation;
the result is mapped by the workstation to the nearest available edge width.
Errors:
   8   GKS not in proper state: GKS should be in one of the states GKOP, WSOP,
         WSAC or SGOP
 425   Edge width scale factor is less than zero

───────────────────────── *FORTRAN Interface* ─────────────────────────
CALL GSEWSC (EDWSF)
Parameters:
Input   EDWSF   edge width scale factor ≥ 0 REAL

SET EDGE COLOUR INDEX   GKOP,WSOP,WSAC,SGOP   L0a
Parameters:
Input   edge colour index $(0..n)$ I
Effect:
The 'current edge colour index' entry in the GKS-3D state list is set equal to the
specified value. This value is used for the display of subsequent FILL AREA SET
3 output primitives created when the 'current edge colour index ASF' entry in the

GKS-3D state list is INDIVIDUAL. This value does not affect the display of subsequent FILL AREA SET 3 output primitives created when the mentioned ASF entry in the GKS-3D state list is BUNDLED.

The colour index is a pointer to the colour tables of the workstations. If the specified colour index is not present in a workstation colour table, a workstation-dependent colour index is used at that workstation.

Errors:

8	GKS not in proper state: GKS should be in one of the states GKOP, WSOP, WSAC or SGOP
92	Colour index is less than zero

――――――――――――――――――― *FORTRAN Interface* ―――――――――――――――――――

CALL GSEDCI (EDCIX)

Parameters:

Input	EDCIX	edge colour index	(0..n)	INTEGER

SET EDGE INDEX   GKOP,WSOP,WSAC,SGOP   L0a

Parameters:

Input	edge index	(1..n)	I

Effect:

The 'current edge index' entry in the GKS-3D state list is set equal to the specified value. This value is used when creating subsequent FILL AREA SET 3 output primitives.

Errors:

8	GKS not in proper state: GKS should be in one of the states GKOP, WSOP, WSAC or SGOP
420	Edge index is invalid

――――――――――――――――――― *FORTRAN Interface* ―――――――――――――――――――

CALL GSEDI (EDIX)

Parameters:

Input	EDIX	edge index	(1..n)	INTEGER

SET EDGE REPRESENTATION   WSOP,WSAC,SGOP   L1a

Parameters:

Input	workstation identifier		N
Input	edge index	(1..n)	I
Input	edge flag	(OFF, ON)	E
Input	edge type	(−n..−1,1..n)	I
Input	edge width scale factor	≥0	R
Input	edge colour index	(0..n)	I

Effect:

In the edge bundle table of the workstation state list, the given edge index is associated with the specified parameters.

The edge bundle table in the workstation state list has at least five predefined entries taken from the workstation description table. Any table entry including the predefined entries may be redefined with this function.

If a FILL AREA SET 3 is displayed with an edge index that is not present in the edge bundle table of a workstation, edge index 1 is used.

Which of the aspects in the entry are used depends upon the way the corresponding aspect source flags are set.

Errors:

7	GKS not in proper state: GKS should be in one of the states WSOP, WSAC or SGOP
20	Specified workstation identifier is invalid
25	Specified workstation is not open
33	Specified workstation is of category MI
35	Specified workstation is of category INPUT
36	Specified workstation is Workstation-Independent Segment Storage
93	Colour index is invalid
420	Edge index is invalid
423	Edge type is equal zero
424	Specified edge type is not supported on this workstation
425	Edge width scale factor is less than zero

———————————————— *FORTRAN Interface* ————————————————

CALL GSEDR (WKID,EDIX,EDFLAG,EDTYPE,EDWSF,EDCIX)
Parameters:

Input	WKID	workstation identifier		INTEGER
Input	EDIX	edge index	$(1..n)$	INTEGER
Input	EDFLAG	edge flag	$(0=\text{off}, 1=\text{on})$	INTEGER
Input	EDTYPE	edge type	$(-n..-1,1..n)$	INTEGER
Input	EDWSF	edge width scale factor	≥ 0	REAL
Input	EDCIX	edge colour index	$(0..n)$	INTEGER

SET ASPECT SOURCE FLAGS 3　　　　　　GKOP,WSOP,WSAC,SGOP　L0a
Parameters:

Input	list of aspect source flags	(BUNDLED, INDIVIDUAL)	$4 \times$ E

Effect:

The aspect source flags (ASFs) in the GKS-3D state list are set equal to the specified values. The elements of the list of ASFs are arranged in the following order: edge flag ASF, edge type ASF, edge width scale factor ASF, edge colour index ASF.

Errors:

8	GKS not in proper state: GKS should be in one of the states GKOP, WSOP, WSAC or SGOP

———————————————— *FORTRAN Interface* ————————————————

CALL GSASF3 (LASF)
Parameters:

Input	LASF(4)	list of aspect source flags	$4 \times$ INTEGER
		$(0=\text{bundled}, 1=\text{individual})$	

6.7　CELL ARRAY 3 Primitive

CELL ARRAY 3 accepts an array of colour indices and generates a raster image on the display surface. The extent of the raster image is given by three points spanning a cell parallelogram in WC3. The cell parallelogram is subdivided by a regular grid aligned with the sides of the parallelogram into parallelograms of equal size called cells, so that the number of cell rows and columns corresponds to the dimensions of the colour index array. Each of these cells

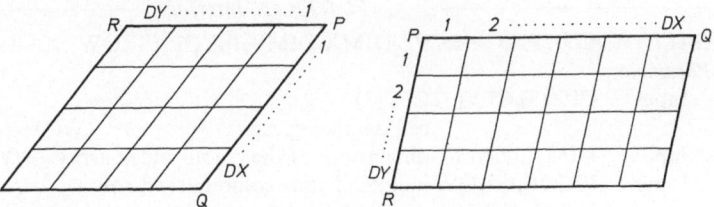

Figure 6.5   Assignment of colour indices to cells

is assigned the respective colour index as indicated in Figure 6.5: Indices (1,1), $(DX,1)$ and $(1,DY)$ are assigned to the cells adjacent to P, Q, and R, respectively.

The grid, defined in WC3, is subject to all transformations which may map the cell parallelograms onto arbitrary quadrangles. The mapping to the pixels on a workstation is done by point sampling as in 2D (cf. Figure III.6.20).

In the case of 2D, the geometry of CELL ARRAY is defined by two points in WC which span a rectangle parallel to the axes in WC. In the case of 3D, three points are needed for the definition of a rectangle. However, as three points generally span a parallelogram, CELL ARRAY 3 accepts parallelograms as well. This was done to avoid superfluous error conditions being created. It does not imply that the use of parallelograms is recommended. Curious effects are possible if the cells of the CELL ARRAY are not closely related to the pixels on the display surface.

It should be noted that each CELL ARRAY 3 primitive lies within one plane.

CELL ARRAY 3   WSAC,SGOP   L0a

Parameters:

Input	cell parallelogram P, Q, R	WC3	$3 \times P3$
Input	dimensions of the colour index array DX, DY	$(1..n)$	$2 \times I$
Input	colour index array	$(0..n)$	$n \times n \times I$

Effect:

A CELL ARRAY 3 primitive is generated as defined by the cell parallelogram corners and the colour index array. The parallelogram is defined by three corner points P, Q, R. The fourth corner point, S, can be obtained by:

$$S = P + ((Q-P) + (R-P)) = Q + R - P$$

The cell dimensions CX, CY are determined by

$$CX = |Q-P|/DX$$
$$CY = |R-P|/DY$$

The colour indices are mapped onto the two-dimensional cell array so that indices (1, 1), (DX, 1), (1, DY) are assigned to the cells adjacent to P, Q, R, respectively. If an index is not present in the colour table at a workstation, a workstation-dependent index is used at that workstation. Look at the definition of CELL ARRAY in Section II.6.6 for further details of mapping of the index array onto pixels at a workstation.

Errors:

5   GKS not in proper state: GKS should be either in the state WSAC or in the state SGOP

91   Dimensions of colour array are invalid

―――――――――――――――― *FORTRAN Interface* ――――――――――

CALL GCA3 (CPX,CPY,CPZ,DIMX,DIMY,ISCOL,ISROW,NCOL,NROW,COLIA)
Parameters:
Input	CPX(3),CPY(3),CPZ(3)			
		cell parallelogram	WC3	$3 \times 3 \times$ REAL
Input	DIMX,DIMY	dimensions of the colour index array	(1..n)	INTEGER
Input	ISCOL,ISROW	indices of start column, start row	(1..n)	INTEGER
Input	NCOL,NROW	number of columns, rows	(1..n)	INTEGER
Input	COLIA(DIMX,DIMY)		(0..n)	
		colour index array		$n \times n \times$ INTEGER

6.8   GENERALIZED DRAWING PRIMITIVE 3 (GDP3)

GENERALIZED DRAWING PRIMITIVE 3 is used, as is its 2D counterpart, to address the special capabilities of workstations. It conveys 3D data to the workstations. This data is properly transformed by GKS, leaving the remaining actions required by this primitive to the workstations which should know how to handle it.

GDP and GDP3 address the same list of non-standard functions. Each GDP has a 3D counterpart, but there may be a GDP3 which has no 2D counterpart. This restriction was necessary to ensure compatibility between GKS and GKS-3D functions as described in Chapter 11.

―――――――――――――――――――――――――――――――――

GENERALIZED DRAWING PRIMITIVE 3(GDP3)   WSAC,SGOP   L0a
Parameters:
Input	number of points	(0..n)	I
Input	points	WC3	$n \times P3$
Input	GDP identifier		N
Input	GDP3 data record		D

Effect:
A GENERALIZED DRAWING PRIMITIVE 3 (GDP3) of the type indicated by the GDP3 identifier is generated on the basis of the given points and the GDP3 data record. The current sets of attribute values, as given by the GKS-3D state list for POLYLINE 3, POLYMARKER 3, TEXT 3, FILL AREA 3, or EDGE, are bound to the primitive. When the GDP3 generates output at the workstation, zero or more of the sets of attributes are used. These are the sets of attributes most appropriate for the specified GDP3 function and are selected for the GDP3 as part of its definition (see workstation description table).

Errors:
5	GKS not in proper state: GKS should be either in the state WSAC or in the state SGOP
100	Number of points is invalid
102	Generalized drawing primitive identifier is invalid
103	Content of generalized drawing primitive data record is invalid
104	At least one active workstation is not able to generate the specified generalized drawing primitive
105	At least one active workstation is not able to generate the specified generalized drawing primitive under the current transformations and clipping rectangle

——————————————— *FORTRAN Interface* ———————————————
CALL GGDP3 (NP,XA,YA,ZA,PRIMID,MXDRA,DRA)
Parameters:

Input	NP	number of points	(0..n)	INTEGER
Input	XA(NP),YA(NP),ZA(NP)			
		points	WC3	$3 \times n \times$ REAL
Input	PRIMID	GDP identifier		INTEGER
Input	MXDRA	dimension of data record array		INTEGER
Input	DRA(MXDRA)	GDP3 data record		$n \times$ CHARACTER*80

7 SEGMENTS

Segments in GKS-3D differ from those in GKS in that they contain exclusively 3D primitives and their attributes. As far as segment generation and manipulation is concerned, the functions of Chapter III.7 apply. For the transformation of segments, two new functions SET SEGMENT TRANSFORMATION 3 and INSERT SEGMENT 3 are provided, which extend the functionality of the respective GKS functions by accepting 3×4 transformation matrices rather than 2×3 matrices as in the case of 2D. The extended transformation matrix has to be recorded in the segment state list.

Table 7.1   Changes to the segment state list (Table III.7.2)

Replace the entry 'segment transformation matrix' by:		
segment transformation matrix	$3 \times 4 \times$ R	1, 0, 0, 0
		0, 1, 0, 0
		0, 0, 1, 0

The segment transformation includes shifting, scaling, rotation and shearing. Utility functions are provided to form a transformation matrix from any number of shift, rotation, and scaling operations.

SET SEGMENT TRANSFORMATION 3   WSOP,WSAC,SGOP   L1a
Parameters:

Input	segment name	N
Input	transformation matrix	$3 \times 4 \times$ R

Effect:
The 'segment transformation matrix' in the segment state list is set equal to the value specified by the parameter. When a segment is displayed, the coordinates of its primitives will be transformed by applying the following matrix multiplication to them:

$$\begin{pmatrix} x' \\ y' \\ z' \end{pmatrix} = \begin{pmatrix} M_{11} & M_{12} & M_{13} & M_{14} \\ M_{21} & M_{22} & M_{23} & M_{24} \\ M_{31} & M_{32} & M_{33} & M_{34} \end{pmatrix} \times \begin{pmatrix} x \\ y \\ z \\ 1 \end{pmatrix}$$

The original coordinates are (x,y,z), the transformed coordinates are (x',y',z'), both in NDC3. The values M_{14}, M_{24}, and M_{34} of the transformation matrix are in NDC3 coordinates, the other values are unitless. For geometric attributes which are vectors (for example, CHARACTER UP VECTOR), the values M_{14}, M_{24}, and M_{34} are replaced by zero.

This function can be used to transform a segment stored on a workstation. The transformation applies to all workstations where the specified segment is stored, even if they are not all active.

The segment transformation (conceptually) takes place in NDC3 space. The segment transformation will be stored in the segment state list and will not affect the contents of the segment. The segment transformation is not cumulative, i.e., it always applies to the segment which was originally created.

N.B.:

Applying the same segment transformation twice to a segment will give identical results. The identity transformation will show the segment in its original geometrical appearance.

Errors:

7	GKS not in proper state: GKS should be in one of the states WSOP, WSAC or SGOP
120	Specified segment name is invalid
122	Specified segment does not exist

───────────────── *FORTRAN Interface* ─────────────────

CALL GSSGT3 (SEGNAM,SEGTM)
Parameters:

Input	SEGNAM	segment name	INTEGER
Input	SEGTM(3,4)	transformation matrix	$3 \times 4 \times$ REAL

The INSERT SEGMENT 3 function not only replaces the clipping information contained in a segment but also all view indices and HLHSR identifiers. These values are replaced by the respective current values in the GKS-3D state list.

───

INSERT SEGMENT 3   WSAC,SGOP   L2a
Parameters:

Input	segment name	N
Input	transformation matrix	$3 \times 4 \times$ R

Effect:

Having been transformed as described below, the primitives contained in the segment are copied either (in state SGOP) into the open segment or (in state WSAC) into the stream of primitives outside segments. In both cases the transformed primitives are sent to all active workstations.

The coordinates of the primitives contained in the inserted segment will be transformed firstly by any segment transformation specified for it, and secondly by applying the following matrix multiplication to them:

$$\begin{pmatrix} x' \\ y' \\ z' \end{pmatrix} = \begin{pmatrix} M_{11} & M_{12} & M_{13} & M_{14} \\ M_{21} & M_{22} & M_{23} & M_{24} \\ M_{31} & M_{32} & M_{33} & M_{34} \end{pmatrix} \times \begin{pmatrix} x \\ y \\ z \\ 1 \end{pmatrix}$$

The original coordinates are (x,y,z), the transformed coordinates are (x',y',z'), both in NDC3. The values M_{14}, M_{24}, and M_{34} of the transformation matrix are NDC3 coordinates, the other values are unitless. For geometric attributes which are vectors (for example, CHARACTER UP VECTOR), the values M_{14}, M_{24}, M_{34} are replaced by zero.

The insert transformation (conceptually) takes place in NDC3 space. Apart from the segment transformation, attributes associated with the inserted segment are ignored.

All clipping indicators, clipping volumes, view indices and HLHSR identifiers in the inserted segment are ignored and replaced by the current values from the GKS-3D state list.

N.B.:

The specified segment must be in the workstation-independent segment storage and not be the open segment. All primitives retain the values of the primitive attributes (e.g., polyline index, text path, pick identifier) which are assigned to them when they are created for their whole lifetime. In particular, when segments are inserted, the values of the primitive attributes within the inserted segments remain unchanged. The values of primitive attributes used to generate subsequent primitives within the segment into which the insertion takes place are unaffected by that insertion.

Errors:

5	GKS not in proper state: GKS should be either in the state WSAC or in the state SGOP
27	Workstation-Independent Segment Storage is not open
120	Specified segment name is invalid
124	Specified segment does not exist on Workstation-Independent Segment Storage
125	Specified segment is open

———————————————— *FORTRAN Interface* ————————————————

CALL GINSG3 (SEGNAM,SEGTM)

Parameters:

Input	SEGNAM	segment name	INTEGER
Input	SEGTM(3,4)	transformation matrix	$3 \times 4 \times$ REAL

———

EVALUATE TRANSFORMATION MATRIX 3

                                    GKOP,WSOP,WSAC,SGOP   L1a

Parameters:

Input	fixed point	WC3 or NDC3	P3
Input	shift vector	WC3 or NDC3	P3
Input	rotation angles $\alpha_x,\alpha_y,\alpha_z$ in radians (positive if anti-clockwise)		$3 \times$ R
Input	scale factors f_x,f_y,f_z		$3 \times$ R
Input	coordinate switch	(WC3,NDC3)	E
Output	transformation matrix		$3 \times 4 \times$ R

Effect:

The transformation defined by fixed point, shift vector, rotation angles around x-, y-, z-axes, and scale factors for x-, y-, z-axes is evaluated and the result is put in the output transformation matrix (for use by INSERT SEGMENT 3 and SET SEGMENT TRANSFORMATION 3). The coordinate switch determines whether the shift vector and fixed point are given in WC3 or NDC3. If WC3 are used, the shift vector and the fixed point are transformed by the current normalization transformation. The order of transformation is: scale, rotate (both relative to the specified fixed point), and shift. The elements M_{14}, M_{24}, and M_{34} of the resulting 3×4 transformation matrix are in NDC3, the other elements are unitless.

Errors:

8   GKS not in proper state: GKS should be in one of the states GKOP, WSOP, WSAC or SGOP

———————————————— *FORTRAN Interface* ————————————————

GALL GEVTM3 (FPX,FPY,FPZ,SVX,SVY,SVZ,ROTX,ROTY,ROTZ, SCX,SCY,SCZ,CSW,NSEGTM)

Parameters:

Input	FPX,FPY,FPZ	fixed point	WC3 or NDC3	$3 \times$ REAL
Input	SVX,SVY,SVZ	shift vector	WC3 or NDC3	$3 \times$ REAL
Input	ROTX,ROTY,ROTZ	rotation angles $\alpha_x,\alpha_y,\alpha_z$ in radians		
		(positive if anti-clockwise)		$3 \times$ REAL
Input	SCX,SCY,SCZ	scale factors f_x, f_y, f_z		$3 \times$ REAL
Input	CSW	coordinate switch ($0=$WC3,$1=$NDC3)		INTEGER
Output	NSEGTM(3,4)	transformation matrix		$3 \times 4 \times$ REAL

ACCUMULATE TRANSFORMATION MATRIX 3

GKOP,WSOP,WSAC,SGOP   L1a

Parameters:

Input	segment transformation matrix		$3 \times 4 \times$ R
Input	fixed point	WC3 or NDC3	P3
Input	shift vector	WC3 or NDC3	P3
Input	rotation angles $\alpha_x,\alpha_y,\alpha_z$ in radians		
	(positive if anti-clockwise)		$3 \times$ R
Input	scale factors f_x,f_y,f_z		$3 \times$ R
Input	coordinate switch	(WC3, NDC3)	E
Output	transformation matrix		$3 \times 4 \times$ R

Effect:

The transformation defined by fixed point, shift vector, rotation angles, and scale factors is composed with the input transformation matrix and the result is returned in the output transformation matrix (for use by INSERT SEGMENT 3 and SET SEGMENT TRANSFORMATION 3). The coordinate switch determines whether the shift vector and fixed point are given in WC3 or NDC3. If WC3 are used, the shift vector and the fixed point are transformed by the current normalization transformation. The order of transformation is: specified input matrix, scale, rotate (both relative to the specified fixed point), and shift. The elements M_{14}, M_{24}, and M_{34} of the 3×4 input matrix and the resulting 3×4 transformation matrix are in NDC3, the other elements are unitless.

Errors:

8   GKS not in proper state: GKS should be in one of the states GKOP, WSOP, WSAG or SGOP

———————————————— *FORTRAN Interface* ————————————————

CALL GACTM3 (OSEGTM,FPX,FPY,FPZ,SVX,SVY,SVZ,ROTX, ROTY,ROTZ,SCX,SCY,SCZ,CSW,NSEGTM)

Parameters:

Input	OSEGTM(3,4)	transformation matrix		$3 \times 4 \times$ REAL
Input	FPX,FPY,FPZ	fixed point	WC3 or NDC3	$3 \times$ REAL

Input	SVX,SVY,SVZ	shift vector WC3 or NDC3	$3 \times$ REAL
Input	ROTX,ROTY,ROTZ	rotation angles $\alpha_x,\alpha_y,\alpha_z$ in radians (positive if anti-clockwise)	$3 \times$ REAL
Input	SCX,SCY,SCZ	scale factors f_x,f_y,f_z	$3 \times$ REAL
Input	CSW	coordinate switch $(0 = WC3, 1 = NDC3)$	INTEGER
Output	NSEGTM(3,4)	transformation matrix	$3 \times 4 \times$ REAL

8 INPUT

The input model and the input classes as described in Chapter III.8 also apply for GKS-3D. The input classes PICK, CHOICE, VALUATOR and TEXT handle non-geometric data and, therefore, are not affected by dimensionality. Only the INITIALISE functions adopt a geometric parameter, echo area, which is extended to a 3D echo volume in the respective INITIALISE 3 functions.

Input classes LOCATOR and STROKE deal with geometric input which has to be extended for GKS-3D. The new input classes are named LOCATOR 3 and STROKE 3 and allow a single point or a sequence of points with 3D coordinate values to be entered. The points are generated in DC3 and are transformed back to WC3. In this transformation the inverses of the workstation transformation, a viewing transformation and a normalization transformation are involved. The workstation transformation is unique for each workstation, the viewing transformation and the normalization transformation are selected according to a priority scheme (cf. Sections 5.6 and III.5.5). Therefore, the measure of LOCATOR 3 and STROKE 3 includes a normalization transformation number and a view index additional to the coordinate values. In detail, the measure of STROKE 3 is determined as follows:

A STROKE 3 measure consists of positions $P_1...P_m$ in world coordinates (WC3), a normalization transformation number N, and a view index I. These measure values are generated from the points $P_1'''...P_m'''$, which are delivered from a physical device in device coordinates (DC3), in the following way:

1. The inverse workstation transformation of the respective workstation is applied to transform each P_i''' in DC3 into P_i'' in NPC.
2. All viewing transformations at the respective workstation whose projection viewport contains all the points $P_1''...P_m''$ are selected. Of those viewing transformations the one with view index I which has the highest view transformation input priority is selected. The inverse of this viewing transformation I is applied to transform each P_i'' in NPC into P_i' in NDC3.
3. All normalization transformations whose viewports contain all the points $P_1'...P_m'$ are selected. Of those normalization transformations the one with the highest viewport input priority is selected. The inverse of this normalization transformation N is applied to transform each P_i' in NDC3 into P_i in WC3.

A LOCATOR 3 measure consists of a position P in world coordinates (WC3), a normalization transformation number N, and a view index I. The measure value P is generated from a point P''', which is delivered from a physical device in device coordinates (DC3), in the same way as the STROKE measure values with a point sequence consisting of one point only (i.e., $m=1$).

As true 3D input devices are rare, it will be usual to generate 3D coordinate values by using 2D input devices. The simulation techniques and complicated prompt and echo types used for this purpose are not addressed in this standard. This is expressed by the fact that GKS-3D only stipulates having prompt and echo type 1 which is implementation-dependent. Further prompt and echo types are defined but not required.

As simulation techniques for 3D input using 2D devices tend to be very clumsy and time consuming, it is important to make this effort only in cases where full 3D input is really needed. But even in a pure 3D system, there are occasions where 2D input is sufficient, e.g., if the viewing window is to be positioned interactively on the viewing plane. In such cases, it would be very convenient if 2D input devices could be used directly rather than having to generate a third coordinate value in a lengthy interaction which will subsequently be discarded.

The use of the 2D input functions of GKS, LOCATOR and STROKE, does not solve this problem as these functions are immediately mapped onto the respective GKS-3D functions, LOCATOR 3 and STROKE 3 (cf. Chapter 11), and are treated identically within the viewing pipeline. This implies that a third coordinate is also needed for LOCATOR and STROKE. However, an implementor is free as how to implement the input functions because no specific prompt and echo types are prescribed. He can provide computationally cheap input techniques, where just $z=ZMIN$ or the z-coordinate of the initial point as set by INITIALISE LOCATOR are used, as well as more comfortable input techniques where any desired 3D point can be selected. Such different input techniques can be connected to different device numbers which will be described in the implementation documentation.

8.1   Initialise Functions

INITIALISE LOCATOR 3   WSOP,WSAC,SGOP   L0b

Parameters:

Input	workstation identifier		N
Input	locator device number	(1..n)	I
Input	initial normalization transformation number	(0..n)	I
Input	initial view index	(0..n)	I
Input	initial locator position	WC3	P3
Input	prompt and echo type	$(-n..-1,1..n)$	I
Input	echo volume	DC3	$6 \times R$
	XMIN < XMAX, YMIN < YMAX, ZMIN ≤ ZMAX		
Input	locator data record		D

Effect:

The parameter values are stored in the workstation state list entry for the specified LOCATOR 3 device. Prompt and echo types see LOCATOR (Section III.8.3).

Errors:

7	GKS not in proper state: GKS should be in one of the states WSOP, WSAC or SGOP
20	Specified workstation identifier is invalid
25	Specified workstation is not open
38	Specified workstation is neither of category INPUT nor of category OUTIN
140	Specified input device is not present on workstation
141	Input device is not in REQUEST mode
144.	Specified prompt and echo type is not supported on this workstation
145	Echo area is outside display space
146	Contents of input data record are invalid
152	Initial value is invalid
406	Box definition is invalid

──────────────────── *FORTRAN Interface* ────────────────────

CALL GINLC3 (WKID,DEVN,INTN,IVWIX,ILOCX,ILOCY,ILOCZ,PE,
EVOL,MXDRA,LOCDR)

Parameters:

Input	WKID	workstation identifier		INTEGER
Input	DEVN	locator device number	$(1..n)$	INTEGER
Input	INTN	initial normalization transformation		
		number	$(0..n)$	INTEGER
Input	IVWIX	initial view index	$(0..n)$	INTEGER
Input	ILOCX,ILOCY,ILOCZ			
		initial locator position	WC3	$3 \times$ REAL
Input	PE	prompt and echo type	$(-n..-1,1..n)$	INTEGER
Input	EVOL(6)	echo volume	DC3	$6 \times$ REAL
		EVOL(1) < EVOL(2), EVOL(3) < EVOL(4), EVOL(5) $\le$ EVOL(6)		
Input	MXDRA	dimension of data record array		INTEGER
Input	LOCDR(MXDRA)			
		locator data record		$n \times$ CHARACTER*80

───

INITIALISE STROKE 3	WSOP,WSAC,SGOP	L0b

Parameters:

Input	workstation identifier		N
Input	stroke device number	$(1..n)$	I
Input	initial normalization transformation number	$(0..n)$	I
Input	initial view index	$(0..n)$	I
Input	number of points in initial stroke	$(0..n)$	I
Input	points in initial stroke	WC3	$n \times$ P3
Input	prompt and echo type	$(-n..-1,1..n)$	I
Input	echo volume	DC3	$6 \times$ R
	XMIN < XMAX, YMIN < YMAX, ZMIN $\le$ ZMAX		
Input	stroke data record		D

Effect:

The parameter values are stored in the workstation state list entry of the specified STROKE 3 device. Prompt and echo types see STROKE (Section III.8.3).

Errors:

7	GKS not in proper state: GKS should be in one of the states WSOP, WSAC or SGOP
20	Specified workstation identifier is invalid
25	Specified workstation is not open
38	Specified workstation is neither of category INPUT nor of category OUTIN
140	Specified input device is not present on workstation
141	Input device is not in REQUEST mode
144	Specified prompt and echo type is not supported on this workstation
145	Echo area is outside display space
146	Contents of input data record are invalid
152	Initial value is invalid
153	Length of initial string is greater than the implementation defined maximum
406	Box definition is invalid

———————————————— *FORTRAN Interface* ————————————————

CALL GINSK3 (WKID,DEVN,INTN,IVWIX,NP,ISX,ISY,ISZ,PE,
EVOL,MXDRA,SKDR)

Parameters:

Input	WKID	workstation identifier		INTEGER
Input	DEVN	stroke device number	$(1..n)$	INTEGER
Input	INTN	initial normalization transformation number	$(0..n)$	INTEGER
Input	IVWIX	initial view index	$(0..n)$	INTEGER
Input	NP	number of points in initial stroke	$(0..n)$	INTEGER
Input	ISX(NP),ISY(NP),ISZ(NP)			
		points in initial stroke	WC3	$3 \times n \times$ REAL
Input	PE	prompt and echo type	$(-n..-1,1..n)$	INTEGER
Input	EVOL(6)	echo volume	DC3	$6 \times$ REAL
	EVOL(1) < EVOL(2), EVOL(3) < EVOL(4), EVOL(5) ≤ EVOL(6)			
Input	MXDRA	dimension of data record array		INTEGER
Input	SKDR(MXDRA)			
		stroke data record		$n \times$ CHARACTER∗80

———

INITIALISE VALUATOR 3		WSOP,WSAC,SGOP	L0b

Parameters:

Input	workstation identifier		N
Input	valuator device number	$(1..n)$	I
Input	initial value		R
Input	prompt and echo type	$(-n..-1,1..n)$	I
Input	echo volume	DC3	$6 \times$ R
	XMIN < XMAX, YMIN < YMAX, ZMIN ≤ ZMAX		
Input	valuator data record		D

Effect:

The parameter values are stored in the workstation state list entry for the specified VALUATOR 3 device. Prompt and echo types see VALUATOR (Section III.8.3).

Errors:

7	GKS not in proper state: GKS should be in one of the states WSOP, WSAC or SGOP
20	Specified workstation identifier is invalid

25   Specified workstation is not open
38   Specified workstation is neither of category INPUT nor of category OUTIN
140   Specified input device is not present on workstation
141   Input device is not in REQUEST mode
144   Specified prompt and echo type is not supported on this workstation
145   Echo area is outside display space
146   Contents of input data record are invalid
152   Initial value is invalid
406   Box definition is invalid

─────────────────── *FORTRAN Interface* ───────────────────

CALL GINVL3 (WKID,DEVN,IVAL,PE,EVOL,LDR,DATREC)
Parameters:

Input	WKID	workstation identifier		INTEGER
Input	DEVN	valutator device number	(1..n)	INTEGER
Input	IVAL	initial value		REAL
Input	PE	prompt and echo type	(−n..−1,1..n)	INTEGER
Input	EVOL(6)	echo volume	DC3	6 × REAL
		EVOL(1) < EVOL(2), EVOL(3) < EVOL(4), EVOL(5) ≤ EVOL(6)		
Input	LDR	dimension of data record array		INTEGER
Input	DATREC(LDR)			
		valuator data record		n × CHARACTER∗80

───

INITIALISE CHOICE 3   WSOP,WSAC,SGOP   L0b
Parameters:

Input	workstation identifier		N
Input	choice device number	(1..n)	I
Input	initial status	(OK,NOCHOICE)	E
Input	initial choice number	(1..n)	I
Input	prompt and echo type	(−n..−1,1..n)	I
Input	echo volume	DC3	6 × R
	XMIN < XMAX, YMIN < YMAX, ZMIN ≤ ZMAX		
Input	choice data record		D

Effect:
The parameter values are stored in the workstation state list entry for the specified CHOICE 3 device. Prompt and echo types see CHOICE (Section III.8.3).
Errors:

7   GKS not in proper state: GKS should be in one of the states WSOP, WSAC
        or SGOP
20   Specified workstation identifier is invalid
25   Specified workstation is not open
38   Specified workstation is neither of category INPUT nor of category OUTIN
140   Specified input device is not present on workstation
141   Input device is not in REQUEST mode
144   Specified prompt and echo type is not supported on this workstation
145   Echo area is outside display space
146   Contents of input data record are invalid
152   Initial value is invalid
406   Box definition is invalid

———————————————— *FORTRAN Interface* ————————————————

CALL GINCH3 (WKID,DEVN,ISTAT,ICHOICE,PE,EVOL,LDR,DATREC)

Parameters:

Input	WKID	workstation identifier		INTEGER
Input	DEVN	choice device number	$(1..n)$	INTEGER
Input	ISTAT	initial status	$(0=$nochoice, $1=$ok$)$	INTEGER
Input	ICHOICE	initial choice number	$(1..n)$	INTEGER
Input	PE	prompt and echo type	$(-n..-1,1..n)$	INTEGER
Input	EVOL(6)	echo volume	DC3	$6\times$REAL
		EVOL(1)$<$EVOL(2), EVOL(3)$<$EVOL(4), EVOL(5)$\leq$EVOL(6)		
Input	LDR	dimension of data record array		INTEGER
Input	DATREC(LDR)			
		choice data record		$n\times$CHARACTER$*80$

INITIALISE PICK 3   WSOP,WSAC,SGOP   L1b

Parameters:

Input	workstation identifier		N
Input	pick device number	$(1..n)$	I
Input	initial status	(OK,NOPICK)	E
Input	initial segment		N
Input	initial pick identifier		N
Input	prompt and echo type	$(-n..-1,1..n)$	I
Input	echo volume	DC3	$6\times$R
	XMIN$<$XMAX, YMIN$<$YMAX, ZMIN$\leq$ZMAX		
Input	pick data record		D

Effect:

The parameter values are stored in the workstation state list entry for the specified PICK 3 device. Prompt and echo types see PICK (Section III.8.3).

Errors:

7	GKS not in proper state: GKS should be in one of the states WSOP, WSAC or SGOP
20	Specified workstation identifier is invalid
25	Specified workstation is not open
38	Specified workstation is neither of category INPUT nor of category OUTIN
140	Specified input device is not present on workstation
141	Input device is not in REQUEST mode
144	Specified prompt and echo type is not supported on this workstation
145	Echo area is outside display space
146	Contents of input data record are invalid
152	Initial value is invalid
406	Box definition is invalid

———————————————— *FORTRAN Interface* ————————————————

CALL GINPK3 (WKID,DEVN,ISTAT,ISEG,IPKID,PE,EVOL,LDR,DATREC)

Parameters:

Input	WKID	workstation identifier		INTEGER
Input	DEVN	pick device number	$(1..n)$	INTEGER
Input	ISTAT	initial status	$(0=$nopick, $1=$ok$)$	INTEGER
Input	ISEG	initial segment		INTEGER
Input	IPKID	initial pick identifier		INTEGER
Input	PE	prompt and echo type	$(-n..-1,1..n)$	INTEGER
Input	EVOL(6)	echo volume	DC3	$6\times$REAL
		EVOL(1)$<$EVOL(2), EVOL(3)$<$EVOL(4), EVOL(5)$\leq$EVOL(6)		

Input	LDR	dimension of data record array		INTEGER
Input	DATREC(LDR)			
		pick data record		n × CHARACTER∗80

INITIALISE STRING 3   WSOP,WSAG,SGOP   L0b

Parameters:

Input	workstation identifier		N
Input	string device number	(1..n)	I
Input	initial string		S
Input	prompt and echo type	(−n.. −1,1..n)	I
Input	echo volume	DC3	6 × R
	XMIN < XMAX, YMIN < YMAX, ZMIN ≤ ZMAX		
Input	string data record		D

Effect:

The parameter values are stored in the workstation state list entry for the specified STRING 3 device. Prompt and echo types see STRING (Section III.8.3).

Errors:

7	GKS not in proper state: GKS should be in one of the states WSOP, WSAC or SGOP
20	Specified workstation identifier is invalid
25	Specified workstation is not open
38	Specified workstation is neither of category INPUT nor of category OUTIN
140	Specified input device is not present on workstation
141	Input device is not in REQUEST mode
144	Specified prompt and echo type is not supported on this workstation
145	Echo area is outside display space
146	Contents of input data record are invalid
152	Initial value is invalid
406	Box definition is invalid

———————————————— *FORTRAN Interface* ————————————————

CALL GINST3 (WKID,DEVN,ISTR,PE,EVOL,LDR,DATREC)

Parameters:

Input	WKID	workstation identifier		INTEGER
Input	DEVN	string device number	(1..n)	INTEGER
Input	ISTR	initial string		CHARACTER∗(∗)
Input	PE	prompt and echo type	(−n.. −1,1..n)	INTEGER
Input	EVOL(6)	echo volume	DC3	6 × REAL
	EVOL(1) < EVOL(2), EVOL(3) < EVOL(4), EVOL(5) ≤ EVOL(6)			
Input	LDR	dimension of data record array		INTEGER
Input	DATREC(LDR)			
		string data record		n × CHARACTER∗80

8.2 Request Input Functions

REQUEST LOCATOR 3   WSOP,WSAC,SGOP   L0b

Parameters:

Input	workstation identifier		N
Input	locator device number	(1..n)	I
Output	status	(OK,NONE)	E
Output	normalization transformation number	(0..n)	I

| Output | view index | | (0..n) | I |
| Output | locator position | | WC3 | P3 |

Effect:

GKS performs a REQUEST on the specified LOCATOR 3 device. If the break facility is invoked by the operator, the status NONE is returned; otherwise OK is returned together with the logical input value which is the current measure of the LOCATOR 3 device. This measure consists of a LOCATOR 3 position in world coordinates, the view index which was used in the conversion from NPC to NDC3, and the normalization transformation number which was used in the conversion from NDC3 to WC3.

Errors:

7	GKS not in proper state: GKS should be in one of the states WSOP, WSAC or SGOP
20	Specified workstation identifier is invalid
25	Specified workstation is not open
38	Specified workstation is neither of category INPUT nor of category OUTIN
140	Specified input device is not present on workstation
141	Input device is not in REQUEST mode

———————————————— *FORTRAN Interface* ————————————————

CALL GRQLC3 (WKID,DEVN,STAT,NTN,VWIX,LOCX,LOCY,LOCZ)

Parameters:

Input	WKID	workstation identifier		INTEGER
Input	DEVN	locator device number	(1..n)	INTEGER
Output	STAT	status	(0=none, 1=ok)	INTEGER
Output	NTN	normalization transformation number	(0..n)	INTEGER
Output	VWIX	view index	(0..n)	INTEGER
Output	LOCX,LOCY,LOCZ			
		locator position	WC3	$3 \times$ REAL

———

REQUEST STROKE 3		WSOP,WSAC,SGOP	L0b

Parameters:

Input	workstation identifier		N
Input	stroke device number	(1..n)	I
Output	status	(OK,NONE)	E
Output	normalization transformation number	(0..n)	I
Output	view index	(0..n)	I
Output	number of points	(0..n)	I
Output	points in stroke	WC3	$n \times$ P3

Effect:

GKS performs a REQUEST on the specified STROKE 3 device. If the break facility is invoked by the operator, the status NONE is returned; otherwise OK is returned together with the logical input value which is the current measure of the STROKE 3 device. This measure consists of a sequence of positions in world coordinates, the view index which was used in the conversion from NPC to NDC3, and the normalization transformation number which was used in the conversion from NDC3 to WC3.

N.B.:

If an operator enters more points than the stroke input buffer size in the workstation state list allows, the additional points are lost. It is anticipated that the operator would be informed of this situation.

Errors:

| 7 | GKS not in proper state: GKS should be in one of the states WSOP, WSAC or SGOP |

20	Specified workstation identifier is invalid
25	Specified workstation is not open
38	Specified workstation is neither of category INPUT nor of category OUTIN
140	Specified input device is not present on workstation
141	Input device is not in REQUEST mode

———————————————— *FORTRAN Interface* ————————————————

CALL GRQSK3 (WKID,DEVN,MXP,STAT,NTN,VWIX,NP,SX,SY,SZ)

Parameters:

Input	WKID	workstation identifier		INTEGER
Input	DEVN	stroke device number	(1..n)	INTEGER
Input	MXP	size of arrays for stroke points	(0..n)	INTEGER
Output	STAT	status	(0 = none, 1 = ok)	INTEGER
Output	NTN	normalization transformation number	(0..n)	INTEGER
Output	VWIX	view index	(0..n)	INTEGER
Output	NP	number of points returned	(0..n)	INTEGER
Output	SX(MXP),SY(MXP),SZ(MXP)			
		points in stroke	WC3	$3 \times n \times$ REAL

8.3 Sample Input Functions

SAMPLE LOCATOR 3		WSOP,WSAC,SGOP	L0c

Parameters:

Input	workstation identifier		N
Input	locator device number	(1..n)	I
Output	normalization transformation number	(0..n)	I
Output	view index	(0..n)	I
Output	locator position	WC3	P3

Effect:

The current measure of the LOCATOR 3 device is returned. This measure consists of a LOCATOR 3 position in world coordinates, the view index which was used in the conversion from NPC to NDC3, and the normalization transformation number which was used in the conversion from NDC3 to WC3.

Errors:

7	GKS not in proper state: GKS should be in one of the states WSOP, WSAC or SGOP
20	Specified workstation identifier is invalid
25	Specified workstation is not open
38	Specified workstation is neither of category INPUT nor of category OUTIN
140	Specified input device is not present on workstation
142	Input device is not in SAMPLE mode

———————————————— *FORTRAN Interface* ————————————————

CALL GSMLC3 (WKID,DEVN,NTN,VWIX,LOCX,LOCY,LOCZ)

Parameters:

Input	WKID	workstation identifier		INTEGER
Input	DEVN	locator device number	(1..n)	INTEGER
Output	NTN	normalization transformation number	(0..n)	INTEGER
Output	VWIX	view index	(0..n)	INTEGER
Output	LOCX,LOCY,LOCZ			
		locator position	WC3	$3 \times$ REAL

SAMPLE STROKE 3   WSOP,WSAC,SGOP   L0c
Parameters:

Input	workstation identifier		N
Input	stroke device number	(1..n)	I
Output	normalization transformation number	(0..n)	I
Output	view index	(0..n)	I
Output	number of points	(0..n)	I
Output	points in stroke	WC3	n × P3

Effect:

The current measure of the STROKE 3 device is returned. This measure consists
. of a sequence of positions in world coordinates, the view index which was used in
the conversion from NPC to NDC3, and the normalization transformation number
which was used in the conversion from NDC3 to WC3.

N.B.:

If an operator enters more points than the stroke input buffer size in the workstation
state list allows, the additional points are lost. It is anticipated that the operator
would be informed of this situation.

Errors:

7	GKS not in proper state: GKS should be in one of the states WSOP, WSAC or SGOP
20	Specified workstation identifier is invalid
25	Specified workstation is not open
38	Specified workstation is neither of category INPUT nor of category OUTIN
140	Specified input device is not present on workstation
142	Input device is not in SAMPLE mode

────────────────────── *FORTRAN Interface* ──────────────────────

CALL GSMSK3 (WKID,DEVN,MXP,NTN,VWIX,NP,SX,SY,SZ)
Parameters:

Input	WKID	workstation identifier		INTEGER
Input	DEVN	stroke device number	(1..n)	INTEGER
Input	MXP	size of arrays for stroke points	(0..n)	INTEGER
Output	NTN	normalization transformation number	(0..n)	INTEGER
Output	VWIX	view index	(0..n)	INTEGER
Output	NP	number of points returned	(0..n)	INTEGER
Output	SX(MXP),SY(MXP),SZ(MXP)			
		points in stroke	WC3	3 × n × REAL

8.4   Event Input Functions

GET LOCATOR 3   WSOP,WSAC;SGOP   L0c
Parameters:

Output	normalization transformation number	(0..n)	I
Output	view index	(0..n)	I
Output	locator position	WC3	P3

Effect:

The LOCATOR 3 value in the current event queue is returned. This value consists
of a LOCATOR 3 position in world coordinates, the view index which was used

in the conversion from NPC to NDC3, and the normalization transformation number which was used in the conversion from NDC3 to WC3.

Errors:

7   GKS not in proper state: GKS should be in one of the states WSOP, WSAC or SGOP

150   No input value of the correct class is in the current event report

———————————————— *FORTRAN Interface* ————————————————

CALL GGTLC3 (NTN,VWIX,LOCX,LOCY,LOCZ)

Parameters:

Output	NTN	normalization transformation number	(0..n)	INTEGER
Output	VWIX	view index	(0..n)	INTEGER
Output	LOCX,LOCY,LOCZ			
		locator position	WC3	3 × REAL

GET STROKE 3   WSOP,WSAC,SGOP   L0c

Parameters:

Output	normalization transformation number	(0..n)	I
Output	view index	(0..n)	I
Output	number of points	(0..n)	I
Output	points in stroke	WC3	n × P3

Effect:

The STROKE 3 value in the current event queue is returned. This value consists of a sequence of positions in world coordinates, the view index which was used in the conversion from NPC to NDC3, and the normalization transformation number which was used in the conversion from NDC3 to WC3.

N.B.:

If an operator enters more points than the stroke input buffer size in the workstation state list allows, the additional points are lost. It is anticipated that the operator would be informed of this situation.

Errors:

7   GKS not in proper state: GKS should be in one of the states WSOP, WSAC or SGOP

150   No input value of the correct class is in the current event report

———————————————— *FORTRAN Interface* ————————————————

CALL GGTSK3 (MXP,NTN,VWIX,NP,SX,SY,SZ)

Parameters:

Input	MXP	size of arrays for stroke points	(0..n)	INTEGER
Output	NTN	normalization transformation number	(0..n)	INTEGER
Output	VWIX	view index	(0..n)	INTEGER
Output	NP	number of points returned	(0..n)	INTEGER
Output	SX(MXP),SY(MXP),SZ(MXP)			
		points in stroke	WC3	3 × n × REAL

9 LIST OF GKS-3D ERROR NUMBERS AND MESSAGES

In addition to the errors listed in Section III.9.6, some new errors may occur in GKS-3D. These errors are numbered from 400 onwards. It is anticipated that there will be a need for more error messages in the future. New error messages will be registered by a registration authority, established by the International Organization for Standardization, and this registration will be similar to the registration of new linetypes or generalized drawing primitives.

9.1 GKS-3D Transformations

400   View up vector and view plane normal are collinear
401   View plane normal is a null vector
402   View up vector is a null vector
403   Projection viewport limits are not within NPC range
404   Projection reference point is between the front and back clipping planes
405   Projection reference point is on the view plane
406   Box definition is invalid
407   Viewport is not within NDC3 unit cube
408   Specified view index is invalid
409   A representation for the specified view index has not been defined on this workstation
410   A representation for the specified view index has not been predefined on this workstation
411   Workstation window limits are not within NPC unit cube
412   Back clipping plane is in front of the front clipping plane
413   View clipping limits are not within NPC range

9.2 GKS-3D Output Attributes

420   Edge index is invalid
421   A representation for the specified edge index has not been defined on this workstation
422   A representation for the specified edge index has not been predefined on this workstation
423   Edge type is equal zero
424   Specified edge type is not supported on this workstation
425   Edge width scale factor is less than zero
426   Pattern reference points are collinear
427   Specified HLHSR mode is not supported on this workstation

428   Specified HLHSR identifier is invalid
429   Specified HLHSR mode is invalid

9.3 GKS-3D Output Primitives

430   Text direction vectors are collinear
431   List of point lists is invalid
432   At least one active workstation is not able to generate the specified gener-
       alized drawing primitive under the current transformations and clipping
       volume

10 INQUIRY FUNCTIONS

As a consequence of the 3D extension of GKS, some entries in the GKS state
list, the workstation state list, and the workstation description table have had
to be added or changed because of the new primitives, attributes, and the third
coordinate introduced for all geometrical entries (cf. Chapter 3). The following
inquiry functions give access to these entries.

10.1 Inquiry Functions for GKS-3D State List

INQUIRE CURRENT PRIMITIVE ATTRIBUTE VALUES 3

GKOP,WSOP,WSAC,SGOP   L0a

Parameters:

Output	error indicator		I
Output	current pattern reference point	WC3	P3
Output	current pattern reference vectors	WC3	$2 \times P3$
Output	current view index	(0..n)	I

Effect:
The inquired values are returned. Possible error numbers: 8.

———————————————— *FORTRAN Interface* ————————————————

CALL GQPRP3(ERRIND,PRPX,PRPY,PRPZ,PRVX,PRVY,PRVZ)

Parameters:

Output	ERRIND error indicator		INTEGER
Output	PRPX,PRPY,PRPZ		
	current pattern reference point	WC3	$3 \times$ REAL
Output	PRVX(2),PRVY(2),PRVZ(2)		
	current pattern reference vectors	WC3	$2 \times 3 \times$ REAL

CALL GQVWI (ERRIND,VWIX)

Parameters:

Output	ERRIND error indicator		INTEGER
Output	VWIX current view index	(0..n)	INTEGER

INQUIRE CURRENT HLHSR IDENTIFIER
GKOP,WSOP,WSAC,SGOP   L1a

Parameters:
Output   error indicator   I
Output   current HLHSR identifier   (0..n)   I
Effect:
The inquired values are returned. Possible error numbers: 8.

———————————————— *FORTRAN Interface* ————————————————

CALL GQHRID (ERRIND,HRID)
Parameters:
Output   ERRIND   error indicator   INTEGER
Output   HRID   current HLHSR identifier   (0..n)   INTEGER

INQUIRE CURRENT INDIVIDUAL ATTRIBUTE VALUES 3
GKOP,WSOP,WSAC,SGOP   L0a

Parameters:
Output   error indicator   I
Output   current edge index   (1..n)   I
Output   current edge flag   (OFF,ON)   E
Output   current edge type   (−n..−1,1..n)   I
Output   current edge width scale factor   ≥0   R
Output   current edge colour index   (0..n)   I
Output   current list of aspect source flags   (BUNDLED,INDIVIDUAL)   4×E
Effect:
The inquired values are returned. Possible error numbers: 8.

———————————————— *FORTRAN Interface* ————————————————

CALL GQEDI (ERRIND,EDIX)
Parameters:
Output   ERRIND   error indicator   INTEGER
Output   EDIX   edge index   (1..n)   INTEGER

CALL GQEDFG (ERRIND,EDFLAG)
Parameters:
Output   ERRIND   error indicator   INTEGER
Output   EDFLAG   edge flag   (0=off, 1=on)   INTEGER

CALL GQEDT (ERRIND,EDTYPE)
Parameters:
Output   ERRIND   error indicator   INTEGER
Output   EDTYPE   edge type   (−n..−1,1..n)   INTEGER

CALL GQEWSC (ERRIND,EDWSF)
Parameters:
Output   ERRIND   error indicator   INTEGER
Output   EDWSF   edge width scale factor   ≥0   REAL

CALL GQEDCI (ERRIND,EDCIX)
Parameters:
Output   ERRIND   error indicator   INTEGER
Output   EDCIX   edge colour index   (0..n)   INTEGER

CALL GQASF3 (ERRIND,LASF)
Parameters:
Output ERRIND   error indicator   INTEGER
Output LASF(4)   list of aspect source flags
                              (0 = bundled, 1 = individual)   4 × INTEGER

INQUIRE NORMALIZATION TRANSFORMATION 3
GKOP,WSOP,WSAC,SGOP L0a

Parameters:

Input	normalization transformation number	(0..n)	I
Output	error indicator		I
Output	window limits	WC3	6 × R
Output	viewport limits	NDC3	6 × R

Effect:
The inquired values are returned. Possible error numbers: 8, 50.

──────────────── *FORTRAN Interface* ────────────────

CALL GQNT3 (NTN,ERRIND,WNLIM,VPLIM)
Parameters:

Input	NTN	normalization transformation number	(0..n)	INTEGER
Output	ERRIND	error indicator		INTEGER
Output	WNLIM(6)	window limits	WC3	6 × REAL
Output	VPLIM(6)	viewport limits	NDC3	6 × REAL

INQUIRE CLIPPING 3   GKOP,WSOP,WSAC,SGOP L0a
Parameters:

Output	error indicator		I
Output	clipping indicator	(CLIP,NOCLIP)	E
Output	clipping volume	NDC3	6 × R

Effect:
The inquired values are returned. Possible error numbers: 8.

──────────────── *FORTRAN Interface* ────────────────

CALL GQCLP3 (ERRIND,CLSW,CLVOL)
Parameters:

Output	ERRIND	error indicator		INTEGER
Output	CLSW	window limits	(0 = noclip, 1 = clip)	INTEGER
Output	CLVOL(6)	clipping volume	NDC3	6 × REAL

10.2 Inquiry Functions for GKS-3D Workstation State List

INQUIRE LIST OF VIEW INDICES   WSOP,WSAC,SGOP L0a
Parameters:

Input	workstation identifier		N
Output	error indicator		I
Output	number of view table entries	(2..n)	I
Output	list of defined view indices	(1..n)	n × 1

Effect:
The inquired values are returned. Possible error numbers: 7, 20, 25, 33, 36.

———————————————— *FORTRAN Interface* ————————————————

CALL GQEVWI (WKID,N,ERRIND,NVWIX,VWIX)

Parameters:

Input	WKID	workstation identifier		INTEGER
Input	N	sequence number of list element requested		INTEGER
Output	ERRIND	error indicator		INTEGER
Output	NVWIX	number of view bundle table entries	(2..n)	INTEGER
Output	VWIX	nth element of list of defined view		
		indices	(1..n)	INTEGER

INQUIRE VIEW REPRESENTATION   WSOP,WSAC,SGOP   L0a

Parameters:

Input	workstation identifier		N
Input	view index	(1..n)	I
Output	error indicator		I
Output	viewing transformation update state	(NOTPENDING,PENDING)	E
Output	requested orientation matrix		$4 \times 4 \times R$
Output	current orientation matrix		$4 \times 4 \times R$
Output	requested view mapping matrix		$4 \times 4 \times R$
Output	current view mapping matrix		$4 \times 4 \times R$
Output	requested view clipping limits	NPC	$6 \times R$
Output	current view clipping limits	NPC	$6 \times R$
Output	requested window clipping indicator	(CLIP,NOCLIP)	E
Output	current window clipping indicator	(CLIP,NOCLIP)	E
Output	requested back clipping indicator	(CLIP,NOCLIP)	E
Output	current back clipping indicator	(CLIP,NOCLIP)	E
Output	requested front clipping indicator	(CLIP,NOCLIP)	E
Output	current front clipping indicator	(CLIP,NOCLIP)	E

Effect:

The inquired values are returned. Possible error numbers: 7, 20, 25, 33, 36, 408, 409.

———————————————— *FORTRAN Interface* ————————————————

CALL GQVWR (WKID,VWIX,CURQ,ERRIND,VWUPD,ORMAT,
VWMAT,PJVPLM,WNCLIP,BKCLIP,FRCLIP)

Parameters:

Input	WKID	workstation identifier		INTEGER
Input	VWIX	view index	(1..n)	INTEGER
Input	CURQ	whether current or requested values are to be returned	(0=current, 1=requested)	INTEGER
Output	ERRIND	error indicator		INTEGER
Output	VWUPD	viewing transformation update state	(0=notpending, 1=pending)	INTEGER
Output	ORMAT(4,4)	orientation matrix		$4 \times 4 \times$ REAL
Output	VWMAT(4,4)	view mapping matrix		$4 \times 4 \times$ REAL
Output	PJVPLM	view clipping limits	NPC	$6 \times$ REAL
Output	WNCLIP	window clipping indicator	(0=noclip, 1=clip)	INTEGER
Output	BKCLIP	back clipping indicator	(0=noclip, 1=clip)	INTEGER
Output	FRCLIP	front clipping indicator	(0=noclip, 1=clip)	INTEGER

INQUIRE WORKSTATION TRANSFORMATION 3

WSOP,WSAC,SGOP   L0a

Parameters:

Input	workstation identifier		N
Output	error indicator		I
Output	workstation transformation		
	update state	(NOTPENDING,PENDING)	E
Output	requested workstation window limits	NPC	$6 \times R$
Output	current workstation window limits	NPC	$6 \times R$
Output	requested workstation viewport limits	DC3	$6 \times R$
Output	current workstation viewport limits	DC3	$6 \times R$

Effect:
The inquired values are returned. Possible error numbers: 7, 20, 25, 33, 36.

————————————— *FORTRAN Interface* —————————————

CALL GQWKT3 (WKID,ERRIND,WTUPD,RWKWN,CWKWN,
RWKVP,CWKVP)

Parameters:

Input	WKID	workstation identifier		INTEGER
Output	ERRIND	error indicator		INTEGER
Output	WTUPD	workstation transformation update state		
		(0 = notpending, 1 = pending)		INTEGER
Output	RWKWN(6)	requested workstation window limits	NPC	$6 \times$ REAL
Output	CWKWN(6)	current workstation window limits	NPC	$6 \times$ REAL
Output	RWKVP(6)	requested workstation viewport limits	DC3	$6 \times$ REAL
Output	CWKVP(6)	current workstation viewport limits	DC3	$6 \times$ REAL

————————————— *FORTRAN Interface* —————————————

INQUIRE TEXT EXTENT 3

WSOP,WSAC,SGOP   L0a

Parameters:

Input	workstation identifier		N
Input	text position	WC3	P3
Input	text direction vectors	WC3	$2 \times P3$
Input	character string		S
Output	error indicator		I
Output	concatenation point	WC3	P3
Output	text extent parallelogram	WC3	$4 \times P3$

Effect:
The inquired values are returned. Possible error numbers: 7, 20, 25, 39, 101.

————————————— *FORTRAN Interface* —————————————

CALL GQTXX3 (WKID,TPX,TPY,TPZ,TRX,TRY,TRZ,STR,ERRIND,
CONPX,CONPY,CONPZ,TXX,TXY,TXZ)

Parameters:

Input	WKID	workstation identifier		INTEGER
Input	TPX,TPY,TPZ	text position	WC3	$3 \times$ REAL

Input	TRX(2),TRY(2),TRZ(2)			
		text direction vectors	WC3	$2 \times 3 \times$ REAL
Input	STR	character string		CHARACTER∗(∗)
Output	ERRIND	error indicator		INTEGER
Output	CONPX,CONPY,CONPZ			
		concatenation point	WC3	$3 \times$ REAL
Output	TXX(4),TXY(4),TXZ(4)			
		text extent parallelogram	WC3	$4 \times 3 \times$ REAL

INQUIRE LIST OF EDGE INDICES   WSOP,WSAC,SGOP   L1a

Parameters:

Input	workstation identifier		N
Output	error indicator		I
Output	number of edge bundle table entries	(5..n)	I
Output	list of defined edge indices	(1..n)	$n \times$ I

Effect:

The inquired values are returned. Possible error numbers: 7, 20, 25, 33, 35, 36.

──────────────────── *FORTRAN Interface* ────────────────────

CALL GQEEDI (WKID,N,ERRIND,NEDBUN,EDBUN)

Parameters:

Input	WKID	workstation identifier		INTEGER
Input	N	sequence number of list element requested		INTEGER
Output	ERRIND	error indicator		INTEGER
Output	NEDBUN	number of edge bundle table entries	(1..n)	INTEGER
Output	EDBUN	nth element of list of defined edge indices	(1..n)	INTEGER

INQUIRE EDGE REPRESENTATION   WSOP,WSAC,SGOP   L1a

Parameters:

Input	workstation identifier		N
Input	edge index	(1..n)	I
Input	type of returned values	(SET,REALIZED)	E
Output	error indicator		I
Output	edge flag	(OFF,ON)	E
Output	edge type	(−n..−1,1..n)	I
Output	edge width scale factor	≥0	R
Output	edge colour index	(0..n)	I

Effect:

The inquired values are returned. Possible error numbers: 7, 20, 25, 33, 35, 36, 420, 421.

──────────────────── *FORTRAN Interface* ────────────────────

CALL GQEDR (WKID,EDIX,INQTYP,ERRIND,EDFLAG,EDTYPE,
    EDWSF,EDCIX)

Parameters:

Input	WKID	workstation identifier		INTEGER
Input	EDIX	edge index	(1..n)	INTEGER
Input	INQTYP	type of returned values	(0=set, 1=realized)	INTEGER

Output	ERRIND	error indicator		INTEGER
Output	EDFLAG	edge flag	$(0 = \text{off}, 1 = \text{on})$	INTEGER
Output	EDTYPE	edge type	$(-n..-1,1..n)$	INTEGER
Output	EDWSF	edge width scale factor	≥ 0	REAL
Output	EDCIX	edge colour index	$(0..n)$	INTEGER

INQUIRE HLHSR MODE   WSOP,WSAC,SGOP   L1a

Parameters:

Input	workstation identifier		N
Output	error indicator		I
Output	HLHSR update state	(NOTPENDING,PENDING)	E
Output	requested HLHSR mode	$(0..n)$	I
Output	current HLHSR mode	$(0..n)$	I

Effect:
The inquired values are returned. Possible error numbers: 7, 20, 25, 39.

───────────────── *FORTRAN Interface* ─────────────────

CALL GQHM (WKID,ERRIND,HMUPD,RHM,CHM)

Parameters:

Input	WKID	workstation identifier		INTEGER
Output	ERRIND	error indicator		INTEGER
Output	HMUPD	HLHSR update state		
			$(0 = \text{notpending}, 1 = \text{pending})$	INTEGER
Output	RHM	requested HLHSR mode	$(0..n)$	INTEGER
Output	CHM	current HLHSR mode	$(0..n)$	INTEGER

INQUIRE LOCATOR DEVICE STATE 3   WSOP,WSAC,SGOP   L0b

Parameters:

Input	workstation identifier		N
Input	locator device number	$(1..n)$	I
Input	type of returned values	(SET,REALIZED)	E
Output	error indicator		I
Output	operating mode	(REQUEST,SAMPLE,EVENT)	E
Output	echo switch	(ECHO,NOECHO)	E
Output	initial normalization transformation number	$(0..n)$	I
Output	initial view index	$(0..n)$	I
Output	initial position	WC3	P3
Output	prompt/echo type	$(-n..-1,1..n)$	I
Output	echo volume	DC3	$6 \times R$
Output	locator data record		D

Effect:
The inquired values are returned. Possible error numbers: 7, 20, 25, 38, 140.

───────────────── *FORTRAN Interface* ─────────────────

CALL GQLCS3 (WKID,LOCDNR,TYPE,MLDR,ERRIND,MODE,ESW,
TNR,VWIX,PX,PY,PZ,PET,EVOL,LDR,DATREC)

Parameters:

Input	WKID	workstation identifier		INTEGER
Input	LOCDNR	locator device number	$(1..n)$	INTEGER
Input	TYPE	type of returned values	$(0 = \text{set}, 1 = \text{realized})$	INTEGER

Input	MLDR	dimension of data record array		INTEGER
Output	ERRIND	error indicator		INTEGER
Output	MODE	operating mode		
		(0 = request, 1 = sample, 2 = event)		INTEGER
Output	ESW	echo switch	(0 = noecho, 1 = echo)	INTEGER
Output	TNR	initial normalization transformation number		
			(0..n)	INTEGER
Output	VWIX	initial view index	(0..n)	INTEGER
Output	PX,PY,PZ	initial position	WC3	3 × REAL
Output	PET	prompt/echo type	(−n.. −1,1..n)	INTEGER
Output	EVOL(6)	echo volume	DC3	6 × REAL
Output	LDR	number of elements returned in data record		INTEGER
Output	DATREC(MLDR)			
		data record		n × CHARACTER*80

INQUIRE STROKE DEVICE STATE 3   WSOP,WSAC,SGOP   L0b

Parameters:

Input	workstation identifier		N
Input	stroke device number	(1..n)	I
Input	type of returned values	(SET,REALIZED)	E
Output	error indicator		I
Output	operating mode	(REQUEST,SAMPLE,EVENT)	E
Output	echo switch	(ECHO,NOECHO)	E
Output	initial normalization transformation number	(0..n)	I
Output	initial view index	(0..n)	I
Output	initial number of points	(0..n)	I
Output	initial points in stroke	WC3	n × P3
Output	prompt/echo type	(−n.. −1,1..n)	I
Output	echo volume	DC3	6 × R
Output	stroke data record		D

Effect:

The inquired values are returned. Possible error numbers: 7, 20, 25, 38, 140.

--------------------- *FORTRAN Interface* ---------------------

CALL GQSKS3 (WKID,SKDNR,TYPE,N,MLDR,ERRIND,MODE,ESW,
TNR,VWIX,NP,PXA,PYA,PZA,PET,EVOL,BUFLEN,LDR,DATREC)

Parameters:

Input	WKID	workstation identifier		INTEGER
Input	SKDNR	stroke device number	(1..n)	INTEGER
Input	TYPE	type of returned values	(0 = set, 1 = realized)	INTEGER
Input	N	maximum number of points		INTEGER
Input	MLDR	size of array for data record		INTEGER
Output	ERRIND	error indicator		INTEGER
Output	MODE	operating mode		
		(0 = request, 1 = sample, 2 = event)		INTEGER
Output	ESW	echo switch	(0 = noecho, 1 = echo)	INTEGER
Output	TNR	initial normalization transformation number		
			(0..n)	INTEGER
Output	VWIX	initial view index	(0..n)	INTEGER
Output	NP	initial number of points returned		INTEGER

Output	PXA(N),PYA(N),PZA(N)			
		points in initial stroke returned	WC3	$3 \times n \times$ REAL
Output	PET	prompt and echo type	$(-n..-1,1..n)$	INTEGER
Output	EVOL(6)	echo volume	DC3	$6 \times$ REAL
Output	BUFLEN	input buffer size		INTEGER
Output	LDR	number of elements returned in data record		INTEGER
Output	DATREC(MLDR)			
		data record		$n \times$ CHARACTER*80

INQUIRE VALUATOR DEVICE STATE 3   WSOP, WSAC, SGOP   L0b

Parameters:

Input	workstation identifier		N
Input	valuator device number	$(1..n)$	I
Output	error indicator		I
Output	operating mode	(REQUEST,SAMPLE,EVENT)	E
Output	echo switch	(ECHO,NOECHO)	E
Output	initial value		R
Output	prompt/echo type	$(-n..-1,1..n)$	I
Output	echo volume	DC3	$6 \times$ R
Output	valuator data record		D

Effect:

The inquired values are returned. Possible error numbers: 7, 20, 25, 38, 140.

———————————— *FORTRAN Interface* ————————————

CALL GQVLS3 (WKID,VLDNR,MLDR,ERRIND,MODE,ESW,IVAL,
PET,EVOL,LOVAL,HIVAL,LDR,DATREC)

Parameters:

Input	WKID	workstation identifier		INTEGER
Input	VLDNR	valuator device number	$(1..n)$	INTEGER
Input	MLDR	size of array for data record		INTEGER
Output	ERRIND	error indicator		INTEGER
Output	MODE	operating mode		
			$(0 =$ request, $1 =$ sample, $2 =$ event$)$	INTEGER
Output	ESW	echo switch	$(0 =$ noecho, $1 =$ echo$)$	INTEGER
Output	IVAL	initial value		REAL
Output	PET	prompt and echo type	$(-n..-1,1..n)$	INTEGER
Output	EVOL(6)	echo volume	DC3	$6 \times$ REAL
Output	LOVAL,HIVAL			
		minimal and maximal value		$2 \times$ REAL
Output	LDR	number of elements returned in data record		INTEGER
Output	DATREC(MLDR)			
		data record		$n \times$ CHARACTER*80

INQUIRE CHOICE DEVICE STATE 3   WSOP, WSAC, SGOP   L0b

Parameters:

Input	workstation identifier		N
Input	choice device number	$(1..n)$	I
Output	error indicator		I
Output	operating mode	(REQUEST,SAMPLE,EVENT)	E
Output	echo switch	(ECHO,NOECHO)	E

Output	initial status	(OK,NOCHOICE)	E
Output	initial choice number	(1..n)	I
Output	prompt/echo type	(−n..−1,1..n)	I
Output	echo volume	DC3	6 × R
Output	choice data record		D

Effect:

The inquired values are returned. Possible error numbers: 7, 20, 25, 38, 140.

───────────────── *FORTRAN Interface* ─────────────────

CALL GQCHS3 (WKID,CHDNR,MLDR,ERRIND,MODE,ESW,
    ISTAT,ICHNR,PET,EVOL,LDR,DATREC)

Parameters:

Input	WKID	workstation identifier		INTEGER
Input	CHDNR	choice device number	(1..n)	INTEGER
Input	MLDR	size of array for data record		INTEGER
Output	ERRIND	error indicator		INTEGER
Output	MODE	operating mode		
		(0 = request, 1 = sample, 2 = event)		INTEGER
Output	ESW	echo switch	(0 = noecho, 1 = echo)	INTEGER
Output	ISTAT	initial status	(0 = ok, 1 = nochoice)	E
Output	ICHNR	initial choice number	(1..n)	INTEGER
Output	PET	prompt and echo type	(−n..−1,1..n)	INTEGER
Output	EVOL(6)	echo volume	DC3	6 × REAL
Output	LDR	number of elements returned in data record		INTEGER
Output	DATREC(MLDR)			
		data record		n × CHARACTER∗80

───

INQUIRE PICK DEVICE STATE 3   WSOP, WSAC, SGOP   L1b

Parameters:

Input	workstation identifier		N
Input	pick device number	(1..n)	I
Input	type of returned values	(SET,REALIZED)	E
Output	error indicator		I
Output	operating mode	(REQUEST,SAMPLE,EVENT)	E
Output	echo switch	(ECHO,NOECHO)	E
Output	initial status	(OK,NOPICK)	E
Output	initial segment		N
Output	initial pick identifier		N
Output	prompt/echo type	(−n..−1,1..n)	I
Output	echo volume	DC3	6 × R
Output	pick data record		D

Effect:

The inquired values are returned. Possible error numbers: 7, 20, 25, 37, 140.

───────────────── *FORTRAN Interface* ─────────────────

CALL GQVLS3 (WKID,PKDNR,TYPE,MLDR,ERRIND,MODE,ESW,
    ISTAT,ISEGNA,IPKID,PET,EVOL,LDR,DATREC)

Parameters:

| Input | WKID | workstation identifier | | INTEGER |
| Input | PKDNR | pick device number | (1..n) | INTEGER |

Input	TYPE	type of returned values	(0 = set, 1 = realized)	INTEGER
Input	MLDR	size of array for data record		INTEGER
Output	ERRIND	error indicator		INTEGER
Output	MODE	operating mode		
			(0 = request, 1 = sample, 2 = event)	INTEGER
Output	ESW	echo switch	(0 = noecho, 1 = echo)	INTEGER
Output	ISTAT	initial status		INTEGER
Output	ISEGNA	initial segment		INTEGER
Output	IPKID	initial pick identifier		INTEGER
Output	PET	prompt and echo type	$(-n..-1,1..n)$	INTEGER
Output	EVOL(6)	echo volume	DC3	$6 \times$ REAL
Output	LDR	number of elements returned in data record		INTEGER
Output	DATREC(MLDR)			
		data record		$n \times$ CHARACTER∗80

INQUIRE STRING DEVICE STATE 3 WSOP, WSAC, SGOP L0b

Parameters:

Input	workstation identifier		N
Input	string device number	(1..n)	I
Output	error indicator		I
Output	operating mode	(REQUEST, SAMPLE, EVENT)	E
Output	echo switch	(ECHO, NOECHO)	E
Output	initial string		S
Output	prompt/echo type	$(-n..-1,1..n)$	I
Output	echo volume	DC3	$6 \times$ R
Output	string data record		D

Effect:
The inquired values are returned. Possible error numbers: 7, 20, 25, 38, 140.

──────────────── *FORTRAN Interface* ────────────────

CALL GQSTS3 (WKID,STDNR,MLDR,ERRIND,MODE,ESW,LOSTR,
ISTR,PET,EVOL,BUFLEN,INIPOS,LDR,DATREC)

Parameters:

Input	WKID	workstation identifier		INTEGER
Input	STDNR	string device number	(1..n)	INTEGER
Input	MLDR	size of array for data record		INTEGER
Output	ERRIND	error indicator		INTEGER
Output	MODE	operating mode		
			(0 = request, 1 = sample, 2 = event)	INTEGER
Output	ESW	echo switch	(0 = noecho, 1 = echo)	INTEGER
Output	LOSTR	number of characters returned		INTEGER
Output	ISTR	initial string		CHARACTER∗(∗)
Output	PET	prompt and echo type	$(-n..-1,1..n)$	INTEGER
Output	EVOL(6)	echo volume	DC3	$6 \times$ REAL
Output	BUFLEN	input buffer size		INTEGER
Output	INIPOS	input cursor position		INTEGER
Output	LDR	number of elements returned in data record		INTEGER
Output	DATEC(MLDR)			
		data record		$n \times$ CHARACTER∗80

10.3   Inquiry Functions for GKS-3D Workstation Description Table

---

INQUIRE DISPLAY SPACE SIZE 3   GKOP,WSOP,WSAC,SGOP   L0a

Parameters:

Input	workstation type		N
Output	error indicator		I
Output	device coordinate units	(METRES,OTHER)	E
Output	display space size in device units	DC3 $>0, >0, \geq 0$	$3 \times R$
Output	display space size in raster units	$(1..n)$	$3 \times I$

Effect:

The inquired values are returned. Possible error numbers: 8, 22, 23, 31, 33, 36.

———————————— *FORTRAN Interface* ————————————

CALL GQDSP3 (WKTYPE,ERRIND,DEVUN,DSDCX,DSDCY,DSDCZ,
DSRUX,DSRUY,DSRUZ)

Parameters:

Input	WKTYPE	workstation type		INTEGER
Output	ERRIND	error indicator		INTEGER
Output	DEVUN	device coordinates units	(0=metres, 1=other)	INTEGER
Output	DSDCX,DSDCY,DSDCZ		DC3 $>0,>0,\geq 0$	$3 \times$ REAL
		display space size in device coordinates		
Output	DSRUX,DSRUY,DSRUZ			
		display space size in raster units	$(1..n)$	$3 \times$ INTEGER

INQUIRE VIEW FACILITIES   GKOP,WSOP,WSAC,SGOP   L0a

Parameters:

Input	workstation type		N
Output	error indicator		I
Output	number of predefined view indices	$(2..n)$	I

Effect:

The inquired values are returned. Possible error numbers: 8, 22, 23, 31, 33, 36.

———————————— *FORTRAN Interface* ————————————

CALL GQPVWF (WKTYPE,ERRIND,NVWIX)

Parameters:

Input	WKTYPE	workstation identifier		INTEGER
Output	ERRIND	error indicator		INTEGER
Output	NVWIX	number of predefined view indices	$(2..n)$	INTEGER

INQUIRE PREDEFINED VIEW REPRESENTATION

Parameters: GKOP,WSOP,WSAC,SGOP   L0a

Input	workstation type		N
Input	predefined view index	$(0..n)$	I
Output	error indicator		I
Output	orientation matrix		$4 \times 4 \times R$
Output	view mapping matrix		$4 \times 4 \times R$
Output	view clipping limits	NPC	$6 \times R$
Output	window clipping indicator	(CLIP,NOCLIP)	E
Output	back clipping indicator	(CLIP,NOCLIP)	E
Output	front clipping indicator	(CLIP,NOCLIP)	E

Effect:
The inquired values are returned. Possible error numbers: 8, 22, 23, 31, 33, 36, 410.

———————————— *FORTRAN Interface* ————————————

CALL GQVWR (WKTYPE,VWIX,ERRIND,ORMAT,VWMAT,
PJVPLM,WNCLIP,BKCLIP,FRCLIP)

Parameters:

Input	WKTYPE	workstation type		INTEGER
Input	VWIX	view index	(0..n)	INTEGER
Output	ERRIND	error indicator		INTEGER
Output	ORMAT(4,4)	orientation matrix		4×4×REAL
Output	VWMAT(4,4)	view mapping matrix		4×4×REAL
Output	PJVPLM	view clipping limits	NPC	6×REAL
Output	WNCLIP	window clipping indicator	(0=noclip, 1=clip)	INTEGER
Output	BKCLIP	back clipping indicator	(0=noclip, 1=clip)	INTEGER
Output	FRCLIP	front clipping indicator	(0=noclip, 1=clip)	INTEGER

INQUIRE HLHSR FACILITIES   GKOP,WSOP,WSAC,SGOP   L1a

Parameters:

Input	workstation type		N
Output	error indicator		I
Output	number of available HLHSR identifiers	(1..n)	I
Output	list of available HLHSR identifiers	(0..n)	n×I
Output	number of available HLHSR modes	(1..n)	I
Output	list of available HLHSR modes	(0..n)	n×I

Effect:
The inquired values are returned. Possible error numbers: 8, 22, 23, 39.

———————————— *FORTRAN Interface* ————————————

CALL GQHRF (WKTYPE,N,ERRIND,NHID,HID,NHM,HM)

Parameters:

Input	WKTYPE	workstation type		INTEGER
Input	N	sequence number of list element requested		INTEGER
Output	ERRIND	error indicator		INTEGER
Output	NHID	number of available HLHSR identifiers	(1..n)	INTEGER
Output	HID	nth element of list of available HLHSR identifiers	(0..n)	INTEGER
Output	NHM	number of available HLHSR modes	(1..n)	INTEGER
Output	HM	nth element of list of available HLHSR modes	(0..n)	INTEGER

INQUIRE EDGE FACILITIES   GKOP,WSOP,WSAC,SGOP   L0a

Parameters:

Input	workstation type		N
Output	error indicator		I
Output	number of available edge types	(4..n)	I
Output	list of available edge types	(−n..−1,1..n)	n×I
Output	number of available edge widths	(0..n)	I
Output	nominal edge width	DC3 >0	R
Output	range of edge widths (minimum, maximum)	DC3 >0	2×R
Output	number of predefined edge indices	(5..n)	I

Effect:
The inquired values are returned. Possible error numbers: 8, 22, 23, 39.

———————————————————— *FORTRAN Interface* ————————————————————

CALL GQEDF (WKTYPE,N,ERRIND,NEDT,EDT,NEDW,NOMEDW,
   MINEDW,MAXEDW,NPEDIX)

Parameters:

Input	WKTYPE	workstation type		INTEGER
Input	N	sequence number of list element requested		INTEGER
Output	ERRIND	error indicator		INTEGER
Output	NEDT	number of available edge types	(4..n)	INTEGER
Output	EDT	nth element of list of edge types	(−n..−1,1..n)	INTEGER
Output	NEDW	number of available edge widths	(0..n)	INTEGER
Output	NOMEDW	nominal edge width	DC3 >0	REAL
Output	MINEDW,MAXEDW			
		range of edge widths	DC3 >0	2 × REAL
		(minimum, maximum)		
Output	NPEDIX	number of predefined edge indices	(5..n)	INTEGER

INQUIRE PREDEFINED EDGE REPRESENTATION
                                    GKOP,WSOP,WSAC,SGOP   L0a

Parameters:

Input	workstation type		N
Input	predefined edge index	(1..n)	I
Output	error indicator		I
Output	edge flag	(OFF,ON)	E
Output	edge type	(−n..−1,1..n)	I
Output	edge width scale factor	≥0	R
Output	edge colour index	(0..n)	I

Effect:

The inquired values are returned. Possible error numbers: 8, 22, 23, 39, 420, 422.

———————————————————— *FORTRAN Interface* ————————————————————

CALL GQPEDR (WKTYPE,PEDIX,ERRIND,EDFLAG,EDTYPE,
   EDWSF,EDCIX)

Parameters:

Input	WKTYPE	workstation type		INTEGER
Input	PEDIX	predefined edge index	(1..n)	INTEGER
Output	ERRIND	error indicator		INTEGER
Output	EDFLAG	edge flag	(0=off, 1=on)	INTEGER
Output	EDTYPE	edge type	(−n..−1,1..n)	INTEGER
Output	EDWSF	edge width scale factor	≥0	REAL
Output	EDCIX	edge colour index	(0..n)	INTEGER

INQUIRE GENERALIZED DRAWING PRIMITIVE 3
                                    GKOP,WSOP,WSAC,SGOP   L0a

Parameters:

Input	workstation type		N
Input	GDP identifier		N
Output	error indicator		I
Output	number of sets of attributes used	(0..5)	I
Output	list of sets of attributes used	(POLYLINE,	
	POLYMARKER, TEXT, FILL AREA, EDGE)		n × E

Effect:

The inquired values are returned. Possible error numbers: 8, 22, 23, 39, 41.

———————————————— *FORTRAN Interface* ————————————————

CALL GQGDP3 (WKTYPE,GDPID,ERRIND,NATTS,LATTS)

Parameters:

Input	WKTYPE	workstation type		INTEGER
Input	GDPID	GDP identifier		INTEGER
Output	ERRIND	error indicator		INTEGER
Output	NATTS	number of sets of attributes used	(0..5)	INTEGER
Output	LATTS(5)	list of sets of attributes used	(0..4)	5 × INTEGER

(0 = polyline, 1 = polymarker, 2 = text,
3 = fill area, 4 = edge)

INQUIRE DYNAMIC MODIFICATION OF WORKSTATION
ATTRIBUTES 3   GKOP,WSOP,WSAC,SGOP   L1a

Parameters:

Input	workstation type		N
Output	error indicator		I
Output	viewing transformation changeable	(IRG,IMM)	E
Output	edge bundle representation changeable	(IRG,IMM)	E
Output	HLHSR mode changeable	(IRG,IMM)	E

Effect:

The inquired values are returned. Possible error numbers: 8, 22, 23, 39.

———————————————— *FORTRAN Interface* ————————————————

CALL GQDWA3 (WKTYPE,ERRIND,VTCHA,EDCHA,HIDCHA)

Parameters:

Input	WKTYPE	workstation type		INTEGER
Output	ERRIND	error indicator		INTEGER
Output	VTCHA	viewing transformation changeable	(0 = irg, 1 = imm)	INTEGER
Output	EDCHA	edge bundle representation changeable	(0 = irg, 1 = imm)	INTEGER
Output	HIDCHA	HLHSR mode changeable	(0 = irg, 1 = imm)	INTEGER

INQUIRE MAXIMUM LENGTH OF WORKSTATION
STATE TABLES 3   GKOP,WSOP,WSAC,SGOP   L0a

Parameters:

Input	workstation type		N
Output	error indicator		I
Output	maximum number of view bundle table entries	(2..n)	I
Output	maximum number of edge bundle table entries	(5..n)	I

Effect:

The inquired values are returned. Possible error numbers: 8, 22, 23, 39.

———————————————— *FORTRAN Interface* ————————————————

CALL GQLWK3 (WKTYPE, ERRIND, MXVTS, MXEDS)

Parameters:

Input	WKTYPE	workstation type		INTEGER
Output	ERRIND	error indicator		INTEGER
Output	MXVTS	maximum number of view bundle table entries	(2..n)	INTEGER
Output	MXEDS	maximum number of edge bundle table entries	(5..n)	INTEGER

INQUIRE DEFAULT LOCATOR DEVICE DATA 3
GKOP,WSOP,WSAC,SGOP   L0b

Parameters:

Input	workstation type		N
Input	logical input device number	$(1..n)$	I
Output	error indicator		I
Output	default initial locator position	WC3	P3
Output	number of available prompt/echo types	$(1..n)$	I
Output	list of available prompt/echo types	$(-n..-1,1..n)$	$n \times I$
Output	default echo volume	DC3	$6 \times R$
Output	default locator data record		D

Effect:

The inquired values are returned. Possible error numbers: 8, 22, 23, 38, 140.

———————————— *FORTRAN Interface* ————————————

CALL GQDLC3 (WKTYPE,DEVN,N,MLDR,ERRIND,DPX,DPY,DPZ,
NPET,PET,EVOL,LDR,DATREC)

Parameters:

Input	WKTYPE	workstation type		INTEGER
Input	DEVN	logical input device number	$(1..n)$	INTEGER
Input	N	sequence number of list element requested		INTEGER
Input	MLDR	size of array for locator data record		INTEGER
Output	ERRIND	error indicator		INTEGER
Output	DPX,DPY,DPZ			
		default initial locator position	WC3	$3 \times REAL$
Output	NPET	number of available prompt/echo types	$(1..n)$	INTEGER
Output	PET	nth element of list of		
		available prompt/echo types	$(-n..-1,1..n)$	INTEGER
Output	EVOL(6)	default echo volume	DC3	$6 \times REAL$
Output	LDR	number of elements returned in data record		INTEGER
Output	DATREC(MLDR)			
		locator data record		$n \times CHARACTER*80$

INQUIRE DEFAULT STROKE DEVICE DATA 3
GKOP,WSOP,WSAC,SGOP   L0b

Parameters:

Input	workstation type		N
Input	logical input device number	$(1..n)$	I
Output	error indicator		I
Output	maximum input buffer size	$(64..n)$	I
Output	number of available prompt/echo types	$(1..n)$	I
Output	list of available prompt/echo types	$(-n..-1,1..n)$	$n \times I$
Output	default echo volume	DC3	$6 \times R$
Output	default stroke data record		D

Effect:

The inquired values are returned. Possible error numbers: 8, 22, 23, 38, 140.

─────────────── *FORTRAN Interface* ───────────────

CALL GQDSK3 (WKTYPE,DEVN,N,MLDR,ERRIND,MXBFSZ,NPET,
PET,EVOL,LDR,DATREC)

Parameters:

Input	WKTYPE	workstation type		INTEGER
Input	DEVN	logical input device number	(1..n)	INTEGER
Input	N	sequence number of list element requested		INTEGER
Input	MLDR	size of array for stroke data record		INTEGER
Output	ERRIND	error indicator		INTEGER
Output	MXBFSZ	maximum input buffer size	(64..n)	INTEGER
Output	NPET	number of available prompt/echo types	(1..n)	INTEGER
Output	PET	nth element of list of available prompt/echo types	(−n..−1,1..n)	INTEGER
Output	EVOL(6)	default echo volume	DC3	6 × REAL
Output	LDR	number of elements returned in data record		INTEGER
Output	DATREC(MLDR)	stroke data record		n × CHARACTER∗80

INQUIRE DEFAULT VALUATOR DEVICE DATA 3
GKOP,WSOP,WSAC,SGOP   L0b

Parameters:

Input	workstation type		N
Input	logical input device number	(1..n)	I
Output	error indicator		I
Output	default initial value		R
Output	number of available prompt/echo types	(1..n)	I
Output	list of available prompt/echo types	(−n..−1,1..n)	n × I
Output	default echo volume	DC3	6 × R
Output	default valuator data record		D

Effect:
The inquired values are returned. Possible error numbers: 8, 22, 23, 38, 140.

─────────────── *FORTRAN Interface* ───────────────

CALL GQDVL3 (WKTYPE,DEVN,N,MLDR,ERRIND,DVAL,NPET,
PET,EVOL,LOVAL,HIVAL,LDR,DATREC)

Parameters:

Input	WKTYPE	workstation type		INTEGER
Input	DEVN	logical input device number	(1..n)	INTEGER
Input	N	sequence number of list element requested		INTEGER
Input	MLDR	size of array for valuator data record		INTEGER
Output	ERRIND	error indicator		INTEGER
Output	DVAL	default initial value		REAL
Output	NPET	number of available prompt/echo types	(1..n)	INTEGER
Output	PET	nth element of list of available prompt/echo types	(−n..−1,1..n)	INTEGER
Output	EVOL(6)	default echo volume	DC3	6 × REAL

Output LOVAL,HIVAL
                        minimal and maximal value   2 × REAL
Output LDR   number of elements returned
                        in data record   INTEGER
Output DATREC(MLDR)
                        valuator data record   n × CHARACTER∗80

INQUIRE DEFAULT CHOICE DEVICE DATA 3
GKOP,WSOP,WSAC,SGOP   L0b

Parameters:

Input	workstation type		N
Input	logical input device number	(1..n)	I
Output	error indicator		I
Output	maximum number of choice alternatives	(1..n)	I
Output	number of available prompt/echo types	(1..n)	I
Output	list of available prompt/echo types	(−n..−1,1..n)	n × I
Output	default echo volume	DC3	6 × R
Output	default choice data record		D

Effect:
The inquired values are returned. Possible error numbers: 8, 22, 23, 38, 140.

----------------------------- *FORTRAN Interface* -----------------------------

CALL GQDCH3 (WKTYPE,DEVN,N,MLDR,ERRIND,MALT,NPET,
    PET,EVOL,LDR,DATREC)

Parameters:

Input	WKTYPE	workstation type		INTEGER
Input	DEVN	logical input device number	(1..n)	INTEGER
Input	N	sequence number of list element requested		INTEGER
Input	MLDR	size of array for choice data record		INTEGER
Output	ERRIND	error indicator		INTEGER
Output	MALT	maximum number of choice alternatives	(1..n)	INTEGER
Output	NPET	number of available prompt/echo types	(1..n)	INTEGER
Output	PET	nth element of list of available prompt/echo types	(−n..−1,1..n)	INTEGER
Output	EVOL(6)	default echo volume	DC3	6 × REAL
Output	LDR	number of elements returned in data record		INTEGER
Output	DATREC(MLDR)	choice data record		n × CHARACTER∗80

INQUIRE DEFAULT PICK DEVICE DATA 3
GKOP,WSOP,WSAC,SGOP   L1b

Parameters:

Input	workstation type		N
Input	logical input device number	(1..n)·	I
Output	error indicator		I
Output	number of available prompt/echo types	(1..n)	I
Output	list of available prompt/echo types	(−n..−1,1..n)	n × I
Output	default echo volume	DC3	6 × R
Output	default pick data record		D

Effect:
The inquired values are returned. Possible error numbers: 8, 22, 23, 37, 140.

——————————————— *FORTRAN Interface* ———————————————

CALL GQDPK3 (WKTYPE,DEVN,N,MLDR,ERRIND,NPET,PET,
    EVOL,LDR,DATREC)

Parameters:

Input	WKTYPE	workstation type		INTEGER
Input	DEVN	logical input device number	$(1..n)$	INTEGER
Input	N	sequence number of list element requested		INTEGER
Input	MLDR	size of array for pick data record		INTEGER
Output	ERRIND	error indicator		INTEGER
Output	NPET	number of available prompt/echo types	$(1..n)$	INTEGER
Output	PET	nth element of list of		
		available prompt/echo types	$(-n..-1,1..n)$	INTEGER
Output	EVOL(6)	default echo volume	DC3	$6 \times$ REAL
Output	LDR	number of elements returned in data record		INTEGER
Output	DATREC(MLDR)			
		pick data record		$n \times$ CHARACTER$*80$

INQUIRE DEFAULT STRING DEVICE DATA 3
GKOP,WSOP,WSAC,SGOP   L0b

Parameters:

Input	workstation type		N
Input	logical input device number	$(1..n)$	I
Output	error indicator		I
Output	maximum string buffer size	$(72..n)$	I
Output	number of available prompt/echo types	$(1..n)$	I
Output	list of available prompt/echo types	$(-n..-1,1..n)$	$n \times$ I
Output	default echo volume	DC3	$6 \times$ R
Output	default string data record		D

Effect:

The inquired values are returned. Possible error numbers: 8, 22, 23, 38, 140.

——————————————— *FORTRAN Interface* ———————————————

CALL GQDST3 (WKTYPE,DEVN,N,MLDR,ERRIND,MBUFF,NPET,
    PET,EVOL,BUFLEN,LDR,DATREC)

Parameters:

Input	WKTYPE	workstation tpe		INTEGER
Input	DEVN	logical input device number	$(1..n)$	INTEGER
Input	N	sequence number of list element requested		INTEGER
Input	MLDR	size of array for string data record		INTEGER
Output	ERRIND	error indicator		INTEGER
Output	MBUFF	maximum string buffer size	$(72..n)$	INTEGER
Output	NPET	number of available prompt/echo types	$(1..n)$	INTEGER
Output	PET	nth element of list of		
		available prompt/echo types	$(-n..-1,1..n)$	INTEGER
Output	EVOL(6)	default echo volume	DC3	$6 \times$ REAL
Output	BUFLEN	buffer length of string		INTEGER
Output	LDR	number of elements returned in data record		INTEGER
Output	DATREC(MLDR)			
		string data record		$n \times$ CHARACTER$*80$

10.4   Inquiry Functions for the Segment State List

INQUIRE SEGMENT ATTRIBUTES 3   WSOP,WSAC,SGOP   L1a
Parameters:

Input	segment name		N
Output	error indicator		I
Input	segment transformation matrix		$3 \times 4 \times R$
Input	visibility	(VISIBLE,INVISIBLE)	E
Input	highlighting	(NORMAL,HIGHLIGHTED)	E
Input	segment priority	[0,1]	R
Input	detectability	(UNDETECTABLE,DETECTABLE)	E

Effect:
The inquired values are returned. Possible error numbers: 7, 120, 122.

--- *FORTRAN Interface* ---

CALL GQSGA3 (SGNA,ERRIND,TM,VIS,HIGH,SGPR,DET)
Parameters:

Input	SGNA	segment name		INTEGER
Output	ERRIND	error indicator		INTEGER
Output	TM(3,4)	segment transformation matrix		$3 \times 4 \times$ REAL
Output	VIS	visibility	(0=invisible, 1=visible)	INTEGER
Output	HIGH	highlighting	(0=normal, 1=highlighted)	INTEGER
Output	SGPR	segment priority	[0,1]	REAL
Output	DET	detectability	(0=undetectable, 1=detectable)	INTEGER

10.5   Pixel Inquiries

INQUIRE PIXEL ARRAY DIMENSIONS 3   WSOP,WSAC,SGOP   L0a
Parameters:

Input	workstation identifier		N
Input	3 points P, Q, R	WC3	$3 \times P3$
Input	view index	(0..n)	I
Output	error indicator		I
Output	dimensions of pixel array DX, DY	(1..n)	$2 \times I$

Effect:
The inquired values are returned. Possible error numbers: 7, 20, 25, 39, 408.

--- *FORTRAN Interface* ---

CALL GQPXD3 (WKID,PX,PY,PZ,QX,QY,QZ,RX,RY,RZ,VWIX,
  ERRIND,DIMX,DIMY)
Parameters:

Input	WKID	workstation identifier		INTEGER
Input	PX,PY,PZ,QX,QY,QZ,RX,RY,RZ			
		3 points	WC3	$9 \times$ REAL
Input	VWIX	view index	(0..n)	INTEGER
Output	ERRIND	error indicator		INTEGER
Output	DIMX,DIMY	dimensions of pixel array	(1..n)	$2 \times$ INTEGER

INQUIRE PIXEL ARRAY 3   WSOP,WSAC,SGOP   L0a

Parameters:

Input	workstation identifier		N
Input	point P	WC3	P3
Input	view index	(0..n)	I
Input	dimensions of colour index array DX, DY	(1..n)	2 × I
Output	error indicator		I
Output	presence of invalid values	(ABSENT,PRESENT)	E
Output	colour index array	(−1..n)	n × n × I

Effect:

The inquired values are returned. Possible error numbers: 7, 20, 25, 39, 40, 91, 408.

———————————— *FORTRAN Interface* ————————————

CALL GQPXA3 (WKID,PX,PY,PZ,VWIX,DIMX,DIMY,ERRIND,
INVLDS,COLIA)

Parameters:

Input	WKID	workstation identifier		INTEGER
Input	PX,PY,PZ	point	WC3	3 × REAL
Input	VWIX	view index	(0..n)	INTEGER
Input	DIMX,DIMY	dimensions of colour index array	(1..n)	2 × INTEGER
Output	ERRIND	error indicator		INTEGER
Output	INVLDS	presence of invalid values	(0=absent, 1=present)	INTEGER
Output	COLIA(DIMX,DIMY)			
		colour index array	(−1..n)	
				n × n × INTEGER

INQUIRE PIXEL 3   WSOP,WSAC,SGOP   L0a

Parameters:

Input	workstation identifier		N
Input	point P	WC3	P3
Input	view index	(0..n)	I
Output	error indicator		I
Output	colour index	(−1..n)	I

Effect:

The inquired values are returned. Possible error numbers: 7, 20, 25, 39, 40, 408.

———————————— *FORTRAN Interface* ————————————

CALL GQPX3 (WKID,PX,PY,PZ,VWIX,ERRIND,COLI)

Parameters:

Input	WKID	workstation identifier		INTEGER
Input	PX,PY,PZ	point P	WC3	3 × REAL
Input	VWIX	view index	(0..n)	INTEGER
Output	ERRIND	error indicator		INTEGER
Output	COLI	colour index	(−1..n)	INTEGER

11 EMBEDDING THE GKS FUNCTIONS INTO GKS-3D

All the GKS functions are also present in GKS-3D and have the same effect in both GKS and GKS-3D. This is easily accomplished for all GKS functions which are not related to geometry, such as OPEN WORKSTATION. All other GKS functions have a counterpart in GKS-3D which has a similar functionality but a different parameter set. The process of embedding consists primarily in mapping the parameter set of a GKS function onto the parameter set of its GKS-3D counterpart. However, this does not necessarily imply that the respective 3D function is really called but it serves to give a precise definition of the effect of the corresponding 2D function in the 3D environment. Furthermore, to ensure that the functionality is not altered, the default settings of the various GKS-3D state lists (cf. Chapter 3) have been chosen appropriately.

As a general rule, 2D output is generated on the $z=0$ plane in WC3, i.e., WC values are converted to WC3 by adding a $z=0$ coordinate.

The 2D transformation functions contain rectangles for window, viewport and workstation window which are converted to cubes with a z-interval of $[-1, 0]$. This particular z-interval has been chosen to ensure that with the default viewing the $z=0$ plane is in front of the cube.

The 2D input classes LOCATOR and STROKE generate 3D values in WC3 just like LOCATOR 3 and STROKE 3. Then the z-coordinates and the view index are discarded and the remaining WC values together with the normalization transformation number are returned as the result. As the z-coordinate is used exclusively for the transformation of 2D input values within a 3D transformation pipeline, it is of importance for a user not to put too much effort in the generation of a z-coordinate which finally is discarded. For this purpose an implementor may provide input devices which obtain z-coordinates from the initial values in the state list rather than from a lengthy user dialogue.

However, if 3D transformation functions are used, it should be recognized that the additional z-value is of importance, especially when selecting the inverse viewing and normalization transformation. It also affects the coordinate values in the case of a projection which is not parallel to the z-axis. No view index is returned with 2D input although 2D input is transformed back by some viewing transformation. Therefore, it is recommended one use 2D input only when viewing transformation 0 has the highest priority.

The GKS functions
— INITIALISE LOCATOR
— INITIALISE STROKE
only set the x- and y-portions of the initial locator position, the points in initial stroke and the echo volume and leave the z-portion in the workstation state list unchanged.

Inquiry functions with geometric parameters just return the x- and y-values and ignore the z-coordinate and any view index.

The following Table 11.1 gives a complete list of the parameter mapping.

Table 11.1   Mapping of GKS functions onto GKS-3D functions

For conciseness, parameters with an identical counterpart in the 3D parameter list have been omitted and functions with similar parameter lists have been grouped together.

POLYLINE	→ POLYLINE 3
POLYMARKER	→ POLYMARKER 3
points (x, y)	→ points (x, y, 0)

TEXT	→ TEXT 3
text position (x, y)	→ text position (x, y, 0)
	→ text direction vectors (1, 0, 0), (0, 1, 0)

FILL AREA	→ FILL AREA 3
points (x, y)	→ points (x, y, 0)

FILL AREA SET	→ FILL AREA SET 3
list of point lists	→ list of point lists
with points (x_i, y_i)	with points $(x_i, y_i, 0)$

N.B.: Currently, FILL AREA SET is not part of GKS. It is anticipated that it will be included in a future revision of GKS.

CELL ARRAY	→ CELL ARRAY 3
cell rectangle (P_x, P_y), (Q_x, Q_y)	→ cell parallelogram $(P_x, P_y, 0)$,
	$(Q_x, P_y, 0)$, $(P_x, Q_y, 0)$

GENERALIZED DRAWING PRIMITIVE

	→ GENERALIZED DRAWING PRIMITIVE 3
points (x, y)	→ points (x, y, 0)

SET PATTERN REFERENCE POINT

	→ SET PATTERN REFERENCE POINT AND VECTORS
pattern reference point (x, y)	→ pattern reference point (x, y, 0)
	→ pattern reference vectors (1,0,0), (0,1,0)

SET WINDOW	→ SET WINDOW 3
window limits XMIN, XMAX,	→ window limits XMIN, XMAX,
YMIN, YMAX	YMIN, YMAX, ZMIN $= -1$, ZMAX $= 0$

SET VIEWPORT	→ SET VIEWPORT 3
viewport limits XMIN, XMAX,	→ viewport limits XMIN, XMAX,
YMIN, YMAX	YMIN, YMAX, ZMIN $= -1$, ZMAX $= 0$

SET WORKSTATION WINDOW	→ SET WORKSTATION WINDOW 3
workstation window limits XMIN,	→ workstation window limits XMIN,
XMAX, YMIN, YMAX	XMAX, YMIN, YMAX,
	ZMIN $= -1$, ZMAX $= 0$

Table 11.1 (continued)

SET WORKSTATION VIEWPORT
workstation viewport limits XMIN,
   XMAX, YMIN, YMAX
	→ SET WORKSTATION VIEWPORT 3
	→ workstation viewport limits XMIN,
	   XMAX, YMIN, YMAX,
	   ZMIN = 0, ZMAX = lz

N.B.: lz is the z-extent of the maximum display volume size entry in the workstation description table.

SET SEGMENT TRANSFORMATION INSERT SEGMENT transformation matrix $$\begin{pmatrix} M_{11} & M_{12} & M_{13} \\ M_{21} & M_{22} & M_{23} \end{pmatrix}$$	→ SET SEGMENT TRANSFORMATION 3 → INSERT SEGMENT 3 → transformation matrix $$\begin{pmatrix} M_{11} & M_{12} & 0 & M_{13} \\ M_{21} & M_{22} & 0 & M_{23} \\ 0 & 0 & 1 & 0 \end{pmatrix}$$

INITIALISE LOCATOR
initial locator position (x, y)
—
 	
echo area XMIN, XMAX,
   YMIN, YMAX
	→ INITIALISE LOCATOR 3
	→ initial locator position (x, y, z)
	→ initial view index 0
	→ echo volume XMIN, XMAX,
	   YMIN, YMAX, ZMIN, ZMAX

N.B.: z, ZMIN, ZMAX are taken from the corresponding entries in the workstation state list which may be the default values or the values set by INITIALISE LOCATOR 3.

INITIALISE STROKE points in initial stroke (x, y)	→ INITIALISE STROKE 3 → points in initial stroke (x, y, z)

N.B.: z is taken from the corresponding entry in the workstation state list, if present, or is set equal to the value corresponding to z=zmax of the workstation window. View index and echo area mapped as above for LOCATOR.

INITIALISE VALUATOR INITIALISE CHOICE INITIALISE PICK INITIALISE STRING	→ INITIALISE VALUATOR 3 → INITIALISE CHOICE 3 → INITIALISE PICK 3 → INITIALISE STRING 3

N.B.: Echo area mapped as above for LOCATOR.

REQUEST LOCATOR SAMPLE LOCATOR GET LOCATOR — locator position (x, y)	→ REQUEST LOCATOR 3 → SAMPLE LOCATOR 3 → GET LOCATOR 3 ← view index ← locator position (x, y, z)

REQUEST STROKE SAMPLE STROKE GET STROKE — points in stroke (x, y)	→ REQUEST STROKE 3 → SAMPLE STROKE 3 → GET STROKE 3 ← view index ← points in stroke (x, y, z)

INQUIRE TEXT EXTENT text position (x, y) — concatenation point (x, y) text extent parallelogram (x_i, y_i)	→ INQUIRE TEXT EXTENT 3 → text position (x, y, 0) → text direction vectors (1, 0, 0), (0, 1, 0) ← concatenation point (x, y, z) ← text extent parallelogram (x_i, y_i, z_i)

Table 11.1 (continued)

INQUIRE GENERALIZED DRAWING PRIMITIVE
  → INQUIRE GENERALIZED DRAWING PRIMITIVE 3
number of sets of attributes used   ← number of sets of attributes used
list of sets of attributes used   ← list of sets of attributes used
  (POLYLINE, POLYMARKER,   (POLYLINE, POLYMARKER, TEXT,
  TEXT, FILL AREA)   FILL AREA, EDGE)

INQUIRE SEGMENT ATTRIBUTES   → INQUIRE SEGMENT ATTRIBUTES 3
transformation matrix   ← transformation matrix

$$\begin{pmatrix} M_{11} & M_{12} & M_{14} \\ M_{21} & M_{22} & M_{24} \end{pmatrix}$$

$$\begin{pmatrix} M_{11} & M_{12} & M_{13} & M_{14} \\ M_{21} & M_{22} & M_{23} & M_{24} \\ M_{31} & M_{32} & M_{33} & M_{34} \end{pmatrix}$$

INQUIRE PIXEL ARRAY DIMENSIONS
  → INQUIRE PIXEL ARRAY DIMENSIONS 3
2 points $(P_x, P_y), (Q_x, Q_y)$ → 3 points $(P_x, P_y, 0), (Q_x, P_y, 0), (P_x, Q_y, 0)$
—   → view index 0

INQUIRE PIXEL ARRAY   → INQUIRE PIXEL ARRAY 3
INQUIRE PIXEL   → INQUIRE PIXEL 3
point (x,y)   → point (x,y,0)
—   → view index 0

---

*N.B.: The following inquiry functions return just the x- and y-values of any 3D point
  or box and ignore any view index:*
INQUIRE NORMALIZATION TRANSFORMATION
  → INQUIRE NORMALIZATION TRANSFORMATION 3
INQUIRE CLIPPING   → INQUIRE CLIPPING 3
INQUIRE WORKSTATION TRANSFORMATION
  → INQUIRE WORKSTATION TRANSFORMATION 3
INQUIRE DISPLAY SPACE SIZE   → INQUIRE DISPLAY VOLUME SIZE
INQUIRE LOCATOR DEVICE STATE
  → INQUIRE LOCATOR DEVICE STATE 3
INQUIRE STROKE DEVICE STATE   → INQUIRE STROKE DEVICE STATE 3
INQUIRE VALUATOR DEVICE STATE
  → INQUIRE VALUATOR DEVICE STATE 3
INQUIRE CHOICE DEVICE STATE   → INQUIRE CHOICE DEVICE STATE 3
INQUIRE PICK DEVICE STATE   → INQUIRE PICK DEVICE STATE 3
INQUIRE STRING DEVICE STATE   → INQUIRE STRING DEVICE STATE 3

INQUIRE DEFAULT LOCATOR DEVICE DATA
  → INQUIRE DEFAULT LOCATOR DEVICE DATA 3
INQUIRE DEFAULT STROKE DEVICE DATA
  → INQUIRE DEFAULT STROKE DEVICE DATA 3
INQUIRE DEFAULT VALUATOR DEVICE DATA
  → INQUIRE DEFAULT VALUATOR DEVICE DATA 3
INQUIRE DEFAULT CHOICE DEVICE DATA
  → INQUIRE DEFAULT CHOICE DEVICE DATA 3
INQUIRE DEFAULT PICK DEVICE DATA
  → INQUIRE DEFAULT PICK DEVICE DATA 3
INQUIRE DEFAULT STRING DEVICE DATA
  → INQUIRE DEFAULT STRING DEVICE DATA 3

---

12 PHIGS

As a successor of the Core, a new proposal called *Programmer's Hierarchical Interactive Graphics Standard (PHIGS)* [ANSI85] has been developed by the working group X3H31 of the American National Standards Institute (ANSI) and has been accepted as a work item by ISO in 1985. PHIGS not only provides 3D functionality but also puts some emphasis on a multilevel hierarchical data structure. This structure contains graphical output primitives, attributes and transformations which can all be edited interactively. Furthermore, substructures can be copied or referenced. By referencing other structures, a multilevel hierarchical structure can be created which is very useful if a subpicture is to occur several times on the display surface where the definition of this subpicture has been stored only once within the data structure. Attributes are stacked when executing a substructure and are restored afterwards. This all allows a higher degree of interaction compared to GKS.

However, the PHIGS proposal has not been accepted unanimously. One objection is that PHIGS is a monolithic system which cannot be broken up into smaller modules from which the application could select those needed in a specific situation. For example, there is no subset provided for pure 2D graphics or for applications using their own data structure for interactive editing instead of the PHIGS data structure. Another point of criticism is that the high-level functionality of the PHIGS data structure is offered at a very low level, leaving most of the housekeeping and consistence checking to the application program rather than to the graphics system.

As PHIGS has been presented to the standardization committees in the *post GKS era,* it has had to define its relationship to the existing GKS standard. The PHIGS document [ANSI85] contains the following statements about its relationship to GKS:
— PHIGS is intended to serve a different clientele than GKS.
— Compatibility with GKS is a highly desirable goal.
— Technical differences will be possible when it suits the needs of the PHIGS clientele and their objectives.
— If PHIGS and GKS have a common function, its functional arguments and language binding, and the effect of any of its attributes will be the same.
— Functionality beyond that provided in GKS will have as its default the GKS functionality whenever possible.

In fact, PHIGS is upward compatible with respect to output primitives, attributes, and input but incompatible with respect to transformations and segmentation.

THE GKS ENVIRONMENT

Part V is devoted to elaborating the various interfaces of GKS within the Computer Graphics environment. The first two chapters outline methods for implementing the GKS standard with the aim of utilizing most existing features of a variety of graphical devices. Furthermore, an outline is given of how the GKS functionality can be realized by using emulation and simulation software to tailor a system to the particular device functions. In Chapter 3, several implementation styles are explained which produce GKS systems in an efficient manner. This chapter also mentions the differences between implementations which are permitted. Chapter 4 deals with the topic of language interfaces. It contains the rules for designing a GKS language binding and gives details for the FORTRAN and PASCAL interface. Chapter 5 is concerned with the interfaces of GKS implementations to graphical devices — a topic which is subject to standardization. This chapter is both important for GKS implementors and those people developing device drivers and connecting them to GKS.

In Chapter 6 we look at the major activities which are happening in the field of graphics metafiles, the aim of them being to standardize the interfaces between different graphics systems for exchanging graphical information. Chapter 7 is devoted to the important processes of checking and proving that the GKS implementations conform to the standard. It can be argued that without a means for validation and certification, standardization is next to useless because its major goal, i.e., the portability of programs, pictures and teaching knowledge, will not be reached. Chapter 8 refers to international efforts to develop a common Computer Graphics terminology and gives a list of the most important international computer graphics terms.

1 MAPPING OUTPUT PRIMITIVES AND ATTRIBUTES TO PHYSICAL WORKSTATIONS

An important concept within the GKS standard is the concept of input/output primitives being capabilities of logical input/output devices. To a certain extent, abstracting from physical devices to logical devices allows a device-independent access to physical devices. However, the implementor of logical input/output devices has to reverse this process of abstraction and has to map the logical devices onto the capabilities of the available physical devices. This chapter describes major aspects of this mapping process for output primitives and attributes. The subsequent chapter will discuss the mapping process for input primitives.

The details of how logical devices are mapped onto physical ones have intentionally been left open within the standard so that the implementor has sufficient freedom to take advantage of specific hardware capabilities and to elaborate on more comfortable features required by the users of a particular implementation. The design decisions taken by the implementor have to be made transparent to the users. The major aspects have to be listed in the workstation description table whereas other decisions have to be documented in the implementation manual.

1.1 POLYLINE Primitive and Attributes

Line drawing facilities will be available on almost all graphical output devices and mapping of POLYLINE, therefore, will be straightforward. Raster devices need a description of linear objects in terms of pixel structures. The conversion of lines to pixels (line-to-scan conversion) will be done within the device or must be provided by the driver. Due to the pixel structure, lines may differ in appearance when drawn horizontally, diagonally, or vertically.

Lines can be drawn with different LINETYPES. The LINETYPES solid, dashed, dotted and dashed-dotted are compulsory; they must be implemented even for devices like colour raster displays which usually use colour to distinguish lines of different classes.

LINETYPE includes some geometric features, e.g., the length of dash and gap for LINETYPE dashed. However, GKS regards LINETYPE as a non-geometric attribute and, deliberately, does not concern itself with this question. On one hand this allows the use of any available hardware capability and, on the other hand, it enables the generation of LINETYPES by software routines which may very tentatively consider the requirements for some applications such as technical drawings and cartography, e.g.:

— LINETYPE patterns which continue over vertices of a POLYLINE or even from one POLYLINE to a subsequent one;
— LINETYPE patterns which are generated for a whole POLYLINE before clipping instead of starting the pattern for the visible parts only;

— ensuring that starting point and endpoint do not lie within a gap by slight modification of the LINETYPE pattern.

If such a comfortable LINETYPE is implemented, it is advisable to assign a new linetype number to it and associate the cheapest method to the compulsory linetypes.

For the LINEWIDTH attribute, the implementor has full freedom to either realize it or not. This is due to the fact that most devices only have a fixed linewidth and can only achieve other linewidths by drawing several lines side by side which may be computationally too expensive, e.g., on vector refresh displays.

1.2   POLYMARKER Primitive and Attributes

The POLYMARKER primitive is a facility which identifies points rather than a symbol facility which allows transformable symbols to be generated. It has been designed so that some hardware character generators may be used provided the symbols dot, plus sign, asterisk, circle, and diagonal cross can be drawn at the centre of a given position.

The clipping convention for POLYMARKER reflects the fact that its, i.e. the POLYMARKER's, purpose is the identification of points. A POLY-MARKER symbol is drawn if, and only if, the marker position is inside the clipping rectangle. If the marker position is inside, but some part of the marker symbol outside the clipping rectangle, clipping may or may not occur.

1.3   TEXT Primitive and Attributes

GKS provides a very comfortable TEXT generation facility which can usually be supported by software text generators only. This full comfort must be present in GKS output levels 1 and 2. However, it may be better to use less flexible built-in capabilities for efficiency reasons. A special TEXT PRECISION attribute allows the selection of cheaper TEXT generation facilities:

— STRING text precision may ignore all geometric attributes except the initial position of the text, thus allowing the use of simple character generators capable of generating text at a fixed size and in a horizontal direction only;
— CHAR text precision evaluates all TEXT attributes to precisely position each character individually. The geometry of each character may be ignored, thus allowing any available generator to be used for each individual character.
— STROKE text precision fully realizes all TEXT attributes. TEXT is transformed and clipped as if the strokes that form the characters were expanded to POLYLINES in WC. However, this does not prevent raster character generating facilities being used, as long as they behave accordingly.

STROKE text precision can usually be realized by a software character generator only. This generator may be included in the GKS nucleus; greater efficiency may be achieved by decentralizing the generator and thus reducing data transfer rates. If decentralized character generators are used, the following rules must be obeyed:

— Font 1, containing the full ASCII-character set (ISO 646) must be present at all workstations with output capabilities. More fonts may be defined within a GKS implementation.
— Not all fonts must be present at each workstation but the same font number must be used to select that particular font at all workstations of a particular installation.
— Not all workstations need to support a specific font with the same text precision. However, if text precision STROKE is required, i.e., in GKS output levels 1 and 2, every workstation must at the very least support STROKE text precision for font 1.

1.4   FILL AREA Primitive and Attributes

The FILL AREA primitive has been modelled around raster devices which possess a true capability to represent areas. Vector devices genuinely cannot generate areas and have to use some simulation technique. Therefore, the implementation of FILL AREA will strongly depend on the type of output device. Four different FILL AREA INTERIOR STYLES have been defined which allow each device type to realize FILL AREA according to its capabilities. The following list gives some typical combinations of INTERIOR STYLE and device classes:

SOLID is intended for colour raster displays; a solid area in a specified colour is generated.

PATTERN is intended for black-and-white and colour raster displays; a solid area is generated, different areas can be distinguished by different definable patterns.

HATCH is intended for plotters and storage tubes; areas are hatched; different areas can be distinguished by different hatch styles selected from a list provided by the implementor.

HOLLOW is intended for vector refresh displays; only the outline of the area is drawn. This is the minimum simulation. It reflects the fact that hatching is computationally expensive in terms of the amount of computer time needed to calculate the hatch lines and in terms of the number of vectors to be drawn. This is important for displays with a limited number of displayable vectors.

1.5   CELL ARRAY Primitive

CELL ARRAY is a typical raster primitive which, in contrast to the FILL AREA primitive, cannot sensibly be simulated on non-raster devices. For those devices, the minimum simulation required is the drawing of the transformed CELL ARRAY boundary.

Whereas the patterns used for FILL AREA generation may or may not be transformed, a CELL ARRAY must fully undergo all transformations. For example, a segment transformation may result in rotation and shearing of the CELL ARRAY. This will include some implementation effort. Furthermore, mapping a transformed CELL ARRAY onto physical pixels includes round-off errors which may become visible due to the limited resolution.

Although there might be problems in transforming CELL ARRAYS, nevertheless, for reasons of consistency, CELL ARRAYS must be defined in WC and it must be possible to transform them. It is left to the application program to select reasonable transformations which do not produce irritating effects.

1.6   GENERALIZED DRAWING PRIMITIVE (GDP)

The GDP provides a means for an implementor of introducing non-standard primitives for his implementation only. The original motivation for having the GDP was to make the output capabilities of some existing workstations accessible, such as circle generator, interpolator, etc. In addition to this, an implementor may decide to provide some special output functions within the driver of a particular workstation which, from the GKS point of view, will be regarded as a GDP. A GDP cannot belong to the GKS nucleus.

The attributes used for a specific GDP may be selected arbitrarily from among the attributes specified for other primitives. However, this choice must be documented in the implementation manual.

1.7   Colour Attribute

Colour is specified as a red, green and blue intensity (RGB), normalized to the interval [0, 1]. This RGB colour model has been chosen to serve the most common colour raster devices.

From the application program's point of view, the RGB model is far from being the best choice. There are other models, such as HLS, HLV [SMIT78] and models based on colour names as used in spoken languages [BERK82], which allow an operator to specify a desired colour more easily and more precisely. These models can be built on top of GKS.

1.8 Transformability of Geometric Aspects of Non-Geometric Attributes

GKS distinguishes between geometric and non-geometric attributes. Geometric attributes are:
— CHARACTER HEIGHT;
— CHARACTER UP VECTOR;
— TEXT PATH;
— TEXT ALIGNMENT;
— PATTERN SIZE;
— PATTERN REFERENCE POINT.

These attributes in conjunction with the attributes
— TEXT FONT AND PRECISION;
— CHARACTER EXPANSION FACTOR;
— CHARACTER SPACING;
— FILL AREA INTERIOR STYLE

define the geometry of the TEXT and FILL AREA primitives in WC. The geometry is subject to the same transformations as the geometric data in the definition of the primitive. For example, if a rectangle is drawn around a TEXT, TEXT should be transformed in such a way that the transformed rectangle is always filled by the TEXT primitive. Transformation requirements may be relaxed by the TEXT PRECISION for TEXT. In the case of FILL AREA, a workstation which can implement a pattern but not transformed patterns may refuse to transform patterns.

However, a closer look at the so-called non-geometric attributes
— LINEWIDTH;
— LINETYPE (length of dash and gap);
— MARKER SIZE;
— FILL AREA INTERIOR STYLE (hatch geometry)

shows that they also contain some geometrical aspects which could be affected by transformations.

LINEWIDTH and MARKER SIZE are specified relatively to a nominal size which is defined in DC. This implies that these geometric aspects cannot be transformed by any transformation but can only be changed by resetting the appropriate entry in a bundle table.

The transformation and clipping of dashing geometry has deliberately been left undefined so that the implementor may make full use of the capabilities of the available hardware and comply with the requirements of his clientele.

Hatching can be well compared to pattern filling and, therefore, hatch lines should be transformed in the same way as patterns. If FILL AREA is transformed but the hatching remains static, a viewer has the impression of looking through a moving outline onto a wall with a stationary wallpaper pattern. However, it is left to the workstation whether hatch lines are transformed or not. Furthermore, the PATTERN REFERENCE POINT can be used so that the same hatch pattern can be positioned in different areas. For example, in cartography, it is annoying if hatch lines are not aligned when the same hatch pattern is used for adjacent areas. In business graphics, hatched rectangles are frequently used where the hatch lines are parallel to a rectangle side. In this case it is important whether the first hatch line coincides with this rectangle side or the hatch lines are centred symmetrically between two rectangle sides.

1.9   Segment Attributes

Segments can be manipulated dynamically. The dynamic capabilities are primarily modelled around the capabilities available at vector refresh displays. Other devices will have serious difficulties in providing the same functionality. The extent to which dynamic changes are supported by the workstation is described in the workstation description table. If dynamic changes require an 'implicit regeneration', they may be postponed as specified by the workstation attribute 'deferral state'.

   If dynamic changes are postponed, the state of the display surface remains undefined for a certain period of time. This intermediate state has deliberately been left undefined so that the implementor is free to take appropriate alternative action. For example, if a line has to be deleted on a storage tube, the implementor may choose to leave the line there and cross it out to indicate a postponed deletion.

   Highlighting is provided by a small class of devices only. Devices without any intensity control may redraw the segment several times (storage tube) or chose a special colour (colour raster displays).

2   MAPPING LOGICAL
ONTO PHYSICAL INPUT DEVICES

2.1   The Role of Logical Input Devices

In order to bring some unification into the great variety of hardware input devices, a small number of well-defined, abstract input devices has been identified. The concept of virtual input devices was enunciated by Wallace [WALL76] as a means whereby interactive graphics applications could be insulated from the peculiarities of the input devices at particular terminals.

   As can be deduced from the popular discussions about the construction of user interfaces [GUED80, SIGG82, PFAF82b], the basic mistake when designing a graphics package is to regard the input and output functions as two

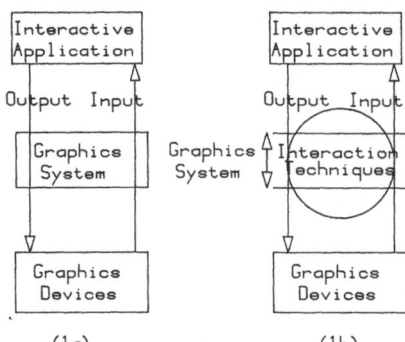

Figure 2.1 Output/input vs. output/interaction

independent concepts rather than seeing how tightly knit they are. Input alone is rather useless for solving interactive problems. Rather than input functions, interaction functions should be defined. Two contradictory approaches are shown in the Figures 2.1a and 2.1b. In Figure 2.1a, input and output functions are kept separate up to a rather high level, leaving both to be coupled together by the application layers. The problem with this approach is that logical input devices at that level hide most of the physical characteristics of actual devices which are needed to create interaction techniques. Both the goals of developing suitable interaction techniques as well as the portability of interactive application programs normally fail if no well-defined access to physical input devices and their characteristics is available. A reason for that is the influence of physical device characteristics on human behaviour. For example, an interaction technique working with a LOCATOR device which is realized on a joystick will not work equally well if the LOCATOR is implemented via a keyboard or a lightpen device.

The original goal for standard input devices was to make their *final* effect the same on all installations (e.g., a LOCATOR should deliver a pair of coordinates); however, the *way* to achieve the final effect is also important, i.e., the interaction technique.

Therefore, another approach must be taken: In Figure 2.1b the interaction techniques have been integrated into the graphics system. Rather than input functions, now it is interaction functions which have been identified. They provide a well-defined standardizable interface which enables application programs to be portable. Their *realization* can be device-dependent since physical input devices instead of logical input devices can be used at this level.

A model containing both, i.e., a fixed set of six logical input devices and the facility to control interaction techniques, has been included in the final versions of GKS. Moreover, the model of input devices has been refined so that it allows control of details at the operator interface, such as the definition and selection of interaction techniques (prompt/echo types) and the grouping of logical input devices [ROSE82]. This, of course, demands appropriate implementation structures. A concept of a GKS implementation which can be moulded to suit actual hardware devices and application and operator needs was described in [PFAF82b].

2.2   Properties of Logical Input Devices

GKS distinguishes between the logical input devices LOCATOR, STROKE, VALUATOR, CHOICE, PICK, and STRING. All these logical devices have certain characteristics which can be controlled by the application program or a dialogue component (such as in [BORU80b] and [BORU82]) which uses parameters. Some of them are:

Simulation: how the implementation uses physical devices to simulate the logical device;

Prompting: how the operator is informed that a physical input device is available for manipulation;

Echo: how the operator is informed of the current logical data value of the device;

Acknowledgement: how the operator is informed that the current logical data value is significant and is being passed on to a REQUEST function or added to the input queue as part of an event report;

Operating mode: (REQUEST, SAMPLE, EVENT);

Initial values: a logical device is given specific initial values each time an interaction begins;

Prompt/echo switch: prompting and echoing information may be switched on or off.

Selecting attribute values for each of these attribute classes yields an instantiation of a logical device.

2.3   Properties of Physical Input Devices

There are not enough logical device attributes to describe interactions with human operators. As well as this, the characteristics of physical devices have to be identified and described in a unified concept. The term "pragmatics" [BAEC82] seems to be adequate to us when describing the physical properties of input tools. Some of these attributes are:

Data contents: the number, type, and meaning of data delivered by an input device.

Category: a generic name describing the type of devices (e.g., joystick representing a group of similar devices).

Number of dimensions a device can handle simultaneously (e.g., a thumb wheel has 1 dimension, tablets have 2 dimensions; 3 dimensions are provided by some joysticks and track balls).

Operating mode: whether a device delivers discrete values (e.g., keyboards) or continuous values (e.g., joysticks, data tablets).

What is sensed: position with tablet and lightpen (absolute values), motion with track ball and mouse (relative movements), pressure with pressure pads and isometric joysticks;

How it is sensed: mechanically with joysticks and thumb wheels, touch-sensitively with touch tablets and touch screens.

It should be noted that many devices are aggregates of more than one different type of simple device. Their power often derives directly from their integration because it cannot be simulated equally well by a collection of independent simple devices (e.g., the four-button puck can be managed with one hand and is, therefore, more powerful than a puck without buttons and a separate, four-button function keyboard).

2.4   The Logical Input Device Model

Every logical input device consists of two components, a measure and a trigger part. These two components are responsible for performing the desired interaction. Taking data from physical devices, they map it onto logical values, i.e., a pair of coordinates, a sequence of points, a real value, an integer number, a segment name and pick identifier, and a character string. The measure part determines how the operator controls the logical data value, while the trigger part determines how the operator indicates that the current value is significant.

The measure part of a logical device is only active when the device is taking part in an interaction (i.e., is enabled). It may be seen as a process which uses the states and changes of state of various physical input devices to calculate a logical data value. It is important to note that a single physical input device may affect the measures of several logical input devices. Figure 2.2 shows a 4-button puck of a data tablet used for controlling the measure parts of a LOCATOR and a CHOICE device. It can simultaneously deliver a pair of coordinates and a choice number between 1 and 15 and at the same time, it may control the trigger process.

The trigger part of a logical device can react in one of two ways: either it fires or it remains quiescent. This reaction depends on the state changes in the physical device. In the above example, the trigger part may be implemented by using the four buttons of the puck. If one of the buttons is depressed the trigger fires.

Many logical input devices may share a common trigger part although the trigger part itself may be seen as an independent process. When the trigger of a logical device fires, it sends a message to all the measure processes it is associated with. The current value of each measure part is dealt with according to the operating state of the logical device:

— In REQUEST mode, the measure process returns its data value to the application program and then stops.

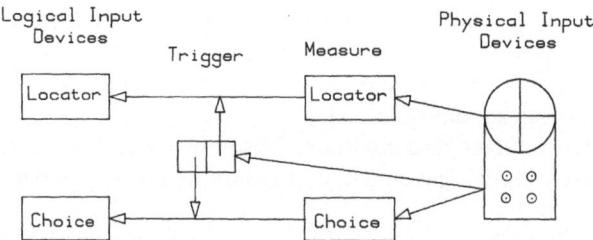

Figure 2.2 Configuration of logical devices on a four-button puck of a data tablet

- In SAMPLE mode, trigger processes are always ignored. The application program may obtain the data value from the measure process whenever it wants.
- In EVENT mode, the measure process attempts to add an event record, containing its identification and data value to the input queue.

If several event reports are generated by a single trigger firing, they are marked as a "group of simultaneous event reports". This grouping together may be determined by the application program during the dequeuing process.

Most ambitious interaction techniques need a means of associating input devices, like the one described in the example above. Such requirements should be part of the description of each interaction technique. During a configuration phase, these associations may be set up. Each association is described as a pair which consists of two logical devices, the second of which refers to the trigger of the first device. The description of the first device is taken from its specification, as described in the next chapter.

2.5 Means of Defining Logical Input Device Realizations

Given the measure trigger model of logical input devices and the attributes introduced above, it is possible to define the binding of logical to physical devices. This definition could be given as input to a configuration generator as described in [PFAF82b]. Using a set of programmed modules, a syntax with the help of which all interaction processes can be described, and some description tables, executable programs can be generated. They implement the desired interaction processes.

Figure 2.3 shows the components of the configuration method. The desired realization of a logical device is described in terms of the logical and physical device attributes required. They are given to the configuration generator in the form of tables. Controlled by these requirement tables and system description tables the generator applies the appropriate productions and replaces symbols by program modules. Eventually, an executable program representing the whole interaction process is generated.

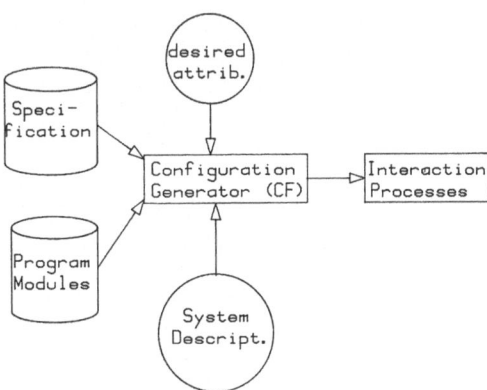

Figure 2.3 Components of the configuration method

Table 2.1 Syntax for the specification of interaction processes

<interaction>	::= <start> <prompting> <adjustment> <stop>
<start>	::=determine source of input data, set initial state of measure process, add measure identification to trigger list. <create echo item>
<prompting>	::=empty|display message|.......
<adjustment>	::= <sample input data> <evaluate logical data> <reaction>
<stop>	::=delete echo, delete prompt, remove measure identification from the trigger list
<create echo item>	::=begin segment, <output primitives>, end segment | .... | ....
<sample input data>	::=read puck (x,y,i) | read lightpen (x,y,display_file_address) | read keyboard (string) | ....
<evaluate logical data>	::= <evaluate measure value>, <evaluate trigger value>
<evaluate measure value>	::=COORDINATE ::= F(x,y) | SEGMENT_NAME,PICK_ID:=P(display_file_ad- dress) | ALTERNATIVE:=i | ....
<evaluate trigger value>	::=TRIGGER=T1(x,y,i) | TRIGGER=T2(x,y,TIME) | ....
<reaction>	::= <update measure value> <update echo>, IF TRIGGER='NOTSET' THEN <adjustment> ELSE <trigger>
<update measure value>	::=LOCATOR:=COORDINATE | PICK:=SEGMENT_NAME,PICK_ID | CHOICE:=ALTERNATIVE | ......
<update echo>	::=shift segment | delete segment, <create echo item> | ... | ...
<trigger> REQUEST: SAMPLE: EVENT:	::=CASE OPERATING MODE OF <acknowledgement>,deliver measure value <adjustment> <acknowledgement>, for each measure id in the trigger list: generate one event report, <adjustment> END

2.5.1 A Syntax for the Specification of Interaction Processes

A syntactic notation has been chosen to describe the interaction processes for two reasons: Firstly, because the syntax could serve as input for a parser which generates the desired executable program. The grammar thus determines the sequence the modules are to be generated in. Secondly, by using this syntax

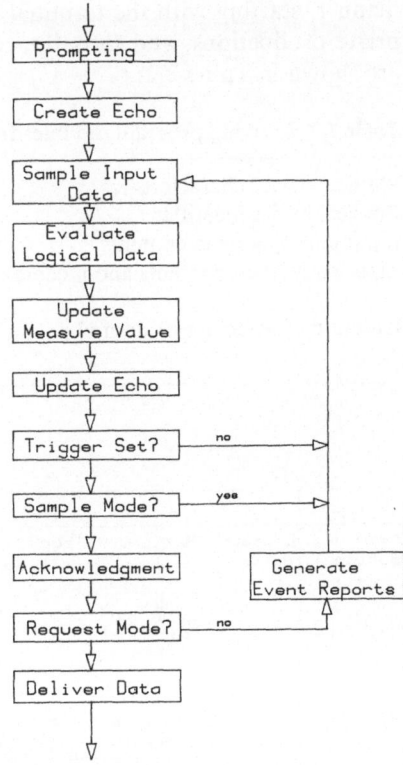

Figure 2.4
Flow diagram of interaction processes

the set of program modules can easily be extended to allow the specification of new interactive processes, simply by defining new productions and (terminal) symbols and developing the corresponding program modules (Table 2.1).

It should be noted that two global states have been defined, namely TRIGGER and OPERATING MODE. The TRIGGER state indicates whether the trigger part for the given device is set, the OPERATING MODE state determines the current operating mode for this device.

The parsing of this syntax leads to the flow diagram in Figure 2.4.

2.5.2 Generating Logical Input Device Implementations

Executable programs which represent interaction processes are generated by a bottom-up parsing of the given syntax. This process is controlled by the user-defined requirement and system property tables. The properties of graphics input and output devices and of all modules used by higher modules are identified once they have been configured. The parser selects the appropriate productions of the syntax above, according to the given tables. The appropriate program modules are chosen and instructions are generated to activate these modules and supply them with parameters. The parsing is performed in a bottom-up manner, starting with the terminal symbols. Some examples of how the appropriate productions, and thus the corresponding program modules, are chosen are shown in Table 2.2:

Table 2.2 Deriving program modules from descriptions

Physical device characteristics	→ Physical device identifier
Physical device identifier	→ Input data types, contents and meanings
Input data types and contents	→ Sample input data function
Input data types, contents and meaning + desired logical input device	
	→ function to evaluate the logical device data
Output device facilities + desired prompt echo type	
	→ functions to create and update the echo

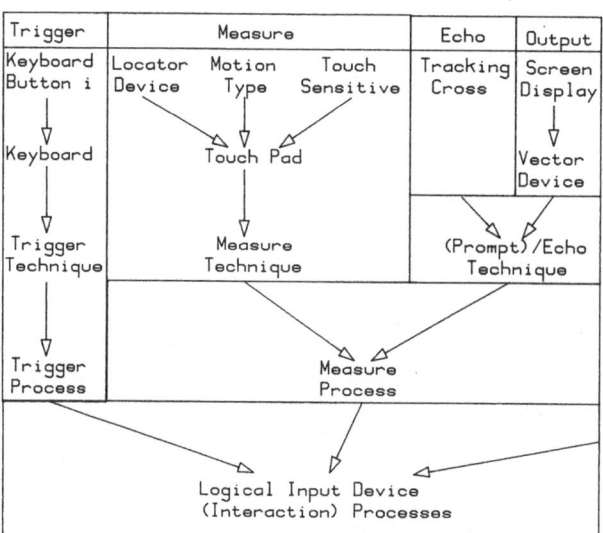

Figure 2.5 Deriving an interaction process from requirements

A small example is given to illustrate how requirements are described and how the interaction process is generated step by step. Starting from the requirements (upper part of Figure 2.5) the physical input device is selected and the corresponding input sampling function is chosen. The format and meaning of the input data obtained from the input device are taken from the interface description tables. Now the simulation module can be selected for the required logical device; this module maps the physical onto the logical data. At the same time, the required prompt/echo technique "tracking cross" and the output device facilities of the given device determine the program module which performs exactly this task. Together with the simulation function and the prompt echo functions the final interaction program can be set up. It should be noted that some details about initialising and terminating the interaction device and also about the handling of the trigger device have been omitted.

2.6 Some Examples of Logical Input Device Realizations

In this section, we give some examples of how logical input devices can be implemented on physical input tools and which simulation software is possibly needed. We also describe some of the device characteristics influencing the operator interface.

2.6.1 LOCATOR and STROKE Devices

The logical input device LOCATOR provides a pair of coordinates and the number of the world coordinate system used. The STROKE device expands this logical data to a sequence of coordinates. Due to the fact that the two logical input devices are related with regard to physical input, we will consider the LOCATOR device further. For a physical input device, the computation from the device to the appropriate world coordinate system has to be done by software. LOCATORs can be implemented on a variety of input devices and some of them are:

Data tablets or digitizers with stylus or hand cursor (puck)
These devices deliver absolute positions rather than movements. Relative movements, however, can easily be simulated by the software storing an actual position, sampling the device position in a given time slice, calculating the differences between the two positions and reporting them whenever a certain time has elapsed or a distance has been exceeded, and finally updating the actual position.

An interesting aspect of the pens (stylus) of data tablets and digitizers is the use of their pressure-sensitive switch. Three states can be distinguished: 'normal state' when the device is on the surface and its position can be determined but its switch is not set, 'push down' when the pen is depressed on the surface in order to indicate positions of interest, 'lift off' when the device is removed from the surface and thus no positions can be sensed.

The same functional behaviour is frequently implemented with a lightpen, a hand cursor, or a mouse if at least one button is associated with them, or with a touch tablet, touch panel, etc.

Lightpens mostly with tip switches
Most lightpens provide a position on a screen which can be used to calculate a position in world coordinates. The advantage of using lightpens is that it is possible to work directly on the output medium; i.e., the operator can pay full attention to the screen and indicate positions on it directly, rather than having to move a screen cursor to the desired position. On the other hand, working with a lightpen can be very tiring for an operator who has to pick

it up, point to a screen position, and put it down again. Therefore, the use of lightpens is expected to decrease in the near future.

Mouse
The mouse is another very popular device because of its simplicity, user friendliness, and inexpensiveness. Based on potentiometers which are adjusted by rollers at the bottom of the mouse, this hand-held device reports relative movements.

While it is very natural to handle (moving the mouse can be directly translated into moving an object) it is not very suitable for precise work.

Track Balls, Joysticks and Thumb Wheels
All three device types are rigidly mounted and have facilities to adjust values. Rather than moving the device itself either a ball is rotated within its mount or a stick is moved either to the left or right, forwards or backwards, or two wheels are turned. Thereby, potentiometers are adjusted and relative movements are reported.

Function Keyboard
Cheap workstations often only have a keyboard as an input device. If a function keyboard is available (the signal resulting from a button being pressed can be sampled), a convenient simulation of a LOCATOR can be done using at least five buttons. Depending on which one is actually pressed, a cursor is moved either to the left or right, up or down. The fifth button is needed to indicate whether the actual cursor position is significant. Four additional buttons might be used for diagonal directions and also for controlling the velocity of the cursor movement.

Alphanumeric Keyboard
At worst, positions can be typed in on a keyboard. While this enables coordinates to be entered very precisely, it is nevertheless a rather inconvenient way of working.

Touch Tablet, Touch Screen
Two less common but innovative and up-and-coming device types should be mentioned briefly. They are touch tablets and touch screens. Some are based on light emitting and sensing diodes, others on sound emitting and reflection measuring techniques, others still measure the changes in electrical capacity, and so on. They all allow an operator to indicate a position with her/his finger or to move the finger over the surface to indicate a motion. These device types provide a very immediate way of interactive working and can therefore be applied especially well for occasional and unskilled users.

2.6.2 VALUATOR

VALUATORS are used to enter real numbers as scalar values. Typical input devices suitable for VALUATOR implementations are rotary and slide potenti-

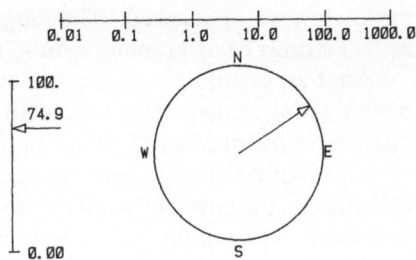

Figure 2.6 Valuator device simulations

ometers. If available, they should be applied in accordance with the semantic interpretation of the values they deliver. For example, a rotary potentiometer should be used to rotate objects, a slide potentiometer to scale them.

With most graphics workstations VALUATORs have to be simulated by some of the devices mentioned in the previous subsection. In this case either one of their two dimensions is used to calculate a scalar value or both dimensions are used to serve two associated VALUATORs.

The simulation might be done in various ways. For example, one of the dials or scales shown in Figure 2.6 is displayed. Using a lightpen, a track ball, a mouse, a hand cursor, or another suitable device, a mark on the scale is moved to a new position or a pointer is turned clockwise or counter-clockwise. The currently indicated value, and possibly the lowest and highest possible values, should be displayed in numeric form. As with the potentiometer types (rotary or slide), the kind of simulation should be in accordance with the semantic interpretation of the values.

Unlike LOCATOR input, VALUATOR values can sensibly be typed in on an alphanumeric keyboard, particularly when highly precise numbers are required.

2.6.3   CHOICE

Most commonly, CHOICE devices are implemented on function keyboards where each button is assigned a choice alternative. The choice alternative is a number between 1 and N, N being either the number of buttons or the number of button combinations. The latter is true for chord devices where an arbitrary number and combination of buttons can be pressed at the same time, thus delivering a combined number. A chord device with 4 buttons can thus produce numbers between 1 and 15. A choice alternative is typically interpreted as a command or an enumeration type value. Such devices are often called 'programmable function keyboard'. Usually, coded overlays are put onto the keyboard to indicate the meaning of the buttons.

More advanced implementations of the CHOICE device use menu techniques. Menus are either displayed on a screen or put on a tablet as an overlay. Using a positioning or a picking device (hand cursor, lightpen, thumb wheels) an alternative is selected. The single choice alternatives are displayed either as text strings or as graphics symbols.

Another solution is to use alphanumeric keyboards to type in text strings. Such a string is then compared with the menu definition. If it matches a choice alternative the number of the choice alternative is reported.

An up-and-coming input device also fits into this scheme, that is, a word recognizer. A number of words is stored internally and speech input is compared with them. The number of the recognized word is delivered.

Another interesting simulation should be mentioned briefly: choice alternatives can be recognized from hand-written patterns entered by the operator. For example, a hand-written symbol 'd' could be interpreted as the command 'delete' after having been recognized as d. Suitable input devices are the hand-held devices mentioned in Section 2.6.1, in particular, the hand cursors, pens and the mouse.

2.6.4   PICK

The only true pick device is the lightpen of vector displays. From a display file address (the address where the display processor stops when the lightpen detects the beam) the identifier is calculated.

In most cases, it is necessary to simulate the PICK and to do that all positioning devices can be used. A cursor is moved to the object which is to be identified and the position is entered. When interpreting an internal display file (segment storage), all output primitives are checked as to whether the position entered lies on or near to them. If several objects are detected the segment priority is used to determine which one is wanted.

Several techniques can be used to accelerate this computation. One is to store a surrounding rectangle or area for each segment in order to avoid searching for segments which cannot have been hit. Another technique is to divide the screen into regions and, for each region, to store the names of those segments contained in it. Then only those segments have to be considered which are included in the region in which the position entered lies.

2.6.5   STRING

The only string device is the alphanumeric keyboard. There is a lot of literature about the ergonomics of keyboards which deals with such aspects as the pressure needed to press a button, the point of contact when a key is accepted, the suitability of delimiter and correction button handling, and the separation of 'dangerous' keys such as clear screen (cf. for example [FRAE77]).

Two simulation types should be mentioned: one is the display of characters and short character sequences on a screen or as overlay of a tablet. The operator composes the text string by identifying the single characters or character sequences by using a particular identification technique.

Another realization is by using pattern recognition of handwritten input. The operator writes as normal on a tablet using a pen. The resulting stream of positions is given to the character recognizer. This then compares the characteristic features of the characters written with a stored dictionary of each character's features. The stored characters have been previously defined by the operator as samples.

3   IMPLEMENTATION ASPECTS

3.1   Feasibility of GKS Implementations

GKS has been defined in a device- and processor-independent way. It is therefore possible to implement GKS on nearly all computers, starting with 16 bit microprocessors, and to support most of the common graphics devices. The only device facilities which cannot be utilized are those which are not covered by the GKS functionality, such as three-dimensional primitives and projection hardware. At the time of writing this book, we know of implementations for the following processor types: CDC, CRAY, DEC, GOULD, IBM, SIEMENS, SPERRY, BULL, NIXDORF, PRIME, APOLLO, AT+T, HEWLETT PACKARD, MOTOROLA, SUN MICRO, INTEL, IBM Personal Computers and Compatibles, and others. More detailed information can be obtained from [GKSVER]. Some of the graphics devices supported by these implementations are: HEWLETT PACKARD plotters and displays, CALCOMP, VERSATEC and TEWIDATA plotters, TEKTRONIX displays and plotters, MEGATEK, DEC VT100, and many others. Depending on the level of GKS, the facilities within the supported level, and the intelligence of the connected graphics devices, the memory sizes needed vary from 4 kbytes to 200 kbytes. The size, of course, also depends on the quality of the particular compiler and the facilities of the available linkage editor.

3.2   Generality of GKS Implementations

The device and processor independence of the GKS definition does not necessarily mean a particular implementation should be independent of the actual graphics devices and processors. On the contrary, GKS installations should be as well adapted to the environment as possible. They should utilize the particular device and processor properties in the best way in order to decrease software overhead and improve execution characteristics. On the other hand, in most cases it would make no sense to implement a new GKS system for every new graphical environment. Three strategies which consider how to develop GKS implementations are briefly discussed.

3.2.1   Environment-Specific Systems

These types of GKS implementations are device- and/or processor-specific as a consequence of their whole design process. That means they have been developed with the very specific installation characteristics of one unique hardware configuration in mind. A particular (set of) graphics device(s) is chosen and thus a set of device functions is determined. The GKS implementation realizes the GKS functions by either using the device functions directly or by emulating them by using existing device functions. An example may clarify this approach.

Let us take a storage tube (e.g., TEKTRONIX 4014) or a graphics device which offers a similar interface (e.g., DEC VT100). In this case POLYLINE and low precision TEXT can be directly mapped by generating the corresponding character codes. As well as this, functions for clearing the screen and entering positions, function codes, and keyboard strings are used. All other GKS output and the attribute functions must be emulated on the basis of lines or characters. For higher GKS levels a segment storage is required to simulate the segment functions and retroactive attribute bundle and workstation transformation modifications. The segment storage may be device-dependent with regard to the function items it stores and to the length of the coordinate data representations.

There are several disadvantages to a pure approach like this. In reality, almost all graphics configurations have more than one type of device. GKS uses the concept of a workstation. Every workstation can be a graphics device or a metafile or a segment storage. A typical interactive system will have a display device, a plotter for hard copying, a metafile for long-term filing, and a segment storage for the transport of segments between the workstations. All these workstations are based on different devices and thus use different device

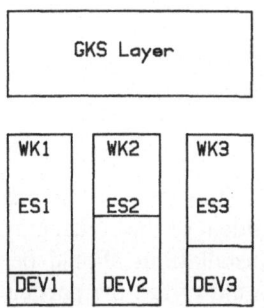

WKi: Workstation i
ESi: Emulation Software i
DEVi: Device i

Figure 3.1 Device-specific implementations

functions. The above approach thus requires emulation software to be dupli-
cated, as is shown in Figure 3.1.

Another major disadvantage is the high costs involved when connecting
a new different device to the system. This would mean the development of
a new workstation with the necessary emulation software (e.g., another device-
dependent segment storage).

To conclude, this approach is only meaningful if very simple GKS installations are intended (level 0 systems with one workstation) and no plans exist
to change the graphics device.

3.2.2 Device-Independent Systems

To overcome the shortcomings mentioned above another approach was considered and that was the development of a DI/DD interface [DIN81]. This separates the device-dependent part (DD) from the device-independent system (DI).
Each particular device defines its own different DI/DD interface. Details of
this approach can be read in Chapter 5. A set of utilities and emulations is
identified, each one performing a transformation step in the mapping process
from logical to physical functions.

The facilities of each particular device are described in a device description
table or can be determined from the respective driver. The DI part uses this
information to select the appropriate simulation and emulation modules and
then maps the GKS functions to the device functions which are actually available. This approach is sketched out in Figure 3.2. It ensures maximum flexibility.

Only one workstation driver is needed to control any graphics device whose
functionality is supported by the DI part. Any new device can be connected
to the system without any modification. Only its facilities must be described
in the table. By adding more utilities, the scope of the implementation can
be expanded with regard to applications as well as to graphics device types.

There are two problems associated with this approach: one is, the generality
of the implementation may lead to some overhead for a particular installation
(devices and applications may be supported that are not needed in a particular
case). The other problem is, the general simulations may not be optimal for

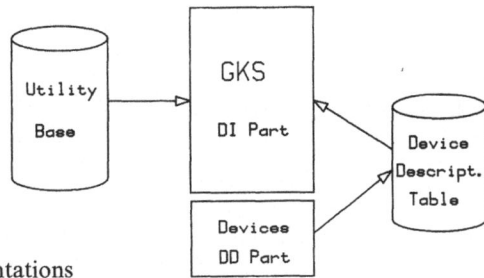

Figure 3.2 Device-independent implementations

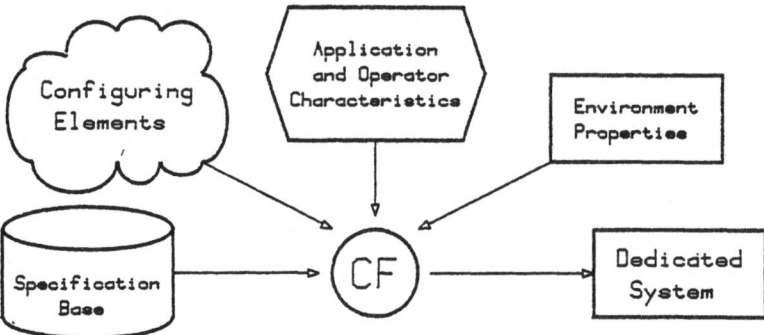

Figure 3.3 Configuration model

certain devices (e.g., a circle might be mapped to lines even if circular arcs are available).

3.2.3   Configurable Systems

One step further in this development is the generation of configurable systems. Because of the large number of different graphics devices and the wide range of application requirements, it does not seem feasible to program a suitable GKS system for each particular case. A multi-purpose GKS implementation (as described above) may be developed so that environment and application-specific GKS installations can be deduced. In [PFAF82a] an approach is described in which a suitable system is automatically generated from a description of the requirements, a set of utility modules, and the specification of the DI part. Figure 3.3 illustrates this approach.

3.3   Some Implementation Concepts

There are four classes of GKS functions which can be distinguished: output, state setting, inquiring about the state, and input functions. They are embedded in a GKS system as shown in Figure 3.4.

3.3.1   Output

One interesting concept is that of the output pipelining. Any output primitive realization can be seen as a sequence of modular steps, transforming the primitive from the logical level to the physical device functions. The intermediate steps are controlled by GKS states (e.g., attributes) which themselves are set prior to the output function activation. One possible transformation sequence for a polyline pipeline is shown in Figure 3.5.

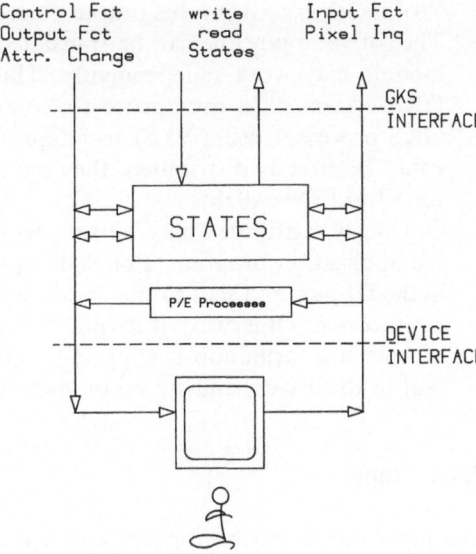

Figure 3.4 Classes of GKS functions

A Polyliné Pipeline

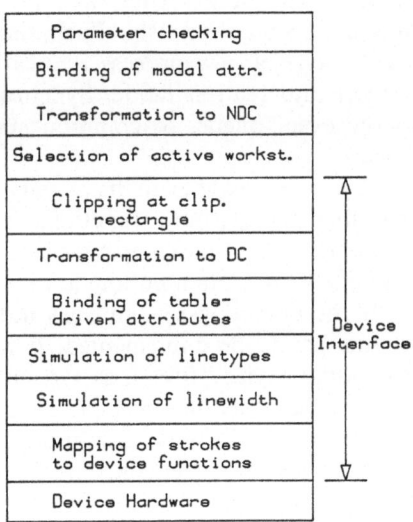

Figure 3.5 Output pipelining

Other valid polyline pipelines can be obtained by exchanging some of these modules without changing the function's effect. The above example addresses a simple device where all attribute emulations and coordinate transformations are performed by software. Other realizations could omit modules in their DI part because the corresponding effect is guaranteed by the device.

A lot of issues arise from this output concept. Some of these are:
— The software pipeline can be translated into hardware pipelines where each module may work independently. This is relevant both for distributing a GKS system on a multiprocessor system and also for designing a special GKS processor using VLSI techniques. While in the first case the modules could be directly distributed, they have to be broken up into smaller pieces for VLSI [ENCA82b].
— Obviously, attributes may be sent to the driver each time they are set by the application program. For code optimising reasons, they may be stored in the DI part and sent to the driver only when a significant output primitive is processed. Otherwise, it might, for example, happen that a large amount of output information is clipped by GKS but the associated attributes are sent to the drivers and stored on metafiles and in the segment storage.

3.3.2 Input

The input model has been dealt with exhaustively in Chapter 2. Here we want to discuss three implementation strategies for asynchronous input (sample and event input).

The most important requirement is the facility of multitasking, i.e., when several processes exist and are active at the same time. If the operating system provides true multitasking, then all input processes and the one output process may exist simultaneously. Each time a logical device is put into sample or event mode, a new process is created. It terminates when the logical device is reset into request mode. Synchronization has to be established for access to the event queue, to common state lists, and to commonly used physical devices.

It is also possible to have only two processes, one handling the output, the other one the input functions. The input process exists as long as at least one logical input device is in sample or event mode. It handles all input devices sequentially (e.g., in a polling loop).

If the operating system does not provide multitasking, an input handling routine has to be implemented. It has to be activated each time an interrupt generating device "fires", as a result of an operator triggering, and each time a given time slice has passed. Then the output process has to be suspended (deactivated and saved). The input handling routine processes the prompting, echoing, acknowledgement, and input data computation for all logical input devices which are currently in event or sample mode. Afterwards, it returns control to the output process again.

3.4 Permitted Differences Between GKS Implementations

A number of details of the standard have been left deliberately unspecified, so as to have the freedom to adapt implementations to different environments and different requirements. In particular, the standard is described in abstract

Table 3.1 Global differences

Functional Scope
  GKS level
Capacity
  Maximum normalization transformation number
  Number of available workstation types
  List of available workstation types
  Maximum number of simultaneously open workstations
  Maximum number of simultaneously active workstations
  Maximum number of workstations associated with a segment
  Maximum size of input queue
  Number of fonts available
  Number of GDPs
  Number of ESCAPE functions
Miscellaneous
  Initial setting of associated source flags (ASFs)
  EMERGENCY CLOSE GKS behaviour
  Value returned by inquiry if information is unavailable
  GKSM format used by each GKSM workstation type
  Font definitions
N.B.:
  The GKS level and the first capacity items are held in the GKS description table,
  and can be determined by an application program. At different GKS levels, certain
  minimal capabilities are defined as in Chapter III.2.

---

terms, so that it can be useful for application programs written in a wide range
of programming languages. In a language binding, the abstract GKS functions
are embedded in a language-dependent layer, according to a number of rules.
These rules are set out in Chapter 4 and are not considered further here. Other
permitted differences fall into two categories:
— Global differences.
— Workstation-dependent differences.

The documentation accompanying a particular implementation should list the
specific choices made in that implementation.

3.4.1   Global Differences

A number of differences are global in the sense that they apply to an implementation as a whole rather than to a particular workstation. These global differences
are itemized below (cf. Table 3.1).

3.4.2   Workstation-Dependent Differences

This group of permitted differences provides for a range of workstations to
be used in a GKS implementation. The major differences in this group are

listed in the Workstation Description Table, specified in Chapter III.3, which forms part of the GKS data structures. Entries in this table can be determined by an application program.

There are restrictions, however, on the values of some entries: at different GKS levels, certain minimal capabilities of a workstation have been defined. In addition, a number of further workstation-dependent differences are listed here.

Control Functions

The following GKS functions can be realized in different ways: MESSAGE, ESCAPE, buffering of deferred actions in deferral modes BNIL, BNIG and ASTI.

Output Functions and Attributes

POLYLINE: The linetype can be either continuous or restarted, at the start of a polyline, at the start of a clipped piece of a polyline and at each vertex of a polyline. Graphical representation of available linetypes (with the restrictions that linetypes 1—4 must be recognizable as solid, dashed, dotted and dashed-dotted, and that other linetypes must have similar appearance on all workstations on which they are available).

POLYMARKER: The available markers can have different graphical representations (with the restrictions that markers 1—5 must be recognizable as dot, plus sign, asterisk, circle and diagonal cross, and that other markers must have similar appearance at all the workstations where they are available).

TEXT: Clipping of STRING and CHAR precision text can vary. In the case of STRING precision, there are different ways in which the current settings of text attributes can be taken into account. For CHAR precision, the evaluation of the attributes CHARACTER HEIGHT, CHARACTER UP VECTOR, CHARACTER EXPANSION FACTOR and TEXT ALIGNMENT can vary.

FILL AREA: There are differences in whether and how the interior styles SOLID, PATTERN and HATCH can be supported and if they are not supported, in the way these interior styles can be simulated (at the very least, the interior style HOLLOW should be supported). It can also vary as to whether patterns and hatching are affected by transformations. Linetype and linewidth vary in the case of interior style HOLLOW.

CELL ARRAY: Simulation can vary (at the very least transformed boundaries of the cell rectangle must be able to be drawn, using implementation-dependent colour, linetype and linewidth).

GDP: Each GDP can be realized in different ways.

All primitives: The colour index used can vary if an output primitive is displayed with a colour index which is not present in the colour table.

Segments
Here, the following can be implemented in different ways:

Picking segments of equal priority.
Display of overlapping segments of equal priority.
Realization of highlighting.

Input Functions
Here, the following can be implemented in different ways:

Realization of logical input devices (for each logical input device, its measure and trigger must be described in terms of the physical devices available at a workstation).
Default prompt/echo realization.
Use of input data record for optional parameters (cf. also Section 3.5).

Inquiry
Here, the following can be implemented in different ways:
Values returned by INQUIRE TEXT EXTENT.
Values returned by PIXEL inquiry functions.
Answers returned by Inquiry when the "REALIZED" flag is set.

3.5   Documentation of an Implementation

A GKS implementation is a module or library written in a programming language which conforms to a GKS language binding. The following rules should be followed when implementing GKS. The objective is to provide all the functions of a particular level of GKS, and none of the functions of higher levels of GKS, in an efficient manner using the facilities available from the host machine and the operating system.

Rule I1
The documentation of a GKS implementation should include a list of all identifiers for procedures, functions, global data aggregates, and files that are visible either to an application program or to the underlying operating system.

On account of this set of identifiers being, in general, a superset of the names specified by the language binding, there can be clashes with names used in programs which have been developed in different implementations of the same language bindings. Therefore, documentation is required to enable potential clashes to be detected in advance (cf. also Chapter 4).

Rule I2
Implementations should not restrict an application program's use of any I/O facilities provided by the host language or operating system. However, implementations should prevent applications bypassing GKS and accessing graphical resources directly.

An implementation will need to assume that it has exclusive control over the graphical resources it is managing. However, as few restrictions as possible should be placed upon the use of other resources.

Rule I3

The documentation of an implementation should specify, for each of the implementation and workstation dependencies, how the dependencies have been resolved.

Several details of the standard have been left deliberately unspecified so as to provide implementors with sufficient freedom to adapt to particular computers and operating systems. Such details are indicated in the text by the words "implementation-dependent". Others have been left unspecified to allow for adaptation to particular graphics devices. They are indicated in the text by the words "workstation-dependent". A list of all such details is given in Section 3.4. The decisions made concerning each of these details should be documented so that the behaviour of application programs may be predicted.

Rule I4

The documentation of each workstation of an implementation should specify how physical input devices and operator actions correspond to the logical input devices at that workstation (if any).

This correspondence is static, and not under the control of the application program and should be documented. Furthermore, it is desirable that workstation implementors should provide a means whereby such correspondences may be changed, perhaps during a GKS configuration phase (cf. also Chapter 2). However, any such means lie outside the scope of the standard.

4   LANGUAGE INTERFACES
AND THEIR IMPLEMENTATION

4.1   Guidelines for the Definition of Language Bindings

The standard is described in abstract terms, in order that it may be useful for applications written in a wide range of programming languages (host languages). Before it can be used by a particular application program written in a particular language, two further stages of specification are required:
— The abstract functions and data types of the standard must be instantiated in terms of the constructs available in the host language.
— The resulting set of language-specific facilities must then be provided using the facilities of a particular machine and operating system.

The aims of the standard are to make application programs portable for different implementations and also to make programming knowledge portable for different languages. Therefore, restrictive rules for the definition of language interfaces have been developed with regard to the language binding (4.1.1) and to its implementations (4.1.2).

4.1.1 Language Binding Rules

A GKS language binding is a document describing the functions that can be accessed by programs written in a specific language. The following rules should be observed when binding GKS to a host language. The aim of a binding is to provide access to the functions and data types of GKS in a natural and efficient manner using the facilities of the host language.

Rule L1
All GKS functions, other than the inquiry functions, must appear atomic to the application program.

This rule forbids the binding to map single GKS functions into sequences of language functions called by the application program, except possibly for inquiry· functions, which in certain language bindings may need to be called once for each element in a structured data type.

Rule L2
The language binding should specify exactly one identifier acceptable to the language for each GKS abstract function name.

The names used for GKS functions in the standard are merely tools for describing the semantics of the standard; they should be replaced by actual identifiers conforming to the restrictions of the host language. There must be a one-to-one mapping from language functions to abstract functions.

Rule L3
The language binding should specify a corresponding data type acceptable to the language for each of the GKS data types. Other data types may be specified as is convenient, in terms of the GKS data types.

The data types used in the standard are merely tools for describing the semantics of it, and they should be replaced by actual data types conforming to the restrictions of the host language.

Rule L4
The language binding should specify, for each GKS abstract function, how the corresponding language function is to be invoked, and the means whereby each of the abstract parameters is transmitted to or from the language function.

The abstract functions will normally be mapped onto language functions or procedures. The parameters will normally be transmitted via a parameter list. The items in such a list may either be, or be references to, items of the data types corresponding to the GKS data types, or aggregates of these types.

Rule L5

The language binding should specify a set of identifiers, acceptable to the language, which may be used by an implementation for internal communication.

An implementation will normally be unable to restrict its use of externally visible identifiers to those specified as a consequence of the preceding rules. Applications should, therefore, avoid using identifiers in this internal set.

4.1.2   Implementation of the Language Interface

A GKS implementation is a module or library written in a programming language which conforms to a GKS language binding. The following rules should be followed when implementing GKS. The aim is to provide access to all the functions of a particular level of GKS, and none of the functions of higher levels of GKS, in an efficient manner, using the facilities available from the host machine and operating system.

Rule I1

The documentation of GKS implementation should include a list of all identifiers for procedures, functions, global data aggregates, and files that are visible either to an application program or to the underlying operating system.

On account of this set of identifiers being, in general, a superset of the names specified by the language binding, programs transported to an implementation from other implementations of the same binding may use names that clash. Documentation is required to enable potential clashes to be detected in advance (cf. also rule L5).

Rule I2

Implementations should not restrict an application program's use of any I/O facilities provided by the host language or operating system. However, implementations should prevent applications bypassing GKS and accessing graphical resources directly.

An implementation will need to assume that it has exclusive control of the graphical resources it is managing. However, as few restrictions as possible should be placed upon the use of other resources.

4.2   The GKS FORTRAN Language Binding

This chapter deals with the GKS language binding for FORTRAN 77 [FORT77]. It is specified as Part I of a separate multi-part standard ISO 8651/1 [ISO 85a]. The complete specification of the GKS FORTRAN subroutines is given together with the specification of the GKS functions in Chapter III. The FORTRAN 77 GKS interface is designed in such a way that GKS application programs can be transported between FORTRAN 77, FORTRAN 77 Subset, and ANSI FORTRAN 66 [FORT66] installations without making many modifications.

In the following, the decisions taken when designing the interface are explained. In doing so, we refer to the rules listed in the previous chapter.

Rule L1

FORTRAN subroutines correspond one-to-one to GKS functions. Each GKS function has a unique FORTRAN subroutine name by which it can be invoked. Some GKS inquiry functions, however, have been split into several FORTRAN subroutines to ease the GKS application programming.

Rule L2

All FORTRAN subroutine names start with the letter 'G'. The remaining letters after the first one are chosen by deriving a unique abbreviation from the single words of the function names. For example, ACTIVATE becomes AC, WORK-STATION becomes WK; hence the FORTRAN subroutine name of ACTI-VATE WORKSTATION becomes GACWK. A complete list of all subroutine names is given in Table 4.1. The method described makes the training of programmers easier since relatively few names have to be memorized to construct all GKS FORTRAN functions. It was therefore preferred to the alternative of providing each GKS function with a more pronounceable name which does not fit into a unique abbreviation concept.

Rule L3

The standard uses several types of parameters most of which cannot be realized directly in FORTRAN. Table 4.2 shows how the types used in the GKS document correspond to their realization in FORTRAN implementations.

Usually, the parameters in the FORTRAN subroutines are in the same order as in the GKS document. For some subroutines, however, there are additional parameters which may interfere with the normal parameter sequence (e.g., maximum array length for arrays being output parameters). This is shown in detail in Appendix 1.

Some of the GKS data types need more special attention beyond that given in Table 4.2:

— The GKS data type STRING is mapped onto the FORTRAN 77 data type CHARACTER*(*). In a FORTRAN 77 Subset implementation CHARACTER*const and an additional parameter N are used where N is the number of characters. IN FORTRAN 66 GKS implementations all occurrences of CHARACTER*const declarations in application programs have to be changed to INTEGER array (M) declarations. The length M of the INTEGER array can be computed as the next whole number greater than [N/K], where K is the number of characters per INTEGER word.
The packing density (number of characters per INTEGER) is the usual one for the particular FORTRAN 66 implementation. This would be the packing density used for the Hollerith string literals.
— The GKS data type ENUMERATION is mapped to INTEGER. The values start with zero. Except for null values, the order of the ENUMERATION alternatives is the same as in the GKS document: null values always appear in the first position (e.g., GNONE, GNCLAS, GNCLIP).

Table 4.1   List of the GKS function names and their FORTRAN abbreviations

Control Functions

GOPKS (ERRFIL,MEMORY)	OPEN GKS
GCLKS	CLOSE GKS
GOPWK (WKID,CONID,WTYPE)	OPEN WORKSTATION
GCLWK (WKID)	CLOSE WORKSTATION
GACWK (WKID)	ACTIVATE WORKSTATION
GDAWK (WKID)	DEACTIVATE WORKSTATION
GCLRWK (WKID,COFL)	CLEAR WORKSTATION
GRSGWK (WKID)	REDRAW ALL SEGMENTS ON WORKSTATION
GUWK (WKID,REGFL)	UPDATE WORKSTATION
GSDS (WKID,DEFMOD,REGMOD)	SET DEFERRAL STATE
GMSG (WKID,MESS)	MESSAGE
GESC (FCTID,IL,IA,MLODR,LODR,ODR)	ESCAPE

Output Functions

GPL (N,PX,PY)	POLYLINE
GPM (N,PX,PY)	POLYMARKER
GTX (X0,Y0,CHARS)	TEXT
GFA (N,PX,PY)	FILL AREA
GCA (PX,PY,QX,QY,N,M,ISC,ISR,DX,DY,COLIA)	CELL ARRAY
GGDP (N,PX,PY,PRIMID,IL,IA)	GENERALIZED DRAWING PRIMITIVE

Output Attributes

GSPLI (INDEX)	SET POLYLINE INDEX
GSLN (LTYPE)	SET LINETYPE
GSLWSC (LWSC)	SET LINEWIDTH SCALE FACTOR
GSPLCI (PLCI)	SET POLYLINE COLOUR INDEX
GSPMI (INDEX)	SET POLYMARKER INDEX
GSMK (MKTYPE)	SET MARKER TYPE
GSMKSC (MKSC)	SET MARKER SIZE SCALE FACTOR

Table 4.1 (continued)

GSPMCI (PMCI)	SET POLYMARKER COLOUR INDEX
GSTXI (INDEX)	SET TEXT INDEX
GSTXFP (FONT,PREC)	SET TEXT FONT AND PRECISION
GSCHXP (CHXP)	SET CHARACTER EXPANSION FACTOR
GSCHSP (CHSP)	SET CHARACTER SPACING
GSTXCI (TXCI)	SET TEXT COLOUR INDEX
GSCHH (CHH)	SET CHARACTER HEIGHT
GSCHUP (CHUX,CHUY)	SET CHARACTER UP VECTOR
GSTXP (TXP)	SET TEXT PATH
GSTXAL (TXALH,TXALV)	SET TEXT ALIGNMENT
GSFAI (INDEX)	SET FILL AREA INDEX
GSFAIS (FAIS)	SET FILL AREA INTERIOR STYLE
GSFASI (FASI)	SET FILL AREA STYLE INDEX
GSFACI (FACI)	SET FILL AREA COLOUR INDEX
GSPA (SZX,SZY)	SET PATTERN SIZE
GSPARF (RFX,RFY)	SET PATTERN REFERENCE POINT
GSASF (LASF)	SET ASPECT SOURCE FLAGS
GSPKID (PCID)	SET PICK IDENTIFIER

Workstation Attributes (Representations)

GSPLR (WKID,PLI,LTYPE,LWIDTH,COLI)	SET POLYLINE REPRESENTATION
GSPMR (WKID,PMI,MTYPE,MSZSF,COLI)	SET POLYMARKER REPRESENTATION
GSTXR (WKID,TXI,FONT,PREC,CHXP,CHSP,COLI)	SET TEXT REPRESENTATION
GSFAR (WKID,FAI,INTS,STYLI,COLI)	SET FILL AREA REPRESENTATION
GSPAR (WKID,PAI,N,MISC,ISR,DX,DY,COLIA)	SET PATTERN REPRESENTATION
GSCR (WKID,CLCR,CG,CB)	SET COLOUR REPRESENTATION

Transformation Functions

GSWN (TNR,XMIN,XMAX,YMIN,YMAX)	SET WINDOW
GSVP (TNR,XMIN,XMAX,YMIN,YMAX)	SET VIEWPORT

Table 4.1 (continued)

GSVPIP (TNR,RTNR,RELPRI)	SET VIEWPORT INPUT PRIORITY
GSELNT (TNR)	SELECT NORMALIZATION TRANSFORMATION
GSCLIP (CLSW)	SET CLIPPING INDICATOR
GSWKWN (WKID,XMIN,XMAX,YMIN,YMAX)	SET WORKSTATION WINDOW
GSWKVP (WKID,XMIN,XMAX,YMIN,YMAX)	SET WORKSTATION VIEWPORT

Segment Functions

GCRSG (SGNA)	CREATE SEGMENT
GCLSG	CLOSE SEGMENT
GRENSG (OLD,NEW)	RENAME SEGMENT
GDSG (SGNA)	DELETE SEGMENT
GDSGWK (WKID,SGNA)	DELETE SEGMENT FROM WORKSTATION
GASGWK (WKID,SGNA)	ASSOCIATE SEGMENT WITH WORKSTATION
GCSGWK (WKID,SGNA)	COPY SEGMENT TO WORKSTATION
GINSG (SGNA,M)	INSERT SEGMENT
GSSGT (SGNA,M)	SET SEGMENT TRANSFORMATION
GSVIS (SGNA,VIS)	SET VISIBILITY
GSHLIT (SGNA,HIL)	SET HIGHLIGHTING
GSSGP (SGNA,PRIOR)	SET SEGMENT PRIORITY
GSDTEC (SGNA,DET)	SET DETECTABILITY

Input Functions

GINLC (WKID,LCDNR,TNR,IPX,IPY, * PET,XMIN,XMAX,YMIN,YMAX,IL,IA)	INITIALISE LOCATOR
GINSK (WKID,SKDNR,TNR,N,IPX,IPY, * PET,XMIN,XMAX,YMIN,YMAX,BUFLEN,INIPOS,IL,IA)	INITIALISE STROKE
GINVL (WKID,VLDNR,IVAL,PET,XMIN, * XMAX,YMIN,YMAX,LOVAL,HIVAL,IL,IA)	INITIALISE VALUATOR
GINCH (WKID,CHDNR,ISTATVAL,PET,XMIN, * XMAX,YMIN,YMAX,IL,IA)	INITIALISE CHOICE

Table 4.1 (continued)

GINPK (WKID,PCDNR,ISTAT,ISGNA,IPCID,PET,	INITIALISE PICK
* XMIN,XMAX,YMIN,YMAX,IL,IA)	
GINST (WKID,STDNR,ZSTR,ISTR,PET,XMIN,	INITIALISE STRING
* XMAX,YMIN,YMAX,IBUFLN,INIPOS,IL,IA)	
GSLCM (WKID,IDNR,MODE,ESW)	SET LOCATOR DEVICE MODE
GSSKM (WKID,IDNR,MODE,ESW)	SET STROKE DEVICE MODE
GSVLM (WKID,IDNR,MODE,ESW)	SET VALUATOR DEVICE MODE
GSCHM (WKID,IDNR,MODE,ESW)	SET CHOICE DEVICE MODE
GSPKM (WKID,IDNR,MODE,ESW)	SET PICK DEVICE MODE
GSSTM (WKID,IDNR,MODE,ESW)	SET STRING DEVICE MODE
GRQLC (WKID,LCDNR,STAT,TNR,PX,PY)	REQUEST LOCATOR
GRQSK (WKID,SKDNR,N,STAT,TNR,NP,PX,PY)	REQUEST STROKE
GRQVL (WKID,VLDNR,STAT,VAL)	REQUEST VALUATOR
GRQCH (WKID,CHDNR,STAT,CHNR)	REQUEST CHOICE
GRQPK (WKID,PCDNR,STAT,SGNA,PCID)	REQUEST PICK
GRQST (WKID,STDNR,STAT,RNCH,CHARS)	REQUEST STRING
GSMLC (WKID,LCDNR,TNR,LPX,LPY)	SAMPLE LOCATOR
GSMSK (WKID,SKDNR,N,TNR,NP,PX,PY)	SAMPLE STROKE
GSMVL (WKID,VLDNR,VAL)	SAMPLE VALUATOR
GSMCH (WKID,CHDNR,STATUS,CHNR)	SAMPLE CHOICE
GSMPK (WKID,PCDNR,STAT,SGNA,PCID)	SAMPLE PICK
GSMST (WKID,STDNR,RNCH,CHARS)	SAMPLE STRING
GWAIT (TOUT,WKID,ICL,IDNR)	AWAIT EVENT
GFLUSH (WKID,ICL,IDNR)	FLUSH DEVICE EVENTS
GGTLC (TNR,LPX,LPY)	GET LOCATOR
GGTSK (N,TNR,NP,PX,PY)	GET STROKE
GGTVL (VAL)	GET VALUATOR
GGTCH (STATUS,CHNR)	GET CHOICE
GGTPK (STAT,SGNA,PCID)	GET PICK
GGTST (RNCH,CHARS)	GET STRING

Table 4.1 (continued)

Metafile Functions

GWITM (WKID,TYPE,NCHS,IL,IA)	WRITE ITEM TO GKSM
GGTITM (WKID,TYPE,IL)	GET ITEM TYPE FROM GKSM
GRDITM (WKID,HL,IOL,IA)	READ ITEM FROM GKSM
GHTM (TYPE,IL,IA)	INTERPRET ITEM

Inquiry Function for Operating State Value

GQOPS (OPSTA)	INQUIRE OPERATING STATE VALUE

Inquiry Function for GKS Description Table

GQLVKS (IERR,JLEVEL)	INQUIRE LEVEL OF GKS
GQEWK (N,IERR,NB,WKTYP)	INQUIRE LIST element OF AVAILABLE WK TYPES
GQWKM (IERR,MXOPWK,MXACWK,MXWKAS)	INQUIRE WORKSTATION MAXIMUM NUMBERS
GQMNTN (IERR,MAXTNR)	INQUIRE MAXIMUM NORM.TRANS. NUMBER

Inquiry Functions for GKS State List

GQOPWK (N,IERR,NB,IWKID)	INQUIRE SET member OF OPEN WORKSTATIONS
GQACWK (N,IERR,NB,IWKID)	INQUIRE SET member OF ACTIVE WORKSTATIONS

Inquire Current Primitive Attribute Values (split into 11 individual subroutines)

GQPLI (IERR,INDEX)	INQUIRE POLYLINE INDEX
GQPMI (IERR,INDEX)	INQUIRE POLYMARKER INDEX
GQTXI (IERR,INDEX)	INQUIRE TEXT INDEX
GQCHH (IERR,CHH)	INQUIRE CHARACTER HEIGHT
GQCHUP (IERR, CHUX,CHUY)	INQUIRE CHARACTER UP VECTOR
GQCHW (IERR,CHW)	INQUIRE CHARACTER WIDTH
GQCHB (IERR,CHBX,CHBY)	INQUIRE CHARACTER BASE VECTOR
GQTXP (IERR,JTXP)	INQUIRE TEXT PATH
GQTXAL (IERR,JTXALH,JTXALV)	INQUIRE TEXT ALIGNMENT
GQFAI (IERR,INDEX)	INQUIRE FILL AREA INDEX

Table 4.1 (continued)

GQPA (IERR,PWX,PWY,PHX,PHY)	INQUIRE PATTERN SIZE
GQPARF (IERR,RFX,RFY)	INQUIRE PATTERN REFERENCE POINT
GQPKID (IERR,IPKID)	INQUIRE PICK IDENTIFIER

Inquire Current Setting of Individual Attributes (split into 14 individual subroutines)

GQLN (IERR,ILTYPE)	INQUIRE LINETYPE
GQLWSC (IERR,RLWID)	INQUIRE LINEWIDTH SCALE FACTOR
GQPLCI (IERR,INDEX)	INQUIRE POLYLINE COLOUR INDEX
GQMK (IERR,IMTYPE)	INQUIRE MARKERTYPE
GQMKSC (IERR,RMSZSF)	INQUIRE MARKER SIZE SCALE FACTOR
GQPMCI (IERR,ICI)	INQUIRE POLYMARKER COLOUR INDEX
GQTXFP (IERR,IFONT,JPREC)	INQUIRE TEXT FONT AND PRECISION
GQCHXP (IERR,CHXP)	INQUIRE CHARACTER EXPANSION FACTOR
GQCHSP (IERR,CHSP)	INQUIRE CHARACTER SPACING
GQTXCI (IERR,ICI)	INQUIRE TEXT COLOUR INDEX
GQFAIS (IERR,JINTS)	INQUIRE FILL AREA INTERIOR STYLE
GQFASI (IERR,ISTYLI)	INQUIRE FILL AREA STYLE INDEX
GQFACI (IERR,ICI)	INQUIRE FILL AREA COLOUR INDEX
GQASF (IERR,LJASF)	INQUIRE ASPECT SOURCE FLAGS
GQCNTN (IERR,ICTNR)	INQUIRE CURRENT NORM.TRANS. NUMBER
GQENTN (N,IERR,NB,INPRIO)	INQUIRE LIST element OF NORM.TRANS. NUMBERS
GQNT (ITNR,IERR,WINDOW,VIEWPT)	INQUIRE NORMALIZATION TRANSFORMATION
GQCLIP (IERR,JCLIPCLRECT)	INQUIRE CLIPPING
GQOPSG (IERR,ISEGNA)	INQUIRE NAME OF OPEN SEGMENT
GQSGUS (N,IERR,NB,ISEGNA)	INQUIRE SET member OF SEGMENT NAMES IN USE
GQSIM (IERR,JFLAG)	INQUIRE MORE SIMULTANEOUS EVENTS

Inquiry Functions for the Workstation State list

GQWKC (IWKID,IERR,ICONID,IWTYPE)	INQUIRE WK CONNECTION AND TYPE
GQWKS (IWKID,IERR,JSTATE)	INQUIRE WORKSTATION STATE
GQWKDU (IWKID,IERR,JDFM,JRGM,JEMPT,JNF)	INQUIRE WK DEFERRAL AND UPDATE STATES

Table 4.1 (continued)

GQEPLI (IWKID,N,IERR,NB,PLI)	INQUIRE LIST element of POLYLINE INDICES
GQPLR (IWKID,IPLI,JTYP,IERR,ILT,RLWSF,ICI)	INQUIRE POLYLINE REPRESENTATION
GQEPMI (IWKID,N,IERR,NB,PMI)	INQUIRE LIST element of POLYMARKER INDICES
GQPMR (IWKID,IPMI,JTYP,IERR,IMT,RMSZS,ICI)	INQUIRE POLYMARKER REPRESENTATION
GQETXI (IWKID,N,IERR,NB,TXI)	INQUIRE LIST element of TEXT INDICES
GQTXR (IWKID,ITXI,JTYP,IERR,IFT,JPREC,CHX,CHSP,ICI)	INQUIRE TEXT REPRESENTATION
GQTXX (IWKID,SX,SY,KSTR,IERR,CPX,CPY,EXRX,EXRY)	INQUIRE TEXT EXTENT (F77)
GQTXXS (IWKID,SX,SY,NCH,KSTR,IERR,CPX,CPY,EX,EX)	INQUIRE TEXT EXTENT (F77-SUBSET)
GQEFAI (IWKID,N,IERR,NB,FAI)	INQUIRE LIST element of FILL AREA INDICES
GQFAR (IWKID,IFAI,JTYP,IERR,JINST,ISTIN,ICI)	INQUIRE FILL AREA REPRESENTATION
GQEPAI (IWKID,N,IERR,NB,PAI)	INQUIRE LIST element of PATTERN INDICES
GQPAR (IWKID,IPAI,JTYPE,NMX,MMX,IERR,N,M,ICIA)	INQUIRE PATTERN REPRESENTATION
GQECI (IWKID,N,IERR,NB,COLI)	INQUIRE LIST element of COLOUR INDICES
GQCR (IWKID,ICI,JTYP,IERR,RR,RG,RB)	INQUIRE COLOUR REPRESENTATION
GQWKT (IWKID,IERR,ITUS,RWINDO,CWINDO,RVIEWP, * CVIEWP)	INQUIRE WORKSTATION TRANSFORMATION
GQSGWK (IWKID,N,IERR,NB,ISEGNA)	INQUIRE SET member of SEGMENT NAMES ON WK
GQLCS (IWKID,ILCDNR,JTYP,MLDR,IERR,JMODE,JESW, * ITNR,IPX,IPY,IPET,EAREA,ILDR,KDR)	INQUIRE LOCATOR DEVICE STATE
GQSKS (IWKID,ISKDNR,JTYP,N,MLDR,IERR,JMODE,JESW, * ITNR,NP,PX,PY,IPET,EAREA,IBUFLN,ILDR,KDR)	INQUIRE STROKE DEVICE STATE
GQVLS (IWKID,JVLDNR,MLDR,IERR,JMODE,JESW, * RIVAL,IPET,EAREA,RLOVAL,RHIVAL,ILDR,KDR)	INQUIRE VALUATOR DEVICE STATE
GQCHS (IWKID,ICHDNR,MLDR,IERR,JMODE,JESW,ISTAT, * ICHNR,IPET,EAREA,ILDR,KDR)	INQUIRE CHOICE DEVICE STATE
GQPKS (IWKID,IPCDNR,JTYP,MLDR,IERR,JMODE,JESW, * JSTAT,ISGNA,IPKID,IPET,EAREA,ILDR,KDR)	INQUIRE PICK DEVICE STATE
GQSTS (IWKID,ISTDNR,MLDR,IERR,JMODJESW, * IRNCH,KISTR,IPET,EAREA,IBUFLN,INIPOS,ILDR,KDR)	INQUIRE STRING DEVICE STATE (F77)

Table 4.1 (continued)

GQSTSS (IWKID,ISTDNR,MNCH,MLDR,IERR,JMOD,JESW, * NRCH,KISTR,IPET,EAREA,IBUFLN,INIPOS,ILDR,KDR)	INQUIRE STRING DEVICE STATE (SUBSET)

Inquiry Functions for Workstation Description Table

GQWKCA (IWTYP,IERR,JWKCAT)	INQUIRE WORKSTATION CATEGORY
GQWKCL (IWTYP,IERR,JVRTYP)	INQUIRE WORKSTATION CLASSIFICATION
GQDSP (IWTYP,IERR,JDCUN,RX,RY,ILX,ILY)	INQUIRE DISPLAY SPACE SIZE
GQDWKA (IWTYP,IERR,JPLBUN,JPMBUN,JTXBUN, * JFABUN,JPAREP,JCOLR,JWKTR)	INQUIRE DYNAMIC MODIFICATION OF WORKSTATION ATTRIBUTES
GQDDS (IWTYP,IERR,JDEFMO,JREGMO)	INQUIRE DEFAULT DEFERRAL STATE VALUE
GQPLF (IWTYP,N,IERR,NLT,LT,NLW,NOMLW, * RLWMIN,RLWMAX,NPPLI)	INQUIRE POLYLINE FACILITIES
GQPPLR (IWTYP,IPLI,IERR,ILN,RLWSF,ICI)	INQUIRE PREDEFINED POLYLINE REPRES.
GQPMF (IWTYP,N,IERR,NMT,MT,NMS,NOMMS, * RMSMIN,RMSMAX,NPPMI)	INQUIRE POLYMARKER FACILITIES
GQPPMR (IWTYP,IPMI,IERR,IMTYP,RMSZ,ICI)	INQUIRE PREDEFINED POLYMARKER REPRES.
GQTXF (IWTYP,N,IERR,NFPP,IFT,JPREC,NCCH, * RMIKH,RMAKH,NCHX,RMIKX,RMAKX,NPTXI)	INQUIRE TEXT FACILITIES
GQPTXR (IWTYP,IPTXI,IERR,IFT,JPR,CHX,CHSP,ICI)	INQUIRE PREDEFINED TEXT REPRES.
GQFAF (IWTYP,NI,NH,IERR,NIS,IS,NHS,IHS,NPFAI)	INQUIRE FILL AREA FACILITIES
GQPFAR (IWTYP,IPFAI,IERR,JINST,IST1,ICI)	INQUIRE PREDEFINED FILL AREA REPRES.
GQPAF (IWTYP,IERR,NPPAI)	INQUIRE PATTERN FACILITIES
GQPPAR (IWTYP,IPPAI,NM,MM,IERR,N,M,ICIA)	INQUIRE PREDEFINED PATTERN REPRES.
GQCF (IWTYP,IERR,NCOLI,JCOLA,NPCI)	INQUIRE COLOUR FACILITIES
GQPCR (IWTYP,IPCI,IERR,RR,RG,RB)	INQUIRE PREDEFINED COLOUR REPRES.
GQEGDP (IWTYP,N,IERR,NGDP,IGDP)	INQUIRE LIST element of AVAILABLE GDPs
GQGDP (IWTYP,IGDP,IERR,NSET,JLSET)	INQUIRE GENERALIZED DRAWING PRIMITIVE
GQLWK (IWTYP,IERR,MPLB,MPMB,MTXB,MFAB,MPAI, * MCOLI)	INQUIRE MAXIMUM LENGTH OF WORKSTATION STATE TABLES
GQSGP (IWTYP,IERR,NSG)	INQUIRE NUMBER OF SEGMENT PRIORITIES

Table 4.1 (continued)

GQDSGA (IWTYP,IERR,JSGTR,JVONOF,JVOFON,JHIGH, *JSGPR,JADD,JSGDEL)	INQUIRE DYNAMIC MODIFICATION OF SEGMENT ATTRIBUTES
GQLI (IWTYP,IERR,NLC,NSK,NVL,NCH,NPK,NST)	INQUIRE NUMBER OF AVAILABLE INPUT DEVICES
GQDLC (IWTYP,IDNR,NP,MLDR,IERR,RIPX,RIPY, *NPL,IPET,EAREA,LDR,KDR)	INQUIRE DEFAULT LOCATOR DEVICE DATA
GQDSK (IWTYP,IDNR,NP,MLDR,IERR,MBFSZ, *NPL,IPET,EAREA,IBUFLN,LDR,KDR)	INQUIRE DEFAULT STROKE DEVICE DATA
GQDVL (IWTYP,IDNR,NP,MLDR,IERR,DVAL, *NPL,IPET,EAREA,RLOVAL,RHIVAL,LDR,KDR)	INQUIRE DEFAULT VALUATOR DEVICE DATA
GQDCH (IWTYP,IDNR,NP,MLDR,IERR,MAXALT, *NPL,IPET,EAREA,LDR,KDR)	INQUIRE DEFAULT CHOICE DEVICE DATA
GQDPK (IWTYP,IDNR,NP,MLDR,IERR, *NPL,IPET,EAREA,LDR,KDR)	INQUIRE DEFAULT PICK DEVICE DATA
GQDST (IWTYP,IDNR,NP,MLDR,IERR,MBFSZ, *NPL,IPET,EAREA,IBUFLN,LDR,KDR)	INQUIRE DEFAULT STRING DEVICE DATA

Inquire Functions for Segment State List

GQASWK (ISGNA,N,IERR,NB,IWKID)	INQUIRE SET member of ASSOCIATED WORKSTAT.
GQSGA (ISGNA,IERR,RSEGM,JVIS,JHIGH,SGPR,JDET)	INQUIRE SEGMENT ATTRIBUTES

Pixel Inquires

GQPXAD (WKID,PX,PY,QX,QY,ERR,N,M)	INQUIRE PIXEL ARRAY DIMENSIONS
GQPXA (WKID,PX,PY,NMX,MMY,ISC,ISR,DX,DY,ERR, INVVAL,COL)	INQUIRY PIXEL ARRAY
GQPX (WKID,PX,PY,ERR,COLI)	INQUIRE PIXEL

Inquiry Function for GKS Error State List

GQIQOV (ERR,WKID,ICL,IDN)	INQUIRE INPUT QUEUE OVERFLOW

Table 4.1 (continued)

Utility Functions	
GEVTM (X0,Y0,DX,DY,PHI,FX,FY,SW,MOUT)	EVALUATE TRANSFORMATION MATRIX
GACTM (MIN,X0,Y0,DX,DY,PHI,FX,FY,SW,MOUT)	ACCUMULATE TRANSFORMATION MATRIX
Error Handling	
GECLKS	EMERGENCY CLOSE GKS
GERHND (ERRNB,FCTID,ERRFIL)	STANDARD ERROR HANDLING PROCEDURE
GERLOG (ERRNB,FCTID,ERRFIL)	STANDARD ERROR LOGGING PROCEDURE
Utility Functions not defined in GKS	
GPREC (IL,IA,RL,RA,NST,KSTR,NLDR,ERRIND,LDR,KDR)	PACK DATA RECORD
GUREC (LDR,KDR,MIL,MRL,MSL,ERRIND,IL,IA, RL,RA,NST,KSTR)	UNPACK DATA RECORD

Table 4.2 Correspondence of the GKS data types to the FORTRAN data types

GKS Data Type	FORTRAN Data Representation
INTEGER	INTEGER
INTEGER ARRAY	1) for arrays of known size: INTEGER giving the length of the INTEGER array, INTEGER array (length). 2) for inquiries of lists or sets of arbitrary size: INTEGER index of requested element (input), INTEGER list or set size (output), INTEGER element requested (output). If the requested element number is zero, only the list or set size is returned. If the size is less than zero or greater than the list or set size, error 502 is generated. Note that the implementation may trap length >1 by using * to dimension the formal argument.
REAL	REAL
REAL ARRAY	INTEGER giving the length of the REAL array, REAL array (length). Note that the implementation may trap length >1 by using * to dimension the formal argument.
const × REAL	1) in non-inquiry functions: List of REALs. 2) REAL array (const) in inquiry functions where const >3.
STRING	1) In a full FORTRAN 77 implementation: INTEGER giving the number of characters returned (for output string argument only), CHARACTER*(*) containing the string. 2) In a FORTRAN 77 Subset implementation: INTEGER giving the number of characters input, INTEGER giving the number of characters returned (for output string argument only), CHARACTER*maxstr containing the string. The quantity 'maxstr' has an 80 character minimum and is defined by the implementation. The number of characters actually used is the minimum of maxstr and the INTEGER giving the number of characters input.
POINT	REAL,REAL giving the X- and Y-values
POINT ARRAY	INTEGER giving the length of the POINT ARRAY, REAL array1(length) containing the X-values, REAL array2(length) containing the Y-values. Note that the implementation may trap length >1 by using * to dimension the formal arguments.
ENUMERATION	INTEGER N.B.: All values are mapped to the range zero to N-1, where N is the number of enumeration alternatives. Except for null values, the order of the enumeration alternatives is the same as in the GKS document: null values always appear in the first position.
LIST	Replaced by list element (or set member in the case of a set) returned by an inquiry function, one at a time. The ordering of the elements (or members) may be altered by any function changing the state lists, but not by inquiry functions.
RECORD	Represented as a set of scalar values and an array of type CHARACTER*80 containing the data. Where the data record is an output parameter, an additional argument 'number of array elements of data record occupied' is needed. The set of scalar values is empty except where the data record contains values which are compulsory in GKS.

Table 4.2 (continued)

GKS Data Type	FORTRAN Data Representation
	N.B.: Data can be read from and written into the data record with the FORTRAN READ and WRITE statements. Special utility functions are defined to pack INTEGER, REAL, and CHARACTER data into the data record and to unpack the data record to the individual data items (GPREC, GUREC). The content of the packed data records is implementation-dependent, but GPREC must perform the inverse function to GUREC and vice versa.
NAME.	INTEGER
	Workstation Identifier, Segment Name, Pick Identifier: An implementation may restrict the range but must at least provide all positive integer values and zero. N.B.: the default value for pick identifier in zero.
	Workstation Type, Connection Identifier, Error File: The set of valid values is implementation dependent.
	GDP Identifier, Escape Identifier: The set of legal values is described in Part I.
	Identification of GKS procedure: The range is below under 'Enumeration types'.

In Table 4.3 a list of FORTRAN names is devised for each enumeration type value. It is not necessary that these mnemonics be used in application programs. Installations should provide convenient means of incorporating the definitions of the names, for example by an INCLUDE or INSERT statement.

— The GKS data type RECORD cannot be conveniently implemented in FORTRAN. Therefore, two special utility functions PACK DATA RECORD and UNPACK DATA RECORD (FORTRAN names: GPREC and GUREC) have been defined to pack any data of the FORTRAN data types INTEGER, REAL and CHARACTER into a CHARACTER*80 array and to unpack the CHARACTER*80 array into the individual data items.

An example is given to illustrate their use: In GKS, the VALUATOR resolution has to be given in the VALUATOR DATA RECORD when the INITIALISE VALUATOR function is invoked. This reads in a FORTRAN program as follows:

```
RA1(1)=0.00001
CALL GPREC (1,EMPTI,1,RA,1,EMPTC,MAXLD,ERRINO,
    ACTLD,D)
CALL GINVL (DISP,VAL1,INITVL,1,EXMIN,EXMAX,EYMIN,
    EYMAX,0.,3.14159,ACTLD,D)
```

It should be noted that if a FORTRAN array is empty, its corresponding length parameter has to be set to '1' to facilitate the use of the adjustable dimension feature. The first element of the array has to be set to an implementation-dependent value signaling invalid data. In the example above, we use the names EMPTI and EMPTC to indicate whether the INTEGER array and the CHARACTER datum are empty. EMPTR would indicate an empty REAL array. The data record D, delivered by the subroutine GPREC, is passed to GKS as an input parameter of the subroutine GINVL when this is called.

The representation of CELL ARRAY, PIXEL ARRAY, and PATTERN allows the user of the routines requiring a cell array parameter to store his data in either a one- or two-dimensional array, and pass any portion of the array as an argument. Two examples should make this clear. It should be noted, however, that passing only part of the array relies on call-by-address parameter passing and the FORTRAN standard array storage convention.

Of course, the user can pass an entire two-dimensional array. In this case the number of columns of the cell array is the same as the first dimension of the FORTRAN array:

```
INTEGER      DX,DY,CELLS(DX,DY)
CALL GCA     X1,Y1,X2,Y2,DX,DY,1,1,DX,DY,CELLS)
```

(1,1)	(2,1)	(3,1)	...	(DX,1)
(1,2)	(2,2)	(3,2)	...	(DX,2)
⋮	⋮	⋮		⋮
(1,DY)	(2,DY)	(3,DY)	...	(DX,DY)

If the user wishes to pass an arbitrary portion of an array he must specify the upper left-hand corner of the portion as the starting address (sx, sy), and the dimensions of the subarray (DX,DY). The dimensions of the whole array are also given (DIMX,DIMY), as they are needed for a proper calculation of addresses.

```
INTEGER      SX,SY,DX,DY,DIMX,DIMY,CELLS(DIMX,DIMY)
DATA         SX/3/SY/6/DX/2/DY/3/
CALL GCA     (X1,Y1,X2,Y2,DIMX,DIMY,SX,SY,DX,DY,CELLS)
```

(1,1)	(2,1)	(3,1)	(4,1)	...	(DIMX,1)
(1,2)	(2,2)	(3,2)	(4,2)	...	(DIMX,2)
⋮	⋮	⋮	⋮		⋮
(1,6)	(2,6)	(3,6)	(4,6)	...	(DIMX,6)
(1,7)	(2,7)	(3,7)	(4,7)	...	(DIMX,7)
(1,8)	(2,8)	(3,8)	(4,8)	...	(DIMX,8)
⋮	⋮	⋮	⋮		⋮
(1,DIMY)	(2,DIMY)	(3,DIMY)	(4,DIMY)	...	(DIMX,DIMY)

All the enumeration types of GKS are mapped to FORTRAN INTEGERS. How GKS scalars and FORTRAN INTEGERS correspond is shown in Table 4.3 in a list of symbolic FORTRAN constants which may be included in any application program. The following section contains a method of mapping GKS enumeration types to FORTRAN variable names. In a full FORTRAN 77 implementation, this mapping could also be accomplished by the PARAMETER statement. However, the following method would ensure compatibility between full FORTRAN 77 and FORTRAN 77 subset. Furthermore, all GKS functions are also given a number for use in the error handling procedures.

It should be noted that due to space limitations, only the DATA statements are listed. All of these variables have to be additionally declared as INTEGERS.

Table 4.3 Mnemonic FORTRAN names for the GKS ENUMERATION type values

INCLUDE FILE containing the mnemonic FORTRAN names and their values for all GKS ENUMERATION type values

aspect source:	bundled, individual	
DATA GBUNDL,GINDIV		/0,1/
clear control flag:	conditionally, always	
DATA GCONDI,GALWAY		/0,1/
clipping indicator:	noclip,clip	
DATA GNCLIP,GCLIP		/0,1/
colour available:	monochrome, colour	
DATA GMONOC,GCOLOR		/0,1/
coordinate switch:	WC, NDC	
DATA GWC,GNDC		/0,1/
deferral mode:	asap, bnil, bnig, asti	
DATA GASAP,GBNIL,GBNIG,GASTI		/0,1,2,3/
detectability:	undetectable, detectable	
DATA GUNDET,GDETEC		/0,1/
device coordinate units:	metres, other	
DATA GMETRE,GOTHU		/0,1/
display surface empty:	notempty, empty	
DATA GNEMPT,GEMPTY		/0,1/
dynamic modification:	irg,imm	
DATA GIRG,GIMM		/0,1/
echo switch:	noecho, echo	
DATA GNECHO,GECHO		/0,1/
fill area interior style:	hollow, solid, pattern, hatch	
DATA GHOLLO,GSOLID,GPATTR,GHATCH		/0,1,2,3/
highlighting:	normal, highlighted	
DATA GNORML,GHILIT		/0,1/
input device status:	none, ok, nopick, nochoice	
DATA GNONE,GOK,GNPICK,GNCHOI		/0,1,2,2/
input class:	none, locator, stroke, valuator, choice, pick; string	
DATA GNCLAS,GLOCAT,GSTROK,GVALUA		/0,1,2,3/
DATA GCHOIC,GPICK,GSTRIN		/4,5,6/
implicit regeneration mode:	suppressed, allowed	
DATA GSUPPD,GALLOW		/0,1/
level of GKS:	L0a, L0b, L0c, L1a, L1b, L1c, L2a, L2b, L2c	
DATA GLOA,GLOB,GLOC,GL1A,GL1B,		/0,1,2,3,4/
DATA GL1C,GL2A,GL2B,GL2C		/5,6,7,8/

Table 4.3 (continued)

INCLUDE FILE containing the mnemonic FORTRAN names and their values for all GKS ENUMERATION type values

new frame action necessary:	no, yes	
DATA GNO,GYES		/0,1/
operating mode:	request, sample, event	
DATA GREQU,GSAMPL,GEVENT		/0,1,2/
operating state value:	GKCL, GKOP, WSOP, WSAC, SGOP	
DATA GGKCL,GGKOP,GWSOP,GWSAC,GSGOP		/0,1,2,3,4/
presence of invalid values:	absent, present	
DATA GABSNT,GPRSNT		/0,1/
regeneration flag:	suppress, perform	
DATA GSUPP,GPERFO		/0,1/
relative input priority:	higher, lower	
DATA GHIGHR,GLOWER		/0,1/
simultaneous events flag:	nomore, more	
DATA GNMORE,GMORE		/0,1/
text alignment horizontal:	normal, left, centre, right	
DATA GAHNOR,GALEFT,GACENT,GARITE		/0,1,2,3/
text alignment vertical:	normal, top, cap, half, base, bottom	
DATA GAVNOR,GATOP,GACAP,GAHALF,GABASE,GABOTT		
		/1,2,3,4,5/
text path:	right, left, up, down	
DATA GRIGHT,GLEFT,GUP,GDOWN		/0,1,2,3/
text precision:	string, char, stroke	
DATA GSTRP,GCHARP,GSTRKP		/0,1,2/
type of returned values:	set,realized	
DATA GSET,GREALI		/0,1/
update state:	notpending, pending	
DATA GNPEND,GPEND		/0,1/
vector raster other type:	vector,raster,other	
DATA GVECTR,GRASTR,GOTHWK		/0,1,2/
visibility:	invisible, visible	
DATA GINVIS,GVISI		/0,1/
workstation category:	output, input, outin, wiss, mo, mi	
DATA GOUTPT,GINPUT,GOUTIN,GWISS,GMO,GMI		/0,1,2,3,4,5/
workstation state:	inactive, active	
DATA GINACT,GACTIV		/0,1/
list of GDP attributes:		
DATA GPLBND,GPMBND,GTXBND,GFABND		/0,1,2,3/
line type:	solid, dashed, dotted, dash-dotted	
DATA GLSOLI,GLDASH,GLDOT,GLDASD		/1,2,3,4/
marker type:	point, plus, asterisk, o-mark, x-mark	
DATA GPOINT,GPLUS,GAST,GOMARK,GXMARK		/1,2,3,4,5/
attribute control flag	current, specified	
DATA GCURNT,GSPEC		/0,1/
polyline/fill area control flag	polyline, fill area	
DATA GPLINE,GFILLA		/0,1/
initial choice prompt flag	off, on	
DATA GPROFF,GPRON		/0,1/

Table 4.3 (continued)

INCLUDE FILE containing the mnemonic FORTRAN names and their values for all GKS ENUMERATION type values

GKS functions (for error handling). The names are the same as the GKS function names except that the sentinel character 'G' is replaced by 'E'.

DATA EOPKS,ECLKS,EOPWK,ECLWK,EACWK,EDAWK	/0,1,2,3,4,5/
DATA ECLRWK,ERSGWK,EUWK,ESDS,EMSG,EESC	/6,7,8,9,10,11/
DATA EPL,EPM,ETX,EFA,ECA,EGDP	/12,13,14,15,16,17/
DATA ESPLI,ESLN,ESLWSC,ESPLCI,ESPMI,ESMK	/18,19,20,21,22,23/
DATA ESMKSC,ESPMCI,ESTXI,ESTXFP,ESCHXP,ESCHSP	/24,25,26,27,28,29/
DATA ESTXCI,ESCHH,ESCHUP,ESTXP,ESTXAL,ESFAI	/30,31,32,33,34,35/
DATA ESFAIS,ESFASI,ESFACI,ESPA,ESPARF,ESASF	/36,37,38,39,40,41/
DATA ESPKID,ESPLR,ESPMR,ESTXR,ESFAR,ESPAR	/42,43,44,45,46,47/
DATA ESCR,ESWN,ESVP,ESVPIP,ESELNT,ESCLIP	/48,49,50,51,52,53/
DATA ESWKWN,ESWKVP,ECRSG,ECLSG,ERENSG,EDSG	/54,55,56,57,58,59/
DATA EDSGWK,EASGWK,ECSGWK,EINSG,ESSGT,ESVIS	/60,61,62,63,64,65/
DATA ESHLIT,ESSGP,ESDTEC,EINLC,EINSK,EINVL	/66,67,68,69,70,71/
DATA EINCH,EINPK,EINST,ESLCM,ESSKM,ESVLM	/72,73,74,75,76,77/
DATA ESCHM,ESPKM,ESSTM,ERQLC,ERQSK,ERQVL	/78,79,80,81,82,83/
DATA ERQCH,ERQPK,ERQST,ESMLC,ESMSK,ESMVL	/84,85,86,87,88,89/
DATA ESMCH,ESMPK,ESMST,EWAIT,EFLUSH,EGTLC	/90,91,92,93,94,95/
DATA EGTSK,EGTVL,EGTCH,EGTPK,EGTST	/96,97,98,99,100/
DATA EWITM,EGTITM,ERDITM,EIITM	/101,102,103,104/
DATA EEVTM,EACTM,EPREC,EUREC	/105,106,107,108/

The following three entries are useful for utilizing the adjustable dimension feature passing 'empty' arrays of length '1' as parameters.

INTEGER	EMPTI	/i.d./
REAL	EMPTR	/i.d./
CHARACTER*1	EMPTC	/i.d./

Note: 'i.d.' means implementation-dependent

Rule L4

Since all GKS functions are mapped to FORTRAN subroutines they can only be invoked by FORTRAN CALLS. The corresponding parameters are passed to and obtained from them according to the FORTRAN parameter passing conventions.

Rule L5

For internal communication purposes, a GKS implementation may need reserved names, e.g., for internal subroutines, functions and common blocks. To avoid any name clashes, it is recommended that internal names should start with the letters 'GK'; other programs should not use such names. GKS installations should provide a means of renaming globally-known internal names when necessary.

Other Features

Every GKS installation has to provide a standard error handling routine, called GERHND. The user may replace this standard error handling routine by his own one using the same name GERHND and the same parameters. A means has to be provided to perform this replacement (e.g., by library management utilities).

4.3   The GKS Pascal Language Binding

4.3.1   General Definitions

This chapter contains the GKS language binding for Pascal [ISO85d]. All of the GKS abstract functions are mapped to Pascal procedures, not always using a one-to-one mapping. The following naming conventions have been adopted:
— enumerated and scalar data types begin with the prefix GT;
— set types begin with the prefix GS;
— arrays begin with GA;
— records begin with GR;
— pointer types begin with GPT;
— constants begin with GC;
— all procedure names begin with the prefix G.

There are a number of implementation-defined characteristics necessary in a Pascal binding. Their implementation must be detailed in the documentation of a GKS system. Those characteristics are:
— the name of the error reporting file (GTerrorfile)
— the maximum length of a string (GCmaxstring)
— the maximum length of a GKS name (GCmaxname)
— the maximum length of an array of points for stroke and output functions in a level 0 Pascal implementation (GCmaxpoint)
— the maximum array sizes for pattern, pixel and cell arrays in a level 0 Pascal implementation (GCmaxDX, GCmaxDY)
— the GKS type, data record for locator, stroke, valuator, choice, pick, string, GDP, escape, and metafile functions
— implementation of conformant array parameters as **var** or value parameters
— data types used for the workstation connection and type parameters
— how separate compilation is achieved
— how the Pascal data types are imported into application programs.

The following Table 4.4 lists a set of abbreviations used in the Pascal language binding:

Table 4.4 Pascal name abbreviations

accumulate	accum
aspect source flags	asf
attribute	attr
buffer	buf
character	char
conditionally	cond
current	curr
defined, default	def
delete	del
description	des
dynamic modification	dmod
evaluate	eval
expansion	expan
fill area	fill (except in procedure name)
identifier	id
initialise	init
inquire	inq
integer	int
level	l (as in level 0a, etc.)
maximum	max
minimum	min
modification	mod
normalization transformation	ntran
number	num
precision	prec
reference	ref
regeneration	regen
representation	rep
request	req
segment	seg
transformation	tran
workstation	ws

The mapping of GKS data types to Pascal data types is shown in the following Table 4.5:

Table 4.5 Mapping of Pascal data types

GKS data type	Pascal data type
integer	integer
real	real
enumerated	enumerated
string	packed conformant array of characters (level 1 Pascal), fixed length string (level 0 Pascal and when component of another data structure)
point	GRpoint = record X,Y : real
point array	GApointarray = array (1..GCmaxpoint) of GRpoint;
name	integer or enumerated types or fixed length string
complex structures	Pascal records and lists
data records	implementation-dependent records

The remaining part of this chapter contains the binding itself. It starts with the definition of the Pascal data types and then lists the Pascal procedure names and parameters.

4.3.2   Pascal Data Types

4.3.2.1   Implementation-Defined Constants

const
```
GCmaxstring =  25;  {length of fixed length strings}
GCmaxname  =  30;  {length of strings representing procedure names}
GCmaxpoint = 100;  {maximum number of points}
GCmaxDX    = 100;  {maximum size of two-dimensional arrays of colour indices}
GCmaxDY    = 100;
GCmaxfile   =  12;  {length of string representing file names}
```

4.3.2.2   Required Constants

```
GCcirclemarker = 4;
GCcrossmarker = 5;
GCdashdotline  = 4;
GCdashedline   = 2;
GCdotmarker    = 1;
GCdottedline    = 3;
GCplusmarker   = 2;
GCsolidline     = 1;
GCstarmarker   = 3;
```

4.3.2.3   General Types

```
GTint0      = 0..MAXINT;
GTint1      = 1..MAXINT;
GTint2      = 2..MAXINT;
GTint3      = 3..MAXINT;
```

4.3.2.4   Names Used by GKS

```
GTWsType  = integer;
GTWsId     = integer;
GTEscapeId = integer;
GTGDPId    = integer;
GTseg      = integer;
GTPickId    = integer;
```

4.3.2.5   GKS Enumerated Types

```
GTasf           = (bundled,indiv);
GTchoiceStatus  = (ChoiceOK,NoChoice);
GTclip          = (clip,noclip);
GTcontrol       = (ClearCond,ClearAlways);
GTcoordSwitch   = (WC,NDC);
```

GTdefer	= (asap,bnig,bnil,asti);
GTdet	= (SegUndet,SegDet);
GTdeviceUnits	= (UnitsMetres,UnitsNotmetres);
GTdisplay	= (ColDisplay,MonoDisplay);
GTDynMod	= (irg,imm);
GTecho	= (Echo,NoEcho);
GTevents	= (MoreEvents,NomoreEvents);
GTgksLevel	= (L0a,L0b,L0c,L1a,L1b,L1c,L2a,L2b,L2c);
GThighlight	= (SegNormal,SegHighlight);
GThorizontal	= (Hnormal,Hleft,Hcentre,Hright);
GTimplicitRegen	= (Suppressed,Allowed);
GTinputClass	= (Locator,Stroke,Valuator,
	Choice,Pick,InputString);
	{The Pick component of this type is only present at levels 1b and 1c}
GTinterior	= (HollowFill,SolidFill,PatternFill,HatchFill);
GTmode	= (ReqInput,SampleInput,EventInput);
GTnfa	= (NfaNotNecessary,NfaNecessary);
GTopst	= (gkcl,gkop,wsop,wsac,sgop);
GTpath	= (RightPath,LeftPath,UpPath,DownPath);
GTpickStatus	= (PickOK,NoPick);
GTpixel	= (ValidCol,InvalidCol);
GTprec	= (StringPrec,CharPrec,StrokePrec);
GTprim	= (Polyline,Polymarker,GKSText,Fill);
GTprimAttr	= (LineType,LineWidth,LineCol,
	MarkerType,MarkerSize,MarkerCol,
	FontPrec,Expan,Spacing,TextCol,
	FillInterior,FillStyleInd,FillCol);
GTpriority	= (HigherPriority,LowerPriority);
GTreturn	= (ValueSet,ValueRealised);
GTsegAttr	= (VisSeg,InvisSeg,
	HighlightedSeg,NormalSeg,
	DetSeg,UndetSeg);
GTstatus	= (StatusOK,StatusNone);
GTsurface	= (empty,notempty);
GTUpdRegen	= (Perform,Postpone);
GTvertical	= (Vnormal,Vtop,Vcap,Vhalf,Vbase,Vbottom);
GTvis	= (SegVis,SegInvis);
GTwsCategory	= (OutputWs,InputWs,OutinWs,WISS,MO,MI);
GTwsClass	= (VectorClass,RasterClass,OtherClass);
GTwsst	= (WsActive,WsInactive);
GTwsTran	= (WsTranNotPending,WsTranPending);

4.3.2.6 Array Types

GAAsf	= **array**[GTPrimAttr] **of** GAasf;
GAColArray	= **array**[1..GCmaxDX,1..GCmaxDY] **of** GTint0;
GAFileName	= **packed array**[1..GCmaxfile] **of** char;
GAInputClass	= **array**[GTInputClass] **of** integer;
GAIntVector	= **array**[1..2] **of** integer;
GAMatrix	= **array**[1..2,1..3] **of** real;

```
GAPrim       = array[GTPrim] of integer;
GAPrimRep    = array[GTPrim] of GRPrimRep;
GAPointArray = array[1..GCmaxpoint] of GRpoint;
GAProcname   = packed array[1..GCmaxname] of char;
GASegMod     = array[GTSegAttr] of GTDynMod;
GAString     = packed array[1..GCmaxstring] of char;
GATextExtent = array[1..4] of GRpoint;
GAVector     = array[1..2] of real;
```

4.3.2.7 Pointer Types

```
GPTint       = →GRint;
GPTfontPrec  = →record
                    fontprec:GRFontPrec;
                    NextFontPrec:GPTFontPrec;
               end;
GPTgdp       = →GRgdp;
GPTseg       = →GRseg;
GPTwsId      = →GRWsId;
GPTwsType    = →GRWsType;
```

4.3.2.8 Set Types

```
GSinterior = set of GTinterior;
GSPrim     = set of GTPrim;
```

4.3.2.9 Record Types

```
GRAlign          = record
                        horizontal: GThorizontal;
                        vertical: GTvertical
                   end;
GRBound          = record
                        LeftBound,RightBound,
                        LowerBound, UpperBound: real;
                   end;
GRChoiceData     = record
                        empty: boolean;
                        {implementation-defined record for initialising choice input}
                   end;
GRCol            = record
                        red,
                        green,
                        blue: real;
                   end;
GRDeferUpd       = record
                        defer: GTdefer;
                        implicitregen: GTImplicitRegen;
                        surface: GTsurface;
                        nfa: GTnfa;
                   end;
```

```
GRDefInput          = record
                        numprompt: integer;
                        promptlist: GPTint;
                        data: GRInputData;
                        area: GRbound;
                          case class: GTInputClass of
                            Locator: (position: GRpoint);
                            Stroke: (strokebuffer: integer);
                            Valuator: (value: real);
                            Choice: (maxchoice: integer);
                            Pick: ( );
                            InputString: (stringbuffer: integer);
                      end;
                              {The Pick component of this type is only present at levels
                              1b and 1c}
GRDisplaySize       = record
                        deviceunits: GTDeviceunits;
                        desize: GAVector;
                        rastersize: GAIntVector;
                      end;
GRDynModWsAttr      = record
                        PrimMod: array[GTPrim] of GTDynMod;
                        ColMod,
                        PatternMod,
                        NTranMod: GTDynMod;
                      end;
GREscapeData        = record
                        {implementation defined for use with escape function}
                        empty: boolean;
                      end;
GRFileData          = record
                        empty: boolean;
                        {implementation defined for use with metafile functions}
                      end;
GRFontPrec          = record
                        font: integer;
                        prec: GTprec;
                      end;
GRGDP               = record
                        GdpId: GTgdpId;
                        NextGdp: GPTgdp;
                      end;
GRGDPdata           = record
                        empty: boolean;
                        {implementation defined for use with gdp function}
                        upvector: GAVector;
                        width: real;
                        basevector: GAVector;
                        path: GTpath;
                        align: GRAlign;
                      end;
```

```
Ghinput                 = record
                            case InputClass:GTInputClass of
                                Locator: (NtranLocator:GTint0;
                                          position:GRpoint);
                                Stroke: (NtranStroke:GTint0;
                                          num:GTint0;
                                          points:GAPointArray);
                                Valuator: (value:real);
                                Choice: (ChoiceStatus:GTChoiceStatus;
                                          choicenum:GTint1);
                                Pick: (PickStatus:GTPickStatus;
                                        seg:GTseg;
                                        pickid:GTPickId);
                                InputString: (stringlength:GTint0;
                                              charstring:GAstring);
                            end;
                            {The Pick component of this type is only present at levels
                            1b and 1c}
GRInputClass            = record
                            case status: GTstatus of
                                StatusOK: (InputClass:GTInputClass);
                                StatusNONE: ( )
                            end;
GRInputData             = record
                            case InputClass: GTInputClass of
                                Locator: (LocatorData:GRLocatorData);
                                Stroke: (strokebufsize:GTint1;
                                         StrokeData:GRStrokeData);
                                Valuator: (lowvalue, highvalue: real;
                                           ValuatorData: GRValuatorData);
                                Choice: (ChoiceData: GRChoiceData);
                                Pick: (PickData:GRPickData);
                                InputString: (stringbufsize:GTint1;
                                              InitialPosition:GTint1;
                                              StringData:GRStringData);
                            end;
                            {The Pick component of this type is only present at levels
                            1b and 1c}
GRInt                   = record
                            int: integer;
                            NextInt: GPTint;
                            end;
GRLocatorData           = record
                            empty: boolean;
                            {implementation-defined record for initialising locator input}
                            end;
GRPickData              = record
                            empty: boolean;
                            {implementation-defined record for initialising pick input}
                            end;
GRPoint                 = record
                            x,y: real;
                            end;
```

```
GRPrimRep          = record
                         Col: GTint0;
                     case Prim: GTPrim of
                         Polyline: (ltype: integer;
                                    width: real);
                         Polymarker: (mtype: integer;
                                      size: real);
                         GKSText: (fontprec: GRFontPrec;
                                   expan, spacing: real);
                         Fill: (interior: GTinterior;
                                styleind: integer);
                     end;

GRPrimAttr         = record
                         PolylineInd: GTint1;
                         PolymarkerInd: GTint1;
                         GKSTextInd: GTint1;
                         FillInd: GTint1;
                         PrimAttr: GRPrimRep;
                         GKSText: GRgksText;
                         PatternWidthVector,PatternHeightVector: GAVector;
                         PatternRefPoint: GRpoint;
                     end;

GRPrimFacil        = record
                         numtypes,
                         numind: integer;
                     case Prim: GTPrim of
                         Polyline: (lines: GPTint;
                                    numwidths: integer;
                                    nominalwidth, minwidth, maxwidth: real);
                         Polymarker: (markers: GPTint;
                                      numsizes: integer;
                                      nominalsize, minsize, maxsize: real);
                         GKSText: (FontPrecs: GPTFontPrec;
                                   numheights: integer;
                                   minheight, maxheight: real;
                                   numexpan: integer;
                                   minexpan, maxexpan: real);
                         Fill: (styles: GSinterior;
                                numhatch: integer;
                                hatches: GPTint);
                     end;

GRSegAttr          = record
                         segtran: GAmatrix;
                         vis: GTvis;
                         highlight: GThighlight;
                         priority: real;
                         det: GTdet;
                     end;

GRSeg              = record
                         SegId: GTseg;
                         NextSeg: GPTseg;
                     end;
```

```
GRStringData      = record
                       empty: boolean;
                       {implementation-defined record for initialising string input}
                    end;
GRStrokeData      = record
                       empty: boolean;
                       {implementation-defined record for initialising stroke input}
                    end;
GRValuatorData    = record
                       empty: boolean;
                       {implementation-defined record for initialising valuator input}
                    end;
GRWsId            = record
                       WsId: GTWsId;
                       nextWs: GPTWsId;
                    end;
GRWsMaxNum        = record
                       maxopenws: GTint1;
                       maxactivews: GTint1;
                       maxwsSeg: GTint1;
                    end;
GRWsType          = record
                       WsType: GTWsTYpe;
                       NextWsType: GPTWsType;
                    end;
```

4.3.2.10   Additional Types for the One-One Mapping

```
GRChoice      = record
                   initialstatus: GTchoiceStatus;
                   initialchoice: GTint1;
                end;
GRFillRep     = record
                   interior: GTinterior;
                   styleind: integer;
                   col: GTint0;
                end;
GRLocator     = record
                   NTranLocator: GTint0;
                   position: GRPoint;
                end;
GRPick        = record
                   initialstatus: GTpickStatus;
                   initialsegment: GTseg;
                   initialpickid: GTint1;
                end;
GRLineRep     = record
                   ltype: integer;
                   width: real;
                   col: GTint0;
                end;
```

```
GRMarkerRep =record
                    mtype: integer;
                    size: real;
                    col: GTint0;
                 end;
GRString      =record
                    stringlength: GTint1;
                    charstring: GAstring;
                 end;
GRStroke      =record
                    NTranStroke: GTint0;
                    num: GTint0;
                    points: GAPointArray;
                 end;
GRTextRep     =record
                    fontprec: GRFontPrec;
                    expan, spacing: real;
                    col: GTint0;
                 end;
```

4.3.3   Pascal Procedures

4.3.3.1   Control Functions

OPEN GKS   **procedure** GOpenGKS (errorfile: GAFileName;
                                  memoryunits: integer);
CLOSE GKS   **procedure** GCloseGKS;
OPEN WORKSTATION   **procedure** GOpenWs (wsid: GTWsId; connid:
                                  GAFileName; wstype: GTWsType);
CLOSE WORKSTATION   **procedure** GCloseWs (wsid: GTWsId);
ACTIVATE WORKSTATION   **procedure** GActivateWs (wsid: GTWsId);
DEACTIVATE WORKSTATION **procedure** GDeactivateWs (wsid: GTWsId);
CLEAR WORKSTATION   **procedure** GClearWs(wsid: GTWsId; controlflag:
                                  GTcontrol);
REDRAW ALL SEGMENTS ON WORKSTATION
                                  procedure GRedrawSegWs (wsid: GTWsId);
UPDATE WORKSTATION   **procedure** GUpdWs (wsid: GTWsId; regenflag:
                                  GTUpdRegen);
SET DEFERRAL STATE   **procedure** GSetDeferSt(wsid: GTWsId; defermode:
                                  GTdefer; regenmode: GTImplicitRegen);
MESSAGE   **procedure** GMessage(wsid: GTWsId; message:
                                  packed array[min..max: GTint1] of CHAR);
MESSAGE LEVEL 0 PASCAL   **procedure** GMessage String(wsid: GTWsId;
                                  stringlength: GTint0; message: GAstring);
ESCAPE   **procedure** GEscape (escapeid: GTEscapeId;
                                  inputdatarec: GREscapeData; **var** outputdatarec:
                                  GREscapeData);
```
```

4.3.3.2   Output Functions

POLYLINE   **procedure** GPolyline(numpoints: GTint2; **var** points:
                                   array[min..max: INTEGER] of GRpoint);
POLYLINE LEVEL 0 PASCAL   **procedure** GPolyline (numpoints: GTint2;
                                   var points: GAPointArray);
POLYMARKER   **procedure** GPolymarker (numpoints: GTint1;
                                   var points: array[min..max: integer] of GRpoint);
POLYMARKER LEVEL 0 PASCAL   **procedure** GPolymarker (numpoints: GTint2;
                                   var points: GAPointArray);
TEXT   **procedure** GText (textposition: GRpoint; charstring:
                                   packed array[min..max: GTint1] of char);
TEXT LEVEL 0 PASCAL   **procedure** GTextString (textposition: GRpoint;
                                   stringlength: GTint0; charstring: GAstring);
FILL AREA   **procedure** GFill (numpoints: GTint3; **var** points:
                                   array[min..max: integer] of GRpoint);
FILL AREA LEVEL 0 PASCAL   **procedure** GFill (numpoints: GTint3; **var** points:
                                   GAPointArray);
CELL ARRAY   **procedure** GCellArray (rectpoint1, rectpoint2:
                                   GRpoint; dx,dy: GTint1; **var** Col: array[min1..
                                   max1: integer; min2..max2: integer] of GTint0);
CELL ARRAY LEVEL 0 PASCAL   **procedure** GCellArray (rectpoint1, rectpoint2:
                                   GRPoint; dx,dy: GTint1; **var** Col: GAColArray);
GENERALIZED DRAWING PRIMITIVE (GDP)   **procedure** Ggdp (numpoints:
                                   GTint0; **var** points: array[min..max: integer] of
                                   GRpoint; gdpid: GTgdpId, datarec: GRgdpData);
GENERALIZED DRAWING PRIMITIVE (GDP) LEVEL 0 PASCAL
                                   procedure Ggdp (numpoints: GTint0;
                                   var points: GAPointArray; gdpid: GTgdpId;
                                   datarec: GRgdpData);

4.3.3.3   Output Attributes

SET POLYLINE INDEX, SET POLYMARKER INDEX, SET TEXT INDEX, SET
FILL AREA INDEX   **procedure** GSetPrimInd (prim: GTPrim; primindind:
                                   GTint1);
SET LINETYPE   **procedure** GSetlineType (linetype: integer);
SET LINEWIDTH SCALE FACTOR   **procedure** GSetLineWidthScale (linewidthscale:
                                   real);
SET POLYLINE COLOUR INDEX   **procedure** GSetLineColInd (linecolind: GTint0);
SET MARKER TYPE   **procedure** GSetMarkerType (markertype: integer);
SET MARKER SIZE SCALE FACTOR   **procedure** GSetMarkerSizeScale
                                   (markersizescale: real);
SET POLYMARKER COLOUR INDEX   **procedure** GSetMarkerColInd
                                   (markercolind: GTint0
SET TEXT FONT AND PRECISION   **procedure** GSetTextFontPrec (textfontprec:
                                   GRFontPrec);
SET CHARACTER EXPANSION FACTOR   **procedure** GSetCharExpan (charexpan:
                                   real);
SET CHARACTER SPACING   **procedure** GSetCharSpacing (charspacing: **real**);
SET TEXT COLOUR INDEX   **procedure** GSetTextColInd (textcolind: GTint0);
SET CHARACTER HEIGHT   **procedure** GSetCharHeight (charheight: real);

SET CHARACTER UP FACTOR **procedure** GSetCharUpVector (charupvector:
                                      GAVector);
SET TEXT PATH   **procedure** GSetTextPath (textpath: GTpath);
SET TEXT ALIGNMENT   **procedure** GSetTextAlign (textalign: GRAlign);
SET FILL AREA INTERIOR STYLE   **procedure** GSetFillIntStyle (fillintstyle:
                                      GTinterior);
SET FILL AREA STYLE INDEX **procedure** GSetFillStyleInd (fillstyleind: integer);
SET FILL AREA COLOUR INDEX   **procedure** GSetFillColInd (fillcolind: GTint0);
SET PATTERN SIZE   **procedure** GSetPatternSize (patternsize: GAVector);
SET PATTERN REFERENCE POINT **procedure** GSetPatternRefPoint (refpoint:
                                      GRpoint);
SET ASPECT SOURCE FLAGS   **procedure** GSetASF (listasf: GAasf);
SET PICK IDENTIFIER   **procedure** GSetPickId (pickid: GTPickId);

4.3.3.4 Workstation Attributes

SET POLYLINE REPRESENTATION, SET POLYMARKER REPRESENTATION,
SET TEXT REPRESENTATION, SET FILL AREA REPRESENTATION
                            procedure GSetPrimRep (prim: GTPrim; wsid:
                            GTWsId; primind: GTint1; primrep: GRPrimRep);
SET PATTERN REPRESENTATION **procedure** GSetPatternRep (wsid: GTWsId;
                            patternind: GTint1; dx,dy: GTint1;
                            var patternarray: array[min1..max1: integer;
                            min2..max2: integer] of GTint0);
SET PATTERN REPRESENTATION LEVEL 0 PASCAL   **procedure** GSetPatternRep
                            (wsid: GTWsId; patternind: GTint1; dx,dy: GTint1;
                            var patternarray: GAColArray);
SET COLOUR REPRESENTATION   **procedure** GSetColRep (wsid: GTWsId; colind:
                            GTint0; col: GRCol);

4.3.3.5 Transformation Functions

SET WINDOW   **procedure** GSetWindow (trannum: GTint1;
                            windowlimits: GRbound);
SET VIEWPORT   **procedure** GSetViewport (trannum: GTint1;
                            viewportlimits: GRbound);
SET VIEWPORT INPUT PRIORITY   **procedure** GSetViewportPriority (trannum,
                            reftrannum: GTint0; relativepriority: GTpriority);
SELECT NORMALIZATION TRANSFORMATION
                            procedure GSelectNTran (trannum: GTint0);
SET CLIPPING INDICATOR   **procedure** GSetClip (clip: GTclip);
SET WORKSTATION WINDOW   **procedure** GSetWsWindow (wsid: GTWsId;
                            wswindowlimits: GRbound);
SET WORKSTATION VIEWPORT   **procedure** GSetWsViewport (wsid: GTWsId;
                            wsviewportlimits: GRbound);

4.3.3.6 Segment Functions

CREATE SEGMENT   **procedure** GCreateSeg (segname: GTseg);
CLOSE SEGMENT   **procedure** GCloseSeg;
RENAME SEGMENT   **procedure** GRenameSeg (oldsegname, newsegname:
                            GTseg);

DELETE SEGMENT   **procedure** GDelSeg (segname: GTseg);
DELETE SEGMENT FROM WORKSTATION   **procedure** GDelSegWs (wsid:
                 GTWsId; segname: GTseg);
ASSOCIATE SEGMENT WITH WORKSTATION   **procedure** GAssocSegWs (wsid:
                 GTWsId; segname: GTseg);
COPY SEGMENT TO WORKSTATION   **procedure** GCopySegWs (wsid: GTWsId;
                 segname: GTseg);
INSERT SEGMENT   **procedure** GInsertSeg (segname: GTseg;
                 tranmatrix: GAmatrix);
SET SEGMENT TRANSFORMATION   **procedure** GSetSegTran (segname: GTseg;
                 tranmatrix: GAmatrix);
SET VISIBILITY   **procedure** GSetVis (segname: GTseg; vis: GTvis);
SET HIGHLIGHTING   **procedure** GSetHighlight (segname: GTseg;
                 highlight: GThighlight);
SET SEGMENT PRIORITY   **procedure** GSetSegPriority (segname: GTseg;
                 segpriority: REAL);
SET DETECTABILITY   **procedure** GSetDet (segname: GTseg;
                 segdet: GTdet);

4.3.3.7 Input Functions

INITIALISE LOCATOR, INITIALISE STROKE, INITIALISE VALUATOR,
INITIALISE CHOICE, INITIALISE PICK, INITIALISE STRING
                 procedure GInitInput (inputclass: GTInputClass; wsid: GTWsId;
                 inputdevicenum: GTint1; initialinput: GRInput; promptechotype:
                 integer; echoarea: GRbound; inputdatarecord: GRInputData
SET LOCATOR MODE, SET STROKE MODE, SET VALUATOR MODE,
SET CHOICE MODE, SET PICK MODE, SET STRING MODE
                 procedure GSetInputMode (inputclass: GTInputClass;
                 wsid: GTWsId; inputdevicenum: GTint1; operatingmode: GTmode;
                 echoswitch: GTecho);
REQUEST LOCATOR, REQUEST STROKE, REQUEST VALUATOR,
REQUEST CHOICE, REQUEST PICK, REQUEST STRING
                 procedure GReqInput (inputclass: GTInputClass; wsid: GTWsId;
                 inputdevicenum: GTint1; **var** status: GTstatus; **var** inputvalue:
                 GRInput);
SAMPLE LOCATOR, SAMPLE STROKE, SAMPLE VALUATOR,
SAMPLE CHOICE, SAMPLE PICK, SAMPLE STRING
                 procedure GSampleInput (inputclass: GTInputClass; wsid: GTWsId;
                 inputdevicenum: GTint1; **var** inputvalue: GRInput);
AWAIT EVENT   **procedure** GAwaitEvent (timeout: real; **var** wsid: GTWsId; **var** class:
                 GRInputClass; **var** inputdevicenum: GTint1);
FLUSH DEVICE EVENTS   **procedure** GFlushDeviceEvents (wsid: GTWsId;
                 inputclass: GTInputClass; inputdevicenum: GTint1);
GET LOCATOR, GET STROKE, GET VALUATOR, GET CHOICE, GET PICK,
GET STRING   **procedure** GGetInput (inputclass: GTInputClass; **var** input:
                 GRinput);

4.3.3.8 Mefafile Functions

WRITE ITEM TO GKSM   **procedure** GWriteItem (wsid: GTWsId; itemtype: integer;
                 itemdatareclength: GTint0; **var** datarec: GRFileData);

GET ITEM TYPE FROM GKSM   **procedure** GGetItemType (wsid: GTWsId;
    var itemtype: integer; **var** itemdatareclength: integer);
READ ITEM FROM GKSM   **procedure** GReadItem (wsid: GTWsId;
   maxitemdatareclength: GTint0; **var** datarec: GRFileData);
INTERPRET ITEM   **procedure** GInterpretItem (itemtype: integer; itemdatareclength:
   GTint0; **var** itemdatarecord: GRFileData);

4.3.3.9   Inquiry Functions

INQUIRE OPERATING STATE VALUE   **procedure** GInqOpSt (**var** opst: GTopst);
INQUIRE LEVEL OF GKS   **procedure** GInqLevelGKS (**var** errorind: integer;
   var levelgks: GTgksLevel);
INQUIRE LIST OF AVAILABLE WORKSTATION TYPES
   procedure GInqListWsTypes (**var** errorind: integer;
   var numwstypes: integer; **var** listwstypes: GPTWsType);
INQUIRE WORKSTATION MAXIMUM NUMBERS   **procedure** GInqWsMaxNum
   (**var** errorind: integer; **var** maxnum: GRWsMaxNum);
INQUIRE MAXIMUM NORMALIZATION TRANSFORMATION NUMBER
   procedure GInqMaxNtranNum (**var** errorind: integer; **var** maxntran:
   GTint1);
INQUIRE SET OF OPEN WORKSTATIONS   **procedure** GInqOpenWs (**var** errorind:
   integer; **var** numopenws: integer; **var** openws: GPTWsId);
INQUIRE SET OF ACTIVE WORKSTATIONS   **procedure** GInqActiveWs
   (**var** errorind: integer; **var** numactivews: integer; **var** activews:
   GPTWsId);
INQUIRE CURRENT PRIMITIVE ATTRIBUTE VALUES
   procedure GInqCurPrimAttr (**var** errorind: integer;
   var PrimAttr: GRPrimAttr);
INQUIRE CURRENT PICK IDENTIFIER   **procedure** GInqCurPickId (**var** errorind:
   integer; **var** curpickid: GTPickId);
INQUIRE CURRENT INDIVIDUAL ATTRIBUTE VALUES
   procedure GInqCurIndivAttr (**var** errorind: integer;
   var indivattr: GAPrimRep; **var** listasf: GAasf);
INQUIRE CURRENT NORMALIZATION TRANSFORMATION NUMBER
   procedure GInqCurNtranNum (**var** errorind: integer;
   var curntrannum: GTint0);
INQUIRE LIST OF NORMALIZATION TRANSFORMATION NUMBERS
   procedure GInqListNtranNum (**var** errorind: integer;
   var ntranlist: GPTint);
INQUIRE NORMALIZATION TRANSFORMATION
   procedure GInqNtran (ntrannum: GTint0; **var** errorind: integer;
   var windowlimits, viewportlimits: GRBound);
INQUIRE CLIPPING   **procedure**GInqClip (**var** errorind: integer; **var** indicator:
   GTclip; **var** clippingrectangle: GRbound);
INQUIRE NAME OF OPEN SEGMENT   **procedure** GInqOpenSeg (**var** errorind:
   integer; **var** segname: GTseg);
INQUIRE SET OF SEGMENT NAMES IN USE   **procedure** GInqSegNames (**var**
   errorind: integer; **var** numsegnames: integer; **var** segnames:
   GPTseg);
INQUIRE MORE SIMULTANEOUS EVENTS   **procedure** GInqMoreEvents (**var**
   errorind: integer; **var** moreevents: GTevents);
INQUIRE WORKSTATION CONNECTION AND TYPE
   procedure GInqWsConnType (wsid: GTWsId; **var** errorind:
   integer; **var** connid: GAFileName; **var** wstype: GTWsType);

INQUIRE WORKSTATION STATE   **procedure** GInqWsSt (wsid: GTWsId;
    var errorind: integer; **var** wsst: GTWsSt);
INQUIRE WORKSTATION DEFERRAL AND UPDATE STATES
    procedure GInqWsDeferUpdSt (wsid: GTWsId;
    var errorind: integer; **var** wssts: GRDeferUpd);
INQUIRE LIST OF POLYLINE INDICES, INQUIRE LIST OF POLYMARKER
INDICES, INQUIRE LIST OF TEXT INDICES, INQUIRE LIST OF FILL AREA
INDICES   **procedure** GInqListPrimInd (wsid: GTWsId; prim: GTPrim;
    var errorind: integer; **var** numprimentries: integer;
    var listdefinedprimind: GPTint);
INQUIRE POLYLINE REPRESENTATION, INQUIRE POLYMARKER
REPRESENTATION, INQUIRE TEXT REPRESENTATION, INQUIRE FILL
AREA REPRESENTATION
    procedure GInqPrimRep (Prim: GTPrim; wsid:
    GTWsId; primind: GTint1; typereturn: GTreturn;
    var errorind: integer; **var** primrep: GRPrimRep);
INQUIRE TEXT EXTENT   **procedure** GInqTextExtent (wsid: GTWsId; textposition:
    GRpoint; charstring: packed array[min..max: GTint1] of char;
    var errorind: integer; **var** concatpoint: GRpoint;
    var textextent: GATextExtent);
INQUIRE TEXT EXTENT LEVEL 0 PASCAL   **procedure** GInqTextStringExtent
    (wsid: GTWsId; textposition: GRpoint; stringlength: GTint0;
    charstring: GAstring; **var** errorind: integer; **var** concatpoint:
    GRpoint; **var** textextent: GATextExtent);
INQUIRE LIST OF PATTERN INDICES   **procedure** GInqListPatternind (wsid:
    GTWsId; **var** errorind: integer; **var** numpatternentries: integer;
    var listpatternind: GPTint);
INQUIRE PATTERN REPRESENTATION   **procedure** GInqPatternRep (wsid:
    GTWsId; patternind: GTint1; typereturn: GTreturn; **var** errorind:
    integer; **var** dx,dy: integer; **var** patternarray: array[min1..max1:
    integer; min2..max2:integer] of integer);
INQUIRE PATTERN REPRESENTATION LEVEL 0 PASCAL
    procedure GInqPatternRep (wsid: GTWsId; patternind: GTint1;
    typereturn: GTreturn; **var** errorind: integer; **var** dx,dy: integer;
    var patternarray: GAColArray);
INQUIRE LIST OF COLOUR INDICES   **procedure** GInqListColInd (wsid: GTWsId;
    var errorind: integer; **var** numcolentries: integer; **var** listcolind: GPTint)
INQUIRE COLOUR REPRESENTATION   **procedure** GinqColRep (wsid: GTWsId;
    colind: GTint0; typereturn: GTreturn; **var** errorind: integer;
    var col: GRCol);
INQUIRE WORKSTATION TRANSFORMATION   **procedure** GInqWsTran (wsid:
    GTWsId; **var** errorind: integer; **var** wstranupdst: GTWsTran;
    var reqwswindow, curwswindow, reqwsviewport, curwsviewport:
    GRbound);
INQUIRE SET OF SEGMENT NAMES ON WORKSTATION
    procedure GInqSegNamesWs (wsid: GTWsId; **var** errorind:
    integer; **var** numsegnames: GTint0; **var** storedsegsws: GPTseg);
INQUIRE LOCATOR DEVICE STATE, INQUIRE STROKE DEVICE STATE,
INQUIRE VALUATOR DEVICE STATE, INQUIRE CHOICE DEVICE STATE,
INQUIRE PICK DEVICE STATE, INQUIRE STRING DEVICE STATE
    procedure GInqlnputDeviceSt (inputclass: GTInputClass; wsid:
    GTWsId; inputdevicenum: GTint1; typereturn: GTreturn;

var errorind: integer; **var** opmode: GTmode; **var** echoswitch:
GTecho; **var** inputdevicest: GRInput; **var** promptecho: integer;
var echoarea: GRBound; **var** inputdatarecord: GRInputData);
INQUIRE WORKSTATION CATEGORY   **procedure** CInqWsCategory (wstype:
GTWsType; **var** errorind: integer; **var** wscategory:
GTWsCategory);
INQUIRE WORKSTATION CLASSIFICATION   **procedure** GInqWsClass (wsytpe:
GTWsType; **var** errorind: integer; **var** wsclass: GTWsClass);
INQUIRE DISPLAY SPACE SIZE   **procedure** GInqDisplaySize (wstype: GTWsType;
var errorind: integer; **var** displaysize: GRDisplaySize);
INQUIRE DYNAMIC MODIFICATION OF WORKSTATION ATTRIBUTES
procedure GInqDynModWsAttr (wstype: GTWsType;
var errorind: integer; **var** dynmod: GRDynModWsAttr);
INQUIRE DEFAULT DEFERRAL STATE VALUES   **procedure** GInqDefDeferSt
(wstype: GTWsType; **var** errorind: integer; **var** defdefermode:
GTDefer; **var** defregenmode: GTImplicitRegen);
INQUIRE POLYLINE FACILITIES, INQUIRE POLYMARKER FACILITIES,
INQUIRE TEXT FACILITIES, INQUIRE FILL AREA FACILITIES
procedure GInqPrimFacil (prim: GTPrim; wstype: GTWsType;
var errorind: integer; **var** primfacil: GRPrimFacil);
INQUIRE PREDEFINED POLYLINE REPRESENTATION, INQUIRE
PREDEFINED POLYMARKER REPRESENTATION, INQUIRE PREDEFINED
TEXT REPRESENTATION, INQUIRE PREDEFINED FILL AREA
REPRESENTATION
procedure GInqPredPrimRep (prim: GTPrim; wstype: GTWsType;
predprimind: GTint1; **var** errorind: integer; **var** primrep:
GRPrimRep);
INQUIRE PATTERN FACILITIES   **procedure** GInqPatternFacil (wstype:
GTWsType; **var** errorind: integer; **var** numpredpatternind: GTint0);
INQUIRE PREDEFINED PATTERN REPRESENTATION
procedure GinqPredPatternRep(wstype:GTWsType; predpatternind:
GTint1; **var** errorind: integer; **var** dx,dy: GTInt1; **var** patternarray:
array[min1..max1:integer; min2..max2:integer] of integer);
INQUIRE PREDEFINED PATTERN REPRESENTATION LEVEL 0 PASCAL
procedure GInqPredPatternRep (wstype: GTWsType;
predpatternind: GTint1; **var** errorind: integer; **var** dx,dy: GTInt1;
var patternarray: GAColArray);
INQUIRE COLOUR FACILITIES   **procedure** GInqColFacil (wstype: GTWsType;
var errorind: integer; **var** numcols: integer; **var** colavail: GTdisplay;
var numpredcolind: integer);
INQUIRE PREDEFINED COLOUR REPRESENTATION
procedure GInqPredColRep (wstype: GTWsType; predcolind:
GTint0; **var** errorind: integer; **var** col: GRCol);
INQUIRE LIST OF AVAILABLE GENERALIZED DRAWING PRIMITIVES
procedure GInqListGDP (wstype: GTWsType; **var** errorind:
integer; **var** numgdp: integer; **var** listgdpid: GPTgdp);
INQUIRE GENERALIZED DRAWING PRIMITIVE   **procedure** GInqGDP
(wstype: GTWsType; gdpid: GTgdpId; **var** errorind: integer;
var numattr: integer; **var** listattr: GSPrim);
INQUIRE MAXIMUM LENGTH OF WORKSTATION STATE TABLES
procedure GInqMaxWsSt (wstype: GTWsType;
var errorind: integer; **var** maxnumprimentries: GAPrim;
var naxnumpatternentries: integer; **var** maxnumcolentries: integer);

INQUIRE NUMBER OF SEGMENT PRIORITIES SUPPORTED
      procedure GInqNumSegPriorities (wstype: GTWSType;
      var errorind: integer; **var** numsegpriorities: integer);

INQUIRE DYNAMIC MODIFICATION OF SEGMENT ATTRIBUTES
      procedure GInqDynModSegAttr (wstype: GTWsType;
      var errorind: integer; **var** segattrchangeable: GASegMod);

INQUIRE NUMBER OF AVAILABLE LOGICAL INPUT DEVICES
      procedure GInqNumInputDevices (wstype: GTWsType;
      var errorind: integer; **var** numinputdevices: GAInputClass);

INQUIRE DEFAULT LOCATOR DEVICE DATA, INQUIRE DEFAULT STROKE
DEVICE DATA, INQUIRE DEFAULT VALUATOR DEVICE DATA, INQUIRE
DEFAULT CHOICE DEVICE DATA, INQUIRE DEFAULT PICK DEVICE DATA,
INQUIRE DEFAULT STRING DEVICE DATA
      procedure GInqDefInputData (inputclass: GTInputClass; wstype:
      GTWsType; inputdevicenum: GTint1; **var** errorind: integer;
      var definputdata: GRDefInput);

INQUIRE SET OF ASSOCIATED WORKSTATIONS **procedure** GInqAssocWs
      (segname: GTseg; **var** errorind: integer; **var** numberassocws:
      GTint1; **var** assocwsid: GPTWsId);

INQUIRE SEGMENT ATTRIBUTES   **procedure** GInqSegAtr (segname: GTseg;
      var errorind: integer; **var** segattr: GRSegAttr);

INQUIRE PIXEL ARRAY DIMENSIONS   **procedure** GInqPixelDim (wsid:
      GTWsId; p,q: GRpoint; **var** errorind: integer; **var** dx,dy: integer);

INQUIRE PIXEL ARRAY   **procedure** GInqPixelArrayDim (wsid: GTWsId; p:
      GRpoint; dx,dy: GTint1; **var** errorind: integer; **var** valid: GTpixel;
      var colindarray: array[minx..maxx: integer; miny..maxy: integer]
      of integer);

INQUIRE PIXEL ARRAY LEVEL 0 PASCAL   **procedure** GInqPixelArrayDim
      (wsid: GTWsId; p: GRpoint; dx,dy: GTint1; **var** errorind: integer;
      var valid: GTpixel; **var** colindarray: GAColArray);

INQUIRE PIXEL **procedure** GInqPixel (wsid: GTWsId; p: GRpoint; **var** errorind:
      integer; **var** colind: integer);

INQUIRE INPUT QUEUE OVERFLOW   **procedure** GInqInputOverflow (**var**
      errorind: integer; **var** wsid: GTWsId; **var** inputclass:
      GTInputClass; **var** inputdevicenum: integer);

4.3.3.10   Utility Functions

EVALUATE TRANSFORMATION MATRIX   **procedure** GEvalTran (fixedpoint:
      GRPoint; shiftvector: GRPoint; rotationangle: real; scale
      GAVector; coordinateswitch: GTCoordSwitch; **var** segtranmatrix:
      GAmatrix);

ACCUMULATE TRANSFORMATION MATRIX   **procedure** GAccumTran
      (insegran: GAmatrix; fixedpoint: GRPoint; shiftvector: GRPoint;
      rotationangle: real; scale: GAVector; coordinateswitch:
      GTCoordSwitch; **var** segtran: GAmatrix);

4.3.3.11   Error Handling

EMERGENCY CLOSE GKS   **procedure** GEmergencyCloseGKS;

ERROR HANDLING   **procedure** GErrorHandling (errornum: integer;
      procid: GAprocname; errorfile: GAFileName);

ERROR LOGGING   **procedure** GErrorLogging (errornum: integer;
      procid: GAprocname; errorfile: GAFileName);

4.3.3.12   Alternative One-One Mapping

In many cases, the Pascal binding uses a many-one mapping of GKS functions to Pascal functions. For a number of these functions an additional one-one mapping has been specified. Table 4.6 lists the many-one functions together with the alternative set of one-one functions.

Table 4.6 Alternative One-one Mapping

Procedure	Alternative Set		
GSetPrimInd	GSetPolylineInd	GSetPolymarkerInd	
	GSetTextInd	GSetFillInd	
GSetPrimRep	GSetPolylineRep	GSetPolymarkerRep	
	GSetTextRep	GSetFillRep	
GInitInput	GInitLocator	GInitStroke	GInitValuator
	GInitChoice	GInitPick	GInitString
GSetInputMode	GSetLocatorMode	GSetStrokeMode	GSetValuatorMode
	GSetChoiceMode	GSetPickMode	GSetStringMode
GReqInput	GReqLocator	GReqStroke	GReqValuator
	GReqChoice	GReqPick	GReqString
GSampleInput	GSampleLocator	GSampleStroke	GSampleValuator
	GSampleChoice	GSamplePick	GSampleString
GGetInput	GGetLocator	GGetStroke	GGetValuator
	GGetChoice	GGetPick	GGetString

SET POLYLINE INDEX   **procedure** GSetPolylineInd (ind: GTint1);
SET POLYMARKER INDEX   **procedure** GSetPolymarkerInd (ind: GTint1);
SET TEXT INDEX   **procedure** GSetTextInd (ind: GTint1);
SET FILL AREA INDEX   **procedure** GSetFillInd (ind: GTint1);
SET POLYLINE REPRESENTATION   **procedure** GSetPolylineRep
                (wsid: GTWsId; ind: GTin1; rep: GRLineRep);
SET POLYMARKER REPRESENTATION   **procedure** GSetPolymarker Rep
                (wsid: GTWsId; ind: GTint1; rep: GRMarkerRep);
SET TEXT REPRESENTATION   **procedure** GSetTextRep
                (wsid: GTWsId; ind:GTint1; rep: GRTextRep);
SET FILL AREA REPRESENTATION   **procedure** GSetFillRep
                (wsid: GTWsId; ind: GTint1; rep: GRFillRep);
INITIALISE LOCATOR   **procedure** GInitLocator (wsid: GTWsId; locdevicenum:
                GTint1; initiallocator:
                GRLocator; promptecho: integer; echoarea: GRBound;
                locatordatarec: GRLocatorData);
INITIALISE STROKE   **procedure** GInitStroke (wsid: GTWsId;
                strokedevicenum: GTint1; initialstroke: GRStroke;
                promptecho: integer; echoarea: GRBound;
                strokebufsize: GTint1; strokedatarec: GRStroke Data);
INITIALISE VALUATOR **procedure** GInitValuator (wsid: GTWsId;
                valdevicenum: GTint1; initialvalue: real;
                promptecho: integer; echoarea: GRBound;
                lowvalue, highvalue: real; valdatarec: GRValuatorData);
INITIALISE CHOICE   **procedure** GInitChoice (wsid: GTWsId; choicedevicenum:
                GTint1; initialchoice: GRChoice; promptecho: integer;
                echoarea: GRBound; choicedatarec: GRChoiceData);

INITIALISE PICK	**procedure** GInitPick (wsid: GTWsId; pickdevicenum: GTint1; initialpick: GRPick; promptecho: integer; echoarea: GRBound; pickdatarec: GRPickData);
INITIALISE STRING	**procedure** GInitString (wsid: GTWsId; stringdevicenum: GTint1; initialstring: GRString; promptecho: integer; echoarea: GRBound; stringbufsize: GTint1; initialposition: GTint1; stringdatarec: GRStringData);
SET LOCATOR MODE	**procedure** GSetLocatorMode (wsid: GTWsId; locdevicenum:GTint1; opmode: GTmode; echoswitch: GTecho);
SET STROKE MODE	**procedure** GSetStrokeMode (wsid: GTWsId; strokedevicenum: GTint1; opmode: GTmode; echoswitch: GTecho);
SET VALUATOR MODE	**procedure** GSetValuatorMode (wsid: GTWsId; valdevicenum: GTint1; opmode: GTmode; echoswitch: GTecho);
SET CHOICE MODE	**procedure** GSetChoiceMode (wsid: GTWsId; choicedevicenum: GTint1; opmode: GTmode; echoswitch: GTecho);
SET PICK MODE	**procedure** GSetPickMode (wsid: GTWsId; pickdevicenum: GTint1; opmode: GTmode; echoswitch: GTecho);
SET STRING MODE	**procedure** GSetStringMode (wsid: GTWsId; stringdevicenum: GTint1; opmode: GTmode; echoswitch: GTecho);
REQUEST LOCATOR	**procedure** GReqLocator (wsid: GTWsId; locdevicenum: GTint1; **var** status: GTstatus; **var** locator: GRLocator);
REQUEST STROKE	**procedure** GReqStroke (wsid: GTWsId; strokedevicenum: GTint1; **var** status: GTstatus; **var** stroke: GRStroke);
REQUEST VALUATOR	**procedure** GReqValuator (wsid: GTWsId; valdevicenum: GTint1; **var** status: GTstatus; **var** value: real);
REQUEST CHOICE	**procedure** GReqChoice (wsid:GTWsId; choicedevicenum: GTint1; **var** status: GTstatus; **var** choice: GRChoice);
REQUEST PICK	**procedure** GReqPick (wsid: GTWsid; pickdevicenum: GTint1; **var** status: GTstatus; **var** pick: GRPick);
REQUEST STRING	**procedure** GReqString (wsid: GTWsId; stringdevicenum: GTint1; **var** status: GTstatus; **var** inputstring: GRString);
SAMPLE LOCATOR	**procedure** GSampleLocator (wsid: GTWsId; locdevicenum: GTint1; **var** locator: GRLocator);
SAMPLE STROKE	**procedure** GSampleStroke (wsid: GTWsId; strokedevicenum: GTint1; **var** stroke: GRStroke);
SAMPLE VALUATOR	**procedure** GSampleValuator (wsid: GTWsId; valdevicenum: GTint1; **var** value: real);
SAMPLE CHOICE	**procedure** GSampleChoice (wsid: GTWsId; choicedevicenum: GTint1; **var** choice: GRChoice);
SAMPLE PICK	**procedure** GSamplePick (wsid: GTWsId; pickdevicenum: GTint1; **var** pick: GRPick);
SAMPLE STRING	**procedure** GSampleString (wsid: GTWsId; stringdevicenum: GTint1; **var** inputstring: GRString);
GET LOCATOR	**procedure** GGetLocator (**var** locator: GRLocator);
GET STROKE	**procedure** GGetStroke (**var** stroke: GRStroke);
GET VALUATOR	**procedure** GGetValuator (**var** value: real);
GET CHOICE	**procedure** GGetChoice (**var** choice: GRChoice);
GET PICK	**procedure** GGetPick (**var** pick: GRPick);

4.4   Other Language Bindings

At the time of writing this book only the FORTRAN 77 and the Pascal language bindings have been internationally discussed and agreed upon. Other language bindings, however, are still under development. The most important ones are the C binding and the ADA binding proposals. They are expected to become standard in 1986 and 1987, respectively. Generally, language bindings may differ in two respects: firstly, how the abstract data types used in the GKS document are mapped onto language data types, and secondly, how the abstract GKS function names and argument lists are mapped onto language functions.

When defining a language binding there is a tradeoff between the number of functions and the number of data types used, depending on the capacity of the language. The FORTRAN language binding represents the one extreme: only the very basic FORTRAN data types can be used and all GKS functions are implemented as FORTRAN subroutines, leaving the error checking and the achievement of the functions' effects to the subroutine-based implementation. The other extreme is a pure specification language using abstract data types, such as the Wide Spectrum Language [BAUE81] or the specification language used by Carson for the PMIG specification [CARS82]. In such a language all GKS functions would correspond to abstract data types and error handling and the effect of the functions would be expressed by means of operations on the data types.

Taking the GKS abstract function SET POLYLINE INDEX (INDEX) as an example, the first solution leads to a FORTRAN subroutine which is called as CALL GSPLI (INDEX). INDEX is an input parameter of type INTEGER. Checking whether INDEX is greater than 1 is left to the implementation as is its effect on the GKS state list. In the second case, POLYLINE INDEX would be an abstract data type which operates on an INTEGER value restricted to the range [1..n]. A further operation is to set the GKS state POLYLINE_ INDEX to the given value. Given a powerful compiler (which would process the specifications), one could simply write 'POLYLINE_INDEX:=4;' in the application program.

The actual implementation of a language interface will obviously depend on the language elements available and on the extensibility of the system, e.g., by macros. The C language binding, for example, has fewer functions than the FORTRAN language binding and uses instead more data types than FORTRAN.

5   INTERFACES TO GRAPHICS DEVICES

5.1   Principles

GKS is based on the concept of abstract workstations. A GKS workstation
represents a unit consisting of zero or one display surfaces and zero or more
input devices, such as a keyboard, tablet and/or lightpen. The workstation presents these devices to the application program as a configuration of abstract
devices, thereby abstracting from the hardware peculiarities. Workstations provide the logical interface through which the application program controls physical devices. Certain special workstations provide facilities for the storage and
exchange of graphical information. In Table 4.3 in Chapter III.4.4 on page 133,
all GKS functions are listed, together with the workstation categories to which
they directly or indirectly apply. Output, attribute, transformation and segment
functions, for example, apply to all output, output/input, and metafile output
workstations, whereas they do not apply to input and metafile input workstations.

Rather than implementing the logical workstation interfaces, GKS systems
will normally realize interfaces to physical devices for the exchange of graphical
data. In order to provide the GKS system with a certain amount of independence
from the various devices, a well-defined interface should be made. Workstations
are based on physical devices of various capabilities and they map the logical
GKS functions to physical device functions. The interaction with physical devices is done via a set of device functions which, together, form the device
interfaces. They address capabilities being directly supported by the low-level
device drivers.

The GKS standard does not define a set of functions for possible device
interfaces, nor the way in which these functions can be used by a GKS implementation. Furthermore, there are no specifications that any interfaces to devices
must be provided at all.

However, there are some good reasons for explicitly providing interfaces to
devices in a GKS implementation and these are:
— Often GKS implementations have to support multiple workstations connected at the same time, or to adjust themselves to different workstations
   in different installations. Using a modular structure and providing interfaces
   helps to reduce the complexity. It enables drivers to be developed independently of the GKS system and of other drivers and even by different teams.
— In many application areas, workstations have to be easily modifiable and
   exchangeable. This can be supported via "connection points" provided by
   well-defined interfaces. This is a most important part which ensures device-
   independence of the major part of a GKS implementation.
— Interfaces provide the means for distributing a GKS system on a multiprocessor system. For example, fully or largely equipped workstations can be implemented on remote microprocessors with local software. Data exchange is
   performed at the interface levels.

— If a GKS implementation is to be certified by testing methods, interfaces are needed to measure the data sent to and received from actual devices. This is explained in Chapter 7.

As well as the implementational aspects, interfaces and their functional elements are also needed to describe or "formally specify" the effect of the GKS functions more completely than the GKS document does. Most of the effect of the GKS functions lies in producing the correct data for a graphical device. This is not such a difficult task if it is performed for abstract workstations of about equal functionality. However, most physically existing graphical devices have different capabilities. The mapping of the logical GKS functions to the various physically existing functions causes the real problem when defining GKS. This problem is dealt with in Chapters 1, 2, and 7 of Part V. Moreover, the interface design as explained in this chapter concerns itself with this task as well.

If can be expected that for the reasons listed above, a small number of device interfaces will evolve reflecting the facilities of typical graphics devices. This is a kind of standardization on a low level: if new graphics devices are developed, their number and kind of functions can be chosen from the existing set. They can then be driven almost directly by existing GKS software.

The following Section 5.2 describes a logical structure within GKS systems. Section 5.3 introduces the background of the DI/DD interface construction. In Section 5.4, we list some DI/DD functions, and in Section 5.5, introduce the description tables which describe the capabilities of device drivers.

Finally, we introduce the efforts within ISO to define a computer graphics interface (CGI) in Section 5.6.

5.2 Separation of the Device-Independent from the Device-Dependent Code Parts

Logically, a GKS system can be subdivided into 3 hierarchically organized subsystems, each one adding a certain functionality to the overall system. As shown in Figure 5.1, we distinguish between the device-dependent, the workstation-dependent, and the workstation-independent parts.

The device-dependent part of a GKS system serves graphics devices at a very low interface (e.g., generating control commands for display processors).

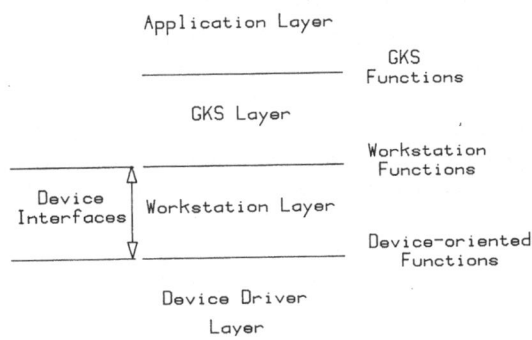

Figure 5.1 Logical structure of GKS systems

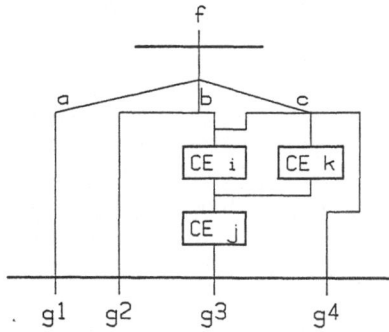

Figure 5.2 Different mappings of the function f to device functions gi

Generally, this level should reduce the various device- and supplier-specific functions to a low-level logical function set. In order to keep the requirements of the device driver construction to a minimum, GKS demands only a very few low-level functions, e.g., draw line, draw pixel, sample input datum, clear screen. Almost no restrictions are placed on extending the device driver function set by new capabilities. One restriction is that those capabilities should fit into the GKS functionality, i.e., GKS functions should be able to utilize them. Some proposals to extend this interface with more sophisticated functions are derived from existing device capabilities and the GKS workstation design. For example, SET COLOUR REPRESENTATION allows the use of colour tables, CREATE and CLOSE SEGMENT supports devices with their own structured display files, and SET SEGMENT TRANSFORMATION utilizes devices with hardware transformation capabilities.

The next logically higher level is constituted by workstations. These establish an additional level of intelligence of graphics functions by introducing device independence [ENCA80]. Software is needed to implement higher logical functions on different device driver functions, such as clipping algorithms, area fill functions, attribute simulations, and logical input devices. Such implementations can be device-independent, i.e., they reduce the higher functions to the minimally required low-level device driver functions. Thus, they can be applied in many different device environments. This is the reason why we call this part of the system the device-independent (DI) part, the device drivers the device-dependent (DD) part, and the interface between the two of them the DI/DD interface. An example of a device-independent implementation of a GKS function on various device-dependent interfaces is shown in Figure 5.2.

The workstation-independent part of GKS finally contains all the functions of a required level, regardless of actual device capabilities and workstation simulations. This level is mainly responsible for the "dynamics" in GKS. All problems of segment handling, dynamic attribute changes, dynamic windowing, etc. may be met by redrawing primitives from a workstation-independent segment storage if no workstation-dependent segment storage is available for that device.

How the effects are achieved is largely hidden from the application programmer and program. Only the differences in the behaviour of the program performance may be visible. For example, the redrawing of pictures may occur at different moments for different workstations or the appearance of attributes may be more or less precise.

An example shows how the effect of the GKS function f, e.g., SET SEG-MENT TRANSFORMATION, can be achieved differently using combinations of the functions gi at three different device interfaces. The gi functions might be SET SEGMENT TRANSFORMATION, DELETE SEGMENT, CLEAR DISPLAY SURFACE, and "draw primitives". In Figure 5.2 the CEi stand for device-independent simulations and utilities, e.g., TRANSFORM COORDI-NATES, READ AND INTERPRET PRIMITIVES FROM SEGMENT STORAGE.

In case a in Figure 5.2, the device driver is able to perform the GKS function f in the way required by GKS. In the second and third case (b and c), the drivers have simpler graphical interfaces than the GKS function at the application layer. The DI part has to analyse the more 'complex' function f, and to map it onto a sequence of 'simpler' functions, g, determined by the real capabilities of the driver. In case b), the combination g2 and g3, in case c) g3 and g4 is used.

5.3   DI/DD Interfaces

As can be deduced from the previous sections, the actual DI/DD interfaces are not fixed at all. They may range from supporting very few and simple functions to providing a fully equipped GKS workstation and in the case of implementations with one workstation, may even be almost identical with the GKS interface. Additionally, they may contain any device-specific functions at all logical levels lower than the GKS level in order to be used by a GKS implementation in a flexible and efficient way.

In order to construct DI/DD interfaces we need both the definitions of the DI/DD function set and the minimal DI/DD interfaces.

5.3.1   DI/DD Function Set

The DI/DD function set consists of an extensible set of functions (given by the names of routines and the list or range of parameters for each routine). Every function defines a possible logical capability of a device driver. The functions are realized directly by the device driver in device-dependent ways.

The DI/DD function set is listed in Section 5.4. It consists of two parts:
— The workstation function set (5.4.1) is a fixed set of functions which is determined by the GKS functions applicable to workstations.
— The device-oriented function set (5.4.2) addresses more device-oriented facilities such as the setting of static unbundled, static bundled, and dynamic unbundled attributes, the drawing of device-specific primitives, the control of physical input devices, etc. It may be extended by any new device-specific function which can be used by a GKS implementation.

5.3.2 Minimal DI/DD Interfaces

Minimal sets of functions can be chosen from the DI/DD function set, according to the device types. Every device driver has to support the corresponding set of required functions. It is ensured that the functions of the minimal interface suffice to implement all GKS functions on top of them. Device types anticipated at the moment are vector types, raster types and input types; they can be combined arbitrarily. Minimal DI/DD interfaces consist of the following functions:

    OPEN DEVICE
    CLOSE DEVICE
    CLEAR SURFACE   (for output type devices)
    LINE   (for vector-output type devices)
    PIXEL   (for raster-output types)
    SAMPLE INPUT DATUM   (for input type devices)

If a device is an aggregate of several types, the functions in this list which refer to these types have to be added together.

5.3.3 Constructing DI/DD Interfaces

Each particular DI/DD interface represents a logical description of the capabilities of a particular device driver, expressed in terms of a number of functions and a DI/DD interface description table. The functions are chosen from the DI/DD function set. A particular DI/DD interface might consist of:
— the workstation function set. All functions of a fully equipped workstation (of a particular GKS level) are supported by the device driver. There is no need for simulation software in the device-independent part. The workstation driver is identical to the device driver and is implemented completely in device-dependent form (DD part). Such solutions are feasible if the graphical device used provides powerful facilities, such as a structured display file (device-dependent segment storage), hardware transformations and clipping, attribute tables, etc. It may also be adopted if device-dependent solutions can be developed without an unreasonable amount of effort and are more powerful than device-independent solutions. This is especially true for remote GKS workstations with slow connection lines to a time-shared host, and for one-workstations systems.
— suitable subsets, chosen from one or both of the workstation function set and the device-oriented function set. In order to provide the application program with powerful workstations on less powerful devices, without implementing special software solutions in device-dependent form, a particular DI/DD interface may omit most of the functions required by a' workstation. Thus, device-independent (DI) solutions can be then realized on top of the device drivers (output, input, attribute simulations, segment handling, redrawing, retroactive attribute changes, and workstation windowing). The term "suitable subset" means that it must at least include the minimal DI/DD interface, and that a duplication of functions at different levels of complexity should be avoided.

5.4   The DI/DD Function Set

5.4.1   The Workstation Function Set

The following list of functions (Table 5.1) has been directly derived from the
GKS functions. Their effect is either the same as in the GKS document or
self-explanatory.

Table 5.1 Workstation function set

Workstation control functions	
OPEN WORKSTATION	CLOSE WORKSTATION
CLEAR WORKSTATION	REDRAW ALL SEGMENTS
UPDATE WORKSTATION	SET DEFERRAL STATE
MESSAGE	ESCAPE

Output functions	
POLYLINE	POLYMARKER
TEXT	FILL AREA
CELL ARRAY	GEN. DRAWING PRIMITIVE

Setting of modal attributes	
SET POLYLINE INDEX	SET POLYMARKER INDEX
SET TEXT INDEX	SET CHARACTER HEIGHT
SET CHARACTER UP VECTOR	SET TEXT PATH
SET FILL AREA INDEX	SET PATTERN SIZE
SET PATTERN REF. POINT	SET PICK IDENTIFIER
SET TEXT ALIGNMENT	SET ATTRIB. SOURCE FLAGS
SET LINETYPE	SET LINEWIDTH SCALE FACTOR
SET POLYLINE COLOUR INDEX	SET MARKER TYPE
SET MARKER SIZE SCALE FAC.	SET POLYMARKER COLOUR INDEX
SET TEXT FONT AND PREC.	SET CHAR EXPANSION FAC.
SET CHARACTER SPACING	SET TEXT COLOUR INDEX
SET INTERIOR STYLE	SET STYLE INDEX
SET FILL AREA COLOUR INDEX	

Setting of attribute bundles (retroactive modification possible)	
SET POLYLINE REPRESENTATION	SET POLYMARKER REPRESEN- TATION
SET TEXT REPRESENTATION	SET FILL AREA REPRESENTATION
SET PATTERN REPRESENTATION	SET COLOUR REPRESENTATION

Transformations and clipping	
SET NORMALIZATION TRANSFORM.	SET CLIPPING RECTANGLE
SET WORKSTATION WINDOW	SET WORKSTATION VIEWPORT

Segmentation functions	
CREATE SEGMENT	CLOSE SEGMENT
RENAME SEGMENT	DELETE SEGMENT

Table 5.1 (continued)

SET SEGMENT TRANSFORMATION	SET VISIBILITY
SET HIGHLIGHTING	SET SEGMENT PRIORITY
SET DETECTABILITY	

Input functions (for input and output/input types only)

INITIALISE <input device>	SET <input device> MODE
REQUEST <input device>	SAMPLE <input device>

Inquire functions

All INQUIRIES except those to the GKS state list

Additional metafile output function

WRITE ITEM TO GKSM

Metafile input functions

GET ITEM TYPE FROM GKSM	READ ITEM FROM GKSM

5.4.2   Device-Oriented Function Set

The device-oriented function set (Table 5.2) has been directly derived from existing low-level device drivers. It, therefore, should not be judged by its conceptual purity but from a pragmatic point of view, i.e. as many device facilities should be utilizable by GKS systems as possible. It is very important to mention that this list of functions can be extended if the need arises. It should serve as a starting point only.

Table 5.2 Device-oriented function set

Device control functions	
OPEN DEVICE	CLOSE DEVICE
CLEAR SURFACE	OUTPUT BUFFER

Output functions	
LINE	LINETO
MOVETO	VECTOR_SET
DRAW_CHARACTER	

The following functions allow raster devices to be controlled on a pixel stream basis; i.e., the raster scan conversion is above the DI/DD interface.

PIXEL	PIXEL STREAM
FILLED RECTANGLE	DRAW PATTERN

Table 5.2 (continued)

Some more static unbundled attributes

The following group of functions is to support some more static unbundled attributes.

SET CURRENT LINEWIDTH   SET CURRENT MARKER SIZE
SET CURRENT CHARACTER SIZE   SET CURRENT CHARACTER
                                      ROTATION
SET CURRENT PATTERN   SET CURRENT COLOUR ATTRIBUTES

Setting of unbundled attribute tables

The following group of functions allows the support of drivers with additional unbundled attribute tables (other than colour and pattern tables such as linetype tables).

SET LINETYPE REPRESENTATION   SET LINEWIDTH REPRESENTATION
SET MARKER TYPE REPRESEN-
    TATION   SET TEXT FONT REPRESENTATION
SET FILL AREA STYLE REPRESEN-
    TATION

Setting of predefined attributes (no modification possible)

Driver-predefined attributes or attribute-combinations may also be used. This is to address specific plotter pens, device-specific linetypes, text fonts, etc.
SET PREDEFINED ATTRIBUTE INDEX

Input control

The following function addresses physical input devices with specific data formats and contents. This allows — together with some segment manipulation functions — the realization of logical input devices above the DI/DD interface.
SAMPLE INPUT DATUM

Segment storage functions

SELECT SEGMENT   GET NEXT RECORD

5.5 DI/DD Interface Description Tables

The capabilities of every GKS device driver are described in the DI/DD interface description table (DIDT). Depending on the GKS implementation it has to be set up each time a new device is connected to or integrated into the system. It may be used for several purposes:
— Implementations may be developed in a device-independent way so that they can adjust themselves to the particular device driver peculiarities [BORU80a]. In their device-independent part, they may use simulation software to increase the device capabilities to the required workstation functions. Of course, this may be limited to certain device types, e.g., a plotter, a storage tube, and a refresh display.

— Implementations may be adjusted to actual device driver capabilities by software adaptations. In this case the DI/DD interface description table will not be available during the running time of GKS programs. Rather it will be used by a system's expert to tailor the implementation. It may also be used as a parameter to control an automated configuration phase. Approaches like this are based on the "conditional code" [SCHO81], source code modelling, or program generation techniques [PFAF82a].

— In every case, the DI/DD interface description table serves as a basis for establishing the workstation description table (WDT). Most of the entries in the DIDT are directly transfered to the WDT. The workstation description tables are completed by the DI part of the GKS implementation according to the simulation facilities available and applicable.

All capabilities lined up in the DI/DD interface description table can be either made available by device hardware or they can at least be performed by the software of the device driver.

A proposed DI/DD interface description table contains the entries listed in Table 5.3. Obviously, its final format and contents have to be laid down by each GKS implementation using it.

Table 5.3 A device description table

Workstation type:
— sequence number
— output/input type
— raster/vector type
Type of device coordinate units
Maximum display surface in length or device units
Default value for deferral and implicit regeneration mode
Availability of primitives:
— Polyline
— Polymarker
— Text
— Fill area
— Pixel array
— Pixel array read back
— others (e.g., line, move, pixel)
Number and table of predefined bundles for:
— Polyline
— Polymarker
— Text
— Fill area
— Pattern
— Colour
Number of intensities and colours
Availability of transformation and clipping: (none, static, dynamic)
Type of attribute handling (static unbundled, static bundled, dynamic unbundled, dynamic bundled)
— Polyline
— Polymarker
— Text

Table 5.3 (continued)

— Fill area
— Pattern
— Colour
Number and list of available linetypes
Number of linewidths and nominal/minimal/maximal linewidths
Number and list of different marker types
Number of marker sizes and nominal/minimal/maximal marker size
Number and list of text fonts and associated precisions
Number of character heights and minimum/maximum character height
Number and list of interior styles
Number and list of hatch styles
Number and list of gdp id's and associated bundle types
Number of segments and segment priorities supported
Technique of attribute modification realized for:
— segment transformation (full matrix, shift, zoom, combinations, not supported)
— visibility (on to off and off to on)
— highlighting
— segment priority
— adding primitives to open segment of lower priority
— segment deletion (direct, inverse overwriting, not supported)
— detectability
Number of logical input devices supported
List of logical input devices supported
— input class
— input device number
— available operating mode
— maximum and default values
— default echo area
— Number and list of prompt/echo types
Number of physical input devices supported
List of physical input devices supported
— connection identification
— data format

It should be mentioned that GKS systems developed for specific devices normally integrate the DI/DD description table into their program code. It therefore is not visible to a user of the system nor is it possible to describe a new (different) device and connect it to the system.

5.6   Computer Graphics Interface

The Computer Graphics Interface (CGI) is a set of basic elements for the control and data exchange between device-independent and device-dependent levels in the graphics pipeline. A special work item was established within ISO WG2 to define the contents of a CGI. The work is based on a proposal called virtual device interface (VDI) [ISO85b].

The computer graphics interface may be implemented as a software to software interface (a procedural binding or a data stream binding) or as a software to hardware interface (a data stream binding).

Commands and data from the CGI are translated by particular graphics device drivers into the form required by an actual input/output device.

The CGI specification is contained in a multipart standard, the parts of which are arranged into 4 groups. The first group consists of part 1: "Overview". It gives a general survey and introduction to the basic concepts and principles of this standard. In Part 1, the different parts of this standard are introduced. The reference models, the relationship to other standards, and the grouping of the functions of the CGI into different areas are outlined. As well as this, references and definitions which are of importance for all other parts of the standard are given in Part 1. Part 1 thus establishes the framework for all the parts of this CGI standard; it does not, however, contain any function content.

The second group consists of Parts 2—9 from the CGI multipart standard and this describes the functionality of the CGI standard. Its functionality is kept separate from the specification of any particular encoding format or language binding.

The third group specifies different encodings of the CGI functions. Encodings are specific representation syntaxes of the functions intended to describe exactly a data stream connecting a graphics system and a device or metafile.

The fourth group of parts in this standard is intended to specify the language bindings of the CGI functions to different programming languages.

Table 5.4 gives a summary of the different parts of the CGI standard.

In the initial version only Parts 1—6 and 10—12 are given, and no language binding is supplied.

Table 5.4 Parts of the CGI Standard

Part No.		Title
1		Overview
2—9		Functional Specifications
	2	Control
	3	Output and Attributes
	4	Sequentation
	5	Input
	6	Raster
	7—9	Reserved for future use
10—19		Encodings
	10	Character Encoding
	11	Binary Encodings
	12	Clear Text Encoding
13—19		Reserved for future use
20 onwards		Language Bindings

5.6.1 Functional Description

The functional description of the CGI functions is contained in parts 2 to 9.

Every part is related to one functional area. Part 2 contains the control functions, such as the virtual device control, display surface control, error handling negotiation and other control functions.

Part 3 consists of the description of functions for the specification of output and attributes.

Part 4 contains the definition of the function related to segmentation.

In Part 5 the input functions are defined.

Part 6 deals with raster functions.

Part 7—9 are reserved for additional functional areas (e.g. GKS-3D, PHIGS). The functionality defined in parts 2—5 is closely related to GKS functions and defined in a way which is compatible to GKS.

5.6.2 Encoding parts

The third group of parts (part 10—12) deals with specific encodings of the CGI functions.

The character encoding specified in Part 10 provides an encoding of minimum size. It conforms to the rules of ISO 646 and ISO 2022 and is particularly suitable for transfer through networks that cannot support binary transfers.

The binary encoding specified in Part 11 provides an encoding which requires the least amount of effort to generate and interpret on many systems.

The clear text encoding specified in Part 12 provides an encoding which can be created, viewed and edited with standard text editors. It is therefore also suitable for transfer through networks which support only transfer of text files, or through data communications links that support only printing characters.

5.6.3 Language Bindings

At present no need of any language binding for the CGI functions has been foreseen. In principle, there are two different approaches possible for the mapping of CGI functions to language procedures: a multiprocedure mapping and a one-procedure mapping. A one-to-one mapping to language procedures is the appropriate solution for language bindings, as in the case of GKS or GKS-3D. However, in most cases the workstation device interface is handled by a one-procedure interface. There is no urgent need to standardize this language interface, however.

If such a need arises, Parts 20 onwards of this standard are reserved for language bindings.

5.6.4   Relationship of CGI to GKS

The CGI including the workstation interface is located between a graphics system and a device or a graphics metafile. On the system side, the CGI has to interface in a directly compatible way with GKS. An extension of the CGI functionality to also cover the additional requirements of GKS-3D and PHIGS can be added at a later stage. On the device side, the CGI must be able to directly support the CGM and GKSM metafiles.

GKS communicates with the devices connected to it via the GKS workstation interface. If the devices are at the functional level of this interface the CGI must be able to support this communication on the same level, i.e. all functions at the workstation interface must be present in the CGI. For more simple devices the GKS workstation functions are transformed into a series of functions at a lower level. Therefore, CGI must also contain lower-level functions. The grouping of CGI functions into functional areas can be directly correlated with the GKS levels. The partitioning of the CGI functions includes the identification of functions related to the GKS workstation interface.

5.6.5   Relationship of CGI to Metafiles

It should be possible to route a CGI data stream into a CGM or GKSM metafile in an unambiguous way without applying complex transformations. Therefore, the CGI output functions are directly equivalent to the CGM output functions. The CGI attribute function set is directly equivalent to the attribute function set of GKS and the CGI segmentation functions are directly equivalent to the GKS ones.

The control functions in the CGI are correlated to the metafile delimiter and descriptor elements of the CGM and GKSM.

The character encoding specified in Part 10 of the CGI standard conforms to the code extension techniques of ISO 2022 and uses the character set defined in ISO 646.

The binary encoding specified in Part 11 of the CGI standard employs the mechanism for representing floating point numbers specified in IEEE project P754 Draft 10.0.

6   METAFILES

6.1   Introduction

Graphics metafiles have been used for a considerable time for storing and transmitting pictures. GKS includes a metafile interface as part of the standard
(cf. Chapter III.11). An appendix of the GKS document gives the definition
of the GKS metafile that can be used together with this interface. However,
it is not part of the ISO standard. Efforts have been started within ISO to
standardize a single graphics metafile. The metafile subgroup of ISO TC97/SC5/
WG2 gave the following general definition of graphics metafiles:
"A graphics metafile is a mechanism for the transfer and storage of graphics
data that is both device- and application-independent".

Additionally, some basic design principles for graphics metafiles were stated:
"The minimal capability of a graphics metafile must include all functions
necessary to describe pictures independently of each other. The pictures
in graphics metafiles must be storable on different media, transportable
between different graphic systems, and displayable on different graphics
devices. The graphics metafile should not require non-sequential access to
graphics primitives in order to display the picture. The basic set of functions
should not preclude the addition of application-dependent data or picture
structure information. The specification of functionality will be kept separate
from the specification of coding formats."

6.2   Graphics Metafiles Proposals

In many application areas, a variety of graphics metafile formats is being used
together with different graphics systems and on different levels of functionality.
The spectrum stretches from very simple and very general designs containing
few graphics primitives and attributes, to very sophisticated data formats for
specific application areas. Examples of graphics metafile proposals are:
— The GKS metafile, developed together with GKS.
— The GSPC metafile, developed by the "Graphics Standards Planning Com-
  mittee" of ACM-SIGGRAPH, 1977 [GSPC79].
— Videotex, a graphics metafile format for routing graphical data to television
  sets connected to the VIDEOTEX network, developed by the Canadian
  Department of Communication, 1980 [BRIE80].
— AGF plotfile, a graphics data exchange format developed at West German
  research centres (and used as the base for the GKS metafile), 1976
  [ENDE78].

The GSPC metafile, the Videotex metafile, the AGF plotfile, as well as lower
levels of the GKS metafile, are very basic formats for the description of pictures.

Another metafile standard should be mentioned. That is the IGES (Initial Graphics Exchange Specification), developed under the supervision of the US National Bureau of Standards, ANSI Standard 1981 [ANSI81]. It is not a graphics metafile, but a product definition data file for the CAD/CAM field. It provides a very complex, application-oriented schema for describing CAD/CAM design objects together with their attributes and properties. Although IGES contains graphics entities, the scope of IGES was considered to be sufficiently distinct from the scope of graphics metafiles, so that up to now both developments were independent of each other. However, CAD files will definitely have an influence on the development of graphics metafiles in the future.

6.3   GKS Metafile

The Graphical Kernel System, GKS, has an interface to a graphics metafile called the GKS Metafile (GKSM). As part of the standard, the document contains a complete definition of the interface to and from the GKSM.

The contents and the format of the GKSM are described in an appendix which is not part of the standard. This division was taken in order to let the standardized graphics metafile develop independently of any specific systems or devices. The metafile interface of GKS, and how the metafile is written or read, has been presented in Chapter III.11.

6.3.1   Contents of the GKS Metafile

The GKS metafile contains two-dimensional pictures. Every picture is represented by a series of data records ("items") which are generated as the result of GKS functions being invoked. The GKS functions are grouped in upward compatible levels with increasing capabilities. Although this is not explicitly stated, the GKS levels induce corresponding GKSM levels. In its simplest form therefore, the GKSM contains only twelve types of records comprising the output primitives polyline, polymarker and text, simple attributes, together with file header, picture header and end record. Higher levels include more elaborate attribute setting functions (e.g., colour, linewidth, text font), raster primitives and segment functions. In addition to the graphics records, the GKSM may also contain non-graphical, application-dependent data.

6.3.2   Format of the GKS Metafile

The GKSM consists of a sequence of logical variable length data records. Every record starts with a key denoting the record type. It is followed by the length of the data record so it can be skipped easily if an interpreter is not interested in a particular record type. The key can be between one and eight bytes long; the data format for real and integer values can be chosen in a flexible way. Internal machine code representation is possible, as well as formatted representation by ASCII strings. Which format a given GKSM uses is specified in the file header, which is the first record of each metafile. The logical data records are arranged one after the other on physical records which have the format of a card image. The complete description of the GKS metafile format is given in the following sections.

6.3.3 Status of the Metafile Definition

The specification of the format and content of a metafile is not part of GKS. However, as a metafile standard does not exist, a specification of a metafile is given in the following which can be used as an implementation guide for a metafile which satisfies all GKS requirements.

6.3.4 File Format and Data Format

The GKS metafile consists of a sequence of logical data records. The file starts with a FILE HEADER in a fixed format which describes the origin of the metafile (author, installation), the format of the following records, and the number representation. The file ends with an END record indicating the logical end of the file. In between these two records the following information is recorded like an audit trail: workstation control records and message records; output primitive records, describing elementary graphics objects; attribute information, including output primitive attributes, segment attributes, and workstation attributes; segment records, describing the segment structure and dynamic segment manipulations; user records. The overall structure of the GKS metafile is shown in Figure 6.1.

All data records, except the file header, have a record header containing: the character string 'GKSM' (optional) which has been introduced to improve the readability of the file and to provide an error control facility; the item type identification number which indicates the kind of information contained in the record; the length of the item. The length of each of these subfields of the record header may be implementation-dependent and is specified in the file header. The content of the item is fully described below for each item type.

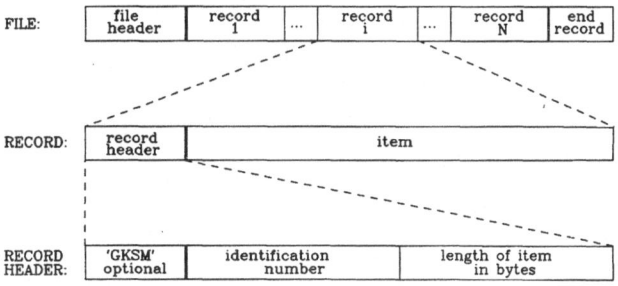

Figure 6.1 GKS metafile structure

The metafile contains characters, integer numbers, and real numbers marked (c), (i), (r) in the record description. Characters in the metafile will be represented according to ISO 646 and ISO 2022 and numbers will be represented according to ISO 6093, using format F1 for integers and format F2 for reals. (Please note: Formats F1 and F2 can be written and read by using FORTRAN formats I and F respectively.)

Real numbers, describing coordinates and length units, will be stored as normalized device coordinates. The workstation transformation, if specified in the application program for the GKSM-OUT workstation, will not be performed but WORKSTATION WINDOW and WORKSTATION VIEWPORT will be stored in data records for later usage. Real numbers may be stored as integers. In this case, transformation parameters are specified in the file header to allow proper transformation of integers into normalized device coordinates.

For economic reasons, numbers can be stored using an internal binary format. As no standard exists for binary number representation, this format will limit the portability of the metafile. The specification of such a binary number representation is outside the scope of this document.

When exchanging metafiles among the different installations, the physical structure of data sets on the specific storage media should be standardized. Such a definition is also outside the scope of this document. However, as an appropriate standard is missing, the following specifications are recommended:

Metafiles should be exchanged using unlabelled 9-track 1600 bpi tapes. Data should be stored in fixed blocks with length 960 bytes, each block composed of 12 physical records of 80 bytes, each byte containing 8 bits.

6.3.5   Generation and Interpretation of Metafile

The generation and interpretation of metafiles is described in Chapter III.11.

6.3.6   Control Items

FILE HEADER | GKSM | N | D | V | H | T | L | I | R | F | RI | ZERO | ONE |

All fields in the file header record have a fixed length. Numbers are formatted according to ISO 6093 FORMAT F1.

General Information:
GKSM	4 bytes	containing string 'GKSM'
N	40 bytes	containing name of author/installation
D	8 bytes	date (year/month/day, eg., 83/03/13)
V	2 bytes	version number: the metafile described here has version number 1

Specification of Field Length:
H	2 bytes	integer specifying how many bytes of the string 'GKSM' are used in the record header. Possible values: 0, 1, 2, 3, 4.
T	2 bytes	length of item type indicator field
L	2 bytes	length of item length indicator field

I   2 bytes   length of field for each integer in the item (applies to all data marked (i) in the record description)

R   2 bytes   length of field for each real in the item (applies to all data marked (r) in the record description)

Specification of Number Representation:

F   2 bytes   Possible values: 1, 2. This applies to all data in the items marked (i) or (r) and to item type and item length:
                            1: all numbers are formatted according to ISO 6093
                            2: all numbers (except in the file header) are stored in an internal binary format

RI   2 bytes   Possible values: 1, 2. This is the number representation for data marked (r):
                            $1 = $ real, $2 = $ integer

ZERO   11 bytes   integer equivalent to 0., if $RI = 2$

ONE   11 bytes   integer equivalent to 1., if $RI = 2$

After the file header, which is in fixed format, all values in the following records are in the format defined by file header. For the following description, the setting:

$$H = 4; \; T = 3; \; F = 1$$

is assumed. In addition to formats (c), (i) and (r), which have already been described, (p) denotes a point represented by a pair of real numbers (2r). The notation allows the single letter to be preceded by an expression, indicating the number of values of that type.

END ITEM | 'GKSM 0' | L |

Last item of every GKS Metafile

CLEAR WORKSTATION | 'GKSM 1' | L | C |

Requests clearing of all active workstations
C(i):   clearing control flag (0 = CONDITIONAL, 1 = ALWAYS)

REDRAW ALL SEGMENTS ON WORKSTATION

                                     | 'GKSM 2' | L |

Requests redrawing of all segments

UPDATE WORKSTATION | 'GKSM 3' | L | R |

Request update
R(i):   regeneration flag (0 = PERFORM, 1 = POSTPONE)

SET DEFERRAL STATE | 'GKSM 4' | L | D | R |

Requests setting of deferral state

D(i):   deferral mode (0=ASAP, 1=BNIG, 2=BNIL, 3=ASTI)
R(i):   implicit regeneration mode (0=ALLOWED, 1=SUPPRESSED)

MESSAGE | 'GKSM 5' | L | N | T |

N(i):   number of characters in string
T(Nc):   string with N characters

ESCAPE | 'GKSM 6' | L | FI | L | M | I | R |

FI(i):   escape function identifier
L(i):   length of integer data in data record
M(i):   length of real data in data record
I(Li):   integer data
R(Mr):   real data

6.3.7 Items for Output Primitives

POLYLINE | 'GKSM 11' | L | N | P |

N(i):   number of points of the polyline
P(Np):   list of points

POLYMARKER | 'GKSM 12' | L | N | P |

N(i):   number of points
P(Np):   list of points

TEXT | 'GKSM 13' | L | P | N | T |

P(p):   starting point of character string
N(i):   number of characters in string
T(Nc):   string with N characters from the set of ISO 646

FILL AREA | 'GKSM 14' | L | N | P |

N(i):   number of points
P(Np):   list of points

CELL ARRAY | 'GKSM 15' | L | P | Q | R | N | M | CT |

P(p),Q(p),R(p):   coordinates of corner points of cell array
N(i):   number of rows in array
M(i):   number of columns in array
CT(MNi):   array of colour indices stored row by row

GENERALIZED DRAWING PRIMITIVE

                         | 'GKSM 16' | L | GI | N | L | M | P | I | R |

GI(i):   GDP identifier
N(i):   number of points

L(i):	length of integer data in data record
M(i):	length of real data in data record
P(Np):	list of points
I(Li):	integer data
R(Mr):	real data

6.3.8 Items for Output Primitive Attributes

POLYLINE INDEX

| 'GKSM 21' | L | M |

M(i):   polyline index

LINETYPE

| 'GKSM 22' | L | T |

T(i):   linetype

LINEWIDTH SCALE FACTOR

| 'GKSM 23' | L | S |

S(r)   linewidth scale factor

POLYLINE COLOUR INDEX

| 'GKSM 24' | L | I |

I(i):   polyline colour index

POLYMARKER INDEX

| 'GKSM 25' | L | M |

M(i):   polymarker index

MARKER TYPE

| 'GKSM 26' | L | T |

T(i):   marker type

MARKER SIZE SCALE FACTOR

| 'GKSM 27' | L | S |

S(r):   marker size scale factor

POLYMARKER COLOUR INDEX

| 'GKSM 28' | L | C |

C(i):   polymarker colour index

TEXT INDEX

| 'GKSM 29' | L | I |

I(i):   text index

TEXT FONT AND PRECISION

| 'GKSM 30' | L | TF | TP |

TF(i):   text font
TP(i):   text precision (0 = STRING, 1 = CHAR, 2 = STROKE)

CHARACTER EXPANSION FACTOR

	'GKSM 31'	L	E

E(r):   character expansion factor

CHARACTER SPACING

	'GKSM 32'	L	S

S(r):   character spacing

TEXT COLOUR INDEX

	'GKSM 33'	L	C

C(i):   text colour index

CHARACTER VECTORS

	'GKSM 34'	L	CH	CW

CH(2r):   character height vector
CW(2r):   character width vector

TEXT PATH

	'GKSM 35'	L	P

P(i):   text path (0 = RIGHT, 1 = LEFT, 2 = UP, 3 = DOWN)

TEXT ALIGNMENT

	'GKSM 36'	L	HA	VA

HA(i):   horizontal alignment (0 = NORMAL, 1 = LEFT, 2 = CENTRE,
                3 = RIGHT)
VA(i):   vertical alignment (0 = NORMAL, 1 = TOP, 2 = CAP, 3 = HALF,
                4 = BASE, 5 = BOTTOM)

FILL AREA INDEX

	'GKSM 37'	L	M

M(i):   fill area index

FILL INTERIOR STYLE

	'GKSM 38'	L	S

S(i):   fill area interior style (0 = HOLLOW, 1 = SOLID, 2 = PATTERN,
                3 = HATCH)

FILL AREA STYLE INDEX

	'GKSM 39'	L	N

N(i):   fill area style index

FILL AREA COLOUR INDEX

	'GKSM 40'	L	C

C(i):   fill area colour index

PATTERN SIZE

	'GKSM 41'	L	PW	PH

PW(2r):   pattern width vector
PH(2r):   pattern up vector

PATTERN REFERENCE POINT

	'GKSM 42'	L	P

P(p) reference point

ASPECT SOURCE FLAGS   `'GKSM 43'` `L` `F`

F(13i):   aspect source flags (0 = BUNDLED, 1 = INDIVIDUAL)

PICK IDENTIFIER   `'GKSM 44'` `L` `P`

P(i):   pick identifier

6.3.9 Items for Workstation Attributes

POLYLINE REPRESENTATION   `'GKSM 51'` `L` `I` `LT` `LW` `CI`

I(i):   polyline index
LT(i):   linetype number
LW(r):   linewidth scale factor
CI(i):   colour index

POLYMARKER REPRESENTATION

`'GKSM 52'` `L` `I` `MT` `MF` `CI`

I(i):   polymarker index
MT(i):   marker type
MF(r):   marker size scale factor
CI(i):   colour index

TEXT REPRESENTATION   `'GKSM 53'` `L` `I` `F` `P` `E` `S` `CI`

I(i):   text index
F(i):   text font
P(i):   text precision (0 = STRING, 1 = CHAR, 2 = STROKE)
E(r):   character expansion factor
S(r):   character spacing
CI(i):   text colour colour index

FILL AREA REPRESENTATION   `'GKSM 54'` `L` `I` `S` `SI` `CI`

I(i):   fill area index
S(i):   interior style (0 = HOLLOW, 1 = SOLID, 2 = PATTERN, 3 = HATCH)
SI(i):   style index
CI(i):   colour index

PATTERN REPRESENTATION   `'GKSM 55'` `L` `I` `N` `M` `CT`

I(i):   pattern index
N(i):   number of columns in array
M(i):   number of rows in array
CT(MNi):   table of colour indices stored row by row

COLOUR REPRESENTATION   `'GKSM 56'` `L` `CI` `RGB`

CI(i):   colour index
RGB(3r):   red/green/blue intensities:

6.3.10   Item for Clipping Rectangle

CLIPPING RECTANGLE | 'GKSM 61' | L | C |

C(4r):   clipping rectangle (XMIN, XMAX, YMIN, YMAX)

6.3.11   Items for Workstation Transformation

WORKSTATION WINDOW | 'GKSM 71' | L | W |

W(4r):   limits of workstation window (XMIN, XMAX, YMIN, YMAX)

WORKSTATION VIEWPORT | 'GKSM 72' | L | V |

V(4r):   limits of workstation viewport (XMIN, XMAX, YMIN, YMAX)

6.3.12   Items for Segment Manipulation

CREATE SEGMENT | 'GKSM 81' | L | S |

S(i):   segment name

CLOSE SEGMENT | 'GKSM 82' | L |

Indicates end of segment

RENAME SEGMENT | 'GKSM 83' | L | SO | SN |

SO(i):   old segment name
SN(i):   new segment name

DELETE SEGMENT | 'GKSM 84' | L | S |

S(i):   segment name

6.3.13   Items for Segment Attributes

SET SEGMENT TRANSFORMATION

| 'GKSM 91' | L | S | M |

S(i):   segment name
M(6r):   transformation matrix (M11,M12,M13,M21,M22,M23,M31,M32,M33)

SET VISIBILITY | 'GKSM 92' | L | S | V |

S(i):   segment name
V(i):   visibility (0 = INVISIBLE, 1 = VISIBLE)

| SET HIGHLIGHTING | 'GKSM 93' | L | S | H |

S(i):   segment name
H(i):   highlighting (0 = NORMAL, 1 = HIGHLIGHTED)

| SET SEGMENT PRIORITY | 'GKSM 94' | L | S | P |

Si(i):   segment name
P(r):   segment priority

| SET DETECTABILITY | 'GKSM 95' | L | S | D |

S(i):   segment name
D(i):   detectability (0 = UNDETECTABLE, 1 = DETECTABLE)

6.3.14   User Items

| USER ITEM | 'GKSMXXX' | L | D |

XXX > 100
D: user data (L bytes)

6.4   The ISO Computer Graphics Metafile CGM

In October 1981, ISO TC97/SC5/WG2 "Computer Graphics" established a metafile subgroup that was given the task of:
— developing a framework in which graphical metafiles can be studied, developed and related to other standards;
— designing a metafile standard proposal and recommending whatever 'work items' would be needed in this area to produce the desired standard.

The metafile subgroup had its first meetings in 1982. The aim of this project was to create a system-independent graphics metafile that can be used with a wide range of systems and devices. The subgroup has based its work on experiences with various metafiles and with GKS and its metafile (e.g., [ENDE80,ROSE80a,REED81]). However, the greatest impact has come from the metafile group of the American National Standards Institute, ANSI X3H33. This group has been developing a national U.S. standard for a metafile that originally was called "Virtual Device Metafile VDM" [ANSI82]. Meanwhile, the ISO metafile project has been named "Computer Graphics — Metafile for the Storage and Transfer of Picture Description Information (CGM)". The CGM is a basic metafile containing static consistent pictures without a picture structure and without a dynamic picture change facility. The CGM is defined in a multipart standard (ISO 8632/1 to ISO8632/4, currently 1985 at DIS stage [ISO85c]). Part 1 of the standard defines the CGM functionality, Part 2 contains a character coding based on ISO 2022 code extension techniques, Part 3 defines a binary coding. In Part 4, a clear text coding which can be written, read and edited in the same way as plain text is specified.

Table 6.1 contains the set of basic CGM elements. It includes output primitives, output primitive attributes, some control elements, and application data. The extent of the functional capabilities coincides with the functions in the lowest GKS level L0a.

The metafile supports two colour models: the direct colour specification using Red-Green-Blue (RGB) values or indirectly by an index pointing to a colour table containing RGB values. There are devices and applications for either one of these models. In the above list, the PIXELS primitive uses only the indirect specification via colour indices, whereas the colour of the other primitives can be specified either by index or by RGB. The selection is done once for a picture with the COLOUR SELECTION MODE element.

The CGM takes the same approach with respect to clipping as the GKS metafile. Primitives can be stored unclipped, but the clipping rectangle is included along with the primitives in the metafile. Clipping can be turned on and off at any time between two primitives.

Since 1986, a project has been under way within ISO that will extend the CGM by functions needed to support the GKSM functionality and at the same time create the GKSM as an ISO standard. The goal is to have one single compatible metafile standard.

Table 6.1 Elements of the basic metafile

Metafile descriptor elements:

METAFILE VERSION	Version of the metafile (there may be more than one version in the future)
METAFILE DESCRIPTION	Description of the metafile contents in free format text (person-readable)
VDC TYPE	VDC = Virtual Device Coordinates, coordinates as reals or integers
INTEGER PRECISION	Related to coding of integers
REAL PRECISION	Related to coding of reals
INDEX PRECISION	Related to coding of index numbers
COLOUR PRECISION	Related to coding of colour values
COLOUR INDEX PRECISION	Related to coding of colour index values
MAXIMUM COLOUR INDEX	Upper bound for colour index value
METAFILE ELEMENT LIST	List of all elements used in a metafile
METAFILE DEFAULTS REPLACEMENT	At BEGIN PICTURE the state of the metafile interpreter will be reset to default values
FONT LIST	Associates font names with text font indices
CHARACTER SET LIST	Associates character sets with character set index values
CHARACTER CODING ANNOUNCER	Coding technique used

Picture descriptor elements:

SCALING MODE	Abstract or metric scaling
COLOUR SELECTION MODE	Indexed or direct colour
LINE WIDTH SPECIFICATION MODE	Absolute or scaled line width specification

Table 6.1 (continued)

MARKER SIZE SPECIFICATION MODE	Absolute or scaled marker size specification
EDGE WIDTH SPECIFICATION MODE	Absolute or scaled edge width specification
VDC EXTENT	Region of interest in VDC space
BACKGROUND COLOUR	Colour of background

Delimiter elements:

BEGIN METAFILE	Start of metafile
END METAFILE	End of metafile
BEGIN PICTURE	Start of picture
BEGIN PICTURE BODY	End of picture descriptor, start of picture body
END PICTURE	End of picture

Control elements:

VDC INTEGER PRECISION	Related to coding of coordinates as integers
VDC REAL PRECISION	Related to coding of coordinates as reals
AUXILIARY COLOUR	Specifies a second colour for output primitives, implementation-dependent
TRANSPARENCY	Sets the transparency indicator to on or off for certain output primitives

Output primitives:

POLYLINE	Vector sequence
DISJOINT POLYLINE	Set of separate lines
POLYMARKER	Set of marker symbols
TEXT, RESTRICTED TEXT APPEND TEXT	Text string
CELL ARRAY	Array of cells of different colours
POLYGON	Filled, hatched or patterned area
POLYGON SET	Set of disjoint areas
GENERALIZED DRAWING PRIMITIVE	GDP as in GKS
RECTANGLE	Rectangle
CIRCLE	Circle
CIRCULAR ARC 3 POINT, CIRCULAR ARC 3 POINT CLOSE, CIRCULAR ARC CENTRE, CIRCULAR ARC CENTRE CLOSE	Circular arcs, as line or area primitive
ELLIPSE	Ellipse
ELLIPTICAL ARC, ELLIPTICAL ARC CLOSE	Elliptical arc, as line or area primitive

Attributes:
Colour:

COLOUR TABLE	Table for associating RGB values with colour indices

Aspect source flags:

ASPECT SOURCE FLAGS	Sets the ASF's

Table 6.1 (continued)

Polyline attributes:
LINEWIDTH	Width of line
LINETYPE	Solid, dash, dot, dash-dot, etc.
LINE COLOUR	Colour, either by index or by RGB values
LINE BUNDLE INDEX	Index of predefined line bundle

Marker attributes:
MARKER TYPE	Type of marker symbol
MARKER SIZE	Height of marker symbol
MARKER COLOUR	Colour, either by index or by RGB values
MARKER BUNDLE INDEX	Index of predefined marker bundle

Text attributes:
CHARACTER HEIGHT	Height of characters
CHARACTER EXPANSION FACTOR	Deviation from nominal width/height ratio
CHARACTER SPACING	Intercharacter space
CHARACTER UP VECTOR	Up-direction of characters
TEXT PATH	LEFT-RIGHT-UP-DOWN
TEXT FONT INDEX	Number of text font
TEXT PRECISION	Degree of fidelity for text attribute evaluation
TEXT ALIGNMENT	Position of text relative to reference point
TEXT COLOUR	Colour, either by index or by RGB values
TEXT BUNDLE INDEX	Index of predefined text bundle
CHARACTER SET INDEX	Selects a character set
ALTERNATE CHARACTER SET INDEX	Selects an alternate character set, e.g., an 8-bit coded one

Fill area attributes:
INTERIOR STYLE	Fill style for area
HATCH INDEX	Selects type of hatching
PATTERN INDEX	Index referring pattern table entry
PATTERN TABLE	Pattern table
PATTERN SIZE	Size of pattern
FILL COLOUR	Colour, either by index or by RGB values
FILL BUNDLE INDEX	Index of predefined fill bundle
EDGE BUNDLE INDEX	Edge bundle index for the edge of area primitives
EDGE TYPE	Solid, dash, dot, dash-dot, etc.
EDGE WIDTH	Line width for edges
EDGE VISIBILITY	Separate drawing of edges switched off or on
FILL REFERENCE POINT	Reference point for area patterns

Other:
ESCAPE	General escape function
MESSAGE	Text that may be used for communication with the operator
APPLICATION DATA	Data generated and processed by the application program

6.5   Levels of Metafiles

The GKSM as well as the CGM includes graphical functions only. On the other hand, there is a need for the integration of graphics metafiles and high-level, application-dependent metafiles, grouped in upward compatible levels. At the highest level, application-dependent files like the IGES file could be based on graphical metafile formats for the graphics parts of their contents. One way of including higher levels of functionality without losing the generality of a simple graphics metafile would be an explicit level structure for metafiles, just as the level structure defined for GKS (cf. Figure 6.1). While the lower three levels in Figure 6.1 are levels with growing graphical functionality, the top level is application-dependent, for example, the CAD information contained in IGES. While only a CAD system can work on the data contained in the CAD level, an interpreter can be designed to extract the graphics information contained in the metafile and to produce a bottom-level metafile. The information contained in the bottom-level metafile then can be displayed on any available graphics output device (cf. Figure 6.2).

LEVEL	CONTENTS
L3 application level	L2+ application oriented data (CAD design objects, their geometry and properties)
L2 definition mechanism	L1+ definition and referencing of subpictures, macros, and text fonts
L1 structured picture	L0+ picture segmentation: naming and transformation of subpictures
L0 picture	graphics primitives graphics attributes

Figure 6.1 Graphics metafile level structure

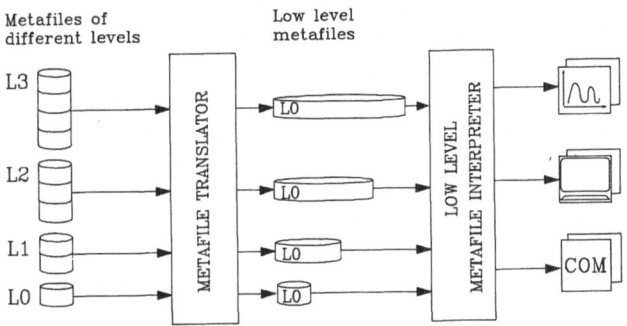

Figure 6.2 Extracting basic graphics information from higher level metafiles

7   CERTIFICATION/VALIDATION OF GKS

7.1   Introduction

Following on from the GKS definition process, there then began the certification process for graphics systems in 1981. A special subgroup for this was set up within ISO/TC97/SC5/WG 2 and the EEC decided to sponsor a number of workshops with the aim of developing a certification/validation scheme and guiding the GKS reviewing process in its final stages. It was recognized that a standard is largely worthless unless there is a procedure to test whether or not the implementations conform to it. Two major aims were identified: the more-or-less informal specification of GKS should be improved and eventually a formal specification of the GKS functions should be developed which could accompany the standard and help implementors of GKS systems with more precise definitions. A sub-subgroup concentrated on the issues arising from such a formal specification for graphics standards. Some of their results are contained in [EEC82d]. In this chapter we focus on the second goal, i.e., to test and ensure that an implementation of GKS adheres to the standard. We refer, however, to the results of formal specification research where appropriate.

From the very beginning, two approaches to the problem were identified and work was undertaken in both areas [EEC81a]. These can be described as the verification approach which uses formal methods to prove formal correctness, and a falsification approach which is based on a suite of test programs [BROD82].

7.1.1   Verifying GKS Implementations

Verification attempts to prove that an implementation is correct, i.e., that it conforms exactly to the standard. The problem of verifying computer software seems hard to solve — especially if larger packages are involved. This is undoubtedly the case with GKS which even at the lowest level covers quite a number of functions and also, since it is defined in a device-independent way, different implementations might look quite different for different devices. Verification could be done by taking a formal specification of GKS, and developing implementations from this specification by a series of program transformations. This is closely connected with program generation techniques [NORM81], [GNAT81]. In the Sections 7.4 and 7.5, we will handle these topics in more detail and show a promising certification concept. This covers both verification and falsification methods and seems to be feasible with a reasonable amount of effort at short notice.

7.1.2   Falsification Approach

Particularly in the area of graphics, no certification procedure will be acceptable without applying testing procedures. We will substantiate this statement later on. Falsification is the attempt to prove that an implementation is incorrect.

In order to do this, a set of test programs is applied and the results produced by the GKS implementation are compared with the expected results. If the two sets of results are not "identical", the GKS implementation being tested is assumed to be incorrect. Of course, this process yields no guarantee of correctness, but confidence is at least inspired in any implementation which survives the rigours of such test procedures. However, several problems remain which we try to solve in this chapter:

— When are two sets of results "identical"? A picture description, e.g., for a storage tube will look quite different from that for a raster plotter.
— How can expected results (reference results) be obtained and how reliable with regard to correctness are they?
— How many test programs have to be applied and which features of GKS have to be tested until a "certificate of correctness" can be issued for a candidate implementation?

Leaving these issues aside until the following sections, the necessity of falsification testing should be emphasized.

— Formal verification of complete packages must be seen as a distant target — yet there is an immediate requirement for some means of validating implementations.
— Formal verification is based on a formal specification of GKS and on program generation techniques. There are and will be GKS implementations which are not derived from a common source and which have been developed completely independently from any certification centre. They will be available as "black boxes" only, i.e. they will not allow any internal checking.
— There are graphics aspects which are not exactly specified by the GKS document but deliberately left open for the implementors' decisions. Examples of this are the appearance of attributes, such as linetypes and of characters. They can only be tested by looking at their visible appearance in pictorial form.
— Formal verification can only cover the part of the system above the device driver implementations. A GKS system however includes device drivers and even device hardware. The correct functioning of the whole system can only be checked by test programs producing pictures and sequences of interactions.

7.2   A Model for Certification

A reference model of the test environment for GKS implementations is shown in Figure 7.1 [BROD81, PFAF81b]. Its main components can be identified as:

— a suite of test programs;
— the implementation under test, termed the candidate implementation;
— a reference implementation;
— a set of results, generated by applying the test suite to the reference implementation;

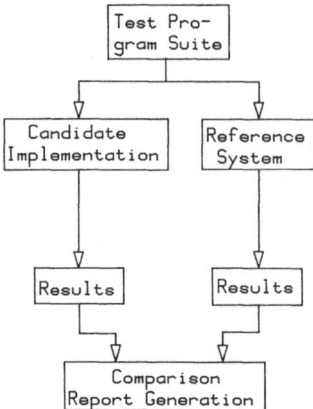

Figure 7.1 Test model

— a set of results, generated by applying the test suite to the candidate implementation;
— a tool for comparing the two sets of results and reporting on them.

7.2.1   Test Programs

The careful design of a test program suite is the most important requirement if tests are to be used successfully in certification. As opposed to verification methods, test methods can never, of course, validate a system completely since testing all the different combinations of functions, parameters, and configurations in GKS implementations would require huge amounts of time and resources. To overcome this drawback, very carefully designed test cases have to be applied to a candidate. In the following, there are some guidelines for the development of test programs; a more detailed list can be found in [MAGU81]:
— employ many test programs containing few tests (then errors can be easily detected);
— identify potential implementation deficiencies and device tests to detect their presence;
— design test programs to cover normal, extreme and erroneous cases;
— ensure that the test suite covers the graphics standard;
— check the order of dependency of functions; e.g., the following calling sequence should produce three errors when it is started in the GKS operating state "workstation active":

CLOSE SEGMENT	error
CREATE SEGMENT (1)	
CREATE SEGMENT (2)	error
CLOSE SEGMENT	
CLOSE SEGMENT	error

Further important aspects when designing the test programs are:
— The test programs should be designed in a language-independent fashion (e.g., in a PASCAL-like notation). Then they can relatively easily be translated into several languages for particular implementation sites. This makes maintainance of the suite of test programs easier.
— To keep the test program suite small, test programs should be defined in a device-independent way as far as possible. If device-dependent features are to be tested (such as attributes), the test programs should adjust themselves to the device by using functions which inquire into the workstation description table.
— Means should be provided to extend the test suite dynamically, because it would give implementors maximal benefit from the certification, and also make it possible to integrate test programs developed at other sites. The test suite should be adapted at certain intervals; all programs have to be classified using a given scheme.

7.2.2 Candidate Implementations

Ideally, candidate implementations should be verified during their development from a GKS specification. Since this is not feasible in most cases such implementations will be provided more or less as "black boxes" so that testing can only take place at their interfaces. As shown in Section 7.5, we also expect implementors to describe their internal program steps — at least on a logical basis, and the elements of the interfaces their implementation is using.

Normally, a GKS implementation covers the whole graphics system between the GKS/application program interface and the graphics devices. As is explained in the next section, this alone is not suitable for a complete testing procedure. An automated testing has to be supported at a functional device interface that is just above the level of the device hardware functions. There we can distinguish between implementations tailored to specific devices and those which are largely device-independent. In the first case, certification with respect to a particular set of devices is required, in the second case it should be checked whether the device-independent part is correct or not, i.e. whether it is able to drive any customer-supplied device drivers.

As should be clear from the GKS workstation concept, implementations of the second kind also contain device drivers: they control virtual (idealized) devices which are similar to the GKS metafile and segment storage workstations. Their adaptation to real devices is done at a lower level in the device-dependent parts. Thus, the two kinds of implementations can be tested by the same means, i.e., comparing picture descriptions for a real device or a virtual device with a suitable reference picture description.

7.2.3 Reference Implementations

The comparison between the reference results and the results produced by a candidate implementation must not be computationally expensive. This means, both sets of results should be on the same logical level, i.e., they should use the same language elements to describe a picture. Three ways of achieving this were identified:

— Reference results can be produced manually. The actual device (real or virtual) determines its interface elements which the candidate implementation uses. In simple cases, the expected output of a test program can be derived from the GKS definition.
— A reference implementation supporting a fixed set of devices may be developed. Test programs are applied to it and the resulting output is stored on a file. If a candidate supports the same set of devices its output can be directly compared; otherwise, it has to have "transformers" connected which map the candidate's device-specific output to the logical level of the reference output.
— Using the candidate description, a reference implementation can be configured from a specification. This should automatically produce output on the same level (i.e., use the same picture description elements) as the candidate output. Details of this are given in Section 7.5.

While the first two methods of producing reference output are rather inflexible and still pose the problem of how to prove their correctness, the third method leaves the candidate unchanged, tests exactly its output, and enables one to prove the correctness of the reference output by formal verification methods.

7.3 Interfaces for Testing

This section will explore which features of a GKS implementation can be tested and identifies the interfaces at which testing can take place. As shown in Figure 7.2, there are three interfaces [EEC81b] at which results from the candidate and reference implementations can be compared.

7.3.1 Application Program Interface

This interface consists of all the GKS functions defined in the standard. It is the appropriate point at which to verify the GKS 'set functions', inquiry functions, input functions and the error handling function. GKS provides well-defined data structures. These provide a detailed record of the current state of a GKS program. Many of the GKS functions are defined in terms of their effect on the state lists. In a first step, a test suite has been developed to check that those state lists are manipulated correctly. The test suite consists of several layers, the lowest one being a one-to-one correspondence to the GKS functions [EEC82a]. These functions either perform the GKS-defined effect or report any errors which have possibly occurred. Thus, in any application program, the GKS function calls can be replaced by the corresponding test function calls without changing the effect of the application program.

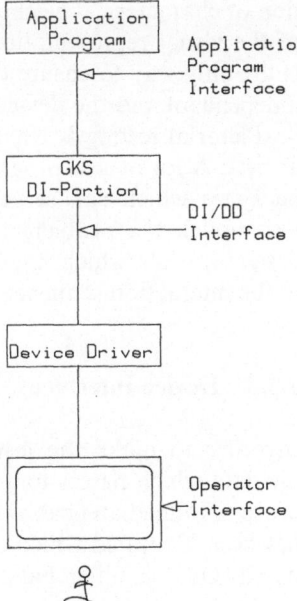

Figure 7.2 Test interfaces

The test functions check themselves. Each one basically consists of the steps:
— the current states of GKS are determined and stored in the test function;
— the GKS function is invoked;
— the corresponding changes of the GKS states are calculated, the state lists stored in the test function are changed, and thus a set of expected results is generated:
— using specially designed test-inquiry functions, it can be checked that the GKS states after the GKS function call are identical with the expected ones. That means, the GKS-defined state changes must have been performed and no other state changes must have occurred.

In higher layers, groups of GKS functions and specific features of GKS are tested with regard to their dependencies.

A similar approach is applied for checking the correct error behaviour. For every GKS function, the GKS system is driven into erroneous situations. The function is called in each of these situations, and it is tested whether the expected errors have occurred and no non-expected errors are reported.

7.3.2   Operator Interface

This is the interface between graphics devices and an operator at which visual output can be checked and input data entered into the system. There are features in GKS which can only be checked by human judgement, such as the representation of characters, the echoing of operator actions, and generally, the suitability of the visual representations. Furthermore, checking at the operator interface is the only way to ensure that the complete system works correctly (the device-independent and the device-dependent parts).

Pictorial testing is what manufacturers of GKS implementations will apply at first. A lot of test programs already exist for GKS as well as other graphics packages which can serve as starting points. With regard to GKS and our test model, the problem is not the quantity of test programs. The art is in designing tests which highlight the appearance of any errors in the picture or in the interaction sequence in order to assist human judgement.

7.3.3   Device Interface

In order to make the testing of pictorial output and input easier, checking the data which passes to and from the physical devices should be an automatic process. Immediately above the level of the pictorial form an interface to devices has been identified which can still be uniquely described and therefore be compared. On the other hand, it became clear very early that the elements of a particular interface cannot be lower (more atomic) than the capabilities of the specific device. For example, if a device provides appropriate clipping hardware, then it should be used together with unclipped coordinates in order to utilize this capability. Obviously then, the correct clipping behaviour cannot be checked at the device interface, but it can be checked that suitable data for defining the clipping rectangle has been passed to the driver.

From a GKS implementation's point of view, the device interface usually also separates the device-independent part (which provides general software for missing device capabilities) from the device-dependent parts (i.e., the device drivers). In this sense, this chapter is related to Chapter 5 (Interfaces to Graphics Devices). Using the definitions of the "device driver function set", "minimal device interfaces", and the "construction of device interfaces" given in Chapter 5, it is obvious that there are a number of device interfaces to actual devices and that their functionality depends on the availability of driver functions.

As will be explained in more detail in Section 7.5, a GKS candidate implementation must identify the particular device interface(s) it is supporting. By determining the elements of an interface, it also fixes the syntax for the description of pictures for that device. Reference pictures using the same syntax can then be produced and a comparison of the two be made.

With regard to the three interfaces, it became clear that each one is suitable in a different way for testing purposes. Certain testing problems can usually be solved at a certain interface relatively easily but cause big problems at another interface. For example, the appearance of a fill area hatch style displayed as strokes or as patterns can best be tested at the operator interface. On the other hand, if importance is laid on the correct computation of coordinates, on a large number of picture sequences, or on large data sets being handled, then the device interface should be used. The different kinds of testing should complement each other.

7.4   Certification by Program Construction

There is a strong relationship between software methodology and the formal specification of a system. Today's software development methodology centres around program specification systems [EEC82c]. Starting from a very short and highly abstract specification, methods of "stepwise refinement" are applied. This is either done automatically (automated program generation) or by guided program transformations where a programmer decomposes higher program constructs into lower ones. The original abstract specification is in a programming form which is language-independent. It does not contain any algorithmic details.

At some stage of the refinement process, a real program is generated, for example, a FORTRAN or PASCAL program. When different program transformations are applied in varying environments (e.g., graphics devices), there will be different end products. This corresponds to the model of device-independent GKS definitions on the one hand, and device-dependent GKS implementations for the peculiarities of a given graphics environment on the other hand.

At some intermediate stage, the program transformation process reaches the last level which is still device-independent; in GKS, this is the functional interface to the device-independent segment storage and the GKS metafile. Both these workstations contain real pictures, but in a completely device-independent fashion. At this stage, a real GKS program might have evolved. This would accept GKS functions and control GKS workstations, all of which have the same capabilities (i.e., they are fully equipped workstations). However, such an implementation is rather useless, since it leaves the real programming work to external workstation drivers (the mapping of logical functions to physical device capabilities), and it does not contain anything really worth proving correct.

Taking the characteristics of actual graphics devices into consideration, the workstation-dependent part can be constructed by further program transformations in either an automated or manual configuring process. This is explained in the next section.

Obviously, there is a logical connection to the reference implementation mentioned in the sections before. In the case of our model, a reference implementation which either implements one particular device-dependent case or which stops at the GKS workstation level (i.e., does not support any real device) would be quite useless. We recognized this fact very early in [PFAF81a] and thus proposed the "configurable reference implementation" approach. This approach was refined in further discussions resulting in the following model.

A suitable syntax for the specification of GKS has been developed and an initial specification undertaken. The terminal symbols of the grammar are atomic modules, such as coordinate transformation, clipping, prompt/echo generation and transformation programs. In addition, the dependencies of basic module calls on specific device capabilities are available in the form of tables. From this specification a real program can be derived by program transformations and this is able to drive a real device. When changing the device properties new, different reference implementations can be generated from the same specification using other parse trees.

The initial reference specification only supports a common set of graphics devices. If a new device is to be supported, or if an implementor finds solutions other than those already contained in the specification, this is extended in an implementor/certifier dialogue.

The certification problem is now split into two aspects:
— The specification has to be correct; this is a process of reaching agreement within a responsible body.
— The generation of programs from the syntax must be proven to be correct. This is made easier by using simple, well-known parsing techniques.

7.5   A Combined Model for Verification and Testing

The intention is to test a candidate GKS implementation, in part, by automatically comparing output from the candidate generated by a "certification workstation", with output from a reference implementation. What information should this output from the implementations, which is input to the comparator, contain? Two objectives in designing this certification data stream were selected [EEC82b]:
— The comparator must not change for varying candidate implementations. The criteria must be derived only from the information contained in the GKS document.
— The comparator should be simple enough to warrant a high degree of confidence that it is correct.

Two immediate consequences of these objectives were:
— Both streams of comparator input has to be at the same logical level. The comparator must not be asked, for example, to determine that a POLYLINE and its dissection into a set of lines are the same.
— The input streams must be compared item by item. These items will usually correspond to GKS functions. Each item in either stream must be self-contained; the comparator must not be expected to maintain a context of attribute values in which to interpret input items.

These consequences imply that the reference implementation must be configurable, i.e., capable of being adapted to imitate the behaviour of the candidate. Clearly, it is impossible to predict in advance all the adaptations which will have to be made. The certification process, however, should not be viewed as static, where certification criteria are imposed and are unchanging. It is rather a dialogue between implementors and certifiers, with the implementors being aided by experience gained from the certification process and vice versa. It is only necessary to start the process by identifying the common adaptations and building a reference implementation capable of performing them. To perform testing based on this approach, three things are required:
— A format must be specified for the certification data stream which the comparator will accept; the comparator must be implemented.

— A format must be specified for the information which describes the candidate to the configurable reference implementation. This information will be supplied by the candidate and used by certifiers to adapt their reference implementation.

— A reference implementation must be constructed. A technique has been identified for doing so.

7.5.1   Format of Certification Data

A certification data stream has many similarities with a graphical metafile, like the one produced and interpreted by the GKS metafile workstation. However, the goals when designing a metafile and a certification data stream are diametrically opposed. A metafile must be as insensitive as possible to differences between implementations, because it will be used to transport information between them. The certification data stream, on the other hand, must be as sensitive as possible to differences between implementations because they are what it will be used to detect.

Input to the comparator must be capable of representing:
a) the GKS output and input primitives;
b) the device-oriented primitives, into which they may be decomposed;
c) the properties which are assigned to these primitives, in terms of coordinates, transformations, and attributes;
d) potentially retro-active modifications of attributes.

In order for the items of comparator input to be self-contained, each primitive should carry with it all the properties it has been assigned. The outline design of the certification data may be expressed as a grammar, using BNF (Table 7.1):

Table 7.1 Grammar for describing certification data

<picture>	::= <item>*
<item>	::= <start> <item name> <prop list> <item>* <end>
<item name>	::= <GKS primitive> | <device primitive> | set attr
<prop list>	::= <prop name>* <value>
<value>	::= <GKS data type> <data>
<prop name>	::= <GKS attr name> | coords | transform | clip rect | pixel array | chars

It should be noted that it is not necessary to specify that the COORDS are in NDC or DC, nor that TRANSFORM maps, for example, from WC to NDC. This information is supplied by the candidate to the reference implementation and does not affect the comparison process. It should be noted also that, as is shown in a later example, this grammar can be used to express the state of a primitive at any stage in its progress from the GKS interface to the device.

7.5.2   Describing the Candidate Implementation

In order for the reference implementation to imitate the operations of the candidate implementation, it must operate with the same workstation description table. Although this ensures that the coordinate spaces will be the same, that the same amounts of resources will be used and that regenerations will occur at appropriate times, this is still not sufficient. The particular set of operations and properties to be applied to the "device" by the candidate will be determined by the "device" capabilities. For example, if the "device" provides linetypes, a LINETYPE property will be applied to it, but if it does not, the POLYLINE primitives will be dissected into sets of lines. Thus, the candidate must supply not only the workstation description table, but also information describing the capabilities of the "device" the workstation is driving. Some of the information required is shown in the example at the end of this section; other information needed was identified by classifying the dependencies flagged in the GKS document.

7.5.3   Reference Implementation

A technique for constructing a reference implementation was identified. In this, we basically distinguish between functions setting GKS states, output functions which — implemented as pipelines — eventually generate output items of a picture description, and input functions which perform interaction sequences in the form of processes (cf. Chapter 2).

The implementation of every function depends on the particular characteristics of a graphics device, while the function's interface remains constant. For some capabilities of a common set of devices the different implementation possibilities have already been identified. They were used for the initial GKS specification. Restricting ourselves to the pipelines of output primitives, the following model was established.

A set of basic modules, such as coordinate transformations, clipping and attribute emulation functions has been identified. Each function is specified using basic modules so that it generates items of the syntax above. Thereby, a skeleton specification is written. Each choice of device capabilities is expressed as a conditional statement. The information from the candidate determines a path through these conditional statements, which, in fact, is a specific pipeline of transformations. The implementation is configured by selecting and permuting these modules.

A Polyline Pipeline

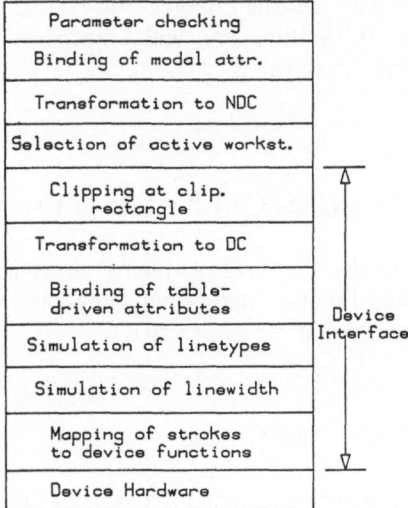

Figure 7.3 A polyline pipeline

In each pipeline, the comparator format's generality is exploited by generating it at the GKS interface. Each step in the transformation and attribute binding pipeline reads the input from preceding stages, identifies the keywords in the stream with which this stage is concerned, alters them and passes the result on to the next stage. For example, one stage might be to apply the TRANSFORM to the COORDS, another might be to replace the POLYLINE INDEX attribute by LINETYPE, LINEWIDTH and COLOUR INDEX attributes.

Besides being useful for the construction of the reference implementation, the specification also provides valuable guidance for implementors, if published.

It should be noted that to ensure that there is confidence in the correctness of the reference implementation, it is important that the executable form of the implementation be as close as possible to the notation used to describe it. This is guaranteed if the steps taken in the program transformation towards a real programming language are very few and simple. The reference implementation does not have to be in the same language as the candidate because its only use is to generate reference output for comparison.

The following pipeline, as shown in Figure 7.3, describes the effect of the GKS output function POLYLINE. At the GKS interface, a picture item is generated containing the name of the item and all relevant attributes, such as coordinates, transformations, clipping rectangle, etc. Each box applies a specific transformation to the elements of the item. For each box, the transformation applied and the changes to the item's data set are described. At every point in the pipeline stream, the actual item contents can be tested. Each capability of a specific candidate device represents such a point in the stream; when certain transformations are applied, others are not. A particular candidate device may, for example, receive a polyline with coordinates being in NDC and the polyline bundle index bound to it. Another one might be controlled by polylines in DC and the linetype and colour index of the current polyline bundle bound to it. A third one will take over the polyline after attribute simulation has been performed.

7.6   GKS Certification in Practice

As the technical problems in certifying GKS have gradually been resolved it has become increasingly appropriate to consider how a certification scheme might operate in practice.

7.6.1   Test Centres

It is expected that for practical reasons, there will be a number of test centres situated at different locations throughout the world. It makes good sense, however, for one central body to have the responsibility of monitoring the test software. Copies of the software would be distributed to all the test centres. This should cause only a few problems if the test software is updated at intervals of say, one year. Certification, of course, could be carried out by any of the centres.

7.6.2   Test Program Suite

The test program suite will have three main parts:
1. application interface tests
2. device interface tests
3. operator interface tests
according to the three interfaces that have been identified for checking. The suite ought to be regarded not as something fixed, but rather as something dynamic: it will be regularly updated to improve the thoroughness of its coverage. The suite will be configurable to GKS implementations of different capabilities, e.g., different GKS levels, different numbers of workstations supported.

Some reference implementation must be available which can be configured according to the different candidate implementations.

The results of applying the test suite to the candidate are evaluated in different ways for the three types of tests. In the case of results from the application interface the test programs themselves can verify the results. For tests conducted at the operator interface the evaluation is done visually, by comparison with certain reference hard-copy output. For tests conducted at the device interface the evaluation is performed automatically by a comparator program which compares the data generated by the candidate and reference implementations.

7.6.3   Certification Procedure

The certification of a candidate GKS implementation might proceed in the following way:
— The implementor contacts the test centre to indicate that he wishes to have his implementation certified.
— The test centre sends the implementor a form, in which he enters full details of his implementation.
— This information enables the test centre to select (generate) an appropriate language version of the test suite and to configure both the test suite and the reference implementation appropriately.
— A set of reference results at the device interface is generated at the test centre, together with suitable pictorial output for checking the operator interface.
— When the implementor indicates he is ready for his implementation to be certified, a representative of the test centre visits the implementor and runs the test suite on the candidate implementation. A comparison of results is made, and a certificate is issued listing any errors detected.
— The implementor may ask to be re-tested at any time and in any case, a certificate would only remain valid for a certain length of time.

7.6.4   Assistance for an Implementor

The implementor may contact the test centre at an early stage in the development of his software. The reference specification, the configured test suite, reference results and comparator can then be made available to him and can be used to assist in the debugging of the implementation. A representative of the test centre would still be responsible for the actual test run for which a certificate is issued.

7.6.5   The Present State of Practical Certification

In 1983, the European Commission made a contract with the GMD, Bonn (Gesellschaft für Mathematik und Datenverarbeitung) [GMD85] which allowed two groups at the universities in Darmstadt and in Leicester to conduct enough tests to start a validation testing service. At the beginning of 1985, the GMD released an initial set of test programs.

It is planned to set up an official certification procedure through the DIN using their DGWK (Deutsche Gesellschaft für Warenkennzeichnung) organisation. The latter would issue the certificate based on test reports provided by the authorized test centre, i.e., the GMD. In the meantime, contacts have been established between the GMD, the EEC and various national standardization groups (or their representative organisations) to adopt the test suite and the test procedures. This should eventually mean that a unique certificate can be issued in any country which would nevertheless have international validity.

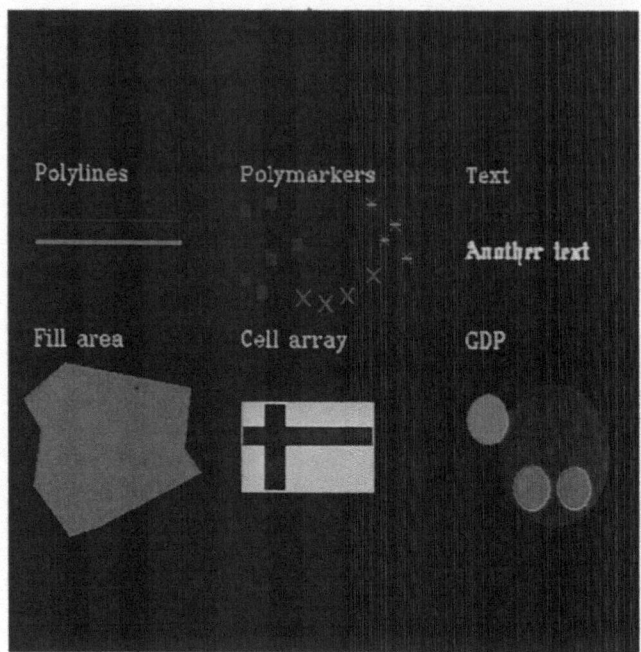

Figure C1 GKS primitives displayed on a colour raster workstation

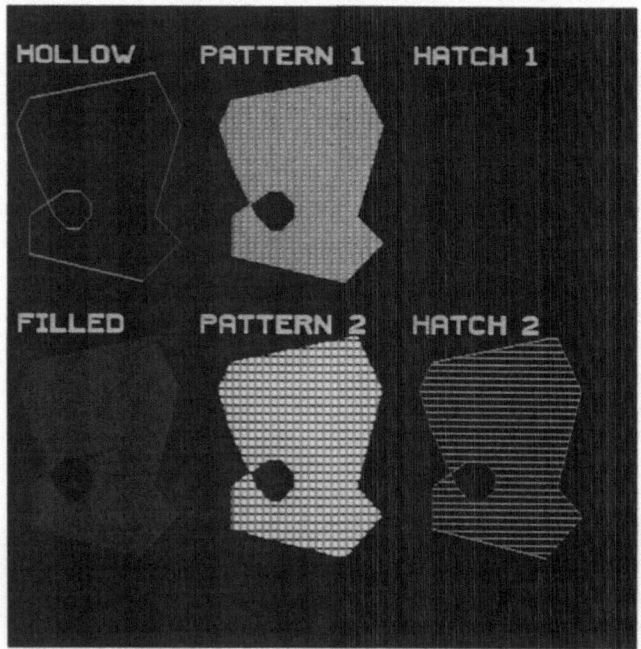

Figure C2 Examples of FILL AREA attributes on a colour raster workstation

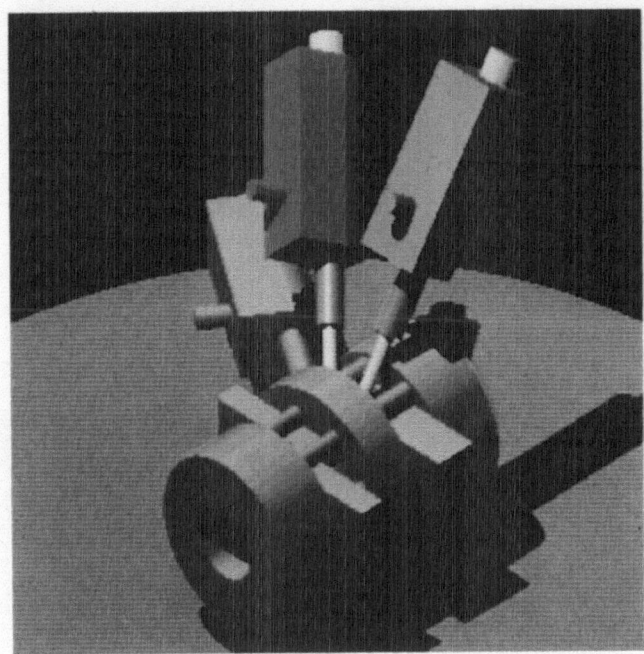

Figure C3 Example of PIXEL ARRAY

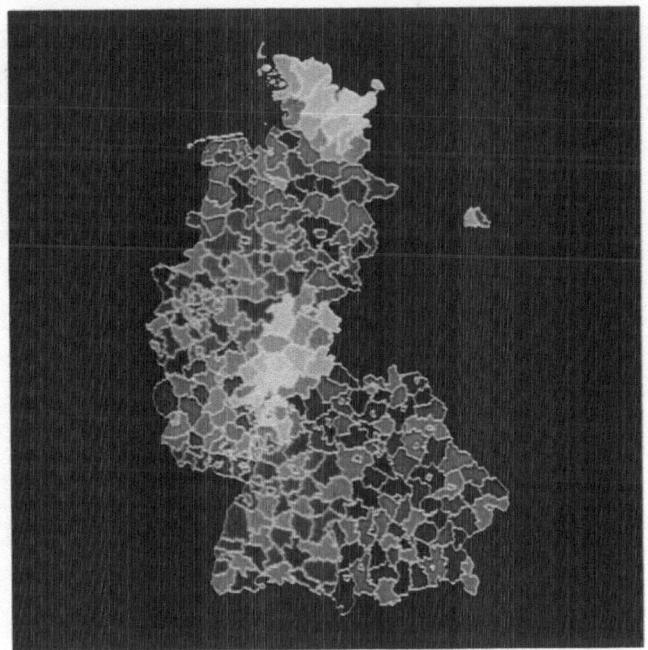

Figure C4 Example of a map with area filling

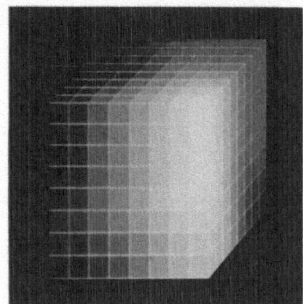

Figure C5 RGB colour model visualized by colour cube

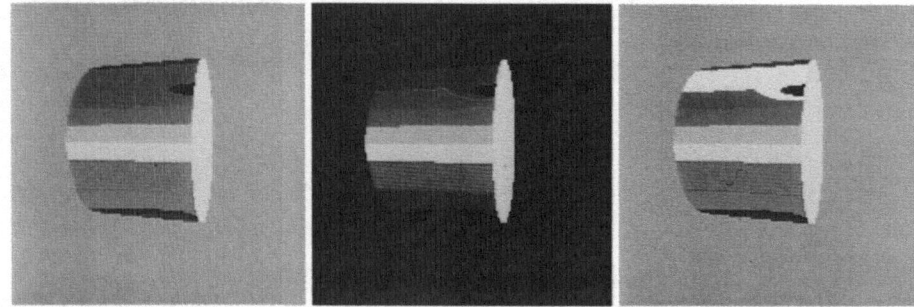

Figure C6 Effect of a change of the colour table on a raster image

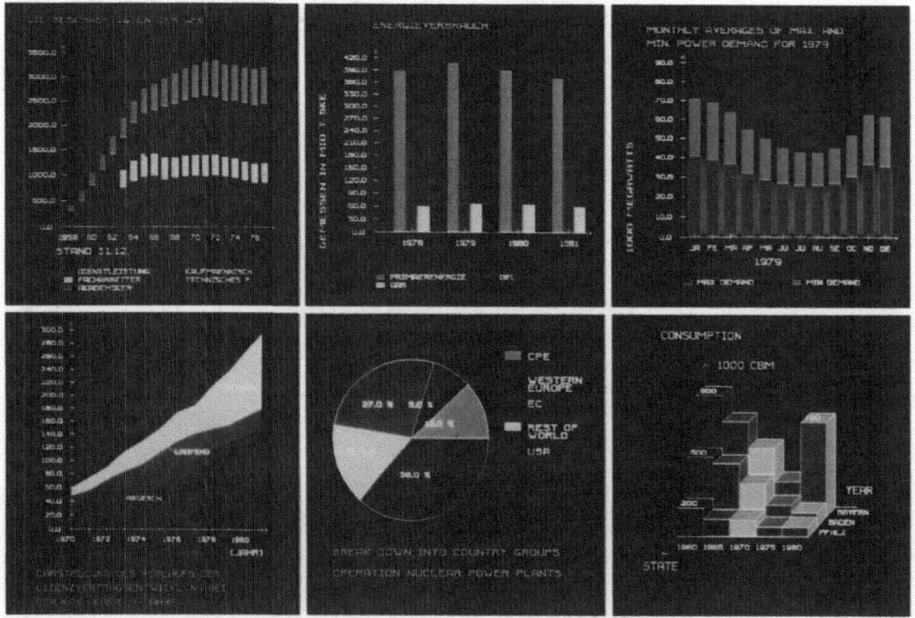

Figure C7 Pictures generated by a business graphics application layer

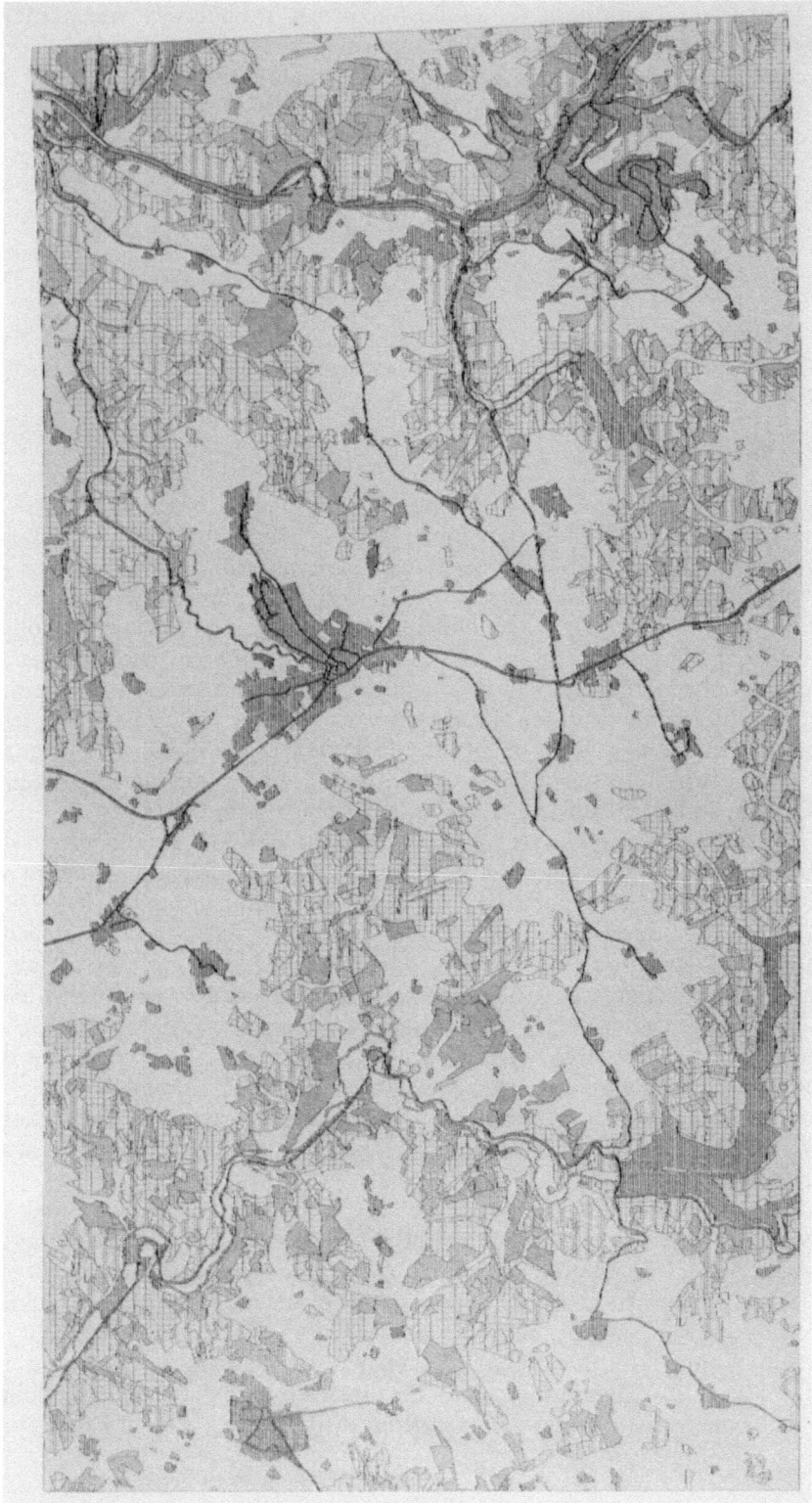

Figure C8 Picture generated by an application layer for mapping

Furthermore, a proposal for a follow-up project is underway, which is trying to find funding for the following developments:
— converting the test suite to languages other than FORTRAN;
— developing a test suite for the Computer Graphics Metafile;
— developing a test suite for the GKS-3D extension.

8   TERMINOLOGY

8.1   Introduction

Human communication needs a common language in order to succeed. Of course, in a new and rapidly developing field like Computer Graphics, different groups will develop their own basis for communication. Many conflicts and misunderstandings in the course of GKS design and review were caused by not having a common language. Different terms were used for the same object, or different objects were given the same name by different people. This was true not only in the international field, where English is used as the main language of communication, but also in various other languages. In order to avoid any difficulties which might arise from designing GKS in two languages at the same time, DIN decided at a very early stage to develop the GKS standard in English, and later translate the finished document into German.

When a task force was set up within TC97 to develop a standardized data processing vocabulary, one of the chapters of the anticipated standard was devoted to a computer graphics vocabulary. The working group ISO TC97/SC5/WG2 took part in this task, commenting on the first draft and recommending changes and additions. This process was influenced to a great extent by the ongoing GKS review. Since a common terminology had to be used (in many cases, it evolved after considerable discussion about the review of GKS), this terminology was also able to serve as a basis for the graphics part of the data processing vocabulary. In 1984, Section 13 "Computer Graphics" of the ISO data processing vocabulary reached the state of an International Standard (ISO 2382/13) [ISO84]. Section 8.2, below, gives the terms and definitions of this standard.

Like every other ISO standard, the data processing vocabulary could only become an International Standard when an approved French translation became available. Therefore, the graphics terms and definitions of Section 13 of ISO 2382 were translated into French. The presence of a French graphics vocabulary was a valuable help for the translation of the GKS document into French. Within DIN, a graphics vocabulary was developed which was used as the basis for the German version of the GKS standard document. The following list contains the German terms together with the English and French ones.

For many of the terms in French and German, there were no existing words suitable so that new terms had to be coined.

The computer graphics vocabulary developed by ISO as an International Standard will contribute considerably in establishing an equal basis for the communication between computer graphics experts. It will facilitate the teaching of computer graphics and it will make international cooperation in this field easier.

8.2 Vocabulary

This section contains the computer graphics terms from ISO 2382/13. For every concept, the English term, the French term, and the German term are given. The English definition of the concept is added. The entries are arranged in alphabetical sequence of the English terms.

ıglish	French	German
3SOLUTE COMMAND .BSOLUTE INSTRUCTION	COMMANDE ABSOLUE	ABSOLUTER BEFEHL

display command that causes the display device to interpret the data following the command absolute coordinates.

3SOLUTE COORDINATE	COORDONNEE ABSOLUE	ABSOLUTE KOORDI-NATE

ıe of the coordinates that identify the position of an addressable point with respect to the origin a specified coordinate system.

3SOLUTE VECTOR	VECTEUR ABSOLU	ABSOLUTER VEKTOR

vector whose start and end points are specified in absolute coordinates.

)DRESSABILITY in Computer Graphics	CAPACITE D'ADRESSAGE	ADRESSBEREICH

e number of addressable points in each axis of a specified device space.

)DRESSABLE POINT	POSITION ADRESSABLE	ADRESSIERBARER PUNKT

ıy point of a device that can be addressed.

MING SYMBOL AIMING CIRCLE AIMING FIELD	CHAMP DE VISEE	ZIELSYMBOL ZIELKREIS PICKBEREICH

ı a display surface, a circle or other pattern of light used to indicate the area in which the presence a lightpen can be detected at a given time.

₁glish	French	German
₁CKGROUND IMAGE STATIC IMAGE	FOND D'IMAGE ARRIERE PLAN D'IMAGE	HINTERGRUNDBILD STATISCHES BILD

₁at part of a display image, such as a form overlay, that is not changed during a particular sequence transactions.

₁ANKING	EXTINCTION	UNSICHTBAR MACHEN

₁e suppression of the display of one or more display elements or segments.

₁INKING	CLIGNOTEMENT	BLINKEN

₁ intentional periodic change in the intensity of one or more display elements or segments.

₁LLIGRAPHIC DISPLAY DEVICE DIRECTED BEAM DISPLAY DEVICE	VISU A BALAYAGE CAVALIER	LINIENGRAPHIKGERÄT KALLIGRAPHISCHES GERÄT

display device in which the display elements of a display image may be generated in any program-₁ntrolled sequence.

₁HARACTER GENERATOR	GENERATEUR DE CARACTERES	ZEICHENGENERATOR

functional unit that converts the coded representation of a character into the graphic representation the character for display.

₁IPPING	DETOURAGE, DECOUPAGE	KLIPPEN

₁moving those parts of display elements that lie outside a given region.

₁DED IMAGE	IMAGE CODEE	KODIERTES BILD

representation of a display image in a form suitable for storage and processing.

₁IOICE DEVICE	SELECTEUR	AUSWÄHLER

₁ input device providing one value from a set of alternatives.

₁MPUTER GRAPHICS	INFOGRAPHIE	COMPUTERGRAPHIK GRAPHISCHE DATEN-VERARBEITUNG

₁thods and techniques for converting data to or from a graphical display via computers.

glish	French	German
)NTROL BALL TRACK BALL	BOULE ROULANTE	ROLLKUGEL

ball, rotatable about its centre that is used as an input device, normally as a locator.

|)ORDINATE GRAPHICS LINE GRAPHICS | INFOGRAPHIE AU TRAIT | KOORDINATEN-GRAPHIK LINIENGRAPHIK |

mputer graphics in which display images are generated from display commands and coordinate ta.

| JRSOR | CURSEUR | SCHREIBMARKE POSITIONSMARKE |

movable, visible mark used to indicate the position on which the next operation will occur on lisplay surface.

| JRVE GENERATOR | GENERATEUR DE COURBES | KURVENGENERATOR |

functional unit that converts a coded representation of a curve into the graphic representation the curve for display.

| :TECTABLE SEGMENT | SEGMENT DETECTABLE | ANSPRECHBARES SEGMENT |

segment that can be detected by a pick device.

| :VICE COORDINATE | COORDONNEE D'APPAREIL | GERÄTEKOORDINATE |

coordinate specified in a coordinate system that is device-dependent.

| :VICE SPACE | ESPACE ECRAN | GERÄTE-KOORDINATENRAUM |

ıe space defined by the complete set of addressable points of a display device.

| :SPLAY | AFFICHAGE | DARSTELLUNG |

visual presentation of data.

| :SPLAY COMMAND DISPLAY INSTRUCTION | COMMANDE D'AFFICHAGE | DARSTELLUNGS-BEFEHL |

command that controls the state or action of a display device.

ıglish	French	German
ˈSPLAY CONSOLE	VISU, VISUEL CONSOLE DE VISUALISATION	GRAPHISCHER ARBEITSPLATZ

console that includes at least one display surface and may also include one or more input devices.

ˈSPLAY ELEMENT GRAPHIC PRIMITIVE OUTPUT PRIMITIVE	ELEMENT GRAPHIQUE PRIMITIVE GRAPHIQUE	GRAPHISCHES GRUNDELEMENT DARSTELLUNGS- ELEMENT

basic graphic element that can be used to construct a display image.

ˈSPLAY IMAGE	IMAGE	GRAPHISCHE DAR- STELLUNG BILD

collection of display elements or segments that are represented together at any one time on a splay surface.

ˈSPLAY SPACE OPERATING SPACE	ESPACE D'AFFICHAGE	BILDBEREICH DARSTELLUNGS- BEREICH

ıat portion of the device space corresponding to the area available for displaying images.

ˈSPLAY SURFACE	SURFACE D'AFFICHAGE SURFACE DE VISUALI- SATION	DARSTELLUNGS- FLÄCHE SICHTFLÄCHE

a display device, that medium on which display images may appear.

ɔT MATRIX CHARACTER GENERATOR	GENERATEUR DE CARACTERES PAR POINTS	RASTER-ZEICHEN- GENERATOR

character generator that generates character images composed of dots.

℞AGGING	ENTRAINEMENT D'IMAGE	NACHZIEHEN

oving one or more segments on a display surface by translating it along a path determined by ocator.

℞UM PLOTTER	TRACEUR A ROULEAU	TROMMELPLOTTER

plotter that draws a display image on a display surface mounted on a rotating drum.

ıglish	French	German
∶HO	ECHO	ECHO

ıe immediate notification of the current values provided by an input device to the operator at ∋ display console.

∟ECTROSTATIC PLOTTER	TRACEUR ELECTRO-STATIQUE	ELEKTROSTATISCHER PLOTTER

raster plotter that uses a row of electrodes to fix the inks electrostatically on the paper.

∟ATBED PLOTTER	TABLE TRACANTE TABLE A TRACER	TISCHPLOTTER ZEICHENTISCH

plotter that draws a display image on a display surface mounted on a flat surface.

∟ICKER	PAPILLOTEMENT	FLICKERN

ı undesirable pulsation of a display image on a cathode ray tube.

ƆREGROUND IMAGE DYNAMIC IMAGE	PREMIER PLAN D'IMAGE	VORDERGRUNDBILD DYNAMISCHES BILD

ıat part of a display image that can be changed for every transaction.

ƆRM FLASH	AFFICHAGE DE GRILLE	FORMULAREINBLEN-DUNG

ıe display of a form overlay.

ƆRM OVERLAY	GRILLE DE SAISIE	FORMULAR

pattern such as a report form, grid or map used as a background image.

ɪDDEN LINE	LIGNE CACHEE	VERDECKTE KANTE

line segment that represents an edge obscured from view in a two-dimensional projection of a ɾee-dimensional object.

ɪGHLIGHTING	MISE EN EVIDENCE	HERVORHEBEN

ɪnphasizing a display element or segment by modifying its visual attributes.

₁AGE REGENERATION	REGENERATION D'IMAGE	BILDWIEDERHOLUNG

ıe sequence of events needed to generate a display image from its representation in storage.

ɪCREMENTAL COORDINATE	COORDONNEE RELATIF	INKREMENTELLE KOORDINATE

relative coordinate where the previously addressed point is the reference point.

ɪCREMENTAL VECTOR	VECTEUR RELATIF	RELATIVER VEKTOR

vector whose end point is specified as a displacement from its start point.

English	French	German

INCREMENT SIZE — **PAS, INCREMENT** — **INKREMENT**

The distance between adjacent addressable points on the display surface.

INKING — **TRACE** — **SPUR ZEICHNEN**

Creating a line by moving a locator over the display surface leaving a trail behind the locator in the manner of a pen drawing a line on paper.

INPUT PRIMITIVE — **PRIMITIVE D'ENTREE** — **EINGABEELEMENT**

An item of data obtained from an input device such as a keyboard, choice device, locator, pick device, stroke device, or valuator.

JOYSTICK — **MANCHE A BALAI** — **STEUERKNÜPPEL**

A lever with at least two degrees of freedom that is used as an input device, normally as a locator.

LIGHTPEN — **PHOTOSTYLE** — **LICHTGRIFFEL**

A light-sensitive pick device that is used by pointing it at the display surface.

LIGHTPEN DETECTION — **DETECTION PAR** — **LICHTGRIFFEL-**
LIGHTPEN HIT — **PHOTOSTYLE** — **DETEKTION**

The sensing by a lightpen of light generated by a display element on a display surface.

LOCATOR — **RELEVEUR DE** — **LOKALISIERER**
 — **COORDONNEES** —

An input device providing coordinates of a position.

MARKER in Computer Graphics — **MARQUE** — **MARKE**

A glyph with a specified appearance which is used to indicate a particular location.

MIRRORING — **REFLEXION** — **SPIEGELN**

Reflection of display elements about a line or plane.

MOUSE — **SOURIS** — **MAUS**

A hand-held locator operated by moving it on a surface.

NORMALIZED DEVICE — **COORDONNEE ECRAN** — **NORMIERTE**
COORDINATE — **NORMEE** — **GERÄTEKOORDINATE**

A coordinate specified in a device-independent intermediate coordinate system normalized to some range, typically 0 to 1.

PANNING — **PANORAMIQUE** — **SCHWENKEN**

Progressively translating the entire display image to give the visual impression of lateral movement of the image.

ıglish	French	German
CK DEVICE	DISPOSITIF DE DESIGNATION	PICKER

ı input device used to specify a particular display element or segment.

| XEL | PIXEL | PIXEL |
| PICTURE ELEMENT | | BILDELEMENT |

ıe smallest element of a display surface that can be independently assigned a colour or intensity.

| _ASMA PANEL | ECRAN A PLASMA | PLASMABILDSCHIRM |
| GAS PANEL | | |

part of a display device that consists of a grid of electrodes in a flat, gas-filled panel.

| _OTTER STEP SIZE | PAS (DE TRACEUR) | PLOTTER-
SCHRITTWEITE |

ıe increment size on a plotter.

| _OTTING HEAD | TETE TRACANTE | ZEICHENKOPF |

ıat part of a plotter used to create marks on a display device.

| ASTER DISPLAY DEVICE | VISU A POINTILLAGE | RASTERGERÄT |

display device in which display images are generated on the display surface by raster graphics.

| ASTER GRAPHICS | INFOGRAPHIE PAR IMAGE | RASTERGRAPHIK |

ımputer graphics in which display images are composed of an array of pixels arranged in rows
d columns.

| ASTER PLOTTER | TRACEUR PAR LIGNE | RASTERPLOTTER |

plotter that generates a display image on a display surface using a line-by-line scanning technique.

| ASTER UNIT | UNITE DE TRAME | RASTEREINHEIT |

ıe unit of measure determined by the distance between adjacent pixels.

| EFRESH | RAFRAICHISSEMENT | BILDWIEDERHOLUNG |

ıe process of repeatedly producing a display image on a display surface so that the image remains
ıble.

| EFRESH RATE | FREQUENCE DE
REFRAICHISSEMENT | BILDWIEDERHOL-
FREQUENZ |

ıe number of times per second at which a display image is produced for refresh.

| ELATIVE COMMAND | COMMANDE RELATIVE | RELATIVER BEFEHL |
| RELATIVE INSTRUCTION | | |

display command that causes the display device to interpret the data following the command
relative coordinates.

English	French	German
RELATIVE COORDINATE	COORDONNEE RELATIVE	RELATIVE KOORDINATE

One of the coordinates that identify the position of an addressable point with respect to some other addressable point.

| ROLLING | DEFILEMENT VERTICAL | ROLLEN |

Scrolling restricted to an upward or downward direction.

| ROTATION | ROTATION | DREHUNG |

Turning display elements about an axis.

| RUBBER BAND | TRACE ELASTIQUE | GUMMIBAND |

A method of echoing a locator position by moving the common ends of a set of straight lines while the other ends remain fixed.

| SCALING | CHANGEMENT D'ECHELLE | SKALIERUNG |

The application of a multiplicative factor to one or more display elements.

| SCROLLING | DEFILEMENT | BLÄTTERN |

Moving a window vertically or horizontally in such a manner that new data appears within the viewport as the old data disappears.

| SEGMENT in Computer Graphics | SEGMENT | SEGMENT |

A collection of display elements that can be manipulated as a whole.

| SHIELDING REVERSE CLIPPING | MASQUAGE | AUSBLENDEN |

Suppression of all or parts of display elements falling within a a specified region.

| SOFT COPY | IMAGE-VIDEO IMAGE SUR ECRAN | BILDSCHIRM- DARSTELLUNG |

A non-permanent display image.

| STORAGE TUBE | TUBE A MEMOIRE | SPEICHERSCHIRM |

A type of cathode ray tube that retains a display image without requiring refresh.

| STROKE CHARACTER GENERATOR | GENERATEUR DE CARACTERES PAR TRAITS | LINIEN-ZEICHEN- GENERATOR |

A character generator that generates character images composed of line segments.

| STROKE DEVICE | LECTEUR DE COURBES | LINIENGEBER |

An input device providing a set of coordinates that records the path of the device.

ιglish	French	German
ιBLET	TABLETTE	TABLETT

special flat surface with a mechanism for indicating positions thereon, normally used as a locator.

| ΙUMB WHEEL | MOLETTE | DAUMENRAD |

wheel, rotatable about its axis, that provides a scalar value.

|) DISPLAY | AFFICHER | DARSTELLEN |
| | VISUALISER | |

) represent data visually.

| ΙACKING | POURSUITE | VERFOLGUNG |

oving a tracking symbol.

| ΙACKING SYMBOL | SYMBOLE DE POURSUITE | VERFOLGUNGSSYMBOL |

symbol on the display surface that indicates the position corresponding to the coordinate data oduced by the locator.

| ΙANSLATION | TRANSLATION | VERSCHIEBUNG |

ιe application of a constant displacement to the position of one or more display elements.

| JMBLING | CULBUTE | TAUMELN |

ynamic display of the rotation of display elements about an axis the orientation of which is contin-ιusly changing in space.

| ΙER COORDINATE | COORDONNEE | ANWENDER- |
| | D'UTILISATEUR | KOORDINATE |

coordinate specified by a user and expressed in a coordiante system that is device-independent.

| ιLUATOR | VALUATEUR | WERTGEBER |

ι input device providing a scalar value.

| ΙCTOR GENERATOR | GENERATEUR DE VECTEURS | VEKTORGENERATOR |

functional unit that generates directed line segments.

| ΙEWPORT | CLOTURE | DARSTELLUNGSFELD |

predefined part of a display space.

| ΙRTUAL PUSH BUTTON | ELEMENT DE MENU | MENÜELEMENT |
| LIGHT BUTTON | TOUCHE VIRTUELLE | |

ιsplay elements used to simulate a function key by means of a pick device.

| ΙRTUAL SPACE | ESPACE VIRTUEL | VIRTUELLER |
| in Computer Graphics | | KOORDINATENRAUM |

space in which the coordinates of the display elements are expressed in a device-independent manner.

ıglish	French	German
INDOW	FENETRE	FENSTER

predefined part of a virtual space.

INDOW/VIEWPORT	TRANSFORMATION	NORMIERUNGS-
TRANSFORMATION	FENETRE CLOTURE	TRANSFORMATION
NORMALIZATION	TRANSFORMATION DE	
TRANSFORMATION	NORMATION	

transformation that maps the boundary and contents of a window into the boundary and interior a viewport.

IRE FRAME	REPRESENTATION FIL	DRAHTRAHMEN-
REPRESENTATION	DE FER	DARSTELLUNG
		DRAHTMODELL

device-independent cartesian coordinate used by the application program for specifying graphical put and output.

| ORLD COORDINATE | COORDONNEE UNIVERSELLE | WELTKOORDINATE |

device independent cartesian coordinate used by the application program for specifying graphical put and output.

| RAPAROUND | BOUCLAGE | UMLAUF |

ıe display at some point on the display surface of the display elements whose coordinates normally outside of the display space.

|)OMING | VARIATION DE FOCALE | ZOOMEN |
| | EFFET DE LOUPE | |

ogressively scaling the entire display image to give the visual impression of movement of one or ore segments toward or away from an observer.

REFERENCES

[ANSI81]   American National Standards Institute:
            Engineering Drawing and Related Documentation Practices — Digital
            Representation for Communication of Product Definition Data (IGES).
            American National Standard ANS Y14.26M (1981).
[ANSI82]   American National Standards Institute:
            Draft Proposed American National Standard for the Virtual Device Meta-
            file.
            Working document X3H3382-15R5 (1982).

[ANSI85]   American National Standards Institute:
            PHIGS Baseline Document.
            Document ANSI/X3H3/85-21 (1985).

[BAEC82]   R. Baecker and W. Buxton:
            Lexical and Pragmatic Considerations of Input Structures.
            Computer System Research Group, University of Toronto, Toronto, Ontario, Canada M5S 1A1 (1982).

[BAUE81]   F.L. Bauer et al.:
            Report on a Wide Spectrum Language for Program Specification and Development (Tentative Version).
            TU München, Institut für Informatik, TUM-I8104 (May 1981).

[BERK82]   T. Berk, L. Brownston, A. Kaufman:
            A Human Factors Study of Colour Notation Systems for Computer Graphics.
            CACM 25(1982) 547-550.

[BO82]   K. Bö:
            IDIGS Reference manual, Version 4.0.
            Document ISO/TC97/SC5/WG2 N151 (1982).

[BONO82]   P. Bono, J. Encarnacao, F.R.A. Hopgood, P. ten Hagen:
            GKS — The first graphics standard.
            IEEE Computer Graphics and Applications 2,5 (1982).

[BORU80a]   H.G. Borufka, H. Kuhlmann, G. Pfaff:
            Implementation of the Graphics Standard Proposal GKS.
            In: P. ten Hagen (ed.): Lecture Notes of Eurographics '80 Tutorials.
            Published by EUROGRAPHICS Association.

[BORU80b]   H.G. Borufka and G. Pfaff:
            The Design of general-purpose Command Interpreter for Man-Machine Communication.
            Proc. IFIP WG 5.2-5.3 Conf., Tokyo (1980) 161-175.

[BORU82]   H.G. Borufka, P. ten Hagen, H. Kuhlmann:
            Defining Interactions by Dialogue Cells.
            IEEE Computer Graphics and Applications (July 1982) 25-33.

[BOS77]   J. van den Bos, L.C. Caruthers, A. van Dam:
            GPGS: A Device-Independent General Purpose Graphic System.
            Proc. Conf. SIGGRAPH 1977, Computer Graphics 11,2 (1977) 112-119.

[BRIE80]   C.D. O'Brien, H. Newman:
            Picture Description Instructions for Geometric and Photographic Image Codings in Videotex Systems.
            Dept. of Communications, Canada (1980).

[BROD81]   K.W. Brodlie:
            Certification Testing at the DI/DD Interface.
            Report G2, Computer Laboratory, University of Leicester (1981).

[BROD82]   K.W. Brodlie, M.C. Maguire, G.E. Pfaff:
            A Practical Strategy for Certifying GKS Implementations.
            Proc. Eurographics '82, North-Holland, Amsterdam (1982).

[CARS82]   S. Carson:
            A Formal Specification of the Programmers Minimal Interface to Graphics.
            X3H3/82-43(1982).

[DIN79]   Deutsches Institut für Normung:
            Proposal of Standard DIN 66252, Information Processing,
            Graphical Kernel System (GKS), Functional Description (1979).

[DIN81]   Deutsches Institut für Normung:
              DI/DD-Interface for GKS (Preliminary Version).
              DIN-NI/UA-5.9/40-81(1981).
[EEC81a]   Report on EEC Workshop on Graphics Certification, Rixensart-Brussels.
              University of Leicester (May 1981).
[EEC81b]   Report on EEC Workshop on Graphics Certification, Darmstadt.
              Report G1, University of Leicester (September 1981).
[EEC82a]   Initial Development of GKS Test Suite.
              Report on EEC Workshop on Graphics Certification, Leicester.
              Report G6, University of Leicester (February 1982).
[EEC82b]   Defining a Device Interface for Certification.
              Report on EEC Workshop on Graphics Certification, Miltenberg/Darm-
              stadt.
              GRIS-Report 82-4, Technische Hochschule Darmstadt (April 1982).
[EEC82c]   Formal Specification of Graphics Software Standards.
              Report on EEC Workshop on Graphics Certification, Steensel/Eindhoven
              (June 82).
[EEC82d]   Testing at the Device Interface.
              Report on EEC Workshop on Graphics Certification, Leicester,
              GRIS-Report 82-11, Technische Hochschule Darmstadt (September 1982).
[EKP84]   G. Enderle, K. Kansy, G. Pfaff:
              Computer Graphics Programming — GKS — The Graphics Standard.
              1. Edition.
              Springer-Verlag Berlin (1984).
[ENCA80]   J. Encarnacao, G. Enderle, K. Kansy, G. Nees, E.G. Schlechtendahl, J.
              Weiss, P. Wißkirchen:
              The Workstation Concept of GKS and the Resulting Conceptual Differ-
              ences to the GSPC Core System.
              Computer Graphics 14,3 (1980) 226-230.
[ENCA81a]   J. Encarnacao, W. Straßer (Eds.):
              Geräteunabhängige graphische Systeme.
              Oldenbourg Verlag, München (1981).
[ENCA81b]   J. Encarnacao:
              Entstehung und Entwicklung des Graphischen Kernsystems GKS.
              In: J. Encarnacao, W. Straßer (Eds.):
              Geräteunabhängige graphische Systeme.
              Oldenbourg Verlag, München (1981) 13-34.
[ENCA82a]   J. Encarnacao, E.G. Schlechtendahl:
              Computer Aided Design, Fundamentals and System Architecture.
              Springer-Verlag Berlin (1982).
[ENCA82b]   J. Encarnacao, R. Lindner, M. Mehl, G. Pfaff, W. Straßer:
              Realisierung des graphischen Standards GKS durch VLSI-Technologie.
              Technische Hochschule Darmstadt, GRIS-Report (1982).
[ENDE78]   G. Enderle, I. Giese, M. Krause, H.P. Meinzer:
              The AGF Plotfile — Towards a Standardization for Storage and Transpor-
              tation of Graphics Information.
              Computer Graphics 12,4 (1978) 92-113.
[ENDE80]   G. Enderle:
              A Distributed Graphics System Based on a Standard Graphics File.
              ASME-PVP Conference, August 1980.
[ENDE81]   G. Enderle, P. ten Hagen:
              GKS Principles and Goals. DIN-NI/UA-5.9/15-81 (1981).

[FORT66]   FORTRAN 66.
            ISO/R 1539 (1972), ANSI X3.9 (1966), DIN 66027 (1979).
[FORT77]   FORTRAN 77.
            ISO 1539 (1980), ANSI X3.9 (1978), DIN 66027 (1980).
[FRAE77]   J. Fraedrich:
            Mensch-Maschine Kommunikation in Leitständen, Teil 1.
            Gesellschaft für Kernforschung mbH Karlsruhe, KFK-PDV 131 (October
            77) Chap. 5.
[GILO72]   W.K. Giloi, J. Encarnacao, W. Kestner:
            APL-G, APL Extended for Graphics.
            Proc. Online '72 (1972).
[GILO78]   W.K. Giloi:
            Interactive Computer Graphics.
            Prentice Hall (1978).
[GINO75]   GINO-F User Manual.
            CAD-Centre, Cambridge (1975).
[GKS85]   International Organization for Standardization:
            Information Processing Systems — Computer Graphics — Graphical Ker-
            nel System (GKS) — Functional Description.
            ISO 7942 (1985).
[GKSVER]   GKS Verein, Kruppstr. 82, D-4300 Essen 1, W. Germany.
[GMD85]   GMD, Dr. Wegner, Postfach 1240, D-5205 St. Augustin 1, W.Germany.
[GNAT81]   R. Gnatz:
            Certification by Program Constructions from Specifications.
            Institut für Informatik der Technischen Universität München.
[GSPC77]   Status Report of The Graphics Standards Planning Committee.
            Computer Graphics 11,3 (1977).
[GSPC79]   GSPC '79, Status Report of The Graphics Standards Planning Committee.
            Computer Graphics 13,3 (1979).
[GUED76]   R.A. Guedj, H.A. Tucker (Eds.):
            Methodology in Computer Graphics.
            Proc. IFIP WG5.2 Workshop SEILLAC I, May 1976.
            North-Holland, Amsterdam (1979).
[GUED80]   R. Guedj et al. (Eds.):
            Methodology of Interaction.
            North-Holland, Amsterdam (1980).
[HAGE79]   P. ten Hagen, F.R.A. Hopgood:
            Towards Compatible Graphic Standards.
            Mathematical Centre Report IN17, Amsterdam 1979.
[HAGE81]   P.J.W. ten Hagen: The GKS Reviewing Process.
            In: J. Encarnacao, W. Straßer (Eds.):
            Geräteunabhängige graphische Systeme.
            Oldenbourg Verlag, München (1981) 75-96.
[HOPG83]   F.R.A Hopgood, D.A. Duce, J.R. Gallop, D.C. Sutcliffe:
            Introduction to the Graphical Kernel System (GKS).
            Academic Press, New York (1983).
[HURW67]   A. Hurwitz, J.P. Citron, J.B. Yeaton:
            GRAF: Graphic Additions to FORTRAN.
            Proc. SJCC (1967).
[ISO80]   International Organization for Standardization:
            ISO/TC97/SC5/WG2 — GKS Review: First Active Issues List.
            Document ISO/TC97/SC5/WG2 — N92 (1980).

[ISO81a]   International Organization for Standardization:
              ISO/TC97/SC5/WG2 — Minutes of experts' meeting in Melbourne, Flor-
              ida, 1981.
              Document ISO TC97/SC5/WG2 — N100 (1981).
[ISO81b]   International Organization for Standardization:
              ISO/TC97/SC5/WG2 — GKS Review: Second Active Issues List.
              Document ISO/TC97/SC5/WG2 — N102 (1981).
[ISO81c]   International Organization for Standardization:
              ISO/TC97/SC5/WG2 — GKS Review: Third Active Issues List.
              Document ISO/TC97/SC5/WG2 — N106 (1981).
[ISO81d]   International Organization for Standardization:
              ISO/TC97/SC5/WG2 — GKS Review: Resolved Issues List.
              Document ISO/TC97/SC5/WG2 — N103 (1981).
[ISO82]   International Organization for Standardization:
              Open Systems Interconnection.
              ISO DIS 7498 (1982).
[ISO83]   International Organization for Standardization:
              Report of 3D Subgroup. Document ISO/TC97/SC5/WG2 N193 (1983).
[ISO84]   International Organization for Standardization:
              Data Processing Vocabulary, Section 13: Computer Graphics.
              ISO 2382/13 (1984).
[ISO85a]   International Organization for Standardization:
              Information Processing Systems — Computer Graphics — Graphical Ker-
              nel System (GKS) — Language Bindings. Part I (FORTRAN).
              ISO DIS 8651/1 (1985).
[ISO85b]   International Organization for Standardization: Information Processing
              Systems – Computer Graphics – Interface Techniques for Dialogues with
              Graphical Devices. Baseline Document.
              ISO/TC97 N1511 (1985)
[ISO85c]   International Organization for Standardization:
              Information Processing Systems — Computer Graphics — Metafile for
              the Storage and Transfer of Picture Description Information.
              ISO DIS 8632 (1985).
[ISO85d]   International Organization for Standardization:
              Information Processing Systems — Computer Graphics — Graphical Ker-
              nel System (GKS) — Language Bindings. Part II (Pascal).
              ISO DIS 8651/2 (1985).
[ISO86]   International Organization for Standardization:
              Information Processing Systems — Computer Graphics — Graphical Ker-
              nel System for Three Dimensions (GKS-3D) — Functional Description.
              ISO/DIS 8805 (1986).
[KANS85a]   K. Kansy:
              GKS-Position today. Proc. SEAS — Spring Technical Meeting 1985, Veld-
              hoven NL (1985) 347-360.
[KANS85b]   K. Kansy:
              3D Extension to GKS. Computer and Graphics (1985) 267-273.
[MAGU81]   M.C. Maguire:
              The Design of Test Programs for the Certification of Graphics Standards.
              Report G3, University of Leicester (November 1981).
[MICH78]   J.C. Michener, J.D. Foley:
              Some Major Issues in the Design of the Core Graphics System.
              Computing Surveys 10,4 (1978) 445-463.

[NAKE72]   F. Nake, A. Rosenfeld (Eds.): Graphic Languages.
Proc. IFIP Working Conference on Graphic Languages, Vancouver, Canada, 1972.
North-Holland, Amsterdam (1972).

[NEWM78]   W.M. Newman, A. v. Dam:
Recent Efforts Towards Graphics Standardization.
Computing Surveys 10,4 (1978) 365-380.

[NORM81]   L.S. Norman:
Software Methodology and Formal Specification Systems.
Research Department Sperry Univac, Blue Bell, Pa 19424 (ANSI-X3H3/81-93).

[PARN75]   D.L. Parnas:
On the Design and Development of Program Families.
TH Darmstadt, FB Informatik, 6100 Darmstadt, Forschungsbericht BS1 75/2.

[PFAF81a]   G. Pfaff:
Certification's Support by a Configurable Reference Implementation of GKS.
Position Paper for EEC Workshop May 1981.
Technische Hochschule Darmstadt (May 1981).

[PFAF81b]   G. Pfaff:
On Testing Methods for the Certification of Graphics Systems.
GRIS-Report 81-3, Technische Hochschule Darmstadt (July 1981).

[PFAF82a]   G. Pfaff, G. Maderlechner:
Tools for Configuring Interactive Picture Processing Systems.
Computer Graphics and Applications (July 1982).

[PFAF82b]   G. Pfaff, H. Kuhlmann, H. Hanusa:
Constructing User Interfaces based on Logical Input Devices.
IEEE, Computers (November 82) 62-68.

[REED81]   T. Reed:
Experiences in the Design and Support of a Graphics Device Driver Interface.
Proc. Eurographics '81, Darmstadt, North-Holland, Amsterdam (1981).

[ROSE80a]   D. Rosenthal:
On the Design of Graphics Metafiles.
ISO TC97/SC5/WG2 N86 (1980).

[ROSE80b]   D. Rosenthal:
Procedure for Technical Comments on GKS.
Document ISO/TC97/SC5/WG2 — N83 (1980).

[ROSE82]   D. Rosenthal, J. Michener, G. Pfaff, R. Kessener, M. Sabin:
The Detailed Semantics of Graphics Input Devices.
Computer Graphics 16,3 (1982) 33-38.

[SCHO81]   J. Schönhut:
Portabilität und Effizienz graphischer Software — ein Widerspruch?
In: J. Encarnacao, W. Straßer (Eds.):
Geräteunabhängige Graphische Systeme.
Oldenburg Verlag, München (1981) 217-233.

[SIGG82]   Graphical Input Interaction Technique (GHT).
Summary of a SIGGRAPH Workshop, Seattle 1982.
Computer Graphics 17,1 (1983) 5-30.

[SMIT71]   D.N. Smith:
GPL/I — A PL/1 Extension for Computer Graphics.
Proc. SJCC (1971).

[SMIT78]   A.R. Smith: Colour Gamut Transform Pairs.
            Proc. SIGGRAPH '78/Computer Graphics 12,3 (1978) 12-19.
[SOOP72]   K. Soop:
            The Design and Use of a PL/1 Based Graphical Programming Language.
            Proc. Online '72 (1972).
[WALL76]   V.L. Wallace:
            The Semantics of Graphics Input Devices.
            Computer Graphics 10,1 (1976) 61-65.
[WIRT71]   Niklaus Wirth:
            The Programming Language PASCAL.
            ACTA INFORMATICA 1 (1971) 35-63.
[WISS78]   P. Wißkirchen, K.H. Klein, P. Seuffert, G. Woetzel:
            Implementation of the Core Graphics System GKS in a Distributed
            Graphics Environment.
            Proc. Int. Conf. Interactive Techniques in CAD, Bologna (1978) 249-254.
[WISS79]   P. Wißkirchen, K. Kansy:
            Experiences with the Implementation of the GKS Standard Proposal.
            Proc. SEAS Spring Technical Meeting, Nijmegen (1979) 135-144.

Index